BRIEF ENCOUNTERS

A DICTIONARY
OF BRIEFS AND PHRASES
FOR COURT REPORTING

compiled by
Laurie Boucke

LAFAYETTE, COLORADO

© Copyright 1995, 1997
by White-Boucke Publishing

First Published August 1995
Reprinted with updates April 1996

Second Edition June 1997
Reprinted February 1999, October 1999, June 2000

ISBN 1-888580-07-0

All rights reserved. The publisher of this work expressly forbids that any part of this publication may be reproduced, stored in a retrieval system, or transmitted in any form or by any means, electronic or otherwise (including CD-ROM/DVD and Internet/WWW pages), without prior written permission.
No liability is assumed with respect to the use of the information herein.

Printed in the United States of America

Library of Congress Cataloging-in-Publication Data
Laurie Boucke
   Brief Encounters : a dictionary of briefs and phrases for court reporting / compiled by Laurie Boucke.–2nd ed.
     p. cm.
ISBN: 1-888580-07-0
     1. Law reporting–United States–Dictionaries.
     2. Shorthand reporting–Dictionaries.
     3. Computer-assisted transcription systems–Dictionaries.
     I. Title.
KF255.B75 1997
653'.18–dc21   97-14159
                                                                                 CIP

www.white-boucke.com

BRIEF ENCOUNTERS

INTRODUCTION

GENERAL

This dictionary is a compilation of conflict-free briefs, phrases, irregular verbs and commonly used words. It contains, for the most part, general vocabulary, as opposed to specialized terminology. None of the entries conflict with each other. Most (aspiring) court reporters rely on briefs and phrases to some degree. For most, there is no other way to write fast and accurately enough to work competently as a Certified Shorthand Reporter (CSR).

Technological advances in the court reporting field have been dramatic since the advent of computer-aided transcription (CAT) in the early sixties. Realtime writing is rapidly becoming the accepted standard. Indeed, the term "realtime" may eventually be eliminated altogether as it becomes the norm. Every student and practicing reporter should therefore strive to write realtime at every opportunity. For those who do not currently work in realtime, it is essential to build a conflict-free dictionary in preparation for the inevitable transition. Whatever system of writing is used, this dictionary will serve as an invaluable tool and trusty companion.

CONFLICT RESOLUTION

The following techniques are employed to avoid conflicts.

- **Stenonyms**
  "Stenonyms" are steno outlines that have the same sound but represent different words. Use TWAIT for *"actuate"* and TWAET for *"activate."*
  In this context, some single-syllable words that resolve conflicts are provided, e.g., KLAO for *"clue"* (avoids conflict with KLAOU for *"conclude"*) and PRAUM for *"prom"* (avoids conflict with PROM for *"promise"*), even though these words are not true briefs.

BRIEF ENCOUNTERS

- **Extra Vowels**
  An extra (nonphonetic) vowel may be added to an outline to avoid conflicts. Use KAENDZ for *"contends"* (avoids conflict with KENDZ for *"can he understand"*).

- **Asterisk**
  When the same outline is used for two different words, an asterisk is used with one of the outlines. In general, the most frequently used word or phrase is written without an asterisk. Use OX for *"objection"* and O*X for *"ox."*
  However, no entry is provided for the asterisked word if it is an uncommon or single-syllable word. For example, a dictionary entry is provided for *"objection"* (OX), but none is given for *"ox"* (O*X).
  Where possible, alternative outlines are given for asterisked entries. Thus, KAENDZ can be used in place of K*ENDZ for *"contends."*

Conflict resolution is not provided for conflicts that can be easily resolved by writing the lesser-used word in full. For example, a dictionary entry is provided for *"upstairs"* (UPS), but none is given for *"ups"* (UP/-S).

GUIDE TO THE DICTIONARY

- **Verbs**
  The principal parts of verbs are provided in the following order:
  first person singular present tense
  third person singular present tense
  present participle
  past tense
  past participle
  (*throw, throws, throwing, threw, thrown*).
  When the past tense and past participle are the same, one form represents both (*have, has, having, had*).
  Some verb forms are found in two locations. *"Are"* is found under "A" for *"are"* and also under "B" as part of the verb *"be,"* (be: *am/are, is, being, was/were, been*).

- **Plurals**
  Regular plural forms of nouns are not included, as they simply involve including a final –S or final –Z with the singular form. Irregular steno plurals and irregular English plurals are provided. Use N–KZ for *"incomes"* (avoids conflict with N–X for *"index"*). Use NOIPS (regularly formed steno plural) for *"notaries public"* (irregular English plural).

- **Phrases**
  Phrases are set in bold italics. Two or more words constitute a phrase. Geographic names are not phrases.

BRIEF ENCOUNTERS

- **Word Families**
  Identical-root "word families" are indented under the root heading where three or more entries occur, as in the family *"vigor, vigorous, vigorously."* In this context, a few entries may be out of strict alphabetical order.
  Prefixes such as "super" are not treated as a word family.

- **Extra Consonants**
  Extra consonants can be used to save one or more strokes. Include an –L with STROUS (*"industrious"*) for STROULS (*"industriously"*) to save a stroke adding the suffix LI (STROUS/LI).

- **Writing Conventions**
  A hyphen is used with vowelless entries to indicate the keyboard location of the consonant(s).
  B– (*"be"*) indicates an initial consonant on the left side of the keyboard.
  –RS (*"remain silent"*) indicates final consonants on the right side of the keyboard).
  N–FRGS (*"information"*) indicates initial and final consonants.
  A slash (/) indicates stroke separation, e.g., BUNL/–G for *"bundling"* (avoids conflict with BUJ for *"budge"*).

- **Multicharacter Combinations**
  i   –FPLT is written as –FMT for words ending in "ment," e.g., SPLAEFMT for *"displacement."*
  ii TKPW– is normally written as initial G–, except when designating DB–, e.g., DBAR for *"debar."*
  iii –PL is normally written as final –M, except when more phonetically logical, e.g., PURPL for *"purple"* and BRUPL for *"abruptly."*
  iv The asterisk is used as an apostrophe in some contractions. Use SH*ES for *"she's."*
  v   *ES is used for the suffix –EST, e.g., M*ES for *"domestic."*
  vi *T is used for the suffix –TH, e.g., WA*IT for *"one-eighth."*
  vii The following lesser-known prefixes and word beginnings are included in this dictionary:
  emb-, emp-, imb-, imm-, imp- = KB–, e.g., KBAK for *"impact."*
  ind- = SDPW–, e.g., SDPWRAOIBL for *"indescribable."*
  jb- = SKPWR–, e.g., JBOX (SKPWROX) for *"jury box."*
  jh- = SKWHR–, e.g., JHOUS (SKWHROUS) for *"jailhouse."*
  jl- = SKWHR–, e.g., JLAOIS (SKWHRAOIS) for *"generalize."*
  sy- = SKWR–, e.g., SYOER (SKWROER) for *"savior."*
  vb- = SPWR–, e.g., VBAOK (SPWRAOK) for *"overbook."*
  z- = S*, e.g., ZIRP (S*IRP) for *"zipper."*

viii The following lesser-known suffixes and word endings are included in this dictionary:
> -cal = –BLG, e.g., NURKL (NURBLG) for *"neurological."*
> -cher = –FRP, e.g., RECHR (REFRP) for *"researcher."*
> -ciousness = –RBS, e.g., VIRBS for *"viciousness."*
> -ism = –FM, e.g., SEFM for *"sexism."*
> -kle = –BLG, e.g., TAKL (TABLG) for *"tackle."*
> -kp = –PBG, e.g., HAOKP (HAOPBG) for *"hookup."*
> -mp = –FRP, e.g., HAMP (HAFRP) for *"hamper."*
> -nk = –FRPBG, e.g., FOENK (FOEFRPBG) for *"phone call."*
> -rv = –FRB, e.g., WERV (WEFRB) for *"Web server."*
> -tional = –LGS, e.g., FUNLGS for *"functional."*
> -tional = –BLGS, e.g., RUXL (RUBLGS) for *"instructional."*
> -v = *F, e.g., SIVL (S*IFL) for *"civil."*

TO STUDENTS . . .

This dictionary does not represent any particular theory. The majority of entries can be used with most common steno theories.

As a student, you will be constantly updating and improving your own dictionary—adding new words, deleting others, shortening the stroke(s) for an entry and thinking of new ways to write faster. The material in this reference work will inspire many new entries and shortcuts.

When adopting a new brief or phrase, practice until you can easily and automatically stroke it. Then gradually incorporate more briefs through repeated practice. Work on a few at a time until you can use them without hesitation.

The most effective way to use this dictionary is in conjunction with realtime writing. The beauty of realtime is that you know immediately if you have made an error or if a stroke you make has already been assigned to another word or phrase. Even if you do not write realtime, your speed-building and progress will be greatly enhanced by using this reference book.

TO THE PROSPECTIVE STUDENT . . .

This dictionary has been compiled to aid your passage through an extremely difficult course of study. There are many misconceptions regarding court reporting studies, some perpetuated by schools themselves. Irrespective of claims that a particular program can be completed in two short years, it is generally acknowledged that approximately four years of applied study, practice and speed-building are required to prepare the average student for the all-important CSR examination.

As you progress through the various stages from basic principles, through multiple voice, to the excruciatingly frustrating process of speed-building, you will find that an accurate and comprehensive dictionary becomes of increasing importance.

BRIEF ENCOUNTERS

EXCELLENCE ACHIEVED

The achievements of three extraordinary practitioners of machine shorthand are included here as a source of inspiration and as an example of what can be accomplished by coordinated human hands and mind.

- **Christine Olson, RPR, RMR, California CSR 2378**
  Christine started court reporting studies at age 20 and passed the CSR 18 months later. She holds Certificates of Proficiency (RPR) and Merit (RMR) and often reports complete trials without assistance. Among the high-profile trials she has reported on her own are the 1988-1989 "Night Stalker" case (People v. Richard Ramirez) and the 1992 Rodney King "beating" case (People v. Powell, et al.). She has also reported (50%) the 1984-1986 "Hillside Strangler" case (People v. Buono), the 1991 Charles Keating case (People v. Keating) and the 1995 O.J. Simpson murder trial (People v. Simpson). Christine makes extensive use of briefs.

- **Carrie A. Hartmann, RPR, Illinois CSR 084-004109**
  Carrie is included here because she has excelled in becoming a certified court reporter despite an overwhelming challenge–Carrie Hartmann is blind. Inspired by her skills as a pianist, she studied court reporting at Southern Illinois University, passed the CSR three years later and earned her RPR in 1997. Carrie has worked for court reporting agencies in Illinois and Florida, doing court and deposition work. Her guide dog Gemini accompanies her on all her assignments. Carrie uses a moderate amount of briefs.

- **Marge Teilhaber, BS, MA, RPR, CM, RDR, NJ CSR XI00856**
  Marge started court reporting (night) school in 1974. She passed the New Jersey CSR and the RPR in 1977, the Certificate of Merit in 1979 and the RDR in 1996.
  Throughout the 1980's, Marge suffered from arthritis, and in 1988 she broke both elbows in a roller skating accident. In 1989, she underwent surgery on both hands to repair extensor tendons. After months of treatment, she returned to work, only to find that she couldn't lift her fingers enough to stroke properly. She wore a device which used a rubber band to lift her ring finger. In 1992, she broke both femurs in a car accident. After months of physical therapy, she had surgery and used a walker for 11 months. In the meantime, her arthritis had worsened, leaving the fingers of both hands bent in opposite directions. She underwent two surgeries and now has artificial knuckles (silicone implant arthroplasties) in seven of the eight knuckle joints.
  She returned to the steno machine in 1995, developed her realtime skills, retook the RPR and resumed her career in 1997. Marge makes extensive use of briefs.

THE COURT REPORTER
by Robert H. Clark, CSR No. 83
Historian - California Court Reporters Association
Historian-Librarian - National Court Reporters Association

If one has occasion to step into any courtroom that is in session, he will see in full working order what is probably in many respects the most important portion of the judicial system. Here he may see the machinery of law in active operation.

There is the dignified judge seated on the bench, calmly hearing the testimony and dispassionately weighing it in mind; the clerk, with his documents spread around him; the bailiff, ready to preserve order and decorum appropriate to the halls of justice; the witness on the stand, timid, bold or indifferent, volubly pouring forth his story at the request of his counsel, or evasively avoiding a reply to an appraising attorney; the counsel on both sides, alert to take advantage of every opportunity, skillfully leading on their own witnesses, or sharply cross-examining those on the other side; the array of attorneys within the bar, watching the proceedings; the jury and crowd of spectators following with interest each detail of the trial. All of these are familiar sights to those who have occasion to visit courtrooms.

But there is still another actor in this diversified drama of right and wrong, of law and equity, of claim and counter-claim. A little to one side you will see the court reporter, with use of pen or shorthand machine, following each spoken word with swift and noiseless movements, recording impartially the words of wisdom, wit and folly, which follow each other in rapid succession.

Witnesses come and go; attorneys question and cross-question, object and argue; the court quietly announces his rulings; one case is ended and another begins, and through it all the court reporter writes, writes and writes, unceasingly and with unslackened speed.

Few of those who look upon the court reporter realize that they are beholding as near an approach to a miracle as unaided human hands and brain have thus far accomplished. There are many who classify a Certified Shorthand Reporter as nothing more than a glorified stenographer. Comparing an eight-year-old child thumping on a toy piano with a concert pianist would have as much credence.

Those unfamiliar with the duties of a court reporter say the pay is high because the reporter is actually working in court only six hours a day. True, but in those six hours very often there is no rest for the court reporter; and if we take the trouble to perform a single act of multiplication, we find those flying fingers have recorded in that short day of apparently easy work, a total of at least 50,000 words. The fabled labors of Hercules sink into insignificance when compared to what a court reporter accomplishes. Every day the stenographer sets down an amount of matter equal to a respectably sized novel.

BRIEF ENCOUNTERS

DICTIONARY

A

a . . . . A
abandon
    abandon. . . . . BAUN
    abandons . . . . BAUNZ
    abandoning . . . . BAUNG
    abandoned . . . . BAUND
abandonment . . . . BAUMT
abbreviate
    abbreviate . . . . BRAOEVT
    abbreviates. . . . . BRAOEVTS
    abbreviating . . . . BRAOEVGT, BRAOEVG
    abbreviated . . . . BRAOEVTD
abbreviation . . . . BRAOEVGS, BRAOEFGS, BREFGS,
                                                                                       BREVGS
abdomen . . . . ABD
abdominal. . . . . ABL, ABLD
abduct
    abduct. . . . . DBUK
    abducts . . . . DBUKZ
    abducting . . . . DBUK/-G
    abducted . . . . DBUKD
abduction. . . . . DBUX
aberrance . . . . BRANS
aberrancy . . . . BRANSZ
aberrant . . . . BRANT
aberration. . . . . BERGS, BRANGS

A

abet
- abet . . . . BOIT
- abets . . . . BOITS
- abetting . . . . BOIGT
- abetted . . . . BOITD

abet
- abetment . . . . BOIMT
- abetter . . . . BOIRT
- abettor . . . . BROIT

abeyance . . . . BAENS

abhor
- abhor . . . . HOER
- abhors . . . . HOERS
- abhorring . . . . HOERG
- abhorred . . . . HOERD

abhor
- abhorrence . . . . HOERNS, HORNZ
- abhorrent . . . . HOERNT, HORNT
- abhorrently . . . . HOERNLT, HORNL

abide
- abide . . . . BAOID
- abides . . . . BAOIDZ
- abiding . . . . BAOIGD
- abided / abode . . . . BAOID/-D / AI/BOED

ability . . . . ABLT
able . . . . AIBL

abnormal
- abnormal . . . . BORL
- abnormalcy . . . . BORLS
- abnormally . . . . BOERL
- abnormality . . . . BORLT

aboard
- aboard . . . . BAORD
- *aboard the* . . . . BAORTD
- *aboard these* . . . . BAORDZ

abolish
- abolish . . . . BLORB
- abolishes . . . . BLORBS
- abolishing . . . . BLORBG
- abolished . . . . BLORBD

abolishment . . . . BLOMT
abomination . . . . BOMGS

abort
- abort . . . . BORT
- aborts . . . . BORTS

BRIEF ENCOUNTERS   A

aborting . . . . BORGT
aborted . . . . BORTD
abortion . . . . BORGS
abortion rights . . . . BRORTS
about
   about . . . . –B
   about an hour . . . . BHOUR
   about half . . . . BHAF
   about half of the . . . . BHAFT
   about half of them . . . . BHAFM
   about half of these . . . . BHAFZ
   about half of those . . . . BHAFS
   about how far . . . . BOUF
   about how fast . . . . BOUFT
   about how large . . . . BOURJ
   about how late . . . . BOULT
   about how long . . . . BOUNG
   about how many . . . . BOUM
   about how many days . . . . BOUMD
   about how many times . . . . BOUMT
   about how much . . . . BOUFP
   about how often . . . . BOUFN
   about how wide . . . . BOID
   about the . . . . –BT
   about the same . . . . BAEM
   about the same time . . . . BAEMT
   about the same time as . . . . BAEMTS
   about these . . . . –BZ
   about those . . . . –BS
   about whom . . . . BHOM
   about whom the . . . . BHOMT
above
   above . . . . BOV
   above the . . . . BOVT
   above them . . . . BOVM, BOFM
   above these . . . . BOVZ
   above those . . . . BOVS
abrasion . . . . BRAEGS
abridge
   abridge . . . . BRAIJ
   abridges . . . . BRAIJS
   abridging . . . . BRAIJ/–G
   abridged . . . . BRAIJD
abridgement . . . . BRAIMT, BRIMT
abroad . . . . BRAOD

A   BRIEF ENCOUNTERS

abrogate
- abrogate . . . . ROEGT
- abrogates . . . . ROEGTS, ROEGZ
- abrogating . . . . ROEGT/-G, ROEG/-G
- abrogated . . . . ROEGTD

abrogation . . . . ROEGS

abrupt
- abrupt . . . . BRUPT
- abruptly . . . . BRUPLT, BRUPL
- abruptness . . . . BRUNS

abscess . . . . ABZ
absence . . . . ABS
absent . . . . ABT

absolute
- absolute . . . . SLU
- absolutely . . . . SLUL
- *absolutely certain* . . . . SLURN
- *absolutely not* . . . . SLUNT
- *absolutely positive* . . . . SLUP
- *absolutely sure* . . . . SLAOUR
- absoluteness . . . . SLUNS

absolutism . . . . SLUFM

absorb
- absorb . . . . SORB
- absorbs . . . . SORBS
- absorbing . . . . SORBG
- absorbed . . . . SORBD

absorbent . . . . SORNT
absorption . . . . SORPGS
abstinence . . . . STIBS, AB/STINS
abstinent . . . . STIBT, AB/STINT
absurd . . . . S*URD
absurdity . . . . SURT
abundance . . . . BAUNS
abundant . . . . BAUNT
abundantly . . . . BAUNL

abuse
- abuse . . . . BAOUS
- abuses . . . . BAOUFS, BAOUSZ
- abusing . . . . BAOUFG
- abused . . . . BAOUFD

abuser . . . . BAOURS

abusive
- abusive . . . . BAOUV
- abusively . . . . BAOUVL

BRIEF ENCOUNTERS A

abusiveness . . . . BAOUVNS
abysmal . . . . ABS/MAL
academia. . . . . KMAOE, DWAOEM
academic . . . . KMEK, KMAEK, DWEM
academically. . . . . KMEKL, DW*EL
academy . . . . KME, DWAD
accelerate
    accelerate . . . . SLERT
    accelerates . . . . SLERTS
    accelerating . . . . SLERGT, SLERG
    accelerated . . . . SLERTD
acceleration. . . . . SLERGS
accelerator . . . . SLOR
accent
    accent . . . . SKWANT
    accents. . . . . SKWANTS
    accenting . . . . SKWANGT
    accented. . . . . SKWANTD
accept
    accept . . . . SEP
    accepts. . . . . SEPS
    accepting . . . . SEPG
    accepted. . . . . SEPD
accept
    acceptability . . . . SEBLT
    acceptable. . . . . SEBL
    acceptably . . . . SAOEBL
    acceptance . . . . SEPZ
access
    access. . . . . KRES, KREF
    accesses. . . . . KREFS
    accessing . . . . KREFG
    accessed. . . . . KREFD
access
    accessibility . . . . KREFBLT
    accessible . . . . KREFBL
    accessory . . . . KRERS, SES/RI
accident
    accident. . . . . SDEN
    accidental. . . . . SDENL
    accidentally. . . . . SDAENL
    accident take place . . . . SDAIP, SDAIPS
    accident took place . . . . SDAOPS
accident happen
    accident happen . . . . SDAP

A   BRIEF ENCOUNTERS

accident happens . . . . SDAPS
accident happening . . . . SDAPG
accident happened . . . . SDAPD
accident occur
    accident occur . . . . SDUR
    accident occurs . . . . SDURS
    accident occurring . . . . SDURG
    accident occurred . . . . SDURD
acclaim
    acclaim . . . . KLAEM
    acclaims . . . . KLAEMS
    acclaiming . . . . KLAEMG
    acclaimed . . . . KLAEMD
acclamation . . . . KLAEMGS
accolade . . . . KLAID
accommodate
    accommodate . . . . KOMT
    accommodates . . . . KOMTS
    accommodating . . . . KOMGT
    accommodated . . . . KOMTD
accommodation . . . . KOMGS, KOJ
accompaniment . . . . KPOIMT, KOEMT
accompany
    accompany . . . . KPOIN, AI/KPAEN
    accompanies . . . . KPOINS, AI/KPAENS
    accompanying . . . . KPOING, KPAENG
    accompanied . . . . KPOIND, KPAEND
accomplice . . . . KPLIS
accomplish
    accomplish . . . . PLIRB
    accomplishes . . . . PLIRBS
    accomplishing . . . . PLIRBG
    accomplished . . . . PLIRBD
accomplishment . . . . PLIRBT, PLIMT
accord
    accord . . . . KWOR
    accords . . . . KWORS
    according . . . . KWORG
    accorded . . . . KWORD
according to
    according to . . . . KRORG, KORGT, KWORGT
    according to the . . . . KRORGT
    according to them . . . . KRORM
    according to these . . . . KORGZ
    according to those . . . . KORGS

ILLEGAL TO PHOTOCOPY   © 1997 White-Boucke Publishing.

account
    account . . . . K-T
    accounts. . . . . K-TS
    accounting . . . . K-GT
    accounted. . . . . K-TD
account
    accountability . . . . K-BLT
    accountable. . . . . K*BL, KABL
    accountant. . . . . KANT
    account payable. . . . . KWAP
    accounts payable . . . . KWAPS
accoutrement. . . . . KAOUMT
accredit
    accredit . . . . KRAED
    accredits . . . . KRAEDZ
    accrediting . . . . KRAEGD
    accredited. . . . . KRAETD
accreditation. . . . . KRA*EGS
accretion . . . . KRAOEGS
accrual . . . . KRUL
accrue
    accrue . . . . KRU
    accrues . . . . KRUS
    accruing . . . . KRU/-G
    accrued. . . . . KRU/-D
accruement. . . . . KR*UMT, KRAO*UMT
accumulate
    accumulate . . . . KAOUM
    accumulates . . . . KAOUMS
    accumulating. . . . . KAOUMG
    accumulated . . . . KAOUMD
accumulation. . . . . KAOUMGS, KAOUJ
accumulative . . . . KAOUV
accumulatively . . . . KAOUVL
accuracy . . . . KRATS
accurate
    accurate. . . . . KRAT
    accurately. . . . . KRAEL
    accurateness . . . . KRANS
    accurate to say . . . . -KTS
    accurate to state. . . . . -KT
accusation. . . . . KAOUGS
accusatorial. . . . . KAOURTS, KAOUS/TORL
accuse
    accuse. . . . . KAOUS

A   BRIEF ENCOUNTERS

accuses	KAOUFS, KAOUSZ
accusing	KAOUFG
accused	KAOUFD
accustom	
accustom	KA*UFM
accustoms	KAUFMS
accustoming	KAUFMG
accustomed	KAUFMD
achievable	KHAOEVBL
achieve	
achieve	KHAOEV
achieves	KHAOEVS
achieving	KHAOEVG
achieved	KHAOEVD
achiever	KHAOEVR
acid	
acid	SD*ID, SID
acidic	SDIK, SIGD
acidity	SDIT, SITD
acknowledge	
acknowledge	NAOJ
acknowledges	NAOJS
acknowledging	NAOJ/-G
acknowledged	NAOJD
acknowledgement	NAOMT
acoustic	
acoustic	KAO*US
acoustical	KAOUFL
acoustically	KAOEFL
acquaint	
acquaint	KWAIN
acquaints	KWAINS
acquainting	KWAING
acquainted	KWAIND
acquaintance	KWAENS, KWAINZ
acquaintanceship	KWHAINS, KWHAENS, KWAIP
acquiesce	
acquiesce	KWAOEF
acquiesces	KWAOEFZ
acquiescing	KWAOEFG
acquiesced	KWAOEFD
acquiescence	KWAOEFS
acquiescent	KWAOEFT
acquire	
acquire	KWAOIR

ILLEGAL TO PHOTOCOPY   8   © 1997 White-Boucke Publishing.

BRIEF ENCOUNTERS   A

acquires	KWAOIRS
acquiring	KWAIORG
acquired	KWAOIRD
acquisition	KWIGS, KWAOIRGS

acquit
- acquit . . . KWI
- acquits . . . KWIS
- acquitting . . . KWIG
- acquitted . . . KWI/-D

acquittal . . . KW-L
acre . . . AEK

across
- across . . . KROS, KROF
- *across the* . . . KROFT
- *across them* . . . KROFM
- *across these* . . . KROFZ

act
- act . . . AK
- acts . . . AKZ
- acting . . . AK/-G
- acted . . . AKD

action . . . AX

activate
- activate . . . TWAET
- activates . . . TWAETS
- activating . . . TWAEGT
- activated . . . TWAETD

activation . . . TWAEGS
activator . . . TWAERT

active
- active . . . TIF, TIV
- actively . . . TIFL, TIVL
- activeness . . . TIFNS, TIVNS

activism . . . TIFM, TIVM
activity . . . TIFT, TIVT
actor . . . AORK
acts and omissions . . . AOM

actual
- actual . . . TWAL
- actuality . . . TWALT
- actually . . . TWAEL

actuarial . . . KHAERL, KHAIRL
actuary . . . KHAER

actuate
- actuate . . . TWAIT, KHAIT

A

actuates	TWAITS, KHAITS
actuating	TWAIGT, KHAIGT
actuated	TWAITD, KHAITD
actuation	TWA*IGS, KHAIGS, TWA*EGS
actuator	TWAIRT
acuity	KWAO*UT
acupressure	KWERB
acupuncture	KWAOUP
acupuncture needle	KWAOUPD
acupuncturist	KWAOUPT

acute
acute	KWAOUT
acutely	KWAOULT
acuteness	KWAOUNS

adamant	DMANT, AD/MANT
adamantly	DMANL, AD/MANLT

adapt
adapt	DAPT
adapts	DAPTS
adapting	DAPGT
adapted	DAPTD

adapt
adaptation	DAPGS
adapter	DRAPT
adaptive	DAVPT
adaptor	DARPT

addenda	DWA
addendum	DWUM

addict
addict	DIKT
addicts	DIKTS, DIKZ
addicting	DIKT/-G
addicted	DIKTD

addiction	DIX
addictive	DIVT

addition
addition	DIGS
additional	DIRBL
additionally	DAOERBL

additive	DAVD

address
address	DRAES
addresses	DRAEFS, DRAESZ
addressing	DRAEFG, DRAEG
addressed	DRAEFD

address
    addressable . . . . DRAEBL
    addressee . . . . DRAOER
    addressor . . . . DRAER
adduct . . . .
    adduct . . . . DAUK
    adducts . . . . DAUKZ
    adducting . . . . DAUK/-G
    adducted . . . . DAUKD
adenoid . . . . DWOI
adept . . . . DAEPT, DWEPT
adequacy . . . . KWATS
adequate . . . . KWAT
adequateness . . . . KWANS
adhere
    adhere . . . . DHAOER, HAO*ER
    adheres . . . . DHAOERS, HAOERZ
    adhering . . . . DHAOERG, HAOERG
    adhered . . . . DHAOERD, HAOERD
adherence . . . . HAOERPBS
adherent . . . . HAOERNT
adhesion . . . . HAOEGS
adhesive
    adhesive . . . . DHAOEV
    adhesively . . . . DHAOEVL
    adhesiveness . . . . DHAOEVNS
ad hoc . . . . DHOK, HAUKD
adjacent . . . . JAIS
adjacent to . . . . JAIFT
adjourn
    adjourn . . . . JOURN
    adjourns . . . . JOURNS
    adjourning . . . . JOURNG
    adjourned . . . . JOURND
adjournment . . . . JOURMT, JAOURMT
adjudicate
    adjudicate . . . . JUD
    adjudicates . . . . JUDZ
    adjudicating . . . . JUGD
    adjudicated . . . . JUD/-D
adjudication . . . . JUX
adjudicative . . . . JUVD
adjunct . . . . JAUNG
adjust
    adjust . . . . JAUF

adjusts	JAUFS
adjusting	JAUFG
adjusted	JAUFD
adjust	
adjustable	JAUFL, JAUFBL
adjustable rate	JAUFLT
adjustable rate mortgage	JAUMT
adjuster	JAUFR
adjustment	JAUFMT, JUFMT
adjuvant	JAOUVT
administer	
administer	M–R
administers	M–RS
administering	M–RG
administered	M–RD
administrate	
administrate	M–RT, MR–T
administrates	M–RTS, MR–TS
administrating	M–RGT, M–RG, MR–GT, MR–G
administrated	M–RTD, MR–TD
administration	M–RGS, MR–GS
administrative	MIV
administratively	MIVL
administrator	MR–R
administrators	MR–RZ
administratrix	MRIX
admissibility	MIFLT
admissible	MIFL
admissibleness	MIFNS
admission	M*IGS, MOIGS, DMIGS
admit	
admit	MIT, DMIT
admits	MITS, DMITS
admitting	MIT/–G, DMIGT
admitted	MITD, DMITD
admittance	MIT/TANS, DMINT, DMINTS
admonish	
admonish	MORB
admonishes	MORBS
admonishing	MORBG
admonished	MORBD
admonishment	MORBT, MORMT
admonition	MOGS
adolescence	DLENS
adolescent	DLENT

BRIEF ENCOUNTERS A

adopt
    adopt..DOPT
    adopts..DOPTS
    adopting..DOPGT
    adopted...DOPTD
adoptive...DOVPT, DOP/TIV
adorable...DOERBL
adorably...DOER/BLI
adoration..DOERGS
adore
    adore..DOER
    adores...DOERS
    adoring..DOERG
    adored...DOERD
adorer...DROER
adrenal
    adrenal..DRAOEN, DRAOENL
    Adrenalin..DREN
    adrenaline.......................................DRENL
adroit
    adroit...DROIT
    adroitly...DROIL, DROILT
    adroitness.......................................DROINS
adult
    adult..DULT
    adulterer..DURLT
    adultery...DRULT
ad valorem...VOERM
advance
    advance..VANS, DWANS
    advances...VANSZ, DWANSZ
    advancing..VANS/-G, DWANG
    advanced...VANS/-D, DWAND
advancement..VAMT, DWAMT
advancer...DWARN
advantage
    advantage..VANG, DWAJ
    advantageous.....................................DWAIJ
    advantageously...................................DWAIL
    advantageousness.................................DWAINS
advent...DWENT
adventure
    adventure..DWUR
    adventures.......................................DWURS
    adventuring......................................DWURG

A BRIEF ENCOUNTERS

adventured	DWURD
adventurer	DWRUR
adventuresome	DWURM
adventurous	DWURZ
adventurousness	DWURNS, DWURNZ
adverb	DWERB
adverbial	DWERBL
adversarial	DWARL
adversary	DWAIR

adverse

adverse	DWER, DWERZ
adversely	DW-RL, DWERL
adverse witness	DWIT
adversity	DW-RT

advertise

advertise	TIZ
advertises	TIFS
advertising	TIFG
advertised	TIFD
advertisement	TIFMT
advice	VIS
advisability	VIBLT
advisable	VIBL

advise

advise	VIZ
advises	VIFS
advising	VIFG
advised	VIFD
advisor	VAOIFR
advocacy	DWOKS

advocate

advocate	VOEK, DWOEK
advocates	VOEKZ, DWOEKZ
advocating	VOEK/-G, DWOEK/-G, DWOEG
advocated	VOEKD, DWOEKD
advocation	VOEX, DWOEX
aerial	A*ERL
aerobic	ROERK
aerodrome	AER/DROEM
aerodynamic	AER/DAM
aeronaut	AER/NAUT
aeronautic	AER/NAUK
aerosol	AERZ
aerospace	AERP
affability	AFBLT

A

affable	AFBL
affably	AEFBL
affair	AIFR
affect	
affect	FAEK
affects	FAEKS
affecting	FAEK/-G, FAEG
affected	FAEKD
affection	AFX
affiant	WAOINT
affidavit	AFD
affiliate	
affiliate	FILT
affiliates	FILTS
affiliating	FILGT
affiliated	FILTD
affiliation	FILGS
affirm	
affirm	AFRM
affirms	AFRMS
affirming	AFRMG
affirmed	AFRMD
affirmation	AFRMGS, AF/MAIGS
affirmative	
affirmative	FRIF
affirmative action	FRIFX, FRIFGS
affirmatively	FRIFL
afford	
afford	FAURD
affords	FAURDZ
affording	FAURGD
afforded	FAURD/-D
affordability	FAURBLT
affordable	FAURBL
affront	
affront	AFRNT, FRAONT
affronts	AFRNTS, FRAONTS
affronting	AFRNGT, AFRNG, FRAONGT, FRAONG
affronted	AFRNTD, FRAONTD
aforethought	AFRT
afraid	FRAID
Africa	
Africa	AFRK
African	AFN
African-American	AEFM

after
- after . . . . AF
- *after all* . . . . AFRL
- *after all the* . . . . AFRLT
- *after all these* . . . . AFRLZ
- *after all those* . . . . AFRLS
- afternoon . . . . AFRN
- *after the* . . . . AFT
- *after them* . . . . AFM
- *after these* . . . . AFZ
- *after those* . . . . AFS
- afterward . . . . AFRD
- afterword . . . . AOFRD

again . . . . GEN
against . . . . GENS
agency . . . . AGS
agenda . . . . JEND
agent . . . . J–
agglomerate
- agglomerate . . . . GLOMT
- agglomerates . . . . GLOMTS
- agglomerating . . . . GLOMGT, GLOMG
- agglomerated . . . . GLOMTD

agglomeration . . . . GLOMGS, GLOJ
aggravate
- aggravate . . . . GRAEVT
- aggravates . . . . GRAEVS, GRAEVTS
- aggravating . . . . GRAEVG, GRAEVGT
- aggravated . . . . GRAEVD, GRAEVTD

aggravation . . . . GRAEVGS
aggregate . . . . AGT, AG/GAT
aggression . . . . GREGS
aggressive
- aggressive . . . . GREV
- aggressively . . . . GREVL
- aggressiveness . . . . GREVNS

aggressor . . . . GRER
agnostic . . . . GAUFT
ago . . . . AG
agree
- agree . . . . GRE
- agrees . . . . GRES
- agreeing . . . . GREG
- agreed . . . . GRED

BRIEF ENCOUNTERS A

agree
- agreeability .... GREBLT
- agreeable .... GREBL
- agreeably .... GRAOEBL
- agreement .... GREMT

agriculture. .... A*G, AIG
ah .... AU
ahead
- ahead. .... HAID
- *ahead of* .... HAIF, HAEF
- *ahead of the*. .... HAIFT, HAEFT
- *ahead of them*. .... HAIFM, HAEFM
- *ahead of these* .... HAIFZ, HAEFZ
- *ahead of those* .... HAIFS, HAEFS

ahold. .... HAOLD
aid and abet
- ***aid and abet***. .... AIB
- ***aids and abets*** .... AIBS
- ***aiding and abetting*** .... AIB/-G
- ***aided and abetted***. .... AIBD

aider and abettor .... AIBT
aiders and abettors. .... AIBTS
AIDS. .... A*IDZ
ailment. .... AIMT
ain't. .... AINT
air
- *air base*. .... AIRB
- aircraft .... AIRK
- airfare. .... AEFR
- airfield. .... AIFLD
- *air force base* .... AIFB
- airline .... AIRL
- *airline pilot*. .... AIRLT
- *air mail*. .... AIRM
- airplane .... AIRP
- airport. .... AIRPT
- *air traffic control* .... FROL
- *air traffic controller*. .... FRORL

air-condition
- air-condition. .... AIRN
- air-conditions. .... AIRNS
- air-conditioning. .... AIRN/-G
- air-conditioned. .... AIRND

air conditioner .... RAIRN
air conditioning .... A*IRNG

© 1997 White-Boucke Publishing.   ILLEGAL TO PHOTOCOPY

A — BRIEF ENCOUNTERS

aisle	YAOIL
Alabama	A*L
alarm	
alarm	LARM
alarms	LARMS
alarming	LARMG
alarmed	LARMD
alarmist	LARMT
Alaska	A*K
album	BLUM, BLAUM
alcohol	
alcohol	KHOL
alcohol and drug	KHAND
alcohol and drugs	KHANDZ
alcoholic	KHOK
alcoholic beverage	KHOB
Alcoholics Anonymous	KHON
alcoholism	KHOFM, KHOM
alcohol or drug	KHORLD
alcohol or drugs	KHORLDZ
alcohol rehabilitation	KHOLGS
alcohol treatment	KHOMT
alert	
alert	LAERT
alerts	LAERTS
alerting	LAERGT
alerted	LAERTD
alfalfa	AL/FAFL
algae	AEG
algebra	
algebra	BRALG, ALG/BRA
algebraic	BRAELG
algebraically	ALG/KLI
Algeria	JAER
Algerian	JAERN
algorithm	GRIFM, ALG/RIFM
alias	AILZ
alibi	AEB
alien	YAEL
alienate	
alienate	YENT
alienates	YENTS
alienating	YENGT, YENG
alienated	YENTD
alienation	YENGS

BRIEF ENCOUNTERS   A

alignment	LAOIMT
alike	LOIK
alimony	LOM
alive	LOIV
all	
all	AUL
all of a sudden	AUFLD
all of the	AUFLT
all of them	AUFM
all of these	AUFLZ
all of those	AUFLS
all right	L-RT
all right, sir	L-RTS
all the	AULT
all these	AULZ
all the while	TWAOIL
all those	AULS
allegation	AELGS
allege	
allege	ALG
alleges	ALGS
alleging	ALG/-G, AELG
alleged	ALGD
alleger	AERLG
allegiance	LAOEJ
allergic	LERJ
allergic to	LERJT
allergy	LAOERJ, L-RJ
alleviate	
alleviate	LAOEVT
alleviates	LAOEVTS
alleviating	LAOEVGT
alleviated	LAOEVTD
alleviation	LAOEVGS
alleviator	LAOEVRT
alley	AEL
alliance	LAOINZ
allocable	LAEBL, AL/KABL
allocate	
allocate	LAET
allocates	LAETS
allocating	LAEGT
allocated	LAETD
allocation	LA*EGS, AL/KAIGS
allocution	KWAOUGS

A — BRIEF ENCOUNTERS

allow
    allow . . . . LOU
    allows . . . . LOUZ
    allowing . . . . LOUG
    allowed . . . . LOU/-D, LO*UD
alluvial . . . . LAOUVL
almond . . . . AUMD
almost . . . . L-M
alone . . . . LAON
along
    along . . . . LAONG
    alongside . . . . LAONGS
    along the . . . . LAONGT
    along these . . . . LAONGZ
a lot
    a lot of . . . . LAOF
    a lot of the . . . . LAOFT
    a lot of them . . . . LAOFM
    a lot of these . . . . LAOFZ
    a lot of those . . . . LAOFS
alphabet
    alphabet . . . . AFL
    alphabetical . . . . AEFL
    alphabetically . . . . AOEFL
alphabetize
    alphabetize . . . . AFLT
    alphabetizes . . . . AFLTS
    alphabetizing . . . . AFLGT, AFLG
    alphabetized . . . . AFLTD
alphanumeric . . . . FAOURK
alphanumerically . . . . FAOURL
already . . . . L-R
also . . . . L-S
altar . . . . A*LT
alter
    alter . . . . ALT
    alters . . . . ALTS
    altering . . . . ALGT
    altered . . . . ALTD
alteration . . . . ALT/RAIGS
alternate
    alternate . . . . NA*ET, ALT/NAIT
    alternates . . . . NAETS, ALT/NAITS
    alternating . . . . NAET/-G, ALT/NAIGT
    alternated . . . . NAETD, ALT/NAITD

alternating current	TURNT
alternation	NA*EGS, ALT/NAEGS
alternative	TERN
alternatively	TERNL

although
    although . . . . AOL
    although the . . . . AOLT
    although these . . . . AOLZ
    although those . . . . AOLS
altitude . . . . TAO*UD, TWAOUD
altogether . . . . L-GT
aluminum . . . . LUM
always . . . . AUZ
Alzheimer's . . . . ALZ
Alzheimer's disease . . . . ALDZ
a.m. . . . . A*M
amalgamate
    amalgamate . . . . MAUG
    amalgamates . . . . MAUGZ
    amalgamating . . . . MAUG/-G
    amalgamated . . . . MAUGD
amalgamation . . . . MAUGS
amaze
    amaze . . . . MAES
    amazes . . . . MAEFS, MAESZ
    amazing . . . . MAEFG
    amazed . . . . MAEFD
amazement . . . . MAEFMT
ambassador . . . . KBOR
amber light . . . . BERLT
ambiance . . . . KBAUNS
ambience . . . . KBINS
ambient . . . . KBINT
ambiguity . . . . MIGT
ambiguous
    ambiguous . . . . MIG
    ambiguously . . . . MILG
    ambiguousness . . . . MIGZ
ambition . . . . BIGS
ambitious . . . . BIRB
ambitiously . . . . BIRBL
ambivalence . . . . BIVL
ambivalent . . . . BIVLT
ambulance . . . . BLANS
ambulant . . . . BLANT

A — BRIEF ENCOUNTERS

ambulation .... BLAIGS
ameliorate
    ameliorate .... MAOELT
    ameliorates .... MAOELTS
    ameliorating .... MAOELGT, MAOELG
    ameliorated .... MAOELTD
amelioration .... MAOELGS
amenable .... MAOEN/-BL
amend
    amend .... AMD
    amends .... AMDZ
    amending .... AMGD
    amended .... AMD/-D
amendment .... AEMT
America
    America .... MERK
    American .... MERN
    American Sign Language .... MERNL
    Americans with Disabilities Act .... MERND
amicus curiae .... MAOEKS
amiable .... YAIBL
ammunition .... NAOUGS
among
    among .... MONG
    among other things .... MOINGS
    among the .... MONGT
    among these .... MONGZ
    among those .... MONGS
amorphous .... MOR/FOUS
amortization .... MORT/SAIGS, AM/TAOIGS
amortize
    amortize .... AM/TAOIZ
    amortizes .... AM/TAOIFS, AM/TAOISZ
    amortizing .... AM/TAOIFG
    amortized .... AM/TAOIFD
amortizement .... TAOIFMT
amount
    amount .... AMT
    amounts .... AMTS
    amounting .... AMGT, AMG
    amounted .... AMTD
amp .... AFRP
ampere .... AEFRP
amphetamine .... FET, FA*ET
amphibian .... FIB/YAN

BRIEF ENCOUNTERS　　　　　　　　　　　　　　　A

ample	AUFRP
amplest	AUFRPT
amply	AUFRPL
amuse	
amuse	MAOUS
amuses	MAOUFS, MAOUSZ
amusing	MAOUFG
amused	MAOUFD
amusement	MAOUFMT
an	AN, AO
anal	AINL
analogies	NALGZ
analogous	GOUS, ANL/GUS, NAL/GUS
analogy	NALG
analyses	NAOELZ
analysis	NALZ, ANL/SIS
analyst	NALTS
analytical	NALT, ANL/LIL
analytically	ANL/LAOEL
analyze	
analyze	NALS
analyzes	NALSZ
analyzing	NALS/-G, NA*LG
analyzed	NALD
analyzer	LAOIRZ
anatomical	NAEMG
anatomy	NAEMT, NAT/M*I
anchor	
anchor	KHOR
anchors	KHORS
anchoring	KHORG
anchored	KHOR/-D
ancient	AINGS
ancillary	SLAIR
and	
and	AND
and a half	NAF
and a quarter	NART
and so forth	SO*RT
and so on and so forth	SO*RNT, SO*RT/SO*RT
and the	ANTD
and these	ANDZ
androgenous	DROJS
androgyny	DROJ
anecdotal	NEK/DOEL

© 1997 White-Boucke Publishing.　　　ILLEGAL TO PHOTOCOPY

anecdote	NEK/DOET
anemia	NOIM
anemic	NO*IK
anesthesia	THAOERB, AEN
anesthesiologist	OELT, THOELT, AEN/YOLT
anesthesiology	OELG, THOELG, AEN/YOLG
anesthetic	THET, AEN/TIK
anesthetist	TH*ES, AEN/T*IS
aneurysm	NURM, AN/RIFM

anger
- anger . . . AING
- angers . . . AINGZ
- angering . . . AING/-G
- angered . . . AINGD

angle
- angle . . . AENL
- angles . . . AENLS
- angling . . . AENLG
- angled . . . AENLD

angrier	RAIRNG
angrier than	RAIRNGT
angry	AIRNG
angstrom	GROM

anguish
- anguish . . . GIRB
- anguishes . . . GIRBS
- anguishing . . . GIRBG
- anguished . . . GIRBD

animosity	MAUS
ankle	AINK
annals	ANLS

annihilate
- annihilate . . . ANLT, NAOIL
- annihilates . . . ANLTS, NAOILS
- annihilating . . . ANLGT, NAOILG
- annihilated . . . ANLTD, NAOILD

annihilation	ANLGS, NAOILGS
annihilator	NAOIRL
anniversary	NAEFRB

announce
- announce . . . NOUNS
- announces . . . NOUFS, NOUNSZ
- announcing . . . NOUFG
- announced . . . NOUFD

announcement	NOUMT

announcer	NOURN
annoy	
annoy	NOI
annoys	NOIS
annoying	NOIG
annoyed	NOI/-D, NO*ID
annoyance	NOINS
annual	YUL
annually	YOIL
annuity	NAOUT
annul	
annul	N*UL
annuls	NULS
annulling	NULG
annulled	NULD
annulment	N*UMT
anoint	
anoint	NOINT
anoints	NOINTS
anointing	NOINGT, NOING
anointed	NOINTD
anomalies	NOM/LIZ
anomalous	NOM/LOUS
anomaly	NOM/LI
anonymity	NIMT, NON/NIMT
anonymous	NOUZ, NON/MOUS
anonymously	NOULS, NOULZ
anorexia	NAORX
another	AOT
another's	AOTS
answer	
answer	ANS
answers	AENS, ANSZ
answering	AENG
answered	AEND
answer	
answering machine	SN-RB
answering service	SNEFRB
answer phone	SNOEN
answer the question	NERB
answer the questions	NERBS
antagonism	TAEFM, GAOIFM
antagonist	
antagonist	TAEFT, GAOIFT
antagonistic	TAEFK, GAOIK, GIK

antagonistically	GAOIFL
antagonize	
antagonize	TAEG, GAOIF
antagonizes	TAEGS, GAOIFS
antagonizing	TAEG/-G, GAOIFG
antagonized	TAEGD, GAOIFD
Antarctica	TARKT
anterior	AOR
anteriorly	AORL
Anthony	THOIN
anthropological	POJ
anthropologist	POLT
anthropology	POLG
anticipate	
anticipate	AEP
anticipates	AEPS
anticipating	AEPG
anticipated	AEPD
anticipation	AEPGS
anticipatory	AEPT
anus	AIN
anxiety	ZAOI
anxious	ZOUS, ANGS
any	
any	NI
any further questions	NIRGS
any good	NIGD
anyhow	NO*U
anymore	NIM
any of	NIF
any of them	NIFM
any of these	NIFZ
any of those	NIFS
anyplace	NAIP
anytime	NIT
anyway	NAI
any way	NI/WAI
anywhere	NIR
anywhere else	NIRLS
anybody	
anybody	NIB
anybody else	NIJ, NIBL
anybody else's	NIJS, NIBLSZ, NIBLS
anyone	
anyone	NIN

BRIEF ENCOUNTERS — A

anyone else	NINL
anyone else's	NINLS
anything	
anything	NIG
anything else	NILGS, NELS
anything further	NIRT
anything like that	NAT/NAT
anything like this	NIS/NIS
anything unusual	THURB
anything unusually	THURBL
aorta	AORT
apart	PAURT
apartment	PARMT
apathetic	
apathetic	AP/THEK
apathetical	AP/THEL
apathetically	AP/THAOEL
apathy	AP/THAOE
apex	AEPX
apologetic	JAOIK
apologize	
apologize	JAOIZ, JAOIS
apologizes	JAOIFS, JAOISZ
apologizing	JAOIFG
apologized	JAOIFD
apology	JAOE
appall	
appall	PAUL
appalls	PAULS
appalling	PAULG
appalled	PAULD
apparatus	PRATS
apparel	PLAER
apparent	PAERNT
apparently	PAERNL
appeal	
appeal	PAEL
appeals	PAELS
appealing	PAELG
appealed	PAELD
appear	
appear	PAER
appears	PAERS
appearing	PAERG
appeared	PAERD

appearance	PAERNS, PAOERNS
appearance fee	PAEFRNS
appease	
appease	PAOEZ
appeases	PAOEFS
appeasing	PAOEFG
appeased	PAOEFD
appeasement	PAEFMT
appellant	PAELT, LANT
appellate	PEL
appellate court	PELT
appellee	PLAOE
append	
append	PAEND
appends	PAENDZ
appending	PAENGD
appended	PAEND/-D
append	
appendage	PAEJ
appendices	PAEXZ
appendicitis	PAETS
appendix	PAEX
applaud	
applaud	PLAUD
applauds	PLAUDZ
applauding	PLAUGD
applauded	PLAUD-/D
appliance	PLAOINS
applicability	PLIBLT
applicable	PLIBL
applicant	PLIKT
application	PLIGS
applicative	PLIV
applicator	PLIRT
applicatory	PLOR
apply	
apply	PLAOI
applies	PLAOIS
applying	PLAOIG
applied	PLAOID
appoint	
appoint	POIN
appoints	POINS
appointing	POING
appointed	POIND

BRIEF ENCOUNTERS A

appointment . . . . POIMT
apportion
    apportion . . . . PAORGS
    apportions . . . . PAORGSZ
    apportioning. . . . . PAORG
    apportioned . . . . PAORGD
appraisable. . . . . PRAEBL, PRAEFBL
appraisal . . . . PRAEL
appraise
    appraise . . . . PRAES
    appraises. . . . . PRAEFS, PRAESZ
    appraising . . . . PRAEFG
    appraised . . . . PRAEFD
appraisement . . . . PRAEFMT
appraiser. . . . . PRAER
appreciate
    appreciate. . . . . PRAOERB
    appreciates . . . . PRAOERBS
    appreciating . . . . PRAOERBG
    appreciated. . . . . PRAOERBD
appreciation . . . . PRAOERBGS
appreciative . . . . PRAOEV
appreciatively . . . . PRAOEVL
apprehend
    apprehend . . . . PRAEND
    apprehends. . . . . PRAENDZ
    apprehending . . . . PRAENGD, PRAENG
    apprehended . . . . PRAEND/-D
apprehensible . . . . PRAENL
apprehension . . . . PRAENGS
apprehensive . . . . PRAEFRB
apprentice. . . . . PRAENT
apprenticeship . . . . PRAEP
approach
    approach. . . . . PROEFP
    approaches . . . . PROEFPS
    approaching. . . . . PROEFPG
    approached . . . . PROEFPD
approachable . . . . PROEFPL
approach light . . . . PROEFPLT
appropriate
    appropriate . . . . PROEPT
    appropriates . . . . PROEPTS
    appropriating. . . . . PROEPGT
    appropriated . . . . PROEPTD

A

appropriation	PROEPGS
approval	PRAOVL, PROVL
approve	
approve	PRAOV
approves	PRAOVS
approving	PRAOVG
approved	PRAOVD
approximate	
approximate	P–
approximates	P–S
approximating	P–G
approximated	P–D
approximately	P–L
approximation	P–GS, PROX
appurtenance	AI/PURNS
appurtenant	AI/PURNT
April	PRIL
apron	PRON
apropos	PRAOP
aquarium	KWAIRM
Arab	
Arab	A*ERB, RAEB
Arabian	A*ERN, AERB/YAN
Arabic	A*ERK
arbitrarily	AERBL, ARBL
arbitrary	AERBT
arbitrate	
arbitrate	ARB
arbitrates	ARBS
arbitrating	ARB/–G
arbitrated	ARBD
arbitration	A*IRBGS, AERBGS
arbitrator	ARBT
arch	
arch	AUFP
arches	AUFPS
arching	AUFPG
arched	AUFPD
archaeological	AERJ, KHOJ
archaeologist	AERLT, KHOLT, ARK/YOLT
archaeology	A*ERLG, KHOLG, ARK/YOLG
architect	ARKT, AERKT
architects	ARKTSZ, AERKTS
architecture	AERK
archival	KAOIVL

BRIEF ENCOUNTERS   A

archive
    archive . . . . KAOIV
    archives . . . . KAOIVS
    archiving . . . . KAOIVG
    archived . . . . KAOIVD
ardent . . . . AERNT
ardently . . . . AERNL
arduous . . . . ARJ
are
    are . . . . R-
    are able . . . . RAIBL
    aren't . . . . R-NT
    are the . . . . R-T
    are you a physician . . . . RUFGS
    are you a physician duly licensed in . . . . RUFGS/DLIND
    are you a physician duly licensed to practice medicine . . . . RUFMD
    are you a physician licensed in . . . . RUFGS/LIND
    are you a physician licensed to practice medicine . . . . RUFM
Argentina . . . . AURGT
Argentinean . . . . AURNG
argue
    argue . . . . AERG
    argues . . . . AERGS, ARGS
    arguing . . . . AERG/-G, ARG/-G
    argued . . . . AERGD, ARGD
argument
    argument . . . . AERMT
    argumentation . . . . AURGS
    argumentative . . . . AURG
arid . . . . AERD
aridity . . . . AERTD
aristocracies . . . . SKROX
aristocracy . . . . SKROK, STROK
aristocrat . . . . SKRAT
Aristotle . . . . STOELT
arithmetic . . . . R*IT
Arizona . . . . A*Z
Arkansas . . . . A*R
army . . . . AERM
around
    around . . . . ARN, ARND
    around the . . . . ARNT
    around these . . . . ARNZ
    around those . . . . ARNS

A

arraign
- arraign . . . RARN
- arraigns . . . RARNS
- arraigning . . . RARNG
- arraigned . . . RARND

arraignment . . . RAIMT

arrange
- arrange . . . ARNG
- arranges . . . ARNGS
- arranging . . . ARNG/-G
- arranged . . . ARNGD

arrangement . . . ARMT
arrearage . . . RAERJ
arrears . . . RAOERZ

arrest
- arrest . . . AR
- arrests . . . ARS
- arresting . . . ARG
- arrested . . . ARD

arrival . . . RAOIVL

arrive
- arrive . . . RAOIV
- arrives . . . RAOIVS
- arriving . . . RAOIVG
- arrived . . . RAOIVD

arrogance . . . GANS
arrogant . . . GANT
arrogantly . . . GANL
arrow . . . RAOR
arson . . . AURS
arsonist . . . AURT
arterial . . . AERL
arteriosclerosis . . . SKLAERT, AERT/SKLOES
artery . . . AERT
arthritic . . . THRIKT
arthritis . . . THRITS
article . . . ARL

articulate
- articulate . . . TARK, TLAET
- articulates . . . TARKZ, TLAETS
- articulating . . . TARK/-G, TLAEGT, TLAEG
- articulated . . . TARKD, TLAETD

articulation . . . TARX, TLAEGS
Aryan . . . AERN

BRIEF ENCOUNTERS   A

as

as	AS, AZ
as a matter	SMAT
as a matter of	SMAF
as a matter of course	SMORK
as a matter of fact	SMAFT
as a matter of law	SMAFL
as a result	SRULT
as a rule	SRUL, SRAOUL
as a whole	SWHOEL
as bad as	SBADS
as best as I can	SBIK
as best as I can recall	SBIRK
as best as I recall	SBIRL
as best as I remember	SBIRM
as big as	SBIGS
as deep	SDAOEP
as deep as	SDAOEPS
as difficult	SD-L
as difficult as	SD-LS
as far as	SFARS
as fast as	SFA*S
as follows	SFOLS
as good as	SGAODZ, SG-S
as great as	SGRAETS
as hard as	SHARDZ
as high as	SHAOIS
as I sit here	SWIR, SWHIR
as I sit here today	SW*IRT, SWHIRT
as I understand	SINDZ
as I understood	SIND
as large as	SLARJS
as little as	SLILS
as long	SLONG
as long as	SLONGS
as low as	SLOEZ
as many as	SM-S
as much	S-FP
as much as	S-FPS, SMUFPS
as much as possible	SPOBL
as near as	SNAERS
as near as possible	SNAERP, SNAERPS
as opposed to	SOPS
as small as	SMAULS
as soon as	SAONS

© 1997 White-Boucke Publishing.   33   ILLEGAL TO PHOTOCOPY

as soon as possible	SAOBL
as the result	SR*ULT
as the results	SRULTS
as well as	SWELS
as we sit here	SWHER
as we sit here today	SWHERT
as we understand	SWENDZ
as wide as	SWAOIDZ
as you sit here	SWOUR, SWHOUR
as you sit here today	SWOURT, SWHOURT
as you were	SURP
asbestos	AOBS, STEB

ascend
ascend	SAEND, SKA*EN
ascends	SAENDZ, SKAENZ
ascending	SAENGD, SKAENG
ascended	SAEND/-D, SKA*END

ascension	SAENGS, SKAENGS
ascent	SKAENT

ascertain
ascertain	SAERN
ascertains	SAERNS
ascertaining	SAERNG
ascertained	SAERND

ascertainable	SAERNL
ascertainment	SAERMT
ASCII	SKWAOE
ashamed	SHOIMD

Asia
Asia	AIZ
Asian	AIGS
Asiatic	AIKT

aside
aside	SOID
aside from	SOIFR, SOIFRD
aside from the	SOIFRT, SOIFRTD

asinine	SNAOIN
asininely	SNAOINL

ask
ask	SK-
asks	SK-S
asking	SK-G
asked	SK-D

asked and answered	SKARND, SKAND
ask the Court	SKORT

BRIEF ENCOUNTERS   A

ask you
    ask you . . . . SKU
    asks you. . . . . SKUZ
    asking you . . . . SKU/-G, SK-G/U
    asked you . . . . SKUD
ask your Honor . . . . SKURN
ASL . . . . ALS
asleep . . . . SLOIP, SLAEP
aspect . . . . SPAK
aspersion . . . . SPAERGS
asphalt . . . . SFAULT
asphyxiate
    asphyxiate. . . . . SFAET
    asphyxiates . . . . SFAETS
    asphyxiating . . . . SFAEGT
    asphyxiated. . . . . SFAETD
asphyxiation . . . . SFAEGS
aspirant . . . . SPIRNT
aspiration . . . . SPAOIRGS, SPRAGS
aspire
    aspire . . . . SPAOIR
    aspires . . . . SPAOIRS
    aspiring. . . . . SPAOIRG
    aspired . . . . SPAOIRD
aspirin . . . . SPRIN
assail
    assail. . . . . SW-L
    assails . . . . SW-LS
    assailing . . . . SW-LG
    assailed . . . . SW-LD
assailant . . . . SAELT, SWAENT, SW-LT
assassin . . . . SNIN
assassinate
    assassinate. . . . . SNAET
    assassinates . . . . SNAETS
    assassinating . . . . SNAEGT
    assassinated . . . . SNAETD
assassination . . . . SNAEGS
assassins. . . . . SNINZ
assault
    assault. . . . . SAULT
    assaults . . . . SAULTS
    assaulting. . . . . SAULGT
    assaulted . . . . SAULTD
assault and battery . . . . SAUB

A BRIEF ENCOUNTERS

assaulter... SAURLT
assault with a deadly weapon .... SWEP, SDWEP
assemblage .... BLAJ
assemble
    assemble .... MEBL
    assembles... MEBLS
    assembling .... MEBLG
    assembled .... MEBLD
assembler .... BLER
assembly .... BLAOE
assent
    assent .... SAENT
    assents .... SAENTS
    assenting .... SAENGT
    assented .... SAENTD
assert
    assert.. SAERT
    asserts .... SAERTS
    asserting .... SAERGT
    asserted .... SAERTD
assert
    assertion .... SAERGS
    assertive... SAEVR, SAEFRB
    assertively .... SAEVRL, SAEFRBL, SAEVL
    assertiveness .... SAEVRNS, SAEFRNS
assess
    assess .... SAES
    assesses.. SAEFS, SAESZ
    assessing .... SAEFG
    assessed.. SAEFD
assessment .... SAEFMT
asset .... SAET
asshole... SHOEL
assign
    assign .... SOIN
    assigns .... SOINS
    assigning... SOING
    assigned .... SOIND
assignment.. SAOIMT
assist
    assist .... S*IS
    assists... SIFS, S*ISZ
    assisting .... SIFG
    assisted .... SIFD

BRIEF ENCOUNTERS   A

assist
    assistance .... SNINS
    assistant .... SNINT
    assistant district attorney .... SDA
associate
    associate .... SOERB
    associates .... SOERBS
    associating .... SOERBG
    associated .... SOERBD
association .... SOERBGS
assorted .... SAORTD
assortment .... SAORMT, SORMT
assuage
    assuage .... SWAIJ
    assuages .... SWAIJS
    assuaging .... SWAIJ/-G
    assuaged .... SWAIJD
assume
    assume .... SAOUM
    assumes .... SAOUMS
    assuming .... SAOUMG
    assumed .... SAOUMD
assumes a fact not in evidence .... SFAEK
assumes facts not in evidence .... SFAEX
assuming a fact not in evidence .... SFAEG, SFAEK/-G
assuming facts not in evidence .... SFAEGZ, SFAEX/-G
assumption .... SUMGS
assumption of risk .... SRIFK, SO*R
assumptive .... SUMT
assurance .... SHAOURNZ
assurances .... SHAOURNSZ
assure
    assure .... SHAO*UR, SHOUR
    assures .... SHAOURS, SHOURS
    assuring .... SHAOURG, SHOURG
    assured .... SHAOURD, SHOURD
asthma .... SMAZ
asthmatic .... SMAKT
astigmatic .... SNIKT, SGIK
astigmatism .... SNIFM, SGIFM
astonish
    astonish .... STIRB
    astonishes .... STIRBS
    astonishing .... STIRB/-G
    astonished .... STIRBD

A BRIEF ENCOUNTERS

astonishingly . . . . STIRBL
astonishment . . . . STIRMT
astound
    astound . . . . STOUN
    astounds . . . . STOUNS
    astounding . . . . STOUNG
    astounded . . . . STOUND
astrologer . . . . STRORLG
astrologist . . . . STROLT
astrology . . . . STROLG
astronomer . . . . STRORM
astronomical . . . . STROM/KAL
astronomically . . . . STROM/KLI
astronomy . . . . STROM
asylum . . . . SAOIM
at
    at . . . . AT
    at a time . . . . TAIT
    at all times . . . . TAULT, TAULTS
    at another time . . . . TAONT
    at any rate . . . . TRAET
    at any time . . . . T-NT
    at home . . . . THOEM
    at last . . . . TLA*S
    at least . . . . TLAES
    at no time . . . . TOENT
    at once . . . . TWUNS
    at one time . . . . TWUNT
    at that particular time . . . . TAPT
    at that time . . . . TAT
    at the . . . . TE
    at the end of counsel table . . . . KAEB/KAEB
    at the present time . . . . TEPT
    at the same time . . . . TAIMT
    at the same time as . . . . TAIMTS
    at the time . . . . TET
    at the time of the accident . . . . TEFKT, SDAOIM
    at the very most . . . . TO*S
    at this particular time . . . . TIPT
    at this time . . . . TIT
    at what time . . . . TWAT
    at which time . . . . TWIT
atheist . . . . A*ET
athlete . . . . TLAOET
athlete's foot . . . . TLAOF

BRIEF ENCOUNTERS   A

athletic	TLEK
Atlanta	TLAN
Atlantic	TLAK
Atlantic Ocean	TLOEGS
ATM	A*MT
atmosphere	SFAER, SFAO*ER
atmospheric	SFAERK, SFAOERK
atom bomb	TBOM

atomic
    atomic . . . . TAUMG
    atomic bomb . . . . TBOEM
    atomic energy . . . . T-RJ

atrocious
    atrocious . . . . TROERB
    atrociously . . . . TROERBL
    atrociousness . . . . TROERNS, TROENS
atrocity . . . . TRO*S, TROFT

atrophy
    atrophy . . . . TROF
    atrophies . . . . TROFS
    atrophying . . . . TROFG
    atrophied . . . . TROFD

AT&T . . . . A*T

attach
    attach . . . . TAFP
    attaches . . . . TAFPS
    attaching . . . . TAFPG
    attached . . . . TAFPD
attachment . . . . TAFMT

attain
    attain . . . . TWAIN
    attains . . . . TWAINS
    attaining . . . . TWAING
    attained . . . . TWAIND
attainability . . . . TWAINLT
attainable . . . . TWAINL
attainder . . . . TWAIRND

attempt
    attempt . . . . TAEMT
    attempts . . . . TAEMTS
    attempting . . . . TAEMGT, TAEMG
    attempted . . . . TAEMTD
    attempted murder . . . . TAERMD

attend
    attend . . . . TAEND

A

attends	TAENDZ
attending	TAENGD, TAENG
attended	TAEND/-D
attendance	TAENZ
attendant	TAENT
attention	TAENGS

attest
attest	TA*ES
attests	TA*ESZ
attesting	TAEFG, TAEFGT
attested	TAEFTD

attest
attestation	TAEFGS
attester	TAEFRT
attestor	TAEFR

attitude	TAOUD
attitudinal	TAOULD

attorney
attorney	TOERN
attorney at law	TOERNL
attorney-client privilege	TOEV, TOERP
attorney-client relationship	TOERL
attorney general	TOERNG
attorneys general	TOERNGS

attractive
attractive	TRAV
attractively	TRAVL
attractiveness	TRAVNS

attributable	TRIBL

attribute
attribute	TRIBT
attributes	TRIBTS
attributing	TRIBGT
attributed	TRIBTD

audacious
audacious	DAIRB
audaciously	DAIRBL
audaciousness	DAIRBS

audacity	DAS, DA*S
audibility	AUBLT
audible	AUBL
audibly	AOEBL
audience	YENS

audio
audio	AOD

audiologist	AULD
audiology	AULG
audio-video	AUVD
audio-visual	AUVL

audit
audit	AUD
audits	AUDZ
auditing	AUGD
audited	AUD/-D, AUTD

audit
audition	AUGS
auditor	AURD
auditorily	AORLD
auditorium	AURM
auditory	AORD

augment
augment	AUGT
augments	AUGTS
augmenting	AUGT/-G
augmented	AUGTD

augmentation	A*UGS
August	AUG
aura	AUR
aural	AURL
Australia	STRAIL
Australian	STRAN, STRAINL
authentic	THENK, THINK

authenticate
authenticate	THAET
authenticates	THAETS
authenticating	THA*EG, THA*EGT
authenticated	THAETD

authentication	THAIGS, THA*EGS
authenticity	THINT

author
author	THAOR
authors	THAORS
authoring	THAORG
authored	THAORD

authoritative
authoritative	THOFRB
authoritatively	THOFRBL
authoritativeness	THOFRNS

authority	THORT
authorization	THORGS

A

authorship . . . . THORP, THAORP
authorize
    authorize . . . . THORS
    authorizes. . . . . THORSZ, THOFS
    authorizing. . . . . THORG, THOFG
    authorized . . . . THORD, THOFD
auto . . . . AOUT
autograph
    autograph. . . . . GRAOF
    autographs. . . . . GRAOFS
    autographing . . . . GRAOFG
    autographed. . . . . GRAOFD
automate
    automate. . . . . AEM
    automates . . . . AEMS
    automating . . . . AEMG
    automated . . . . AEMD, AUMTD
automatic . . . . AUMT
automation. . . . . AUMGS, AUJ, AEMGS
automobile . . . . AUB
automotive. . . . . AUV
autonomous. . . . . TON/MOUS
autonomy . . . . AUT/M*I, TON/M*I
autopsy . . . . AUP
auxiliary. . . . . AUX
availability . . . . VAIBLT
available . . . . VAIBL
avalanche. . . . . VAFP
avant-garde . . . . VAUNGD
avenge
    avenge. . . . . VAEJ
    avenges . . . . VAEJS
    avenging . . . . VAEJ/-G
    avenged . . . . VAEJD
avenger . . . . VAERJ
avenue. . . . . AV
average
    average. . . . . AVRJ, AFRJ
    averages. . . . . AVRJS, AFRJS
    averaging . . . . AVRJ/-G, AFRJ/-G
    averaged . . . . AVRJD, AFRJD
averse
    averse. . . . . WERS
    aversely. . . . . WERLS
    averseness. . . . . WERNS

BRIEF ENCOUNTERS   A

```
aversion . . . . . . . . . . . . . . . . . . . . . . . . . . . . . . . . . WERGS, AVRGS
avert
    avert . . . . . . . . . . . . . . . . . . . . . . . . . . . . . . . . . . . . . . . . . WERT
    averts . . . . . . . . . . . . . . . . . . . . . . . . . . . . . . . . . . . . . . . . WERTS
    averting. . . . . . . . . . . . . . . . . . . . . . . . . . . . . . . . . . . . . . WERGT
    averted . . . . . . . . . . . . . . . . . . . . . . . . . . . . . . . . . . . . . . WERTD
aviation. . . . . . . . . . . . . . . . . . . . . . . . . . . . . . . . . . . . . . . . . AIVGS
avid . . . . . . . . . . . . . . . . . . . . . . . . . . . . . . . . . . . . . . . . . . . . . AVD
avidly. . . . . . . . . . . . . . . . . . . . . . . . . . . . . . . . . . . . . . . . . . . AVLD
avocado. . . . . . . . . . . . . . . . . . . . . . . . . . . . . . . . . . . . . . . . . AUFD
avoid
    avoid. . . . . . . . . . . . . . . . . . . . . . . . . . . . . . . . . . . . . . . . . . WOI
    avoids . . . . . . . . . . . . . . . . . . . . . . . . . . . . . . . . . . . . . . . . WOIS
    avoiding. . . . . . . . . . . . . . . . . . . . . . . . . . . . . . . . . . . . . . WOIG
    avoided . . . . . . . . . . . . . . . . . . . . . . . . . . . . . . . . . . . . . . WOID
avoidable . . . . . . . . . . . . . . . . . . . . . . . . . . . . . . . . . . . . . . WOIBL
avoidance. . . . . . . . . . . . . . . . . . . . . . . . . . . . . . . . . . . . . WOINS
await
    await . . . . . . . . . . . . . . . . . . . . . . . . . . . . . . . . . . . . . . . . WOIT
    awaits . . . . . . . . . . . . . . . . . . . . . . . . . . . . . . . . . . . . . . WOITS
    awaiting. . . . . . . . . . . . . . . . . . . . . . . . . . . . . . . . . . . . . WOIGT
    awaited . . . . . . . . . . . . . . . . . . . . . . . . . . . . . . . . . . . . WOITD
awake
    awake . . . . . . . . . . . . . . . . . . . . . . . . . . . . . . . . . . . . . . WOIK
    awakes . . . . . . . . . . . . . . . . . . . . . . . . . . . . . . . . . . . . WOIKS
    awaking . . . . . . . . . . . . . . . . . . . . . . . . . . . . . . . . . WOIK/-G
    awoke . . . . . . . . . . . . . . . . . . . . . . . . . . . . . . . . . . . . . WAOK
    awaked . . . . . . . . . . . . . . . . . . . . . . . . . . . . . . . . . . . WOIKD
awaken
    awaken. . . . . . . . . . . . . . . . . . . . . . . . . . . . . . . . . . . . WAEN
    awakens . . . . . . . . . . . . . . . . . . . . . . . . . . . . . . . . . WAENS
    awakening. . . . . . . . . . . . . . . . . . . . . . . . . . . . . . . WAENG
    awakened . . . . . . . . . . . . . . . . . . . . . . . . . . . . . . . WAEND
award
    award. . . . . . . . . . . . . . . . . . . . . . . . . . . . . . . . . . . . WAURD
    awards . . . . . . . . . . . . . . . . . . . . . . . . . . . . . . . . . WAURDZ
    awarding . . . . . . . . . . . . . . . . . . . . . . . . . . . . . . WAURGD
    awarded . . . . . . . . . . . . . . . . . . . . . . . . . . . . . WAURD/-D
aware . . . . . . . . . . . . . . . . . . . . . . . . . . . . . . . . . . . . . . . . WAIR
awareness . . . . . . . . . . . . . . . . . . . . . . . . . . . . . . . . WAIRNS
away . . . . . . . . . . . . . . . . . . . . . . . . . . . . . . . . . . . . . . . . . . WA
awe. . . . . . . . . . . . . . . . . . . . . . . . . . . . . . . . . . . . . . . . . . A*U
awful . . . . . . . . . . . . . . . . . . . . . . . . . . . . . . . . . . . . . . . . AUFL
awkward . . . . . . . . . . . . . . . . . . . . . . . . . . . . . . . . . . . AUKD
awning . . . . . . . . . . . . . . . . . . . . . . . . . . . . . . . . . . . . . AUNG
```

axes	A*XZ, KPISZ, SKWISZ
axial	AXL
axis	KPIS, SKWIS
azimuth	ZUT

B

babe	BAEB
baby	BAIB
bachelor	BLAFP
back	
back	BAK
backache	BAIK
back and forth	BO*RT
background	BAUG
backlog	BLAUG
back of them	BAFM
back of these	BAFZ
back of those	BAFS
backup	BAUP
backward	BAURD
backyard	BARD
back up	
back up	BUP
backs up	BUPS
backing up	BUPG
backed up	BUPD
bacteria	BAKT, BAEKT
bacterial	BARL, BAOERL
bacterium	BAOERM
bad faith	B-F
badly	BALD
baggage	BAUJ
Bahamas	BHAM, BHAMS
bailiff	BIF, BLIF
baker	BAIRK, BAERK
bakers	BAIRKZ, BAERKS
balance	
balance	BAL
balances	BALS
balancing	BALG
balanced	BAL/-D
balcony	BLOIN
balk	
balk	BAUK
balks	BAUKS
balking	BAUK/-G
balked	BAUKD
Balkan	BLAUK

ballad	BLALD
ballet	BLAI
ballistic	BLIK
balloon	
balloon	BLAON
balloons	BLAONS
ballooning	BLAONG
ballooned	BLAOND
ballot	BLAOT
ballpark	BAP
ballpark figure	BAPG
Baltimore	BAULT
banal	BANL
banality	BANLT
Bangladesh	DERB
banish	
banish	B-RB
banishes	B-RBS
banishing	B-RBG
banished	B-RBD
banishment	BAMT
bank	
bank	BANK
bank account	BANT, BANKT
banker	BRANK
bankruptcy	BRUPS
bankrupt	
bankrupt	BRUP
bankrupts	BRUPZ
bankrupting	BRUPG
bankrupted	BRUPD
banquet	KWET
banter	
banter	BAERNT
banters	BAERNTS
bantering	BAERNGT, BAERNG
bantered	BAERNTD
baptism	BIFM
baptize	
baptize	BAPT
baptizes	BAPTS
baptizing	BAPGT
baptized	BAPTD
barb	BAURB, BA*RB
barber	BAERB

BRIEF ENCOUNTERS   B

```
barbiturates ........................................ BRIFP
bare
    bare ............................................ BAIR
    bareback ....................................... BAIRB
    barely ......................................... BAIRL
bargain
    bargain ........................................ BAURG
    bargains ...................................... BAURGS
    bargaining .................................. BAURG/-G
    bargained ..................................... BAURGD
barium .............................................. BAIRM
barnyard .................................... BRARD, BARND
barometer ........................................... BROMT
*barometric pressure* ................................ BREP
baron ................................................ BRON
barracks ............................................ BAIRX
barrage
    barrage ......................................... BRAJ
    barrages ....................................... BRAJS
    barraging .................................... BRAJ/-G
    barraged ....................................... BRAJD
barrel .............................................. BAERL
barren
    barren ......................................... BAIRN
    barrenly ...................................... BAIRNL
    barrenness .................................... BAIRNS
barricade
    barricade ..................................... BAIRKD
    barricades ................................... BAIRKDZ
    barricading ................................ BAIRKD/-G
    barricaded ................................. BAIRKD/-D
barroom ............................................. BR-RM
baseball ........................................... BAEBL
*baseball bat* ..................................... BAEBLT
basement ........................................... BAIMT
basic .............................................. BAIFK
basically .......................................... BAIFL
basis ................................................ BAZ
bask
    bask ........................................... BAFK
    basks ......................................... BAFKS
    basking ..................................... BAFK/-G
    basked ........................................ BAFKD
basket ..................................... BAEFK, BAFKT
basketball ........................................ BAUBL
```

© 1997 White-Boucke Publishing.   ILLEGAL TO PHOTOCOPY

B — BRIEF ENCOUNTERS

bastard... BAFRD
bath
    bathrobe.. BROEB
    bathroom.. BARM
    bathtub... BAUB
batter
    batter.. BAERT
    batters... BAERTS
    battering....................................... BAERGT
    battered.. BAERTD
batterer... BRAERT
battery.. BRAET
battle
    battle.. BALT
    battles... BALTS
    battling.. BALGT
    battled... BALTD
battleground................................ BALGTD, BALGD
bawdy... BA*UD
bazaar... ZBAR
bazooka... ZAOK
B.C... B*K
be
    am / are...................................... AM / R–
    is... S–
    being.. B–G
    was / were................................... WUZ / W–R
    been... B–N
be
    be... B–
    be able...................................... BAIBL
    be consistent................................ B–NT
    be like....................................... BLAOIK
    be on time................................... BAOIM
    be ready..................................... B–RD
    be seated.................................... BAOETD
    be the....................................... B–T
    be those..................................... B–S
bear
    bear... BAER
    bears.. BAERS
    bearing.. BAERG
    bore... BOER
    borne / born............................... BOERN / BORN

BRIEF ENCOUNTERS   B

bear
    bearable .... BAERBL
    bearably .... BAOERBL
    bearer .... BRA*ER, BRAIR
    bearing in mind .... BAERMGD, BAERMD/-G
    bear in mind .... BAERMD
beat
    beat .... BAET
    beats .... BAETS
    beating .... BAEGT
    beat .... BAET
    beaten .... BAENT
beater .... BAOERT
beautician .... BAOUGS
beautiful .... BAOUF
beautifully .... BAOUFL
beauty .... BAOUT
because
    because .... BAUZ
    because of .... BAUF
    because of the .... BAUFT
    because of them .... BAUFM
    because of these .... BAUFZ
    because of those .... BAUFS
become
    become .... B-K
    becomes .... B-KS
    becoming .... B-K/-G
    became .... BAIM
    become .... B-K
bedlam· .... BLAM
bedroom .... BERM
been .... B-N
beeper .... BAOERP
befall
    befall .... BE/FAUL
    befalls .... BE/FAULS
    befalling .... BE/FAULG
    befell .... BE/FEL
    befallen .... BE/FAUNL
before
    before .... B-FR
    beforehand .... B-FRND
    before the .... B-FRT
    before them .... B-FRM

B — BRIEF ENCOUNTERS

before these . . . . B–FRZ
before those . . . . B–FRS
begin
   begin . . . . GIN
   begins . . . . GINS
   beginning . . . . GING
   began . . . . GAN
   begun . . . . G*UN, BUN
beginner . . . . GIRN
begrudge
   begrudge . . . . BRUJ
   begrudges . . . . BRUJS
   begrudging . . . . BRUJ/-G
   begrudged . . . . BRUJD
begrudger . . . . BRURJ
begrudgingly . . . . BRULG, BRUJ/LI
beg your pardon
   beg your pardon . . . . GURP
   begs your pardon . . . . GURPS
   begging your pardon . . . . GURPG
   begged your pardon . . . . GURPD
behalf
   behalf . . . . BAF
   behalf of the . . . . BAFT
   behalf of them . . . . B–FM
   behalf of these . . . . B–FZ
behave
   behave . . . . BAIV
   behaves . . . . BAIVS
   behaving . . . . BAIVG
   behaved . . . . BAIVD
behavior . . . . BAIVR, BAIFR
behavioral . . . . BAIVRL, BAIFRL
behemoth . . . . BAO*ET
behest . . . . BH*ES
behind
   behind . . . . BIND
   behind the . . . . BINTD
   behind these . . . . BINDZ
behold
   behold . . . . BHOLD, BHOL
   beholds . . . . BHOLDZ, BHOLS
   beholding . . . . BHOLGD, BHOLG
   beheld . . . . BHELD, BHEL
being . . . . B–G

BRIEF ENCOUNTERS — B

belabor
    belabor . . . . BLAIB
    belabors . . . . BLAIBS
    belaboring . . . . BLAIBG
    belabored . . . . BLAIBD
belated . . . . BLAITD
Belgian . . . . BELGS
Belgium . . . . BELG
behoove
    behoove . . . . BAOV
    behooves . . . . BAOVS
    behooving . . . . BAOVG
    behooved . . . . BAOVD
beleaguer
    beleaguer . . . . BLAOERG
    beleaguers . . . . BLAOERGS
    beleaguering . . . . BLAOERG/-G
    beleaguered . . . . BLAOERGD
belief . . . . BLAOEF
believable . . . . BLAOEVBL, BLAOEFBL, BLEFBL
believe
    believe . . . . BLAOEV
    believes . . . . BLAOEVS
    believing . . . . BLAOEVG
    believed . . . . BLAOEVD
believe
    believe it or not . . . . BLORNT
    believe me . . . . BLAOEVM
    believe them . . . . BLAOEFM
belittle
    belittle . . . . BLIL
    belittles . . . . BLILS
    belittling . . . . BLILG
    belittled . . . . BLILD
belittler . . . . BLIRL
belligerence . . . . BLIJS
belligerency . . . . BLIJSZ, BLIJZ
belligerent . . . . BLIJ
belong
    belong . . . . BLONG
    belongs . . . . BLONGZ
    belonging . . . . BLONG/-G
    belonged . . . . BLONGD
belongings . . . . BLONGS
beloved . . . . BLOVD

B — BRIEF ENCOUNTERS

below. . . . . BLO
bench . . . . BEFP
bench warrant. . . . . BARNT
bend
    bend . . . . BEND
    bends. . . . . BENDZ
    bending . . . . BENGD, BENG
    bent. . . . . BENT
bender. . . . . BERND
beneath . . . . NAO*ET
beneficial. . . . . BERBL
beneficiary . . . . BERB
benefit
    benefit . . . . BEF
    benefits. . . . . BEFS
    benefiting . . . . BEFG
    benefited. . . . . BEFD
benefit of the doubt . . . . BEFT, BOUFD
benevolence. . . . . BEFL
benevolent. . . . . BEFLT
Benzedrine . . . . BENS
bequeath
    bequeath . . . . KWAOET, KWAO*ET
    bequeaths. . . . . KWAOETS, KWAO*ETS
    bequeathing . . . . KWAOEGT, KWAO*EGT
    bequeathed . . . . KWAOETD, KWAO*ETD
bequeathal . . . . KWAOELT, KWAO*ELT
bequeathment. . . . . KWAOEMT
bereave
    bereave . . . . BAOEV
    bereaves . . . . BAOEVS
    bereaving. . . . . BAOEVG
    bereaved / bereft. . . . . BAOEVD / BREFT
bereavement. . . . . RAOEVMT, BAOEVMT
Bermuda. . . . . BERMD, BAOUMD
berry . . . . BRER
berserk . . . . BERZ
beseech
    beseech . . . . SAOEFP
    beseeches. . . . . SAOEFPS
    beseeching . . . . SAOEFPG
    beseeched / besought. . . . . SAOEFPD / BE/SAUT
beside . . . . BES
besiege
    besiege. . . . . BAOEJ

BRIEF ENCOUNTERS   B

besieges . . . . BAOEJS
besieging . . . . BAOEJ/-G
besieged . . . . BAOEJD
besieger . . . . BAOERJ
best
   best . . . . B*ES
   best evidence . . . . BEVD
   best evidence rule . . . . BEVLD
   best of my ability . . . . BIBLT, BEBLT
   best of my knowledge . . . . BEJ
   best of my memory . . . . BIRM
   best of my recollection . . . . BEX
   best of your ability . . . . BURLT
   best of your knowledge . . . . BURJ
   best of your memory . . . . BURM
   best of your recollection . . . . BURX
   best seller . . . . BLERL
   best selling . . . . BLELG
   best selling book . . . . BLEB
bet
   bet . . . . BET
   bets . . . . BETS
   betting . . . . BEGT
   bet . . . . BET
betray
   betray . . . . BRAE
   betrays . . . . BRAES
   betraying . . . . BRAE/-G
   betrayed . . . . BRAE/-D
betrayal . . . . BRAEL
betrayer . . . . BRAER
better
   better . . . . BERT
   betters . . . . BERTS
   bettering . . . . BERGT
   bettered . . . . BERTD
better
   Better Business Bureau . . . . BERBZ
   betterment . . . . BERMT
   better off . . . . BROF
   better than . . . . BERN
   better than the . . . . BERNT
   better than these . . . . BERNZ
   better than those . . . . BERNS
bettor . . . . BOERT

B   BRIEF ENCOUNTERS

between
- between . . . . TWAOEN
- *between the* . . . . TWAOENT
- *between them* . . . . TWAOEM
- *between these* . . . . TWAOENZ
- *between those* . . . . TWAOENS

beyond
- beyond . . . . YOND
- *beyond all reasonable doubt* . . . . Y-RLD
- *beyond any reasonable doubt* . . . . YIRD
- *beyond a reasonable doubt* . . . . Y-RD
- *beyond every reasonable doubt* . . . . YERD
- *beyond the* . . . . YONTD
- *beyond the scope* . . . . YOEP
- *beyond the scope of* . . . . YOEFP
- *beyond the scope of the* . . . . YOEFPT
- *beyond the scope of these* . . . . YOEFPZ
- *beyond the scope of those* . . . . YOEFPS

bias
- bias . . . . BAOIZ, BAOIF, BAS
- biases . . . . BAOIFS, BAF/-S
- biasing . . . . BAOIFG, BAFG
- biased . . . . BAOIFD, BAFD

bias or prejudice . . . . BOP
Bible . . . . BAOIBL
Bible school . . . . BAOL
biblical . . . . BIBL
biceps . . . . BEPS

bicker
- bicker . . . . BIRK
- bickers . . . . BIRKS
- bickering . . . . BIRK/-G
- bickered . . . . BIRKD

bicycle
- bicycle . . . . BOIK
- bicycles . . . . BOIKS
- bicycling . . . . BOIK/-G
- bicycled . . . . BOIKD

bicycler . . . . BOIRK

bid
- bid . . . . BID
- bids . . . . BIDZ
- bidding . . . . BIGD
- bid / bade . . . . BID / BAID
- bid / bidden . . . . BID / BID/-N

BRIEF ENCOUNTERS   B

```
bidder ............................................... BRID
bide
    bide ............................................ BAO*ID
    bides........................................... BAO*IDZ
    biding.......................................... BAO*IGD
    bided / bode ........................... BAO*ID/-D / BOED
bifocal ..................................... BAOIFL, BOEKL
bifurcate
    bifurcate ......................................... BIFT
    bifurcates................................... BIFTS, BIFZ
    bifurcating................................... BIFGT, BIFG
    bifurcated ................................... BIFTD, BIFD
bifurcation ......................................... BIFGS
big
    bigger ........................................... BIRG
    bigger than ..................................... BIRNG
    bigger than the................................. BIRNGT
    biggest ......................................... B*IGS
bigot
    bigot............................................. BIGT
    bigoted ......................................... BIGTD
    bigotry ......................................... BRIGT
bilateral........................................... BLARL
bilaterally ....................................... BLAOERL
bilingual ........................................... BLINL
bill
    billiard ball .................................... BLIBL
    billings......................................... BILGS
    Billings........................................ B*ILGS
    bill of attainder............................... BAIRND
    bill of health................................... B*ELT
    bill of lading................................. BLAIGD
    bill of rights ................................... BIRTS
    bill of sale ..................................... BLAEL
    bills of attainder ............................ BAIRNDZ
    bills of health ................................. B*ELTS
    bills of lading ............................... BLAIGDZ
    bills of rights................................. BIRTSZ
    bills of sale .................................. BLAELS
billion
    billion ............................................ B-L
    billion dollar.................................... B-LD
    billion of these ................................. B-LZ
    billionth.................................. B-LT, B*ILT
```

bind
    bind .... BAOIN, BAOIND
    binds .... BAOINS, BAOINDZ
    binding .... BAOING, BAOINGD
    bound .... BOUN
binder .... BAOIRN, BAOIRND
bindle .... BINL
binge
    binge .... BIJ
    binges .... BIJS
    binging .... BIJ/-G
    binged .... BIJD
bio .... BO
biographer .... BAEFR, BOG/FER
biography .... BAEF, BOG/FI
biologist .... BOLGT
biology .... BOLG
biopsy .... BOIP
bipartisan .... BAURN
bipartisanship .... BAURP, BARP
birth
    birth control .... BROEL
    birthday .... BOIFD, BIRTD
    birthday party .... BOIFP, BOIFPD
    birthplace .... BIRP
biscuit .... BIFK, BIFKT
bite
    bite .... BAOIT
    bites .... BAOITS
    biting .... BAOIGT
    bit .... BIT
    bit / bitten .... BIT / BINT
bitter
    bitter .... BIRT
    bitterly .... BIRLT
    bitterness .... B*IRNS
blabber
    blabber .... BLARB
    blabbers .... BLARBS
    blabbering .... BLARB/-G
    blabbered .... BLARBD
black
    black and blue .... BLAUB
    black and white .... BLIT
    black ass .... BLAS

blackbird	BLIRD
black belt	BLABLT
blackboard	BLORD
blacker	BLARK
black man	BLAN
black market	BLAERK
black men	BLEN
black or white	BLORT
black person	BLERN
black woman	BLOM
black women	BLIM

blackball
    blackball . . . . BLAUL, BLABL
    blackballs . . . . BLAULS, BLABLS
    blackballing . . . . BLAULG, BLABLG
    blackballed . . . . BLAULD, BLABLD
blackmail
    blackmail . . . . BLAIL
    blackmails . . . . BLAILS
    blackmailing . . . . BLAILG
    blackmailed . . . . BLAILD
blackmailer . . . . BLAIRL
bladder . . . . BLAD, BLARD
blandly . . . . BLANL
blank
    blank . . . . BLANG
    blanks . . . . BLANGS
    blanking . . . . BLANG/-G
    blanked . . . . BLANGD
blanket
    blanket . . . . BLAENK
    blankets . . . . BLAENKS
    blanketing . . . . BLAENK/-G
    blanketed . . . . BLAENKD
blasé . . . . BLAUZ
blasphemous . . . . FOUM, FOUMS
blasphemy . . . . FAOEM
blast
    blast . . . . BLAFT
    blasts . . . . BLAFTS
    blasting . . . . BLAFGT, BLA*GS
    blasted . . . . BLAFTD
blatancy . . . . BLAINS, BLAITS
blatant . . . . BLAIT
blatantly . . . . BLAINL

bleak . . . . BLAEK
bleed
    bleed . . . . BLAOED
    bleeds . . . . BLAOEDZ
    bleeding . . . . BLAOEGD
    bled . . . . BLED
bleeder . . . . BLAOERD
bleeding-heart . . . . BLART
blemish
    blemish . . . . BLEM
    blemishes . . . . BLEMS
    blemishing . . . . BLEMG
    blemished . . . . BLEMD
blemisher . . . . BLERM
blender . . . . BLERND
bless
    bless . . . . BLEF, BLES
    blesses . . . . BLEFS, BLESZ
    blessing . . . . BLEFG
    blessed . . . . BLEFD
blind
    blind . . . . BLAOIN
    blinds . . . . BLAOINZ
    blinding . . . . BLAOING
    blinded . . . . BLAOIND
blindfold
    blindfold . . . . BLOEL, BLAOIFL
    blindfolds . . . . BLOELS, BLAOIFLS
    blindfolding . . . . BLOELG, BLAOIFLG
    blindfolded . . . . BLOELD, BLAOIFLD
blindly . . . . BLAOINL, BLAOINLD
blindness . . . . BLAOINS
blink
    blink . . . . BLING, BLINK
    blinks . . . . BLINGS, BLINKS
    blinking . . . . BLING/-G, BLINK/-G
    blinked . . . . BLINGD, BLINKD
blinker . . . . BLIRNG
blister
    blister . . . . BLIS, BLIFR
    blisters . . . . BLIFS, BLIFRS
    blistering . . . . BLIFG, BLIFRG
    blistered . . . . BLIFD, BLIFRD
blizzard . . . . BLIZ
blockade . . . . BLAED

BRIEF ENCOUNTERS   B

blockage . . . . BLOJ
blocking . . . . BLOG
blood
   blood alcohol . . . . BLOL
   blood alcohol level . . . . BLEVL
   blood count . . . . BLAOK
   blood evidence . . . . BLEVD, BLUVD
   blood group . . . . BLAOP
   blood poisoning . . . . BLOIG
   blood pressure . . . . BLUP
   blood test . . . . BLUT, BL*ES
   blood transfusion . . . . BLAOUGS, BLAOUFGS
   blood type . . . . BLAOIP
   blood vessel . . . . BLUFL
blossom
   blossom . . . . BLOFM, BLOS
   blossoms . . . . BLOFMS, BLOSZ
   blossoming . . . . BLOFMG
   blossomed . . . . BLOFMD
blow
   blow . . . . BLOE
   blows . . . . BLOES
   blowing . . . . BLOEG
   blew . . . . BLU, BLAO*U
   blown . . . . BLOEN
blow
   blower . . . . BLOER
   blowjob . . . . BLOEJ
   blowout . . . . BLOUT
   blowup . . . . BLO*EP
blow up
   blow up . . . . BLOEP
   blows up . . . . BLOEPS
   blowing up . . . . BLOEPG
   blew up . . . . BLAO*UP, BL*UP
bludgeon
   bludgeon . . . . BLUJ
   bludgeons . . . . BLUJS
   bludgeoning . . . . BLUJ/-G
   bludgeoned . . . . BLUJD
bludgeoner . . . . BLURJ
blue
   blue . . . . BLAOU
   blue book . . . . BLAOUB
   blue-collar . . . . BLAOUK

blue-collar worker . . . . BLAOURK
blue jeans . . . . BLAOUJ, BLAOUJS
blueprint
    blueprint. . . . . BLAOUP
    blueprints . . . . BLAOUPS
    blueprinting . . . . BLAOUPG
    blueprinted . . . . BLAOUPD
bluish. . . . . BLAOURB
blunder
    blunder. . . . . BLUN
    blunders . . . . BLUNS
    blundering . . . . BLUNG
    blundered . . . . BLUND
blunderer . . . . BLURN, BLURND
bluntly. . . . . BLUNL, BLUNLT
board
    boarding school. . . . . BRAOL
    board of directors . . . . BREX
    Board of Education. . . . . BREJ
    board of regents. BRAOEJ, BRAOEJS
    board of supervisors . . . . BR–FR, BROFR
    board of trustees. . . . . BRUF
    board room . . . . BAORM
boastful. . . . . BOEFLT
bobble
    bobble . . . . BOBL
    bobbles. . . . . BOBLS
    bobbling . . . . BOBLG
    bobbled . . . . BOBLD
bodily
    bodily. . . . . BOL
    bodily harm . . . . BA*RM, B–RM
    bodily injury. . . . . B–J, BO*J
body . . . . BOD
boggle
    boggle . . . . BO*LG
    boggles . . . . BOLGS
    boggling . . . . BOLG/–G
    boggled . . . . BOLGD
boggler. . . . . BORLG
boiler
    boiler. . . . . BOIRL
    boilerplate . . . . BOIRP
    boiler room . . . . BOIRM

boisterous
    boisterous . . . . BO*IS
    boisterously . . . . BO*ILS, BO*IL
    boisterousness . . . . BOINS
bolder . . . . BOERLD
boldface
    boldface . . . . BOEFL
    boldfaces . . . . BOEFLS
    boldfacing . . . . BOEFLG
    boldfaced . . . . BOEFLD
Bolivia . . . . BLIV
Bolivian . . . . BLIVN
bomb
    bomb . . . . BOEM
    bombs . . . . BOEMS
    bombing . . . . BOEMG
    bombed . . . . BOEMD
bombard
    bombard . . . . BORMD
    bombards . . . . BORMDZ
    bombarding . . . . BORMGD, BORMG
    bombarded . . . . BORMD/-D
bombardier . . . . BOERMD
bombardment . . . . BOMT, BOEMT
bomber . . . . BORM
bona fide . . . . BOFD
bondage . . . . BOJ
bony . . . . BOIN
book
    booking . . . . BAOG
    bookkeeper . . . . BAOP, BAORP
    bookkeeping . . . . BAOPG
    booklet . . . . BLET
boondoggle . . . . BAOND
bootleg . . . . BLEG
border
    border . . . . BROERD
    borders . . . . BROERDZ
    bordering . . . . BROERGD
    bordered . . . . BROERD/-D
boredom . . . . BOERM
borough . . . . BROUG
borrow
    borrow . . . . BOR
    borrows . . . . BORS

borrowing. . . . . BORG
borrowed. . . . . BOR/-D
borrower . . . . BROR
Bosnia . . . . BOZ
Bosnia-Herzegovina . . . . BHOZ, BLOZ
Bosnian . . . . BONZ
Boston. . . . . BOFN
bother
    bother . . . . BOFR
    bothers. . . . . BOFRS
    bothering . . . . BOFRG
    bothered. . . . . BOFRD
bothersome . . . . BOFRM
both of
    both of . . . . BOEF
    both of the . . . . BOEFT
    both of them . . . . BOEFM
    both of these . . . . BOEFZ
    both of those . . . . BOEFS
bottle
    bottle. . . . . BOT
    bottles . . . . BOTS
    bottling . . . . BOGT
    bottled. . . . . BOTD
bottom
    bottom . . . . BOM
    bottoms. . . . . BOMS
    bottoming . . . . BOMG
    bottomed. . . . . BOMD
bottom line . . . . BLAOIM, BLAO*IN
bought. . . . . BAUT
bouillon . . . . BAO*UL
boulder. . . . . BOURLD
boulevard . . . . BL-FD, BL-VD
bound
    bound . . . . BOUN
    bounds . . . . BOUNZ, BOUNDZ
    bounding. . . . . BOUNGD
    bounded . . . . BOUND
boundary . . . . BOURND
bourbon. . . . . BOURB
bowler. . . . . BOURL
bowling ball . . . . BOUBL
boxer. . . . . BORX

BRIEF ENCOUNTERS   B

boycott
    boycott . . . . BOIKT
    boycotts . . . . BOIKTS
    boycotting . . . . BOIKT/-G
    boycotted . . . . BOIKTD
boycotter. . . . . BOIRKT
boyfriend . . . . BOIF
bracket
    bracket. . . . . BRAKT
    brackets. . . . . BRAKTS
    bracketing . . . . BRAKT/-G
    bracketed. . . . . BRAKTD
braggart. . . . . BRAGT
braille . . . . BRAIL
brailler. . . . . BRAIRL
brainless . . . . BRAINL
brainstorm . . . . BRORM
brainwash
    brainwash . . . . BRAIRB
    brainwashes. . . . . BRAIRBS
    brainwashing . . . . BRAIRBG
    brainwashed . . . . BRAIRBD
brake fluid . . . . BRAIFK
brake light . . . . BRAILT
branch
    branch . . . . BRAFP
    branches. . . . . BRAFPS
    branching . . . . BRAFPG
    branched . . . . BRAFPD
bravado . . . . BRAVD
brave
    brave . . . . BRAIV
    bravely . . . . BRAIVL
    braveness . . . . BRAIVNS
    braver. . . . . BRAIVR
    braver than. . . . . BRAIVRN, BRAIFRN
    braver than the . . . . BRAIVRNT, BRAIFRNT
    braver than these. . . . . BRAIVRNZ, BRAIFRNZ
    braver than those. . . . . BRAIVRNS, BRAIFRNS
brazen
    brazen . . . . BRAEZ
    brazenly . . . . BRAELZ
    brazenness . . . . BRAENZ
Brazil . . . . BRAZ
Brazilian . . . . BRANZ, BRALZ

B   BRIEF ENCOUNTERS

breach of contract . . . . BRAEFPT
breadth . . . . BR*ETD, BRA*ET
break
    break . . . . BRAEK
    breaks . . . . BRAEKS
    breaking . . . . BRAEG
    broke . . . . BROEK
    broken . . . . BROEN
break
    breakable . . . . BRAEBL
    breakage . . . . BRAEJ
    break and enter . . . . BRAEN
    breakdown . . . . BRAEKD
    breaker . . . . BRAERK
    breakfast . . . . BREFS
    breaking and entering . . . . BRAENG
breath analyzer . . . . BLAOIRS
breed
    breed . . . . BRAOED
    breeds . . . . BRAOEDZ
    breeding . . . . BRAOEGD
    bred . . . . BRED
breeder . . . . BRAOERD
brevity . . . . BREVT
brewer . . . . BRAOUR
bribery . . . . BROIB
bridal . . . . BRAOILD
bridle
    bridle . . . . BRELD
    bridles . . . . BRELDZ
    bridling . . . . BRELGD
    bridled . . . . BRELD/-D
briefcase . . . . BRAOEFK
brigade . . . . BRIGD
brighten
    brighten . . . . BRAOIN, BRAOINT
    brightens . . . . BRAOINS, BRAOINTS
    brightening . . . . BRAOING, BRAOINGT
    brightened . . . . BRAOIND, BRAOINTD
bright
    brightener . . . . BRAOIRN, BRAOIRNT
    brighter . . . . BRAOIRT
    brightest . . . . BRAOITS
brilliance . . . . BRILS
brilliancy . . . . BRILZ, BRILSZ

BRIEF ENCOUNTERS B

brilliant	BRIL
bring	
bring	BRI
brings	BRIS
bringing	BRIG
brought	BRAUT
bring up	
bring up	BRIP
brings up	BRIPS
bringing up	BRIPG
brought up	BRAUP
Britain	BRIN, BRINT
British	BRIRB
British Isles	BRAOIL, BRAOILS
brittle	BRILT
broaden	
broaden	BROND
broadens	BRONDZ
broadening	BRONGD
broadened	BROND/-D
broadly	BROLD
broadcast	
broadcast	BRAUD
broadcasts	BRAUDZ
broadcasting	BRAUGD, BRAUG
broadcast	BRAUD
broadcaster	BRAURD
brochure	BRUR
broken	BROEN
broker	
broker	BROER, BROERK
brokers	BROERS, BROERKS
brokering	BROERG, BROERK/-G
brokered	BROER/-D, BROERKD
brokerage	BROERJ
Bronx	BRONGS
brothel	BROFL, BRO*LT
brother	
brother	BRO
brotherhood	BRORD
brother-in-law	BROL
brotherly	BRORL, BROERL
brothers-in-law	BROLS
browner	BROURN
brownest	BROUNS

B — BRIEF ENCOUNTERS

brunch . . . . BRUN
brunette. . . . . BRAOUNT
brusque . . . . BRUFK
brusquely . . . . BRUFKL
brutal. . . . . BRAOUL, BRUL
brutality . . . . BRAOULT, BRULT
bubble
    bubble . . . . BUBL
    bubbles. . . . . BUBLS
    bubbling . . . . BUBL/-G
    bubbled . . . . BUBLD
bucket . . . . BUKT
buckle
    buckle . . . . BUKL
    buckles. . . . . BUKLS
    buckling. . . . . BUKL/-G
    buckled . . . . BUKLD
budget
    budget. . . . . BOIJ
    budgets. . . . . BOIJS
    budgeting . . . . BOIG
    budgeted. . . . . BOIJD
buffet . . . . BAOUFT
Buick. . . . . BAOUK
build
    build . . . . BILD
    builds . . . . BILDZ
    building . . . . BILGD, B-LG
    built. . . . . BILT
builder. . . . . BIRLD
bulb . . . . BLUB
bulge
    bulge . . . . BULG
    bulges . . . . BULGS
    bulging . . . . BULG/-G
    bulged . . . . BULGD
bulimia. . . . . BLAOEM
bulimic . . . . BLAOEMG
bulk . . . . BLUK
bulky. . . . . BLOIK
bullet . . . . BULT
bulletin . . . . BLIN
bulletin board . . . . BLIB
bulletproof
    bulletproof . . . . BLAOF

bulletproofs	BLAOFS
bulletproofing	BLAOFG
bulletproofed	BLAOFD
bulletproof glass	BLAOVG
bulletproof vest	BLAOV
bullion	BAOUL
bumper sticker	BUBS
bumper to bumper	BUB
bumper-to-bumper traffic	BUBT

bunch
bunch	B–FP
bunches	B–FPS
bunching	B–FPG
bunched	B–FPD
bunches of stuff	BUFTS
bunch of stuff	BUFT

bundle
bundle	BUNL
bundles	BUNLS
bundling	BUNL/–G
bundled	BUNLD

bunk
bunk	BUNG
bunks	BUNGS
bunking	BUNG/–G
bunked	BUNGD

burden
burden	BURD
burdens	BURDZ
burdening	BURGD
burdened	BURD/–D
burden of proof	BRAOF, BURP
burden of proving	BRAOFG, BURPG

bureau
bureau	BUR
bureaucracy	BROK
bureaucrat	BURK
bureaucratic	BRAK
bureaucrats	BURKZ

burgeon
burgeon	BERJ
burgeons	BERJS
burgeoning	BERJ/–G
burgeoned	BERJD
burglar	BLAR

burglarize
    burglarize . . . . BLAF
    burglarizes. . . . . BLAFS
    burglarizing . . . . BLAFG
    burglarized . . . . BLAFD
burglary
    burglary . . . . BLAER
    burglary in the first degree. . . . . BLAEFD
    burglary in the second degree . . . . BLAEND
burner . . . . BRURN
burrito . . . . BRAOET
burro . . . . BROE
burrow
    burrow . . . . BRO*E
    burrows . . . . BROEZ
    burrowing. . . . . BROEG
    burrowed . . . . BROED
burst
    burst . . . . BURS, B*URS
    bursts. . . . . BURSZ, B*URSZ
    bursting . . . . BURGS, B*URGS
    burst . . . . BURS, B*URS
bury
    bury. . . . . BRU
    buries. . . . . BRUS
    burying . . . . BRU/-G
    buried . . . . BRUD
bushel . . . . BURBL
busier. . . . . B-RZ
busiest . . . . B*IS
business
    business . . . . BIZ
    businesses. . . . . BISZ
    businessman . . . . BAM
    businessmen. . . . . BEM
    business or occupation. . . . . BORK
    businesswoman. . . . . BO*M, BA*M
    businesswomen. . . . . B*IM, B*EM
bus station . . . . BUFGS
busy
    busy. . . . . B-Z
    busies. . . . . B-FS
    busying . . . . B-FG
    busied . . . . B-FD
but . . . . BU

BRIEF ENCOUNTERS — B

butcher
    butcher . . . . BRUFP
    butchers . . . . BRUFPS
    butchering . . . . BRUFPG
    butchered . . . . BRUFPD
butler . . . . BLERT
butter
    butter . . . . BURT
    butters . . . . BURTS
    buttering . . . . BURGT
    buttered . . . . BURTD
but the . . . . BUT
button
    button . . . . BON
    buttons . . . . BONS
    buttoning . . . . BONG
    buttoned . . . . BON/–D
buy
    buy . . . . BAOI
    buys . . . . BAOIS
    buying . . . . BAOIG
    bought . . . . BAUT
buyer . . . . BAOIR
buyer's market . . . . BAOIRM
buzzard . . . . BUFRD
buzzer . . . . BURZ
by
    by . . . . BI
    by means of . . . . BIM
    by means of the . . . . BIMT
    by means of these . . . . BIMZ
    by means of those . . . . BIMS
    by reason . . . . BIRN
    by reason of the . . . . BIRNT
    by reason of these . . . . BIRNZ
    by reason of those . . . . BIRNS
    by the way . . . . BAE
    by virtue of . . . . BIFR
    by virtue of the . . . . BIFRT
    by virtue of the fact . . . . BIFRK
    by virtue of them . . . . BIFRM
    by virtue of these . . . . BIFRZ
    by virtue of those . . . . BIFRS
bylaw . . . . BLAU

bypass
- bypass . . . . BIP
- bypasses . . . . BIPS
- bypassing . . . . BIPG
- bypassed . . . . BIPD

C

cabal	KAUBL
cabaret	KBRAI
cabin	
cabin	KBIN
cabinet	KABT
cabins	KBINZ
caboose	KBAOS
cackle	
cackle	KAKL
cackles	KAKLS
cackling	KALG, KAKL/-G
cackled	KAKLD
cadaver	DAFR, DAVR
cafeteria	KAEFT, KAEFRT
Cairo	KRO
cajole	
cajole	JOL
cajoles	JOLS
cajoling	JOLG
cajoled	JOLD
calamity	KLAMT
Cal.App.	
Cal.App.	KLAUP
Cal.App.2d.	KLEND
Cal.App.3d.	KLIRD
calculate	
calculate	KLAET, KAELT
calculates	KLAETS, KAELTS
calculating	KLAEGT, KAELGT
calculated	KLAETD, KAELTD
calculation	KLAEGS, KAL/KLAIGS
calculator	KLAERT, KAERLT
calculus	KL-S
calendar	KALD
California	KRA*
call	
caller	KAURL
Caller ID	KAURLD
calling for speculation	KLAIGS/-G
calling your attention	KAURGS
calls for speculation	KLAIGS
call your attention	KAURT

C — BRIEF ENCOUNTERS

    call your first witness .... KWINS/KWINS
    call your next witness .... KWEX/KWEX
calligrapher .... KLIFR, KLIG/FER
calligraphy .... KLAOEF, KLIG/FI
call up
    call up .... KAUP
    calls up .... KAUPS
    calling up .... KAUPG
    called up .... KAUPD
calm
    calm .... KAUM
    calms .... KAUMS
    calming .... KAUMG
    calmed .... KAUMD
calmer .... KAURM
Cambodia .... KBOED
Cambodian .... KBOEND
camera
    camera .... KAERM
    cameraman .... KAM/MAN
    camerawoman .... KWOM, KAM/WOM
camouflage
    camouflage .... FLAJ
    camouflages .... FLAJS
    camouflaging .... FLAJ/-G
    camouflaged .... FLAJD
campaign
    campaign .... KPAIN
    campaigns .... KPAINS
    campaigning .... KPAIN/-G
    campaigned .... KPAIND
campaigner .... KPRAIN
campus .... KPUS
can
    can .... K-
    can be .... K-B
    can believe .... K-BL
    can feel .... K-FL
    can have .... K-F
    can have been .... K-FB
    can not .... KWO*T
    cannot .... KWOT, K-/NOT
    can recall .... K*RL
    can recollect .... K-RK
    can remember .... K-RM

BRIEF ENCOUNTERS   C

can't	K-NT
can understand	K-NDZ
can want	K-PT
Canada	KRAND
Canadian	KRAEND
canal	KANL
canary	KA/NAIR
cancel	
cancel	KAEL
cancels	KAELS
canceling	KAELG
canceled	KAELD
cancellation	KAELGS
cancer	KAERN
cancerous	KAERNZ
candid	KA*ND
candidly	KANLD, KAND/LI
candle	KAENL
candlelight	KANLT, KAENLT
candor	KAOND
can he	
can he	KE
can he be	KEB
can he believe	KEBL
can he ever	KEFR, KEVR
can he feel	KEFL
can he get	KEGT
can he have	KEF
can he live	KEV
can he recall	KERL
can he recollect	KERK
can he remember	KERM
can he say	KES
can he see	KEZ
can he think	KENG
can he understand	KENDZ
can I	
can I	KI
can I be	KIB
can I believe	KIBL
can I ever	KIFR, KIVR
can I feel	KIFL
can I get	KIGT
can I go	KIG
can I have	KIF

C

can I live	KIV
can I mean	KIM
can I mean to	KIMT
can I mean to say	KIMTS
can I recall	K*IRL
can I recollect	KIRK
can I remember	KIRM
can I say	KIS
can I see	KIZ
can I understand	KINDZ
can I want	KIPT
cannabis	KBIZ
cannon	KWON
cannot	KWOT, K-/NOT
can't	K-NT
canvas	KWAS
canvass	
canvass	KWAF
canvasses	KWAFS
canvassing	KWAFG
canvassed	KWAFD
can you	
can you	KU
can you be	KUB
can you believe	KUBL
can you ever	KUVR
can you feel	KUFL
can you get	K*UGT
can you go	KUG
can you imagine	KUJ
can you live	KUV
can you please	KUP
can you please tell	KUPT
can you please tell us	KUPTS
can you recall	KURL
can you recollect	KURK
can you remember	KURM
can you repeat	KURP
can you repeat the	KURPT
can you repeat the question	KURPTS
can you rephrase	KUFR
can you rephrase the	KUFRT
can you rephrase the question	KUFRTS
can you say	KUS
can you see	KUZ, K*US

BRIEF ENCOUNTERS C

can you tell	KUT
can you tell us	KUTS
can you think	KUNG
can you understand	KUNDZ
capability	KPAIBLT, KAIBLT
capable	KPAIBL
capably	KPAEBL

capacitate
- capacitate . . . KPAFT
- capacitates . . . KPAFTS
- capacitating . . . KPAFGT
- capacitated . . . KPAFTD

capacitor	KPRAFT
capacity	KPA*S
caper	KAIRP
capillary	KPLAIR

capital
- capital . . . KAEP, KPAL
- *capital gain* . . . KPALG
- *capital gains* . . . KPALGZ
- capitalism . . . KAFM, KAEFM
- capitalist . . . KAEPT, KL*IS
- capitalization . . . KAEPGS, KLAOIFGS
- *capital punishment* . . . KPUMT

capitalize
- capitalize . . . KLAOIZ
- capitalizes . . . KLAOIFS, KLAOISZ
- capitalizing . . . KLAOIFG
- capitalized . . . KLAOIFD

capitol	KPOL
Capitol Hill	KPOIL

capitulate
- capitulate . . . KPIFP
- capitulates . . . KPIFPS
- capitulating . . . KPIFPG
- capitulated . . . KPIFPD
- capitulation . . . KPIFPGS

cappuccino	KPAFP
caprice	KPRAOES

capricious
- capricious . . . KPRIRB, KPRAOERB
- capriciously . . . KPRIRBL, KPRAOERBL
- capriciousness . . . KPRINS, KPRAOENS

capsulate
- capsulate . . . KPAFL

© 1997 White-Boucke Publishing.   75   ILLEGAL TO PHOTOCOPY

capsulates	KPAFLS
capsulating	KPAFLG
capsulated	KPAFLD
capsulation	KPAFLGS
capsule	KP-FL
capsulization	KP-FLGS

capsulize
capsulize	KP-FLZ
capsulizes	KP-FLSZ
capsulizing	KP-FLG
capsulized	KP-FLD

captain	KAPT

caption
caption	KAPGS
captions	KAPGSZ
captioning	KAPGS/-G
captioned	KAPGS/-D, KAPGD

captive	KPIV
captivity	KPIVT

capture
capture	KPUR
captures	KPURS
capturing	KPURG
captured	KPURD

car alarm	KLAURM
carat	KRA*T

carbon
carbon	KBON
carbon dioxide	KBOX, KBO*D
carbon monoxide	KBOM

carcinogen	SKROG
carcinoma	SKROEM
cardboard	KBORD
cardiac	KAURK
cardiac arrest	KAURKT
cardigan	KARGD
cardiologist	KAURLT, KARD/YOLT
cardiology	KAURLG, KARD/YOLG
cardiovascular	KAUFRB
care and treatment	KAIRMT

careen
careen	KRAOEN
careens	KRAOENS
careening	KRAOENG
careened	KRAOEND

BRIEF ENCOUNTERS   C

career .... KRAOER
careful
    careful .... KAIF
    carefully .... KAIFL
    carefulness .... KAIFRNS
careless .... KAIRLS
caret .... KR*ET, KRA*ET
cargo .... KARG
Caribbean .... KRAOEB, KRIB/YAN
carjack
    carjack .... KAURJ
    carjacks .... KAURJS
    carjacking .... KAURJ/-G
    carjacked .... KAURJD
carjacker .... KRAURJ
carload .... KARLD
carnage .... KARJ
carotid .... KROTD
carpal
    carpal .... KPARL
    carpal tunnel .... KPARLT, KUNL
    carpal tunnel syndrome .... KPARLTS, KUNLS
carpenter .... KRARP
carpentry .... KAERPT
car pool .... KPAO*L
car-pool
    car-pool .... KPAOL
    car-pools .... KPAOLS
    car-pooling .... KPAOLG
    car-pooled .... KPAOLD
car-pooler .... KPRAOL
car-pool lane .... KPLAEN
carpus .... KARPS
carriage .... KAIRJ
carrier .... KRA*ER
carrot .... KAERT
carry
    carry .... KAER
    carries .... KAERS
    carrying .... KAERG
    carried .... KAERD
carryover .... KROEVR
cartilage .... KLART
cartridge .... KRAJ
carton .... KRAONT

case in point	KOINT
cast	
cast	KAFT
casts	KAFS
casting	KAFG
cast	KAFT
castle	KAFL
castrate	
castrate	KRAIF
castrates	KRAIFS
castrating	KRAIFG
castrated	KRAIFD
castration	KRAIFGS
casual	
casual	KARBL
casually	KAERBL
casualty	KARBLT
CAT	KA*T
cataclysm	KLIFM
cataclysmal	KLIFL
cataclysmic	KLIZ, KLIFK
catalog	
catalog	KLAOG
catalogs	KLAOGS
cataloging	KLAOG/-G
cataloged	KLAOGD
cataloger	KLAORG
catalyst	KLIS
cat and mouse	KMOUZ
catapult	
catapult	PULT
catapults	PULTS
catapulting	PULGT
catapulted	PULTD
cataract	KAKT
catastrophe	STRAOF, STROF
catastrophes	STRAOFS, STROFZ
catastrophic	STRAOFK, STROFK
catastrophically	STRAOFL, STROFL
catch	
catch	KAFP
catches	KAFPS
catching	KAFPG
caught	KAUT
catcher	KRAFP

BRIEF ENCOUNTERS　　　　　　　　　　　　　　　　　　C

categorical
    categorical.. KOIRK
    categorically..................................... KOIRL
    categorically speaking...................... KOIRLS, KOIRLG
categorize
    categorize............................. KROIZ, KAT/GRAOIZ
    categorizes .... KROIFS, KAT/GRAOIFS
    categorizing......................... KROIFG, KAT/GRAOIFG
    categorized .... KROIFD, KAT/GRAOIFD
category .... KOIR, KAGT
catharsis .... THAURS
cathartic .... THAURKT
catheter .... THERT
Catholic .... KA*LT
Catholicism... KLAFM
caulk .... KAUK
causal... KAUFL, KAULZ
causative .... KAUV
cause
    cause .... KAUS, KAUZ
    causes..................................... KAUFS, KAUSZ
    causing .... KAUFG
    caused... KAUFD
cause of
    cause of....................................... KA*UFS
    cause of action................................. KAUX
    cause of the .... KAUFT
    cause of them .... KAUFM
    cause of these.................................. KAUFZ
    causes of action .... KAUXZ
caution
    caution .... KAUGS
    cautions....................................... KAUGSZ
    cautioning .... KAUGS/-G, KAUG
    cautioned .... KAUGD, KAUD
cautionary .... KRAUGS
cautious... KAURB
cautiously... KAURBL
cavalier
    cavalier .... KAVRL
    cavalierly .... KAEVRL
    cavalierness .... KAVRLS
cavalry.. KRAVL
caveat .... KAEVT
caveat emptor................................... KAEVPT

C

BRIEF ENCOUNTERS

cavern . . . . KAVRN, KAFRN
cavernous . . . . KAVRNS, KAFRNS
caverns . . . . KAVRNZ, KAFRNZ
cavort
    cavort . . . . KWOERT
    cavorts . . . . KWOERTS
    cavorting . . . . KWOERGT
    cavorted . . . . KWOERTD
CD-ROM . . . . DROM
cease
    cease . . . . SAOES
    ceases . . . . SAOEFS, SAOESZ
    ceasing . . . . SAOEFG
    ceased . . . . SAOEFD
Celsius . . . . SELZ
celebrate
    celebrate . . . . SBRAIT
    celebrates . . . . SBRAITS
    celebrating . . . . SBRAIGT
    celebrated . . . . SBRAITD
celebration . . . . SBRAIGS
celebrity . . . . SLEB
celestial . . . . SLES
cell
    cell . . . . KREL
    cellophane . . . . SFAIN
    cell phone . . . . SLOEN
    cell phones . . . . SLOENZ
    cellular . . . . SLER
    cellular call . . . . SLERK, SLAUL
    cellular phone . . . . SLERP
cement
    cement . . . . SEMT
    cements . . . . SEMTS
    cementing . . . . SEMGT
    cemented . . . . SEMTD
cemetery . . . . KRAEMT
censor
    censor . . . . SNUR
    censors . . . . SNURS
    censoring . . . . SNURG
    censored . . . . SNURD
censorship . . . . SNURP, SHORP
census . . . . SKRENS

BRIEF ENCOUNTERS C

center
    center .... SNER
    centers .... SNERS
    centering .... SNERG
    centered .... SNERD
center
    center field .... SNEFLD
    center fielder .... SNEFRLD
    centerfold .... SNOLD
    center lane .... SLAEN
    centerline .... SLAOIN
    center line .... SLOIN
    center of .... SNEF
    center of attention .... SNEFGS
    center of the .... SNEFT
    center of them .... SNEFM
    center of these .... SNEFZ
    centerpiece .... SNERP
    center stage .... SNAIJ
centigrade .... SGRAID
centimeter .... SMAOERT, KR-M
central
    central .... STRAL
    Central America .... STRERK
    Central American .... STRARN
    Central Intelligence Agency .... STEJ, KRAI/KRAI
    centralization .... STRALGS
    centrally .... STRAEL
    central nervous system .... KR-NS
centralize
    centralize .... STRALS
    centralizes .... STRALSZ
    centralizing .... STRALG
    centralized .... STRALD
centric .... STRENK
centrifugal
    centrifugal .... STRIF
    centrifugal force .... STRORZ
    centrifugally .... STRIFL
centrifuge .... STRAOUJ
centrism .... STRIFM
centrist .... STRIFT
centuries .... SENZ
century .... SEN
CEO .... KRAOE

cereal	KRAOERL
cerebellum	SPWLUM
cerebral	SPWRAL
cerebral palsy	SPWRALS, SPWRALZ
cerebrum	SPWRUM
ceremonial	SMOENL
ceremonious	SMOENZ, SMOUS
ceremony	SMOEN

certain
- certain . . . . SERN
- certainly . . . . SERNL
- certainty . . . . SERNT

certifiable	SFAOIBL
certifiably	SFAOEBL
certificate	SER
certificates	SER/–S
certification	SERGS
certified public accountant	SPOUNT, SPAE/SPAE
certifier	SFAOIR

certify
- certify . . . . SFAOI
- certifies . . . . SFAOIS
- certifying . . . . SFAOIG
- certified . . . . SFAOID

certiorari	SHAIRB, SERS/RAIR
cervical	SR–FL
cervix	SR–FX
Cesarean	SAIRN
Cesarean section	SAIRNGS
chain of command	KHAMD
chain of custody	KH*UD

chair
- chairman . . . . KHAIRM
- *chairman of the board* . . . . KHAIRB
- chairperson . . . . KHAIRP
- chairwoman . . . . KHAM

challenge
- challenge . . . . KHAJ
- challenges . . . . KHAJS
- challenging . . . . KHAJ/–G
- challenged . . . . KHAJD

challenge for cause	KHAUS
challenger	KHAERJ
chamber	KHAIM
chamber of commerce	KHARK

BRIEF ENCOUNTERS   C

champerty	KHERP
champion	KHAON
championship	KHAONZ, KHAOP
change	
change	KHAIJ, KHAING
changes	KHAIJS, KHAINGS
changing	KHAIJ/-G, KHAIG
changed	KHAIJD, KHAINGD
change of venue	KHAV, KHAOUV
channel	
channel	KHANL
channels	KHANLS
channeling	KHANL/-G
channeled	KHANLD
chaos	KAOS
chaotic	KAOKT
chapter	KHAPT
character	
character	KARK
characteristic	KARKT
characterization	KARGS, KRAOIFGS
characterize	
characterize	KRAOIZ
characterizes	KRAOIFS
characterizing	KRAOIFG
characterized	KRAOIFD
chargeable	KHARBL
charge the jury	KHAURJ
chariot	KHOT
charisma	KRIZ
charismatic	KRAMT, KRIZ/TIK
charitable	KHAIRBL
charity	KHAIRT
charlatan	SHARL
charlatanism	SHAFM
Charlotte	SHARLT
charter	
charter	KHAERT
charters	KHAERTS
chartering	KHAERGT
chartered	KHAERTD
chase	
chase	KHAIS
chases	KHAIFS, KHAISZ
chasing	KHAIFG

chased . . . . KHAIFD
chastise
    chastise . . . . KHAOIS
    chastises . . . . KHAOIFS, KHAOISZ
    chastising . . . . KHAOIFG
    chastised . . . . KHAOIFD
chastisement . . . . KHAOIFMT
chastiser . . . . KHAOIFR, KHAOIFRS
chattel . . . . KHALT
chauvinism . . . . SHOEFM, SHOEVM
chauvinist . . . . SHOEFT, SHOEVT
chauvinistic . . . . SHOEFK, SHOEVK
cheap
    cheaper . . . . KHAERP
    cheapest . . . . KHAEPS
    cheaply . . . . KHAEPL
    cheapness . . . . KHAENS
cheapen
    cheapen . . . . KHAOEN
    cheapens . . . . KHAOENS
    cheapening . . . . KHAOENG
    cheapened . . . . KHAOEND
cheater . . . . KHAOERT
check
    checkbook . . . . KHEB
    checker . . . . KHERK
    checkers . . . . KHERKZ
    checkpoint . . . . KHOINT, KHEPT
    checkpoints . . . . KHOINTS, KHEPT/-S
    checkroom . . . . KHAOM
check out
    check out . . . . KHOUT
    checks out . . . . KHOUTS
    checking out . . . . KHOUGT
    checked out . . . . KHOUTD
check up
    check up . . . . KHUP
    checks up . . . . KHUPS
    checking up . . . . KHUPG
    checked up . . . . KHUPD
checkup . . . . KHEP
checkups . . . . KHEPZ
cheer
    cheerful . . . . KHAOEFRL, KHOIF
    cheerfully . . . . KHOIFL

BRIEF ENCOUNTERS   C

cheerily	KHAOERL
cheerleader	KHAOERLD
cheer up	
cheer up	KHAOERP
cheers up	KHAOERPS
cheering up	KHAOERPG
cheered up	KHAOERPD
chemical	
chemical	KHEM
chemical weapon	KWEP
chemical weapons	KWEPZ
chemistry	KHEMZ
chemotherapy	KAOEM, KAOEMT
cherish	
cherish	KHER
cherishes	KHERS
cherishing	KHERG
cherished	KHERD
Chevrolet	SHEV
Chevy	SHAEV
chic	SHAO*EK
Chicago	KHIG, KH*I
chicken pox	KHAUX, KHOKZ
chief	
Chief Executive Officer	KHOFR, KRAOE/KRAOE
Chief Justice	KH–J, KR–J
chiefly	KHAOEFL
chief of staff	KHAFT
chiefs of staff	KHAFTS
chieftain	KHAOEFT
child	
child abuse	KHAOUS
childbearing	KHAERG
child birth	KH*IRT
childhood	KHAOD
childish	KHAOIRB
childlike	KHAOIK
child molestation	KHOELGS
child molester	KHOERL
childproof	KHAOF
children	KHIRN
children's	KHIRNS
child's	KHAOILDZ
child support	KHORT
child support payment	KHORMT, KHORM

C

Chile	KHAE
Chilean	KHAEN
China	KHAOIN
Chinatown	KHAOINT, KHOUN
Chinese	KHAOEZ, KH-Z
chiropractic	KAOIRT
chiropractor	KAOIR

chisel
- chisel . . . . KHILZ
- chisels . . . . KHIFZ, KHISZ
- chiseling . . . . KHIFG
- chiseled . . . . KHIZ/-D, KHILZ/-D

chiseler	KHIRLZ
chiselers	KHIRLSZ
chloroform	KLORM
chocolate	KHOKT
cholesterol	KLES, KL*ES

choose
- choose . . . . KHAOS
- chooses . . . . KHAOFS, KHAOSZ
- choosing . . . . KHAOFG
- chose . . . . KHOES
- chosen . . . . KHOEFN, KHOENS

chopper	KHORP
choppy	KHOIP

choreograph
- choreograph . . . . KRAUF
- choreographs . . . . KRAUFS
- choreographing . . . . KRAUFG
- choreographed . . . . KRAUFD

choreographer	KRAURG
choreography	KRAUG
CHP	KH*P

christen
- christen . . . . KRIFN
- christens . . . . KRIFNS
- christening . . . . KRIFNG
- christened . . . . KRIFND

Christian	KRIN
Christianity	KRINT

Christmas
- Christmas . . . . KROIM
- ***Christmas Eve*** . . . . KRAOEV, KROIVM
- ***Christmas tree*** . . . . KROIMT

chromosome	ZOEM, SMOEM

BRIEF ENCOUNTERS   C

```
chronic .................................................. KRONK
chronically ............................................... KRONL
chronicle
    chronicle ....................................... KRON, KROKL
    chronicles ..................................... KRONS, KROKLS
    chronicling ............................. KRON/-G, KROKL/-G
    chronicled .................................... KROND, KROKLD
chuckle
    chuckle ............................................... KHUKL
    chuckles ............................................. KHUKLS
    chuckling ................................... KHULG, KHUKL/-G
    chuckled ............................................. KHUKLD
church .................................................. KHUFP
CIA ....................................................... KRAI
cigar ..................................................... SGAR
cigarette
    cigarette ...................................... SGRET, S-G
    *cigarette smoke* .................................... SGROEK
    *cigarette smoker* ................................... SGROERK
cinch
    cinch ................................................. KRIFP
    cinches .............................................. KRIFPS
    cinching ............................................. KRIFPG
    cinched .............................................. KRIFPD
Cincinnati .............................................. SNAIT
cinema
    cinema ................................................ SN-M
    cinematographer ......................... SMAURG, SNAURG
    cinematography ............................. SMAUG, SNAUG
cinnamon ................................................. SNON
cipher .................................................. SAOIFR
circle
    circle ......................................... S*IRL, KRIRL
    circles ............................................... SIRLS
    circling .............................................. SIRLG
    circled ............................................... SIRLD
circuit
    circuit ............................................... SKRIT
    circuits ............................................. SKRITS
    circuiting ........................................... SKRIGT
    circuited ............................................ SKRITD
circuit
    *circuit board* ..................................... SKBORD
    *circuit breaker* .................................. SKBRAERK
    *circuit court* ..................................... SKOURT
```

Circuit Court	SKRORT
circuitry	SKRAOERT
circular	SLAR

circulate
circulate	SL-
circulates	SL-Z
circulating	SL-G
circulated	SL-D
circulation	SL-GS
circulatory	SLORT, SIRKT

circumcise
circumcise	SKMAOIS
circumcises	SKMAOIFS, SKMAOISZ
circumcising	SKMAOIFG
circumcised	SKMAOIFD
circumcision	SKMIGS
circumference	SFRENS, SK-FRNS
circumferential	SFRENL, SK-FRNL
circumstance	SIRK
circumstantial	SIRKL, S-RBL
circumstantial evidence	SKEVD
circus	SKRUS
citation	KRAOIGS

cite
cite	KRAOIT
cites	KRAOITS
citing	KRAOIGT
cited	KRAOITD
citizen	SIZ
citizenship	SHIZ

city
city	STI
city attorney	STIRN
City Attorney's Office	STOFS
City of Los Angeles	SLAX

civil
civil	SIVL
civilian	SIVNL
civility	SIVLT, SIFLT
civilization	SIFGS, SIVGS
civil law	SLA
civil liberties	SIBTS
civil rights	SIRTS
claimant	KLAIMT
clairvoyance	KLOINS

BRIEF ENCOUNTERS   C

clairvoyant... KLOINT
clamber
    clamber.. KLAEB
    clambers.. KLAEBS
    clambering.. KLAEBG
    clambered... KLAEBD
clamor
    clamor.. KLARM
    clamors.. KLARMS
    clamoring.. KLARMG
    clamored.. KLARMD
clamorous... KLOUS
clandestine... KLAND
clap
    clap... KLAP
    claps... KLAPZ
    clapping.. KLAPG
    clapped.. KLAPD
clarification.. KLAIFGS
clarify
    clarify.. KLAIF
    clarifies... KLAIFS
    clarifying.. KLAIFG
    clarified... KLAIFD
clarity.. KLAIRT
clasp
    clasp.. KL-PS
    clasps... KL-PZ
    clasping... KL-PG
    clasped.. KL-PD
class
    class action .... KLAGS
    class action lawsuit .... KLAUT
    classic... KLAFK
    classification...................................... KLAFGS
    classroom... KLAOM
classify
    classify.. KLAF
    classifies.. KLAFS
    classifying... KLAFG
    classified.. KLAFD
claustrophobia................................. KLA*US, KLAUF
claustrophobic.. KLAUFK
clavicle.. KLAFL, KLAVL

© 1997 White-Boucke Publishing.   89   ILLEGAL TO PHOTOCOPY

clean
    cleaner . . . . KLAOERN
    cleaner than . . . . KLAOERNT
    cleanliness. . . . . KLENLS
    cleanly . . . . KLENL
clean up
    clean up . . . . KLAOEP
    cleans up . . . . KLAOEPS
    cleaning up . . . . KLAOEPG
    cleaned up . . . . KLAOEPD
clean up the . . . . KLAOEPT
clean up these . . . . KLAOEPZ
clear
    clearance . . . . KLAOERNS
    clear-cut . . . . KLAOERK, KLAOERKT
    clearly. . . . . KLAOERL
clear up
    clear up . . . . KLAOERP
    clears up. . . . . KLAOERPS
    clearing up . . . . KLAOERPG
    cleared up. . . . . KLAOERPD
clear up the. . . . . KLAOERPT
clear up these . . . . KLAOERPZ
cleavage. . . . . KLAOEVJ
cleave
    cleave . . . . KLAOEV
    cleaves. . . . . KLAOEVS
    cleaving . . . . KLAOEVG
    cleaved / cleft / clove . . . . KLAOEVD / KLEFT / KLOEV
    cleaved / cleft / cloven . . . . KLAOEVD / KLEFT / KLOEVN
clemency . . . . KLEM
clench
    clench. . . . . KLEFP
    clenches . . . . KLEFPS
    clenching. . . . . KLEFPG
    clenched . . . . KLEFPD
clergy . . . . KLERJ
clerical . . . . KLERL
Cleveland . . . . KLAOEVLD, KLAOEFLD
clever
    clever. . . . . KLEVR
    cleverly. . . . . KLEVRL
    cleverness. . . . . KLEVRNS
cliché. . . . . KLIRB
client . . . . KLAOI

BRIEF ENCOUNTERS   C

clientele	KLEL
climate	KLIMT
clime	KLOIM
clinch	
clinch	KLIFP
clinches	KLIFPS
clinching	KLIFPG
clinched	KLIFPD
clincher	KLIFRP
cling	
cling	KLING
clings	KLINGZ
clinging	KLING/-G
clung	KLUNG
clinic	KLIN
clinical	KLINL
clipper	KLIRP
close	
close	KLOES
closes	KLOEFS, KLOESZ
closing	KLOEFG
closed	KLOEFD
close	
close by	KLOEB
close by the	KLOEBT
close by these	KLOEBZ
close by those	KLOEBS
closed-captioned	KLOEPD
closed-captioning	KLOEPG
closed circuit	KLOEKT
closed-circuit TV	KLOEVK
closer	KLOERS
closer than	KLOERNS, KLOERN
closer than the	KLOERNTS, KLOERNT
closest	KLOEFT, KLO*ES
close-up	KLOEP
closet	KLOZ, KLOS
closure	KLO*UR
cloture	KLOET
clue	KLAO
cluster	
cluster	KLUFR
clusters	KLUFRS
clustering	KLUFRG
clustered	KLUFRD

C — BRIEF ENCOUNTERS

Co.	KOFPLT
coagulate	
coagulate	KWAG
coagulates	KWAGZ
coagulating	KWAG/-G
coagulated	KWAGD
coagulation	KWAGS
coalition	KOLGS
coast	
coastal	KOEFL
coaster	KOEFR
coast guard	*KOEFGD*
cocaine	KRAEN
coccyx	SKOX
cochlea	
cochlea	KLA
cochlear	KLAER
cochlear implant	*KLAERN*
cocktail	KOKT
coconspirator	SKPOIRT, SKPIRT
C.O.D.	KROD
code section	*K-X*
codicil	SKOD
co-ed	KO*ED, KW*ED
coerce	
coerce	KWOEF, KO*ERS
coerces	KWOEFS, KOEFS
coercing	KWOEFG, KOEFG
coerced	KWOEFD, KOEFD
coercer	KWOEFR
coercible	KWOEFBL
coercion	KOERGS
coercive	
coercive	KWOEV
coercively	KWOEVL
coerciveness	KWOEVNS
coffee	KOEF
coffer	KAUFR
coffin	KAUFN
cogency	KOEJS
cogent	KOEJ
cognitive	KOV
cognitively	KOVL
cognizance	KOGS, KOGZ
cognizant	KOGT

BRIEF ENCOUNTERS   C

cohabit
    cohabit .... KWABT
    cohabits .... KWABTS
    cohabiting .... KWABT/-G, KWABGT
    cohabited .... KWABTD
cohabitation...................................... KWABGS
coherence .... KWERNZ, KW*ERNS
coherency .... KWERNSZ
coherent .... KWERNT
coherently .... KWERNLT, KWERNL
cohesion .... KWAOEGS
cohesive
    cohesive .... KWAOEV
    cohesively .... KWAOEVL
    cohesiveness............................... KWAOEVNS
cohort... KWORT
coincidence....................................... KWINZ
coincidental...................................... KWINL
coincidentally................................... KWAOENL
collaborate
    collaborate .... KLAB
    collaborates................................... KLABS
    collaborating.................................. KLABG
    collaborated .... KLABD
collaboration .... KLAEX
collage .... KLAJ
collapse
    collapse .... KLAPS
    collapses................................... KLAPSZ
    collapsing .... KLAPS/-G, KLAPGS
    collapsed .... KLAPS/-D
collapsible .... KLABL
collar .... KLAR
collarbone .... KLARN
collate
    collate .... KLAIT
    collates .... KLAITS
    collating .... KLAIGT
    collated .... KLAITD
collateral .... KLARL
collation...................................... KLA*IGS
colleague .... KLAOEG
collect
    collect .... KLEK
    collects...................................... KLEKZ

C — BRIEF ENCOUNTERS

```
collecting ............................ KLEK/-G, KLEG
collected ............................................ KLEKD
collect
    collectable ..................................... KLEBL
    collectible ..................................... KLIBL
    collection ....................................... KLEX
    collective ....................................... KLEV
    collective bargaining ................... KLEFB, KLEVB
    collective bargaining agreement ........ KLEFMT, KLEVMT
    collectively ................................... KLEVL
    collectivism ............................ KLEVM, KLEFM
    collector ............................. KLERKT, KLEKT
college ............................................. KLEJ
collide
    collide ........................................ KLAOID
    collides ..................................... KLAOIDZ
    colliding .................................... KLAOIGD
    collided ................................... KLAOID/-D
collie ............................................. KLAOE
collision ........................................... KLIGS
colloid ............................................. KLOID
colloquial ............................ KWAOEL, KLOEKL
colloquy .......................................... KWAOE
collude
    collude ................................. KL-D, KLAO*U
    colludes ............................. KL-DZ, KLAO*US
    colluding ................... KL-GD, KLAO*UG, KLAOUGD
    colluded .............. KL-D/-D, KLAO*UD, KLAOUD/-D
collusion ............................ KL-GS, KLAO*UGS
Colombia ........................................... KLOM
Colombian ................................ KLO*M, KLOB
colon .............................................. KLON
colonel ............................................. KOL
colonies ......................................... KLOINZ
colony ............................................ KLOIN
color
    color .......................................... KLOR
    colors ........................................ KLORS
    coloring ...................................... KLORG
    colored ....................................... KLORD
color
    coloration ................................... KLORGS
    colorblind ........................... KLORB, KLORND
    colorful ..................................... KLOFRL
    colorless ..................................... KLORL
```

BRIEF ENCOUNTERS   C

Colorado .... KRO*
Columbia .... KL*UM
column .... KLUM
columnist... KLUMT
COM.. KROM
coma .... KO*EM, KMO
combat
    combat.. KBAT
    combats....................................... KBATS
    combating .... KBAGT
    combated..................................... KBATD
combat
    combative .... KBAV
    combatively .... KBAVL
    combativeness .... KBAVNS
    combattant................................... KBANT
combination.. KBAIGS
combine
    combine .... KBAOIN
    combines .... KBAOINS
    combining..................................... KBAOING
    combined .... KBAOIND
combustibility .... KBUBLT
combustible.. KBUBL
combustion.. KBUGS
come
    come .... KOM
    comes... KOMS
    coming.................................. KOMG, KOG
    came .... KAIM
    come .... KOM
comedian .... KMAOED
comedy.. KOMD
come out
    come out..................................... KMOU
    comes out .... KMOUS
    coming out .... KMOUG
    came out..................................... KMOUD
comet .... KMET
come up
    come up .... KMUP
    comes up..................................... KMUPS
    coming up .... KMUPG
    came up .... KMUPD
comeuppance..................................... KMUPZ

© 1997 White-Boucke Publishing.   ILLEGAL TO PHOTOCOPY

comfort
- comfort ... K–FRT
- comforts ... K–FRTS
- comforting ... K–FRGT
- comforted ... K–FRTD
comfortable ... K–FRBL
comfortably ... KEFRBL
comforter ... KR–FRT
comma ... KMA
command
- command ... KMAN
- commands ... KMANS
- commanding ... KMANG
- commanded ... KMAND
command
- commander ... KMARND, KMARN
- ***commander in chief*** ... KMAOEF
- ***commanders in chief*** ... KMAOEFS
- commandment ... KMANT, KMAMT
commemorate
- commemorate ... KMEM
- commemorates ... KMEMS
- commemorating ... KMEMG
- commemorated ... KMEMD
commemoration ... KMEMGS, KMEJ
commence
- commence ... KMENS
- commences ... KMEFS, KMENSZ
- commencing ... KMEFG
- commenced ... KMEFD
commencement ... KMEMT
commend
- commend ... KMEND
- commends ... KMENDZ
- commending ... KMENGD
- commended ... KMEND/–D
commendable ... KMENL
commensurable ... KMRABL
commensurably ... KMRAEBL
commensurate ... KMRAT
commensuration ... KMENGS
comment
- comment ... KMENT
- comments ... KMENTS
- commenting ... KMENGT, KMENG

BRIEF ENCOUNTERS C

commented	KMENTD
commentator	KMERNT
commerce	KMERS
commercial	
commercial	KMERL
commercialism	KMEFM
commercialization	KMERLGS
commercially	KMAOERL
commiserate	
commiserate	KMRAET
commiserates	KMRAETS
commiserating	KMRAEGT
commiserated	KMRAETD
commiseration	KMRAEGS
commissary	KMAR
commission	
commission	KMIGS
commissions	KMIGSZ
commissioning	KMIG
commissioned	KMIGD
commissioner	KMIRGS
commit	
commit	KMIT
commits	KMITS
committing	KMIGT
committed	KMITD
commit	
commitment	KMIMT
committable	KMIBL
committal	KMILT
committee	KMAOET
commodity	KMOD
common	
common	KMON
commoner	KMORN
common ground	KMONGD
common law	KMOL
common-law	KMAUL
common-law marriage	KMAERJ
commonly	KMONL
common sense	KMENZ
commonsense	KM*ENZ
commonwealth	KWELT
commotion	KMOEGS
communal	KMAOUNL, KMUNL

communally . . . . KMAOENL
communicability . . . . KMUBLT
communicable. . . . . KMUBL
communicate
    communicate . . . . KMUN
    communicates . . . . KMUNS
    communicating . . . . KMUNG
    communicated . . . . KMUND
communication . . . . KMUNGS
communicative
    communicative. . . . . KMUV
    communicatively. . . . . KMUVL
    communicativeness . . . . KMUVNS
communicator . . . . KMURN
communion. . . . . KMAOUNGS
communique . . . . KMAI
communism. . . . . KMAOUFM, KMOUFM
communist . . . . KMAOUFT, KMOUFT, KMUFT
community
    community. . . . . KMUNT, KMAOUNT
    community college . . . . KMUNK
    community property. . . . . KPROT
compact
    compact. . . . . KPAK
    compacts . . . . KPAKZ
    compacting . . . . KPAK/-G, KPAG
    compacted . . . . KPAKD
compaction. . . . . KPAX
compactor . . . . KPARK
companion . . . . KPAN
companions . . . . KPANZ
company . . . . KPAEN
comparability. . . . . KPARBLT, KPAIRBLT
comparable . . . . KPARBL, KPAIRBL
comparably . . . . KPAERBL
comparative. . . . . KPAV, KPAIV
comparatively. . . . . KPAVL, KPAIVL
compare
    compare . . . . KPAIR
    compares. . . . . KPAIRS
    comparing . . . . KPAIRG
    compared . . . . KPAIRD
comparison . . . . KPAIRN
compartment . . . . KPARMT
compass. . . . . KPAS

BRIEF ENCOUNTERS   C

compassion
    compassion .... KPARB, KPAGS
    compassionate .... KPARBT, KPAGT
    compassionately. .... KPAERBLT
compatibility .... KPABLT
compatible .... KPABL
compel
    compel. .... KMEL
    compels .... KMELS
    compelling .... KMELG
    compelled. .... KMELD
compensate
    compensate .... KPEN
    compensates. .... KPENS
    compensating .... KPENG
    compensated. .... KPEND
compensation .... KPENGS
compensatory
    compensatory .... KPRENT
    compensatory damage .... K-D, KPRENTD
    compensatory damages .... K-DZ, KPRENTDZ, KPRENDZ
compete
    compete. .... KPAOET
    competes .... KPAOETS
    competing .... KPAOEGT
    competed. .... KPAOETD
competence. .... KPES
competency .... KPAES
competent. .... KPE
competently. .... KPELT
competition. .... KPEGS
competitive
    competitive. .... KPEV
    competitively. .... KPEVL
    competitiveness. .... KPEVNS
competitor. .... KPRET
compilation. .... KPILGS
compile
    compile .... KPIL
    compiles. .... KPILS
    compiling .... KPILG
    compiled .... KPILD
compiler. .... KPIRL
complacence .... KPLAENZ
complacency .... KPLAENSZ

complacent . . . . KPLA*ENT
complain
    complain . . . . KPLAIN
    complains . . . . KPLAINS
    complaining . . . . KPLAING
    complained . . . . KPLAIND
complainant . . . . KPLAINT
complaint . . . . PLAINT
complaisance . . . . KPLAENS
complaisant . . . . KPLAENT
complaisantly . . . . KPLAENL
complement
    complement . . . . KPLEMT
    complements . . . . KPLEMTS
    complementing . . . . KPLEMGT, KPLEMG
    complemented . . . . KPLEMTD
complementary . . . . KPLERMT
complete
    complete . . . . PLET
    completes . . . . PLETS
    completing . . . . PLEGT
    completed . . . . PLETD
completely . . . . KPLEL
completeness . . . . PLENS
completion . . . . PLEGS, PLAOEGS
complex . . . . KPLEX
compliance . . . . KPLAOINS
compliancy . . . . KPLAOINSZ
compliant . . . . KPLAOINT
compliantly . . . . KPLAOINL, KPLAOINLT
complicate
    complicate . . . . KPLIK, KPLIKT
    complicates . . . . KPLIKZ, KPLIKTS
    complicating . . . . KPLIK/-G, KPLIKT/-G, KPLIG
    complicated . . . . KPLIKD, KPLIKTD
complication . . . . KPLIX, KPLIGS
compliment
    compliment . . . . KPLIM, KPLIMT
    compliments . . . . KPLIMS, KPLIMTS
    complimenting . . . . KPLIMG, KPLIMGT
    complimented . . . . KPLIMD, KPLIMTD
comply
    comply . . . . KPLAOI
    complies . . . . KPLAOIS
    complying . . . . KPLAOIG

BRIEF ENCOUNTERS   C

complied . . . . KPLAOID
component . . . . KPOENT
comport
    comport . . . . KP-RT
    comports . . . . KP-RTS
    comporting . . . . KP-RGT
    comported . . . . KP-RTD
comportment . . . . KP-MT
compose
    compose. . . . . KPOES
    composes . . . . KPOEFS, KPOESZ
    composing . . . . KPOEFG
    composed. . . . . KPOEFD
composer . . . . KPOER
composite. . . . . KPOS, KPO*S
composition . . . . KPOGS, KPOEGS
compost
    compost . . . . KPOEFT
    composts . . . . KPOEFTS
    composting . . . . KPOEFGT
    composted . . . . KPOEFTD
composure . . . . KPOUR
compound
    compound . . . . KPOUN
    compounds. . . . . KPOUNS
    compounding . . . . KPOUNG
    compounded . . . . KPOUND
compoundable. . . . . KPOUNL
compound interest . . . . KPINT
comprehend
    comprehend . . . . KPREN
    comprehends. . . . . KPRENS
    comprehending . . . . KPRENG
    comprehended. . . . . KPREND
comprehensibility . . . . KPRENLT
comprehensible . . . . KPRENL
comprehension . . . . KPRENGS
comprehensive
    comprehensive . . . . KPREV
    comprehensively . . . . KPREVL
    comprehensiveness . . . . KPREVNS
comprise
    comprise . . . . KPRAOIS
    comprises . . . . KPRAOIFS, KPRAOISZ
    comprising. . . . . KPRAOIFG

comprised	KPRAOIFD
compromise	
compromise	KM-, KPROM
compromises	KM-S, KPROMS
compromising	KM-G, KPROMG
compromised	KM-D, KPROMD
compromiser	KM-R, KPRORM
comptroller	KROERL
compulsion	KPULGS
ompulsive	
compulsive	KPUV
compulsively	KPUVL
compulsiveness	KPUVNS
compulsory	KPULS, KPURLS
compunction	KP*UNGS
computability	KP-BLT
computable	KP-BL
computation	KPUGS, KPAOUGS
compute	
compute	KP-T, KPAOUT
computes	KP-TS, KPAOUTS
computing	KP-GT, KPAOUGT
computed	KP-TD, KPAOUTD
computer	KPR-
computerize	
computerize	KPR-R
computerizes	KPR-RS
computerizing	KPR-RG
computerized	KPR-RD
conceal	
conceal	SKAOEL
conceals	SKAOELS
concealing	SKAOELG
concealed	SKAOELD
conceal	
concealable	SKAOEBL
concealer	SKAOERL
concealment	SKAOEMT
concede	
concede	SKAOED
concedes	SKAOEDZ
conceding	SKAOEGD
conceded	SKAOED/-D
conceit	SKAOET
conceivability	SKAOEVLT, SKAOEVBLT

BRIEF ENCOUNTERS   C

conceivable	SKAOEVL
conceivableness	SKAOEVNS
conceivably	SKAOEVBL

conceive
conceive	SKAOEV
conceives	SKAOEVS
conceiving	SKAOEVG
conceived	SKAOEVD

concentrate
concentrate	SKRAENT
concentrates	SKRAENTS
concentrating	SKRAENG, SKRAENGT
concentrated	SKRAENTD

concentration	SKRAENGS
concept	SKEP
conception	SKEPGS

concern
concern	KERN, K-RN
concerns	KERNS, K-RNS
concerning	KERNG, K-RNG
concerned	KERND, K-RND

concert	SKERT
concession	SKEGS
concierge	SERJ
conciliable	SKIBL

conciliate
conciliate	SKILT
conciliates	SKILTS
conciliating	SKILGT, SKILG
conciliated	SKILTD

conciliation	SKILGS
conciliatory	SKIRLT

conclude
conclude	KLAOU
concludes	KLAOUS
concluding	KLAOUG
concluded	KLAOUD

conclusion
conclusion	KLAOUGS
conclusion of law	KLAOUL
conclusions of law	KLAOULS

conclusive
conclusive	KLAOUF, KLAOUV
conclusively	KLAOUFL, KLAOUVL
conclusiveness	KLAOUFNS, KLAOUVNS

© 1997 White-Boucke Publishing.   103   ILLEGAL TO PHOTOCOPY

concoct
- concoct . . . KWOK
- concocts . . . KWOKZ
- concocting . . . KWOK/-G
- concocted . . . KWOKD

concoct
- concocter . . . KWORK
- concoction . . . KWOX
- concoctive . . . KWOVK

concourse . . . KROURS
concrete . . . KRET, KRAOET
concur
- concur . . . KRUR
- concurs . . . KRURS
- concurring . . . KRURG
- concurred . . . KRURD

concur
- concurrence . . . KRUNS
- concurrent . . . KRUNT
- concurrently . . . KRUNL

concussion . . . KUNGS
condemn
- condemn . . . KEM
- condemns . . . KEMS
- condemning . . . KEMG
- condemned . . . KEMD

condemnation . . . KEMGS, KEJ
condescend
- condescend . . . SKEND
- condescends . . . SKENDZ
- condescending . . . SKENGD
- condescended . . . SKEND/-D

condescension . . . SKENGS
condiment . . . KWOMT
condition
- condition . . . K-N
- conditions . . . K-NS
- conditioning . . . K-NG
- conditioned . . . K-ND

condo . . . KOND
condom . . . KMOM
condominium . . . KMIM
conduct
- conduct . . . KUK
- conducts . . . KUKZ

BRIEF ENCOUNTERS   C

conducting .... KUK/-G
conducted .... KUKD
conduction .... KUX
conductor .... KURKT
conduit .... DWAOUT
confer
    confer .... K-FR
    confers .... K-FRS
    conferring .... K-FRG
    conferred .... K-FRD
conference .... K-FRNS
conference call .... K-FRK
confess
    confess .... FES
    confesses .... FEFZ
    confessing .... FEFG
    confessed .... FEFD
confession .... FEGS
confide
    confide .... KWAOI
    confides .... KWAOIS
    confiding .... KWAOIG
    confided .... KWAOID
confidence .... K-FD
confident
    confident .... K-FT
    confidential .... K-FLT
    confidentiality .... KEFLT
configuration .... FWIGS
confine
    confine .... KWAOIN
    confines .... KWAOINS
    confining .... KWAOING
    confined .... KWAOIND
confinement .... KWAOIMT
confirm
    confirm .... KWIRM
    confirms .... KWIRMS
    confirming .... KWIRMG
    confirmed .... KWIRMD
confirmation .... KWIRGS, KWIRMGS, KWIRJ
confiscate
    confiscate .... SFAIK
    confiscates .... SFAIKZ
    confiscating .... SFAIK/-G, SFAIG

C   BRIEF ENCOUNTERS

confiscated . . . . SFAIKD
confiscation . . . . SFAIX
confiscatory . . . . SFAIKT, SFOR
conflict
    conflict . . . . KIKT
    conflicts . . . . KIKTS
    conflicting . . . . KIKT/–G
    conflicted . . . . KIKTD
conflict of interest . . . . KINT
conform
    conform . . . . KWORM
    conforms . . . . KWORMS
    conforming . . . . KWORMG
    conformed . . . . KWORMD
conformation . . . . KWORGS, KWORMGS
confound
    confound . . . . KWOUN
    confounds . . . . KWOUNS
    confounding . . . . KWOUNG
    confounded . . . . KWOUND
confront
    confront . . . . KRONT
    confronts . . . . KRONTS
    confronting . . . . KRONGT
    confronted . . . . KRONTD
confrontation . . . . KRONGS
confuse
    confuse . . . . KWUS
    confuses . . . . KWUFS, KWUSZ
    confusing . . . . KWUFG
    confused . . . . KWUFD
confusion . . . . KWUGS, KWUFGS
congenial . . . . JAOENL
congeniality . . . . JAOENT, JAOENLT
congenital . . . . K–JT
congenitally . . . . KEJT
congest
    congest . . . . GEFT
    congests . . . . GEFTS
    congesting . . . . GEFGT
    congested . . . . GEFTD
congestion . . . . GEGS
congestive . . . . GEV
conglomerate
    conglomerate . . . . KLOMT

BRIEF ENCOUNTERS — C

```
conglomerates .................................. KLOMTS
conglomerating ........................ KLOMGT, KLOMG
conglomerated .................................. KLOMTD
conglomeration ..................................... KLOJ
congratulate
    congratulate................................... GLAIT
    congratulates ................................ GLAITS
    congratulating ............................... GLAIGT
    congratulated................................ GLAITD
congratulations .................................. GLAIGS
congratulatory .......................... GLAIRT, GLORT
congress
    congress ...................................... KONG
    congressional ................................. KRAL
    congressman ................................. KRAM
    congressmen ................................. KREM
    congresswoman ............................. KWAM
    congresswomen............................. KWEM
congruence ..................................... GRAOUNS
congruency ................................... GRAOUNSZ
congruent ...................................... GRAOUNT
congruently .................................... GRAOUNLT
congruity........................................ GRAOUT
congruous ...................................... GRAOUS
connect
    connect ........................................ KEK
    connects....................................... KEKZ
    connecting..................................... KEK/-G
    connected...................................... KEKD
connect
    connection ..................................... KEX
    connective .................................... KEVK
    connectively .................................. KEVL
    connectivity ................................... KEVT
    connector ..................................... KEKT
Connecticut ....................................... KR*T
conniption ....................................... KIPGS
connoisseur..................................... KWOUR
conquer
    conquer....................................... KWUR
    conquers...................................... KWURS
    conquering ................................... KWURG
    conquered.................................... KWURD
conquerable ................................... KWURBL
conqueror ..................................... KWRUR
```

© 1997 White-Boucke Publishing. ILLEGAL TO PHOTOCOPY

conscience . . . . K-RB
conscientious
    conscientious . . . . K-RBS
    conscientiously . . . . K-RBLS
    conscientiousness . . . . K-RBSZ
conscious . . . . KONS
consciousness . . . . KONSZ
consecutive
    consecutive . . . . SK-V
    consecutively . . . . SK-VL
    consecutiveness . . . . SK-VNS, SKEVNS
consensual . . . . SKENL
consensus . . . . SKENS
consent
    consent . . . . SKENT
    consents . . . . SKENTS
    consenting . . . . SKENGT, SKENG
    consented . . . . SKENTD
consequence . . . . KWENS
consequent . . . . KWENT
consequently . . . . KWENL
conservation . . . . SKEFRBGS
conservatism . . . . SKEFM
conservative . . . . SKEFT
conservator . . . . SKEFRT
conservatorship . . . . SKEFRP
conserve
    conserve . . . . SKEFRB
    conserves . . . . SKEFRBS
    conserving . . . . SKEFRBG
    conserved . . . . SKEFRBD
consider
    consider . . . . K-R
    considers . . . . K-RS
    considering . . . . K-RG
    considered . . . . K-RD
consider
    considerable . . . . K-RL
    considerate . . . . K-RT
    consideration . . . . K-RGS
consign
    consign . . . . SKAOIN
    consigns . . . . SKAOINS
    consigning . . . . SKAOING
    consigned . . . . SKAOIND

BRIEF ENCOUNTERS   C

consignment . . . . SKAOIMT
consignor . . . . SKAOIRN
consist
    consist. . . . . SKIFT
    consists. . . . . SKIFTS, SKIFS
    consisting . . . . SKIFGT, SKIFG
    consisted. . . . . SKIFTD, SKIFD
consistency . . . . SKINTS
consistent . . . . SKINT
consistently . . . . SKINL
consolable. . . . . SKOEBL
consolation . . . . SKOELGS
console
    console. . . . . SKOEL
    consoles . . . . SKOELS
    consoling . . . . SKOELG
    consoled. . . . . SKOELD
consolidate
    consolidate . . . . SDAIT
    consolidates. . . . . SDAITS
    consolidating . . . . SDAIGT
    consolidated . . . . SDAITD
consolidation . . . . SDAIGS
consortium . . . . SKOERB, SKORM
conspicuous
    conspicuous. . . . . SKPIK
    conspicuously. . . . . SKPIL
    conspicuousness. . . . . SKPINS
conspiracy . . . . SPIR
conspirator. . . . . SPRIR, SPRIRT
conspire
    conspire . . . . SKPAOIR
    conspires. . . . . SKPAOIRS
    conspiring . . . . SKPAOIRG
    conspired . . . . SKPAOIRD
constancy . . . . SKANTS
constant. . . . . SKANT
constantly . . . . SKANL
constellation . . . . STLAEGS
constipate
    constipate . . . . SKPAIT
    constipates . . . . SKPAITS
    constipating . . . . SKPAIGT, SKPAIG
    constipated . . . . SKPAITD
constipation. . . . . SKPAIGS

constituency . . . . SWENS
constituent. . . . . SWENT
constitute
    constitute. . . . . KAOT
    constitutes. . . . . KAOTS
    constituting . . . . KAOGT
    constituted. . . . . KAOTD
constitution
    constitution . . . . KAOGS
    constitutional . . . . KAOLGS
    constitutional amendment . . . . KAOMT
    constitutionality . . . . KAOLGT
    constitutionally . . . . KAOULGS
    constitutional right . . . . KAORT
constrain
    constrain. . . . . SKRAIN
    constrains . . . . SKRAINS
    constraining. . . . . SKRAING
    constrained . . . . SKRAIND
constraint. . . . . SKRAINT, KRAINT
constrict
    constrict . . . . STRIKT
    constricts. . . . . STRIKTS
    constricting. . . . . STRIKT/-G
    constricted. . . . . STRIKTD
constriction . . . . STRIX
construct
    construct . . . . KRUK
    constructs . . . . KRUKZ
    constructing . . . . KRUK/-G, KRUG
    constructed . . . . KRUKD
construction. . . . . KRUX
constructive
    constructive . . . . KRUV
    constructively . . . . KRUVL
    constructiveness. . . . . KRUVNS
    constructive notice. . . . . KRUF, STRUF
construe
    construe. . . . . SKRU
    construes . . . . SKRU/-S
    construing . . . . SKRUG
    construed. . . . . SKRUD
consul
    consul . . . . SKWUL
    consular. . . . . SKWURL

BRIEF ENCOUNTERS   C

consulate . . . . SKWULT
consulate general. . . . . SKWULG, SKWULGT
consulates general . . . . SKWULGS, SKWULGTS
consulship. . . . . SKWIP
consult
    consult . . . . SKULT
    consults . . . . SKULTS
    consulting. . . . . SKULGT, SKULG
    consulted . . . . SKULTD
consultant . . . . SKUNT, SKUNLT
consultation . . . . SKULGS
consultatory . . . . SKURLT
consume
    consume . . . . SKAOM, SKAO*UM
    consumes. . . . . SKAOMS, SKAOUMS
    consuming. . . . . SKAOMG, SKAOUMG
    consumed . . . . SKAOMD, SKAOUMD
consumer. . . . . SKAORM, SKAOURM
consummate
    consummate . . . . KMAIT
    consummates . . . . KMAITS
    consummating. . . . . KMAIGT
    consummated . . . . KMAITD
consummation. . . . . KMAIGS
consumption . . . . SKUMGS, SKUJ
contact
    contact . . . . KAK
    contacts. . . . . KAKS
    contacting . . . . KAK/-G, KAG
    contacted. . . . . KAKD
contagious. . . . . TAIJ
contain
    contain . . . . TAIN
    contains . . . . TAINS
    containing. . . . . TAING
    contained . . . . TAIND
contain
    containable . . . . TAINL
    container. . . . . TAIRN
    containment . . . . TA*IMT
contaminant. . . . . TAMT
contaminate
    contaminate. . . . . TAM
    contaminates . . . . TAMS
    contaminating . . . . TAMG

© 1997 White-Boucke Publishing.   ILLEGAL TO PHOTOCOPY

contaminated . . . . TAMD
contamination . . . . TAMGS, TAJ
contemplate
    contemplate . . . . KPLAIT
    contemplates . . . . KPLAITS
    contemplating . . . . KPLAIGT
    contemplated . . . . KPLAITD
contemplation . . . . KPLAIGS
contemplative
    contemplative . . . . KPLAIV
    contemplatively . . . . KPLAIVL
    contemplativeness . . . . KPLAIVNS
contemplator . . . . KPLAIRT
contemporaneity . . . . KRAENT
contemporaneous
    contemporaneous . . . . KRAENS
    contemporaneously . . . . KRAENL
    contemporaneousness . . . . KRAENSZ
contemporarily . . . . KRAERL
contemporary . . . . KRAER
contempt . . . . KEMT
contempt of court . . . . KERMT
contend
    contend . . . . KEND
    contends . . . . K*ENDZ, KAENDZ
    contending . . . . KENGD
    contended . . . . KEND/-D
content . . . . KET
contention . . . . KENGS
contest
    contest . . . . K*ES
    contests . . . . KEFS, K*ESZ
    contesting . . . . KEFG
    contested . . . . KEFD
contestable . . . . KEFBL
contestation . . . . KEGS
context . . . . K*EX, KOFRNX
continent . . . . NENT
continental . . . . NENL
contingency . . . . TIJS
contingent . . . . TIJ
continual . . . . KONL
continually . . . . KOENL
continuation . . . . KONGS

continue
- continue . . . . KONT
- continues . . . . KONTS
- continuing . . . . KONGT
- continued . . . . KONTD

continuity . . . . KAOUNT, KWOUT
continuous . . . . KOUS
continuously . . . . KOULS
contraband . . . . KBAND

contract
- contract . . . . KR–T
- contracts . . . . KR–TS
- contracting . . . . KR–GT
- contracted . . . . KR–TD

contraction . . . . KRAX
contractor . . . . KR–RT

contradict
- contradict . . . . KRIK
- contradicts . . . . KRIKZ
- contradicting . . . . KRIK/–G
- contradicted . . . . KRIKD

contradiction . . . . KRIX
contrary . . . . KRAIR
contrary to . . . . KRAIRT

contrast
- contrast . . . . KRAS
- contrasts . . . . KRAFS
- contrasting . . . . KRAFG
- contrasted . . . . KRAFD

contravene
- contravene . . . . KREVN
- contravenes . . . . KREVNS
- contravening . . . . KREVNG
- contravened . . . . KREVND

contravention . . . . KREVNGS

contribute
- contribute . . . . KRIBT
- contributes . . . . KRIBTS
- contributing . . . . KRIBGT
- contributed . . . . KRIBTD

contribution . . . . KRAOUX

contributor
- contributor . . . . KRIRB
- contributory . . . . KRIRBT
- ***contributory negligence*** . . . . KRIJ

C

BRIEF ENCOUNTERS

contrivance	KRAOIVNS, TRAOIVNS
contrive	
contrive	KRAOIV, TRAOIV
contrives	KRAOIVS, TRAOIVS
contriving	KRAOIVG, TRAOIVG
contrived	KRAOIVD, TRAOIVD
contriver	KRAOIVR, TRAOIVR
control	
control	KROL
controls	KROLS
controlling	KROLG
controlled	KROLD
control	
controllable	KROBL
controlled substance	KRUB
controller	KRORL
controversial	TROVL
controversy	TROV
controvert	
controvert	TROVT
controverts	TROVTS
controverting	TROVGT, TROVG
controverted	TROVTD
controvertible	TROVBL
contusion	TAOGS
convalesce	
convalesce	KWLES
convalesces	KWLEFS, KWLESZ
convalescing	KWLEFG
convalesced	KWLEFD
convalescent	
convalescent	KWLET
convalescent home	KWLOEM
convalescent hospital	KWLOP, KWHOP
convalescence	KWLENS
convene	
convene	KWAO*EN
convenes	KWAOENZ
convening	KWAOENG
convened	KWAOEND
convener	KWAOERN
convenience	VAOENS
convenient	VAOENT
conveniently	VAOENLT

ILLEGAL TO PHOTOCOPY © 1997 White-Boucke Publishing.

BRIEF ENCOUNTERS   C

convention
    convention. . . . . KWENGS
    conventional . . . . KWENLGS, KW*ENL, KW-NL
    conventionally. . . . . KWAOENLGS, KWAO*ENL
converge
    converge . . . . KWERJ
    converges . . . . KWERJS
    converging . . . . KWERJ/-G
    converged . . . . KWERJD
convergence . . . . KWERNS
conversation . . . . K-FRGS
converse
    converse . . . . KWERS
    converses . . . . KWEFS, KWERSZ
    conversing . . . . KWEFG
    conversed . . . . KWEFD
conversion. . . . . KWERGS
convert
    convert . . . . KWERT
    converts . . . . KWERTS
    converting . . . . KWERGT
    converted . . . . KWERTD
converter. . . . . KWRERT
convertible . . . . KWERBL
convey
    convey. . . . . KWAI
    conveys . . . . KWAIS
    conveying . . . . KWAIG
    conveyed . . . . KWAID
conveyance . . . . KWA*INS
conveyor . . . . KWAIR
conveyor belt . . . . KWAIRB
convict
    convict. . . . . KWIKT
    convicts . . . . KWIKTS, KWIKZ
    convicting. . . . . KWIKT/-G, KWIK/-G
    convicted . . . . KWIKTD, KWIKD
conviction. . . . . KWIX
convince
    convince. . . . . KWINS
    convinces . . . . KWIFS, KWINSZ
    convincing . . . . KWIFG
    convinced. . . . . KWIFD
convoluted . . . . VOULTD
convolution . . . . VOULGS

C

convoy	KWOI

convulse

convulse	KWULS
convulses	KWUFLS, KWULSZ
convulsing	KWUFLG
convulsed	KWUFLD
convulsion	KWULGS

convulsive

convulsive	KWUV
convulsively	KWUVL
convulsiveness	KWUVNS
cooker	KAORK
coolant	KAOLT
cooler	KAORL
co-op	KWOP

cooperate

cooperate	KAOPT
cooperates	KAOPTS
cooperating	KAOPGT, KAOPG
cooperated	KAOPTD
cooperation	KAOPGS
cooperative	KAOVP
cooperatively	KAOVPL

co-opt

co-opt	KWOPT
co-opts	KWOPTS
co-opting	KWOPGT
co-opted	KWOPTD

coordinate

coordinate	KAORN, KAORNT
coordinates	KAORNS, KAORNTS
coordinating	KAORNG, KAORNGT
coordinated	KAORND, KAORNTD
coordination	KAORNGS
coordinator	KRAORD
copper	KRORP
copulation	KOPGS

copy

copy	KPAOE
copies	KPAOES
copying	KPAOEG
copied	KPAOE/-D

copyright

copyright	KPAOERT
copyrights	KPAOERTS

BRIEF ENCOUNTERS   C

copyrighting	KPAOERGT, KPAOERG
copyrighted	KPAOERTD
coral	KOERL
cornea	KR-N

corner
corner	KRORN
corners	KRORNS
cornering	KRORNG
cornered	KRORND

coronary
coronary	KOIRN
coronary bypass surgery	KOIRPS
coronary heart disease	KOIRD
coronation	KORNGS

coroner
coroner	KR-RN
coroner's office	KR-FS
coroner's report	KR-RNT, KRORT

Corp.	KORP
corporate	KORPT
corporation	KORPGS
corps	KOERP
corpse	KORPS
corral	KRA*L

correct
correct	KREK
corrects	KREKZ
correcting	KREK/-G, KREG
corrected	KREKD

correct
correction	KREX
correctional	KRELGS, KREXL
corrective	KREV
correctively	KREVL
correctly	KR*EL, KRELG
correct me if I misunderstood	KRAOD
correct me if I'm mistaken	KRAIM
correct me if I'm wrong	KRONG
correctness	KRENS
corrector	KRERK

correlate
correlate	KORL
correlates	KORLS
correlating	KORLG
correlated	KORLD

correlation	KORLGS
correspond	
correspond	KOR
corresponds	KORZ
corresponding	KORG
corresponded	KOR/-D
correspondence	KORNS
correspondent	KORNT
corridor	KOERD
corroborate	
corroborate	KROB
corroborates	KROBS
corroborating	KROB/-G
corroborated	KROBD
corroboration	KROX
corroborative	KROV
corroborator	KROR, KROBT
corrode	
corrode	KROED
corrodes	KROEDZ
corroding	KROEGD
corroded	KROED/-D
corrosion	KROEGS
corrupt	
corrupt	KRUP, KRUPT
corrupts	KRUPS, KRUPTS
corrupting	KRUPG, KRUPGT
corrupted	KRUPD, KRUPTD
corruptible	KRUBL
corruption	KRUPGS
Corvette	KOVRT
cosign	
cosign	KAOIN
cosigns	KAOINZ
cosigning	KAOING
cosigned	KAOIN/-D
cosign	
cosignatories	SKIGS
cosignatory	SKIG
cosigner	KAOIRN
cosine	KWOIN, KAO*IN
cosmetic	KOS, KOZ
cosmetologist	KMOLT
cosmetology	KMOLG
cosmopolitan	KPOLT

BRIEF ENCOUNTERS   C

cost
    cost .... KOFT
    costs .... KOFTS, KOFS
    costing .... KOFGT, KOFG
    cost .... KOFT
costume .... KOFM
coterie .... KOERT
cottage .... KAJ
cotton .... KROT
cough
    cough .... KOF
    coughs .... KOFZ
    coughing .... KOF/-G
    coughed .... KOFD
cougher .... KOFR
could
    could .... KO, KOULD
    could assume a fact not in evidence .... KO/SFAEK
    could assume facts not in evidence .... KO/SFAEX
    could be .... KOUB
    could believe .... KOUBL
    could believe the .... KOUBLT
    could be the .... KOUBT
    could be these .... KOUBZ
    could be those .... KOUBS
    could feel .... KOUFL
    could feel the .... KOUFLT
    could have .... KOUF
    could have been .... KOUFB
    could have been the .... KOUFBT
    could have believed .... KOUFBLD
    could have believed the .... KOUFBLTD
    could have gone .... KOUFG
    could have had .... KOUFD
    could have had the .... KOUFTD
    could have recalled .... KOUFRLD
    could have recalled the .... KOUFRLTD
    could have recollected .... KOUFRKD
    could have recollected the .... KOUFRKTD
    could have remembered .... KOUFRMD
    could have remembered the .... KOUFRMTD
    could have the .... KOUFT
    couldn't .... KUNT
    could recall .... KOURL
    could recall the .... KOURLT

could recollect . . . . KOURK
could recollect the . . . . KOURKT
could remember . . . . KOURM
could remember the . . . . KOURMT
could understand . . . . KOUNDZ
could you please . . . . KOUP
could you please tell . . . . KOUPT
could you please tell us . . . . KOUPTS
could you repeat . . . . KOURP
could you repeat the . . . . KOURPT
could you repeat the question . . . . KOURPTS
could you rephrase . . . . KOUFR
could you rephrase the . . . . KOUFRT
could you rephrase the question . . . . KOUFRTS
could you tell . . . . KOUT
could you tell us . . . . KOUTS
council
    council. . . . . KOUNS
    councilman . . . . KOUM
    councilor. . . . . KOUNLS, KOUNS/LOR
    councilwoman. . . . . KWOUM
counsel
    counsel . . . . KOUN
    counsels . . . . KOUNZ
    counseling. . . . . KOUNG
    counseled . . . . KOUND
counselor. . . . . KOUNL
counselors . . . . KOUNLZ
counsel table. . . . . KAEB
counter
    counter . . . . KOURNT, KOURN
    counters . . . . KOURNTS, KOURNS
    countering. . . . . KOURNGT, KOURNG
    countered . . . . KOURNTD, KOURND
counter
    counterclockwise . . . . KOUNK
    counteroffer . . . . KRAUFR
    counterpart. . . . . KPART
    counterproductive . . . . KPRUV
    counterproductively . . . . KPRUVL
    counterproposal. . . . . KROEP
counteract
    counteract . . . . KRAKT
    counteracts. . . . . KRAKTS
    counteracting . . . . KRAKT/-G, KRAGT

BRIEF ENCOUNTERS   C

```
counteracted .................................. KRAKTD
counterfeit
    counterfeit ................................. KIFT
    counterfeits ................................ KIFTS
    counterfeiting .............................. KIFGT
    counterfeited ............................... KIFTD
counterfeiter ................................... KIFRT
country ......................................... KUN
countryside ......................... K*UND, KROID, KAOID
county
    county ...................................... KROIN
    county jail ................................. KAIL
    County of Los Angeles ....................... KLAX
couple
    couple ...................................... KUPL
    couples ..................................... KUPLZ
    coupling .................................... KUPLG
    coupled ..................................... KUPLD
coupon .......................................... KRAOUP
courage .................................. KOURJ, KURJ
courageous ...................................... KRAIJ
course of action ................................ KORX
court
    court and jury .............................. KORJ
    courthouse .................................. KROUS
    Court instructs the jury .................... K-J
    court of appeals ............................ KORPL
    court of law ................................ KORLT
    court of original jurisdiction .............. KORJD
    court of record ............................. KROERD
    court reporter ..................... KROER, KROERT
    court reporting ............................. KROERG
    court reporting school ...................... KRAOL
    courtroom ................................... KRAOM
    court ruling ............. KRAOULG, KRULG, KOURLG
    courts of appeal ............................ KORMS
    courts of record ............................ KROERDZ
    courtyard ................................... KRORD
court-martial
    court-martial ............................... KO*URM
    court-martials .............................. KOURMS
    court-martialing ............................ KOURMG
    court-martialed ............................. KOURMD
courts-martial .................................. KOURMZ
cousin .......................................... KUFN
```

covenant	KOFNT, KOVNT
cover	
cover	KOVR
covers	KOVRS
covering	KOVRG
covered	KOVRD
coverage	KOVRJ
coverup	KOVRP
coward	KOURD
cowardly	KOURLD
cower	
cower	KOUR
cowers	KOURZ
cowering	KOURG
cowered	KOUR/-D
CPA	SPAE
cracker	KRAERK
crackle	
crackle	KRAKL
crackles	KRAKLS
crackling	KRALG, KRAKL/-G
crackled	KRAKLD
cradle	
cradle	KRAELD
cradles	KRAELDZ
cradling	KRAELGD
cradled	KRAELD/-D
crafty	KRAEFT
cranial	KRAINL
crater	KRAERT
craze	KRAEZ
crazy	KRAIZ
create	
create	KRI
creates	KRIS
creating	KRIG
created	KRID
creation	KRIGS
creative	
creative	KRIV
creatively	KRIVL
creativeness	KRIVNS
creativity	KRIVT
creator	KRIR
creature	KRAOEFP

BRIEF ENCOUNTERS C

credence . . . . KRAOENZ
credential . . . . KRENL
credibility . . . . KREBLT
credible . . . . KREBL
credible evidence . . . . KREVD
credibly . . . . KRAOEBL
credit
    credit . . . . KRED
    credits . . . . KREDZ
    crediting . . . . KREGD
    credited . . . . KRED/-D, KRETD
credit
    credit bureau . . . . KREB
    credit card . . . . KRARD
    creditor . . . . KRERD
    credit union . . . . KRAOUN
    creditworthiness . . . . KWORNS
    creditworthy . . . . KWO*RT
credulous . . . . KREJ
creep
    creep . . . . KRAOEP
    creeps . . . . KRAOEPS
    creeping . . . . KRAOEPG
    crept . . . . KREPT
cremate
    cremate . . . . KRAOEMT
    cremates . . . . KRAOEMTS
    cremating . . . . KRAOEMGT
    cremated . . . . KRAOEMTD
crematorium . . . . KROERM
crevice . . . . KREVS
crime scene . . . . KRAEM
criminal
    criminal . . . . KR-L
    criminalist . . . . KRIFLT, KRIFMT
    criminality . . . . KR-LT
    criminal law . . . . KRA
    criminal lawyer . . . . KLAUR
criteria . . . . KAOER
criterion . . . . KAOERN
crisis . . . . KRAOISZ
critic
    critic . . . . KRIFT
    critical . . . . KRIL
    critically . . . . KRAOEL

```
criticism ......................................... KRIFM
criticize
    criticize ...................................... KRIF
    criticizes ..................................... KRIFS
    criticizing .................................... KRIFG
    criticized ..................................... KRIFD
critter ........................................... KRIRT
croquet ........................................... KROEKT
*croquet ball* .................................... KROEBL
cross
    cross ......................................... KROSZ
    crosses ....................................... KROFS
    crossing ...................................... KROFG
    crossed ....................................... KROFD
cross-examination ................................. KR–X
CROSS-EXAMINATION ................................. KR–X/KR–X
cross-examine
    cross-examine ................................. KR–K
    cross-examines ................................ KR–KZ
    cross-examining ........................ KR–K/–G, KR–G
    cross-examined ................................ KR–KD
crossly ........................................... KROFL
crosswalk ......................................... KRAUK
crow
    crow .......................................... KROE
    crows ......................................... KROES
    crowing ....................................... KROEG
    crowed ........................................ KROE/–D
    crowed / crew ......................... KROE/–D / KRAOU
crowbar ........................................... KROEB
crucifix .................................... KRUFX, KRAOUFX
crucifixion ............................... KRUFGS, KRAOUFGS
crucify
    crucify ....................................... KRUZ
    crucifies ..................................... KRUFS
    crucifying .................................... KRUFG
    crucified ..................................... KRUFD
*cruel and unusual punishment* .................... KRUMT
cruelty ........................................... KRAOULT
cruise
    cruise ........................................ KRAOUZ
    cruises .............................. KRAOUFS, KRAOUSZ
    cruising ...................................... KRAOUFG
    cruised ....................................... KRAOUFD
```

BRIEF ENCOUNTERS   C

crunch
    crunch . . . . KRUN
    crunches . . . . KRUNZ
    crunching . . . . KRUNG
    crunched . . . . KRUND
crusade
    crusade . . . . KRAID
    crusades . . . . KRAIDZ
    crusading . . . . KRAIGD
    crusaded . . . . KRAID/-D
crusader . . . . KRAIRD
crystal . . . . STLAL, KRIFL
crystalline . . . . STLAOEN
Cuba . . . . KBA
Cuban . . . . KBAN
cubic
    cubic . . . . KBIK
    cubic centimeter . . . . SKMAOERT
    cubic feet . . . . KBAOET
    cubic foot . . . . KBAOT
    cubic inch . . . . KBIFP
    cubic meter . . . . KMAOERT
cubicle . . . . KAOUBL
cucumber . . . . KAOUK
cucumbers . . . . KAOUKZ
cul-de-sac . . . . KULD
culprit . . . . KPRIT
cultivate
    cultivate . . . . KUVL
    cultivates . . . . KUVLS
    cultivating . . . . KUVLG
    cultivated . . . . KUVLD
cultivation . . . . KUVLGS, KULGS
cultivator . . . . KUVRLT, KUVRL
cultural . . . . KOUL
culture . . . . KOULT
cupboard . . . . KUBD
cupid . . . . KAOUPD
curability . . . . KAOURBLT
curable . . . . KAOURBL
curiosity . . . . KAOURT
curious . . . . KAOURZ
currant . . . . KAURNT
currencies . . . . KURNZ/-S
currency . . . . KURNZ

C   BRIEF ENCOUNTERS

```
current............................................. KURNT
currently........................................... KURNL
curriculum.......................................... KLIM
curriculum vitae................................... KR-V
curtail
    curtail......................................... KRAIL
    curtails....................................... KRAILS
    curtailing..................................... KRAILG
    curtailed...................................... KRAILD
curtailment........................................ KRAIMT
curtain................................... KURN, KRURT
curtains........................... KURN/-S, KRURTS
curvature......................................... KUFRBT
curve
    curve.......................................... KUFRB
    curves........................................ KUFRBS
    curving....................................... KUFRBG
    curved........................................ KUFRBD
cushion
    cushion......................................... KUGS
    cushions...................................... KUGSZ
    cushioning............................... KUGS/-G
    cushioned..................................... KUGD
cusp............................................... KUPZ
cusps.............................................. KUPSZ
custodial......................................... STOELD
custodian.......................................... KUND
custodians.................................... KUND/-S
custody............................................. KUD
custom
    custom......................................... KUFM
    customarily................... KMAIRL, KMAERL
    customary.......................... KMAIR, KMAER
    customer....................................... KMER
    customers.................................... KMERZ
    customer service.......................... KMEFRB
    customer service department.......... KMEFRBT
    customization............... KMUFMGS, KMUFGS
customize
    customize..................................... KMUFM
    customizes.................................. KMUFMS
    customizing................................. KMUFMG
    customized.................................. KMUFMD
cut
    cut............................................ K*UT
```

ILLEGAL TO PHOTOCOPY   © 1997 White-Boucke Publishing.

BRIEF ENCOUNTERS   C

```
cuts ............................................. K*UTS
cutting ........................................... KUGT
cut ............................................... K*UT
cyanide ......................................... KRAOIND
cyber ........................................... SAOIRB
cyberspace ..................................... SAOIRBS
cycle
    cycle ................................... SAOIL, SAOIKL
    cycles .................................. SAOILS, SAOIKLS
    cycling ............................... SAOILG, SAOIKL/-G
    cycled ................................ SAOILD, SAOIKLD
    cycler ................................ SAOIRL, SAOIRKL
cyclic ............................................ SKLIK
cyclical .......................................... SKLIL
cylinder .......................................... SLIND
cylindrical ....................................... SLINL
cyclist ...................................... SAOIK, SKL*IS
cyclone .......................................... SKLOEN
cynical .................................... SNINL, SIN/KAL
cynicism .................................... SIFM, SIN/SIFM
cystitis ......................................... STAOITS
cytoplasm ........................................ SPLAFM
Czech ............................................ ZHEK
Czechoslovakia ..................................... ZEK
Czechoslovakian .................................. ZHEN
```

© 1997 White-Boucke Publishing.   ILLEGAL TO PHOTOCOPY

D

D.A.	DA
daddy	DOID
dagger	DARG
daily	DAIL
dairy	DA*IR
dais	DAES
Dallas	DLAS
damage	
damage	DAJ
damages	DAJS
damaging	DAJ/-G
damaged	DAJD
dancer	DARNS
Dane	DAEN
Danes	DAENZ
Danish	DAERB
danger	
danger	D-, DAIRN
dangerous	DROUS
dangerously	DROULS
dangerous weapon	DWAP
dangle	
dangle	DANL
dangles	DANLS
dangling	DANL/-G
dangled	DANLD
darker	
darker	DRARK
darker than	DRARN
darker than the	DRARNT
darker than these	DRARNZ
darker than those	DRARNS
darkness	DARNZ, DAURNS
D.A.'s office	DAFS
data	DAT
database	D-B
daughter	
daughter	DAUT
daughter-in-law	DAURL
daughters-in-law	DAURLS
day	
day care	DAIRK

BRIEF ENCOUNTERS — D

daylight	DAOILT, DAILT
day of	DAIF
day of the	DAIFT
day of the month	DAIFM
day of these	DAIFZ
day of the week	DAIFK
day or night	DAORNT
days of the month	DAIFMS
days of the week	DAIFKS
daytime	DAIMT, DAOIM
dB	D*B, DAOEB

dead
- dead . . . DAED
- deadline . . . DLOIN
- deadly . . . DELD
- *deadly weapon* . . . DWEP

deadlock
- deadlock . . . DLOK
- deadlocks . . . DLOKS
- deadlocking . . . DLOK/-G
- deadlocked . . . DLOKD

deaf
- deaf . . . DAEF
- *deaf and hard of hearing* . . . DHARD, DHARGD, DHAR
- *deaf and hard-of-hearing people* . . . DHARP
- deaf-blind . . . DAEFB, DEFB
- deaf-blindness . . . DAEFBS, DEFBS
- deafly . . . DAEFL
- deafness . . . DAEFNZ, DEFNZ
- *deaf or hard of hearing* . . . DHAORD, DHAORGD, DHOR, DHORD, DHORGD
- *deaf or hard-of-hearing people* . . . DHAOERP
- *deaf or hard-of-hearing person* . . . DHORP

deafen
- deafen . . . DAEFN
- deafens . . . DAEFNS
- deafening . . . DAEFNG
- deafened . . . DAEFND

deal
- deal . . . DAOEL
- deals . . . DAOELS
- dealing . . . DAOELG
- dealt . . . DELT

dealer . . . DLER
dealership . . . DLERP

D BRIEF ENCOUNTERS

death row. . . . . DROE
death warrant . . . . DWARNT
debacle . . . . DBAK
debar
    debar. . . . . DBAR
    debars . . . . DBARS
    debarring . . . . DBARG
    debarred . . . . DBAR/-D
debase
    debase . . . . DBAES
    debases . . . . DBAEFS, DBAESZ
    debasing. . . . . DBAEFG
    debased . . . . DBAEFD
debasement . . . . DBAEFMT
debatable . . . . DB-BL
debate
    debate . . . . DB-T
    debates . . . . DB-TS
    debating. . . . . DB-GT
    debated . . . . DB-TD
debater. . . . . DB-RT
debauch
    debauch . . . . DBAUFP
    debauches . . . . DBAUFPS
    debauching. . . . . DBAUFPG
    debauched . . . . DBAUFPD
debauchery. . . . . DBRAUFP
debenture . . . . DBUR
debilitate
    debilitate . . . . DBLAET
    debilitates . . . . DBLAETS
    debilitating . . . . DBLAEGT
    debilitated . . . . DBLAETD
debilitation . . . . DBLAEGS
debilitative . . . . DBLAEV
debilities . . . . DBLIT/-S
debility. . . . . DBLIT
debit
    debit . . . . DIBT
    debits . . . . DIBTS
    debiting . . . . DIBT/-G
    debited . . . . DIBTD
debrief
    debrief. . . . . DBAOEF
    debriefs . . . . DBAOEFS

BRIEF ENCOUNTERS D

debriefing . . . . DBAOEFG
debriefed . . . . DBAOEFD
debris . . . . DBRI
debtor . . . . DERBT
debug
   debug . . . . DBUG
   debugs . . . . DBUGZ
   debugging . . . . DBUG/-G
   debugged . . . . DBUGD
debunk
   debunk . . . . DBUNK
   debunks . . . . DBUNKS
   debunking . . . . DBUNK/-G
   debunked . . . . DBUNKD
debut
   debut . . . . DBAOU
   debuts . . . . DBAOUS
   debuting . . . . DBAOUG
   debuted . . . . DBAOUD
decade . . . . DAID
decease
   decease . . . . SDAOES, DAOES
   deceases . . . . SDAOEFS, DAOEFS
   deceasing . . . . SDAOEFG, DAOEFG
   deceased . . . . SDAOEFD, DAOEFD
decedent . . . . DAOENT
deceive
   deceive . . . . DAOEV, SDAOEV
   deceives . . . . DAOEVS, SDAOEVS
   deceiving . . . . DAOEVG, SDAOEVG
   deceived . . . . DAOEVD, SDAOEVD
deceiver . . . . SDAOEFR
December . . . . DEZ
decency . . . . SDAOENS
decent . . . . SDAOENT
decently . . . . SDAOENLT, SDAOENL
deception . . . . SDEPGS
deceptive
   deceptive . . . . SDEVP
   deceptively . . . . SDEVPL
   deceptiveness . . . . SDEVNS
decibel . . . . SDIBL
decide
   decide . . . . SDI
   decides . . . . SDIS

deciding	SDIG
decided	SDID
decidedly	SDILD
decimal	SDAUL, SDMAUL

decipher
decipher	SDAOIFR
deciphers	SDAOIFRS
deciphering	SDAOIFRG
deciphered	SDAOIFRD

decipherable	SDAOIFL, SDAOIFRBL
decipherment	SDAOIFMT
decision	SDIGS

decisive
decisive	SDIV
decisively	SDIVL
decisiveness	SDIVNS

declarable	DLAIRBL
declarant	DLAIRNT
declaration	DLAIRGS
declarative	DLAV
declaratory	DLORT
declaratory judgment	DLORNT, DLORMT, DLUMT

declare
declare	DLAIR
declares	DLAIRS
declaring	DLAIRG
declared	DLAIRD

declassifiable	DLAFBL
declassification	DLAFGS

declassify
declassify	DLAF
declassifies	DLAFS
declassifying	DLAFG
declassified	DLAFD

declension	DLENGS
declination	DLINGS

decline
decline	DLAOIN
declines	DLAOINS
declining	DLAOING
declined	DLAOIND

decline to
decline to	DLAOINT
decline to do	DLAOINTD
decline to go	DLAOINGT

BRIEF ENCOUNTERS — D

decline to say	DLAOINTS
decoder	DROED
decorate	
decorate	DRAIT
decorates	DRAITS
decorating	DRAIGT
decorated	DRAITD
decoration	DRA*IGS
decorative	
decorative	DRAIF
decoratively	DRAIFL
decorativeness	DRAIFNS
decorator	DRAIRT
decorum	DOERM
decrease	
decrease	DRAOES
decreases	DRAOEFS, DRAOESZ
decreasing	DRAOEFG
decreased	DRAOEFD
decree	
decree	KRE
decrees	KREZ
decreeing	KRE/-G
decreed	KRE/-D
decrepit	DREPT
deduct	
deduct	DEKT
deducts	DEKTS
deducting	DEKT/-G
deducted	DEKTD
deduction	DUX
deeper	
deeper	DAOERP
deeper than	DAOERN
deeper than the	DAOERNT
deeper than these	DAOERNZ
deeper than those	DAOERNS
defamation	DWAFGS
defamatory	DWORT
defame	
defame	DWAIM
defames	DWAIMS
defaming	DWAIMG
defamed	DWAIMD

default
    default . . . . DWALT, DWAULT
    defaults . . . . DWALTS, DWAULTS
    defaulting . . . . DWALGT, DWAULGT
    defaulted . . . . DWALTD, DWAULTD
defeat
    defeat. . . . . DWAOET
    defeats . . . . DWAOETS
    defeating . . . . DWAOEGT
    defeated . . . . DWAOETD
defeatism . . . . DWAOEFM
defeatist . . . . DWAOEFT
defect
    defect. . . . . DWEK
    defects . . . . DWEKZ
    defecting. . . . . DWEK/–G, DWEG
    defected . . . . DWEKD
defect
    defection. . . . . DWEX
    defective. . . . . DWEV
    defectively . . . . DWEVL
    defectiveness . . . . DWEVNS
    defector. . . . . DWERK
defend
    defend. . . . . D–F, DWEN
    defends . . . . D–FZ, DWENZ
    defending . . . . D–FG, DWENG
    defended . . . . D–FD, DWEND
defend
    defendant . . . . D–FT
    defendant's exhibit . . . . D–X
    defender. . . . . D–FR, D–FRD
defense . . . . D–FS
defensibility . . . . D–FLT, DWENLT
defensible. . . . . D–FL, DWENL
defensibly . . . . DWAOENL
defensive
    defensive . . . . D–VS
    defensively . . . . D–VL
    defensiveness. . . . . D–VNS
defer
    defer . . . . DEFR
    defers. . . . . DEFRS
    deferring. . . . . DEFRG
    deferred . . . . DEFRD

defer
  deference . . . . DEFRNS
  deferent . . . . DEFRNT
  deferential . . . . DEFRNL
  deferment . . . . DEFRMT, DEFMT
defiance . . . . DWAOINZ
defiant . . . . DWAOINT
defiantly . . . . DWAOINLT
deficiency . . . . DWAOERB
deficient . . . . DWIRBT
deficiently . . . . DWIRBLT
deficit . . . . SDEFT
defile
  defile . . . . DWAOIL
  defiles . . . . DWAOILS
  defiling . . . . DWAOILG
  defiled . . . . DWAOILD
defilement . . . . DWAOIMT
defiler . . . . DWAOIRL
definable . . . . DWABL
define
  define . . . . DWAOIN
  defines . . . . DWAOINS
  defining . . . . DWAOING
  defined . . . . DWAOIND
definite
  definite . . . . DAF
  definitely . . . . DAFL
  definiteness . . . . DAFNS
definition . . . . DEFGS, DAFGS
definitive
  definitive . . . . DAV
  definitively . . . . DAVL
  definitiveness . . . . DAVNS
deflect
  deflect . . . . FLEKT
  deflects . . . . FLEKTS
  deflecting . . . . FLEKT/-G, FLEG
  deflected . . . . FLEKTD
deflect
  deflection . . . . FLEGS
  deflective . . . . FLEV
  deflector . . . . FLERKT, FLERK
  deflectors . . . . FLERKTS, FLERKZ

deform
- deform . . . DWORM
- deforms . . . DWORMS
- deforming . . . DWORMG
- deformed . . . DWORMD

deformity . . . DWORMT

defraud
- defraud . . . DRAUD, DWAUD
- defrauds . . . DRAUDZ, DWAUDZ
- defrauding . . . DRAUGD, DWAUGD
- defrauded . . . DRAUD/-D, DWAUD/-D

defrauder . . . DRAURD, DWAURD

defrost
- defrost . . . DRO*S, DROFT
- defrosts . . . DRO*SZ, DROFTS
- defrosting . . . DROFGT
- defrosted . . . DROFTD

defroster . . . DROFRT

defunct . . . DWUNG, DWUNGT

defund
- defund . . . DWUN
- defunds . . . DWUNS
- defunding . . . DWUN/-G
- defunded . . . DWUND

defy
- defy . . . DWAOI
- defies . . . DWAOI/-S
- defying . . . DWAOIG
- defied . . . DWAOID

degenerate
- degenerate . . . JAIRT
- degenerates . . . JAIRTS
- degenerating . . . JAIRGT, JAIRG
- degenerated . . . JAIRTD

degenerately . . . JAIRLT
degenerateness . . . JAIRNS
degeneration . . . JAIRGS
degenerative . . . JAIV
degeneratively . . . JAIVL
degradation . . . DEGS

degrade
- degrade . . . DRAID
- degrades . . . DRAIDZ
- degrading . . . DRAIGD
- degraded . . . DRAID/-D

degree
- degree . . . . DRE
- *degree of* . . . . DREF
- *degree of medical certainty* . . . . DREFM, DREM
- *degree of the* . . . . DREFT
- *degree of these* . . . . DREFZ

dehumanization . . . . DAOUMGS

dehumanize
- dehumanize . . . . DAO*UM
- dehumanizes . . . . DAOUMS
- dehumanizing . . . . DAOUMG
- dehumanized . . . . DAOUMD

dehydrate
- dehydrate . . . . DWAOIT
- dehydrates . . . . DWAOITS
- dehydrating . . . . DWAOIGT
- dehydrated . . . . DWAOITD

dehydration . . . . DWAOIGS

Delaware . . . . DWE, D*E/D*E

delay
- delay . . . . DLAI
- delays . . . . DLAIS
- delaying . . . . DLAIG
- delayed . . . . DLAID

delegate
- delegate . . . . DELGT
- delegates . . . . DELGTS
- delegating . . . . DELGT/-G
- delegated . . . . DELGTD

delegation . . . . DELGS

delete
- delete . . . . DLAOET
- deletes . . . . DLAOETS
- deleting . . . . DLAOEGT, DLAOEG
- deleted . . . . DLAOETD

deleterious
- deleterious . . . . DLERT
- deleteriously . . . . DLERL
- deleteriousness . . . . DLERTS

deletion . . . . DLAOEGS

deliberate
- deliberate . . . . DLIB
- deliberates . . . . DLIBS
- deliberating . . . . DLIBG
- deliberated . . . . DLIBD

D   BRIEF ENCOUNTERS

deliberately . . . . DLIBL
deliberation . . . . DLIBGS
deliberative. . . . . DLIBT
delicate . . . . DLIKT
delight
    delight. . . . . DLAOIT
    delights. . . . . DLAOITS
    delighting . . . . DLAOIGT
    delighted . . . . DLAOITD
delightful . . . . DLAOIF
delightfully . . . . DLAOIFL
delimit
    delimit . . . . DLIMT, DL*IM
    delimits . . . . DLIMTS, DLIMS
    delimiting. . . . . DLIMGT, DLIMG
    delimited . . . . DLIMTD, DLIMD
delineate
    delineate . . . . DLAET, DLIN/YAIT
    delineates. . . . . DLAETS, DLIN/YAITS
    delineating . . . . DLAEGT, DLIN/YAIGT
    delineated . . . . DLAETD, DLIN/YAITD
delineation. . . . . DLAEGS, DLIN/YAIGS
delinquency . . . . DLIN
delinquent . . . . DLINT
delirious. . . . . DLIR, DLAOERS
delirium . . . . DLUM, DLIRM
deliver
    deliver. . . . . DLIVR, DLIFR
    delivers . . . . DLIVRS, DLIFRS
    delivering . . . . DLIVRG, DLIFRG
    delivered . . . . DLIVRD, DLIFRD
deliver
    deliverable . . . . DLIVRL, DLIVRBL
    deliverance . . . . DLIVRNS, DLIFRNS
    delivery. . . . . DLOIVR
delta. . . . . DAELT
deltoid. . . . . DLOID
delude
    delude . . . . DLAOU
    deludes . . . . DLAOUS
    deluding. . . . . DLAOUG
    deluded . . . . DLAOUD
deluge
    deluge . . . . DLAOUJ, DLUJ
    deluges. . . . . DLAOUJS, DLUJS

BRIEF ENCOUNTERS D

deluging . . . . DLAOUJ/-G, DLUJ/-G
deluged . . . . DLAOUJD, DLUJD
delusion . . . . DLAOUGS
delusional . . . . DLAOUL, DLAOURBL
delusive . . . . DLAOUV
delusively . . . . DLAOUVL
deluxe . . . . DLUX
delve
    delve . . . . DLEV
    delves . . . . DLEVS
    delving . . . . DLEVG
    delved . . . . DLEVD
demand
    demand . . . . MAND, DMAN
    demands . . . . MANDZ, DMANS
    demanding . . . . MAND/-G, DMANG
    demanded . . . . MAND/-D, DMAND
demean
    demean . . . . DMAOEN
    demeans . . . . DMAOENS
    demeaning . . . . DMAOENG
    demeaned . . . . DMAOEND
demeanor . . . . DOM, DMAOERN
demented . . . . DMENTD
dementia . . . . DMERB
demise . . . . DMAOIS
democracy . . . . MAUK, DMOK
democrat . . . . DAEM, DMAT
democratic . . . . DAEMT, DEMT, DMAKT
demographer . . . . DRAEFR
demographic . . . . DRAF
demographically . . . . DRAFL
demography . . . . DRAEF
demolish
    demolish . . . . DMORB, DORB
    demolishes . . . . DMORBS, DORBS
    demolishing . . . . DMORBG, DORB/-G
    demolished . . . . DMORBD, DORBD
demonstrate
    demonstrate . . . . DEM
    demonstrates . . . . DEMS
    demonstrating . . . . DEMG
    demonstrated . . . . DEMD
demonstration . . . . DEMGS, DEJ

demote
    demote . . . . DMOET
    demotes . . . . DMOETS
    demoting . . . . DMOEGT
    demoted . . . . DMOETD
demotion . . . . DMOEGS
demur
    demur . . . . DMUR
    demurs . . . . DMURS
    demurring . . . . DMURG
    demurred . . . . DMURD
demure
    demure . . . . DMAOUR
    demurely . . . . DMAOURL
    demureness . . . . DMAOURNS
demurrer . . . . DMRUR
denial . . . . D-NL
Denmark . . . . DAERK
denominator . . . . DMAIRT, DOM/NAIRT
denounce
    denounce . . . . DOUNZ
    denounces . . . . DOUFS
    denouncing . . . . DOUFG
    denounced . . . . DOUFD
denouncement . . . . DOUFMT
denouncer . . . . DOURNZ, DOURNS
dental . . . . DENL
dental school . . . . DAOL
dentist . . . . D-NTS
dentistry . . . . D-RNT
Denver . . . . DEVRN, DEFRN
deny
    deny . . . . D-N
    denies . . . . D-NS
    denying . . . . D-NG
    denied . . . . D-ND
deodorant . . . . DOED
depart
    depart . . . . DPART
    departs . . . . DPARTS
    departing . . . . DPARGT, DPARG
    departed . . . . DPARTD
department
    department . . . . D-PT, DARMT
    departmental . . . . DARL, D-PT/AL

BRIEF ENCOUNTERS   D

departmentalization . . . . DAP/SAIGS
Department of Education . . . . DAEGS
department of motor vehicles . . . . DMV/DMV
Department of Motor Vehicles . . . . D-V/D-V
departmentalize
    departmentalize. . . . . DAP
    departmentalizes . . . . DAPS
    departmentalizing . . . . DAPG
    departmentalized. . . . . DAPD
departure . . . . DPAUR
depend
    depend. . . . . DEND
    depends. . . . . D*ENDZ, DAENDZ
    depending . . . . DENGD, DENG
    depended . . . . DEND/-D
depend
    dependable . . . . DAEBL
    dependence . . . . DAENS
    dependency . . . . DAENSZ
    dependent . . . . DAENT
depict
    depict. . . . . DWIK, DWIKT
    depicts . . . . DWIKZ, DWIKTS
    depicting . . . . DWIK/-G, DWIKT/-G
    depicted. . . . . DWIKD, DWIKTD
depiction . . . . DWIX
deplete
    deplete. . . . . DPLAOET
    depletes . . . . DPLAOETS
    depleting . . . . DPLAOEGT
    depleted . . . . DPLAOETD
depletion . . . . DPLAOEGS
deplorable. . . . . PLOERBL, PLORBL
deplore
    deplore . . . . PLOER
    deplores . . . . PLOERS
    deploring. . . . . PLOERG
    deplored . . . . PLOERD
deploy
    deploy . . . . DLOI, DPLOI
    deploys. . . . . DLOIS, DPLOIS
    deploying . . . . DLOIG, DPLOIG
    deployed . . . . DLOI/-D, DPLOID
deployment . . . . DLOIMT, DPLOIMT
depo . . . . DPO

deponent . . . . DPOENT
deport
    deport . . . . DPORT
    deports . . . . DPORTS
    deporting . . . . DPORGT, DPORG
    deported . . . . DPORTD
deportation . . . . DPORGS
depose
    depose . . . . DPOES
    deposes . . . . DPOEFS, DPOESZ
    deposing . . . . DPOEFG
    deposed . . . . DPOEFD
deposit
    deposit . . . . POFT
    deposits . . . . POFTS
    depositing . . . . POFGT, POFG
    deposited . . . . POFTD
deposition . . . . DEPGS
depot . . . . DPOT
deprave
    deprave . . . . DRAIV
    depraves . . . . DRAIVS
    depraving . . . . DRAIVG
    depraved . . . . DRAIVD
depravedly . . . . DRAIVLD
depravity . . . . DRAVT
deprecate
    deprecate . . . . DRAIK
    deprecates . . . . DRAIKZ
    deprecating . . . . DRAIG
    deprecated . . . . DRAIKD
deprecation . . . . DRAIX
depreciate
    depreciate . . . . DRAOERB
    depreciates . . . . DRAOERBS
    depreciating . . . . DRAOERBG
    depreciated . . . . DRAOERBD
depreciation . . . . DRAOERBGS
depress
    depress . . . . D-P
    depresses . . . . D-PS
    depressing . . . . D-PG
    depressed . . . . D-PD
depress
    depressant . . . . D*PT, DRANT

BRIEF ENCOUNTERS — D

depression	D-PGS
depressive	D-VP
depressor	DR-P
deprivation	PRAOIVGS
deprive	
deprive	PRAOIV
deprives	PRAOIVS
depriving	PRAOIVG
deprived	PRAOIVD
deputize	
deputize	DEPZ
deputizes	DEPSZ
deputizing	DEPG
deputized	DEPD
deputy	DEP
Deputy District Attorney	**DAEP**
derail	
derail	DRAIL
derails	DRAILS
derailing	DRAILG
derailed	DRAILD
derailment	DRAIMT
derange	
derange	DRAEN, DARNG
deranges	DRAENS, DARNGS
deranging	DRAENG, DARNG/-G
deranged	DRAEND, DARNGD
derangement	DRAEMT
derelict	DERLT
dereliction	DERLGS
deride	
deride	DRID
derides	DRIDZ
deriding	DRIGD
derided	DRID/-D
derision	DRIGS
derisory	DRAOIZ
derivation	DRIFGS, DRIVGS
derivative	DRIVT, DRAOIVT
derive	
derive	DRIF, DRAOIV
derives	DRIFS, DRAOIVS
deriving	DRIFG, DRAOIVG
derived	DRIFD, DRAOIVD
derogatory	DROG

descend
- descend . . . . SDEND
- descends . . . . SDENDZ
- descending . . . . SDENGD
- descended . . . . SDEND/-D

descendant . . . . SDAENT
descent . . . . SDENT
describable . . . . DRAOIBL

describe
- describe . . . . DRAOIB
- describes . . . . DRAOIBS
- describing . . . . DRAOIBG
- described . . . . DRAOIBD

description . . . . DRIPGS

descriptive
- descriptive . . . . DRIVP
- descriptively . . . . DRIVPL
- descriptiveness . . . . DRIVNS

desecrate
- desecrate . . . . SKRAIT
- desecrates . . . . SKRAITS
- desecrating . . . . SKRAIGT
- desecrated . . . . SKRAITD

desecration . . . . SKRAIGS

desert
- desert . . . . SDERT
- deserts . . . . SDERTS
- deserting . . . . SDERGT
- deserted . . . . SDERTD

deserter . . . . SDRERT
desertion . . . . SDERGS

deserve
- deserve . . . . SDEFRB
- deserves . . . . SDEFRBS
- deserving . . . . SDEFRBG
- deserved . . . . SDEFRBD

design
- design . . . . SDAOIN
- designs . . . . SDAOINS
- designing . . . . SDAOING
- designed . . . . SDAOIND

designate
- designate . . . . SDEGT
- designates . . . . SDEGTS
- designating . . . . SDEGT/-G

BRIEF ENCOUNTERS   D

designated	SDEGTD
designation	SDEGS
designer	SDAOIRN
desirability	SDIRBLT, SDAOIRBLT
desirable	SDIRBL, SDAOIRBL

desire
desire	SDIR, SDAOIR
desires	SDIRS, SDAOIRS
desiring	SDIRG, SDAOIRG
desired	SDIRD, SDAOIRD

desirous	SDROUS

desist
desist	SDIF, SDIFT
desists	SDIFS, SDIFTS
desisting	SDIFG, SDIFGT
desisted	SDIFD, SDIFTD

desk
desk	DEFK
desk light	DEFLT
desktop	D–T

desolate	SDOLT
desolation	SDOLGS

desperate
desperate	SPRAT, SPRAET
desperately	SPRAL, SPRAEL
desperateness	SPRANS, SPRAENS

desperation	SPRAGS, SPRAEGS
despicable	SPEBL, SPIKL

despise
despise	SDPAOIS
despises	SDPAOIFS, SDPAOISZ
despising	SDPAOIFG
despised	SDPAOIFD

despite	SDPAOIT
dessert	DERT
destination	SNAIGS
destinies	SNIZ
destiny	SNI
destitute	DAOT
destituteness	DAONS
destitution	DAOGS, DAOUGS

destroy
destroy	STROI
destroys	STROIS
destroying	STROIG

D   BRIEF ENCOUNTERS

```
    destroyed ..................................... STROID
destroyer........................................ STROIR
destructibility................................ SDRUBLT, DRUBLT
destructible.................................. SDRUBL, DRUBL
destruction...................................... SDRUX
destructive
    destructive................................... SDRUV
    destructively................................ SDRUVL
    destructiveness.............................. SDRUVNS
destructivity................................... SDRUVT
detach
    detach ....................................... DAFP
    detaches...................................... DAFPS
    detaching..................................... DAFPG
    detached ..................................... DAFPD
detachment ...................................... DAFMT
detail
    detail ....................................... DAEL
    details ...................................... DAELS
    detailing .................................... DAELG
    detailed ..................................... DAELD
detain
    detain........................................ DAIN
    detains ...................................... DAINS
    detaining..................................... DAING
    detained ..................................... DAIND
detainment ...................................... DAINT
detect
    detect ....................................... D-KT
    detects....................................... D-KTS
    detecting..................................... D-KT/-G
    detected...................................... D-KTD
detect
    detective .................................... D-K
    detectives.................................... D-KZ
    detector ..................................... D-RK
    detectors .................................... D-RKZ
detention ....................................... DENGS
deteriorate
    deteriorate .................................. DRAET
    deteriorates.................................. DRAETS
    deteriorating................................. DRAEGT
    deteriorated ................................. DRAETD
deterioration.................................... DRAEGS
determination ................................... DERGS
```

determine
- determine .... DER
- determines .... DERS
- determining .... DERG
- determined .... DERD

deterrent .... TERNT

detonate
- detonate .... DWAET, DET/NAIT
- detonates .... DWAETS, DET/NAITS
- detonating .... DWAEGT, DET/NAIGT
- detonated .... DWAETD, DET/NAITD

detonation .... DWAEGS, DET/NAIGS
detonator .... DWAERT, DET/NAIRT

detract
- detract .... DRAK
- detracts .... DRAKZ
- detracting .... DRAK/-G
- detracted .... DRAKD

detraction .... DRAX
detractor .... DRAEK
detriment .... DRIMT
detrimental .... DRINL
Detroit .... TROIT
devaluation .... DWALGS

devalue
- devalue .... DWAL
- devalues .... DWALS
- devaluing .... DWALG
- devalued .... DWALD

devastate
- devastate .... SDEVT
- devastates .... SDEVTS, SDEVS
- devastating .... SDEVGT, SDEVG
- devastated .... SDEVTD, SDEVD

devastation .... SDEVGS
devastator .... SDEVRT

develop
- develop .... DWOP
- develops .... DWOPS
- developing .... DWOPG
- developed .... DWOPD

develop
- developer .... DWORP
- development .... DWOMT
- developmental .... DWOL

deviance	DWAOENS
deviancy	DWAOENSZ
deviant	DWAOENT
deviate	
deviate	DWAIT
deviates	DWAITS
deviating	DWAIGT
deviated	DWAITD
deviation	DWAIGS
device	DWAOIS
devise	
devise	DWAOIZ
devises	DWAOIFS
devising	DWAOIFG
devised	DWAOIFD
devoid	DWOID
devoid of	DWOIF
devolution	DWOFLGS, DWOVLGS, DWEFLGS, DWEVLGS
devolve	
devolve	DWOFL, DWOVL
devolves	DWOFLS, DWOVLS
devolving	DWOFLG, DWOVLG
devolved	DWOFLD, DWOVLD
devolvement	DWOFMT, DWOVMT, DWEFMT, DWEVMT
devote	
devote	DWOET
devotes	DWOETS
devoting	DWOEGT
devoted	DWOETD
devotion	DWOEGS
devour	
devour	DWOUR
devours	DWOURS
devouring	DWOURG
devoured	DWOURD
devout	
devout	DWOUT
devoutly	DWOULT
devoutness	DWOUNS
Dexedrine	DEX
diabetes	DAOIB
diabetic	DAOIBT

BRIEF ENCOUNTERS — D

diagnose
    diagnose .... D-G
    diagnoses .... D-GZ
    diagnosing .... D-G/-G
    diagnosed .... D-GD
diagnosis .... D-GS
diagnostic .... D-GT
diagnostician .... D-G/TIGS, DIGTS
diagonal .... DAG
diagram
    diagram .... DRAM
    diagrams .... DRAMS
    diagraming .... DRAMG
    diagramed .... DRAMD
dialect .... DLEKT
dialogue .... DLOG
dialysis .... DAL
diameter .... DAOIRMT
diamond .... DAOIMD
Diane .... DWAN
diaper .... DAOIP, DAOIRP
diaphragm .... DAOIRM, DAOIFRM
diarrhea .... DRAOE
diary .... DIR
dictate
    dictate .... DAIK
    dictates .... DAIKZ
    dictating .... DAIK/-G
    dictated .... DAIKD
dictation .... DAIX
dictionary .... DRAIR
didactic .... DAKT
did assume a fact not in evidence .... DID/SFAEK
did assume facts not in evidence .... DID/SFAEX
did he
    did he .... DE*
    did he believe .... DEBL
    did he do .... DED
    did he ever .... DEVR
    did he feel .... DEFL
    did he get .... DEGT
    did he go .... DEG
    did he have .... DEF
    did he know .... D*EN
    did he live .... DEV

did he recall	DERL
did he recollect	DERK
did he remember	DERM
did he say	DES
did he see	D*ES
did he tell	DET
did he understand	DENDZ
did he want	DEPT

did I

did I	DI
did I believe	DIBL
did I ever	DIVR
did I have	DIF
did I live	DIV
did I recall	DIRL
did I recollect	DIRK
did I remember	DIRM
did I see	DIZ
did I understand	DINDZ
did I want	DIPT
didn't	D-NT

did she

did she	SDE
did she believe	SDEBL
did she do	SDED
did she ever	SDEFR, SDEVR
did she feel	SDEFL
did she get	SD*EGT
did she go	SDEG
did she happen	SDEP
did she have	SDEF
did she imagine	SDEJ
did she live	SDEV
did she mean	SDEM
did she mean to	SDEMT
did she mean to say	SDEMTS
did she recall	SDERL
did she recollect	SDERK
did she remember	SDERM
did she say	SDES
did she see	SDEZ, SD*ES
did she tell	SDET
did she think	SDENG
did she want	SDEPT

BRIEF ENCOUNTERS   D

did you
  did you .... DU
  did you believe .... DUBL
  did you do .... DUD
  did you ever .... DUVR, DUFR
  did you feel .... DUFL
  did you get .... DUGT
  did you give .... GUD
  did you give her .... GUFR
  did you give him .... GUFM
  did you give them .... GEFM
  did you go .... DUG
  did you have .... DUF
  did you imagine .... DUJ
  did you know .... DUN
  did you live .... DUV
  did you mean .... DUM
  did you mean to .... DUMT
  did you mean to say .... DUMTS
  did you recall .... DURL
  did you recollect .... DURK
  did you remember .... DURM
  did you say .... DUS
  did you see .... D*US
  did you tell .... DUT
  did you think .... DUNG
  did you think so .... DUNGS
  did you understand .... DUNDZ
  did you want .... DUPT
diesel .... SDAOEL
diesel fuel .... SDAOEFL
diet
  diet .... DAET
  diets .... DAETS
  dieting .... DAEGT
  dieted .... DAETD
dietary .... DA*ERT
dieter .... DAERT
difference .... DIFS, DIFRNS
different
  different .... DIFT
  differential .... DIFRNL
  differentiation .... DIFGS, DAEFGS
  differently .... DIFL
  different than .... DIFRN

different than them. . . . . DIFM
different than these . . . . DIFRNZ
differentiate
    differentiate . . . . DAEFT
    differentiates. . . . . DAEFTS
    differentiating . . . . DAEFGT, DAEFG
    differentiated. . . . . DAEFTD
difficult. . . . . D-L
difficulty . . . . D-LT
diffuse
    diffuse . . . . DWAOUS
    diffuses. . . . . DWAOUFS, DWAOUSZ
    diffusing. . . . . DWAOUFG
    diffused . . . . DWAOUFD
diffusion. . . . . DWAOUGS
dig
    dig . . . . DIG
    digs . . . . DIGZ
    digging. . . . . DIG/-G
    dug . . . . D*UG
digest
    digest. . . . . D-J
    digests . . . . D-JZ
    digesting . . . . D-J/-G
    digested . . . . D-JD
digestion. . . . . D-JS
digestive
    digestive. . . . . D-VJ
    digestives . . . . D-VJZ
    digestive system . . . . D-VJS
digger. . . . . DIRG
digit . . . . DIJ
digital . . . . DIJT
dignity . . . . DIGT
digress
    digress . . . . GRESZ
    digresses . . . . GREFS
    digressing. . . . . GREFG
    digressed . . . . GREFD
digression. . . . . GR*EGS, GR-GS
dilapidate
    dilapidate . . . . DLAP
    dilapidates . . . . DLAPS
    dilapidating . . . . DLAPG
    dilapidated . . . . DLAPD

BRIEF ENCOUNTERS   D

dilapidation .... DLAPGS
dilate
    dilate .... DLAIT
    dilates .... DLAITS
    dilating .... DLAIGT
    dilated .... DLAITD
dilation .... DLAIGS
dilemma .... DLEM
diligence .... DILG, DIL/JENS
diligent .... DILT, DIL/JENT
diligently .... DLIL, DIL/JENL
dilute
    dilute .... DLAOUT
    dilutes .... DLAOUTS
    diluting .... DLAOUGT
    diluted .... DLAOUTD
dilution .... DILGS
dime .... DWAOIM
dimmer .... D*IRM
diminish
    diminish .... MIRB
    diminishes .... MIRBS
    diminishing .... MIRB/-G
    diminished .... MIRBD
diner .... DAOIRN
dining room .... D-RM
dinner .... DIRN
dinnertime .... DIRNT
dinosaur .... DAUR
diploma .... PLOEM
diplomat .... PLOEMT
diode .... DWOED
dioxide .... DWOKD
diplomacy .... PLOEMZ
direct
    direct .... DREK
    directs .... DREKZ
    directing .... DREK/-G, DREG
    directed .... DREKD
direct
    direct current .... DRURNT
    direct evidence .... DREVD
    direct examination .... DR-X
    DIRECT EXAMINATION .... DR-X/DR-X
    directing your attention .... DURGS

D   BRIEF ENCOUNTERS

    direction . . . . DREX
    directional . . . . DREXL
    directive . . . . DREV
    directly . . . . DREL
    directness . . . . DRENS
    director . . . . DRERK
    directory . . . . DRERKT, DREKT
    direct your attention . . . . DURT
dirty . . . . DOIRT
disability . . . . SDABLT, SDAIBLT
disable
    disable . . . . DAIBL, SDAIBL
    disables . . . . DAIBLS, SDAIBLS
    disabling . . . . DAIBLG, SDAIBLG
    disabled . . . . DAIBLD, SDAIBLD
disadvantage
    disadvantage . . . . SAJ
    disadvantages . . . . SAJZ
    disadvantaging . . . . SAJ/–G
    disadvantaged . . . . SAJD
disadvantageous . . . . SAJS
disagree
    disagree . . . . SGRE
    disagrees . . . . SGRES
    disagreeing . . . . SGREG
    disagreed . . . . SGRED
disagreeable . . . . SGREBL
disagreement . . . . SGREMT
disallow
    disallow . . . . DLOU
    disallows . . . . DLOUS
    disallowing . . . . DLOUG
    disallowed . . . . DLOUD
disallowable . . . . DLOUBL
disallowance . . . . DLOUNS
disappear
    disappear . . . . SPAER
    disappears . . . . SPAERS
    disappearing . . . . SPAERG
    disappeared . . . . SPAERD
disappearance . . . . SPAERNS
disappoint
    disappoint . . . . SPOIN
    disappoints . . . . SPOINS
    disappointing . . . . SPOING

BRIEF ENCOUNTERS — D

```
disappointed ................................. SPOIND
disappointment ............................... SPOIMT
disapproval ........................... SPRAOVL, SPROVL
disapprove
    disapprove ............................... SPRAOV
    disapproves .............................. SPRAOVS
    disapproving ............................. SPRAOVG
    disapproved .............................. SPRAOVD
disarm
    disarm ..................................... DARM
    disarms .................................... DARMS
    disarming .................................. DARMG
    disarmed ................................... DARMD
disarrange
    disarrange ................................. SARNG
    disarranges ................................ SARNGS
    disarranging ............................. SARNG/-G
    disarranged ................................ SARNGD
disarrangement ................................. SARMT
disarray ....................................... DRAI
disassociate
    disassociate ..................... SDOERBT, SDORB
    disassociates .................. SDOERBTS, SDORBS
    disassociating ................. SDOERBGT, SDORBG
    disassociated .................. SDOERBTD, SDORBD
disassociation ................... SDO*ERBGS, SDORBGS
disaster ............................... SDAFT, SDA*S
disastrous .................................. SDRO*US
disavow
    disavow ..................................... SDOU
    disavows .................................... SDOUS
    disavowing .................................. SDOUG
    disavowed ................................... SDOUD
disavowal ..................................... SDOUL
disband
    disband ........................... SBAND, DBAND
    disbands ......................... SBANDZ, DBANDZ
    disbanding ..................... SBAND/-G, DBANGD
    disbanded .................... SBAND/-D, DBAND/-D
disbar
    disbar ...................................... SBAR
    disbars ..................................... SBARS
    disbarring .................................. SBARG
    disbarred ................................... SBARD
disbarment ................................... SBARMT
```

disbelief	SBLAOEF
disbelieve	
disbelieve	SBLAOEV
disbelieves	SBLAOEVS
disbelieving	SBLAOEVG
disbelieved	SBLAOEVD
disburse	
disburse	SDBURS
disburses	SDBURSZ
disbursing	SDBURG
disbursed	SDBURD
disbursement	SDBURMT, BURMT
discard	
discard	DARD
discards	DARDZ
discarding	DARGD
discarded	DARD/-D
discern	
discern	DERN
discerns	DERNS
discerning	DERNG
discerned	DERND
discernible	DERNL
discernment	DERNT
discharge	
discharge	DARJ
discharges	DARJS
discharging	DARJ/-G
discharged	DARJD
discharger	DRARJ
disciple	SDIP
disciplinarian	SPLIRN
disciplinary	SPLAIR
discipline	
discipline	SPLIN
disciplines	SPLINS
disciplining	SPLING
disciplined	SPLIND
disclaim	
disclaim	SKLAIM
disclaims	SKLAIMS
disclaiming	SKLAIMG
disclaimed	SKLAIMD
disclaimer	SKLAIRM

BRIEF ENCOUNTERS D

disclose
- disclose .... SKLOES
- discloses .... SKLOEFS, SKLOESZ
- disclosing .... SKLOEFG
- disclosed.. SKLOEFD

disclosure... SKLOUR
disco .... DWOE

discolor
- discolor .... SKLOR
- discolors.. SKLORS
- discoloring .... SKLORG
- discolored.. SKLORD

discoloration .... SKLORGS

discomfit
- discomfit... SKOMT
- discomfits .... SKOMTS
- discomfiting... SKOMGT
- discomfited .... SKOMTD

discomfiture .... SFUR
discomfort... SK-FRT

disconnect
- disconnect .... SKEK
- disconnects... SKEKZ
- disconnecting.............................. SKEK/-G, SKEG
- disconnected... SKEKD

disconnection .... SKEX
discontinuation.. SKONGS

discontinue
- discontinue.. SKONT
- discontinues.. SKONTS
- discontinuing.............................. SKONGT, SKONG
- discontinued.. SKONTD

discord
- discord... SKRORD
- discordance .... SKORNZ
- discordant .... SKORNT
- discordantly .... SKORNL

discount
- discount... SKOUNT
- discounts.. SKOUNTS
- discounting .... SKOUNGT, SKOUNG
- discounted... SKOUNTD

discourage
- discourage .... SKOURJ, DURJ
- discourages............................... SKOURJS, DURJS

© 1997 White-Boucke Publishing. ILLEGAL TO PHOTOCOPY

discouraging	SKOURJ/-G, DURJ/-G
discouraged	SKOURJD, DURJD
discouragement	SKOURMT, DURMT
discourse	SKOURS

discover
discover	SKOVR
discovers	SKOVRS
discovering	SKOVRG
discovered	SKOVRD

discovery	SKOIVR

discredit
discredit	SKRED
discredits	SKREDZ
discrediting	SKREGD
discredited	SKRED/-D

discreet	SKRAOET
discreetly	SKRAOELT, SKRAOEL
discrepancy	SKREP

discrete
discrete	SKRAET
discretely	SKRAELT, SKRAEL
discreteness	SKRAENS

discretion	SKREGS
discretionary	SKRAER

discriminate
discriminate	SKRIM
discriminates	SKRIMS
discriminating	SKRIMG
discriminated	SKRIMD

discrimination	SKRIMGS, SKRIJ
discriminatory	SKROIMT

discuss
discuss	SKUS
discusses	SKUFS, SKUSZ
discussing	SKUFG
discussed	SKUFD

discussion	SKUGS

disdain
disdain	SDAIN
disdains	SDAINS
disdaining	SDAING
disdained	SDAIND

disease	D-Z

disembark
disembark	DBARK

disembarks . . . . DBARKS
disembarking . . . . DBARK/-G
disembarked . . . . DBARKD
disembarkation . . . . DBARGS
disenchant
   disenchant . . . . SHANT
   disenchants . . . . SHANTS
   disenchanting . . . . SHANGT
   disenchanted . . . . SHANTD
disenchantment . . . . SHAMT
disengage
   disengage . . . . DAIJ, DAEJ
   disengages . . . . DAIJS, DAEJS
   disengaging . . . . DAIJ/-G, DAEJ/-G
   disengaged . . . . DAIJD, DAEJD
disengagement . . . . DAIJT, DAEJT
disentangle
   disentangle . . . . DANG
   disentangles . . . . DANGS
   disentangling . . . . DANG/-G
   disentangled . . . . DANGD
disentanglement . . . . DANGT
disfavor . . . . SFAIVR
disfigure
   disfigure . . . . SFIG
   disfigures . . . . SFIGZ
   disfiguring . . . . SFIG/-G
   disfigured . . . . SFIGD
disfigurement . . . . SFIMT
disgrace
   disgrace . . . . SGRAIS
   disgraces . . . . SGRAIFS, SGRAISZ
   disgracing . . . . SGRAIFG
   disgraced . . . . SGRAIFD
disgraceful . . . . SGRAIF
disgracefully . . . . SGRAIFL
disgruntle
   disgruntle . . . . SGRUN
   disgruntles . . . . SGRUNS
   disgruntling . . . . SGRUNG
   disgruntled . . . . SGRUND
disgruntlement . . . . SGRUMT
disguise
   disguise . . . . SGAOIS
   disguises . . . . SGAOIFS, SGAOISZ

disguising . . . . SGAOIFG
disguised. . . . . SGAOIFD
disgust
    disgust. . . . . SGUF, SGUFT
    disgusts . . . . SGUFS, SGUFTS
    disgusting . . . . SGUFG, SGUFGT
    disgusted . . . . SGUFD, SGUFTD
disharmony . . . . DHARM
dishearten
    dishearten . . . . SHARN, DHARN
    disheartens . . . . SHARNS, DHARNS
    disheartening. . . . . SHARNG, DHARNG
    disheartened . . . . SHARND, DHARND
dishevel
    dishevel . . . . SDEVL, DHEVL
    dishevels. . . . . SDEVLS, DHEVLS
    disheveling . . . . SDEVLG, DHEVLG
    disheveled. . . . . SDEVLD, DHEVLD
dishonest
    dishonest. . . . . SHONS
    dishonestly. . . . . SHONLS
    dishonesty . . . . SHOENS, SHO*NS
dishonor
    dishonor . . . . SHON
    dishonors. . . . . SHONZ
    dishonoring . . . . SHONG
    dishonored. . . . . SHOND
dishonor
    dishonorable. . . . . SHONL
    dishonorable discharge. . . . . SHONLD
    dishonorably . . . . SHOENL
dishwasher . . . . DWARB
disillusion
    disillusion . . . . DLU
    disillusions . . . . DLUS
    disillusioning. . . . . DLUG
    disillusioned . . . . DLUD
disillusionment. . . . . DLUT
disinformation . . . . SN-FGS, D-FGS
disinherit
    disinherit. . . . . SHERT
    disinherits. . . . . SHERTS
    disinheriting . . . . SHERGT
    disinherited . . . . SHERTD

disintegrate
    disintegrate. . . . . SDIN, SDRAIT
    disintegrates . . . . SDINS, SDRAITS
    disintegrating . . . . SDING, SDRAIGT
    disintegrated. . . . . SDIND, SDRAITD
disintegration . . . . SDINGS, SDRAIGS
disinterest . . . . DINT
disinterested . . . . DINTD
disjoint
    disjoint . . . . DOINT
    disjoints . . . . DOINTS
    disjointing. . . . . DOINGT
    disjointed . . . . DOINTD
diskette . . . . SKET
dislike
    dislike. . . . . SLAOIK
    dislikes . . . . SLAOIKS
    disliking. . . . . SLAOIK/-G, SLAOIG
    disliked . . . . SLAOIKD
dislocate
    dislocate. . . . . SLOEK
    dislocates . . . . SLOEKZ
    dislocating . . . . SLOEK/-G
    dislocated . . . . SLOEKD
dislocation . . . . SLOEX
dislodge
    dislodge . . . . SLOJ
    dislodges. . . . . SLOJS
    dislodging . . . . SLOJ/-G
    dislodged . . . . SLOJD
disloyal . . . . SLOIL
disloyalty . . . . SLOILT
dismantle
    dismantle. . . . . SMANL
    dismantles . . . . SMANLS
    dismantling . . . . SMANLG
    dismantled. . . . . SMANLD
dismay
    dismay. . . . . SMAI
    dismays . . . . SMAIS
    dismaying. . . . . SMAIG
    dismayed . . . . SMAID
dismember
    dismember . . . . SMEB
    dismembers . . . . SMEBS

dismembering	SMEB/-G
dismembered	SMEBD
dismemberment	SMEMT

dismiss
dismiss	SMIS
dismisses	SMIFS
dismissing	SMIFG
dismissed	SMIFD
dismissal	SMIFL

dismount
dismount	SMOUNT
dismounts	SMOUNTS
dismounting	SMOUNGT
dismounted	SMOUNTD
disobedience	SBAOENS
disobedient	SBAOENT
disobediently	SBAOENL, SBAOENLT

disobey
disobey	SBAI
disobeys	SBAIS
disobeying	SBAIG
disobeyed	SBAID
disobeyer	SBAIR
disorder	DORD
disorderly	DORLD
disorganization	DORGS

disorganize
disorganize	DORG
disorganizes	DORGZ
disorganizing	DORG/-G
disorganized	DORGD

disorient
disorient	DORN
disorients	DORNS
disorienting	DORNG
disoriented	DORND

disorientate
disorientate	DORNT
disorientates	DORNTS
disorientating	DORNGT
disorientated	DORNTD
disorientation	DORNGS

disparage
disparage	SPAIRJ
disparages	SPAIRJS

BRIEF ENCOUNTERS — D

disparaging .... SPAIRJ/-G
disparaged .... SPAIRJD
disparate...................................... SPAERT
disparity .... SPAIRT
dispatch
    dispatch .... SPAFP
    dispatches................................. SPAFPS
    dispatching .... SPAFPG
    dispatched .... SPAFPD
dispatcher..................................... SPRAFP
dispel
    dispel .... SDPEL
    dispels .... SDPELS
    dispelling................................. SDPELG
    dispelled .... SDPELD
dispensability .... SPENLT, SDPENLT
dispensable .... SPENL, SDPENL
dispensation .... SDPENGS
dispensary..................................... SDPERNL
dispense
    dispense .... SDPENS
    dispenses......................... SDPEFS, SDPENSZ
    dispensing................................. SDPEFG
    dispensed .... SDPEFD
dispersal .... SPERLS, SDPERLS, SDPERL
disperse
    disperse............................ SPERS, SDPER
    disperses .... SPERSZ, SDPERS
    dispersing .... SPERG, SDPERG
    dispersed .... SPERD, SDPERD
dispersion .... SDPERGS, SP*ERGS
displace
    displace .... SPLAES
    displaces .... SPLAEFS, SPLAESZ
    displacing .... SPLAEFG
    displaced.................................. SPLAEFD
displacement .... SPLAEFMT, SPLAEMT, SPLAIMT
display
    display.................................... SPLAI
    displays .... SPLAIZ
    displaying .... SPLAIG
    displayed .... SPLAID
displease
    displease .... SPLES
    displeases .... SPLEFS, SPLESZ

D — BRIEF ENCOUNTERS

displeasing	SPLEFG
displeased	SPLEFD
displeasure	SPLERB
disposability	SPOEFBLT
disposable	SPOEFBL
disposal	SPOEFL
dispose	
dispose	SDPOES
disposes	SDPOEFS
disposing	SDPOEFG
disposed	SDPOEFD
disposition	SPOGS, SDPOGS
disproportion	
disproportion	SPRORGS
disproportional	SPRORLGS
disproportionate	SPRORNT
disproportionately	SPRORNL
disprove	
disprove	SPROV
disproves	SPROVS
disproving	SPROVG
disproved	SPROVD
disputability	SPAOUBLT
disputable	SPAOUBL
dispute	
dispute	SPAOUT
disputes	SPAOUTS
disputing	SPAOUGT
disputed	SPAOUTD
disqualification	SKW–FGS
disqualifier	SKW–FR
disqualify	
disqualify	SKW–F
disqualifies	SKW–FS
disqualifying	SKW–FG
disqualified	SKW–FD
disquiet	SKWAET
disregard	
disregard	DRAR
disregards	DRARS
disregarding	DRARG
disregarded	DRARD
disrespect	
disrespect	D–RP
disrespects	D–RPS

BRIEF ENCOUNTERS — D

disrespecting	D-RPG
disrespected	D-RPD
disrespectful	D-RL

disrobe
disrobe	DROEB
disrobes	DROEBS
disrobing	DROEBG
disrobed	DROEBD

disrober	DROERB
disrobement	DROEMT

disrupt
disrupt	DRUP
disrupts	DRUPS
disrupting	DRUPG
disrupted	DRUPD

disrupt
disrupter	DRURP
disruption	DRUPGS
disruptive	DRUV
disruptively	DRUVL

dissatisfaction	SDAFX
dissatisfactorily	SDAEFL
dissatisfactory	SDAEF

dissatisfy
dissatisfy	SDAF
dissatisfies	SDAFS
dissatisfying	SDAFG
dissatisfied	SDAFD

dissect
dissect	SDEK
dissects	SDEKZ
dissecting	SDEK/-G
dissected	SDEKD

dissection	SDEX

disseminate
disseminate	SDIM
disseminates	SDIMS
disseminating	SDIMG
disseminated	SDIMD

dissemination	SDIMGS, SDIJ
dissension	SD-NGS, D-NGS

dissent
dissent	SD-N
dissents	SD-NS
dissenting	SD-NG

D   BRIEF ENCOUNTERS

dissented	SD-ND
dissenter	SD-RN
disservice	SD-VS
dissimilar	SD*IM
dissimilarity	SDIMT
dissipate	
dissipate	SPAET
dissipates	SPAETS
dissipating	SPAEGT
dissipated	SPAETD
dissipation	SPAEGS
dissociate	
dissociate	SDOERB
dissociates	SDOERBS
dissociating	SDOERBG
dissociated	SDOERBD
dissociation	SDOERBGS
dissociative	SDOEV
dissolution	DOLGS, DOFLGS, SDLAOUGS
dissolve	
dissolve	DOFL
dissolves	DOFLS
dissolving	DOFLG
dissolved	DOFLD
dissuade	
dissuade	DWAED
dissuades	DWAEDZ
dissuading	DWAEGD
dissuaded	DWAED/-D
dissuasion	DWA*EGS
dissuasive	DWAEV
dissuasively	DWAEVL
distance	
distance	SDANS
distances	SDANSZ
distancing	SDANG
distanced	SDAND
distant	SDANT
distantly	SDANL
distaste	
distaste	STA*IS
distasteful	STAIFL
distastefulness	STAIFNS
distemper	SDEFRP

BRIEF ENCOUNTERS D

distend
    distend . . . . STIND
    distends . . . . STINDZ
    distending . . . . STINGD
    distended . . . . STIND/-D
distention . . . . STINGS
distill
    distill . . . . SDIL
    distills . . . . SDILS
    distilling . . . . SDILG
    distilled . . . . SDIL/-D
distill
    distillation . . . . SDILGS, SDLAIGS
    distiller . . . . SDIRL
    distillery . . . . SDRIL
distinct . . . . DING, DINGT
distinction . . . . DINGS
distinguish
    distinguish . . . . DWIRB
    distinguishes . . . . DWIRBS
    distinguishing . . . . DWIRBG
    distinguished . . . . DWIRBD
distinguishable . . . . DWIRBL
distort
    distort . . . . DORT
    distorts . . . . DORTS
    distorting . . . . DORGT
    distorted . . . . DORTD
distortion . . . . SDORGS
distract
    distract . . . . SDRAK
    distracts . . . . SDRAKZ
    distracting . . . . SDRAK/-G, SDRAG
    distracted . . . . SDRAKD
distraction . . . . SDRAX
distraught . . . . SDRAUT, STRAUT
distress
    distress . . . . SDREF, SDRES
    distresses . . . . SDREFS, SDRESZ
    distressing . . . . SDREFG
    distressed . . . . SDREFD
distressful . . . . SDREFL
distribute
    distribute . . . . DRIB
    distributes . . . . DRIBS

D

distributing	DRIB/-G
distributed	DRIBD
distribution	DRAOUGS, DRAOUX
distributor	DRIBT
distributorship	DRIRP, DRIB/TORP

district
    district . . . . DRIK, DRIKT
    district attorney . . . . DAO
    District Attorney's Office . . . . DAOFS
    district court . . . . DRORT
    District of Columbia . . . . D-KD, D*K/D*K, DRIK/KLUM

distrust
    distrust . . . . SDRUF, STR*US
    distrusts . . . . SDRUFS, STRUFS
    distrusting . . . . SDRUFG, STRUFG
    distrusted . . . . SDRUFD, STRUFD

disturb
    disturb . . . . DURB
    disturbs . . . . DURBS
    disturbing . . . . DURB/-G
    disturbed . . . . DURBD

disturbance . . . . DURNS
disunity . . . . DAOUNT

diverge
    diverge . . . . DWERJ
    diverges . . . . DWERJZ
    diverging . . . . DWERJ/-G, DWERG
    diverged . . . . DWERJD

divergence . . . . DWERNS, DWERJS
divergency . . . . DWERNZ
divergent . . . . DWERNT
diverse . . . . DWERS
diversification . . . . DWEVRGS, DWEFGS

diversify
    diversify . . . . DWEVR
    diversifies . . . . DWEVRS, DWEVS
    diversifying . . . . DWEVRG, DWEVG
    diversified . . . . DWEVRD, DWEVD

diversity . . . . DW*ERS

divest
    divest . . . . DWES, DWEF
    divests . . . . DWESZ, DWEFS
    divesting . . . . DWEGS, DWEFG
    divested . . . . DWES/-D, DWEFD

divestiture . . . . DW*UR, DWAOUR

divide
- divide . . . . DWI
- divides . . . . DWIS
- dividing . . . . DWIG
- divided . . . . DWID

divided by . . . . DWIBD
dividend . . . . DIVD
divider . . . . DWIR
divine . . . . DWAO*IN, DWOIN
divinely . . . . DWAOINL, DWOINL
divinity . . . . DWINT
divisibility . . . . DWIBLT
divisible . . . . DWIBL
division . . . . DWIGS
divisive
- divisive . . . . DWIV
- divisively . . . . DWIVL
- divisiveness . . . . DWIVNS

divorce
- divorce . . . . DWORS
- divorces . . . . DWOFS, DWORSZ
- divorcing . . . . DWOFG
- divorced . . . . DWOFD

divulge
- divulge . . . . DWULG
- divulges . . . . DWULGS
- divulging . . . . DWULG/-G
- divulged . . . . DWULGD

dizzier . . . . SDIRZ
dizziest . . . . SD*IZ
dizzily . . . . SDILZ
dizziness . . . . SDINZ
dizzy . . . . SDIZ
DJ . . . . D*J
DMV . . . . D-V, DM-V
DNA . . . . DAE
DNA evidence . . . . DAEVD
do
- do . . . . DO
- does . . . . DUZ
- doing . . . . DOG
- did . . . . DID
- done . . . . DOEN

docile . . . . SDOIL
docility . . . . SDOILT

docket
- docket .... DOKT
- dockets .... DOKTS
- docketing .... DOKT/-G, DOGT
- docketed .... DOKTD

doctor
- doctor .... D-R
- doctors .... D-RS
- doctoring .... D-RG
- doctored .... D-RD

doctoral .... DORL
doctorate .... D-RT

document
- document .... D-MT
- documents .... D-MTS
- documenting .... D-MGT, D-MG
- documented .... D-MTD

documentation .... DAOUJ, D-MGS
dodger .... DORJ

does
- does .... DUZ
- *does he feel* .... DAOEFL
- doesn't .... DUNT

dog .... DAUG

dogma
- dogma .... DAUM
- dogmatic .... DAUMT
- dogmatically .... DAUL
- dogmatism .... DAUFM
- dogmatist .... DAUFMT

do-gooder .... DAORGD

do I
- *do I believe* .... DOIBL
- *do I ever* .... DOIVR, DOIFR
- *do I feel* .... DOIFL
- *do I get* .... DOIGT
- *do I go* .... DOIG
- *do I happen* .... DOIP
- *do I have* .... DOIF
- *do I imagine* .... DOIJ
- *do I know* .... DOIN
- *do I live* .... DOIV
- *do I mean* .... DOIM
- *do I mean to* .... DOIMT
- *do I mean to say* .... DOIMTS

do I recall .... DOIRL
do I recall the .... DOIRLT
do I recollect .... DOIRK
do I recollect the .... DOIRKT
do I remember. .... DOIRM
do I remember the .... DOIRMT
do I say. .... DOIS
do I see. .... DOIZ
do I think .... DOING
do I think so .... DOINGS
do I understand .... DOINDZ
do I want. .... DOIPT
doily .... DO*IL
doing. .... DOG
doings. .... DOGS
dollar. .... DLAR
dolly
    dolly. .... DLOL
    dollies. .... DLOLS
    dollying .... DLOLG
    dollied .... DLOLD
domain. .... DMAIN
domestic .... M*ES, DMEFK
domestically .... M*ELS
domesticate
    domesticate .... DMEFT, DM*ES
    domesticates .... DMEFTS, DM*ESZ
    domesticating .... DMEFG, DM*ES/-G
    domesticated .... DMEFTD, DM*ES/-D
domestication .... DMEFGS, DM*EGS
domesticity .... DMIFT
domicile
    domicile .... SDAOIL
    domiciles. .... SDAOILS
    domiciling .... SDAOILG
    domiciled. .... SDAOILD
dominance. .... DOMS
dominant .... DAMT, DO*MT
dominate
    dominate. .... DOMT, DMAIT
    dominates .... DOMTS, DMAITS
    dominating. .... DOMGT, DOMG, DMAIGT
    dominated. .... DOMTD, DMAITD
domination .... DOMGS, DMAIGS

domineer
    domineer . . . . DMAOER
    domineers . . . . DMAOERS
    domineering . . . . DMAOERG
    domineered . . . . DMAOERD
Dominican Republic . . . . DREB
domino . . . . DMOE
donate
    donate . . . . DOENT
    donates . . . . DOENTS
    donating . . . . DOENGT, DOENG
    donated . . . . DOENTD
donation . . . . DOENGS
done . . . . DOEN
donor . . . . DOERN
do not . . . . Y–T
don't . . . . DONT
doom and gloom . . . . DLAOM
dormant . . . . DORMT
dorsal . . . . DORLS
dosage . . . . DOEJ
double
    double . . . . DOUBL
    doubles . . . . DOUBLS
    doubling . . . . DOUBLG
    doubled . . . . DOUBLD
double-cross
    double-cross . . . . DROS
    double-crosses . . . . DROFS
    double-crossing . . . . DROFG
    double-crossed . . . . DROFD
double
    double-crosser . . . . DROFR
    double jeopardy . . . . DUBLG, DUBLD
    double vision . . . . DOUBLGS, DUVGS
doubt
    doubtful . . . . DOUF
    doubtfully . . . . DOUFL
    doubtfulness . . . . DOUFNS
    doubtless . . . . DOULS
dovetail
    dovetail . . . . DOVT
    dovetails . . . . DOVTS
    dovetailing . . . . DOVGT
    dovetailed . . . . DOVTD

BRIEF ENCOUNTERS   D

down
    down . . . . DOUN
    downhill . . . . DWIL
    downstairs . . . . DOUNS, DWOUNZ
    down the . . . . DOUNT
    downtown . . . . DWOUN
    downward . . . . DWAORD, DAORD
    downwardly . . . . DWAORLD, DWAORL, DAORLD,
                                                                                  DAORL
download
    download . . . . DOUNL
    downloads . . . . DOUNLS
    downloading . . . . DOUNLG
    downloaded . . . . DOUNLD
do you
    do you . . . . DOU
    do you believe . . . . DAOUBL
    do you do . . . . DAOUD
    do you ever . . . . DAOUFR, DAOUVR
    do you feel . . . . DAOUFL
    do you get . . . . DAOUGT
    do you go . . . . DAOUG
    do you have . . . . DAOUF
    do you know . . . . DAOUN
    do you live . . . . DAOUV
    do you mean . . . . DAOUM
    do you mean to . . . . DAOUMT
    do you mean to say . . . . DAOUMTS
    do you mind . . . . DOUMD
    do you recall . . . . DAOURL
    do you recall the . . . . DAOURLT
    do you recollect . . . . DAOURK
    do you recollect the . . . . DAOURKT
    do you remember . . . . DAOURM
    do you remember the . . . . DAOURMT
    do you say . . . . DAOUS
    do you see . . . . DAOUZ
    do you think . . . . DAOUNG
    do you think so . . . . DAOUNGS
    do you understand . . . . DAOUNDZ
    do you waive . . . . DAIV
    do you waive further reading . . . . DRAOED
    do you want . . . . DAOUPT
dozen . . . . DOZ
Dr. . . . . DR-, DR-FPLT

dragon. . . . . DRAON
drainage . . . . DRAIJ
drama
    drama. . . . . DRAUM
    dramatic. . . . . DRAUMT, DRAMT
    dramatization . . . . DRAMGS, DRAJ, DRIMGS, DRIJ
dramatize
    dramatize. . . . . DRIM
    dramatizes . . . . DRIMS
    dramatizing. . . . . DRIMG
    dramatized . . . . DRIMD
draperies . . . . DRAIRPS
drastic. . . . . DRAFK
drastically . . . . DRAEFK, DRAOEFK, DRAEFL
draw
    draw . . . . DRAU
    draws . . . . DRAUS
    drawing. . . . . DRAUG
    drew. . . . . DRAOU
    drawn . . . . DRAUN
draw
    drawback. . . . . DRAUB
    drawer. . . . . DRAUR
    drawing board . . . . DRAUBD
    drawing your attention. . . . . DRAURGS
    draw your attention. . . . . DRAURT
dreadful
    dreadful . . . . DRAEFLD
    dreadfully . . . . DRAOEFL, DRAOEFLD
    dreadfulness . . . . DRAEFNS, DREFNS
dream
    dream. . . . . DRAOEM
    dreams . . . . DRAOEMS
    dreaming. . . . . DRAOEMG
    dreamed / dreamt . . . . DRAOEMD / DREMT
dreamer. . . . . DRAOERM
drearily . . . . DRERL
dreariness. . . . . DRERNS
dreary . . . . DRER
drench
    drench . . . . DREFP
    drenches. . . . . DREFPS
    drenching . . . . DREFPG
    drenched. . . . . DREFPD

BRIEF ENCOUNTERS   D

dress
    dress . . . . DRESZ
    dresses . . . . DREFS
    dressing . . . . DREFG
    dressed . . . . DREFD
dresser . . . . DRERS
dressing room . . . . DR–M, DRAOM
dress up
    dress up . . . . DREP
    dresses up . . . . DREPS
    dressing up . . . . DREPG
    dressed up . . . . DREPD
drier
    drier . . . . DRAOIR
    drier than . . . . DRAOIRN
    drier than the . . . . DRAOIRNT
    drier than these . . . . DRAOIRNZ
    drier than those . . . . DRAOIRNS
drink
    drink . . . . DRING, DRINK
    drinks . . . . DRINGS, DRINKS
    drinking . . . . DRING/–G, DRINK/–G
    drank . . . . DRANG, DRANK
    drunk . . . . DRUNG, DRUNK
drinker . . . . DRIRNG
drive
    drive . . . . DRI
    drives . . . . DRIS
    driving . . . . DRIG
    drove . . . . DRO
    driven . . . . DRIN
drive
    driver . . . . DRIR
    driver's door . . . . DRIRD
    driver's license . . . . DL–
    driver's license no. . . . . DL*N
    driver's license number . . . . DL–N
    driver's seat . . . . DRAOET
    drive under the influence . . . . DRUFL, DOI/DOI
    driveway . . . . DROI
    drive while intoxicated . . . . DWOK
driving under the influence . . . . DRUFLG, DOI/–G
driving while intoxicated . . . . DROK, DWOG
drizzle
    drizzle . . . . DRIFL

drizzles. . . . . DRIFLS
drizzling. . . . . DRIFLG
drizzled . . . . DRIFLD
drudgery. . . . . DRURJ
drug
   drug and alcohol . . . . DROL
   drug lord . . . . DLORD
   drug or alcohol . . . . DRORL
   drug or intoxicant . . . . DROKT
   drugs and alcohol . . . . DROLS
   drugs or alcohol. . . . . DRORLS
   drugs or intoxicants . . . . DROKTS
   drugstore . . . . DROR
   drug traffic . . . . DRUFK
   drug trafficking . . . . DRUFG, DRAFG
drummer . . . . DRURM
drunkard . . . . DRUN
dry
   dry cleaner . . . . DLAOERN
   dryer. . . . . DROIR
   dryly . . . . DRAO*IL
dry clean
   dry clean . . . . DLAOEN
   dry cleans. . . . . DLAOENZ
   dry cleaning . . . . DLAOENG
   dry cleaned. . . . . DLAOEND
dual . . . . DWAOL
duality. . . . . DWAOLT, DWAOULT
dubious
   dubious . . . . DAOUB
   dubiously . . . . DAOUBLS
   dubiousness . . . . DAOUBS, DAOUNS
due
   due. . . . . DAOU
   due course. . . . . DAOURS
   due diligence . . . . DAOULG, DAOD
   due process . . . . DAOP
   due process clause . . . . DAOK
   due process of law. . . . . DAOFPL
   due process rights . . . . DAORZ, DAORTS
duel
   duel . . . . DWAOUL
   duels . . . . DWAOULS
   dueling. . . . . DWAOULG
   dueled . . . . DWAOULD

BRIEF ENCOUNTERS — D

dueler	DWAOURL
duet	DWET
D.U.I.	DOI
duly	
duly	DAOUL
duly licensed in	DLIND
duly licensed to practice	DLIP, DLIPT
duly licensed to practice medicine	DLIM
dune	DAON, DAO*UN
dunes	DAONZ, DAOUNZ
duo	DWAO
duodenum	DWOD
duplicate	
duplicate	DUP
duplicates	DUPS
duplicating	DUPG
duplicated	DUPD
duplication	DUPGS
durability	DURBLT
durable	DURBL
duration	DRAIGS
during	
during	DUR, DURG
during the	DRURG, DURGT
during the course of	DROURS
during the course of the trial	DRAOIL
during the course of this trial	DRAOILT
during the period	DURPT
during these	DURZ
during these periods	DURPZ
during this period	DURP
during those	DURS
during those periods	DURPS
dust	
dust	DUFT
dusts	DUFTS
dusting	DUFGT
dusted	DUFTD
dutiful	DAOF
dutifully	DAOFL
duty	DAOUT
dwarf	
dwarf	DWAR
dwarfs	DWARS
dwarfing	DWARG

D   BRIEF ENCOUNTERS

```
    dwarfed ...................................... DWARD
dwell
    dwell......................................... DWEL
    dwells ....................................... DWELS
    dwelling...................................... DWELG
    dwelled / dwelt ..................... DWELD / DWELT
D.W.I. ........................................... DW*I
dwindle
    dwindle ...................................... DWINL
    dwindles...................................... DWINLS
    dwindling .................................... DWINLG
    dwindled ..................................... DWINLD
dyer ............................................. DAO*IR
dynamic........................................... DWAM
dynamically........................... DWAEL, DWANL
dynamite ......................................... DMAOIT
dysfunction ...................................... SFUNGS
dysfunctional............................ SFUNL, SFUNLGS
dyslexia ......................................... SDLEX
dyslexic ......................................... SDLEK
```

E

each
- *each of* . . . . AOEF, YAOEF
- *each of the* . . . . AOEFT, AOEFPT, YAOEFPT
- *each of them* . . . . AOEFM, YAOEFPL
- *each of these* . . . . AOEFZ, AOEFPZ, YAOEFPZ
- *each of those* . . . . AOEFPS, YAOEFPS
- *each other* . . . . YAOEFP

eager
- eager . . . . AOERG
- eagerly . . . . AOERLG
- eagerness . . . . AOERNS

eagle . . . . AOEG, AO*ELG
eardrum . . . . AOERM
earlier . . . . YERL
earliest . . . . ERLS
early . . . . ERL
ear plug . . . . AOERP
earring . . . . AOERNG
earthquake . . . . KWEK
ease . . . . AEZ
easement . . . . AOEFMT
easier . . . . YAEZ, YAOEZ

east
- eastbound . . . . AOEB
- easterly . . . . AOERL
- eastern . . . . AOERN
- easterner . . . . RAOERN
- *east side* . . . . EDZ
- eastward . . . . AOERD

Easter . . . . AO*ERS
easy . . . . AOEZ

eat
- eat . . . . AOET
- eats . . . . AOETS
- eating . . . . AOEGT
- ate . . . . AET
- eaten . . . . AOENT

eater . . . . AOERT
ebullience . . . . BAOULS
ebulliency . . . . BAOULSZ
ebullient . . . . BAOULT
ebullition . . . . BAOULGS

E — BRIEF ENCOUNTERS

echelon	ERBL
echo	
echo	KHOE
echoes	KHOEZ
echoing	KHOEG
echoed	KHOED
ecologist	KOELT
ecology	KOLG, KOELG
economic	
economic	KMIK
economical	KMIL
economically	KMAOEL
economic development	KMOMT
economist	KMIFT, KM*IS
economize	
economize	KMAOIZ, KMAOIS
economizes	KMAOIFS, KMAOISZ
economizing	KMAOIFG
economized	KMAOIFD
economy	KMI
ecstasy	STAOE
ecstatic	STEKT
ecstatically	STEKL
Ecuador	KWAOR
Ecuadoran	KWAORN
eczema	ZAOEM
edict	DAOEK, DAOEKT
edification	EFGS, ED/F-X
edit	
edit	Y*IT, YAOIT
edits	YITS, YAOITS
editing	YIGT, YAOIGT
edited	YITD, YAOITD
edit	
edition	YIGS
editor	YIRT, YAOIRT
editorial	YAOIRL
educate	
educate	JAET
educates	JAETS
educating	JAEGT
educated	JAETD
education	
education	JAEGS
educational	JAEL

BRIEF ENCOUNTERS   E

educationally . . . . JAOEL
educator . . . . JAERT
effect
    effect . . . . FEK
    effects . . . . FEKS
    effecting . . . . FEK/-G, FEG
    effected . . . . FEKD
effective
    effective . . . . FEV
    effectively . . . . FEVL
    effectiveness . . . . FEVNS
effectuate
    effectuate . . . . FAEKT
    effectuates . . . . FAEKTS
    effectuating . . . . FAEKT/-G
    effectuated . . . . FAEKTD
effectuation . . . . FAEGS, EFX
efficiency . . . . FIRBS
efficient . . . . FIRB
efficiently . . . . F*IRBL
effort . . . . EFRT
ego
    ego . . . . GOE
    egoist . . . . GOEFT
    egomaniac . . . . GOM
    egotism . . . . GOEFM
    egotistic . . . . GOEK
    egotistical . . . . GOL
egregious . . . . GRAOEJ
Egypt . . . . JIPT
Egyptian . . . . JIPGS
eight
    eight of the . . . . AIFT
    eight of them . . . . AIFM
    eight of these . . . . AIFZ
    eight of those . . . . AIFS
    eight-time . . . . YAOIM
    eight times . . . . YAOIMS
    eighty . . . . Y*I, AOIGT
    eighty of the . . . . YIFT
    eighty of them . . . . YIFM
    eighty of these . . . . YIFZ
    eighty of those . . . . YIFS
Eisenhower . . . . SNAUR

E

either
    either . . . . ET, *ET
    either of them . . . . EFM
    either of these . . . . EFZ
    either of those . . . . EFS
ejaculate
    ejaculate . . . . JAL
    ejaculates . . . . JALS
    ejaculating . . . . JALG
    ejaculated . . . . JALD
ejaculation . . . . JALGS
EKG . . . . AOEJ
elaborate
    elaborate . . . . LAEB
    elaborates . . . . LAEBS
    elaborating . . . . LAEB/–G
    elaborated . . . . LAEBD
elaboration . . . . LAEBGS
elapse
    elapse . . . . LAEP
    elapses . . . . LAEPS
    elapsing . . . . LAEPG
    elapsed . . . . LAEPD
elastic . . . . LAFKT
El Salvador . . . . SAFL
elbow
    elbow . . . . EBL
    elbows . . . . EBLS
    elbowing . . . . EBLG
    elbowed . . . . EBLD
elder . . . . ERLD
elderly . . . . AOERLD
electric
    electric . . . . LEKT
    electrical . . . . LAL, LEK/KAL
    electrically . . . . LAOEL
    electrician . . . . LIRGS, LEK/TRIGS
    electricity . . . . LIKT, LEK/TR*IS
electrify
    electrify . . . . FAOI, LEK/FAOI
    electrifies . . . . FAOIZ, LEK/FAOIS
    electrifying . . . . FAOIG, LEK/FAOIG
    electrified . . . . FAOID, LEK/FAOID
electrocardiogram . . . . AOEJD

electrocute
    electrocute . . . . L-KT, LEK/KAOUT
    electrocutes . . . . L-KTS, LEK/KAOUTS
    electrocuting . . . . L-KT/-G, LEK/KAOUGT
    electrocuted . . . . L-KTD, LEK/KAOUTD
electrocution . . . . L-GS, LEK/KAOUGS
electron
    electron . . . . TRON
    electronic . . . . TRONG
    electronically . . . . TRONL, TRAOENG
elegance . . . . ELGS
elegant . . . . ELGT
elegantly . . . . ELG
element . . . . L-MT
elementary . . . . L-RMT
elevate
    elevate . . . . VAIT
    elevates . . . . VAITS
    elevating . . . . VAIGT
    elevated . . . . VAITD
elevation . . . . VAEGS
elevator . . . . VAERT
eleven . . . . LEVN
eleventh . . . . LEVNT
elicit
    elicit . . . . E/LIF, E/LIFT
    elicits . . . . E/LIFS, E/LIFTS
    eliciting . . . . E/LIFG, E/LIFGT
    elicited . . . . E/LIFD, E/LIFTD
elicitation . . . . E/LIFGS
elicitor . . . . E/LIFR
eligibility . . . . JEBLT
eligible . . . . JEBL
eliminate
    eliminate . . . . LIM
    eliminates . . . . LIMS
    eliminating . . . . LIMG
    eliminated . . . . LIMD
elimination . . . . LIMGS
elite . . . . LAOET
elitism . . . . LAOEFM
elongate
    elongate . . . . LAUNT
    elongates . . . . LAUNTS
    elongating . . . . LAUNGT, LAUNG

E

elongated	LAUNTD
elongation	LAUNGS
elude	
elude	LAO*UD
eludes	LAOUDZ
eluding	LAOUGD
eluded	LAOUD/-D
elusive	
elusive	LAOUF
elusively	LAOUFL
elusiveness	LAOUFNS, LAOUVNS
e-mail	
e-mail	E/MAIL
e-mails	E/MAILS
e-mailing	E/MAILG
e-mailed	E/MAILD
e-mailer	E/MAIRL
emancipate	
emancipate	MAEP
emancipates	MAEPS
emancipating	MAEPG
emancipated	MAEPD
emancipation	MAEPGS
embalm	
embalm	KBAUM
embalms	KBAUMS
embalming	KBAUMG
embalmed	KBAUMD
embalmer	KBAURM
embalmment	KBAUMT
embank	
embank	KBANG
embanks	KBANGS
embanking	KBANG/-G
embanked	KBANGD
embankment	KBANGT
embargo	
embargo	KBARG
embargoes	KBARGS
embargoing	KBARG/-G
embargoed	KBARGD
embark	
embark	KBAERK
embarks	KBAERKZ
embarking	KBAERK/-G, KBAERG

embarked . . . . KBAERKD
embarkation . . . . KBAERX
embarrass
   embarrass. . . . . KBAERS
   embarrasses. . . . . KBAEFS, KBAERSZ
   embarrassing. . . . . KBAEFG
   embarrassed . . . . KBAEFD
embarrassment . . . . KBAEFMT
embassy. . . . . KBAOE
embattle
   embattle. . . . . KBALT
   embattles . . . . KBALTS
   embattling . . . . KBALGT
   embattled. . . . . KBALTD
embellish
   embellish . . . . KBEL, BLERB
   embellishes. . . . . KBELS, BLERBS
   embellishing. . . . . KBELG, BLERBG
   embellished . . . . KBELD, BLERBD
embellishment . . . . KBELT, BLEMT
embezzle
   embezzle . . . . KBEBL, KBEFL
   embezzles. . . . . KBEBLS, KBEFLS
   embezzling . . . . KBEBLG, KBEFLG
   embezzled . . . . KBEBLD, KBEFLD
embezzlement . . . . KBEFMT, KBEBLT
embezzler. . . . . KBERBL, KBEFRL
embodiment. . . . . KBOMT
embody
   embody . . . . KBOD
   embodies . . . . KBODZ
   embodying. . . . . KBOGD
   embodied . . . . KBOD/-D
embolism. . . . . KBLIFM
emboss
   emboss . . . . KBAUS
   embosses. . . . . KBAUFS, KBAUSZ
   embossing . . . . KBAUFG
   embossed. . . . . KBAUFD
embosser . . . . KBAUFR
embossment. . . . . KBAUFMT
embrace
   embrace . . . . KBRAIS
   embraces . . . . KBRAISZ, KBRAIFS
   embracing . . . . KBRAIFG

E — BRIEF ENCOUNTERS

embraced	KBRAIFD
embroider	
embroider	KBROIRD
embroiders	KBROIRDZ
embroidering	KBROIRGD, KBROIRG
embroidered	KBROIRD/-D
embroidery	KBROIR
embroil	
embroil	KBROIL
embroils	KBROILS
embroiling	KBROILG
embroiled	KBROILD
embryo	KBROE
emerge	
emerge	MAOERJ
emerges	MAOERJS
emerging	MAOERJ/-G
emerged	MAOERJD
emergence	MAOERNS
emergency	M-RJ
emergency room	M-RM, MAOM, ERM
emergent	MAOERJT, MERNT
emeritus	AOERMT
emigrate	
emigrate	KBRAET
emigrates	KBRAETS
emigrating	KBRAEGT
emigrated	KBRAETD
emigration	KBRA*EGS
eminence	KBEMS, KBENZ, EM/NENS
eminent	KB*EMT, KBENT, EM/NENT
eminently	KBENL, EM/NENL
emission	AOEMGS
emit	
emit	AOEMT
emits	AOEMTS
emitting	AOEMGT
emitted	AOEMTD
emitter	E/MIRT
emotional	MORBL
emotionally	MOERBL
empathetic	KBHEK, EM/THEK
empathetically	KBHEL, EM/THEL
empathize	
empathize	KBHAOIS, KBHAOIZ

BRIEF ENCOUNTERS　　　　　　　　　　　　　　　　　E

```
empathizes . . . . . . . . . . . . . . . . . . . . . . . . . KBHAOIFS, KBHAOISZ
empathizing . . . . . . . . . . . . . . . . . . . . . . . . . . . . . . . . KBHAOIFG
empathized . . . . . . . . . . . . . . . . . . . . . . . . . . . . . . . . KBHAOIFD
emphasis . . . . . . . . . . . . . . . . . . . . . . . . . . . . . . . . . . . . . . . KBIS
emphasize
    emphasize . . . . . . . . . . . . . . . . . . . . . . . . . . . . . . . . . KBAOIS
    emphasizes . . . . . . . . . . . . . . . . . . . . . . . . KBAOIFS, KBAOISZ
    emphasizing . . . . . . . . . . . . . . . . . . . . . . . . . . . . . . . KBAOIFG
    emphasized . . . . . . . . . . . . . . . . . . . . . . . . . . . . . . . KBAOIFD
emphatic . . . . . . . . . . . . . . . . . . . . . . . . . . . . . . . . . . . . . . KBAFT
emphatically . . . . . . . . . . . . . . . . . . . . . . . . . . . KBAFL, KBAFLT
emphysema . . . . . . . . . . . . . . . . . . . . . . . . . . . . . . . . . KBAOEM
empire . . . . . . . . . . . . . . . . . . . . . . . . . . . . . . . . . . . . . . KBAOIR
empiric . . . . . . . . . . . . . . . . . . . . . . . . . . . . . . . . . . . . . . KBIRK
empirical . . . . . . . . . . . . . . . . . . . . . . . . . . . . . . . . . . . . . KBIRL
employ
    employ . . . . . . . . . . . . . . . . . . . . . . . . . . PLOI, PEM, KBLOI
    employs . . . . . . . . . . . . . . . . . . . . . . . . PLOIS, PEMS, KBLOIS
    employing . . . . . . . . . . . . . . . . . . . . . . . PLOIG, PEMG, KBLOIG
    employed . . . . . . . . . . . . . . . . . . . . . . . PLOID, PEMD, KBLOID
employ
    employability . . . . . . . . . . . . . . . . . . . . . . PLOIBLT, KBLOIBLT
    employable . . . . . . . . . . . . . . . . . . . . . . . . . PLOIBL, KBLOIBL
    employee . . . . . . . . . . . . . . . . . . . . . . . . . . . . PLOE, KBLAOE
    employer . . . . . . . . . . . . . . . . . . . . . . . . . . . . . PLOIR, KBLOIR
    employment . . . . . . . . . . . . . . . . . . . . . . . . PLOIMT, KBLOIMT
emporium . . . . . . . . . . . . . . . . . . . . . . . . . . . . . . . . . . . KBORM
empower
    empower . . . . . . . . . . . . . . . . . . . . . . . . . . . . . . . . . . KBAUR
    empowers . . . . . . . . . . . . . . . . . . . . . . . . . . . . . . . . KBAURS
    empowering . . . . . . . . . . . . . . . . . . . . . . . . . . . . . . . KBAURG
    empowered . . . . . . . . . . . . . . . . . . . . . . . . . . . . . . . KBAURD
empowerment . . . . . . . . . . . . . . . . . . . . . . . . . . . . . . KBAURMT
emptiness . . . . . . . . . . . . . . . . . . . . . . . . . . . . . . . . . . EM/TINS
empty
    empty . . . . . . . . . . . . . . . . . . . . . . . . . . . . . . . . . . . . . . EMT
    empties . . . . . . . . . . . . . . . . . . . . . . . . . . . . . . . . . . . . EMTS
    emptying . . . . . . . . . . . . . . . . . . . . . . . . . . . . . . . . . . EMGT
    emptied . . . . . . . . . . . . . . . . . . . . . . . . . . . . . . . . . . . EMTD
emulate
    emulate . . . . . . . . . . . . . . . . . . . . . . . . . . . . . . . . . MAOULT
    emulates . . . . . . . . . . . . . . . . . . . . . . . . . . . . . . . . MAOULTS
    emulating . . . . . . . . . . . . . . . . . . . . . . . . MAOULGT, MAOULG
    emulated . . . . . . . . . . . . . . . . . . . . . . . . . . . . . . . MAOULTD
emulation . . . . . . . . . . . . . . . . . . . . . . . . . . . . . . . . . MAOULGS
```

enable
- enable . . . . NABL, NA*IBL
- enables . . . . NABLS, NAIBLS
- enabling . . . . NABLG, NAIBLG
- enabled . . . . NABLD, NAIBLD

enact
- enact . . . . NAKT
- enacts . . . . NAKTS
- enacting . . . . NAKT/–G, NAK/–G
- enacted . . . . NAKTD

enactment . . . . NAMT
enamel . . . . NAM/EL

enchant
- enchant . . . . KHAENT
- enchants . . . . KHAENTS
- enchanting . . . . KHAENGT
- enchanted . . . . KHAENTD

enchantment . . . . KHAEMT

enclose
- enclose . . . . KLO
- encloses . . . . KLOFS
- enclosing . . . . KLOFG
- enclosed . . . . KLOFD

enclosure . . . . KLOUR

encompass
- encompass . . . . NUFRP
- encompasses . . . . NUFRPS
- encompassing . . . . NUFRPG
- encompassed . . . . NUFRPD

encompassment . . . . NUMT

encounter
- encounter . . . . KROUNT
- encounters . . . . KROUNTS
- encountering . . . . KROUNGT
- encountered . . . . KROUNTD

encourage
- encourage . . . . NURJ
- encourages . . . . NURJS
- encouraging . . . . NURJ/–G
- encouraged . . . . NURJD

encouragement . . . . NURMT

encroach
- encroach . . . . KROEFP
- encroaches . . . . KROEFPS
- encroaching . . . . KROEFPG

BRIEF ENCOUNTERS   E

encroached	KROEFPD
encroachment	KROEMT, KROEFMT
encrypt	
encrypt	KRIP
encrypts	KRIPS
encrypting	KRIPG
encrypted	KRIPD
encryption	KRIPGS
encumber	
encumber	KBUM
encumbers	KBUMZ
encumbering	KBUMG
encumbered	KBUMD
encumbrance	KBUMS
encyclopedia	SKLOP, SKLAOEP
encyclopedic	SKLOPG, SKLAOEPG
encyclopedism	SKLOFM, SKLAOEFM
encyclopedist	SKLOPT, SKLAOEPT
endanger	
endanger	DAERN
endangers	DAERNS
endangering	DAERNG
endangered	DAERND
endangered species	DAERNDZ
endangerment	DAERMT
endeavor	
endeavor	SPWEFR, SPWEVR
endeavors	SPWEFRS, SPWEVRS
endeavoring	SPWEFRG, SPWEVRG
endeavored	SPWEFRD, SPWEVRD
endocrine	KREN
endorse	
endorse	SPWORS, SPWOF
endorses	SPWORSZ, SPWOFS
endorsing	SPWORG, SPWOFG
endorsed	SPWORD, SPWOFD
endorsement	SPWORMT, SPWOFMT
endow	
endow	SPWOU
endows	SPWOUS
endowing	SPWOUG
endowed	SPWOUD
endowment	SPWOUMT
endurance	SPWURNS, SPWAOURNS

endure
    endure . . . . SPWAOUR, SPWUR
    endures . . . . SPWAOURS, SPWURS
    enduring . . . . SPWAOURG, SPWURG
    endured . . . . SPWAOURD, SPWURD
enemy. . . . . NAOEM
energize
    energize . . . . NAOIRJ
    energizes. . . . . NAOIRJS
    energizing. . . . . NAOIRJ/–G
    energized . . . . NAOIRJD
energizer. . . . . NRAOIRJ
energy . . . . N–RJ
enforce
    enforce . . . . NOF
    enforces. . . . . NOFS
    enforcing . . . . NOFG
    enforced . . . . NOFD
enforce
    enforceability. . . . . NOFBLT
    enforceable . . . . NOFBL
    enforcement . . . . NO*FMT, NO*MT
    enforcer . . . . NOEFR
engage
    engage. . . . . GAEJ
    engages . . . . GAEJS
    engaging . . . . GAEJ/–G
    engaged . . . . GAEJD
engagement. . . . . GAEMT
engine . . . . N–J
engineer
    engineer . . . . JER
    engineers . . . . JERS
    engineering . . . . JERG
    engineered . . . . JERD
England. . . . . ENG, GLAUND
English. . . . . GLIRB
engross
    engross . . . . GROESZ, GROEF
    engrosses . . . . GROEFS
    engrossing . . . . GROEFG
    engrossed. . . . . GROEFD
engrossment . . . . GROEMT, GROEFMT
enhance
    enhance. . . . . HANS

BRIEF ENCOUNTERS   E

enhances .... HANSZ
  enhancing .... HANS/-G, HAFG
  enhanced .... HANS/-D, HAFD
enhancement .... HAMT
enjoy
  enjoy .... GOI
  enjoys .... GOIS
  enjoying .... GOIG
  enjoyed .... GOID
enjoy
  enjoyable .... GOIBL
  enjoyer .... GROI
  enjoyment .... GOIMT
enlarge
  enlarge .... NARJ
  enlarges .... NARJS
  enlarging .... NARJ-/G
  enlarged .... NARJD
enlargement .... NARMT
enmesh
  enmesh .... KBERB
  enmeshes .... KBERBS
  enmeshing .... KBERBG
  enmeshed .... KBERBD
enormity .... NORMT
enormous .... NORMS
enough
  enough .... NUF
  enough of the .... NUFT
  enough of them .... N*UFM
  enough of these .... NUFZ
  enough of those .... NUFS
enrichment .... RIFMT
enslavement .... SLAIFMT, SLAIVMT
ensure
  ensure .... SNAOUR
  ensures .... SNAOURS
  ensuring .... SNAOURG
  ensured .... SNAOURD
entail
  entail .... SPWAIL
  entails .... SPWAILS
  entailing .... SPWAILG
  entailed .... SPWAILD

entangle
- entangle . . . . SPWANG
- entangles . . . . SPWANGS
- entangling . . . . SPWANG/-G
- entangled . . . . SPWANGD

entanglement . . . . SPWAMT

enter
- enter . . . . SPWER
- enters . . . . SPWERS
- entering . . . . SPWERG
- entered . . . . SPWERD

enter into
- *enter into* . . . . SPWAO
- *enters into* . . . . SPWAOS
- *entering into* . . . . SPWAOG
- *entered into* . . . . SPWAOD

enter into
- *enter into the* . . . . SPWAOT
- *enter into them* . . . . SPWAOM
- *enter into these* . . . . SPWAOZ

enterprise . . . . SPW-PS
enterpriser . . . . SPW-RPS
enterprising . . . . SPW-PG

entertain
- entertain . . . . SPWRAIN
- entertains . . . . SPWRAINS
- entertaining . . . . SPWRAING
- entertained . . . . SPWRAIND

entertainer . . . . SPWRAIRN
entertainment . . . . SPWRAIMT

enthrall
- enthrall . . . . SPWRAUL
- enthralls . . . . SPWRAULS
- enthralling . . . . SPWRAULG
- enthralled . . . . SPWRAULD

enthrone
- enthrone . . . . SPWROEN
- enthrones . . . . SPWROENS
- enthroning . . . . SPWROENG
- enthroned . . . . SPWROEND

enthuse
- enthuse . . . . THAOU, THAOUS
- enthuses . . . . THAOUSZ, THAOUFS
- enthusing . . . . THAOUFG
- enthused . . . . THAOUFD

enthusiasm	THUFM
enthusiast	
enthusiast	THUFT
enthusiastic	THUK
enthusiastically	THUL
entice	
entice	SPWAOIS
entices	SPWAOIFS, SPWAOISZ
enticing	SPWAOIFG
enticed	SPWAOIFD
enticement	SPWAOIFMT, SPWAOIMT
entire	
entire	SPWAOIR
entirely	SPWAOIRL
entirety	SPWAOIRT
entitle	
entitle	SPWIL, SPWAOIL, SPWAOILT
entitles	SPWILS, SPWAOILS, SPWAOILTS
entitling	SPWILG, SPWAOILG, SPWAOILGT
entitled	SPWILD, SPWAOILD, SPWAOILTD
entitled to	SPWILTD
entitlement	SPWILT, SPWIMT, SPWAO*IMT, TAOIMT
entity	SPW-T
entomb	
entomb	SPWAOUM
entombs	SPWAOUMS
entombing	SPWAOUMG
entombed	SPWAOUMD
entourage	TAOURJ, SPWROURJ
entrails	SPWRAILS
entrain	
entrain	SPWRAEN
entrains	SPWRAENS
entraining	SPWRAENG
entrained	SPWRAEND
entrance	SPWRANS
entrant	SPWRANT
entrap	
entrap	SPWRAP
entraps	SPWRAPS
entrapping	SPWRAPG
entrapped	SPWRAPD
entrapment	TRAMT, SPWRAMT

entreat
    entreat . . . . SPWRAOET
    entreats. . . . . SPWRAOETS
    entreating . . . . SPWRAOEGT
    entreated. . . . . SPWRAOETD
entreatment. . . . . SPWRAOEMT
entree . . . . SPWRAI
entrench
    entrench . . . . NEFP, SPWREFP
    entrenches. . . . . NEFPS, SPWREFPS
    entrenching. . . . . NEFPG, SPWREFPG
    entrenched . . . . NEFPD, SPWREFPD
entrenchment . . . . NEFMT, SPWREMT, SPWREFMT
entrepreneur
    entrepreneur. . . . . SPWRUR
    entrepreneurial . . . . SPWRURL
    entrepreneurship. . . . . SPWRURP
entrust
    entrust. . . . . SPWRUFT
    entrusts. . . . . SPWRUFTS, SPWRUFS
    entrusting . . . . SPWRUFGT, SPWRUFG
    entrusted. . . . . SPWRUFTD, SPWRUFD
entry . . . . SPWRI
enumerate
    enumerate . . . . RAET
    enumerates. . . . . RAETS
    enumerating . . . . RAEGT
    enumerated. . . . . RAETD
enumeration . . . . RAEGS
enunciation. . . . . N*UNGS, NINGS
envelope
    envelope. . . . . N-VL
    envelopes. . . . . N-VLS
    enveloping . . . . N-VLG
    enveloped. . . . . N-VLD
envelopment . . . . N-MT
environment
    environment . . . . VAOIRMT, VIRMT
    environmental. . . . . VIRNL
    environmentalist. . . . . VIRNT
    environmentally. . . . . VAOERNL
    Environmental Protection Agency . . . . AOEPG, AOEP/AOEP
enzymatic . . . . ZAMT, ZAOIMT
enzyme . . . . ZAOIM
epidemic. . . . . EPD

BRIEF ENCOUNTERS E

epiglottis	GLOT
epilepsy	LEPS
epileptic	LEPG
epitome	AOEPT

equal
- equal . . . . KWAL
- equals . . . . KWALS
- equaling . . . . KWALG
- equaled . . . . KWALD

equal
- equality . . . . KWAELT
- equalization . . . . KWALGS, KWAELGS
- equally . . . . KWAEL

equate
- equate . . . . KWAIT
- equates . . . . KWAITS
- equating . . . . KWAIGT
- equated . . . . KWAITD

equation . . . . KWAIGS

equip
- equip . . . . KWIP
- equips . . . . KWIPS
- equipping . . . . KWIPG
- equipped . . . . KWIPD

equipment . . . . KWIMT
equitable . . . . KWIBLT
equity . . . . EKT, KWEKT
equivalence . . . . KWIVS, KWIVNS
equivalency . . . . KWIVSZ

equivalent
- equivalent . . . . KWIV
- equivalents . . . . KWIVZ
- *equivalent to* . . . . KWIVT
- *equivalent to those* . . . . KWIVTS

equivocate
- equivocate . . . . KWAEK, KWAEV
- equivocates . . . . KWAEKZ, KWAEVS
- equivocating . . . . KWAEK/-G, KWAEG, KWAEVG
- equivocated . . . . KWAEKD, KWAEVD

equivocation . . . . KWAEX, KWAEVGS
eroticism . . . . ROFMT

err
- err . . . . *ER
- errs . . . . *ERS
- erring . . . . *ERG

© 1997 White-Boucke Publishing.   ILLEGAL TO PHOTOCOPY

erred	*ERD
err	
errand	AERND
errant	ERNT
erroneous	ROEN
erroneously	ROENL
error	ROR
errors and omissions	AOEM
erupt	
erupt	RUP
erupts	RUPS
erupting	RUPG
erupted	RUPD
eruption	RUPGS
escalate	
escalate	SKLAIT
escalates	SKLAITS
escalating	SKLAIGT
escalated	SKLAITD
escalation	SKLAIGS
escalator	SKLAIRT
escape	
escape	SKAIP
escapes	SKAIPS
escaping	SKAIPG
escaped	SKAIPD
escapee	SKAOEP
escheat	SKHAOET
escort	
escort	SKOERT
escorts	SKOERTS
escorting	SKOERGT
escorted	SKOERTD
escrow	SKROE
Eskimo	SKWO
esophagus	SOF, SOFG, SOF/GUS
especially	EPS, SPAOERBL
espionage	SPAOEJ
essential	SERB
essentially	SERBL
establish	
establish	BLIRB
establishes	BLIRBS
establishing	BLIRBG
established	BLIRBD

establishment	BLIMT
estate	STAET

esteem
esteem	STAOEM
esteems	STAOEMS
esteeming	STAOEMG
esteemed	STAOEMD
esthetic	STHEKT

estimate
estimate	STIMT
estimates	STIMTS
estimating	STIMGT, STIMG
estimated	STIMTD
estimation	STIMGS

estop
estop	STAUP
estops	STAUPS
estopping	STAUPG
estopped	STAUPD
estoppel	STAUPL

estrange
estrange	STRAEJ
estranges	STRAEJS
estranging	STRAEJ/-G, STRAEG
estranged	STRAEJD
estrangement	STRAEMT
estrogen	STREG
et al.	AELT
et cetera	ETS
eternal	TAOERNL
eternity	TAOERNT
ether	AO*ET
ethereal	AO*ELT

ethic
ethic	TH*EK
ethically	THELG
ethics	THEX
Ethiopia	TYOEP
Ethiopian	TYOEN
ethnicity	TH*IS

eulogize
eulogize	YAOIZ
eulogizes	YAOISZ, YAOIFS
eulogizing	YAOIFG
eulogized	YAOIFD

E — BRIEF ENCOUNTERS

eulogy . . . . YAOULG
euphemism . . . . YAOUFM
Europe . . . . YURP
European . . . . YURN
evacuate
    evacuate . . . . VAEK
    evacuates . . . . VAEKZ
    evacuating . . . . VAEK/-G, VAEG
    evacuated . . . . VAEKD
evacuation . . . . VAEX
evade
    evade . . . . VAID
    evades . . . . VAIDZ
    evading . . . . VAIGD
    evaded . . . . VAID/-D
evaluate
    evaluate . . . . VAELT
    evaluates . . . . VAELTS
    evaluating . . . . VAELGT
    evaluated . . . . VAELTD
evaluation . . . . VAELGS
evaporate
    evaporate . . . . VAP
    evaporates . . . . VAPS
    evaporating . . . . VAPG
    evaporated . . . . VAPD
evaporation . . . . VAPGS
evasive
    evasive . . . . VAIV
    evasively . . . . VAIVL
    evasiveness . . . . VAIVNS, VAIFNS
even
    even . . . . AOEN
    evens . . . . AOENZ
    evening . . . . AOENG
    evened . . . . AOEND
even
    even . . . . AOEN
    evenly . . . . AOENL
    evenness . . . . AOENS
event . . . . FEN
events . . . . FENZ
eventual
    eventual . . . . VENL, EVL
    eventuality . . . . VENLT

eventually	VAOENL
ever	EVR, EFR

every
every	EV
everybody	EVRB, EFRB
everybody else	EFRBL
everybody else's	EFRBLS
everyday	EFRD
everyone	EVRN, EFRN
everyone else	EFRNL
everyone else's	EFRNLS
everyone of these	EFRNZ
everyone's	EFRNS
everything	EVRG, EFRG
everything else	EFRLG
every time	EVRT
everywhere	WREF
everywhere else	WREFL

evidence
evidence	EVD
Evidence Code	EK
Evidence Code Section	*EX

evident
evident	EVT
evidentially	EV/DENL
evidentiary	EVRD
evidently	EVLT

evil	AOEVL
evilness	AOEVNS
evolution	VOFLGS, VAOULGS

evolve
evolve	VOFL
evolves	VOFLS
evolving	VOFLG
evolved	VOFLD

exacerbate
exacerbate	KPAEB
exacerbates	KPAEBS
exacerbating	KPAEBG
exacerbated	KPAEBD
exacerbation	KPAEX

exact
exact	ZAK
exacts	ZAKS
exacting	ZAK/-G

exacted .... ZAKD
exactly .... ZAL
exaggerate
    exaggerate .... KPAJ
    exaggerates .... KPAJS
    exaggerating .... KPAJ/-G
    exaggerated .... KPAJD
exaggeration .... KPAEJ
exalt
    exalt .... KPALT
    exalts .... KPALTS
    exalting .... KPALGT
    exalted .... KPALTD
exaltation .... KPALGS
exam
    exam .... KPAM
    examination .... KP-GS
    examination room .... KPAOM
    examiner .... KP*ER
examine
    examine .... KP-
    examines .... KP-S
    examining .... KP-G
    examined .... KP-D
example .... KP-L
exasperate
    exasperate .... KPAP
    exasperates .... KPAPS
    exasperating .... KPAPG
    exasperated .... KPAPD
exasperation .... KPAPGS
excavate
    excavate .... SKWAIT
    excavates .... SKWAITS
    excavating .... SKWAIGT
    excavated .... SKWAITD
excavation .... SKWAIGS
excavator .... SKWAIRT
exceed
    exceed .... KPAOED
    exceeds .... KPAOEDZ
    exceeding .... KPAOEGD
    exceeded .... KPAOED/-D
exceedingly .... KPAOELGD
excellence .... KPLENS

BRIEF ENCOUNTERS — E

Excellency . . . . KPLENSZ
excellent . . . . KPLENT
excellently . . . . KPLENL
except
    except . . . . KPEP
    exception . . . . KPEPGS
    except the . . . . KPEPT
    except them . . . . KPEM
    except these . . . . KPEPZ
    except those . . . . KPEPS
excess
    excess . . . . KPESZ
    excessive . . . . KPEF
    excessively . . . . KPEFL
    excessiveness . . . . KPEFNS
exchange
    exchange . . . . KPAING
    exchanges . . . . KPAINGS
    exchanging . . . . KPAING/-G
    exchanged . . . . KPAINGD
exchange
    exchangeability . . . . KPAINLT, KPAINT
    exchangeable . . . . KPAINL
    exchanger . . . . KPAIRNG
excise
    excise . . . . KPAOIS
    excises . . . . KPAOIFS, KPAOISZ
    excising . . . . KPAOIFG
    excised . . . . KPAOIFD
excision . . . . KPIGS
excitability . . . . KPAOIBLT
excitable . . . . KPAOIBL
excite
    excite . . . . KPAOIT
    excites . . . . KPAOITS
    exciting . . . . KPAOIGT
    excited . . . . KPAOITD
excitedly . . . . KPAOILTD
excitement . . . . KPAOIMT
exclaim
    exclaim . . . . SKLAEM
    exclaims . . . . SKLAEMS
    exclaiming . . . . SKLAEMG
    exclaimed . . . . SKLAEMD
exclamation . . . . SKLAEMGS, SKLAEJ

E BRIEF ENCOUNTERS

exclamation mark................................... SKLARK
exclude
    exclude .... SKLU, SKLAOU
    excludes............................... SKLUS, SKLAOUS
    excluding.............................. SKLUG, SKLAOUG
    excluded .... SKLUD, SKLAOUD
exclusion
    exclusion.............................. SKLUGS, SKLAOUGS
    exclusionary .... SKLURN
exclusionary rule......................... SKLURNL, SKLURL
exclusive
    exclusive .... SKLUV, SKLAOUV
    exclusively .... SKLUVL, SKLAOUVL
    exclusiveness....................... SKLUVNS, SKLAOUVNS
    exclusive of the .... SKLUFT
    exclusive of them .... SKLUFM
    exclusive of these .... SKLUFZ
    exclusive of those .... SKLUFS
exclusivity .... SKLUVT, SKLAOUVT
excommunicate
    excommunicate .... KPAOUN
    excommunicates............................... KPAOUNS
    excommunicating .... KPAOUNG
    excommunicated .... KPAOUND
excommunication .... KPAOUNGS
excrete
    excrete...................................... KPRAOET
    excretes .... KPRAOETS
    excreting .... KPRAOEGT
    excreted................................... KPRAOETD
excretion .... KPRAOEGS
excruciating .... SKRAOURB
exculpable.. KPUBL
exculpate
    exculpate .... KPAIT
    exculpates..................................... KPAITS
    exculpating .... KPAIGT
    exculpated..................................... KPAITD
exculpation .... KPAIGS
exculpatory .... KPUPT, KPUP
exculpatory evidence .... KPEVD, KPUVP
excursion .... SKURGS
excusable....................................... SKAOUBL
excuse
    excuse...................................... SKAOUS

excuses . . . . SKAOUFS, SKAOUSZ
excusing . . . . SKAOUFG
excused . . . . SKAOUFD
excuse me. . . . . SKAOUM
exec. . . . . KPEK
executable . . . . SKUBL
execute
   execute . . . . SKUT
   executes. . . . . SKUTS
   executing. . . . . SKUGT, SKUG
   executed . . . . SKUTD
executer. . . . . SKRUT
execution. . . . . SKAOUGS
executioner . . . . SKAOURGS
executive . . . . SKUV
executor. . . . . SKOR
executrix . . . . SKRIX
exemplary. . . . . KPLEM
exemplification . . . . KPLEFMGS, KPLEMGS, KPEFMGS
exemplify
   exemplify. . . . . KPEFM, EM/FI
   exemplifies . . . . KPEFMS, EM/FIS
   exemplifying. . . . . KPEFMG, EM/FIG
   exemplified. . . . . KPEFMD, EM/FID
exempt
   exempt . . . . KPEMT
   exempts. . . . . KPEMTS
   exempting . . . . KPEMGT, KPEMG
   exempted. . . . . KPEMTD
exemption. . . . . KPEJ, KPEMGS
exercise
   exercise . . . . KP-R
   exercises . . . . KP-RS
   exercising. . . . . KP-RG
   exercised . . . . KP-RD
exhale
   exhale . . . . KPAIL
   exhales . . . . KPAILS
   exhaling. . . . . KPAILG
   exhaled . . . . KPAILD
exhaust
   exhaust . . . . KPAUF, KPAUS
   exhausts. . . . . KPAUFS
   exhausting . . . . KPAUFG
   exhausted. . . . . KPAUFD

E

exhaust
    exhaustion . . . . KPAUGS
    exhaustive . . . . KPAUV
    exhaustively . . . . KPAUVL
exhibit
    exhibit. . . . . KPIBT, KPIB
    exhibits . . . . KPIBTS, KPIBS
    exhibiting . . . . KPIBGT, KPIBG
    exhibited . . . . KPIBTD, KPIBD
exhibit
    exhibition. . . . . KPIX
    exhibitionism . . . . KPIFM
    exhibitor . . . . KPIRB
exhilarate
    exhilarate . . . . ZIL, KPILT
    exhilarates . . . . ZILS, KPILTS
    exhilarating . . . . ZILG, KPILGT
    exhilarated . . . . ZILD, KPILTD
exhilaration . . . . ZILGS, KPILGTS
exhilarative . . . . ZIV
exhilarator . . . . ZIRLT, KPIRLT
exhort
    exhort . . . . KPORT
    exhorts. . . . . KPORTS
    exhorting . . . . KPORGT, KPORG
    exhorted. . . . . KPORTD
exhortation. . . . . KPORGS
exile
    exile . . . . KPAOIL
    exiles . . . . KPAOILS
    exiling. . . . . KPAOILG
    exiled . . . . KPAOILD
exist
    exist . . . . KP*IS, KPIF
    exists . . . . KP*ISZ, KPIFS
    existing. . . . . KPIFGT, KPIFG
    existed . . . . KPIFTD, KPIFD
existence. . . . . KPINS
existent . . . . KPENT
exit
    exit . . . . KPIT
    exits . . . . KPITS
    exiting . . . . KPIGT, KPIG
    exited . . . . KPITD

BRIEF ENCOUNTERS E

exonerate
    exonerate . . . . KPON
    exonerates . . . . KPONS
    exonerating . . . . KPONG
    exonerated . . . . KPOND
exoneration . . . . KPONGS
exorbitance . . . . KPORBS
exorbitant . . . . KPORBT, KPORB
exorbitantly . . . . KPORBL
exotic . . . . KPOT
expand
    expand . . . . SPAND, KPAND
    expands . . . . SPANDZ, KPANDZ
    expanding . . . . SPANGD, KPANGD
    expanded . . . . SPAND/-D, KPAND/-D
expanded memory . . . . SPAM
expanse . . . . SPANS
expansion . . . . SPANGS, KPANGS
expansive
    expansive . . . . SPAV
    expansively . . . . SPAVL
    expansiveness . . . . SPAVNS, SPAFNS
expansivity . . . . SPAVT
ex parte . . . . KPAERT
expect
    expect . . . . KP-PT
    expects . . . . KP-PTS
    expecting . . . . KP-PGT, KP-PG
    expected . . . . KP-PTD
expect
    expectance . . . . KP-NS
    expectancy . . . . KP-NSZ
    expectation . . . . KP-PGS
expedience . . . . SPAOENS
expediency . . . . SPAOENSZ
expedient . . . . SPAOENT
expediently . . . . SPAOENLT
expedite
    expedite . . . . SPAOET
    expedites . . . . SPAOETS
    expediting . . . . SPAOEGT
    expedited . . . . SPAOETD
expedition . . . . SPEGS, SPAOEGS
expeditious
    expeditious . . . . SP*ERB, SPAO*ERB

E

expeditiously	SP*ERBL, SPAO*ERBL
expeditiousness	SP*ERNS, SPAO*ERNS

expel
expel	SKPEL
expels	SKPELS
expelling	SKPELG
expelled	SKPELD

expend
expend	SKPEN
expends	SKPENS
expending	SKPENG
expended	SKPEND

expendable	SKPENL
expenditure	SPEFP, SKPEFP
expense	SPENS
expensive	SPEV

experience
experience	SPERNS
experiences	SPERNSZ
experiencing	SPERNS/-G, SPERNG
experienced	SPERNS/-D, SPERND

experiential	SPERNLT

experiment
experiment	SPERMT
experiments	SPERMTS
experimenting	SPERMGT, SPERMG
experimented	SPERMTD

experimental	SPERNL
experimentation	SPERGS

expert
expert	SPERT
expert in the field	SP-F
expertise	SPAOEZ
expert testimony	SP-T, SP-M
expert witness	SPWIN, SW-NS

expiration	KPRAIGS

expire
expire	KPAOIR
expires	KPAOIRS
expiring	KPAOIRG
expired	KPAOIRD

explain
explain	SPLAIN
explains	SPLAINS
explaining	SPLAING

BRIEF ENCOUNTERS   E

explained	SPLAIND
explanation	SPLAINGS, SPLANGS
explanatory	SPLANT
expletive	SPLAOEV
expletive deleted	SPLAOEVD
explicit	PLIFT
explicitly	PLIFL

explode
explode	SPLOED
explodes	SPLOEDZ
exploding	SPLOEGD
exploded	SPLOED/-D

exploit
exploit	SPLOIT
exploits	SPLOITS
exploiting	SPLOIGT, SPLOIG
exploited	SPLOITD

exploit
exploitable	SPLOIBL
exploitation	SPLOIGS
exploiter	SPLOIRT
exploitive	SPLOIVT

exploration	SPLOERGS
exploratory	SPLOERT

explore
explore	SPLOER
explores	SPLOERS
exploring	SPLOERG
explored	SPLOERD

explosion	SPLOEGS

explosive
explosive	SPLOIF, SPLOIV
explosive device	SPLOIFD, SPLOIVD
explosively	SPLOIFL, SPLOIVL
explosiveness	SPLOIFNS, SPLOIVNS

exponent
exponent	SPOENT, SKPOENT
exponential	SPOENL, SKPOENL
exponentially	SPAOENL, SKPAOENL

export
export	SPOERT, KPOERT
exports	SPOERTS, KPOERTS
exporting	SPOERGT, KPOERGT, KPOERG
exported	SPOERTD, KPOERTD

export
- exportable . . . . SPOERBL, KPOERBL
- exportation . . . . SPOERGS, KPOERGS
- exporter . . . . SPROERT, KPROERT

expose
- expose . . . . SKPOES
- exposes . . . . SKPOEFS, SKPOESZ
- exposing . . . . SKPOEFG
- exposed . . . . SKPOEFD

exposé . . . . SKPAI
exposition . . . . SKPOEGS, SKPOGS
ex post facto . . . . KPOFT
exposure . . . . SKPOUR, SKPOURS

expound
- expound . . . . SPOUN
- expounds . . . . SPOUNS
- expounding . . . . SPOUNG
- expounded . . . . SPOUND

express
- express . . . . KPREF, KPRES
- expresses . . . . KPRESZ, KPREFS
- expressing . . . . KPREFG
- expressed . . . . KPREFD

express
- expression . . . . KPREGS
- expressive . . . . SPREV, SKPREV
- expressively . . . . SPREVL, SKPREVL
- expressiveness . . . . SPREVNS, SKPREVNS
- expressly . . . . SPREL, KPREL
- expressway . . . . KPROI

expulsion . . . . SPULGS

expunge
- expunge . . . . SKPUNG
- expunges . . . . SKPUNGS
- expunging . . . . SKPUNG/-G
- expunged . . . . SKPUNGD

exquisite
- exquisite . . . . SKWIZ
- exquisitely . . . . SKWILZ
- exquisiteness . . . . SKWINZ

extant . . . . STA*NT

extemporaneous
- extemporaneous . . . . STEFRP
- extemporaneously . . . . STEFRPL
- extemporaneousness . . . . STEFRPS

BRIEF ENCOUNTERS   E

extend
    extend . . . . STEN
    extends . . . . STENS
    extending . . . . STENG
    extended . . . . STEND
extended memory . . . . SKEM
extension . . . . STENGS
extensive
    extensive . . . . STEV
    extensively . . . . STEVL
    extensiveness . . . . STEVNS, STEFNS
extent . . . . STENT
exterior
    exterior . . . . KPAOR
    exteriority. . . . . KPAORT
    exteriorly . . . . KPAORL
exterminate
    exterminate . . . . STERMT
    exterminates. . . . . STERMTS
    exterminating. . . . . STERMGT, STERMG
    exterminated . . . . STERMTD
extermination . . . . STERGS
external. . . . . STERNL
externally . . . . STAERNL, STAOERNL
extinct . . . . KPINGT, KPING
extinction . . . . KPINGS
extinguish
    extinguish . . . . TWIRB
    extinguishes . . . . TWIRBS
    extinguishing. . . . . TWIRBG
    extinguished . . . . TWIRBD
extinguishable . . . . TWIRBL
extinguisher. . . . . TWRIRB
extol
    extol. . . . . KPOEL
    extols . . . . KPOELS
    extolling . . . . KPOELG
    extolled . . . . KPOELD
extoller . . . . KPOERL
extort
    extort. . . . . STORT
    extorts . . . . STORTS
    extorting . . . . STORGT
    extorted . . . . STORTD
extorter . . . . STRORT

extortion	STORGS
extra	KPRA

extract
extract	STRAK
extracts	STRAKZ
extracting	STRAK/-G
extracted	STRAKD

extraction	STRAX
extraditable	KPRAOIBL

extradite
extradite	KPRAOIT
extradites	KPRAOITS
extraditing	KPRAOIGT
extradited	KPRAOITD

extradition	KPRIGS

extraneous
extraneous	STRAEN
extraneously	STRAENL
extraneousness	STRAENS

extraordinarily	STRAORLD
extraordinariness	STRAORNS
extraordinary	STRAORD

extrapolate
extrapolate	KPRAP
extrapolates	KPRAPS
extrapolating	KPRAPG
extrapolated	KPRAPD

extrapolation	KPRAPGS
extrapolator	KPRARP
extravagance	STRAVS, STRAVG
extravagant	STRAVT, STRAVGT
extravaganza	STRAVZ
extreme	STREM
extremely	STREL
extremism	STREFM
extremist	STREFT
extremity	STREMT

extricate
extricate	KPRAET, KPRAIT
extricates	KPRAETS, KPRAITS
extricating	KPRAEGT, KPRAIGT
extricated	KPRAETD, KPRAITD

extrication	KPRAEGS
extrinsic	KPRIN
extrinsically	KPRINL

BRIEF ENCOUNTERS — E

extrovert . . . . KPROEFRT, KPROEVRT
extroverted . . . . KPROEFRTD, KPROEVRTD
extrude
    extrude . . . . KPRAOUD
    extrudes. . . . . KPRAOUDZ
    extruding . . . . KPRAOUGD
    extruded . . . . KPRAOUD/-D
extrusion . . . . KPRAOUGS
exuberance. . . . . KPAOUBS
exuberant. . . . . KPAOUBT, KPAOUB
exuberantly . . . . KPAOUBLT, KPAOUBL
exult
    exult. . . . . KPULT
    exults . . . . KPULTS
    exulting . . . . KPULGT
    exulted . . . . KPULTD
exultation . . . . KP*ULGS
eye
    eye. . . . . AOI
    eyes . . . . AOIZ
    eyeing . . . . AOIG
    eyed. . . . . AOI/-D, AO*ID
eye
    eyeball . . . . AOIBL
    eye care . . . . AOIK
    eye care specialist . . . . AOIKT
    eye doctor. . . . . AOIRD
    eyeful . . . . AOIFL

F

FAA	FAI
fabric	FRIB
fabulous	
fabulous	FAB
fabulously	FABLS
fabulousness	FABS
facet	FAFT
faceted	FAFTD
facetious	
facetious	FAERB
facetiously	FAERBL
facetiousness	FAERBS, FAERNS
facial	FAIRBL
facilitate	
facilitate	FAF
facilitates	FAFS
facilitating	FAFG
facilitated	FAFD
facilitation	FAFGS
facilitator	FA*FR
facility	FAFLT
fact	
fact	FAK
faction	FA*X, FWAX
factory	FAOKT
facts	FAKZ
facts and circumstances	FARKS
factual	FAUK
factor	
factor	FAOK, FAKT
factors	FAOKS, FAKTS
factoring	FAOK/-G, FAOG, FAKT/-G
factored	FAOKD, FAKTD
faculty	FULT
fade-out	FOUT
faggot	FAGT
Fahrenheit	FAIRNT
failure	FLUR
fair	
fair and impartial	FAP
fair and reasonable	FAIRNL
fairground	FAIRGD

BRIEF ENCOUNTERS F

fairly	FAIRL
fair market	FAERK, FAIRM
fair market value	FAEV, FAEFRB
fairness	FAIRNS
fair preponderance	FAIRP
fair preponderance of the evidence	FAIRPD
fair statement	FAIRMT
fair to say	FAIRTS, -FRTS
fair to state	FAIRT, -FRT
fair trial	FRAOIL
faithful	FAIF
faithfully	FAIFL

fall
fall	FAUL
falls	FAULS
falling	FAULG
fell	FEL
fallen	FAUNL

fallacious	FLAIRB
fallaciously	FLAIRBL
fallibility	FABLT
fallible	FABL
Fallopian	FLOEP
Fallopian tube	FLOEPT
false alarm	FLAURM
false imprisonment	FIFMT
falsification	FALGS

falter
falter	FARLT
falters	FARLTS
faltering	FARLGT, FARLG
faltered	FARLTD

familial	FLIL
familiar	FAM
familiarity	FAMT
family	FAEM
family room	FAERM
famished	FARBD
famous	FOUS
fancy	FAENS
fantastic	FAFK
fantastically	FAFL
fantasy	FAENT
faraway	FWAR
far away	FWAI

© 1997 White-Boucke Publishing.   213   ILLEGAL TO PHOTOCOPY

F   BRIEF ENCOUNTERS

farewell.. FAERL
farmer... FRARM
farther
    farther.. FA*RT
    farther than .... FARN
    farther than the............................... FARNT
    farther than these .... FARNZ
    farther than those .... FARNS
farthest.. FA*ERS
fascinate
    fascinate...................................... SFAIT
    fascinates..................................... SFAITS
    fascinating.................................... SFAIGT
    fascinated..................................... SFAITD
fascination... SFAIGS
fascism .... FAFM
fascist .... FARBT
fasten
    fasten... FAEFN
    fastens.. FAEFNS
    fastening .... FAEFNG
    fastened....................................... FAEFND
fastener .... FRAEFN
faster
    faster .... FA*RS, FAFR
    faster than .... FAFRN
    faster than the................................ FAFRNT
    faster than them .... FAFRM
    faster than these .... FAFRNZ
    faster than those .... FAFRNS
fast food .... FAOF, FAOFD
fast food restaurant .... FAOFT, FAOFRD
fatal
    fatal.. FAILT
    fatality .... FALT
    fatally... FAELT
father
    father...................................... FA, FAU
    fatherhood .... FAUD
    father-in-law .... FANL
    fathers-in-law .... FANLS
fathom
    fathom .... FAOM
    fathoms....................................... FAOMS
    fathoming .... FAOMG

BRIEF ENCOUNTERS   F

```
        fathomed. . . . . . . . . . . . . . . . . . . . . . . . . . . . . . . . . . . . . . FAOMD
fatigue
        fatigue. . . . . . . . . . . . . . . . . . . . . . . . . . . . . . . . . . . . . . . . FAOEG
        fatigues . . . . . . . . . . . . . . . . . . . . . . . . . . . . . . . . . . . . . . FAOEGS
        fatiguing . . . . . . . . . . . . . . . . . . . . . . . . . . . . . . . . . . . . FAOEG/-G
        fatigued . . . . . . . . . . . . . . . . . . . . . . . . . . . . . . . . . . . . . . FAOEGD
faucet. . . . . . . . . . . . . . . . . . . . . . . . . . . . . . . . . . . . . . . . . . . . . . . FAUFT
*faux pas* . . . . . . . . . . . . . . . . . . . . . . . . . . . . . . . . . . . . . . . . . . . . . FOEP
favor
        favor. . . . . . . . . . . . . . . . . . . . . . . . . . . . . . . . . . . . . . . . . . FAIVR
        favors . . . . . . . . . . . . . . . . . . . . . . . . . . . . . . . . . . . . . . . . FAIVRS
        favoring. . . . . . . . . . . . . . . . . . . . . . . . . . . . . . . . . . . . . . FAIVRG
        favored . . . . . . . . . . . . . . . . . . . . . . . . . . . . . . . . . . . . . . FAIVRD
favorable . . . . . . . . . . . . . . . . . . . . . . . . . . . . . . . . . . . . . . . . . FAIVRBL
fax . . . . . . . . . . . . . . . . . . . . . . . . . . . . . . . . . . . . . . . . . . . . . . . . FAX
FBI . . . . . . . . . . . . . . . . . . . . . . . . . . . . . . . . . . . . . . . . . . . . . . . . FIB
FCC . . . . . . . . . . . . . . . . . . . . . . . . . . . . . . . . . . . . . . . . . . . . . . FAOEK
fear
        fearful . . . . . . . . . . . . . . . . . . . . . . . . . . . . . . . . . . . . . . . . FAOEF
        fearfully. . . . . . . . . . . . . . . . . . . . . . . . . . . . FAOEFL, FAOEFRL
        fearless. . . . . . . . . . . . . . . . . . . . . . . . . . . . . . . . . . . . . . FAOERL
        fearsome . . . . . . . . . . . . . . . . . . . . . . . . . . . . . . . . . . . . FAOERM
feasibility. . . . . . . . . . . . . . . . . . . . . . . . . . . . . . . . . . . . . . FAOEFBLT
feasible . . . . . . . . . . . . . . . . . . . . . . . . . . . . . . . . . FAOEZ, FAOEFBL
feasibly. . . . . . . . . . . . . . . . . . . . . . . . . . . . . . . . . . . . . . . . . FAOELZ
feather
        feather . . . . . . . . . . . . . . . . . . . . . . . . . . . . . . . . . . . . . . . F*ERT
        feathers. . . . . . . . . . . . . . . . . . . . . . . . . . . . . . . . . . . . . . F*ERTS
        feathering . . . . . . . . . . . . . . . . . . . . . . . . . . . . . . . . . . . . F*ERGT
        feathered . . . . . . . . . . . . . . . . . . . . . . . . . . . . . . . . . . . . F*ERTD
feature
        feature . . . . . . . . . . . . . . . . . . . . . . . . . . . . . . . . . . . . . . FAOEFP
        features . . . . . . . . . . . . . . . . . . . . . . . . . . . . . . . . . . . . FAOEFPS
        featuring. . . . . . . . . . . . . . . . . . . . . . . . . . . . . . . . . . . . FAOEFPG
        featured . . . . . . . . . . . . . . . . . . . . . . . . . . . . . . . . . . . . FAOEFPD
feature
        *feature of the*. . . . . . . . . . . . . . . . . . . . . . . . . . . . . . . . FAOEFPT
        *feature of them*. . . . . . . . . . . . . . . . . . . . . . . . . . . . . . . FAOEFM
        *feature of these* . . . . . . . . . . . . . . . . . . . . . . . . . . . . . FAOEFPZ
February . . . . . . . . . . . . . . . . . . . . . . . . . . . . . . . . . . . . . . . . . . FEB
federal
        federal . . . . . . . . . . . . . . . . . . . . . . . . . . . . . . . . . . . . . . . FRAL
        *Federal Aviation Administration* . . . . . . . . . . . . . . . FAIVGS, FAI/FAI
        *Federal Bureau of Investigation* . . . . . . . . . . . . . . . FAO*EB, FIB/FIB
        *Federal Communications Commission* . . . . . . . . . FAOUNGS, FAOEKS
```

federal government	FRALG
federalism	FRAFM, FRAEFM
federalist	FRALT, FRAEFT
federalization	FRAELGS
federal law	FLA
federal laws	FLAZ
federally	FRAEL
federal regulation	FRALGS

federalize
federalize	FR-L
federalizes	FR-LS
federalizing	FR-LG
federalized	FR-LD

federation	FRAIGS
feeble	FAOEBL

feed
feed	FAOED
feeds	FAOEDZ
feeding	FAOED/-G
fed	FED

feedback	FAOEB

feel
feel	FAOEL
feels	FAOELS
feeling	FAOELG
felt	FELT

feisty	FAO*IS
feline	FLAOIN
fellatio	FLAERB
fellow	FLEL
fellowship	FLEP

felon
felon	FLON
felonious	FLOIS, FLOENS
feloniously	FLOINL, FLOIL, FLOILS
felony	FLOIN

female	FAEL
feminine	FEM
feminism	FEFM
feminist	FEMT, FEFT
femur	FERM
fender	FERND

ferment
ferment	FERMT
ferments	FERMTS

BRIEF ENCOUNTERS   F

fermenting .... FERMGT, FERMG
fermented................................... FERMTD
fermentation .... FERMGS, FERJ
ferocious
    ferocious...................................... FROERB
    ferociously................................... FROERBL
    ferociousness .... FROERBS
ferret
    ferret .... FERT
    ferrets.. FERTS
    ferreting..................................... FERT/-G
    ferreted...................................... FERTD
fertile .... FERL
fertility .... FERLT
fertilization .... FERLGS
fervent
    fervent .... FERNT, FEVRNT
    fervently .... FERNL, FEVRNL
    ferventness .... FERNZ, FEVRNZ
fervor .... FEFRB
festival... FIVL
fetal.. FAOELT
fetish .... FERB
fetus .... FAOETS
few
    few... FAOU
    fewer... FAOUR
    fewer than .... FAOURN
    fewer than the .... FAOURNT
    fewer than these............................ FAOURNZ
    few of the .... FAOUFT
    few of them................................. FAOUFM
    few of these .... FAOUFZ
    few of those .... FAOUFS
fiance... FAE
fiancee................................... FA*E, FWAE
fiasco .... FWAS
fiber .... FAOIB
fiberglass.................................... FAOIBG
fickle .... FIKL
fiction .... F*IX
fidelity .... FELTD
fidget
    fidget.. FIJ
    fidgets.. FIJS

F

fidgeting	FIJ/-G
fidgeted	FIJD
fiduciary	FURB, FAOURB
fierceness	FAOERNS
Fifth Amendment	FAEMT
Fifth Amendment right	FAERMT
fifty	VI

fight
fight	FAOIT
fights	FAOITS
fighting	FAOIGT
fought	FAUT

fighter	FAOIRT
figment	FIMT

figure
figure	FIG
figures	FIGS
figuring	FIG/-G
figured	FIGD

Fiji	FAOEJ
Fijian	FAOENG, FAOEFRNG
filament	FLIMT
Filipino	FWIP
filer	FAOIRL

film
film	FIM
films	FIMS
filming	FIMG
filmed	FIMD

filter
filter	FIRLT
filters	FIRLTS
filtering	FIRLGT
filtered	FIRLTD

filtration	FILGTS, FIRLGS

finagle
finagle	FAIG
finagles	FAIGZ
finagling	FAIG/-G
finagled	FAIGD

finagler	FRAIG

final
final	FAOINL
finality	FAOINLT
final judgment	FAOIJ

BRIEF ENCOUNTERS — F

finally	FAENL
finale	FAINL
finalize	
finalize	FINL
finalizes	FINLS
finalizing	FINL/-G
finalized	FINLD
finance	
finance	F-N
finances	F-NS
financing	F-NG
financed	F-ND
financial	F-NL
financier	F-RN
find	
find	FAOIND
finds	FAOINDZ
finding	FAOINGD
found	FOUN
finding of fact	FIFK
findings of fact	FIFKS
finer	FAOIRN
finely	FOINL
finger	
finger	FIRNG
fingernail	FIRN
fingerprint	F-P
fingerspell	SFEL
fingerspelling	SFELG
fingertip	FINT
finish	
finish	FIN
finishes	FINS
finishing	FING
finished	FIND
finite	FAOINT
Finland	FWAN, FWAND
Finn	FWIN
Finnish	FWIRB
fire	
fire alarm	FLARM
firearm	FAOIRM
fireball	FAOIRBL
fire department	FEPT
fire departments	FEPT/-S

F   BRIEF ENCOUNTERS

fire extinguisher . . . . F–Z
fire hydrant . . . . FAOIRNT
fireman . . . . FRAN
firemen . . . . FREN
fireplace . . . . FAOIRP
fire station . . . . FAIGS
fire truck . . . . FAOIRK, FRUK
first
    first . . . . F*IRS
    First Amendment . . . . FIRMT
    First Amendment right . . . . FRIRMT
    first class . . . . FLAS
    first degree . . . . F–D
    first-degree burn . . . . F–BD
    first-degree murder . . . . F–MD
    firsthand . . . . FRAND
    First Lady . . . . FLAED
    first of all . . . . FR–FL
    first time . . . . FIRT
fiscal
    fiscal . . . . SKAL
    fiscally . . . . SKLI
    fiscal year . . . . SKARL, SKALG
fisher . . . . FRIRB
fissure . . . . FIRZ
five
    fivefold . . . . FAOIFLD, FAOIVLD
    five of the . . . . FAOIFT
    five of them . . . . FAOIFM
    five of these . . . . FAOIFZ, FAOIVZ
    five of those . . . . FAOIVS
    five-piece . . . . FAOIVP
    five-time . . . . FAOIM
    five times . . . . FAOIMS
fixation . . . . FAIX
flabbergast
    flabbergast . . . . FLABT
    flabbergasts . . . . FLABTS
    flabbergasting . . . . FLABT/–G
    flabbergasted . . . . FLABTD
flaccid
    flaccid . . . . FLAFD
    flaccidity . . . . FLAFT, FLAFTD
    flaccidly . . . . FLAFL, FLAFLD
    flaccidness . . . . FLAFNS

BRIEF ENCOUNTERS   F

flagrant	FLAEGT, FLAEG, FLAGT
flagrantly	FLAELG, FLALG
flamboyance	FLOINZ
flamboyancy	FLOINSZ
flamboyant	FLOINT
flammable	FLABL
flammable liquid	FLID
flashlight	FLARBT, FLARBLT
flatly	FLALT
flatten	
flatten	FLANT
flattens	FLANTS
flattening	FLANGT
flattened	FLANTD
flatter	
flatter	FLAERT
flatters	FLAERTS
flattering	FLAERGT
flattered	FLAERTD
flatulence	FLAFP
flatulent	FLAFPT
flawless	FLAULS
flawlessly	FLAUL
flee	
flee	FLAOE
flees	FLAOEZ
fleeing	FLAOEG
fled	FLED
flexibility	FLEBLT
flexible	FLEBL
flexion	FL*EX, FL-X, FLEFN
flick	
flick	FL*IK, FLOIK
flicks	FL*IKS, FLOIKS
flicking	FL*IK/-G, FL*IG, FLOIK/-G, FLOIG
flicked	FL*IKD, FLOIKD
flicker	
flicker	FLIRK
flickers	FLIRKS
flickering	FLIRK/-G
flickered	FLIRKD
flight school	FLAOL
flight simulator	FLAIRT
flimsy	FLIM

flinch
- flinch . . . FLIFP
- flinches . . . FLIFPS
- flinching . . . FLIFPG
- flinched . . . FLIFPD

fling
- fling . . . FLING
- flings . . . FLINGS
- flinging . . . FLING/-G
- flung . . . FLUNG

flip out
- *flip out* . . . FLOUP
- *flips out* . . . FLOUPS
- *flipping out* . . . FLOUPG
- *flipped out* . . . FLOUPD

flippant . . . FLIPT
flirtation . . . FLIRGS
floodgate . . . FLAOGTD
floodgates . . . FLAOGTDZ
floodlight . . . FLAOLT
floppy . . . FLOIP
floppy disk . . . FLOIPD
Florida . . . FL*
florist . . . FLORT
flotation . . . FLOEGS

flounder
- flounder . . . FLOUN
- flounders . . . FLOUNZ
- floundering . . . FLOUNG
- floundered . . . FLOUND

fluoridate
- fluoridate . . . FLAOURT
- fluoridates . . . FLAOURTS
- fluoridating . . . FLAOURGT
- fluoridated . . . FLAOURTD

fluoridation . . . FLORGS, FLAOURGS

flourish
- flourish . . . FLOURB
- flourishes . . . FLOURBS
- flourishing . . . FLOURBG
- flourished . . . FLOURBD

flu . . . FL*U

fluctuate
- fluctuate . . . FLUK
- fluctuates . . . FLUKZ

BRIEF ENCOUNTERS   F

fluctuating . . . . FLUK/-G
fluctuated . . . . FLUKD
fluctuation . . . . FLUGS
fluency . . . . FLAOUNZ, FLUNS
fluent . . . . FLAOUNT, FLUNT
fluently . . . . FLAOUNL, FLUNL
fluid . . . . FLAOUD
fluidity . . . . FLAOUTD
flummox
   flummox . . . . FLUM
   flummoxes . . . . FLUMS
   flummoxing . . . . FLUMG
   flummoxed . . . . FLUMD
fluoresce
   fluoresce . . . . FLOURS
   fluoresces . . . . FLOUFS, FLOURSZ
   fluorescing . . . . FLOUFG
   fluoresced . . . . FLOUFD
fluorescence . . . . FLENS, FLORS
fluorescent
   fluorescent . . . . FLENT, FLES, FLOR
   fluorescent light . . . . FLENLT, FLORLT
   fluorescent lighting . . . . FLENLGT, FLORLGT
fluster
   fluster . . . . FLUFR
   flusters . . . . FLUFRS
   flustering . . . . FLUFRG
   flustered . . . . FLUFRD
flutter
   flutter . . . . FLURT
   flutters . . . . FLURTS
   fluttering . . . . FLURGT
   fluttered . . . . FLURTD
fly
   fly . . . . FLAOI
   flies . . . . FLAOIS
   flying . . . . FLAOIG
   flew . . . . FLAOU
   flown . . . . FLOEN
focal . . . . FOEFL, FOEKL
focal point . . . . FOEFP, FOEFLT
focus
   focus . . . . FOEF
   focuses . . . . FOEFS
   focussing . . . . FOEFG

focussed	FOEFD
fogey	FOEG
foggy	FAUG
foible	FOIBL

foist
foist	FOIF
foists	FOIFS
foisting	FOIFG
foisted	FOIFD

folder	FORLD
foliage	FOEJ

follow
follow	FOL
follows	FOLS
following	FOLG
followed	FOL/-D
follower	FO*RL

follow up
follow up	FLUP
follows up	FLUPS
following up	FLUPG
followed up	FLUPD
follow up the	FLUPT

foment
foment	FOEMT
foments	FOEMTS
fomenting	FOEMGT
fomented	FOEMTD
fomentation	FOEMGS

fondle
fondle	FO*NL
fondles	FONLS
fondling	FONL/-G, FO*NLG
fondled	FONLD

food poisoning	FAOP, FAOPG

fool
foolhardy	FAORLD
foolish	FAORB
foolishly	FAORBL
foolishness	FAORNS
foolproof	FLAOF

foot
footage	FAOJ
football	FAOBL
football game	FAOBLG

BRIEF ENCOUNTERS   *F*

```
    footnote ........................................ FAON
    foot-pound ..................................... FAOPD
    footprint ...................................... FRINT
for
    for ............................................ FOR
    for example .................................... FR-X
    for identification ............................. FOID
    for instance ................................... FRINS
    for probable cause ............................. FRAUZ
    for probable cause only ........................ FOEZ
    for sale ....................................... SFAEL
    for sale sign .................................. SFAELS
    for the most part ...................... FORPT, FR-MT
    for the purpose ................................ FORP
    for the purposes of ............................ FORPS
    for the record ................................. FRORD
    for the record, please ................. FORDZ, FRORDZ
    for the truth .................................. FR*UT
    for the truth of the matter .................... FRUT
    for the truth of the matter asserted ........... FRUTS
forage
    forage ......................................... FAURJ
    forages ........................................ FAURJS
    foraging ............................... FAURJ/-G, FAURG
    foraged ........................................ FAURJD
forager .......................................... FRAURJ
forbid
    forbid .................................. FORBD, FOERBD
    forbids ............................... FORBDZ, FOERBDZ
    forbidding ........................... FORBGD, FOERBD/-G
    forbade / forbad .................... FOR/BAID / FO*R/BAD
    forbidden / forbid ................... FORND / FORBD
force
    force .......................................... FORS
    forces ................................... FOFS, FORSZ
    forcing ........................................ FOFG
    forced ......................................... FOFD
forceful ......................................... FOFL
forceps ................................... FREP, FREPS
fore
    fore ........................................... FOER
    forearm ........................................ FROERM
    foreclosure .................................... FLOERK
    foreground ..................................... FOERGD
    forehead ....................................... FOERD
```

F

forelady	FRAED
foreman	FRAM
foremost	FOERMT
foreperson	FOERP

forecast
forecast	F–RK, FOER/KAF
forecasts	F–RKZ, FOER/KAFS
forecasting	F–RK/–G, F–RG, FOER/KAFG
forecast / forecasted	F–RK, FOER/KAF / F–RKD, FOER/KAFD

forecaster	FR–RK, FOER/KAFR

foreclose
foreclose	FOERK
forecloses	FOERKS
foreclosing	FOERK/–G
foreclosed	FOERKD

forego
forego	FOERG, FRO
foregoes	FOERGS, FROS
foregoing	FOERG/–G, FRO/–G
forewent	FROENT, FRENT
foregone	FOERNG, FRON

foreign	FORN
foreigner	FRORN
forensic	FRENS
forensic evidence	FREVD

forest
forest	FR*ES
forestation	FREFGS
forester	FREFRS
foresters	FREFRSZ
forestry	FR*ERS
forest ranger	FREJ

forever	FREFR, FREVR

forfeit
forfeit	FOFT
forfeits	FOFTS
forfeiting	FOFGT
forfeited	FOFTD

forfeiture	FOFRT
forgery	FOERJ

forget
forget	FERG, FORG
forgets	FERGS, FORGS
forgetting	FERG/–G, FORG/–G

BRIEF ENCOUNTERS   F

forgot	FORGT
forgotten	FOERN
forgettable	FERBL
forgetfulness	FERNS, FERG/FL-NS
forgivable	FRIVL, GIVL
forgive	
forgive	FRIV, FOR/GIV
forgives	FRIVS, FOR/GIVS
forgiving	FRIVG, FO*R/GIVG
forgave	FRAEV, FOR/GAEV
forgiven	FRIVN, FRIFN, FOR/GIVN
forgiveness	FRIVNS, GIVNS
formal	FOM
formality	FOMT
formally	FAL
format	
format	FORMT
formats	FORMTS
formatting	FORMGT
formatted	FORMTD
formation	FORMGS
former	FOERM
formerly	FOERL
fornication	FORNGS
forsake	
forsake	FRAIK
forsakes	FRAIKS
forsaking	FRAIK/-G
forsook	FRAOK
forsaken	FRAIK/-N, FRA*IN
forte	FOERT
forth	
forthcoming	FUMG
forthright	FRAO*IT
forthrightly	FRAO*ILT
forthrightness	FRAO*ITS
forthwith	FOF
fortunate	FORNT, KHAOUNT
fortunately	FORL, FORNL, KHAOUNL
fortune	KHAOUN
forty	
forty	FRI
forty of the	FRIFT
forty of them	FRIFM
forty of these	FRIFZ

forty of those . . . . FRIFS
forum . . . . FRUM
forward . . . . FARD
fossil . . . . FOIFL
foster
    foster . . . . FOFR
    fosters . . . . FOFRS
    fostering . . . . FOFRG
    fostered . . . . FOFRD
foster parent . . . . FOFRP
found
    found. . . . . FOUN
    founds . . . . FOUNS
    founding . . . . FOUNG
    found. . . . . FOUN
    founded . . . . FOUND
found
    foundation . . . . FOUNGS
    foundational . . . . FOUNLGS, FOUNL
    founder . . . . FOURN, FOURND
fountain . . . . FOUNT
four
    four. . . . . FOUR
    fourfold. . . . . FOUFRLD
    four of the . . . . FOUFT
    four of them. . . . . FOUFM
    four of these . . . . FOUFZ
    four of those . . . . FOUFS
    four-piece. . . . . FOURP
    foursome . . . . FOURM
    four-time. . . . . FRAOIM
    four times . . . . FRAOIMS
foyer. . . . . FOIR
fraction . . . . FRAX
fracture
    fracture . . . . FRAK, FRAKT
    fractures . . . . FRAKZ, FRAKTS
    fracturing . . . . FRAKT/-G, FRAK/-G, FRAG
    fractured . . . . FRAKD, FRAKTD
fragile. . . . . FRAJ
fragility. . . . . FRAJT
fragment
    fragment . . . . FRAMT
    fragments . . . . FRAMTS
    fragmenting. . . . . FRAMGT

BRIEF ENCOUNTERS F

fragmented	FRAMTD
fragmentation	FRAMGS, FRAGS
fragrance	FRAIGTS, FRA*IGS
fragrant	FRAIGT
framework	FRAIRK
frantic	FRANT
frantically	FRANLT, FRANL
fraternity	FRAENT

fraud
fraudulence	FRAUNS
fraudulent	FRAULT
fraudulently	FRAUL

free
free	FRE, FRAO*E
frees	FRES, FRAOES
freeing	FRE/-G, FRAOEG
freed	FRE/-D, FRAOED

free
freebie	FRAOEB
freedom	FREM, FRAOEM
freeway	FOI

freckle
freckle	FREKL
freckles	FREKLS
freckling	FREKL/-G
freckled	FREKLD

freelance
freelance	FLANS
freelances	FLANSZ
freelancing	FLANS/-G, FLANGS
freelanced	FLANS/-D
freelancer	FLARNS

freeload
freeload	FLOD
freeloads	FLODZ
freeloading	FLOD/-G
freeloaded	FLOD/-D
freeloader	FLORD

freeze
freeze	FRAOEZ
freezes	FRAOEFS, FRAOESZ
freezing	FRAOEFG
froze	FROEZ
frozen	FROENZ
freezer	FRAOERZ

F — BRIEF ENCOUNTERS

freight	FRAIT
French	FREFP
frenzy	FRENZ
frequencies	FREKSZ
frequency	FREKZ
frequent	
frequent	FREK
frequents	FREKS
frequenting	FREK/-G, FREG
frequented	FREKD
frequently	FREL
friar	FRAR
friction	FRIGS
Friday	FRID
fridge	FR*IJ
friendly	FRENL
friendship	FRIP
frighten	
frighten	FRAOINT, FRAOIN
frightens	FRAOINTS, FRAOINS
frightening	FRAOINGT, FRAOING
frightened	FRAOINTD, FRAOIND
frightful	FRAOIFL
frightfully	FRAOEFL
fringe	FRING
frivolity	FRIFLT
frivolous	FRIFLS
from	
from	FR–
from a	FRA
from her	FRER
from him	FRIM
from it	FRIT
from the	FR–T
from them	FR–M
from these	FR–Z
from those	FR–S
from time to time	FRIMT
from us	FRUS
from you	FRU
front	
frontage	FROJ
frontage road	FROEJ, FROJD
frontal	FRONL
front door	FROND

front of the	FROFT
front of them	FROFM
front of these	FROFZ
front of those	FROFS
front room	FR-RM, FRAOM
front seat	FROIT
front yard	FRARD
frostbite	FRAOIB, FRAOIBT

frugal
    frugal . . . . FRAOUG
    frugality . . . . FRAOULT
    frugally . . . . FRAOUL
    frugalness . . . . FRAOUNS

fruitful	FRAOUF
fruitfully	FRAOUFL, FRUFL

frustrate
    frustrate . . . . FRUF
    frustrates . . . . FRUFS
    frustrating . . . . FRUFG
    frustrated . . . . FRUFD

frustration	FRUFGS
fryer	FRAOIR
fugitive	FAOUJ

fulfill
    fulfill . . . . F-FL
    fulfills . . . . F-FLS
    fulfilling . . . . F-FLG
    fulfilled . . . . F-FLD

fulfillment	FUFMT
full time	FUMT
fully	FL*I

fumigate
    fumigate . . . . FAOUMT
    fumigates . . . . FAOUMTS
    fumigating . . . . FAOUMGT
    fumigated . . . . FAOUMTD

fumigation	FAOUMGS
fumigator	FAOURMT

function
    function . . . . FUNGS
    functions . . . . FUNGSZ
    functioning . . . . FUNGS/-G
    functioned . . . . FUNGS/-D

functional	FUNLGS

F BRIEF ENCOUNTERS

fund
- fundamental ... FENL
- fundamentalist ... FENLT
- fundamentally ... FAOENL
- fund-raiser ... FRAEFR
- fund-raising ... FRAEFG

funeral ... FAOURNL

funnel
- funnel ... FUNL
- funnels ... FUNLS
- funneling ... FUNL/-G
- funneled ... FUNLD

funny ... FOIN

fur
- fur ... F*UR, FWUR
- *fur ball* ... FURBL
- *fur coat* ... FURKT

furious
- furious ... FAOURS
- furiously ... FAOURLS
- furiousness ... FAOURNS

furnish
- furnish ... FURN
- furnishes ... FURNS
- furnishing ... FURNG
- furnished ... FURND

furniture ... FURNT
furor ... FROR

further
- further ... FURT
- furthers ... FURTS
- furthering ... FURGT
- furthered ... FURTD

further
- furtherance ... FRAENS
- furthermore ... F*URM, FRURM
- *further reading* ... FRAEG

further stipulate
- *further stipulate* ... FOIP
- *further stipulates* ... FOIPS
- *further stipulating* ... FOIPG
- *further stipulated* ... FOIPD

further stipulation ... FOIPGS
fury ... FRAOUR
fuselage ... SLAUJ

futile	FAOULT
futility	F–LT
future	FUT
fuzzy	FOIZ

G

gadget	GAJ
gage	GAIG
gainful	GAIF
gainfully	GAIFL
galactic	GLAK
galaxy	GLAX
gallant	GLANT
gallantly	GLANL
gallbladder	GAUB
gallery	GLAL
gallon	GAL
gallop	
gallop	GLOP
gallops	GLOPS
galloping	GLOPG
galloped	GLOPD
galvanization	GAVGS
galvanize	
galvanize	GAV
galvanizes	GAVS
galvanizing	GAVG
galvanized	GAVD
galvanizer	GAVR
gamble	
gamble	GABL
gambles	GABLS
gambling	GABLG
gambled	GABLD
gambler	GRABL
gamut	GUMT
garage	
garage	GRAJ
garages	GRAJS
garaging	GRAJ/-G
garaged	GRAJD
garage sale	GRAJZ
garage sales	GRAJSZ
garbage	GARJ
garbage truck	GARJT
garden	
garden	GAERN
gardens	GAERNS

BRIEF ENCOUNTERS   G

gardening	GAERNG
gardened	GAERND
gardener	GRAERN
garlic	GARL
garment	GARMT
garment bag	**GAERMT**
garnish	
garnish	GARN
garnishes	GARNS
garnishing	GARNG
garnished	GARND
garnishment	GAMT
gasoline	GLAEN
gasp	
gasp	GAFP
gasps	GAFPS
gasping	GAFPG
gasped	GAFPD
gas station	**GAGS**
gather	
gather	GAFR, GAT
gathers	GAFRS, GATS
gathering	GAFRG, GAGT
gathered	GAFRD, GATD
gauge	
gauge	GAIJ
gauges	GAIJS
gauging	GAIJ/-G
gauged	GAIJD
gauntlet	GAUNL
gavel	GAVL
gave up	**GAEP, GUPD**
Geiger counter	**GAOIRG**
gender	JERND
gene	
gene	GAOEN
genealogist	GAOENT
genealogy	GAOENL
general	
general	JEN
generality	JENLT
generally	JENL
general manager	**J-M**
generalization	JENLGS, JL-GS, JLAOIGS

G   BRIEF ENCOUNTERS

generalize
- generalize. . . . . JLAOIS
- generalizes. . . . . JLAOIFS, JLAOISZ
- generalizing . . . . JLAOIFG
- generalized. . . . . JLAOIFD

generate
- generate . . . . JAIT
- generates. . . . . JAITS
- generating . . . . JAIGT
- generated . . . . JAITD

generation . . . . JAIGS, JENGS
generic. . . . . GERK
generically. . . . . GERL
generosity. . . . . JOS, JOFT
generous . . . . JOUS
generously . . . . JOULS
genesis. . . . . JENSZ, GENSZ
geneticist . . . . JIFT
genetic. . . . . GENT
genetically . . . . GENLT
genital . . . . GAENL
genius . . . . JAOENZ

gentle
- gentle. . . . . GENL
- gentleman. . . . . JA
- gentleman's . . . . JAS
- gentlemen. . . . . JE
- ***gentlemen of the jury*** . . . . JERJ
- gentlemen's. . . . . JES

genuine
- genuine . . . . JAOUN
- genuinely . . . . JAOUNL
- genuineness. . . . . JAOUNS

genus . . . . GAOENZ
geographer . . . . J-FR

geographic
- geographic . . . . J-FK
- geographical. . . . . J-FL
- geographically . . . . JAOEFL

geography. . . . . J-F
geologist . . . . JOELT
geology. . . . . JOELG
geometric. . . . . JAOEK
geometrically. . . . . JAOEKL
geometry. . . . . JOEMT, JAOEMT

BRIEF ENCOUNTERS   G

Georgia	GA*
geriatric	GERT
German	JOIM
germane	JAIM
Germany	JOIRM
germinate	
germinate	JERMT
germinates	JERMTS
germinating	JERMGT, JERMG
germinated	JERMTD
germination	JERGS
gestate	
gestate	JEGT
gestates	JEGTS
gestating	JEGT/-G
gestated	JEGTD
gestation	JEGS
gesticulate	
gesticulate	J-LT
gesticulates	J-LTS
gesticulating	J-LGT, J-LG
gesticulated	J-LTD
gesticulation	J-LGS
gesture	
gesture	GER
gestures	GERS
gesturing	GERG
gestured	GERD
get	
get	GET
gets	GETS
getting	GEGT
got	GOT
gotten / got	GOEN / GOT
get a fair trial	GRAOIL
geyser	GAOIRS
Ghana	GHAN
ghetto	GHET
ghoul	
ghoul	GAOUL
ghoulish	GAOURB
ghoulishly	GAOURBL
ghoulishness	GAOURBS
GI	GI
giant	JAOINT

G — BRIEF ENCOUNTERS

gibberish	GIB
gigabit	GIBT
gigabyte	GIGT
giggle	
giggle	GILG
giggles	GILGS
giggling	GILG/-G
giggled	GILGD
gigs	GIGZ
gimmick	GIMG
ginger	JIRNG
giraffe	JAF
girlfriend	GL-F, GOIF
Girl Scout	GLOUT
GIs	GIZ
give	
give	GIV
gives	GIVS
giving	GIVG
gave	GAEV
given	GIVN
give up	
give up	GUP
gives up	GUPS
giving up	GUPG
gave up	GUPD, GAEP
give	
give up the	GUPT
give up these	GUPZ
give us your name	GURN
glacial	GLAIRBL
glacier	GLAIRB
glad	
glad	GLAD
gladder	GLARD
gladdest	GLA*S
gladly	GLALD
gladness	GLADZ
glamorous	GLAMS
glamour	GLAM
glance	
glance	GLANS, GLAF
glances	GLANSZ, GLAFZ
glancing	GLANGS, GLAFG
glanced	GLANS/-D, GLAFD

BRIEF ENCOUNTERS　　　　　　　　　　　　　　　　　　　G

glaucoma	GLAUK
gleeful	GLAOEF
gleefully	GLAOEFL
glimpse	
glimpse	GLIP
glimpses	GLIPS
glimpsing	GLIPG
glimpsed	GLIPD
glisten	
glisten	GLIFN
glistens	GLIFNS
glistening	GLIFNG
glistened	GLIFND
global	GLOEBL
globalization	GLOEBLGS
glorification	GLORGS, GLOFGS
glorify	
glorify	GLOF
glorifies	GLOFS
glorifying	GLOFG
glorified	GLOFD
glorious	GLOUS, GLORZ
gloriously	GLOULS, GLORLZ
glory	GLOR
glossy	GLOIS
glove compartment	GLOVMT
glucose	GLAOUK
gnosis	GOENSZ
go	
go	GO
goes	GOES
going	GOG
went	WENT
gone	GON
go	
go ahead	GED
goes out	GOUTS
going out	GOUGT
going to	GOGT
go out	GOUT
god	
godfather	GOF, GAUF
godfathers	GOFZ, GAUFS
godsend	GOND
gofer	GO*EFR

G — BRIEF ENCOUNTERS

golden . . . . GONLD
golf
    golf . . . . GOFL
    golf bag . . . . GOFB
    golf ball . . . . GOFBL
    golf club . . . . GOFK
    golf course . . . . GOURS
    golfer . . . . GOFRL
gonad . . . . GOEND
goner . . . . GOERN
good
    good . . . . G–
    good afternoon . . . . GAFRN
    good evening . . . . GAOENG
    good faith . . . . G–F
    goodies . . . . GAOEDZ, GAOEZ
    good looking . . . . G–LG
    good luck . . . . G–L, GLUK
    good morning . . . . G–M, GORNG
    goodness . . . . G–NS
    good night . . . . G–N
    goods . . . . G–Z
    Good Samaritan . . . . GAIRM
    goodwill . . . . GAOL
    goody . . . . GAOED
goofball . . . . GAOFBL, GAOBL
gorgeous . . . . GORJS
gorilla . . . . GORL, GLA
goriness . . . . GOIRNS
gory . . . . GOIR
gospel . . . . GOS
gossip
    gossip . . . . GIP
    gossips . . . . GIPS
    gossiping . . . . GIPG
    gossiped . . . . GIPD
gossiper . . . . GIRP
gotten . . . . GOEN
gourmet . . . . GOURMT
govern
    govern . . . . GOFRN, GOVRN
    governs . . . . GOFRNS, GOVRNS
    governing . . . . GOFRNG, GOVRNG
    governed . . . . GOFRND, GOVRND

BRIEF ENCOUNTERS   G

government
    government .... GOVT
    governmental .... GOVRL, GOVLT
    Government's Exhibit .... GEX
governor
    governor .... GOFR
    governors .... GOFRZ
    governorship .... GORP
    governor's office .... GOFS, GOFRS
gracious .... GRAIRB
graciously .... GRAIRBL
grader .... GRAIRD
gradual
    gradual .... GRAUL
    gradually .... GRAOEL
    gradualness .... GRAUNS
graduate
    graduate .... GRAU
    graduates .... GRAUS
    graduating .... GRAUG
    graduated .... GRAUD
    graduate school .... GRAOL
graduation .... GRAUGS
graffiti .... GRAEFT
grammar .... GRAR
grammatical .... GRAMT
grammatically .... GRAEMT
grand
    grandchild .... GAOILD
    grandchildren .... GHIRN, GHRIRN
    grandfather .... GR-FR
    grand jury .... GR-J
    grand jury's .... GR-JZ
    grandma .... GR-M
    grandmother .... GROER
    grandpa .... GR-P
    grandparent .... GR-PT
    grand theft .... GREFT
granule .... GRANL, GRUL
grapefruit .... GRAIPT
graphic .... GRAFK
graphically .... GRAFL, GRAEFK
grapple
    grapple .... GRAP
    grapples .... GRAPS

© 1997 White-Boucke Publishing.   ILLEGAL TO PHOTOCOPY

grappling	GRAPG
grappled	GRAPD
grassroots	GRAOTS
grateful	GRAIF
gratefully	GRAIFL
gratification	GRAFGS, GRIFGS, GRAEFGS
gratifier	GRIFR, GRAEFR

gratify
gratify	GRIF, GRAEF
gratifies	GRIFS, GRAEFS
gratifying	GRIFG, GRAEFG
gratified	GRIFD, GRAEFD

gratitude	GRAOUD
gratuitous	GRAT

grave
gravely	GRAIVL
graveness	GRAIVNS
graveyard	GRARD, GRAIVD

gravitation	GRAVGS
gravity	GRAVT
gravy	GRAEV

gray
gray	GRAI
grays	GRAI/-S, GRA*IS
graying	GRAI/-G, GRA*IG
grayed	GRAI/-D, GRA*ID

gray matter	GRAIMT

great
great	GRAET
great bodily harm	GARM
Great Britain	GRINT
great deal	GRAEL
greatest	GRA*ETS, GRAETS
great extent	GRAEX
greatly	GRAELT, GRAILT
greatness	GRAENS

greater
greater	GRAERT
greater than	GRAERNT
greater than or equal to	GRAOEKL
greater than the	GRAERNTD
greater than these	GRAERNZ
greater than those	GRAERNTS

green
green card	GRAOERD

BRIEF ENCOUNTERS — G

```
        greener ....................................... GRAOERN
        greener than the ............................. GRAOERNT
        greener than these ........................... GRAOERNZ
        greener than those ........................... GRAOERNS
        greenhouse effect ................................. GREF
        green light ...................................... GR-LT
gregarious
        gregarious ........................................ GRAIR
        gregariously .................................... GRAIRL
        gregariousness ................................. GRAIRNS
Grenada .............................................. GRAEND
grenade .................................................. GREN
grey
        grey ............................................... GRAE
        greys ............................................. GRAEZ
        greying ........................................... GRAEG
        greyed ............................................ GRAED
gridlock ................................................. GLOK
grievance ............................. GRAOEFNS, GRAOEVNS
grimace
        grimace ............................................ GRIS
        grimaces .......................................... GRISZ
        grimacing ...................................... GRIS/-G
        grimaced ....................................... GRIS/-D
grind
        grind .................................. GRAOIN, GRAOIND
        grinds .............................. GRAOINS, GRAOINDZ
        grinding ............................ GRAOING, GRAOINGD
        ground ........................................... GROUND
grisly .................................................. GRILZ
gristle ................................................ GRIFLT
gristly ................................................. GRIFL
grizzly .................................................. GRIZ
grocer ................................................. GRO*R
grocery store ........................................... GROR
grosser ............................................... GRORSZ
grossly ................................................ GROLS
grouchy ............................................... GROIFP
groundless
        groundless ...................................... GROUNL
        groundlessly ................................... GROUNLS
        groundlessness ..................... GROUNS, GROUNLZ
group therapy ....................................... GRAOUPT
grow
        grow .............................................. GROE
```

grows	GROES
growing	GROEG
grew	GRAOU
grown	GROUN

gruesome
gruesome	GRAOUM
gruesomely	GRAOUNL
gruesomeness	GRAOUMS

grumble
grumble	GRUM
grumbles	GRUMS
grumbling	GRUMG
grumbled	GRUMD

grumbler	GRURM
grumpy	GROIFRP
Guam	GAUM

guarantee
guarantee	GARNT
guarantees	GARNTS
guaranteeing	GARNGT
guaranteed	GARNTD

guarantor	GRORNT, GAURNT
guaranty	GIRNT
guardian	GAURND
guardianship	GARP
Guatemala	GAUT
Guatemalan	GAUN
gubernatorial	GAOUB
gubernatorial candidate	GAOUBD
guerilla	GREL

guess
guess	GES
guesses	GEFS
guessing	GEFG
guessed	GEFD

guesstimate
guesstimate	GEMT
guesstimates	GEMTS
guesstimating	GEMGT, GEMG
guesstimated	GEMTD

guesstimation	GEMGS
guidance	GID, GAOINS
guide dog	GAUG
guideline	GLAOIN, GLIN
guilt or innocence	GOINS

BRIEF ENCOUNTERS G

guilty
    guilty .... G-LT
    guilty of .... GUF
    guilty of the .... GUFT
    guilty or innocent .... GOIT, GOINT
    guilty or not .... G-NT
    guilty or not guilty .... G-NG
guitar .... GIRT
guitarist .... GIS, G*IS
gulch .... GUFP, GLUFP
gulf .... GUFL
gullibility .... GUBLT
gullible .... GUBL
gullibly .... GAOEBL
gulp
    gulp .... GLUP
    gulps .... GLUPS
    gulping .... GLUPG
    gulped .... GLUPD
gumption .... GUMGS
gun
    gun barrel .... GUNL
    gun control .... GROL
    gunfire .... GAOIR
    gunpowder .... GAURP
    gunshot .... G-S, GHOT, GURBT
gurgle
    gurgle .... GURG, GURL
    gurgles .... GURGS, GURLS
    gurgling .... GURG/-G, GURLG
    gurgled .... GURGD, GURLD
guru .... GAOUR
gustation .... GUGS
gutter .... GURT
Guyana .... GAOIG
guzzle
    guzzle .... GUZ
    guzzles .... GUSZ
    guzzling .... GUZ/-G
    guzzled .... GUZ/-D
gym
    gym .... GIM
    gymnasium .... GIMZ
    gymnasiums .... GIMSZ
    gymnast .... G*IMT

G

gymnastic	GIMT
gymnastically	GAOELT
gynecologist	GOLT
gynecology	GOLG
gyroscope	JAOIRP, JOEP
gyroscopic	JAOIRPG, JOEPG

H

habeas corpus	HAIB, HAIBS
habit	
habit	HABT
habitual	HABL
habitually	HAEBL
habituate	
habituate	HAET
habituates	HAETS
habituating	HAEGT
habituated	HAETD
habituation	HAEGS
hacker	HAERK
had	
had been	H-B
had believed	H-BLD
had felt	H-FLT
had had	H-D
had imagined	H-JD
had lived	H-VD
had meant	H-MT
had meant to say	H-MTS
hadn't	H-NT
had recalled	H-RLD
had recalled the	H-RLTD
had recollected	H-RKD
had recollected the	H-RKTD
had remembered	H-RMD
had remembered the	H-RMTD
had seen	H-Z
had understood	H-ND
had wanted	H-PTD
hair	
hair	HAIR
hairball	HAIRBL
hairbrush	HAIRB
haircut	HAIRK
hairpin	
hairpin	HAIRP
hairpin bend	HAIRPD
hairpin turn	HAIRPT
Haiti	HOIT
Haitian	HOIRB

H

half
- half . . . HAF
- *half hour* . . . FAUR
- *half of the* . . . HAFT
- *half of them* . . . HAFM
- *half of these* . . . HAFZ
- *half of those* . . . HAFS

Halloween . . . HAOEN

hallucinate
- hallucinate . . . HAOUL
- hallucinates . . . HAOULS
- hallucinating . . . HAOULG
- hallucinated . . . HAOULD

hallucination . . . HAOULGS

halve
- halve . . . HAV
- halves . . . HAVS
- halving . . . HAVG
- halved . . . HAVD

hammer
- hammer . . . HAERM
- hammers . . . HAERMS
- hammering . . . HAERMG
- hammered . . . HAERMD

hamper
- hamper . . . HAFRP
- hampers . . . HAFRPS
- hampering . . . HAFRPG
- hampered . . . HAFRPD

hand
- handball . . . H-BL
- handbook . . . HAOB
- handgun . . . H-G
- handler . . . HARNL
- handout . . . HO*UT, HAND/O*UT
- handwriting . . . HARNG
- handwritten . . . HARN
- handy . . . HAEND

handcuff
- handcuff . . . HUF
- handcuffs . . . HUFS
- handcuffing . . . HUFG
- handcuffed . . . HUFD

handicap
- handicap . . . H-K

BRIEF ENCOUNTERS — H

handicaps . . . . H–KS
handicapping . . . . H–K/–G
handicapped . . . . H–KD
handle
  handle . . . . HANL
  handles . . . . HANLS
  handling . . . . HANLG
  handled . . . . HANLD
hang
  hang . . . . HANG
  hangs . . . . HANGS
  hanging . . . . HANG/–G
  hung / hanged . . . . HUNG / HANG/–D
hanger . . . . HA*RNG
haphazard
  haphazard . . . . ZARD
  haphazardly . . . . ZARL
  haphazardness . . . . ZARNS
happen
  happen . . . . HAP
  happens . . . . HAPS
  happening . . . . HAPG
  happened . . . . HAPD
happenings . . . . HAPGS
happenstance . . . . HAPZ
happier . . . . HAERP
happily . . . . HAEPL
happiness . . . . HAEPS, HAENS
happy . . . . HAEP
harangue
  harangue . . . . HAURNG
  harangues . . . . HAURNGS
  haranguing . . . . HAURNG/–G
  harangued . . . . HAURNGD
harass
  harass . . . . HARS
  harasses . . . . HARSZ
  harassing . . . . HARS/–G
  harassed . . . . HARS/–D
harassment . . . . HARMT
harbor
  harbor . . . . HAORB
  harbors . . . . HAORBS
  harboring . . . . HAORB/–G
  harbored . . . . HAORBD

H

hard
- hardbound . . . . HABD
- hardly . . . . HARL
- **hard of hearing**. . . . . HARGD, HARG
- hardship . . . . H–RP
- hardware . . . . WHAER, DWAER
- hardwood . . . . DWAOD
- **hardwood floor** . . . . DWAOFD

harden
- harden. . . . . HARND
- hardens . . . . HARNDZ
- hardening . . . . HARNGD
- hardened . . . . HARND/–D

harem . . . . HAIRM
Harley . . . . HAERL
Harley-Davidson . . . . HAERLD
harmonious . . . . HARMZ
harness . . . . HARNS

harsh
- harsh. . . . . HAURB
- harshly. . . . . HAURBL
- harshness . . . . HAURNS

Harvard. . . . . HAVRD

has
- **has been** . . . . HAB
- has-been . . . . HA*B
- **has had** . . . . H–D
- hasn't . . . . HANT

hassle
- hassle. . . . . HAFL
- hassles. . . . . HAFLS
- hassling . . . . HAFLG
- hassled. . . . . HAFLD

hatchet. . . . . HAFPT
hateful. . . . . HAIFL
hatefully. . . . . HAOEFL
haughtiness . . . . HAUNS
haughty. . . . . HAUT
haunch. . . . . HAUFP
Havana . . . . HAFRN, HAVRN

have
- have . . . . V–
- has . . . . HAS, HAZ
- having . . . . V–G
- had . . . . HAD

BRIEF ENCOUNTERS   H

have
- have a seat . . . . VAET
- have been . . . . V-B
- have been had . . . . V-BD
- have been the . . . . V-BT
- have believed . . . . V-BLD
- have felt . . . . V-FLT
- have got . . . . V-GT
- have had . . . . V-D
- have happened . . . . V-PD
- have imagined . . . . V-JD
- have lived . . . . V-VD
- have meant . . . . V-MT
- have meant to say . . . . V-MTS
- haven't . . . . V-NT
- have recalled . . . . V-RLD
- have recalled the . . . . V-RLTD
- have recollected . . . . V-RKD
- have recollected the . . . . V-RKTD
- have remembered . . . . V-RMD
- have remembered the . . . . V-RMTD
- have the . . . . V-T
- have these . . . . V-TSZ
- have those . . . . V-TS
- have understood . . . . V-ND
- have wanted . . . . V-PTD

have you
- have you . . . . VU
- have you been . . . . VUB
- have you believed . . . . VUBLD
- have you ever . . . . VUFR, VUVR
- have you ever been . . . . VUFRB, VUVRB
- have you ever been convicted of a felony . . . . FLEVR, FLEFR
- have you ever had . . . . VUFRD, VUVRD
- have you felt . . . . VUFLT
- have you gone . . . . VUG
- have you got . . . . VUGT
- have you had . . . . VUD
- have you happened . . . . VUPD
- have you imagined . . . . VUJD
- have you lived . . . . VUVD
- have you meant . . . . VUMT
- have you not . . . . VUNT
- have you recalled . . . . VURLD
- have you recalled the . . . . VURLTD

have you recollected	VURKD
have you recollected the	VURKTD
have you remembered	VURMD
have you remembered the	VURMTD
have you said	VUS
have you seen	VUZ
have you told	VUT
have you told us	VUTS
have you understood	VUND
have you wanted	VUPTD
havoc	HAFK, HAVK
Hawaii	H*I
hazard	HAFRD
he	
he	HE
he believe	HEBL
he believed	HEBLD
he believes	HEBLS
he believing	HEBLG
he can	HEK
he can't	HEKT, HEK/-NT, HE/K-NT
he could	HEKD
he couldn't	HEKTD, HEKD/-NT, HE/KUNT
he'd	H*ED
he ever	HEFR, HEVR
he feel	HEFL
he feeling	HEFLG
he feels	HEFLS
he felt	HEFLT
he get	HEGT
he gets	HEGTS
he go	HEG
he goes	HEGS
he have	HEF
he is	HES
he isn't	HES/-NT, HE/S-NT
he'll	H*EL
he recall	HERL
he recalled	HERLD
he recalling	HERLG
he recalls	HERLS
he recollect	HERK
he recollected	HERKD
he recollects	HERKS
he remember	HERM

BRIEF ENCOUNTERS H

he remembered	HERMD
he remembering	HERMG
he remembers	HERMS
he's	H*ES
he shall	H*ERB
he should	HERBD
he shouldn't	HERBTD, HERBD/-NT, HE/SH-NT
he think	HENG
he thinks	HENGS
he thinks so	HENGSZ
he understands	HENDZ
he understood	HEND
he want	HEPT
he wanted	HEPTD
he wanting	HEPGT
he wants	HEPTS
he was	HEFS
he wasn't	HEFT, HEFS/-NT, HE/WUNT
he were	HERP
he weren't	HERPT, HERP/-NT, HE/W-RNT
he would	H*ELD
he wouldn't	HELTD, HELD/N-T, HE/WONT
he would say	HELDZ

head
head	HAED
headache	HAIK
headlight	HAELT
headphone	HAEFD
headquartered	HAURD
headquarters	HAURS

healer	HAOERL

health
health	H*ELT
health and safety	H*ELTS, HAIFT
healthier	H*ERLT
healthy	HA*ELT

hear
hear	HEAR
hears	HEARS
hearing	HEARG
heard	HEARD

hearing
hearing aid	HAERGD, HIRD
hearing dog	HAUG
hearing impaired	HIRM, HIRMD, HIRP

hearing impairment	HIRMT
hearing loss	HAERLG
hearing person	HAERPG
hearing people	HAOERPG
hearing-sighted	HAERTD
hearsay	H–S

heart

heart attack	HARKT, HAURK
heart surgery	HARJ
heartwarming	TWAERM

heat of passion	HAGS
heaven	HEVN
heavenly	HEVNL
heavily	HEVL
heaviness	HEVNS
heavy	HEV
he be	HEB
he had	HED
Hebrew	HAOEB

heckle

heckle	H*EKL
heckles	HEKLS
heckling	HEKL/–G
heckled	HEKLD

hedonism	HOFM
height	HAOIT

heighten

heighten	HAOIN, HAOINT
heightens	HAOINS, HAOINTS
heightening	HAOING, HAOINGT
heightened	HAOIN/–D, HAOINTD

heinous	HAINS

heir

heir	HA*IR, HIR
heir apparent	HAIRNT, HA*IRP
heir presumptive	HA*IRPT

helicopter	KOPT
helmet	HEMT

help

help	HEP
helps	HEPS
helping	HEPG
helped	HEPD

helper	H*ERP
hematoma	HAOEMT

hemisphere	HAOEFR
hemorrhage	
hemorrhage	HERJ
hemorrhages	HERJS
hemorrhaging	HERJ/-G
hemorrhaged	HERJD
her	HER
herbal	HERBL
here	
here	HAOER
hereabout	HAOERBT
hereby	HAOERB
herein	HAOERN
hereto	HAOERT
heretofore	HAOERFT, HEFRT
hereditary	HA*IRD
heretic	HAIRKT
heritage	HAERJ
hermit	HERMT
hernia	HAERN
herniate	
herniate	HAERNT
herniates	HAERNTS
herniating	HAERNGT, HAERNG
herniated	HAERNTD
herniation	HAERNGS, HERNGS
hero	
hero	HAOE
heroic	HAOEK, HAOERK
heroin	HERN
heroine	H*ERN
heroism	HAOEFM
herpes	HERPS
herself	H*ERS, HERSZ
hertz	H*ERTS
hesitate	
hesitate	HEZ
hesitates	HEFZ
hesitating	HEFG
hesitated	HEFD
hesitation	HEFGS
heterogeneous	HAOENS, HET/JAOENS
heterosexual	H-T, HET
heterosexuality	HELT
hiatus	HAUTS

H

hibernate
- hibernate . . . . HAOIB
- hibernates . . . . HAOIBS
- hibernating . . . . HAOIB/-G
- hibernated . . . . HAOIB/-D

hibernation . . . . HAOIBGS

hide
- hide . . . . HAOID
- hides . . . . HAOIDZ
- hiding . . . . HAOIGD
- hid . . . . HID
- hidden . . . . HIND

hierarchial . . . . HAOIRL
hierarchy . . . . HAOIRK
hieroglyph . . . . GLIF
hieroglyphic . . . . GLIFK, GLIFG

high
- highball . . . . HAOIBL
- *high school* . . . . HAOL
- *High School* . . . . HAO*L
- highway . . . . HOI
- *highway patrol* . . . . HOIP

higher
- higher . . . . HAO*IR
- *higher than* . . . . HAOIRN
- *higher than the* . . . . HAO*IRNT
- *higher than them* . . . . HAOIRM
- *higher than these* . . . . HAOIRNZ
- *higher than those* . . . . HAOIRNS

highlight
- highlight . . . . HAOILT
- highlights . . . . HAOILTS
- highlighting . . . . HAOILGT
- highlighted . . . . HAOILTD

hijack
- hijack . . . . HAOIJ
- hijacks . . . . HAOIJS
- hijacking . . . . HAOIJ/-G
- hijacked . . . . HAOIJD

hijacker . . . . HAOIRJ
him . . . . HIM
himself . . . . HOIM, HOIMS

hinder
- hinder . . . . HIRND
- hinders . . . . HIRNDZ

hindering	HIRNGD
hindered	HIRND/-D
hinderance	HIRNS

hinge
hinge	HIJ
hinges	HIJS
hinging	HIJ/-G
hinged	HIJD

Hindi	HAOEND
hireling	HAOIRLG
his	HIS
His Honor	HIRN
His Honor's	HIRNZ
Hispanic	HAIP
Hispanic male	HAIM

historic
historic	HIFK
historical	HIFL
historically	HAOEFK

history	HIFT

hit
hit	HIT
hits	HITS
hitting	HIGT
hit	HIT

hither	H*IT
hitherto	H*IRT
hitter	HIRT

hoard
hoard	HAORD
hoards	HAORDZ
hoarding	HAORGD
hoarded	HAORD/-D

hoarse	HAORS

hobble
hobble	HOBL
hobbles	HOBLS
hobbling	HOBLG
hobbled	HOBLD

hobby	HOIB
hobo	HOEB
hobos	HOEBZ
hockey	HOIK
hocus pocus	HOEK

hoist
- hoist ... HO*IS, HOIFT
- hoists ... HO*ISZ, HOIFTS
- hoisting ... HOIFG, HOIFGT
- hoisted ... HOIFD, HOIFTD

hold
- hold ... HOLD, HOL
- holds ... HOLDZ, HOLS
- holding ... HOLGD, HOLG
- held ... HELD

holdup ... HUPD, HOLD/*UP
holey ... HO*EL
holiday ... HOILD
Holland ... HAUN

holler
- holler ... HAURL
- hollers ... HAURLS
- hollering ... HAURLG
- hollered ... HAURLD

hollow
- hollow ... HO*L
- hollows ... HO*LS
- hollowing ... HO*LG
- hollowed ... HO*LD

Hollywood ... HOIL
holy ... HO*IL
homage ... HAUM

home
- *home business* ... HOEBS
- *home equity* ... HOEKT
- *home improvement* ... HOVMT
- homeowner ... HOERN
- homeowners ... HOERNZ
- *homeowners association* ... HOERNGS
- *home ownership* ... HOERP
- hometown ... HOEMT
- homework ... HOERK

homicide ... HOM
homogeneous ... HAOEMS, HOEM/JAOENS
homogenize
- homogenize ... MOJ
- homogenizes ... MOJS
- homogenizing ... MOJ/-G
- homogenized ... MOJD

homogenous ... HOJZ, MOJZ, MOJ/NOUS

BRIEF ENCOUNTERS H

Homo sapiens. . . . . SAIP
homosexual. . . . . H-L
homosexuality . . . . H-LT
Honda. . . . . HAUND
Honduran. . . . . HOURN
Honduras. . . . . HOURND
honest
    honest. . . . . HONS
    honestly. . . . . HOENL, HONS/LI
    honesty . . . . HO*NS
honeymoon . . . . HAOUN
honor
    honor . . . . HON
    honors. . . . . HONZ
    honoring . . . . HONG
    honored. . . . . HOND
honorable. . . . . HONL
hoodlum . . . . HAOM
hooker. . . . . HAORK
hookup. . . . . HAOKP, HAOK/*UP
hooligan. . . . . HAOLG
horizon
    horizon . . . . HORZ, ZON
    horizontal. . . . . ZONL
    horizontally . . . . ZOENL, ZAOENL
hormonal . . . . HOERNL, HOERL
hormone . . . . HOERM
horrific. . . . . HORK, HOFK
horror . . . . HOR
horrors . . . . HOR/-S
horsepower . . . . HORP
horticultural . . . . HORL
horticulture. . . . . HORT
horticulturist . . . . HORLT
hospitable . . . . HIBL
hospital . . . . HOPT
hospitality. . . . . HOFPT
hospitalization . . . . HOPGS, HOFGS
hospitalize
    hospitalize . . . . HOF
    hospitalizes. . . . . HOFS
    hospitalizing . . . . HOFG
    hospitalized . . . . HOFD
host
    host. . . . . HO*S

H   BRIEF ENCOUNTERS

```
hosts . . . . . . . . . . . . . . . . . . . . . . . . . . . . . . . . . . . . . . . HO*SZ
    hosting . . . . . . . . . . . . . . . . . . . . . . . . . . . . . . . . . . . HOFGT
    hosted . . . . . . . . . . . . . . . . . . . . . . . . . . . . . . . . . . . . HOFTD
hostage . . . . . . . . . . . . . . . . . . . . . . . . . . . . . . . HOJ, HAUJ
hostile . . . . . . . . . . . . . . . . . . . . . . . . . . . . . . . . . . . . . . . HOFL
```
hostile witness . . . . HIN
```
hostility . . . . . . . . . . . . . . . . . . . . . . . . . . . . . . . HOFT, HOFLT
hotel . . . . . . . . . . . . . . . . . . . . . . . . . . . . . . . . . HOLT, HOELT
hotter
    hotter . . . . . . . . . . . . . . . . . . . . . . . . . . . . . . . . . . . . . HAURT
```
   hotter than . . . . HAURN
   hotter than the . . . . HAURNT
   hotter than these . . . . HAURNZ
```
hour
    hour . . . . . . . . . . . . . . . . . . . . . . . . . . . . . . . . . . . . . . . HOUR
```
   hour ago . . . . HOURG
   hourly . . . . HOURL
   hours ago . . . . HOURGS
```
house
    household . . . . . . . . . . . . . . . . . . . . . . . . . . . . . . . . HOUFLD
    housekeeper . . . . . . . . . . . . . . . . . . . . . . . . . . . . . . . . HURP
    housekeeping . . . . . . . . . . . . . . . . . . . . . . . . . . . . . . . HUPG
    housewife . . . . . . . . . . . . . . . . . . . . . . . . . . . . . . . . . HAOIF
    housework . . . . . . . . . . . . . . . . . . . . . . . . . . . . . . . . HOURK
how
```
   how about . . . . HOUB
   how about the . . . . HOUBT
   how about these . . . . HOUBZ
   how about those . . . . HOUBS
   how bad . . . . HOUBD
   how big . . . . HOUG
   how can . . . . HOUK
   how can the . . . . HOUKT
   how can these . . . . HOUKZ
   how can those . . . . HOUKS
   how come . . . . HO*UK
   how could . . . . HOUKD
   how'd . . . . HO*UD
   how do you plead . . . . HOUPD
   how do you spell . . . . HOUP
   how else . . . . HOULS
   however . . . . HOUFR, HOUVR
   how far . . . . HOUF
   how fast . . . . HOUFT
   how good . . . . HOUGD

BRIEF ENCOUNTERS   H

how great	HOUGT
how hard	HOURD, WHARD
how is	HOUZ
how large	HOURJ
how late	HOULT
how long	HOUNG
how many	HOUM
how many days	HOUMD
how many of the	HOUFMT
how many of them	HOUFM
how many of these	HOUMZ, HOUFMZ
how many of those	HOUMS, HOUFMS
how many times	HOUMT
how much	HOUFP
how much of the	HOUFPT
how often	HOUFN
how old	HOELD
how're	HO*UR
how's	HO*US
how shall	HOURB
how should	HOURBD
how soon	HAON
how the	HOUT
how was	HOUFS
how were	HOURP
how wide	HOID
how would	HOULD
Hugh	HAOUG
Hughes	HAOUZ
huh	HU
human	
human	HAOUM
humanism	HAOUFM
humanity	HAOUMT
human nature	HAOUFP
human rights	HAOURTS
humble	HUBL
humid	HAOUMD
humidity	HAOUMTD
humiliation	HAOUMGS
humility	HAOULT
humongous	HAOUMG
humor	
humor	HAOURM
humors	HAOURMS

H

humoring	HAOURMG
humored	HAOURMD
humorist	HAOURMT
humorous	HAOURMZ |//

hundred
- hundred . . . HUN
- *hundred dollar* . . . HUND
- *hundred of the* . . . HUFT
- *hundred of them* . . . HUFM
- *hundred of these* . . . HUFZ

Hungarian	HAIRN
Hungary	HAUNG
hunger	H-NG
hung jury	HURJ
hungry	H-RNG, HURNG
hunter	HURNT
hurricane	HURK
hurricanes	HURKZ

hurry
- hurry . . . HUR
- hurries . . . HURS
- hurrying . . . HURG
- hurried . . . HURD

hurt
- hurt . . . HURT
- hurts . . . HURTS
- hurting . . . HURGT
- hurt . . . HURT

hurtle
- hurtle . . . HURLT
- hurtles . . . HURLTS
- hurtling . . . HURLGT
- hurtled . . . HURLTD

husband	HUZ
hybrid	HAOIBD
hydrant	HAOIRNT
hydraulic	DRAUK
hydrologist	DROLT
hydrology	DROLG
hyper	HAOIRP
hyphen	HOIF
hypnosis	SNOP
hypnotic	SNOPG, SNOPK
hypnotist	SNOPT
hypocrisy	PAUK

hypocrite	KRIT
hypocritical	KRILT
hypodermic	HAOIM
hypotheses	H-PS
hypothesis	H-P

hypothesize
hypothesize	H-PT
hypothesizes	H-PTS
hypothesizing	H-PGT
hypothesized	H-PT/-D, H*PTD

hypothetical	HIPT
hysteria	ST*ER

hysteric
hysteric	STERK
hysterical	ST*ERL, STERKL
hysterically	STAO*ERL

Hz	H-RZ, H*ERZ

I

I	I
I am	IM
I believe	IBL
I believed	IBLD
I believe so	IBLS
I believing	IBLG
I can	IK
I cannot	YANT
I can't	IKT, YA
I could	IKD
I could not	YUNT
I couldn't	IKTD, YU
I'd	AOID
I did not	YINT
I didn't	YI
I do not	YONT
I don't	YO
I feel	IFL
I feeling	IFLG
I felt	IFLT
I get	IGT
I go	IG
I had	ID
I hadn't	ID/–NT
I have	IF
I have been	IFB
I have believed	IFBLD
I have had	IFD
I have known	IFN
I haven't	IFT
I'll	AOIL
I'm	AOIM
I mean	*IM
I mean to	*IMT
I mean to say	IMTS
I object	IB
I objected	IBD
I objected to	IBTD
I object to	IBT
I offer	IFR
I offered	IFRD

BRIEF ENCOUNTERS   I

I offered it	IFRTD
I offer in evidence	IFRND
I offering	IFRG
I offer it	IFRT
I recall	IRL
I recalled	IRLD
I recalling	IRLG
I remember	IRM
I remembered	IRMD
I remembering	IRMG
I respect	*IRP
I respected	IRPD
I respecting	IRPG
I should	IRBD
I shouldn't	IRBTD
I think	ING
I think so	INGS
I understand	INDZ
I've	AOIV
I've been	AOIVB
I've had	AOIVD
I've known	IVN
I want	IPT
I wanted	IPTD
I wanting	IPGT
I was	IFS
I were	IRP
I would	ILD
I would not	YAONT
I wouldn't	ILTD, YAO
I would say	ILDZ
IBM	AOIB

I can't

I can't	YA, IKT
I can't be	YAB
I can't believe	YABL
I can't believe so	YABLS
I can't do	YAD
I can't ever	YAFR, YAVR
I can't feel	YAFL
I can't get	YAGT
I can't go	YAG
I can't have	YAF
I can't have been	YAFB
I can't have had	YAFD

© 1997 White-Boucke Publishing.   ILLEGAL TO PHOTOCOPY

BRIEF ENCOUNTERS

I can't imagine	YAJ
I can't know	YAN
I can't live	YAV
I can't recall	YARL
I can't recollect	YARK
I can't remember	YARM
I can't say	YAS
I can't see	YAZ
I can't tell	YAT
I can't think	YANG
I can't understand	YANDZ
I can't want	YAPT
ice cream	SKRAEM
ice cube	YAOUB

I couldn't

I couldn't	YU, IKTD
I couldn't be	YUB
I couldn't believe	YUBL
I couldn't do	YUD
I couldn't ever	YUFR, YUVR
I couldn't feel	YUFL
I couldn't get	YUGT
I couldn't go	YUG
I couldn't have	YUF
I couldn't have been	YUFB
I couldn't have had	YUFD
I couldn't imagine	YUJ
I couldn't know	Y*UN
I couldn't live	YUV
I couldn't mean	Y*UM
I couldn't recall	YURL
I couldn't recollect	YURK
I couldn't remember	YURM
I couldn't say	YUS
I couldn't see	YUZ, Y*US
I couldn't tell	YUT
I couldn't think	Y*UNG
I couldn't understand	YUNDZ
I couldn't want	YUPT
I.D.	*ID
Idaho	DHOE, *ID/*ID

idea

idea	Y-D
ideal	Y-L
idealist	YILT

BRIEF ENCOUNTERS *I*

idealize
    idealize .... DLAOIS, DLAOIZ
    idealizes .... DLAOIFS, DLAOISZ
    idealizing .... DLAOIFG
    idealized .... DLAOIFD
identical .... OIK
identically .... OIKL
identifiable .... OIFL, OIFBL
identifiably .... AOEFBL
identification .... OIFGS
identify
    identify .... OIF
    identifies .... OIFS
    identifying .... OIFG
    identified .... OIFD
identity .... OIT
ideologist .... YOLT
ideology .... YOLG, Y-LG
I didn't
    I didn't .... YI
    I didn't believe .... YIBL
    I didn't believe so .... YIBLS
    I didn't do .... YID
    I didn't ever .... YIFR, YIVR
    I didn't feel .... YIFL
    I didn't get .... Y*IGT
    I didn't go .... YIG
    I didn't have .... YIF
    I didn't imagine .... YIJ
    I didn't know .... YIN
    I didn't live .... YIV
    I didn't mean .... YIM
    I didn't mean to .... YIMT
    I didn't mean to say .... YIMTS
    I didn't recall .... YIRL
    I didn't recall the .... YIRLT
    I didn't recollect .... YIRK
    I didn't recollect the .... YIRKT
    I didn't remember .... YIRM
    I didn't remember the .... YIRMT
    I didn't say .... YIS
    I didn't see .... YIZ, Y*IS
    I didn't tell .... YIT
    I didn't think .... YING
    I didn't think so .... YINGS

© 1997 White-Boucke Publishing.   ILLEGAL TO PHOTOCOPY

BRIEF ENCOUNTERS

I didn't understand	YINDZ
I didn't want	YIPT
idiocy	YOIZ
idiot	YOIT
idiotic	YOK
idle	AOILD
idol	DOLD
idolize	
idolize	DL–Z
idolizes	DL–FS, DL–SZ
idolizing	DL–FG
idolized	DL–FD
I don't	
I don't	YO
I don't believe	YOBL
I don't believe so	YOBLS
I don't do	YOD
I don't ever	YOEFR, YOEVR
I don't feel	YOFL
I don't get	YOGT
I don't go	YOG
I don't have	YOF
I don't imagine	YOJ
I don't know	YON
I don't live	YOV
I don't mean	YOM
I don't mean to	YOMT
I don't mean to say	YOMTS
I don't recall	YORL
I don't recall the	YORLT
I don't recollect	YORK
I don't recollect the	YORKT
I don't remember	YORM
I don't remember the	YORMT
I don't say	YOS
I don't see	YOZ, YO*S
I don't think	YONG
I don't think so	YONGS
I don't understand	YONDZ
I don't want	YOPT
if	F–
if he	
if he	FE
if he believed	FEBLD
if he believes	FEBLS

BRIEF ENCOUNTERS

if he can't	FEKT, FE/K-NT
if he could	F*EKD
if he couldn't	FEKTD, FEKD/-NT, FE/KUNT
if he ever	FEFR, FEVR
if he feels	FEFLS
if he felt	FEFLT
if he gets	FEGTS
if he goes	F*EGS
if he got	FEGT
if he hadn't	FED/-NT
if he happened	FEPD
if he happens	FEPS
if he imagined	FEJD
if he imagines	FEJS
if he lived	FEVD
if he lives	FEVS
if he recalled	FERLD
if he recalled the	FERLTD
if he recalls	FERLS
if he recollected	FERKD
if he recollected the	FERKTD
if he recollects	FERKS
if he remembered	FERMD
if he remembers	FERMS
if he says	FESZ
if he sees	FEZ
if he should	FERBD
if he shouldn't	FERBTD, FERBD/-NT, FE/SH-NT
if he thinks	FENGS
if he thinks so	FENGSZ
if he wanted	FEPTD
if he wants	FEPTS
if he was	FEFS
if he wasn't	FEFS/-NT, FE/WUNT
if he were	FERP
if he weren't	FERPT, FERP/-NT, FE/W-RNT
if he would	FELD
if he wouldn't	FELD/-NT, FE/WONT

if I

if I	FI
if I believe	FIBL
if I believed	FIBLD
if I can	FIK
if I can't	FIKT, FIK/-NT, FI/K-NT
if I could	FIKD

I

BRIEF ENCOUNTERS

if I couldn't	FIKTD, FIKD/-NT, FI/KUNT
if I ever	FIFR, FIVR
if I feel	FIFL
if I felt	FIFLT
if I had	FID
if I hadn't	FID/-NT, FI/H-NT
if I happen	FIP
if I happened	FIPD
if I live	FIV
if I lived	FIVD
if I recall	FIRL
if I recalled	FIRLD
if I recollect	FIRK
if I recollected	FIRKD
if I remember	F*IRM
if I remembered	F*IRMD
if I say	FIS
if I see	FIZ
if I should	FIRBD
if I shouldn't	FIRBTD, FIRBD/-NT, FI/SH-NT
if I understand	FINDZ
if I want	FIPT
if I wanted	FIPTD
if I was	FIFS
if I wasn't	FIFS/-NT, FI/WUNT
if I were	FIRP
if I weren't	FIRPT, FIRP/-NT, FI/W-RNT
if I would	F*ILD
if I wouldn't	FILD/-NT, FI/WONT
if I would say	FILDZ
if it please the Court	FLOURT
if the	F-T
if the Court please	KLAOEZ

if you

if you	FU
if you are	FUR
if you aren't	FUR/-NT, FU/R-NT
if you believe	FUBL
if you believed	FUBLD
if you can	FUK
if you can't	FUKT, FUK/-NT, FU/K-NT
if you could	FUKD
if you couldn't	FUKTD, FUKD/-NT, FU/KUNT
if you ever	FUFR, FUVR
if you feel	FUFL

BRIEF ENCOUNTERS

if you felt	FUFLT
if you get	FUGT
if you go	FUG
if you had	FUD
if you hadn't	FUD/-NT, FU/H-NT
if you happen	FUP
if you happened	FUPD
if you have	FUF
if you have been	FUFB
if you have had	FUFD
if you have known	FUFN
if you haven't	FUFT, FUF/-NT, FU/V-NT
if you imagine	F*UJ
if you imagined	FUJD
if you know	FAOUN, FUN
if you live	FUV
if you lived	FUVD
if you mean	FUM
if you mean to	F*UMT
if you mean to say	FUMTS
if you recall	FURL
if you recalled	FURLD
if you recalled the	FURLTD
if you recall the	FURLT
if you recollect	FURK
if you recollected	FURKD
if you recollected the	FURKTD
if you remember	FURM
if you remembered	FURMD
if you remembered the	FURMTD
if you remember the	FURMT
if you say	FUS
if you see	F*US
if you shall	F*URB
if you should	FURBD
if you shouldn't	FURBTD, FURBD/-NT, FU/SH-NT
if you think	FUNG
if you think so	FUNGZ
if you want	FUPT
if you wanted	FUPTD
if you were	FURP
if you weren't	FURPT, FURP/-NT, FU/W-RNT
if you will	FUL
if you would	FULD
if you wouldn't	FULTD, FULD/-NT, FU/WONT

igloo	GLAO

ignite

ignite	GAOIT
ignites	GAOITS
igniting	GAOIGT
ignited	GAOITD
ignition	GIGS, GAOIGS
ignorance	GORNZ, IGS
ignorant	GORNT
ignorantly	GORNLT, GORNL

ignore

ignore	GOR
ignores	GORS
ignoring	GORG
ignored	GORD

illegal

illegal	ILG
illegality	ILGT, IL/LELT
illegally	AOELG, ILG/LI
illegitimacy	IL/JIS, IL/JITS
illegitimate	IL/JIT
illegitimately	IL/JILT

illicit

illicit	IL/LIFT
illicitly	IL/LIFL
illicitness	IL/LIFNS
Illinois	*IL
illiteracy	IL/LIRTS
illiterate	IL/LIRT
illiterateness	IL/LIRNS

illuminate

illuminate	LAOUM, LAOUMT
illuminates	LAOUMS, LAOUMTS
illuminating	LAOUMG, LAOUMGT
illuminated	LAOUMD, LAOUMTD
illumination	LAOUJ, LAOUMGS
illusion	ILGS

illustrate

illustrate	STRAET
illustrates	STRAETS
illustrating	STRAEGT
illustrated	STRAETD
illustration	STRAEGS
illustrative	STRAEV
illustrator	STRAERT

BRIEF ENCOUNTERS

image	IJ
imaginary	MAEJ
imagination	MAJS
imagine	
imagine	MAJ
imagines	MAJZ
imagining	MAJ/-G
imagined	MAJD
imbalance	KBAL
imbed	
imbed	KBED
imbeds	KBEDZ
imbedding	KBEGD
imbedded	KBED/-D
imbibe	
imbibe	KBAOIB
imbibes	KBAOIBS
imbibing	KBAOIBG
imbibed	KBAOIBD
imbue	
imbue	KBAOU
imbues	KBAOUS
imbuing	KBAOUG
imbued	KBAOUD
imitate	
imitate	KBAET
imitates	KBAETS
imitating	KBAEGT
imitated	KBAETD
imitation	KBAEGS
immanent	KBAMT
immaterial	IMT
immature	
immature	KBA*UR
immaturely	KBAURL
immatureness	KBAURNS
immaturity	KBAURT
immediacy	MAOEDZ
immediate	
immediate	MAOED
immediately	MAOELD
immediateness	MAOENTS
immerse	
immerse	KBERS
immerses	KBERSZ

immersing	KBERS/-G
immersed	KBERS/-D
immersion	KBERGS
immigrant	KBRANT

immigrate
immigrate	KBRAIT
immigrates	KBRAITS
immigrating	KBRAIGT
immigrated	KBRAITD

immigration	KBRAIGS
Immigration & Naturalization Service	**KBRAINGS**
imminent	KBIMT
imminently	KBINL

immolate
immolate	KBOELT
immolates	KBOELTS
immolating	KBOELGT, KBOELG
immolated	KBOELTD

immolation	KBOELGS
immoral	KBORL
immortal	KBORLT
immortality	KBOERLT
immovable	KBOVL
immune	MAOUN
immunity	MAOUNT, MUNT

impact
impact	KBAK
impacts	KBAKS
impacting	KBAK/-G, KBAG
impacted	KBAKD

impair
impair	KBAIR
impairs	KBAIRS
impairing	KBAIRG
impaired	KBAIRD

impaired vision	**KBIGS**
impairment	KBAIRMT

impale
impale	KBAIL
impales	KBAILS
impaling	KBAILG
impaled	KBAILD

impalement	KBAIMT, KBAILT
impalpable	KBABL

BRIEF ENCOUNTERS

impanel
    impanel .... KBANL
    impanels .... KBANLS
    impaneling .... KBANLG
    impaneled .... KBANLD
impart
    impart .... KBART
    imparts .... KBARTS
    imparting .... KBARGT
    imparted .... KBARTD
impartial
    impartial .... KBARBL
    impartiality .... KBARBLT
    impartially .... KBAERBL
impasse .... KBAS
impassion
    impassion .... KBARB, KBAGS
    impassions .... KBARBS, KBAGSZ
    impassioning .... KBARBG, KBAGS/-G
    impassioned .... KBARBD, KBAGD
impassive
    impassive .... KBIV, KBIF
    impassively .... KBIVL, KBIFL
    impassiveness .... KBIVNS, KBIFNS
    impassivity .... KBIVT, KBIFT
impatience .... KBAIRB, KBAIRBS
impatient .... KBAIRBT
impatiently .... KBAIRBL
impeach
    impeach .... KBAOEFP
    impeaches .... KBAOEFPS
    impeaching .... KBAOEFPG
    impeached .... KBAOEFPD
impeachment .... PAOEMT, PAOEFMT, KBAOEMT
impeccable .... KBEK
impedance .... KBAOEND, KBAOENDZ
impede
    impede .... KBAOED
    impedes .... KBAOEDZ
    impeding .... KBAOEGD
    impeded .... KBAOED/-D
impediment .... KBEMT
impel
    impel .... KB*EL, KBIL
    impels .... KB*ELS, KBILS

impelling	KB*ELG, KBILG
impelled	KB*ELD, KBILD
impend	
impend	KBEN
impends	KBENS
impending	KBENG
impended	KBEND
impenetrable	KBRENL
imperative	
imperative	KBRIV
imperatively	KBRIVL
imperativeness	KBRIVNS, KBIFNS
imperfect	KBER
imperfection	KBEFRGS
imperial	KBAOERL
imperialism	KBAOEFM
imperil	
imperil	KBERL
imperils	KBERLS
imperiling	KBERLG
imperiled	KBERLD
imperilment	KBERMT
impermissibility	KBIBLT
impermissible	KBIBL
impersonal	KBERNL
impersonate	
impersonate	KBERN
impersonates	KBERNS
impersonating	KBERNG
impersonated	KBERND
impersonation	KBERNGS
impersonator	KBERNT
impertinence	KBERTS
impertinency	KBERTSZ
impertinent	KBERT
impertinently	KBERLT
impervious	
impervious	KBEFRB
imperviously	KBEFRBL
imperviousness	KBEFRBS
impetuous	
impetuous	KBEFP
impetuously	KBEFPL
impetuousness	KBEFNS
impetus	KBUS

BRIEF ENCOUNTERS

impinge
    impinge . . . . KBIJ
    impinges . . . . KBIJS
    impinging . . . . KBIJ/-G
    impinged . . . . KBIJD
implant
    implant . . . . KBLANT
    implants . . . . KBLANTS
    implanting . . . . KBLANGT
    implanted . . . . KBLANTD
implantation . . . . KBLANGS
implausibility . . . . KBLAUFT
implausible . . . . KBLAUS, KBLAUZ
implausibleness . . . . KBLAUNS
implausibly . . . . KBLAULS, KBLAULZ
implement
    implement . . . . KBLEM, KBLEMT
    implements . . . . KBLEMS, KBLEMTS
    implementing . . . . KBLEMG, KBLEMGT
    implemented . . . . KBLEMD, KBLEMTD
implementation . . . . KBLEMGS, KBLEJ
implicate
    implicate . . . . KBLIK
    implicates . . . . KBLIKZ
    implicating . . . . KBLIK/-G
    implicated . . . . KBLIKD
implication . . . . KBLIX
implicit
    implicit . . . . KBLIS, KBLIFT
    implicitly . . . . KBLIFL
    implicitness . . . . KBLINS
implode
    implode . . . . KBLOED
    implodes . . . . KBLOEDZ
    imploding . . . . KBLOEGD
    imploded . . . . KBLOED/-D
implore
    implore . . . . KBLOER
    implores . . . . KBLOERS
    imploring . . . . KBLOERG
    implored . . . . KBLOERD
implosion . . . . KBLOEGS
imply
    imply . . . . KBLAOI
    implies . . . . KBLAOIS

implying	KBLAOIG
implied	KBLAOID
impolite	
impolite	KBLAOIT
impolitely	KBLAOILT, KBLAOIL
impoliteness	KBLAOINS
impolitic	KBLOK
imponderable	KBONL, KBOND/RABL
import	
import	KBORT
imports	KBORTS
importing	KBORGT
imported	KBORTD
importance	PORNS
important	PORNT
importantly	PORNL
importation	KBORGS
importune	KBOR/TAOUN
impose	
impose	KBOES
imposes	KBOEFS, KBOESZ
imposing	KBOEFG
imposed	KBOEFD
imposition	KBOGS
impossibility	KBOBLT
impossible	KBOBL
impossibly	KBOEBL
imposter	KBOFT, KBO*S
impotence	KBOENS
impotency	KBAOENS, KBOENSZ
impotent	KBOENT
impound	
impound	KBOUN
impounds	KBOUNS
impounding	KBOUNG
impounded	KBOUND
impoverish	
impoverish	KBOVR, KBOFR
impoverishes	KBOVRS, KBOFRS
impoverishing	KBOVRG, KBOFRG
impoverished	KBOVRD, KBOFRD
impoverishment	KBOVMT, KBOFMT
impracticable	KBRAL
impractical	
impractical	KBRAK

BRIEF ENCOUNTERS I

impracticality	KBRAKT
impracticalness	KBRANS
impregnable	KBREL, KBREG/NABL

impregnate

impregnate	KBREG
impregnates	KBREGZ
impregnating	KBREG/-G
impregnated	KBREGD
impregnation	KBRAEGS

impress

impress	KBREF, KBRES
impresses	KBREFS
impressing	KBREFG
impressed	KBREFD
impression	KBREGS

impressive

impressive	KBREV
impressively	KBREVL
impressiveness	KBREVNS, KBREFNS

imprint

imprint	KBRINT
imprints	KBRINTS
imprinting	KBRINGT
imprinted	KBRINTD

imprison

imprison	KBRIZ, KBRIS
imprisons	KBRIFS, KBRISZ
imprisoning	KBRIFG
imprisoned	KBRIFD
imprisonment	KBRIMT, PRIFMT
improbability	KBROBLT
improbable	KBROBL
improbably	KBROEBL
impromptu	KBROM
improper	KBROR
improperly	KBRORL
impropriety	KBRAOIT

improve

improve	KBROV
improves	KBROVS
improving	KBROVG
improved	KBROVD
improvement	KBROVMT, PROVMT
improvisation	KBROVGS, KBROFGS

improvise
- improvise . . . KBRO
- improvises . . . KBROS
- improvising . . . KBROG
- improvised . . . KBROD

imprudence . . . KBRAOUNS
imprudent . . . KBRAOUNT
impudence . . . PAOUNS
impudency . . . PAOUNSZ
impudent . . . PAOUNT
impudently . . . PAOUNLT

impugn
- impugn . . . KBAOUN
- impugns . . . KBAOUNS
- impugning . . . KBAOUNG
- impugned . . . KBAOUND

impulse . . . KBULS

impulsive
- impulsive . . . KBUV, KBUF
- impulsively . . . KBUVL, KBUFL
- impulsiveness . . . KBUVNS, KBUFNS

impunity . . . KBAOUNT
impure . . . KBAOUR
impureness . . . KBAOURNS
impurity . . . KBAOURT
imputation . . . KBAOUGS

impute
- impute . . . KBAOUT
- imputes . . . KBAOUTS
- imputing . . . KBAOUGT
- imputed . . . KBAOUTD

in
- in . . . N-
- *in accordance* . . . NAK
- *in addition* . . . NIGS
- *in and out* . . . NOUT
- *in and out of* . . . NOUF
- *in and out of the* . . . NOUFT
- *in and out of these* . . . NOUFZ
- *in and out of those* . . . NOUFTS
- *in an effort* . . . NEFRT
- *in any* . . . N-N
- *in any case* . . . NAIS
- *in any event* . . . NINT
- *in any way, shape, manner or form* . . . NOFRM

BRIEF ENCOUNTERS

in any way, shape or form	NOFM
inasmuch as	SNUFPS, IN/S-FPS
in case	NAES
in case of emergency	KERJ
in custody	NUD
in each	NAOEFP
in each of the	NAOEFPT
in each of them	NAOEFM
in each of these	NAOEFPZ
in each of those	NAOEFPS
in effect	NEFKT
in emergency	NERJ
in evidence	NEVD
in fact	N-FT
in front of	FROF
in lieu of	N-/LAOUF
in lieu of the	N-/LAOUVFT
in liminie	NLAOEM
in liminie motion	LAOEMGS, NAOEMGS
in my opinion	NAOIP
in order	NORD
in order to	NORTD
in other words	NORDZ
in reference	NREFRNS
in reference to	NREFRNT
in regard	NRAR, NRARD
in regard to	NRARTD
in respect	NR-P
in respect to	NR-PT
insofar	NOFR
insofar as	NOFRZ, IN/SOFRS
in spite of	SPAOIF
in spite of the	SPAOIFT
in spite of them	SPAOIFM
in spite of these	SPAOIFZ
in spite of those	SPAOIFS
in that	NAT
in that event	NAFT
in that regard	NARD
in the	N-T
in the afternoon	NAFRN
in the evening	NAOENG
in the first place	FIRPS
in them	NEM
in the meantime	MAOENT

© 1997 White-Boucke Publishing.

in the morning	NORNG
in there	NER
in terms of	NERM
in terms of the	NERMT
in terms of these	NERMZ
in terms of those	NERMS
in these	NEZ
in this	NIS
in this action	NAX
in this case	NIK
in this event	NIFT
in those	NOS, NOZ
in toto	SPWOET
in view of	N-/VAOUF
in view of the	N-/VAOUFT
in view of them	N-/VAOUFM
in view of these	N-/VAOUFZ
in view of those	N-/VAOUFS
in your mind	NURMD
in your opinion	NURP
in your own words	NURND, NURNDZ
inability	NABLT
inaccuracy	NAEX
inaccurate	NAEK
inactive	NAV, NAK/TIV
inactiveness	NAVNS, NAK/TIVNS
inactivate	
inactivate	NAEVT, NAEFT
inactivates	NAEVTS, NAEFTS
inactivating	NAEVGT, NAEFGT
inactivated	NAEVTD, NAEFTD
inactivation	NAEVGS, NAEFGS
inactivity	NAVT, NAK/TIVT
inadequacy	DWAS
inadequate	DWAT
inadequately	DWAELT
inadmissibility	NIFLT
inadmissible	NIFL
inadvertence	VERNS
inadvertent	VERNT
inadvertently	VERNL
inane	NAIN
inanely	NAINL
inappropriate	NOEPT
inappropriateness	NOEPS

BRIEF ENCOUNTERS *I*

inapt	NAPT
inasmuch as	SNUFPS, IN/S-FPS
inaudibility	NAUBLT
inaudible	NAUBL
inaugural	NAURL, NAURLG
inaugurate	
inaugurate	NAUG
inaugurates	NAUGZ
inaugurating	NAUG/-G
inaugurated	NAUGD
inauguration	NAUGS
Inc.	*ING, OING
incandescent light	NANLT
incarcerate	
incarcerate	KRAIT
incarcerates	KRAITS
incarcerating	KRAIGT
incarcerated	KRAITD
incarceration	KRAIGS
incarnate	
incarnate	KARN, KARNT
incarnates	KARNS, KARNTS
incarnating	KARNG, KARNGT
incarnated	KARND, KARNTD
incarnation	KARNGS
incendiary	SNAER
incendiary device	SNAERD
incentive	SNEV
inception	SNEPGS
incest	SN*ES
inch	
inch	N-FP
inches	N-FPS
inching	N-FPG
inched	N-FPD
incidence	DINZ
incidences	DINSZ
incident	
incident	DIN
incidental	DINL
incidentally	DAINL, DAOENL
incision	SNIGS
incisor	SNAOIRZ
incite	
incite	SNAO*IT

© 1997 White-Boucke Publishing.

incites.	SNAOITS
inciting	SNAOIGT
incited	SNAOITD
incitement	SNAOIMT
inclement	KLEMT
inclination.	KLINGS, KLAOINGS

incline
incline.	KLAOIN
inclines	KLAOINS
inclining	KLAOING
inclined.	KLAOIND

include
include	KLU
includes	KLUS
including.	KLUG
included	KLUD
including the	KLUGT
including these	KLUGZ

inclusion.	KLUGS

inclusive
inclusive	KLUV, KLUF
inclusively	KLUVL, KLUFL
inclusiveness.	KLUVNS, KLUFNS
incoherence	IN/KWERNZ
incoherency	IN/KWERNSZ
incoherent	IN/KWERNT
incoherently	IN/KWERNL

income
income.	N-K
incomes	N-KZ
income tax	N-KT

incommunicado	IN/KMAOUN
incomparability.	IN/KPARBLT
incomparable.	IN/KPARBL
incomparably.	IN/KPAERBL
incompatibility.	IN/KPABLT
incompatible	IN/KPABL
incompetence.	IPS
incompetency.	IPSZ
incompetent.	IP
incompetent, irrelevant and immaterial.	NIPT

incomplete
incomplete.	IN/PLET
incompletely.	IN/PLEL
incompleteness	IN/PLENS

BRIEF ENCOUNTERS

incompletion	IN/PLEGS, IN/PLAOEGS
incomprehensible	IN/KPRENL
inconceivable	IN/SKAOEVL, IN/SKAOEVBL
inconclusive	IN/KLAOUF, IN/KLAOUV
incongruence	IN/GRAOUNS
incongruent	IN/GRAOUNT
incongruous	IN/GRAOUS
inconsequence	IN/KWENS
inconsequent	IN/KWENT
inconsequently	IN/KWENL
inconsiderable	IN/K-RL
inconsiderate	IN/K-RT
inconsistencies	NIKTSZ
inconsistency	NIKTS
inconsistent	NIKT
inconsolable	IN/SKOEBL
inconstant	IN/SKANT
incontestable	IN/KEFBL
incontrovertibility	IN/TROFLT, IN/TROVLT
incontrovertible	IN/TROFL, IN/TROVL
incontrovertibleness	IN/TROVNS, IN/TROFNS
incontrovertibly	IN/TROEFL, IN/TROEVL
inconvenience	IN/VAOENS
inconvenient	IN/VAOENT
incorporate	
incorporate	NORP
incorporates	NORPS
incorporating	NORPG
incorporated	NORPD
incorporation	NORPGS
incorrect	IN/KREK
incorrectly	IN/KREL
incorrigibility	NORJT
incorrigible	NORJ
increase	
increase	SPWRAOES
increases	SPWRAOEFS, SPWRAOESZ
increasing	SPWRAOEFG
increased	SPWRAOEFD
incredible	IN/KREBL
incredulous	IN/KREJ
increment	KREMT
incriminate	
incriminate	KRIMT, KRIM
incriminates	KRIMTS, KRIMS

incriminating	KRIMGT, KRIMG
incriminated	KRIMTD, KRIMD
incrimination	KRIMGS, KRIJS
incubate	
incubate	KAOUBT
incubates	KAOUBTS
incubating	KAOUBGT
incubated	KAOUBTD
incubation	KAOUBGS
incubator	KAOURBT
incumbency	KUMS
incumbent	KUMT
incur	
incur	KBUR
incurred	KBURZ
incurring	KBURG
incurred	KBURD
incurability	IN/KURBLT
incurable	IN/KURBL
indebted	SDPWETD, SDPWET
indebtedness	SDPWETS
indecency	SDPWAOENS
indecent	SDPWAOENT
indecently	SDPWAOENL
indecision	SDPWIGS
indecisive	
indecisive	SDPWIV
indecisively	SDPWIVL
indecisiveness	SDPWIVNS
indeed	N–D
indeed the	N–TD
indefensibility	SDPWEFLT
indefensible	SDPWEFL
indefinite	
indefinite	SDPWAF
indefinitely	SDPWAFL
indefiniteness	SDPWAFNS
indelible	SPWEBL
indelibly	SPWAOEBL
indemnification	NEMGS
indemnify	
indemnify	N*EM
indemnifies	NEMS
indemnifying	NEMG
indemnified	NEMD

BRIEF ENCOUNTERS

indemnity	NEMT
independence	N–PS
independent	N–PT
independently	N–PL
indescribability	SDPWRAOIBLT
indescribable	SDPWRAOIBL
indestructibility	SDPWRUBLT
indestructible	SDPWRUBL
indeterminate	SPWERMT

index
index	N–X
indexes	N–XZ
indexing	N–X/–G
indexed	N–X/–D, N–KD

India	DWIND
Indiana	DWIN, *IN/*IN
Indianapolis	NAP/LIS

indicate
indicate	KAIT
indicates	KAITS
indicating	KAIGT
indicated	KAITD

indication	KAIGS
indicative	KAIV
indicatively	KAIVL
indicator	KAIRT

indict
indict	DIT, DAOIT
indicts	DITS, DAOITS
indicting	DIT/–G, DAOIGT
indicted	DITD, DAOITD

indictment	DIMT, DAOIMT
indifference	SPWIFRNS, SPWIFS
indifferent	SPWIFRNT, SPWIFT
indifferently	SPWIFRNL, SPWIFL
indigence	JINS
indigenous	SDPWIJS
indigent	JIJ, JINT, SDPWIJ
indigents	JIJS, JINTS, SDPWIJZ
indigestion	SPWEGS
indignant	SPWINT
indignantly	SPWINLT, SPWINL
indignation	SPWINGS
indignity	SPWIGT

indirect
    indirect . . . . SPWREK
    indirect evidence . . . . SPWREVD, SDREVD, SDPWREVD
    indirectly . . . . SPWREL
    indirectness . . . . SPWRENS
indiscreet . . . . IN/SKRAOET
indiscreetly . . . . IN/SKRAOEL
indiscrete . . . . IN/SKRAET
indiscretion . . . . IN/SKREGS
indiscriminate . . . . IN/SKRIM
indiscrimination . . . . IN/SKRIJ
indispensable . . . . IND/SPENL
indispose . . . . IN/SDPOES
indisposition . . . . IN/SDPOGS
indisputable . . . . IN/SPAOUBL
indistinct . . . . NING, NINGT, SDWIT, SDINGT
indistinguishable . . . . SDWIRBL
individual
    individual . . . . VID
    individuality . . . . VILTD
    individually . . . . VILD
indoctrinate
    indoctrinate . . . . SPWOKT
    indoctrinates . . . . SPWOKTS
    indoctrinating . . . . SPWOKT/-G
    indoctrinated . . . . SPWOKTD
indoctrination . . . . SPWO*X, SPWORX, SPWOGS
Indonesia
    Indonesia . . . . DAOEZ
    Indonesian . . . . DAOENZ
    Indonesians . . . . DAOENSZ
indoor . . . . SPWAOR
induce
    induce . . . . SPWAOUS
    induces . . . . SPWAOUFS, SPWAOUSZ
    inducing . . . . SPWAOUFG
    induced . . . . SPWAOUFD
inducement . . . . SPWAOUMT, SPWAOUFMT
induct
    induct . . . . SPWUK
    inducts . . . . SPWUKZ
    inducting . . . . SKWUK/-G, SPWUG
    inducted . . . . SPWUKD
induction . . . . SPWUX

BRIEF ENCOUNTERS

indulge
    indulge . . . . SPWULG
    indulges. . . . . SPWULGS
    indulging. . . . . SPWULG/-G
    indulged . . . . SPWULGD
indulgence. . . . . SPWUNS
indulgent . . . . SPWULT
industrial
    industrial . . . . STRIL
    industrialist. . . . . STRILT
    industrialization. . . . . STRILGS
industrialize
    industrialize. . . . . STRAOIS, STRAOIZ
    industrializes . . . . STRAOIFS, STRAOISZ
    industrializing. . . . . STRAOIFG
    industrialized . . . . STRAOIFD
industrious
    industrious . . . . STROUS
    industriously . . . . STROULS
    industriousness. . . . . STROUNS
industry. . . . . STRI
inebriate
    inebriate . . . . BRAIT, NAOEB
    inebriates. . . . . BRAITS, NAOEBS
    inebriating . . . . BRAIGT, NAOEB/-G
    inebriated . . . . BRAITD, NAOEBD
inebriation. . . . . BRAIGS, NAOEGS
ineffective
    ineffective. . . . . IN/FEV
    ineffectively. . . . . IN/FEVL
    ineffectiveness . . . . IN/FEVNS
inefficiency. . . . . IN/FIRBS
inefficient. . . . . IN/FIRB
ineligibility. . . . . NEBLT
ineligible . . . . NEBL
inept . . . . NEPT
ineptitude . . . . NEPTD
inequality. . . . . IN/KWAELT
inequity . . . . NEKT
inert. . . . . NERT
inertia. . . . . NERZ, NER/SHA
inessential. . . . . IN/SERB
inevitability. . . . . NEVBLT, NEFBLT
inevitable . . . . NEVBL
inevitably . . . . NAOEVBL

BRIEF ENCOUNTERS

inexact	IN/ZAK
inexcusable	IN/SKAOUBL
inexorability	NEX/RABLT
inexorable	NEX/RABL
inexorably	NEX/RAEBL
inexpensive	IN/SPEV
inexperience	NERNS
inexperienced	NERND
inextinguishable	IN/TWIRBL
infallibility	IN/FABLT
infallible	IN/FABL
infant	FANT
infarct	
infarct	FAURK, N-FRKT
infarcted	FAURKD, N-FRKTD
infarction	FAURX, N-FRX
infatuate	
infatuate	FAFP
infatuates	FAFPS
infatuating	FAFPG
infatuated	FAFPD
infatuation	FAFPGS
infect	
infect	NEFK
infects	NEFKZ
infecting	NEFK/-G, NEFG
infected	NEFKD
infection	NEFX, NEFGS
infer	
infer	N-FR
infers	N-FRS
inferring	N-FRG
inferred	N-FRD
inference	N-FRNS
inferior	
inferior	FAOR
inferiority	FAORT
inferiorly	FAORL
infinite	IN/FINT
infinity	IN/FOINT
inflame	
inflame	FLAM
inflames	FLAMS
inflaming	FLAMG
inflamed	FLAMD

BRIEF ENCOUNTERS

inflammation. . . . . FLAMGS
inflammatory. . . . . FLAMT
inflatable . . . . FLAIBL
inflate
    inflate . . . . FLAIT
    inflates. . . . . FLAITS
    inflating . . . . FLAIGT
    inflated . . . . FLAITD
inflation. . . . . FLAIGS
inflationary. . . . . FLAIRGS
inflict
    inflict. . . . . FLIK
    inflicts . . . . FLIKZ
    inflicting . . . . FLIK/-G, FLIG
    inflicted . . . . FLIKD
infliction. . . . . FLIX
influence
    influence. . . . . FLU
    influences . . . . FLUS
    influencing . . . . FLUG
    influenced. . . . . FLUD
influential. . . . . FLURBL
influx. . . . . NUX
info . . . . FO
inform
    inform . . . . N-F
    informs. . . . . N-FS
    informing . . . . N-FG
    informed. . . . . N-FD
informal . . . . N-FL
informality. . . . . N-FLT
informant. . . . . NANT
information . . . . N-FGS
informative . . . . NIV
informer . . . . NR-F
infrared. . . . . FRAERD
infrastructure . . . . FRUR
infrequent . . . . IN/FREK
infringe
    infringe . . . . FRIJ
    infringes. . . . . FRIJS
    infringing. . . . . FRIJ/-G
    infringed. . . . . FRIJD
infringement . . . . FRIJT

infuriate
- infuriate . . . . FAOURT
- infuriates . . . . FAOURTS
- infuriating . . . . FAOURGT
- infuriated . . . . FAOURTD

ingenuity . . . . JAOUNT

ingenuous
- ingenuous . . . . JOUNS
- ingenuously . . . . JOUNL
- ingenuousness . . . . JOUNZ

ingest
- ingest . . . . IN/J*ES
- ingests . . . . IN/JEFTS, IN/J*ESZ
- ingesting . . . . IN/JEFGT
- ingested . . . . IN/JEFTD

ingratiate
- ingratiate . . . . GRAIRBT
- ingratiates . . . . GRAIRBTS
- ingratiating . . . . GRAIRBGT
- ingratiated . . . . GRAIRBTD

ingratiation . . . . GRAIRBGS
ingredient . . . . GRENT

inhabit
- inhabit . . . . NABT
- inhabits . . . . NABTS
- inhabiting . . . . NABT/-G
- inhabited . . . . NABTD

inhalation . . . . HALGS, NAELGS

inhale
- inhale . . . . NA*EL
- inhales . . . . NAELS
- inhaling . . . . NAELG
- inhaled . . . . NAELD

inherent . . . . HERNT
inherently . . . . HERNL

inherit
- inherit . . . . HERT
- inherits . . . . HERTS
- inheriting . . . . HERGT
- inherited . . . . HERTD

inheritance . . . . HERNS

inhibit
- inhibit . . . . NIBT
- inhibits . . . . NIBTS
- inhibiting . . . . NIBT/-G

BRIEF ENCOUNTERS

inhibited	NIBTD
inhibition	BIX
initial	
initial	NIRB
initials	NIRBS
initialing	NIRB/-G
initialed	NIRBD
initially	NIRBL
initiate	
initiate	NIRBT
initiates	NIRBTS
initiating	NIRBGT
initiated	NIRBTD
initiation	NIRBGS
initiative	NIVT
injunction	NUNGS
injure	
injure	JIR
injures	JIRS
injuring	JIRG
injured	JIRD
injury	JAOUR
injustice	NUS, JUNS, IN/JUS
ink	
ink	IFRNG
inks	IFRNGS
inking	IFRNG/-G
inked	IFRNGD
inmate	NAIT
innate	
innate	NAET
innately	NAELT
innateness	NAENS
inner	N*R
inning	N*G
innocence	N-NS
innocent	
innocent	N-NT
innocently	N-NLT, N-NL
innocent or guilty	NORG
innovate	
innovate	NOEVT
innovates	NOEVTS
innovating	NOEVGT
innovated	NOEVTD

innovation	NOEVGS
innovative	NOEV
innovator	NOEVRT
innuendo	YEND
innuendoes	YENDZ
inoperable	NOPBL, NOP/-BL, NOP/RABL
inorganic	NANK
inpatient	NAIRB, NAIRBT

inquire

inquire	KWIR
inquires	KWIRS
inquiring	KWIRG
inquired	KWIRD
inquiry	KWAER
inquisition	IN/KWIGS
I.N.S.	*INS
insane	SNAIN
insanely	SNAINL
insanity	SNANT
insatiable	IN/SAIRBL
inscription	SKRIPGS
insect	SNEKT
insecure	NUR
insecurity	NURT

insert

insert	SNERT
inserts	SNERTS
inserting	SNERGT
inserted	SNERTD
insertion	SNERGS

inside

inside	SNAOI
inside of	SNAOIF
inside of the	SNAOIFT
inside of them	SNAOIFM
inside of these	SNAOIFZ
inside of those	SNAOIFS
insider	SNOIR
inside the	SNAOIT
inside them	SNAOIM
inside these	SNAOIZ
inside those	SNAOIS

insidious

insidious	SDUS
insidiously	SDULS

BRIEF ENCOUNTERS

insidiousness	SDUNS
insight	SNOIT
insignia	SNIG/YA
insignificance	SNIGZ
insignificant	SNIG
insincere	SNAO*ER
insincerity	SNAOERT
insinuate	
insinuate	SINT
insinuates	SINTS
insinuating	SINT/-G
insinuated	SINTD
insinuation	S*INGS, SIN/WAIGS
insipid	
insipid	SNIBD
insipidly	SNIBLD
insipidness	SNIBLDZ
insipidity	SNIBTD, SNIBT
insist	
insist	SN*IS
insists	SNIFZ, SN*ISZ
insisting	SNIFG
insisted	SNIFD
insistence	STINS
insistent	ST*INT
insistently	STINL
insobriety	IN/SOBT, IN/SOEBT
insofar	NOFR
insofar as	NOFRZ, IN/SOFRS
insolubility	SNOBLT
insoluble	SNOBL
insomnia	SNOM, IN/SOM
inspect	
inspect	SPEK
inspects	SPEKZ
inspecting	SPEK/-G, SPEG
inspected	SPEKD
inspection	SPEX
inspector	SPERK
inspiration	SNIRGS, SNAOIRGS
inspirational	SNIRL, SNAOIRL
inspire	
inspire	SNAOIR
inspires	SNAOIRS
inspiring	SNAOIRG

inspired	SNAOIRD
instability	SNABLT
install	
install	SNAUL
installs	SNAULS
installing	SNAULG
installed	SNAULD
installation	SNAULGS
installment	SNAUMT
instance	SNANS
instant	
instant	STANT
instantaneous	TAENS
instantaneously	TAENL
instantaneousness	TAENSZ
instantly	SNANL
instead	
instead	STED
instead of	STEF
instead of the	STEFT
instead of them	STEFM
instead of these	STEFZ
instead of those	STEFS
instigate	
instigate	SGAIT
instigates	SGAITS
instigating	SGAIGT
instigated	SGAITD
instigation	SGAIGS
instinct	
instinct	STINGT
instinctive	STIV
instinctively	STIVL
instinctual	STUL
instinctually	STOIL
institute	
institute	TAOUT
institutes	TAOUTS
instituting	TAOUGT
instituted	TAOUTD
institution	TAOUGS
institutionalization	TAOULGS
institutionalize	
institutionalize	TAOUL
institutionalizes	TAOULS

BRIEF ENCOUNTERS / I

institutionalizing . . . . TAOULG
institutionalized . . . . TAOUL/-D
instruct
   instruct . . . . RUK
   instructs. . . . . RUKZ
   instructing. . . . . RUK/-G
   instructed. . . . . RUKD
instruct
   instruction . . . . RUX
   instructional . . . . RUXL
   instructive . . . . RUV
   instructively . . . . RUVL
   instructiveness . . . . RUVNS
   instructor . . . . RURK
instruct the jury
   instruct the jury . . . . STRUJ
   instructs the jury . . . . STRUJS
   instructing the jury . . . . STRUJ/-G
   instructed the jury . . . . STRUJD
instrument
   instrument . . . . STRUMT
   instrumental . . . . STRUL
   instrumentality. . . . . STRULT
   instrumentation . . . . STRUMGS
insubordinate . . . . IN/SBORN
insubordinately . . . . IN/SBORNL
insubordination . . . . IN/SBORNGS
insubstantial . . . . IN/STANL
insufferable . . . . IN/SUFRBL
insufficiency . . . . SNUFZ
insufficient
   insufficient . . . . SNUF
   insufficient evidence . . . . SNUVD
   insufficiently . . . . SNUFL
   insufficient proof. . . . . SNAOF
insulate
   insulate . . . . SLAIT
   insulates . . . . SLAITS
   insulating. . . . . SLAIGT
   insulated . . . . SLAITD
insulation. . . . . SLAIGS
insulator. . . . . SLAIRT
insulin . . . . SLIN
insult
   insult . . . . SNUL, SNULT

insults	SNULS, SNULTS
insulting	SNULG, SNULGT
insulted	SNULD, SNULTD
insurability	SHURBLT
insurable	SHURBL
insurance	
insurance	SHURNS
insurance agent	SHURJ
insurance company	SHURK
insurance coverage	SHUVRNS
insurance policy	SHURP
insure	
insure	SHUR
insures	SHURS
insuring	SHURG
insured	SHURD
insurer	SHOIR, SH*UR
insurgence	SNURNS
insurgency	SNURNSZ
insurgent	SNURNT
insurgently	SNURNL
insurmountable	SNOUNL, IN/SMOUNL
insusceptibility	IN/STIBLT
insusceptible	IN/STIBL
intangible	SPWANL
intangibly	SPWAENL
integral	SPWRALG, SPW-RL
integrate	
integrate	GRAIT
integrates	GRAITS
integrating	GRAIGT
integrated	GRAITD
integration	GRAIGS
integrity	SPWEGT
intellect	
intellect	SPW-
intellectual	SPWUL
intellectually	SPWAOEL
intelligence	TEJS
intelligencia	TEJZ, JENZ
intelligent	TEJ
intelligibility	JIBLT
intelligible	JIBL
intensification	SPWEFGS

BRIEF ENCOUNTERS

intensify
    intensify . . . . SPWEF
    intensifies . . . . SPWEFS
    intensifying . . . . SPWEFG
    intensified . . . . SPWEFD
intensive
    intensive . . . . SPWEV
    intensive care . . . . SPWEVK
    intensively . . . . SPWEVL
    intensiveness . . . . SPWEVNS
intent
    intent . . . . SPWENT
    intentional . . . . SPWENL
    intentionally . . . . SPWOINL
    intentioned . . . . SPWENGD
    intently . . . . SPWENLT
interact
    interact . . . . SPWRAK
    interacts . . . . SPWRAKZ
    interacting . . . . SPWRAK/-G, SPWRAG
    interacted . . . . SPWRAKD
interaction . . . . SPWRAX
interactive . . . . SPWRAV
inter alia . . . . SPWRAIL
intercept
    intercept . . . . SNEPT, SNEP
    intercepts . . . . SNEPTS, SNEPS
    intercepting . . . . SNEPGT, SNEPG
    intercepted . . . . SNEPTD, SNEPD
interception . . . . SN*EPGS
interceptor . . . . SNERPT
interchange
    interchange . . . . SPWRAIJ
    interchanges . . . . SPWRAIJS
    interchanging . . . . SPWRAIJ/-G
    interchanged . . . . SPWRAIJD
interchange
    interchangeability . . . . SPWAIBLT
    interchangeable . . . . SPWAIBL
    interchangeableness . . . . SPWAINS
interconnect
    interconnect . . . . SPWREKT
    interconnects . . . . SPWREKTS
    interconnecting . . . . SPWREKT/-G, SPWREG
    interconnected . . . . SPWREKTD

I   BRIEF ENCOUNTERS

interconnection . . . . SPWREX
intercourse . . . . SPWOURS
interest
    interest . . . . TR–
    interests . . . . TR–S
    interesting . . . . TR–G
    interested . . . . TR–D
interest
    interestingly . . . . TR–LG
    interest of justice . . . . TR–J
    interest rate . . . . TR–RT
interfere
    interfere . . . . SPWR–FR, SPW–FR
    interferes . . . . SPWR–FRS, SPW–FRS
    interfering . . . . SPWR–FRG, SPW–FRG
    interfered . . . . SPWR–FRD, SPW–FRD
interference . . . . SPWR–FRNS, SPW–FRNS
interim . . . . SPWRIM
interior . . . . NAOR
interiorly . . . . NAORL
interlock
    interlock . . . . SPWLAUK
    interlocks . . . . SPWLAUKS
    interlocking . . . . SPWLAUK/–G, SPWLAUG
    interlocked . . . . SPWLAUKD
interlocutory . . . . SPWLOK
interlocutory decree . . . . SPWLOKD
interlope
    interlope . . . . SPWLOEP
    interlopes . . . . SPWLOEPS
    interloping . . . . SPWLOEPG
    interloped . . . . SPWLOEPD
interloper . . . . SPWLOERP
interlude . . . . TLAOUD, SPWLAOUD
intermediary . . . . SPWAOERD
intermediate . . . . SPWAOED
intermission . . . . SPWR–MGS
intermittence . . . . SPWRIMS, SPWR–MS
intermittent . . . . SPWRIMT, SPWR–MT
intermittently . . . . SPWRILT, SPWR–L
intern
    intern . . . . SPWERN
    internal . . . . SPWERNL
    internally . . . . SPWAERNL
    Internal Revenue Service . . . . IRSZ, IRS/IRS

ILLEGAL TO PHOTOCOPY   © 1997 White-Boucke Publishing.

BRIEF ENCOUNTERS

international	SPW-L
Internet	SPW-NT
internist	SPWERNT
internship	SPWERP

interpolate
interpolate	SPWLAIT
interpolates	SPWLAITS
interpolating	SPWLAIGT, SPWLAIG
interpolated	SPWLAITD
interpolation	SPWLAIGS

interpose
interpose	SPWERPS
interposes	SPWERPSZ
interposing	SPWERPG
interposed	SPWERPD
interposer	SPWRERPS
interposition	SPWERPGS

interpret
interpret	TERP
interprets	TERPS
interpreting	TERPG
interpreted	TERPD
interpretation	TERPGS
interpreter	TRERP

interrelate
interrelate	SPWERLT
interrelates	SPWERLTS
interrelating	SPWERLGT
interrelated	SPWERLTD

interrogate
interrogate	SPWERGT
interrogates	SPWERGTS
interrogating	SPWERGT/-G
interrogated	SPWERGTD
interrogation	SPWERGS
interrogative	TROG
interrogator	SPWRERGT
interrogatory	ROG

interrupt
interrupt	TRUPT, TRUP
interrupts	TRUPTS, TRUPS
interrupting	TRUPGT, TRUPG
interrupted	TRUPTD, TRUPD
interrupter	TRURP
interruption	TRUPGS

intersect
- intersect . . . SPWEK
- intersects . . . SPWEKS
- intersecting . . . SPWEK/-G, SPWEG
- intersected . . . SPWEKD

intersection . . . SPW-GS, SPW-X
interstate . . . SPWAIT
interstitial . . . SPWIRBL
intertwine
- intertwine . . . SPWRAOIN
- intertwines . . . SPWRAOINS
- intertwining . . . SPWRAOING
- intertwined . . . SPWRAOIND

interval . . . SPW-FL, SPW-VL
intervene
- intervene . . . SPW-VN
- intervenes . . . SPW-VNS
- intervening . . . SPW-VNG
- intervened . . . SPW-VND

intervention . . . SPW-VNGS
interview
- interview . . . SPWUF
- interviews . . . SPWUFS
- interviewing . . . SPWUFG
- interviewed . . . SPWUFD

interviewee . . . SPWAOE, SPWRAOE
interviewer . . . SPWUFR, SPWRUFR
inter vivos . . . SPWIV
inter vivos trust . . . SPWIVT
intestate . . . SPW*ES, SPWEFT
intestinal . . . SPWEL, SPWELS
intestine . . . SPWES
intimacy . . . SPWAOEM
intimate
- intimate . . . SPWEM
- intimates . . . SPWEMS
- intimating . . . SPWEMG
- intimated . . . SPWEMD

intimation . . . SPWEMGS, SPWEJ
intimidate
- intimidate . . . SPWIM
- intimidates . . . SPWIMS
- intimidating . . . SPWIMG
- intimidated . . . SPWIMD

intimidation . . . SPWIMGS, SPWIJ

BRIEF ENCOUNTERS

into
    into . . . . NAO
    into the . . . . NAOT
    into them . . . . NAOM
    into these. . . . . NAOZ
intolerability . . . . SPWOBLT
intolerable . . . . SPWOBL
intolerableness . . . . SPWONS
intolerably . . . . SPWOEBL
intolerance . . . . SPWORNS
intolerant . . . . SPWORNT
intolerantly . . . . SPWORNLT
intonation . . . . SPWOEGS, SPWOENGS
intone
    intone . . . . SPWOEN
    intones . . . . SPWOENS
    intoning . . . . SPWOENG
    intoned . . . . SPWOEND
in toto . . . . SPWOET
intoxicant . . . . SPWANT
intoxicate
    intoxicate . . . . SPWOK
    intoxicates . . . . SPWOKZ
    intoxicating . . . . SPWOK/-G, SPWOG
    intoxicated . . . . SPWOKD
intoxication . . . . SPWOX
intransigent . . . . SPWRANZ
intrastate . . . . SPWRAET
intravenous
    intravenous . . . . SPWAOEN, SPWRAOEN
    intravenous injection . . . . SPWREGS
    intravenous feeding . . . . SPWAOEF, SPWRAOEF
    intravenously . . . . SPWRAOENL
intrepid . . . . SPWREPD
intrepidly . . . . SPWRELD
intricacy . . . . SPWRIKS
intricate . . . . SPWRIK
intrigue
    intrigue . . . . SPWRAOEG
    intrigues . . . . SPWRAOEGS
    intriguing . . . . SPWRAOEG/-G
    intrigued . . . . SPWRAOEGD
intrinsic . . . . SPWRINS, SPWRIN
intrinsically . . . . SPWRINL

introduce
- introduce . . . . DRAO
- introduces . . . . DRAOS
- introducing . . . . DRAOG
- introduced . . . . DRAOD

introduction . . . . DRAOGS, DRUX
introductory . . . . DRAORK, DRURK

introspect
- introspect . . . . SPWROPT
- introspection . . . . SPWROPGS
- introspective . . . . SPWROVP
- introspectively . . . . SPWROVPL
- introspectiveness . . . . SPWROVNS, SPWRONS

introversion . . . . TROEFRGS, SPWROFRGS

introvert
- introvert . . . . TROEFRT, SPWROFRT
- introverts . . . . TROEFRTS, SPWROFRTS
- introverting . . . . TROEFRGT, SPWROFRGT
- introverted . . . . TROEFRTD, SPWROFRTD

intrude
- intrude . . . . TRAOUD, SPWRAOUD
- intrudes . . . . TRAOUDZ, SPWRAOUDZ
- intruding . . . . TRAOUGD, SPWRAOUGD
- intruded . . . . TRAOUD/-D, SPWRAOUD/-D

intruder . . . . TRAOURD, SPWRAOURD
intrusion . . . . TRAOUGS, SPWRAOUGS

intrusive
- intrusive . . . . TRAOUV, SPWRAOUV
- intrusively . . . . TRAOUVL, SPWRAOUVL
- intrusiveness . . . . TRAOUVNS, SPWRAOUVNS

intuition . . . . SPWAOUGS

intuitive
- intuitive . . . . SPWAOUV
- intuitively . . . . SPWAOUVL
- intuitiveness . . . . SPWAOUVNS

invade
- invade . . . . VAED
- invades . . . . VAEDZ
- invading . . . . VAEGD
- invaded . . . . VAED/-D

invader . . . . VA*ERD
invalid . . . . IN/VALD
invalidity . . . . IN/VALTD
invaluable . . . . IN/VABL
invariable . . . . VARBL

BRIEF ENCOUNTERS   *I*

invariably	VAOERBL
invasion	VA*EGS
invasive	VAEV
invective	
invective	VEVK
invectively	VEVL
invectiveness	VEVNS
invent	
invent	NEVT
invents	NEVTS
inventing	NEVGT, NEVG
invented	NEVTD
invention	VENGS, NEVGS
inventory	VEN
inversion	N−VRGS, NERGS
invert	
invert	N−VRT, N*ERT
inverts	N−VRTS, NERTS
inverting	N−VRGT, NERGT
inverted	N−VRTD, NERTD
invertor	NR−VRT
invest	
invest	VEF
invests	VEFS
investing	VEFG
invested	VEFD
investigate	
investigate	GAIT
investigates	GAITS
investigating	GAIGT
investigated	GAITD
investigating officer	GAIFR
investigation	GAIGS
investigative	GAIV
investigator	
investigator	GAIRT
investigatorial	GAIRL, GAERL
investigatory	GAERT
investment	VEFMT
investor	VEFR
invigorate	
invigorate	VIGT
invigorates	VIGTS
invigorating	VIGT/−G
invigorated	VIGTD

© 1997 White-Boucke Publishing.   ILLEGAL TO PHOTOCOPY

invigoration	V*IGS, VOIGS
invisibility	NIFBLT
invisible	NIFBL
invitation	VAOIGS
invite	
invite	VAOIT
invites	VAOITS
inviting	VAOIGT
invited	VAOITD
invocation	NOEFGS
invoice	
invoice	VOI
invoices	VOIZ
invoicing	VOIG
invoiced	VOI/-D
invoke	
invoke	NOEF
invokes	NOEFS
invoking	NOEFG
invoked	NOEFD
invoking the rule	NOEVL, NOEFL
involuntary	VOIN
involuntary manslaughter	VOIM
involve	
involve	VOF
involves	VOFS
involving	VOFG
involved	VOFD
involvement	VOFMT
iodine	AOIND
ion	AOIN
ionization	AOINGS
iota	AOIT
Iowa	A*I
ipso facto	IPS/FAK
Iran	RA*N
Iranian	RA*EN
Iraq	AOIRK
Iraqi	AOERK
irate	AOIRT
irately	AOIRLT
Ireland	AOIRL, AOIRLD
iris	AOIRZ
Irish	AOIRB
ironic	AOIRNK

BRIEF ENCOUNTERS *I*

irony	OIRN
irrational	IR/RAL
irrationally	IR/RAEL
irregardless	IR/RARL
irregular	IRG
irregularity	IRGT
irrelevance	*IRS
irrelevancy	IRZ
irrelevant	
irrelevant	IR
irrelevant and immaterial	IRMT
irrelevantly	IRLT
irresistibility	RIFBLT, IR/RIBLT
irresistible	RIFBL, IR/RIBL
irrespective	IRPT
irresponsibility	RONT
irresponsible	RONL
irresponsibleness	RONS
irreverence	IVS
irreverent	IVT
irreverently	IVLT
irrigate	
irrigate	RIRT
irrigates	RIRTS
irrigating	RIRGT
irrigated	RIRTD
irrigation	RIRGS
irritability	IRBLT
irritable	IRBL
irritant	IRNT
irritate	
irritate	IRT
irritates	IRTS
irritating	IRT/-G
irritated	IRTD
irritation	IRGS
IRS	IRS
is	S-
is it	
is it	ST-
is it accurate to say	ST-KTS
is it accurate to state	ST-KT
is it a fact	ST-FK
is it correct	ST-RK
is it fair	SFAIR

© 1997 White-Boucke Publishing.

I

is it fair to	SFAIRT
is it fair to do	SFAIRTD, SFAIRD
is it fair to say	SFAIRTS, ST-FRTS
is it fair to state	ST-FRT
is it happening	ST-PG
is it not	STON
is it not a fact	STOFK
is it not correct	STORKT
is it not right	STOR
is it not so	STOS
is it not true	STRON
is it right	ST-R, ST-RT
is it so	S-TS
is it the	ST-T
is it true	STRU
is it your wish and desire	SWAOIR
Islam	SLAUM
Islamic	SLAUMG

isn't

isn't	S-NT
isn't it a fact	SNIFT
isn't it correct	SNIRK
isn't it right	SNIRT
isn't it so	SN-S
isn't it true	SNU
isn't that	SNA
isn't that a fact	SNAFT
isn't that correct	SNARK
isn't that right	SNART
isn't that right, sir	SNARTS
isn't that so	SNAS
isn't that true	SNAU

isolate

isolate	ZOELT
isolates	ZOELTS
isolating	ZOELGT, ZOELG
isolated	ZOELTD

isolation

isolation	ZOELGS, SOELGS
isolationism	ZOEFM, ZOEFMT
isolationist	ZOEFLT
Israel	IZ
Israeli	ILZ
issuance	IRBNS

BRIEF ENCOUNTERS *I*

issue
    issue . . . . IRB
    issues . . . . IRBS
    issuing . . . . IRB/-G
    issued . . . . IRB/-D
issue of fact . . . . SHAOUFT
issues of fact . . . . SHAOUFTS
is that
    is that . . . . STHA
    is that a fact . . . . STHAF, STHAFT
    is that all . . . . STHAUL
    is that all right . . . . STL-RT
    is that can . . . . STHAK
    is that can't . . . . STHAKT, STHAK/-NT, STHA/K-NT
    is that correct . . . . STHARK
    is that correct? . . . . STHARKT
    is that could . . . . STHAKD
    is that couldn't . . . . STHAKTD, STHAKD/-NT, STHA/KUNT
    is that ever . . . . STHAFR, STHAVR
    is that feeling . . . . STHAFLG
    is that feels . . . . STHAFLS
    is that felt . . . . STHAFLT
    is that gets . . . . STHAGTS
    is that goes . . . . STHAGS
    is that got . . . . STHAGT
    is that had . . . . STHAD
    is that hadn't . . . . STHAD/-NT, STHA/H-NT
    is that is . . . . STHAS
    is that isn't . . . . STHAS/-NT, STHA/S-NT
    is that means . . . . STHAMS
    is that means to . . . . STHAMT
    is that means to say . . . . STHAMTS
    is that not . . . . STHANT
    is that right . . . . STHART
    is that shall . . . . STHARB
    is that should . . . . STHARBD
    is that shouldn't . . . . STHARBTD, STHARBD/-NT, STHA/SH-NT
    is that so . . . . STHAZ
    is that the . . . . STHAT
    is that true . . . . STHRAU
    is that wanted . . . . STHAPTD
    is that was . . . . STHAFS
    is that wasn't . . . . STHAFS/-NT, STHA/WUNT
    is that will . . . . STHAL
    is that would . . . . STHALD

is that wouldn't	STHALTD, STHALD/-NT, STHA/WONT
is that would say	STHALDZ
is that you are	STHAUR
is that your	STHA*UR
is that your recollection	STHAURX

is that he

is that he	STHAE
is that he believed	STHAEBLD
is that he believes	STHAEBLS
is that he can	STHAEK
is that he can't	STHAEKT, STHAEK/-NT, STHAE/K-NT
is that he could	STHAEKD
is that he couldn't	STHAEKTD, STHAEKD/-NT, STHAE/KUNT
is that he ever	STHAEFR, STHAEVR
is that he feels	STHAEFLS
is that he felt	STHAEFLT
is that he gets	STHAEGTS
is that he goes	STHAEGS
is that he got	STHAEGT
is that he had	STHAED
is that he hadn't	STHAED/-NT, STHAE/H-NT
is that he happened	STHAEPD
is that he happens	STHAEPS
is that he is	STHAES
is that he isn't	STHAES/-NT, STHAE/S-NT
is that he knows	STHAENS
is that he lived	STHAEVD
is that he lives	STHAEVS
is that he means	STHAEMS
is that he means to	STHAEMT
is that he means to say	STHAEMTS
is that he recalled	STHAERLD
is that he recalls	STHAERLS
is that he recollected	STHAERKD
is that he recollects	STHAERKS
is that he remembered	STHAERMD
is that he remembers	STHAERMS
is that he says	STHAESZ
is that he sees	STHAEZ
is that he shall	STHAERB
is that he should	STHAERBD
is that he shouldn't	STHAERBTD, STHAERBD/-NT, STHAE/SH-NT
is that he thinks	STHAENGS

BRIEF ENCOUNTERS

is that he thinks so	STHAENGSZ
is that he understands	STHAENDZ
is that he understood	STHAEND
is that he wanted	STHAEPTD
is that he wants	STHAEPTS
is that he was	STHAEFS
is that he wasn't	STHAEFT, STHAEFS/-NT, STHAE/WUNT
is that he will	STHAEL
is that he would	STHAELD
is that he wouldn't	STHAELTD, STHAELD/-NT, STHAE/WONT
is that he would say	STHAELDZ

is that I

is that I	STHAI
is that I am	STHAIM
is that I believe	STHAIBL
is that I believed	STHAIBLD
is that I can	STHAIK
is that I can't	STHAIKT, STHAIK/-NT, STHAI/K-NT
is that I could	STHAIKD
is that I couldn't	STHAIKTD, STHAIKD/-NT, STHAI/KUNT
is that I ever	STHAIFR, STHAIVR
is that I feel	STHAIFL
is that I felt	STHAIFLT
is that I get	STHAIGT
is that I go	STHAIG
is that I had	STHAID
is that I hadn't	STHAID/-NT, STHAI/H-NT
is that I happen	STHAIP
is that I happened	STHAIPD
is that I have	STHAIF
is that I have been	STHAIFB
is that I have had	STHAIFD
is that I have known	STHAIFN
is that I haven't	STHAIFT, STHAIF/-NT, STHAI/V-NT
is that I know	STHAIN
is that I live	STHAIV
is that I lived	STHAIVD
is that I mean	STHA*IM
is that I mean to	STHAIMT
is that I mean to say	STHAIMTS
is that I recall	STHAIRL
is that I recalled	STHAIRLD

is that I recollect	STHAIRK
is that I recollected	STHAIRKD
is that I remember	STHAIRM
is that I remembered	STHAIRMD
is that I say	STHAIS
is that I see	STHAIZ
is that I shall	STHAIRB
is that I should	STHAIRBD
is that I shouldn't	STHAIRBTD, STHAIRBD/-NT, STHAI/SH-NT
is that I think	STHAING
is that I think so	STHAINGS
is that I understand	STHAINDZ
is that I understood	STHAIND
is that I want	STHAIPT
is that I wanted	STHAIPTD
is that I was	STHAIFS
is that I wasn't	STHAIFS/-NT, STHAI/WUNT
is that I will	STHAIL
is that I would	STHAILD
is that I wouldn't	STHAILTD, STHAILD/-NT, STHAI/WONT
is that I would say	STHAILDZ

is that you

is that you	STHAU
is that you are	STHAUR
is that you aren't	STHAURNT, STHAUR/-NT, STAU/R-NT
is that you believe	STHAUBL
is that you believed	STHAUBLD
is that you can	STHAUK
is that you can't	STHAUKT, STAUK/-NT, STAU/K-NT
is that you could	STHAUKD
is that you couldn't	STHAUKTD, STHAUKD/-NT, STHAU/KUNT
is that you ever	STHAUFR, STHAUVR
is that you feel	STHAUFL
is that you felt	STHAUFLT
is that you get	STHAUGT
is that you go	STHAUG
is that you had	STHAUD
is that you hadn't	STHAUD/-NT, STHAU/H-NT
is that you happen	STHAUP
is that you happened	STHAUPD
is that you have	STHAUF

BRIEF ENCOUNTERS I

is that you have been	STHAUFB
is that you have had	STHAUFD
is that you have known	STHAUFN
is that you haven't	STHAUFT, STHAUF/-NT, STHAU/V-NT
is that you know	STHAUN
is that you live	STHAUV
is that you lived	STHAUVD
is that you mean	STHAUM
is that you mean to	STHAUMT
is that you mean to say	STHAUMTS
is that you recall	STHAURL
is that you recalled	STHAURLD
is that you recollect	STHAURK
is that you recollected	STHAURKD
is that you remember	STHAURM
is that you remembered	STHAURMD
is that you say	STHAUS
is that you see	STHAUZ
is that you shall	STHAURB
is that you should	STHAURBD
is that you shouldn't	STHAURBTD, STHAURBD/-NT, STHAU/SH-NT
is that you think	STHAUNG
is that you think so	STHAUNGS
is that you understand	STHAUNDZ
is that you understood	STHAUND
is that you want	STHAUPT
is that you wanted	STHAUPTD
is that you were	STHAURP
is that you weren't	STHAURPT, STHAURP/-NT, STHAU/W-RNT
is that you will	STHA*UL
is that you would	STHAULD
is that you wouldn't	STHAULTD, STHAULD/-NT, STHAU/WONT
is that you would say	STHAULDZ
is the	S-T

is there

is there	STHR-
is there anything	STHR-G
is there anything else	STHR-LGS, STHR-LG
is there is	STHR-S

is this

is this	STH-

© 1997 White-Boucke Publishing.   ILLEGAL TO PHOTOCOPY

I   BRIEF ENCOUNTERS

is this is . . . . STH-S
is this the . . . . STH-T
is this true . . . . STHU
is to
    is to. . . . . STO
    is to be. . . . . STOB
    is to believe. . . . . STOBL
    is to do . . . . STOD
    is to do so . . . . STODZ
    is to feel . . . . STOFL
    is to get . . . . STOGT
    is to have . . . . STOF
    is to have been . . . . STOFB
    is to have had . . . . STOFD
    is to have known. . . . . STOFN
    is to go . . . . STOG
    is to live. . . . . STOV
    is to recall. . . . . STORL
    is to see. . . . . STOZ
    is to the. . . . . STOT
    is to think . . . . STONG
    is to understand . . . . STONDZ
    is to want. . . . . STOPT
is what
    is what. . . . . SWHA
    is what can . . . . SWHAK
    is what can't . . . . SWHAKT, SWHAK/-NT,
                                                                                                    SWHA/K-NT
    is what could. . . . . SWHAKD
    is what couldn't . . . . SWHAKTD, SWHAKD/-NT,
                                                                                                    SWHA/KUNT
    is what feels. . . . . SWHAFLS
    is what felt. . . . . SWHAFLT
    is what gets . . . . SWHAGTS
    is what goes . . . . SWHAGS
    is what got . . . . SWHAGT
    is what had. . . . . SWHAD
    is what hadn't . . . . SWHAD/-NT, SWHA/H-NT
    is what happened. . . . . SWHAPD
    is what happens. . . . . SWHAPS
    is what is . . . . SWHAS
    is what isn't. . . . . SWHAS/-NT, SWHA/S-NT
    is what means. . . . . SWHAMS
    is what means to. . . . . SWHAMT
    is what means to say . . . . SWHAMTS

BRIEF ENCOUNTERS

is what recalled	SWHARLD
is what recalls	SWHARLS
is what says	SWHASZ
is what sees	SWHAZ
is what shall	SWHARB
is what should	SWHARBD
is what shouldn't	SWHARBTD, SWHARBD/-NT, SWHA/SH-NT
is what the	SWHAT
is what wanted	SWHAPTD
is what wants	SWHAPTS
is what was	SWHAFS
is what wasn't	SWHAFT, SWHAFS/-NT, SWHA/WUNT
is what will	SWHAL
is what would	SWHALD
is what wouldn't	SWHALTD, SWHALD/-NT, SWHA/WONT
is what would say	SWHALDZ

is what he

is what he	SWHAE
is what he believed	SWHAEBLD
is what he believes	SWHAEBLS
is what he can	SWHAEK
is what he can't	SWHAEKT, SWAEK/-NT, SWAE/K-NT
is what he could	SWHAEKD
is what he couldn't	SWHAEKTD, SWHAEKD/-NT, SWHAE/KUNT
is what he ever	SWHAEFR, SWHAEVR
is what he feels	SWHAEFLS
is what he felt	SWHAEFLT
is what he gets	SWHAEGTS
is what he goes	SWHAEGS
is what he got	SWHAEGT
is what he had	SWHAED
is what he hadn't	SWHAED/-NT, SWHAE/H-NT
is what he happened	SWHAEPD
is what he happens	SWHAEPS
is what he imagined	SWAEJD
is what he imagines	SWHAEJS
is what he is	SWHAES
is what he isn't	SWHAES/-NT, SWHAE/S-NT
is what he knows	SWHAENS
is what he lived	SWHAEVD

BRIEF ENCOUNTERS

  is what he lives .... SWHAEVS
  is what he means .... SWHAEMS
  is what he means to .... SWHAEMT
  is what he means to say .... SWHAEMTS
  is what he recalled .... SWHAERLD
  is what he recalls .... SWHAERLS
  is what he recollected .... SWHAERKD
  is what he recollects .... SWHAERKS
  is what he remembered .... SWHAERMD
  is what he remembers .... SWHAERMS
  is what he says .... SWHAESZ
  is what he sees .... SWHAEZ
  is what he shall .... SWHAERB
  is what he should .... SWHAERBD
  is what he shouldn't .... SWHAERBTD, SWHAERBD/-NT,
                                                SWHAE/SH-NT
  is what he thinks .... SWHAENGS
  is what he understands .... SWHAENDZ
  is what he understood .... SWHAEND
  is what he wanted .... SWHAEPTD
  is what he wants .... SWHAEPTS
  is what he was .... SWHAEFS
  is what he wasn't .... SWHAEFT, SWHAEFS/-NT,
                                                SWHAE/WUNT
  is what he will .... SWHAEL
  is what he would .... SWHAELD
  is what he wouldn't .... SWHAELTD, SWHAELD/-NT,
                                                SWHAE/WONT
  is what he would say .... SWHAELDZ
is what I
  is what I .... SWHAI
  is what I am .... SWHAIM
  is what I believe .... SWHAIBL
  is what I believed .... SWHAIBLD
  is what I can .... SWHAIK
  is what I can't .... SWHAIKT, SWHAIK/-NT, SWHAI/K-NT
  is what I could .... SWHAIKD
  is what I couldn't .... SWHAIKTD, SWHAIKD/-NT,
                                                SWHAI/KUNT
  is what I ever .... SWHAIFR, SWHAIVR
  is what I feel .... SWHAIFL
  is what I felt .... SWHAIFLT
  is what I get .... SWHAIGT
  is what I go .... SWHAIG
  is what I had .... SWHAID

BRIEF ENCOUNTERS

is what I hadn't	SWHAID/-NT, SWHAI/H-NT
is what I happen	SWHAIP
is what I happened	SWHAIPD
is what I have	SWHAIF
is what I have been	SWHAIFB
is what I have had	SWHAIFD
is what I have known	SWHAIFN
is what I haven't	SWHAIFT, SWHAIF/-NT, SWHAI/V-NT
is what I imagine	SWHAIJ
is what I imagined	SWHAIJD
is what I know	SWHAIN
is what I live	SWHAIV
is what I lived	SWHAIVD
is what I mean	SWHA*IM
is what I mean to	SWHAIMT
is what I mean to say	SWHAIMTS
is what I recall	SWHAIRL
is what I recalled	SWHAIRLD
is what I recollect	SWHAIRK
is what I recollected	SWHAIRKD
is what I remember	SWHAIRM
is what I remembered	SWHAIRMD
is what I say	SWHAIS
is what I see	SWHAIZ
is what I shall	SWHAIRB
is what I should	SWHAIRBD
is what I shouldn't	SWHAIRBTD, SWHAIRBD/-NT, SWHAI/SH-NT
is what I think	SWHAING
is what I understand	SWHAINDZ
is what I understood	SWHAIND
is what I want	SWHAIPT
is what I wanted	SWHAIPTD
is what I was	SWHAIFS
is what I wasn't	SWHAIFS/-NT, SWHAI/WUNT
is what I will	SWHAIL
is what I would	SWHAILD
is what I wouldn't	SWHAILTD, SWHAILD/-NT, SWHAI/WONT
is what I would say	SWHAILDZ
is what you	
is what you	SWHAU
is what you are	SWHAUR

I   BRIEF ENCOUNTERS

is what you aren't	SWHAURNT, SWHAUR/-NT, SWHAU/R-NT
is what you believe	SWHAUBL
is what you believed	SWHAUBLD
is what you can	SWHAUK
is what you can't	SWHAUKT, SWHAUK/-NT, SWHAU/K-NT
is what you could	SWHAUKD
is what you couldn't	SWHAUKTD, SWHAUKD/-NT, SWHAU/KUNT
is what you ever	SWHAUFR, SWHAUVR
is what you feel	SWHAUFL
is what you felt	SWHAUFLT
is what you get	SWHAUGT
is what you go	SWHAUG
is what you had	SWHAUD
is what you hadn't	SWHAUD/-NT, SWHAU/H-NT
is what you happen	SWHAUP
is what you happened	SWHAUPD
is what you have	SWHAUF
is what you have been	SWHAUFB
is what you have had	SWHAUFD
is what you have known	SWHAUFN
is what you haven't	SWHAUFT, SWHAUF/-NT, SWHAU/V-NT
is what you imagine	SWHAUJ
is what you imagined	SWHAUJD
is what you know	SWHAUN
is what you live	SWHAUV
is what you lived	SWHAUVD
is what you mean	SWHAUM
is what you mean to	SWHAUMT
is what you mean to say	SWHAUMTS
is what you recall	SWHAURL
is what you recalled	SWHAURLD
is what you recollect	SWHAURK
is what you recollected	SWHAURKD
is what you remember	SWHAURM
is what you remembered	SWHAURMD
is what you say	SWHAUS
is what you see	SWHAUZ
is what you shall	SWHAURB
is what you should	SWHAURBD
is what you shouldn't	SWHAURBTD, SWHAURBD/-NT, SWHAU/SH-NT

BRIEF ENCOUNTERS

    is what you think . . . . SWHAUNG
    is what you understand . . . . SWHAUNDZ
    is what you understood . . . . SWHAUND
    is what you want . . . . SWHAUPT
    is what you wanted . . . . SWHAUPTD
    is what you were . . . . SWHAURP
    is what you weren't . . . . SWHAURPT, SWHAURP/-NT,
                                                     SWHAU/W-RNT
    is what you will . . . . SWHAUL
    is what you would . . . . SWHAULD
    is what you wouldn't . . . . SWHAULTD, SWHAULD/-NT,
                                                     SWHAU/WONT
    is what you would say . . . . SWHAULDZ
is when . . . . SWH-
is when he
    is when he . . . . SWHE
    is when he believed . . . . SWHEBLD
    is when he believes . . . . SWHEBLS
    is when he can . . . . SWHEK
    is when he can't . . . . SWHEKT, SWHEK/-NT, SWHE/K-NT
    is when he could . . . . SWHEKD
    is when he couldn't . . . . SWHEKTD, SWHEKD/-NT,
                                                     SWHE/KUNT
    is when he ever . . . . SWHEFR, SWHEVR
    is when he feels . . . . SWHEFLS
    is when he felt . . . . SWHEFLT
    is when he gets . . . . SWHEGTS
    is when he goes . . . . SWHEGS
    is when he got . . . . SWHEGT
    is when he had . . . . SWHED
    is when he hadn't . . . . SWHED/-NT, SWHE/H-NT
    is when he happened . . . . SWHEPD
    is when he happens . . . . SWHEPS
    is when he imagined . . . . SWHEJD
    is when he imagines . . . . SWHEJS
    is when he is . . . . SWHES
    is when he isn't . . . . SWHES/-NT, SWHE/S-NT
    is when he knows . . . . SWHENS
    is when he lived . . . . SWHEVD
    is when he lives . . . . SWHEVS
    is when he means . . . . SWHEMS
    is when he means to . . . . SWHEMT
    is when he means to say . . . . SWHEMTS
    is when he recalled . . . . SWHERLD
    is when he recalls . . . . SWHERLS

is when he recollected	SWHERKD
is when he recollects	SWHERKS
is when he remembered	SWHERMD
is when he remembers	SWHERMS
is when he says	SWHESZ
is when he sees	SWHEZ
is when he shall	SWHERB
is when he should	SWHERBD
is when he shouldn't	SWHERBTD, SWHERBD/-NT, SWHE/SH-NT
is when he thinks	SWHENGS
is when he thinks so	SWHENGSZ
is when he understands	SWHENDZ
is when he understood	SWHEND
is when he wanted	SWHEPTD
is when he wants	SWHEPTS
is when he was	SWHEFS
is when he wasn't	SWHEFS/-NT, SWHE/WUNT
is when he will	SWHEL
is when he would	SWHELD
is when he wouldn't	SWHELTD, SWHELD/-NT, SWHE/WONT
is when he would say	SWHELDZ

is when I

is when I	SWHI
is when I am	SWHIM
is when I believe	SWHIBL
is when I believed	SWHIBLD
is when I can	SWHIK
is when I can't	SWHIKT, SWHIK/-NT, SWHI/K-NT
is when I could	SWHIKD
is when I couldn't	SWHIKTD, SWHIKD/-NT, SWHI/KUNT
is when I ever	SWHIFR, SWHIVR
is when I feel	SWHIFL
is when I felt	SWHIFLT
is when I get	SWHIGT
is when I go	SWHIG
is when I had	SWHID
is when I hadn't	SWHID/-NT, SWHI/H-NT
is when I happen	SWHIP
is when I happened	SWHIPD
is when I have	SWHIF
is when I have been	SWHIFB
is when I have believed	SWHIFBLD

BRIEF ENCOUNTERS

is when I have had . . . . SWHIFD
is when I have known . . . . SWHIFN
is when I haven't . . . . SWHIFT, SWHIF/-NT, SWHI/V-NT
is when I imagine . . . . SWHIJ
is when I imagined . . . . SWHIJD
is when I know . . . . SWHIN
is when I live . . . . SWHIV
is when I lived . . . . SWHIVD
is when I mean . . . . SWH*IM
is when I mean to . . . . SWHIMT
is when I mean to say . . . . SWHIMTS
is when I recall . . . . SWHIRL
is when I recalled . . . . SWHIRLD
is when I recollect . . . . SWHIRK
is when I recollected . . . . SWHIRKD
is when I remember . . . . SWHIRM
is when I remembered . . . . SWHIRMD
is when I say . . . . SWHIS
is when I see . . . . SWHIZ
is when I shall . . . . SWHIRB
is when I should . . . . SWHIRBD
is when I shouldn't . . . . SWHIRBTD, SWHIRBD/-NT, SWHI/SH-NT
is when I think . . . . SWHING
is when I think so . . . . SWHINGS
is when I understand . . . . SWHINDZ
is when I understood . . . . SWHIND
is when I want . . . . SWHIPT
is when I wanted . . . . SWHIPTD
is when I was . . . . SWHIFS
is when I wasn't . . . . SWHIFS/-NT, SWHI/WUNT
is when I will . . . . SWHIL
is when I would . . . . SWHILD
is when I wouldn't . . . . SWHILTD, SWHILD/-NT, SWHI/WONT
is when I would say . . . . SWHILDZ
is when the . . . . SWH-T
is when you
   is when you . . . . SWHU
   is when you are . . . . SWHUR
   is when you aren't . . . . SWHURNT, SWHUR/-NT, SWHU/R-NT
   is when you believe . . . . SWHUBL
   is when you believed . . . . SWHUBLD
   is when you can . . . . SWHUK
   is when you can't . . . . SWHUKT, SWHUK/-NT, SWHU/K-NT
   is when you could . . . . SWHUKD

is when you couldn't	SWHUKTD, SWHUKD/-NT, SWHU/KUNT
is when you ever	SWHUFR, SWHUVR
is when you feel	SWHUFL
is when you felt	SWHUFLT
is when you get	SWHUGT
is when you go	SWHUG
is when you had	SWHUD
is when you hadn't	SWHUD/-NT, SWHU/H-NT
is when you happen	SWHUP
is when you happened	SWHUPD
is when you have	SWHUF
is when you have been	SWHUFB
is when you have had	SWHUFD
is when you have known	SWHUFN
is when you haven't	SWHUFT, SWHUF/-NT, SWHU/V-NT
is when you imagine	SWHUJ
is when you imagined	SWHUJD
is when you know	SWHUN
is when you live	SWHUV
is when you lived	SWHUVD
is when you mean	SWHUM
is when you mean to	SWHUMT
is when you mean to say	SWHUMTS
is when you recall	SWHURL
is when you recalled	SWHURLD
is when you recollect	SWHURK
is when you recollected	SWHURKD
is when you remember	SWHURM
is when you remembered	SWHURMD
is when you say	SWHUS
is when you see	SWHUZ
is when you shall	SWHURB
is when you should	SWHURBD
is when you shouldn't	SWHURBTD, SWHURBD/-NT, SWHU/SH-NT
is when you think	SWHUNG
is when you think so	SWHUNGS
is when you understand	SWHUNDZ
is when you understood	SWHUND
is when you want	SWHUPT
is when you wanted	SWHUPTD
is when you were	SWHURP

BRIEF ENCOUNTERS

is when you weren't	SWHURPT, SWHURP/-NT, SWHU/W-RNT
is when you will	SWHUL
is when you would	SWHULD
is when you wouldn't	SWHULTD, SWHULD/-NT, SWHU/WONT
is when you would say	SWHULDZ

is where he

is where he	SWRE
is where he believed	SWREBLD
is where he believes	SWREBLS
is where he can	SWREK
is where he can't	SWREKT, SWREK/-NT, SWRE/K-NT
is where he could	SWREKD
is where he couldn't	SWREKTD, SWREKD/-NT, SWRE/KUNT
is where he ever	SWREFR, SWREVR
is where he feels	SWREFLS
is where he felt	SWREFLT
is where he gets	SWREGTS
is where he goes	SWREGS
is where he got	SWREGT
is where he had	SWRED
is where he hadn't	SWRED/-NT, SWRE/H-NT
is where he happened	SWREPD
is where he happens	SWREPS
is where he imagined	SWREJD
is where he imagines	SWREJS
is where he is	SWRES
is where he isn't	SWRES/-NT, SWRE/S-NT
is where he knows	SWRENS
is where he lived	SWREVD
is where he lives	SWREVS
is where he means	SWREMS
is where he means to	SWREMT
is where he means to say	SWREMTS
is where he recalled	SWRERLD
is where he recalls	SWRERLS
is where he recollected	SWRERKD
is where he recollects	SWRERKS
is where he remembered	SWRERMD
is where he remembers	SWRERMS
is where he says	SWRESZ
is where he sees	SWREZ
is where he shall	SWRERB

I

is where he should	SWRERBD
is where he shouldn't	SWRERBTD, SWRERBD/-NT, SWRE/SH-NT
is where he thinks	SWRENGS
is where he thinks so	SWRENGSZ
is where he understands	SWRENDZ
is where he understood	SWREND
is where he wanted	SWREPTD
is where he wants	SWREPTS
is where he was	SWREFS
is where he wasn't	SWREFT, SWREFS/-NT, SWRE/WUNT
is where he will	SWREL
is where he would	SWRELD
is where he wouldn't	SWRELTD, SWRELD/-NT, SWRE/WONT
is where he would say	SWRELDZ

is where I

is where I	SWRI
is where I am	SWRIM
is where I believe	SWRIBL
is where I believed	SWRIBLD
is where I can	SWRIK
is where I can't	SWRIKT, SWRIK/-NT, SWRI/K-NT
is where I could	SWRIKD
is where I couldn't	SWRIKTD, SWRIKD/-NT, SWRI/KUNT
is where I feel	SWRIFL
is where I felt	SWRIFLT
is where I get	SWRIGT
is where I go	SWRIG
is where I had	SWRID
is where I hadn't	SWRID/-NT, SWRI/H-NT
is where I happen	SWRIP
is where I happened	SWRIPD
is where I have	SWRIF
is where I have been	SWRIFB
is where I have had	SWRIFD
is where I have known	SWRIFN
is where I haven't	SWRIFT, SWRIF/-NT, SWRI/V-NT
is where I imagine	SWRIJ
is where I imagined	SWRIJD
is where I know	SWRIN
is where I live	SWRIV
is where I lived	SWRIVD
is where I mean	SWR*IM
is where I mean to	SWRIMT

BRIEF ENCOUNTERS   *I*

is where I mean to say	SWRIMTS
is where I recall	SWRIRL
is where I recalled	SWRIRLD
is where I recollect	SWRIRK
is where I recollected	SWRIRKD
is where I remember	SWRIRM
is where I remembered	SWRIRMD
is where I say	SWRIS
is where I see	SWRIZ
is where I shall	SWRIRB
is where I should	SWRIRBD
is where I shouldn't	SWRIRBTD, SWRIRBD/-NT, SWRI/SH-NT
is where I think	SWRING
is where I think so	SWRINGS
is where I understand	SWRINDZ
is where I understood	SWRIND
is where I want	SWRIPT
is where I wanted	SWRIPTD
is where I was	SWRIFS
is where I wasn't	SWRIFS/-NT, SWRI/WUNT
is where I will	SWRIL
is where I would	SWRILD
is where I wouldn't	SWRILTD, SWRILD/-NT, SWRI/WONT
is where I would say	SWRILDZ
is where you	
is where you	SWRU
is where you are	SWRUR
is where you aren't	SWRURNT, SWRUR/-NT, SWRU/R-NT
is where you believe	SWRUBL
is where you believed	SWRUBLD
is where you can	SWRUK
is where you can't	SWRUKT, SWRUK/-NT, SWRU/K-NT
is where you could	SWRUKD
is where you couldn't	SWRUKTD, SWRUKD/-NT, SWRU/KUNT
is where you ever	SWRUFR, SWRUVR
is where you feel	SWRUFL
is where you felt	SWRUFLT
is where you get	SWRUGT
is where you go	SWRUG
is where you had	SWRUD
is where you hadn't	SWRUD/-NT, SWRU/H-NT
is where you happen	SWRUP
is where you happened	SWRUPD

is where you have.	SWRUF
is where you have been	SWRUFB
is where you have had	SWRUFD
is where you have known	SWRUFN
is where you haven't	SWRUFT, SWRUF/-NT, SWRU/V-NT
is where you imagine.	SWRUJ
is where you imagined.	SWRUJD
is where you know	SWRUN
is where you live	SWRUV
is where you lived	SWRUVD
is where you mean.	SWRUM
is where you mean to.	SWRUMT
is where you mean to say	SWRUMTS
is where you recall	SWRURL
is where you recalled.	SWRURLD
is where you recollect	SWRURK
is where you recollected	SWRURKD
is where you remember	SWRURM
is where you remembered.	SWRURMD
is where you say	SWRUS
is where you see	SWRUZ
is where you shall.	SWRURB
is where you should	SWRURBD
is where you shouldn't	SWRURBTD, SWRURBD/-NT, SWRU/SH-NT
is where you think	SWRUNG
is where you think so	SWRUNGS
is where you understand	SWRUNDZ
is where you understood.	SWRUND
is where you want	SWRUPT
is where you wanted.	SWRUPTD
is where you were	SWRURP
is where you weren't	SWRURPT, SWRURP/-NT, SWRU/W-RNT
is where you will.	SWRUL
is where you would.	SWRULD
is where you wouldn't	SWRULTD, SWRULD/-NT, SWRU/WONT
is where you would say.	SWRULDZ
is whether he	
is whether he.	SWHRE
is whether he believed.	SWHREBLD
is whether he believes	SWHREBLS
is whether he can.	SWHREK

BRIEF ENCOUNTERS

is whether he can't	SWHREKT, SWHREK/-NT, SWHRE/K-NT
is whether he could	SWHREKD
is whether he couldn't	SWHREKTD, SWHREKD/-NT, SWHRE/KUNT
is whether he ever	SWHREFR, SWHREVR
is whether he feels	SWHREFLS
is whether he felt	SWHREFLT
is whether he gets	SWHREGTS
is whether he goes	SWHREGS
is whether he got	SWHREGT
is whether he had	SWHRED
is whether he hadn't	SWHRED/-NT, SWHRE/H-NT
is whether he happened	SWHREPD
is whether he happens	SWHREPS
is whether he imagined	SWHREJD
is whether he imagines	SWHREJS
is whether he is	SWHRES
is whether he isn't	SWHRES/-NT, SWHRE/S-NT
is whether he knows	SWHRENS
is whether he lived	SWHREVD
is whether he lives	SWHREVS
is whether he means	SWHREMS
is whether he means to	SWHREMT
is whether he means to say	SWHREMTS
is whether he recalled	SWHRERLD
is whether he recalls	SWHRERLS
is whether he recollected	SWHRERKD
is whether he recollects	SWHRERKS
is whether he remembered	SWHRERMD
is whether he remembers	SWHRERMS
is whether he says	SWHRESZ
is whether he sees	SWHREZ
is whether he shall	SWHRERB
is whether he should	SWHRERBD
is whether he shouldn't	SWHRERBTD, SWHRERBD/-NT, SWHRE/SH-NT
is whether he thinks	SWHRENGS
is whether he thinks so	SWHRENGSZ
is whether he understands	SWHRENDZ
is whether he understood	SWHREND
is whether he wanted	SWHREPTD
is whether he wants	SWHREPTS
is whether he was	SWHREFS

is whether he wasn't	SWHREFT, SWHREFS/-NT, SWHRE/WUNT
is whether he will	SWHREL
is whether he would	SWHRELD
is whether he wouldn't	SWHRELTD, SWHRELD/-NT, SWHRE/WONT
is whether he would say	SWHRELDZ

is whether I

is whether I	SWHRI
is whether I am	SWHRIM
is whether I believe	SWHRIBL
is whether I believed	SWHRIBLD
is whether I can	SWHRIK
is whether I can't	SWHRIKT, SWHRIK/-NT, SWHRI/K-NT
is whether I could	SWHRIKD
is whether I couldn't	SWHRIKTD, SWHRIKD/-NT, SWHRI/KUNT
is whether I ever	SWHRIFR, SWHRIVR
is whether I feel	SWHRIFL
is whether I felt	SWHRIFLT
is whether I get	SWHRIGT
is whether I go	SWHRIG
is whether I had	SWHRID
is whether I hadn't	SWHRID/-NT, SWHRI/H-NT
is whether I happen	SWHRIP
is whether I happened	SWHRIPD
is whether I have	SWHRIF
is whether I have been	SWHRIFB
is whether I have had	SWHRIFD
is whether I have known	SWHRIFN
is whether I haven't	SWHRIFT, SWHRIF/-NT, SWHRI/V-NT
is whether I imagine	SWHRIJ
is whether I imagined	SWHRIJD
is whether I know	SWHRIN
is whether I live	SWHRIV
is whether I lived	SWHRIVD
is whether I mean	SWHR*IM
is whether I mean to	SWHRIMT
is whether I mean to say	SWHRIMTS
is whether I recall	SWHRIRL
is whether I recalled	SWHRIRLD
is whether I recollect	SWHRIRK
is whether I recollected	SWHRIRKD

BRIEF ENCOUNTERS

I

is whether I remember	SWHRIRM
is whether I remembered	SWHRIRMD
is whether I say	SWHRIS
is whether I see	SWHRIZ
is whether I shall	SWHRIRB
is whether I should	SWHRIRBD
is whether I shouldn't	SWHRIRBTD, SWHRIRBD/-NT, SWHRI/SH-NT
is whether I think	SWHRING
is whether I think so	SWHRINGS
is whether I understand	SWHRINDZ
is whether I understood	SWHRIND
is whether I want	SWHRIPT
is whether I wanted	SWHRIPTD
is whether I was	SWHRIFS
is whether I wasn't	SWHRIFS/-NT, SWHRI/WUNT
is whether I will	SWHRIL
is whether I would	SWHRILD
is whether I wouldn't	SWHRILTD, ,SWHRILD/-NT, SWHRI/WONT
is whether I would say	SWHRILDZ
is whether or not	SWHRORNT
is whether or not he	
is whether or not he	SWHROE
is whether or not he believed	SWHROEBLD
is whether or not he believes	SWHROEBLS
is whether or not he can	SWHROEK
is whether or not he can't	SWHROEKT, SWHROEK/-NT, SWHROE/K-NT
is whether or not he could	SWHROEKD
is whether or not he couldn't	SWHROEKTD, SWHROEKD/-NT, SWHROE/KUNT
is whether or not he ever	SWHROEFR, SWHROEVR
is whether or not he feels	SWHROEFLS
is whether or not he felt	SWHROEFLT
is whether or not he gets	SWHROEGTS
is whether or not he goes	SWHROEGS
is whether or not he got	SWHROEGT
is whether or not he had	SWHROED
is whether or not he hadn't	SWHROED/-NT, SWHROE/H-NT
is whether or not he happened	SWHROEPD
is whether or not he happens	SWHROEPS
is whether or not he imagined	SWHROEJD
is whether or not he imagines	SWHROEJS
is whether or not he is	SWHROES

is whether or not he isn't	SWHROES/-NT, SWHROE/S-NT
is whether or not he knows	SWHROENS
is whether or not he lived	SWHROEVD
is whether or not he lives	SWHROEVS
is whether or not he means	SWHROEMS
is whether or not he means to	SWHROEMT
is whether or not he means to say	SWHROEMTS
is whether or not he recalled	SWHROERLD
is whether or not he recalls	SWHROERLS
is whether or not he recollected	SWHROERKD
is whether or not he recollects	SWHROERKS
is whether or not he remembered	SWHROERMD
is whether or not he remembers	SWHROERMS
is whether or not he says	SWHROESZ
is whether or not he sees	SWHROEZ
is whether or not he shall	SWHROERB
is whether or not he should	SWHROERBD
is whether or not he shouldn't	SWHROERBTD, SWHROERBD/-NT, SWHROE/SH-NT
is whether or not he thinks	SWHROENGS
is whether or not he thinks so	SWHROENGSZ
is whether or not he understands	SWHROENDZ
is whether or not he understood	SWHROEND
is whether or not he wanted	SWHROEPTD
is whether or not he wants	SWHROEPTS
is whether or not he was	SWHROEFS
is whether or not he wasn't	SWHROEFT, SWHROEFS/-NT, SWHROE/WUNT
is whether or not he will	SWHROEL
is whether or not he would	SWHROELD
is whether or not he wouldn't	SWHROELTD, SWHROELD/-NT, SWHROE/WONT
is whether or not he would say	SWHROELDZ
is whether or not I	
is whether or not I	SWHROI
is whether or not I am	SWHROIM
is whether or not I believe	SWHROIBL
is whether or not I believed	SWHROIBLD
is whether or not I can	SWHROIK
is whether or not I can't	SWHROIKT, SWHROIK/-NT, SWHROI/K-NT
is whether or not I could	SWHROIKD
is whether or not I couldn't	SWHROIKTD, SWHROIKD/-NT, SWHROI/KUNT
is whether or not I ever	SWHROIFR, SWHROIVR

BRIEF ENCOUNTERS *I*

is whether or not I feel . . . . SWHROIFL
is whether or not I felt . . . . SWHROIFLT
is whether or not I get . . . . SWHROIGT
is whether or not I go . . . . SWHROIG
is whether or not I had . . . . SWHROID
is whether or not I hadn't . . . . SWHROID/-NT, SWHROI/H-NT
is whether or not I happen . . . . SWHROIP
is whether or not I happened . . . . SWHROIPD
is whether or not I have . . . . SWHROIF
is whether or not I have been . . . . SWHROIFB
is whether or not I have had . . . . SWHROIFD
is whether or not I have known . . . . SWHROIFN
is whether or not I haven't . . . . SWHROIFT, SWHROIF/-NT, SWHROI/V-NT
is whether or not I imagine . . . . SWHROIJ
is whether or not I imagined . . . . SWHROIJD
is whether or not I know . . . . SWHROIN
is whether or not I live . . . . SWHROIV
is whether or not I lived . . . . SWHROIVD
is whether or not I mean . . . . SWHRO*IM
is whether or not I mean to . . . . SWHROIMT
is whether or not I mean to say . . . . SWHROIMTS
is whether or not I recall . . . . SWHROIRL
is whether or not I recalled . . . . SWHROIRLD
is whether or not I recollect . . . . SWHROIRK
is whether or not I recollected . . . . SWHROIRKD
is whether or not I remember . . . . SWHROIRM
is whether or not I remembered . . . . SWHROIRMD
is whether or not I say . . . . SWHROIS
is whether or not I see . . . . SWHROIZ
is whether or not I shall . . . . SWHROIRB
is whether or not I should . . . . SWHROIRBD
is whether or not I shouldn't . . . . SWHROIRBTD, SWHROIRBD/-NT, SWHROI/SH-NT
is whether or not I think . . . . SWHROING
is whether or not I think so . . . . SWHROINGS
is whether or not I understand . . . . SWHROINDZ
is whether or not I understood . . . . SWHROIND
is whether or not I want . . . . SWHROIPT
is whether or not I wanted . . . . SWHROIPTD
is whether or not I was . . . . SWHROIFS
is whether or not I wasn't . . . . SWHROIFS/-NT, SWHROI/WUNT
is whether or not I will . . . . SWHROIL
is whether or not I would . . . . SWHROILD

BRIEF ENCOUNTERS

is whether or not I wouldn't . . . . SWHROILTD, SWHROILD/-NT, SWHROI/WONT
is whether or not I would say . . . . SWHROILDZ
is whether or not you
    is whether or not you . . . . SWHROU
    is whether or not you are . . . . SWHROUR
    is whether or not you aren't . . . . SWHROURNT, SWHROUR/-NT, SWHROU/R-NT
    is whether or not you believe . . . . SWHROUBL
    is whether or not you believed . . . . SWHROUBLD
    is whether or not you can . . . . SWHROUK
    is whether or not you can't . . . . SWHROUKT, SWHROUK/-NT, SWHROU/K-NT
    is whether or not you could . . . . SWHROU/KUNT
    is whether or not you couldn't . . . . . . SWHROUKTD, SWHROUKD/-NT, SWHROUKD
    is whether or not you ever . . . . SWHROUFR, SWHROUVR
    is whether or not you feel . . . . SWHROUFL
    is whether or not you felt . . . . SWHROUFLT
    is whether or not you get . . . . SWHROUGT
    is whether or not you go . . . . SWHROUG
    is whether or not you had . . . . SWHROUD
    is whether or not you hadn't . . . . SWHROUD/-NT, SWHROU/H-NT
    is whether or not you happen . . . . SWHROUP
    is whether or not you happened . . . . SWHROUPD
    is whether or not you have . . . . SWHROUF
    is whether or not you have been . . . . SWHROUFB
    is whether or not you have had . . . . SWHROUFD
    is whether or not you have known . . . . SWHROUFN
    is whether or not you haven't . . . . SWHROUFT, SWHROUF/-NT, SWHROU/V-NT
    is whether or not you imagine . . . . SWHROUJ
    is whether or not you imagined . . . . SWHROUJD
    is whether or not you know . . . . SWHROUN
    is whether or not you live . . . . SWHROUV
    is whether or not you lived . . . . SWHROUVD
    is whether or not you mean . . . . SWHROUM
    is whether or not you mean to . . . . SWHROUMT
    is whether or not you mean to say . . . . SWHROUMTS
    is whether or not you recall . . . . SWHROURL
    is whether or not you recalled . . . . SWHROURLD
    is whether or not you recollect . . . . SWHROURK
    is whether or not you recollected . . . . SWHROURKD
    is whether or not you remember . . . . SWHROURM
    is whether or not you remembered . . . . SWHROURMD

BRIEF ENCOUNTERS

is whether or not you say	SWHROUS
is whether or not you see	SWHROUZ
is whether or not you shall	SWHROURB
is whether or not you should	SWHROURBD
is whether or not you shouldn't	SWHROURBTD, SWHROURBD/-NT, SWHROU/SH-NT
is whether or not you think	SWHROUNG
is whether or not you think so	SWHROUNGS
is whether or not you understand	SWHROUNDZ
is whether or not you understood	SWHROUND
is whether or not you want	SWHROUPT
is whether or not you wanted	SWHROUPTD
is whether or not you were	SWHROURP
is whether or not you weren't	SWHROURPT, SWHROURP/-NT, SWHROU/W-RNT
is whether or not you will	SWHROUL
is whether or not you would	SWHROULD
is whether or not you wouldn't	SWHROULTD, SWHROULD/-NT, SWHROU/WONT
is whether or not you would say	SWHROULDZ

is whether you

is whether you	SWHRU
is whether you are	SWHRUR
is whether you aren't	SWHRURNT, SWHRUR/-NT, SWHRU/R-NT
is whether you believe	SWHRUBL
is whether you believed	SWHRUBLD
is whether you can	SWHRUK
is whether you can't	SWHRUKT, SWHRUK/-NT, SWHRU/K-NT
is whether you could	SWHRUKD
is whether you couldn't	SWHRUKTD, SWHRUKD/-NT, SWHRU/KUNT
is whether you ever	SWHRUFR, SWHRUVR
is whether you feel	SWHRUFL
is whether you felt	SWHRUFLT
is whether you get	SWHRUGT
is whether you go	SWHRUG
is whether you had	SWHRUD
is whether you hadn't	SWHRUD/-NT, SWHRU/H-NT
is whether you happen	SWHRUP
is whether you happened	SWHRUPD
is whether you have	SWHRUF
is whether you have been	SWHRUFB
is whether you have had	SWHRUFD

I

BRIEF ENCOUNTERS

is whether you have known	SWHRUFN
is whether you haven't	SWHRUFT, SWHRUF/-NT, SWHRU/V-NT
is whether you imagine	SWHRUJ
is whether you imagined	SWHRUJD
is whether you know	SWHRUN
is whether you live	SWHRUV
is whether you lived	SWHRUVD
is whether you mean	SWHRUM
is whether you mean to	SWHRUMT
is whether you mean to say	SWHRUMTS
is whether you recall	SWHRURL
is whether you recalled	SWHRURLD
is whether you recollect	SWHRURK
is whether you recollected	SWHRURKD
is whether you remember	SWHRURM
is whether you remembered	SWHRURMD
is whether you say	SWHRUS
is whether you see	SWHRUZ
is whether you shall	SWHRURB
is whether you should	SWHRURBD
is whether you shouldn't	SWHRURBTD, SWHRURBD/-NT, SWHRU/SH-NT
is whether you think	SWHRUNG
is whether you think so	SWHRUNGS
is whether you understand	SWHRUNDZ
is whether you understood	SWHRUND
is whether you want	SWHRUPT
is whether you wanted	SWHRUPTD
is whether you were	SWHRURP
is whether you weren't	SWHRURPT, SWHRURP/-NT, SWHRU/W-RNT
is whether you will	SWHRUL
is whether you would	SWHRULD
is whether you wouldn't	SWHRULTD, SWHRULD/-NT, SWHRU/WONT
is whether you would say	SWHRULDZ

it

it	IT
it be	T-B
it can	T-K
it can't	T-KT
it could	T-KD
it'd	ITD
it feel	T-FL

BRIEF ENCOUNTERS

it feeling	T-FLG
it feels	T-FLS
it felt	T-FLT
it go	T-G
it goes	T-GS
it get	T-GT
it gets	T-GTS
it had	T-D
it happen	T-P
it happened	T-PD
it happening	T-PG
it happens	T-PS
it have	T-F
it have been	T-FB
it have had	T-FD
it have happened	T-FPD
it is	T-S
it'll	ILT
it means	T-MS
it meant	T-MT
it recall	T-RL
it recalled	T-RLD
it recalling	T-RLG
it recalls	T-RLS
its	ITS
it's	*ITS
it says	T-SZ
it seemed to me	SMED
it seems to me	SME
it shall	T-RB
it should	T-RBD
it was	T-FS
it were	T-RP
it weren't	T-RPT
it will	T-L
it would	T-LD
it wouldn't	T-LTD
item	TUM
itinerary	TRAIR
itself	ISZ

it would

it would	T-LD
it would be	TWOUB
it would have	TWOUF
it would have been	TWOUFB

I

it would have had	TWOUFD
it would seem to me	T−LD/SME

I wouldn't

I wouldn't	YAO, ILTD
I wouldn't believe	YAOBL
I wouldn't believe so	YAOBLS
I wouldn't do	YAOD
I wouldn't feel	YAOFL
I wouldn't get	YAOGT
I wouldn't go	YAOG
I wouldn't have	YAOF
I wouldn't have been	YAOFB
I wouldn't have had	YAOFD
I wouldn't have known	YAOFN
I wouldn't imagine	YAOJ
I wouldn't know	YAON
I wouldn't live	YAOV
I wouldn't mean	YAOM
I wouldn't mean to	YAOMT
I wouldn't mean to say	YAOMTS
I wouldn't recall	YAORL
I wouldn't recollect	YAORK
I wouldn't remember	YAORM
I wouldn't say	YAOS
I wouldn't see	YAOZ, Y*AOS
I wouldn't think	YAONG
I wouldn't think so	YAONGS
I wouldn't understand	YAONDZ
I wouldn't want	YAOPT

J

jabber
- jabber . . . JARB
- jabbers . . . JARBS
- jabbering . . . JARB/-G
- jabbered . . . JARBD

jackal . . . JAKL
jacket . . . JAKT
Jacksonville . . . JAVL
jailer . . . JAIRL
jailhouse . . . JHOUS

Jamaica
- Jamaica . . . JAEK
- Jamaican . . . JAEN
- Jamaicans . . . JAENZ

janitor . . . JANT
January . . . JAN
Japan . . . JAP
Japanese . . . JAPS, JAOEPZ
jargon . . . JAURG
jaundice . . . JAUN
jaundiced . . . JAUND
jealous . . . J-L
jealousy . . . J-LS

jeopardize
- jeopardize . . . JEPD
- jeopardizes . . . JEFS
- jeopardizing . . . JEFG
- jeopardized . . . JEFD

jeopardy . . . JEP
Jerusalem . . . JAOUM

jest
- jest . . . J*ES
- jests . . . JEFTS, J*ESZ
- jesting . . . JEFGT
- jested . . . JEFTD

jettison
- jettison . . . JOIT
- jettisons . . . JOITS
- jettisoning . . . JOIGT
- jettisoned . . . JOITD

jewel
- jewel . . . JAOUL

jeweler	J-RL
jewelry	JAOURL
Jewish	JAOURB

jinx
jinx	JINGS
jinxes	JINGSZ
jinxing	JINGS/-G
jinxed	JINGS/-D, JINGD

jobless	JOBLS
jogger	JORG
Johannesburg	JANS/BURG
joinder	JO*IND, JO*IRND

joint
jointly	JOINLT, JOINL
joint tenancy	JAENS
joint tenant	JAENT
joint venture	JOIV

joker	JOERK
Jordan	JORD
Jordanian	JORND
Joseph	JOEF

journal
journal	JOURL, JOURNL
journalism	JOURM
journalist	JOURT
journalistic	JOURK
journalistically	JAOERK, JOURK/LI

journey
journey	JOIRN
journeys	JOIRNS
journeying	JOIRNG
journeyed	JOIRND

jovial
jovial	JOEVL
joviality	JOEVLT
jovially	JAOEVL

joy
joyful	JOIF
joyfully	JOIFL
joyfulness	JOIFNS
joyless	JOIL

Jr.	J*R
Juan	WAUN
jubilance	JAOUBLS
jubilancy	JAOUBLSZ

BRIEF ENCOUNTERS — J

jubilant	JAOUBLT
jubilantly	JAOUBL
jubilee	JAOUB
judgment	JUMT
judicial	JURBL
judicial district	JURBLD, J-D, JIK, JUK
judiciary	JAIR
judicious	JURB
juggle	
juggle	JULG
juggles	JULGZ
juggling	JULG/-G
juggled	JULGD
juggler	JURLG
jugular	JARL, JAUR
jugular vein	JAUV
July	JUL
jump	
jump	JUM
jumps	JUMS
jumping	JUMG
jumped	JUMD
junction	JUNGS
June	JUN
jungle	JUNL
junior	J-R
junior high school	JAOL
junket	JUNGT
Jupiter	JAOUPT
Jurassic	JARK
jurat	JAT
jurisdiction	JURD
jurisdictional	JURLD
jurisprudence	JURP
jurisprudent	JURPT
jurisprudential	JURPLT
jurist	JIRT
juror	JAOR
jury	
jury	JUR
jury box	JBOX
jury instruction	JURK
jury nullification	JULGS
jury room	JURM
jury selection	JURGS

jury trial . . . . JURT
just
   just a bit . . . . JIBT
   just about . . . . JUB
   just about the . . . . JUBT
   just a minute . . . . JIMT, JAMT
   just a moment . . . . JOMT
   just a second . . . . JEK
   just cause . . . . JAUZ
justice
   justice . . . . JUS
   justice department . . . . J–PT
   justice of the peace . . . . J–P
justifiable . . . . JUBL
justifiably . . . . JAOEBL
justification . . . . JUFGS, JUFX
justify
   justify . . . . JUF
   justifies . . . . JUFS
   justifying . . . . JUFG
   justified . . . . JUFD
juvenile
   juvenile . . . . JUFL, JUVL
   juvenile delinquent . . . . JUFLD, JUVLD
   juvenile hall . . . . JAUL
juxtapose
   juxtapose . . . . JUP
   juxtaposes . . . . JUPS
   juxtaposing . . . . JUPG
   juxtaposed . . . . JUPD
juxtaposition . . . . JUPGS

K

Kaiser	KAOIZ
kangaroo	GRAO
kangaroo court	GRAORT
Kansas	K*S
kaput	KPUT
karat	KA*ERT
karate	KRAUT
keep	
keep	KAOEP
keeps	KAOEPS
keeping	KAOEPG
kept	KEPT
keeper	KERP, KAOERP
kelvin	KEVNL
kennel	KENL
Kentucky	KAO*I
kernel	KERNL
kerosine	KERZ
ketchup	KEFP
kettle	KELT
keyboard	KAOEB
keynote	
keynote	KOENT, KAOET
keynote address	KOENTD, KAOETD
keynoter	KOERNT
keynote speaker	KAOERNT
keynote speech	KOENTS
kg	K-G
kHz	K-Z, KH*ERZ
kibbutz	KBUTS
kidder	KIRD
kidnap	
kidnap	KIP
kidnaps	KIPS
kidnapping	KIPG
kidnapped	KIPD
kidnapper	KIRP
kidney	KAOEND
killer	KIRL
kilo	
kilo	KLOE
kilogram	K-LG

kilohertz . . . . KHERZ
kilometer . . . . K–M
kilos . . . . KLOEZ
kind
    kindly . . . . KAOINLD, KAOINL
    kindness . . . . KAOINS
    kind of . . . . KAOIF
    kinds of . . . . KAOIFS
    kinds of the . . . . KAOIFTS
kindergarten . . . . KIND
kindergartens . . . . KIND/–S
kindergartner . . . . KIRND
kindle
    kindle . . . . KINL
    kindles . . . . KINLS
    kindling . . . . KINLG
    kindled . . . . KINLD
kingdom . . . . KINGD
kiss
    kiss . . . . KISZ
    kisses . . . . KIFS
    kissing . . . . KIFG
    kissed . . . . KIFD
kitchen . . . . KIFP
kitchen door . . . . KIFPD
Kleenex . . . . KLAOEX
knave . . . . NAEV
knead
    knead . . . . NAED
    kneads . . . . NAEDZ
    kneading . . . . NAEGD
    kneaded . . . . NAED/–D
knee
    knee . . . . NAOE
    knees . . . . NAOEZ
    kneeing . . . . NAOE/–G
    kneed . . . . NAOE/–D
kneel
    kneel . . . . NAOEL
    kneels . . . . NAOELS
    kneeling . . . . NAOELG
    knelt / kneeled . . . . NELT / NAOEL/–D
knit
    knit . . . . N*IT
    knits . . . . NITS

BRIEF ENCOUNTERS K

knitting . . . . NIGT
knit / knitted . . . . N*IT / NITD
knot
    knot. . . . . NO*T
    knots. . . . . NOTS
    knotting. . . . . NOGT
    knotted . . . . NOTD
knotty . . . . NOT/TI
know
    know. . . . . NOE
    knows . . . . NOES
    knowing. . . . . NOEG
    knew. . . . . NAOU
    known. . . . . NOEN
know
    knowingly. . . . . NOELG
    knowledge . . . . NOJ
    knowledgeable. . . . . N–BL, JOBL
knuckle
    knuckle . . . . NUKL
    knuckles. . . . . NUKLS
    knuckling . . . . NUKL/-G
    knuckled . . . . NUKLD
koala. . . . . KWAUL
Koran . . . . KRAN
Korea
    Korea. . . . . KRAE
    Korean. . . . . KRA*EN
    Koreans . . . . KRAENZ
kosher . . . . KOERB
Ku Klux Klan. . . . . KLAOUK
Kuwait . . . . KWUT

L

L.A.
    L.A. .... LA
    L.A.P.D. .... LAPD
    L.A. Police Department .... LAPT

labor
    labor .... LAIB
    labors .... LAIBS
    laboring .... LAIB/-G
    labored .... LAIBD

labor
    laboratory .... LABT
    laborer .... LAIRB
    laborious .... LOUBS, LAIB/ROUS

labyrinth .... R*INT

lacerate
    lacerate .... LAFRT
    lacerates .... LAFRTS
    lacerating .... LAFRGT
    lacerated .... LAFRTD

laceration .... LARGS
laches .... LAFPS

lack
    lacking in foundation .... LOUNGS/-G
    lack of foundation .... LOUNGS
    lacks foundation .... LOUNGSZ

ladder .... LAERD

lade
    lade .... LA*ID
    lades .... LA*IDZ
    lading .... LA*IGD
    laded .... LA*ID/-D
    laden / laded .... LAIND / LA*ID/-D

ladies and gentlemen .... LAIJ
ladies and gentlemen of the jury .... LAIRJ
lady .... LAED
Lafayette .... LAFT
lager .... LARG
lagers .... LARG/-S
lagoon .... GLAON

lament
    lament .... LAMT
    laments .... LAMTS

BRIEF ENCOUNTERS — L

lamenting	LAMGT, LAMG
lamented	LAMTD
lamentation	LAMGTS, LEMGS
laminate	
laminate	LAIMT
laminates	LAIMTS
laminating	LAIMGT, LAIMG
laminated	LAIMTD
lamination	LAMGS, LAIMGS
landfill	LAFN
landlord	LAORD
landscape	
landscape	SKLAIP
landscapes	SKLAIPS
landscaping	SKLAIPG
landscaped	SKLAIPD
landscaper	SKLAIRP
language	LANG
larceny	LARS
large print	LIRNT
largess	LARGZ, LARJS
larynx	LAIRNGS
laser	LAIRZ
last will and testament	WA*S
Las Vegas	L–V
late	
lately	LAILT
later	LAIRT
later than	LAIRNT
later than the	LAERNT, LAIRNTD
later than these	LAIRNZ
latest	LAITS
latent	
latent	LAENT
latent fingerprint	LAIF
latent print	LAIP
lateral	LARL
laterally	LAERL
Latin	
Latin	LAN
Latin America	LERK
Latin American	LAERN
Latino	LAT
latitude	LATD
latrine	TRAOEN

L   BRIEF ENCOUNTERS

latter	LART
laudable	LAUBL
laughable	LAFBL
laughter	LAFT
launch	
launch	LAUFP
launches	LAUFPS
launching	LAUFPG
launched	LAUFPD
launder	
launder	LAUND
launders	LAUNDZ
laundering	LAUNGD
laundered	LAUND/-D
laundry	LAURND
lavatory	LAVT
lavender	LAVN
law	
law and order	LAURD
law clerk	LAURK
law enforcement	LAUMT
law enforcement officer	LAIFR
law firm	LIRM
lawful	LAUF
lawfully	LAUFL
lawless	LAUL
lawlessness	LAUNS
lawmaker	LAURM
law officer	LAUFR
law of the	LAUFT
law of the land	LAUFLD
law of these	LAUFZ
law of those	LAUFS
law school	LAOL
Law School	LAO*L
law schools	LAOLZ
lawsuit	LAUT
lawyer	LAUR
lay	
lay	LAI
lays	LAI/-S
laying	LAIG
laid	LAID
laze	
laze	LAEZ

BRIEF ENCOUNTERS — L

lazes	LAEFS
lazing	LAEFG
lazed	LAEFD
lazier	LAERZ
lazy	LAIZ

lead
lead	LAOED
leads	LAOEDZ
leading	LAOEGD
led	LED

leach	LA*EFP

lead
leader	LERD, LAOERD
leadership	LERP
leading and suggestive	LUG
leading question	L–K
leaflet	LAOEFT

leap
leap	LAOEP
leaps	LAOEPS
leaping	LAOEPG
leaped / leapt	LAOEPD / LAEPT

learning disability	LABLT
learning disabled	LABL, LABLD
leather	LEFR

leave
leave	LAOEV
leaves	LAOEVS
leaving	LAOEVG
left	LEFT

leave to amend	LAMD, LEMD
Lebanese	LEBZ
Lebanon	LEB

lecture
lecture	LURKT
lectures	LURKTS
lecturing	LURKT/–G, LURG
lectured	LURKTD

left
left-hand	LEFD
left-handed	LEFTD
left-hand lane	L–NL
left-hand side	L–NDZ
left-hand turn	L–NT
left lane	L–L

left leg	LEFLG
left side	L-DZ
left turn	-LT
legacy	LEGZ

legal
    legal . . . . LEL
    legal blindness . . . . LEBS
    legalese . . . . LAOEZ
    legality . . . . LELT
    legalization . . . . LOIFGS
    legally . . . . LAEL
    legally blind . . . . LEBD, LELD

legalize
    legalize . . . . LOIZ
    legalizes . . . . LOIFS
    legalizing . . . . LOIFG
    legalized . . . . LOIFD

legend	LEJD
legibility	LEBLT
legible	LEBL
legion	LAO*EJ

legislate
    legislate . . . . LAEG
    legislates . . . . LAEGZ
    legislating . . . . LAEG/-G
    legislated . . . . LAEGD

legislation	LAEGS
legislative	LAEV
legislatively	LAEVL
legislator	LOR
legislators	LORZ
legislature	LUR
legitimacy	JITS
legitimate	JIT
legitimately	JILT
legitimization	J-MGS

legitimize
    legitimize . . . . J-MT, JIT/MAOIZ
    legitimizes . . . . J-MTS, JIT/MAOIFS
    legitimizing . . . . J-MGT, J-MG, JIT/MAOIFG
    legitimized . . . . J-MTD, JIT/MAOIFD

leisure	LERB
leisurely	LERBL
lemon	LEM

BRIEF ENCOUNTERS   **L**

```
lend
    lend  . . . . . . . . . . . . . . . . . . . . . . . . . . . . . . . . . . . . . . . . . LEND
    lends  . . . . . . . . . . . . . . . . . . . . . . . . . . . . . . . . . . . . . . . LENDZ
    lending . . . . . . . . . . . . . . . . . . . . . . . . . . . . . . . . . . . . . . LENGD
    lent  . . . . . . . . . . . . . . . . . . . . . . . . . . . . . . . . . . . . . . . . . LENT
lender . . . . . . . . . . . . . . . . . . . . . . . . . . . . . . . . . . . . . . . . . . . L*ERND
length . . . . . . . . . . . . . . . . . . . . . . . . . . . . . . . . . . . . . . . . . . . . LENG
lengthier  . . . . . . . . . . . . . . . . . . . . . . . . . . . . . . . . . L*ERNG, LERNT
leniency . . . . . . . . . . . . . . . . . . . . . . . . . . . . . . . . . . . . . . . LAOENTS
lenient  . . . . . . . . . . . . . . . . . . . . . . . . . . . . . . . . . . . . . . . . LAOENT
leniently . . . . . . . . . . . . . . . . . . . . . . . . . . . . . . . . . . . . . . LAOENLT
lentil . . . . . . . . . . . . . . . . . . . . . . . . . . . . . . . . . . . . . . . . . . . . LENL
leopard . . . . . . . . . . . . . . . . . . . . . . . . . . . . . . . . . . . . . . . . . . LEPD
lessen
    lessen  . . . . . . . . . . . . . . . . . . . . . . . . . . . . . . . . . . L-FN, L*EN
    lessens . . . . . . . . . . . . . . . . . . . . . . . . . . . . . . . . . L-FNS, L*ENS
    lessening . . . . . . . . . . . . . . . . . . . . . . . . . . . . . . . L-FNG, L*ENG
    lessened  . . . . . . . . . . . . . . . . . . . . . . . . . . . . . . . L-FND, L*END
lesson . . . . . . . . . . . . . . . . . . . . . . . . . . . . . . . . . . . . . . . . . . . LEFN
*less than* . . . . . . . . . . . . . . . . . . . . . . . . . . . . . . . . . . . . . . . . . LEN
*less than or equal to* . . . . . . . . . . . . . . . . . . . . . . . . . . . . . . . LAOEKL
let
    let . . . . . . . . . . . . . . . . . . . . . . . . . . . . . . . . . . . . . . . . . . . . LET
    lets . . . . . . . . . . . . . . . . . . . . . . . . . . . . . . . . . . . . . . . . . . LETS
    letting . . . . . . . . . . . . . . . . . . . . . . . . . . . . . . . . . . . . . . . . LEGT
    let . . . . . . . . . . . . . . . . . . . . . . . . . . . . . . . . . . . . . . . . . . . . LET
let
    *let me ask you that*  . . . . . . . . . . . . . . . . . . . . . . . . . . . . . . SKLAT
    *let me ask you this*  . . . . . . . . . . . . . . . . . . . . . . . . . . . . . . SKLIS
    *let's* . . . . . . . . . . . . . . . . . . . . . . . . . . . . . . . . . . . . . . . . L*ETS
    *let the record further reflect* . . . . . . . . . . . . . . . . . . . . . . . . LOFRT
    *let the record reflect* . . . . . . . . . . . . . . . . . . . . . . . . . . . . . . LORT
    *let the record show* . . . . . . . . . . . . . . . . . . . . . . . . . . . . . . LORS
    *let the record so reflect* . . . . . . . . . . . . . . . . . . . . . . . . . . . LORTS
    *let us know*  . . . . . . . . . . . . . . . . . . . . . . . . . . . . . . . . . . . . LUN
lethal . . . . . . . . . . . . . . . . . . . . . . . . . . . . . . . . . . . . . . . . . . LAO*ET
lethally . . . . . . . . . . . . . . . . . . . . . . . . . . . . . . . . . . . . . . . . LAO*ELT
lethargic . . . . . . . . . . . . . . . . . . . . . . . . . . . . . . . . . . . . . . . THARJ
lethargy . . . . . . . . . . . . . . . . . . . . . . . . . . . . . . . . . . . . . . . . THERJ
letter
    letter . . . . . . . . . . . . . . . . . . . . . . . . . . . . . . . . . . . . . . . . . . LERT
    *letter of credit*  . . . . . . . . . . . . . . . . . . . . . . . . . . . . . . . . . LERKD
    *letter of the law*  . . . . . . . . . . . . . . . . . . . . . . . . . . . . . . . . . LERL
    *letters of credit*  . . . . . . . . . . . . . . . . . . . . . . . . . . . . . . . LERKDZ
leukemia . . . . . . . . . . . . . . . . . . . . . . . . . . . . . . . . . . . . . . . . LOUM
```

L BRIEF ENCOUNTERS

levity	LEVT
liability	LAOIBLT
liable	LAOIBL
libel	LAOIB
liberal	
liberal	LIBL
liberalism	LIFM
liberally	LAOEBL
liberalize	
liberalize	LIBZ
liberalizes	LIFS, LIBSZ
liberalizing	LIFG
liberalized	LIFD
liberate	
liberate	LIB
liberates	LIBS
liberating	LIB/-G
liberated	LIBD
liberation	LIBGS
Liberia	LAOER
Liberian	LAOERN
liberty	LIBT
librarian	LAIRN
library	LAOIRB
license	
license	LINS
licensed in	LIND
license plate	L-P
lie	
lie	LAOI
lies	LAOIZ
lying	LAOIG
lay	LAI
lain	LAIN
Liechtenstein	LAOIFP
lie detector	LAOIRK
lie detector test	LAOIRKT
lieu of	
lieu of the	LAOUFT
lieu of them	LAOUFM
lieu of these	LAOUFZ
lieu of those	LAOUFS
lieutenant	LAOUNT
lieutenant general	LAOUNGT

BRIEF ENCOUNTERS   L

life
    lifeboat .... LAOIFBT
    lifeguard .... LAOIFGD
    life jacket .... LAOIFKT
    lifeless .... LAOIFL
    lifelike .... FLAOIK
    lifelong .... FLONG
    lifestyle .... LAOIFLT
    lifetime .... LAOIFM
ligament .... LIGT
light
    light .... LAOIT
    lights .... LAOITS
    lighting .... LAOIGT
    lighted / lit .... LAOITD / LIT
light
    lighter .... LAOIRT
    light-hearted .... LARTD
    light-heartedly .... LARLTD
    lightly .... LAOILT
    lightning .... LOINGT, LOING
    light of the .... LAOIFT
    light of these .... LAOIFZ
lighten
    lighten .... LAOINT
    lightens .... LAOINTS
    lightening .... LAOINGT
    lightened .... LAOINTD
likely .... LAOIL
likewise .... LOIS
liminie .... LAOEM
limit
    limit .... LIMT
    limits .... LIMTS
    limiting .... LIMGT
    limited .... LIMTD
limitation .... LIMGTS
limousine .... ZAOEN
line up
    line up .... LAOIP
    lines up .... LAOIPS
    lining up .... LAOIPG
    lined up .... LAOIPD
lineup .... LOIP, LAO*IP
line up the .... LAOIPT

linger
    linger . . . . LIRNG
    lingers . . . . LIRNGS
    lingering . . . . LIRNG/-G
    lingered . . . . LIRNGD
linguist . . . . LING
linguistic . . . . LINGT
linoleum . . . . LINL
lintel . . . . LINLT
lipid . . . . PID
lipoid . . . . PO*ID
lipread . . . . LIRP
lipreading . . . . LIRPG
liqueur . . . . LIRK
liqueurs . . . . LIRKZ
liquid . . . . KLID
liquidate
    liquidate . . . . KLAE
    liquidates . . . . KLAES
    liquidating . . . . KLAEG
    liquidated . . . . KLAED
liquidation . . . . KLA*EGS, KLAIX
liquor
    liquor . . . . LIR
    liquors . . . . LIRZ
    liquor store . . . . LIRS
    liquor stores . . . . LIRSZ
list
    list . . . . L-FT
    lists . . . . L-FTS
    listing . . . . L-FGT, L-FG
    listed . . . . L-FTD
listen
    listen . . . . L-N
    listens . . . . L-NS
    listening . . . . L-NG
    listened . . . . L-N/-D
listener . . . . L-RN
listings . . . . L-FGS
liter . . . . LAOERT
literacy . . . . LITS, LAOETS
literal . . . . LIRL
literally . . . . LIRLT, LAOERL
literate . . . . LURT
literature . . . . LIRT

BRIEF ENCOUNTERS L

lithium	L*IT
litigate	
litigate	LIG
litigates	LIGZ
litigating	LIG/-G
litigated	LIGD
litigation	LIGS
little	LIL
little bit	LILT
livelihood	LAOD
lively	LAOIVL
livid	LOIVD
living room	LIVM
lobby	
lobby	LOIB
lobbies	LOIBS
lobbying	LOIB/-G
lobbied	LOIBD
lobbyer	LOIRB, LOIB/ER
lobbyist	LOIBT
local	
local	LOL, LOEKL
locale	LO*L
locality	LOLT
localization	LOLGS
locally	LOEL, LOIKL
locate	
locate	LOEKT, LOEK
locates	LOEKTS, LOEKZ
locating	LOEKT/-G, LOEK/-G
located	LOEKTD, LOEKD
location	LOEX
locational	LOEXL
locker	LORK
locker room	LORM
locomotive	LOEVK
lodger	LORJ
logger	LORG
logic	
logic	L-J
logical	LAJ
logically	LOIJ
logistic	L-JT
logo	LOEG
logos	LOEGZ

loiter
- loiter . . . LOIT
- loiters . . . LOITS
- loitering . . . LOIGT
- loitered . . . LOITD

loiterer . . . LOIRT
London . . . LOND
lone
- lone . . . LON, LO*EN
- lonely . . . LOENL
- loner . . . LORN, LO*ERN

long
- *long distance* . . . L-D
- longer . . . LORNG
- longest . . . LONGS
- longevity . . . JEVT
- longitude . . . LONT
- longitudinal . . . LONL
- long-term . . . LERM
- *long time* . . . LONGT

look at
- *look at* . . . LAOKT
- *looks at* . . . LAOKTS
- *looking at* . . . LAOKT/-G
- *looked at* . . . LAOKTD

looker . . . LAORK
looking . . . LAOG
look like
- *look like* . . . KLAOIK
- *looks like* . . . KLAOIKS
- *looking like* . . . KLAOIK/-G, KLAOIG
- *looked like* . . . KLAOIKD

look out
- *look out* . . . LOUT
- *looks out* . . . LOUTS
- *looking out* . . . LOUGT
- *looked out* . . . LOUTD

loose
- loose . . . LAOS
- looser . . . LAORS
- loosely . . . LAOLS

looter . . . LAORT
lordship . . . LORP
Los Angeles . . . LOGS
Los Angeles Police Department . . . LEPT

BRIEF ENCOUNTERS   **L**

lose
- lose .... LAOZ
- loses .... LAOSZ
- losing .... LAOZ/-G, LAOGZ, LAOFG
- lost .... LO*S

loser .... LAORZ
loss of vision .... LOVGS
lot(s) of
- *lot of* .... LOF
- *lots of* .... LOFS
- *lots of them* .... LOFM
- *lots of these* .... LOFZ
- *lots of those* .... LOEFS

lottery .... LOERT
lotto .... LOET
loud
- louder .... LOURD
- *louder than* .... LOURN, LOURND
- *louder than the* .... LOURNT, LOURNTD
- *louder than these* .... LOURNZ
- *louder than those* .... LOURNS
- loudest .... LOUDZ
- loudly .... LOULD

Louisiana .... LA*
Louisville .... LAOUV
lounge
- lounge .... LOUJ, LOUNG
- lounges .... LOUJS, LOUNGZ
- lounging .... LOUJ/-G, LOUNG/-G
- lounged .... LOUJD, LOUNGD

lounger .... LOURJ
lovable .... LOVBL
lovely .... LOVL
lower
- lower .... LOER
- lowers .... LOERS
- lowering .... LOERG
- lowered .... LOERD

lower than
- *lower than* .... LOERN
- *lower than the* .... LOERNT
- *lower than these* .... LOERNZ
- *lower than those* .... LOERNS

low-fat .... LOEFT
loyalist .... LOIFT

loyalty	LOILT
lozenge	LOZ
lubricant	LUBT
lubricate	
lubricate	LAOUBT
lubricates	LAOUBTS
lubricating	LAOUBT/-G
lubricated	LAOUBTD
lubrication	LAOUX
lucency	LAOUSZ
lucent	LAOUS
lucently	LAOULS
lucid	
lucid	LAOUFD
lucidity	LAOUFTD, LAOUTD
lucidly	LAOUFLD
luck	
luckily	LUKL
luckless	LUKLS
lucky	L*UK, KLAOEK
lucrative	LAOUKT
lucratively	LAOUL
ludicrous	LUD
luggage	LAUG
lumbar	L*UM, L*UB
lunacy	LAOUNZ
lunar	LAOURN
lunatic	LAOUNG
lunch	
lunch	LUFP
lunches	LUFPS
lunching	LUFPG
lunched	LUFPD
lunchroom	LUFM, LURM
lunchtime	LUFPT
lunge	
lunge	LUJ
lunges	LUJS
lunging	LUJ/-G
lunged	LUJD
lurid	LURD
luscious	
luscious	LURBS
lusciously	LURBL
lusciousness	LURNS, L*UNS

Luxembourg	LOURG
luxurious	LOURS, LUX/ROUS
luxury	LUX
lymph	YIFRP
lynch	
lynch	LIFP
lynches	LIFPS
lynching	LIFPG
lynched	LIFPD
lyric	L*IRK, LAOERK
lyrical	L*IRL

M

macabre	KMAB, MA/KAB
machine	
machine	M–RB
machine gun	M–RBG
machine guns	M–RBGZ
machinery	M–RN
machinist	MIFT, M–RBT
magnanimity	MAG/NIMT
magnet	MAEGT
magnetic	MAEKT, MAG/NEK
magnification	MAFGS
magnificence	SMAGS
magnificent	SMAG, SMAGT
magnificently	SMALG
magnitude	MAOUGD
mahogany	MOG/N*I
maiden	MA*END
Maine	M*E
mainland	MAINLD
maintain	
maintain	MAEN
maintains	MAENS
maintaining	MAENG
maintained	MAEND
maintenance	MAENT
majesty	MAJT
major	MAIJ
majority	MAIJT, JOIRT
make	
make	MAIK
makes	MAIKS
making	MAIK/–G, MAIG
made	MAED
make-up	MAUP
maladjusted	MAUFD
maladjustment	MAUFMT
Malasia	
Malaysia	MALS
Malaysian	MANZ
Malaysians	MANSZ
male Hispanic	MAIP
malevolence	MEVNS, MEFNS

BRIEF ENCOUNTERS — M

malevolent	MEVNT, MEFNT
malevolently	MEVL
malfeasance	MAFZ, MAL/FAOEZ
malice	LIS
malice aforethought	M-FT
malicious	LIRB
maliciously	LIRBL
malignancy	MALG
malignant	MALGT

malpractice
- malpractice . . . M-P
- ***malpractice insurance*** . . . M-PS
- ***malpractice lawsuit*** . . . M-PT

mammoth	MA*MT
man	MAN

manage
- manage . . . MANG
- manages . . . MANGZ
- managing . . . MANG/-G
- managed . . . MANGD

manage
- management . . . M-GT
- manager . . . M-G
- managerial . . . M-LG

mandamus	MAMD, MAND/MUS

mandate
- mandate . . . MA*ENT
- mandates . . . MAENTS
- mandating . . . MAENGT
- mandated . . . MAENTD

mandatory	MARND
mandible	MABL

maneuver
- maneuver . . . MAOUVR
- maneuvers . . . MAOUVRS
- maneuvering . . . MAOUVRG
- maneuvered . . . MAOUVRD

maneuverability	MAOUVRLT
maneuverable	MAOUVRL
Manhattan	MANT
maniac	MAINK
manic	MANK

manifest
- manifest . . . MEFT
- manifests . . . MEFTS

manifesting	MEFGT
manifested	MEFTD
manifestation	MEFGS

manipulate
manipulate	MIP
manipulates	MIPS
manipulating	MIPG
manipulated	MIPD

manipulation	MIPGS
manipulative	MIVP
manipulator	M*IRP
mannequin	KWIN, MAN/KIN
mannequins	KWIN/-S, MAN/KINS
manner	MARN
mannerly	MARNL
manor	MAORN
man's	MANS
manslaughter	MALT
manual	MANL
manually	MAENL

manufacture
manufacture	M-FR
manufactures	M-FRS
manufacturing	M-FRG
manufactured	M-FRD

manufacturer	MR-FR
manure	MAOUR
manuscript	SKRIMT

many
many	M-
many of the	M-VT
many of them	M-VM
many of these	M-FZ
many of those	M-FS

march
march	MAUFP
marches	MAUFPS
marching	MAUFPG
marched	MAUFPD

March	MAR
margarita	MAURGT
margin	MARJ
marginal	M-RL, MAURJ
marijuana	MAIRN
marina	RAOEN/NA

marine
- marine .... RAOEN
- Marine .... RAO*EN
- *Marine Corps* .... RAOENG
- Marines .... RAOENS

marital .... MAERT, MAERLT
maritime .... MAERMT
marked for identification .... MOID
market
- market .... MAERK
- markets .... MAERKS
- marketing .... MAERK/-G
- marketed .... MAERKD

marketplace .... MAERP
marriage .... MAERJ, MAIRJ
marry
- marry .... MAER
- marries .... MAERS
- marrying .... MAERG
- married .... MAERD

marshal .... MAURBL
martial .... MARL
martial law .... MA*URL
marvel
- marvel .... MAVRL
- marvels .... MAFRLZ
- marveling .... MAFRLG
- marveled .... MAFRLD

marvelous .... MAFRLS, MAVRLS
Maryland .... M*D
mascot .... SKWOT
masculine .... SKLIN
masculinity .... SKLINT
mask
- mask .... MAF, MAFK
- masks .... MAFS, MAFKS
- masking .... MAFG
- masked .... MAFD, MAFKD

masquerade
- masquerade .... SKRAED
- masquerades .... SKRAEDZ
- masquerading .... SKRAEGD, SKRAEG
- masqueraded .... SKRAED/-D

Massachusetts .... MA*

M

massacre
- massacre . . . . SKER, MAS/KER
- massacres . . . . SKERS, MAS/KERS
- massacring . . . . SKERG, MAS/KERG
- massacred . . . . SKERD, MAS/KERD

massage
- massage . . . . MAUJ
- massages . . . . MAUJS
- massaging . . . . MAUJ/-G
- massaged . . . . MAUJD

massive
- massive . . . . MAV
- massively . . . . MAVL
- massiveness . . . . MAVNS

mastectomy . . . . MEKT

master
- master . . . . MAFR
- masters . . . . MAFRS
- mastering . . . . MAFRG
- mastered . . . . MAFRD

master
- ***master bedroom*** . . . . MARM
- masterful . . . . MAFRL
- masterfully . . . . MAOEFRL
- masterpiece . . . . MAFRP

masturbate
- masturbate . . . . MAURB, MURBT
- masturbates . . . . MAURBS, MURBTS
- masturbating . . . . MAURBG, MURBGT
- masturbated . . . . MAURBD, MURBTD

masturbation . . . . MAURBGS, MURBGS

material
- material . . . . TERL
- materiality . . . . TERLT
- materialization . . . . TERLGS

maternal . . . . MAERNL

mathematic
- mathematical . . . . MA*LT, MA*T/KAL
- mathematically . . . . MA*ELT, MA*T/KLI
- mathematics . . . . MA*T/MA*T

matter
- matter . . . . MART
- matters . . . . MARTS
- mattering . . . . MARGT
- mattered . . . . MARTD

BRIEF ENCOUNTERS M

matter
    matter of fact . . . . MAFT
    matter-of-factly . . . . MAFLT, MAEFL
    matter-of-factness . . . . MAFNS, MAEFNS
    matters of fact . . . . MAFTS
mature
    mature . . . . MAUR
    matures . . . . MAURS
    maturing . . . . MAURG
    matured . . . . MAURD
maturely . . . . MAURL
matureness . . . . MAURNS
maturity . . . . MAURT
mausoleum . . . . MAUM
maverick . . . . MAVRK
maximum . . . . MAX
may
    may . . . . MAI
    May . . . . MA*I
    may feel . . . . MAIFL
    may have . . . . MAIF
    may have been . . . . MAIFB
    may have had . . . . MAIFD
    may have the . . . . MAIFT
    may I approach . . . . MOEFP
    may I approach the bench . . . . MOEFP/BEFP
    may I approach the witness . . . . MOEFP/MOEFP, MOEFP/W-NS
    may I have a moment . . . . MAI/MOEM, MOEM/MOEM
    may I proceed . . . . MAOIG
    may I respectfully . . . . MAIRP
    may not . . . . MAINT
    may remember . . . . MAIRM
    may the record reflect . . . . MORT
    may the record show . . . . MORS
    may understand . . . . MAINDZ
    may want . . . . MAIPT
    may we approach . . . . MAOEFP
    may we approach the bench . . . . MAOEFP/BEFP
maybe . . . . MAIB
mayhem . . . . MAEM
mayor
    mayor . . . . MAIR
    Mayor . . . . MA*IR
    mayoral . . . . MAIRL
M.D. . . . . M-D

M — BRIEF ENCOUNTERS

me	ME
mea culpa	MUKL
meager	MAOERG
meagerly	MAOERLG

mean
- mean . . . MAEN
- means . . . MAENS
- meaning . . . MAENG
- meant . . . MENT

mean
- meaner . . . MAOERN
- ***meaner than*** . . . MAOERNT
- ***meaner than those*** . . . MAOERNTS
- meaningful . . . MAOEFL
- mean-spirited . . . MIRTD
- meanwhile . . . MAOENL

meander
- meander . . . MAERN, MAOERND
- meanders . . . MAERNS, MAOERNDZ
- meandering . . . MAERNG, MAOERNGD
- meandered . . . MAERND, MAOERND/-D

measles	MAOEZ
measurable	MURBL
measurably	MOIRBL, MAOERBL

measure
- measure . . . MUR
- measures . . . MURS
- measuring . . . MURG
- measured . . . MUR/-D

measurement	MURMT
meatball	MAEBL
mechanic	M-K
mechanical	M-KL, M-K/KAL
mechanism	MEFM
medal	MAELD

meddle
- meddle . . . MELD
- meddles . . . MELDZ
- meddling . . . MELGD
- meddled . . . MELD/-D

meddler	MERLD
media	YAOED, DYA
mediation	MAOEGS

medical
- medical . . . MEL

BRIEF ENCOUNTERS M

medical evidence	MEVD
medically	M*EL
medical malpractice	M*M, MAMT
medical school	MAOL
medication	MEGS
medicinal	M–NL
medicine	M–N
mediocre	YOEG, YOEKT, MAOED/YOEK
mediocrity	YOKT, MAOED/YOKT
Mediterranean	MED/YAN
medium	MAOEM
meekly	MAOEKL

meet
meet	MAOET
meets	MAOETS
meeting	MAOEGT
met	MET

mega-
mega-	MEG
megabit	MIBT
megabyte	MEGT
megacycle	SMEG
megahertz	MEGZ

melody	MEL/DI

member
member	MEB
member of the board	MEBD
membership	MEP
memberships	MEPZ
members of the board	MEBDZ
members of the jury	MEJ

membrane	BRAEM
memento	MEMT

memo
memo	MOE
memoranda	MEMD
memorandum	MUM

memory	MEM
men	MEN
Meniere's disease	MAIND
meningitis	JAOIT
menopausal	MAUFL
menopause	MAUZ
men's	MENS

M BRIEF ENCOUNTERS

mental
- mental .... MENL
- mentality .... MENLT
- mentally .... MOINL

mention
- mention .... MENGS
- mentions .... MENGSZ
- mentioning .... MENG
- mentioned .... MENGD

Mercedes .... MERDZ
merchandise .... M–DZ
merchant .... M–FPT
merciful .... MEFRL, MEFRS
merciless .... MERLS
mercy .... MERS
merely .... MAOERL
meridian .... MERD, MERD/YAN
meridians .... MERD/–S

merit
- merit .... MERT
- merits .... MERTS
- meriting .... MERGT
- merited .... MERTD

meritorious .... MERT/YOUS
meritoriousness .... MERT/YOUNS
merry-go-round .... MERG
message .... MEFP
messenger .... MEFRP
Messrs. .... MERZ
metabolic .... BLOLG, BL*IK, MET/BLIK
metabolism .... BLIFM, MET/BLIFM

metabolize
- metabolize .... BLAOIZ, BLAOIS
- metabolizes .... BLAOIFS, BLAOISZ
- metabolizing .... BLAOIFG
- metabolized .... BLAOIFD

metal
- metal .... MAELT
- metallurgist .... TLURT
- metallurgy .... TLURG, MET/LURJ

meter .... MAOERT
methamphetamine .... MAEFM

method
- method .... MEF
- methodical .... MEFK

ILLEGAL TO PHOTOCOPY   366   © 1997 White-Boucke Publishing.

BRIEF ENCOUNTERS   *M*

methodically . . . . MAOEFK
methodology . . . . MEFL
meticulous
    meticulous . . . . TLOUS
    meticulously . . . . TLOULS
    meticulousness . . . . TLOUNS
metric . . . . MERKT
metropolis . . . . MET/POLS
metropolitan . . . . MET/POLT
Mexican . . . . M*EX
Mexicans . . . . MEXZ
Mexico . . . . MEX
Miami . . . . YAM
Michael . . . . MAOIKL
Michigan . . . . M*I
microfilm . . . . M-FM
microphone . . . . M-F
microphones . . . . M-F/-S
microscope . . . . MAOIRK
microscopic . . . . MAOIRP
microwave
    microwave . . . . MAIV
    microwaves . . . . MAIVS
    microwaving . . . . MAIVG
    microwaved . . . . MAIVD
microwave oven . . . . MOVN
middle
    middle . . . . MILD
    Middle East . . . . MAO*ELS
    Middle Eastern . . . . MAOERNZ
    middle of . . . . MIFLD
    middle of the . . . . MIFLTD
    middle of them . . . . MIFM
    middle of these . . . . MIFLZ
    middle of those . . . . MIFLS
Mideast
    Mideast . . . . DAO*ES
    Mideastern . . . . DAO*ERN
    Mideasterner . . . . DRAOERN
midget . . . . MIJ
midnight . . . . MAOINT
midst . . . . M*ID
midterm . . . . MERM
midway . . . . DWAI
Midwest . . . . DW*ES, DWEFT

M   BRIEF ENCOUNTERS

midwife . . . . DWAOIF
midwifery . . . . DWIF
midwives . . . . DWAOIVS
miff
    miff . . . . MOIF
    miffs . . . . MOIFS
    miffing . . . . MOIFG
    miffed . . . . MOIFD
might
    might be . . . . MIB
    might have . . . . MIF
    might have been . . . . MIFB
    might have had . . . . MIFD
    might have known . . . . MIFN
    might want . . . . MIPT
migrate
    migrate . . . . MAO*IG
    migrates . . . . MAOIGZ
    migrating . . . . MAOIG/-G
    migrated . . . . MAOIGD
migration . . . . MAOIGS
mile(s)
    mileage . . . . MAOIJ
    mile-an-hour . . . . MIR
    mile per gallon . . . . MIRPG
    mile-per-hour . . . . MIRP
    miles an hour . . . . MIRS
    miles per hour . . . . MIRPS
military . . . . MILT
military retirement . . . . MAOIRMT
milk
    milk . . . . MOIL
    milks . . . . MOILS
    milking . . . . MOILG
    milked . . . . MOILD
milligram . . . . M*LG
millimeter . . . . M-M
million
    million . . . . M-L
    million dollar . . . . M-LD
    millionth . . . . M-LT, M*ILT
Milwaukee . . . . MIL/WAUK
mimicry . . . . MIMG
miner . . . . MAOIRN
mineral . . . . MIRNL

minestrone	STROEN
mingle	
mingle	MING
mingles	MINGS
mingling	MING/-G
mingled	MINGD
miniature	MIRNT
minimal	MINL
minimum	MIM
Minneapolis	MIN/YAP
Minnesota	M*N
minor	MOIRN
minority	MOIRNT, MOINT
minus	MOIN
minuscule	SKAOUL
minute	MIN
minutia	MAOURB
miracle	MIRK, MIRKL
miracles	MIRKZ, MIRKLZ
miraculous	MIRKLS, MIRK/LOUS
miraculously	MOIRKL, MIRK/LI
mirage	MIRJ, MRAJ
Miranda	MIRND
mirror	
mirror	MOIR, M*IR
mirrors	MOIRS, MIRZ
mirroring	MOIRG, MIRG
mirrored	MOIRD, MIRD
misappropriate	
misappropriate	MOEPT
misappropriates	MOEPTS
misappropriating	MOEPGT
misappropriated	MOEPTD
misappropriation	MOEPGS
miscarriage	SKAIRJ, SKAERJ
miscarry	
miscarry	SKAER
miscarries	SKAERS
miscarrying	SKAERG
miscarried	SKAERD
miscellaneous	MIFK
mischief	SKHIF
mischievous	SKHAOEV, SKHAOEVS
miscommunication	SKMUNGS

M

misconduct
- misconduct . . . SKUK
- misconducts . . . SKUKS
- misconducting . . . SKUK/-G
- misconducted . . . SKUKD

misdemeanor . . . MIDZ
miser . . . MAOIRZ
miserable . . . M-BL, MIFBL
miserably . . . MAOEBL, MAOEFBL
miserly . . . MAOIRLZ
misery . . . MIZ
misfeasance . . . MIFZ, SFAOEZ, MIS/FAOEZ
misguidance . . . SGAOINS, SGINS

misguide
- misguide . . . SGAOID, SGI
- misguides . . . SGAOIDZ, SGIS
- misguiding . . . SGAOIGD, SGIG
- misguided . . . SGAOID/-D, SGID

mishandle
- mishandle . . . SHANL
- mishandles . . . SHANLS
- mishandling . . . SHANLG
- mishandled . . . SHANLD

mishap . . . SHAP
misinformation . . . M-FGS

misinterpret
- misinterpret . . . MERP
- misinterprets . . . MERPS
- misinterpreting . . . MERPG
- misinterpreted . . . MERPD

misinterpretation . . . MERPGS
misjoinder . . . MOIRND, MIS/JOIRND

misjudge
- misjudge . . . MUJ
- misjudges . . . MUJS
- misjudging . . . MUJ/-G
- misjudged . . . MUJD

misjudgment . . . MUJT

mislead
- mislead . . . SLAOED
- misleads . . . SLAOEDZ
- misleading . . . SLAOEGD
- misled . . . MIS/LED

misnomer . . . SNOERM, SNOEM
misquotation . . . SKWOEGS

BRIEF ENCOUNTERS — M

misquote
    misquote .... SKWOET
    misquotes .... SKWOETS
    misquoting .... SKWOEGT
    misquoted .... SKWOETD
misrepresent
    misrepresent .... M*EP
    misrepresents .... MEPS
    misrepresenting .... MEPG
    misrepresented .... MEPD
misrepresentation .... MEPGS
Miss .... M–S
miss
    miss .... MISZ
    misses .... MAOIFS
    missing .... MAOIFG
    missed .... MAOIFD
missile .... MAOIFL
Mississippi .... M*S
Missouri .... MO*
mistake
    mistake .... MAEK
    mistakes .... MAEKS
    mistaking .... MAEK/-G, MAEG
    mistook .... MIS/TAOK, STAOK
    mistaken .... MAEFN
mistakenly .... MAEFNL
mistrial .... STRAOIL
misunderstand
    misunderstand .... MUND
    misunderstands .... MUNDZ
    misunderstanding .... MUNGD, MUNG
    misunderstood .... MUNTD, MAOND
mobility .... MOEBLT
model
    model .... MOELD
    models .... MOELDZ
    modeling .... MOELGD
    modeled .... MOELD/-D
modem .... MOEMD
modern .... MOERND
modernization .... MOERNGS
modernize
    modernize .... MORNS
    modernizes .... MORNSZ

M   BRIEF ENCOUNTERS

modernizing .... MORNS/-G
modernized .... MORNS/-D, MORND
modesty .... MOD/STI
modification .... MOFGS
modify
    modify .... MOF
    modifies .... MOFS
    modifying .... MOFG
    modified .... MOFD
moisten
    moisten .... MOI
    moistens .... MOIS
    moistening .... MOIG
    moistened .... MOI/-D
moisture .... MOIRT
molestation .... MOELGS
moment
    moment .... MOEMT, MOMT
    moment ago .... MOEMG
    momentous .... MOEMS, MUMTS
    moments ago .... MOEMGS
    momentum .... MOEM, MUMT
mommy .... MOIM
monarchy .... MAURNG, MAURNK
Monday .... MOND
monetarily .... MOENL
monetary .... MOENT
money .... MUN, MON
money order .... MORD
Mongolia .... MOUNG
Mongoloid .... MAUNG
monitor
    monitor .... MONT
    monitors .... MONTS
    monitoring .... MONT/-G
    monitored .... MONTD
monopolist .... NAUPT
monopolization .... NAUPGS
monopolize
    monopolize .... NAUP
    monopolizes .... NAUPS
    monopolizing .... NAUPG
    monopolized .... NAUPD
monopoly .... NAUPL, NOP/LI
monotone .... MAUNT

BRIEF ENCOUNTERS — M

montage	MAUT
Montana	M*T
month	MO
monthly	MONL
monument	M–NT, MON/YAOUMT, MON/YUMT
monumental	M–NLT, MAOUNL, MON/MENL
moocher	MAOFRP

moonlight
- moonlight ... MAONL, MAONLT
- moonlights ... MAONLS, MAONLTS
- moonlighting ... MAONLG, MAONLG
- moonlighted ... MAONLD, MAONLTD

moral
- moral ... MORL
- morality ... MORLT
- morals ... MORLZ

morale	MAORL
morbid	MOERBD

more
- more ... MOR
- *more or less* ... MORLS
- moreover ... MROEVR
- mores ... MORZ
- *more than* ... MOERN
- *more than the* ... MOERNT
- *more than them* ... MOERM
- *more than these* ... MOERNZ
- *more than those* ... MOERNS

Mormon	MORM
morning	MORNG
Morocco	MAORK
Moroccan	MAORNG
morphine	MOFRB
mortal	MAORLT
mortality	MAORT, MO*RLT, MOERLT

mortgage
- mortgage ... MO*RT
- mortgages ... MORTS
- mortgaging ... MORGT
- mortgaged ... MORTD

mortgagee	MAOEJ
mortgagor	MOERJ
mortification	MORGS
mortuary	TWAIR, MORT/WAIR
Moscow	SKWOU

M — BRIEF ENCOUNTERS

moslem . . . . MOFM
mosquito . . . . SKWAOET
most
    most . . . . MO*ES, MO*S
    mostly . . . . MOL, MOLS
    most of . . . . MOEF
    most of all . . . . MOEFL
    most of the . . . . MOEFT
    most of them . . . . MOEFM
    most of these . . . . MOEFZ
    most of those . . . . MOEFS
motel . . . . MOELT
mother
    mother . . . . MOER
    motherfucker . . . . MUFR
    motherhood . . . . MOERD
    mother-in-law . . . . MOERL
    mothers-in-law . . . . MOERLS
motif . . . . TAOEF
motion
    motion . . . . MOEGS
    motion denied . . . . MOD
    motion granted . . . . MOG
    motion in liminie . . . . MAOEMGS
    motion of the . . . . MOFT
    motion of these . . . . MOFZ
    motion to dismiss . . . . MODZ
    motion to exclude . . . . MAOUD
    motion to strike . . . . MOETS, MOTS
    motion to suppress . . . . MOZ
motivate
    motivate . . . . MOEVT
    motivates . . . . MOEVTS
    motivating . . . . MOEVGT, MOEVG
    motivated . . . . MOEVTD
motivation . . . . MOEVGS
motivational . . . . MOEVL
motivator . . . . MOEVRT
motive . . . . MOEV
motor
    motor . . . . MOERT
    motorcycle . . . . MOIK
    motor vehicle . . . . MOEK
motto . . . . MOT
mountain . . . . M–T

BRIEF ENCOUNTERS   M

mourner	MROURN
mousetrap	MOUP
movability	MOVBLT, MOFBLT
movable	MOVBL, MOFBL
move	
movement	MOVMT, MOFMT
mover	MOVR, MOFR
move to strike	MAOK
movie	MAOEV
mow	
mow	MOU
mows	MOUZ
mowing	MOUG
mowed	MOUD
mowed / mown	MOUD / MOUN
Mozambique	ZAM
Mr.	
Mr.	MR-, MR-FPLT
Mr. and Mrs.	MR-RS
Mr. Chairman	MR-FP
Mr. Foreman	MR-FM
Mr. Foreperson	MR-FRP
Mr. or Mrs.	MR*RS
Mr. President	MR-PT
Mr. Secretary	MRAEK
Mr. Speaker	MR-K
Mr. Vice President	MR-VP
MRI	MR*I
Ms.	
Ms.	M-Z
Ms. Chairperson	M-FPZ
Ms. Foreperson	M-FRPZ
Ms. President	M-PZ
Ms. Secretary	M-KZ, MRAEKZ
Ms. Speaker	MR-KZ
Ms. Vice President	M-VPZ
much	
much	MUFP
much of the	MUFPT
much of these	MUFPZ
much of those	MUFPS
mucous	MAOUK
mucus	MOUK, MAOUKS
muffle	
muffle	M*UFL

M   BRIEF ENCOUNTERS

    muffles. . . . . M*UFLS
    muffling. . . . . M*UFLG
    muffled . . . . M*UFLD
muffler. . . . . MRUFL, MR*UFL
multicultural. . . . . MOURL
multiculturalism . . . . MOUFM
multimedia . . . . MAOEMD
multiple . . . . M*ULT, MOIP
multiple sclerosis. . . . . SKLOEM
municipal. . . . . MUP
municipal court. . . . . MUPT
munition. . . . . MAO*UNGS
mural . . . . MAOURL
murder
    murder . . . . MURD
    murders. . . . . MURDZ
    murdering . . . . MURGD
    murdered . . . . MURD/-D
    murderer . . . . MRURD
    murder in the first degree. . . . . M-FD
    murder in the second degree . . . . M-KD
muscle
    muscle. . . . . MUFL
    muscles . . . . MUFLS
    muscling . . . . MUFLG
    muscled . . . . MUFLD
museum . . . . MAOUM
mushroom
    mushroom. . . . . SHRAOM
    mushrooms . . . . SHRAOMS
    mushrooming. . . . . SHRAOMG
    mushroomed . . . . SHRAOMD
music
    music . . . . MAOUF
    musical . . . . MAOUFK
    musicality . . . . MAOUFKT
    musically . . . . MAOUFL
    musician. . . . . MAOUGS
muslim . . . . MUFM
mussel. . . . . M-FL
must
    must. . . . . M*US
    must be. . . . . MUB
    must have been . . . . MUFB

must have had	MUFD
must have known	MUFN
must recall	MURL
mustache	MUS
mutant	TAOUNT
mutate	
mutate	TAOUMT
mutates	TAOUMTS
mutating	TAOUMG, TAOUMGT
mutated	TAOUMTD
mutation	TAOUMGS, MAIGS
mutative	TAOUVT
mutilate	
mutilate	MAOLT
mutilates	MAOLTS
mutilating	MAOLGT
mutilated	MAOLTD
mutilation	MAOLGS
mutual	
mutual	MAOUFP
mutual fund	MAOUFPD
mutuality	MAOUFPT
mutually	MAOUFPL
muzzle	
muzzle	MUZ
muzzles	MUZ/-S
muzzling	MUZ/-G
muzzled	MUZ/-D
my	
my	MI
my mind	MIND
my opinion	MAOIP
my reason	MIRN
my reasoning	MIRNG
myopia	MAOP
myopic	MAOPG, MAOPK
myriad	MAOERD
myself	MAOIZ
mysteries	STRAOEZ
mysterious	
mysterious	STRAOES, STRO*US
mysteriously	STRAOEL
mysteriousness	STRAOENS
mystery	STRAOE

N

nacho... NAUFP
naive
    naive... NAOEV
    naively....................................... NAOEVL
    naivete .... NAOEVT
naked.. NAIKD
name and occupation .... NOUPGS
namely... NAEM
narcissism.. NARMS
narcissistic...................................... NARTS
Narcissus... NARSZ
narcotic.. NARKT
narrate
    narrate....................................... NAIRT
    narrates...................................... NAIRTS
    narrating..................................... NAIRGT
    narrated...................................... NAIRTD
narration... NAIRGS
narrative... NAIVT
narrow
    narrow.. NAIR
    narrows....................................... NAIRS
    narrowing..................................... NAIRG
    narrowed...................................... NAIRD
narrow
    narrower...................................... NA*IR
    narrowly...................................... NAIRL
    narrowness.................................... NAIRNS
nasal.. NAILZ
natal.. NAILT
national
    national...................................... NARBL
    National Captioning Institute.......................... NAPGS
    nationalism .... NAFM
    nationalistic .... NAFK
    nationality................................... NARBLT
    nationally.................................... NAERBL
native.. NAIF
Native American............................... NAIRM, NAIRN
natural
    natural....................................... NAL
    naturalization .... NALGS

naturally . . . . NAEL
nature
    nature . . . . NAIFP
    nature of the . . . . NAIFPT
    nature of them. . . . . NAIFM
    nature of these . . . . NAIFPZ
    nature of those . . . . NAIFPS
naughty . . . . NAUT
nausea . . . . NAUZ
nauseate
    nauseate . . . . NAURBT
    nauseates . . . . NAURBTS
    nauseating . . . . NAURBGT
    nauseated . . . . NAURBTD
nauseous . . . . NAURB
nautical . . . . NAULT
    nautical mile . . . . NAUMT
naval . . . . NAIVL
navel . . . . NAEVL
navigate
    navigate . . . . NAFGT
    navigates . . . . NAFGTS
    navigating . . . . NAFGT/-G, NAFG
    navigated . . . . NAFGTD
navigation . . . . NAFGS
navigator . . . . NAFRGT
navy . . . . NAIV
near
    near . . . . NAOER
    nearby . . . . NAOERB
    nearest . . . . NERS
    nearly . . . . NAERL
    nearness . . . . NAOERNS
    nearsighted . . . . NAOERTD
    near the . . . . NAOERT
    near them . . . . NAOERM
    near these . . . . NAOERZ
Nebraska . . . . N*E
nebulous
    nebulous . . . . NEB
    nebulously . . . . NEBLS
    nebulousness . . . . NEBLZ
necessarily . . . . NEFL
necessary . . . . NES
nefarious . . . . NAIFRS

negate
- negate . . . . NAIG
- negates . . . . NAIGZ
- negating . . . . NAIG/-G
- negated . . . . NAIGD

negation . . . . NEGS

negative
- negative . . . . NEG
- negatively . . . . NAIFL, NAEFL
- negatives . . . . NEGZ

negativity . . . . NAIGT, NAEGT

neglect
- neglect . . . . GLEKT, GLEK
- neglects . . . . GLEKTS, GLEKS
- neglecting . . . . GLEKT/-G, GLEG
- neglected . . . . GLEKTD, GLEKD

neglectful
- neglectful . . . . GLEFL
- neglectfully . . . . GLAEFL, GLOIFL
- neglectfulness . . . . GLEFNS

negligence . . . . NEJS
negligent . . . . NEJ, NEJT
negotiable . . . . NOERBL

negotiate
- negotiate . . . . NOERB
- negotiates . . . . NOERBS
- negotiating . . . . NOERBG
- negotiated . . . . NOERBD

negotiation . . . . NOERBGS

Negro
- Negro . . . . NAOEG
- Negroid . . . . GROID
- Negroes . . . . NAOEGZ

neighbor
- neighbor . . . . NAIB
- neighborhood . . . . NAIBD
- neighborly . . . . NAEBL

neither . . . . NE, N*ET
nemesis . . . . NEMZ
neon light . . . . NAOELT
nepotism . . . . NEP

nervous
- nervous . . . . NEFS
- ***nervous breakdown*** . . . . N-B
- nervously . . . . NEFLS

BRIEF ENCOUNTERS — N

nervousness . . . . NEFNS
nervous system . . . . N-S
Netherlands . . . . NELTS, N*ELTS
network
    network . . . . TWORK
    networks . . . . TWORKS
    networking . . . . TWORK/-G
    networked . . . . TWORKD
neurological . . . . NURL
neurologically . . . . NAOURL
neuron . . . . NAOURN
neuroses . . . . NAOURSZ
neurosis . . . . NAOURS
neurotic . . . . NAOURKT
neuter
    neuter . . . . NAOURT
    neuters . . . . NAOURTS
    neutering . . . . NAOURGT
    neutered . . . . NAOURTD
Nevada . . . . N-V
never . . . . NEFR, NEVR
nevertheless . . . . NEFRL, NEFRLS
new
    new . . . . NU
    Newark . . . . NAOURK
    newborn . . . . NAOUB
    New Guinea . . . . NAOUG
    New Hampshire . . . . H*N
    New Jersey . . . . N*J
    newly . . . . NAOUL
    New Mexico . . . . N*M
    New Orleans . . . . NAOENS
    newspaper . . . . NAOUP
    New York . . . . NORK
    New York City . . . . NO*RKS
    New York Times . . . . NORKT
    New Zealand . . . . N-Z
    New Zealander . . . . N-RLZ
    New Zealanders . . . . N-RLSZ
newer
    newer . . . . NAOUR
    newer than . . . . NAO*URN
    newer than the . . . . NAOURNT
    newer than them . . . . NAOURM
    newer than these . . . . NAOURZ

newer than those	NAO*URS
news conference	NAOUFRNS
next	NEX

nibble
nibble	N*IBL
nibbles	N*IBLS, NIBLZ
nibbling	NIBL/-G
nibbled	NIBLD

nicer
nicer	NAOIRS
nicer than	NAOIRN
nicer than the	NAOIRNT
nicer than these	NAOIRNZ
nicer than those	NAOIRNS

nick
nick	NIRK
nicks	NIRKZ
nicking	NIRK/-G
nicked	NIRKD

nickel	NIKL
Niger	NAOIRG
Nigerian	NAOERJ

night
night-light	NAOILT
nightmare	NAER
night school	NAOL
nighttime	NAOIM

nine
nine of the	NAOIFT
nine of them	NAOIFM
nine of these	NAOIFZ
nine of those	NAOIFS
nine-time	NAO*IM
nine times	NAOIMS
ninety	NAOI

nitrogen	NAOIJ
nitrous	NAOIR
nitrous oxide	NAOIRD, NAUX

no
no	NO
no,	NORBGS
no.	NOFPLT
no audible response	NAUBLS
no contest	NOEK
no evidence	NOEVD

BRIEF ENCOUNTERS N

no further questions	NOURGS
no idea	NOID
no ideas	NOIDZ
no, ma'am	NAM
no more	NOM
no objection	NOEX
no place	NOEPL, NO*P
no proper	NOP
no, sir	NORS
no such	NOUFP
no, your Honor	NURN
Nobel Prize	NAOIZ

nobody
nobody	NOEB
nobody else	NOBL
nobody else's	NOBLS
nocturnal	NURNL
noel	NO*EL
nolo contendere	NOELD
nomenclature	KLAIFP

nominate
nominate	NOMT
nominates	NOMTS
nominating	NOMGT, NOMG
nominated	NOMTD
nomination	NOMGS
nonchalance	SLAUNS
nonchalant	SLAUNT
nonchalantly	SLAUNL
noncompliance	NLAOINS
non compos mentis	NENTS

none
none	NUN
none of the	NUNT
none of them	NUFM
none of these	NUNZ
none of those	NUNS
none of your business	NURBS
nonetheless	NUNL, NUNLS
nonfat	NOEFT
nonfeasance	NOFZ, NON/FAOEZ
nonprofit	N-P
nonresponsive	N-RP
nonsense	NAUNS
nonsensical	NAUNL

N

non sui juris	NAOEJ
noontime	NAONT
normal	
normal	NOL
normality	NOILT
normalization	NORLGS, NO*LGS
normally	NOIL
north	
North America	NA
North American	NARN
northbound	NORB
North Carolina	N*K
North Dakota	N*D
northeast	NAO*ES
northeasterly	NAOERL
northeastern	NAOERN
northeasterner	NRAOERN
northerly	NORL
northern	NORN
northerner	NRORN
north side	N–DZ
northwest	N*ES
northwesterly	NERL
northwestern	NERN
northwesterner	NRERN
Norway	NAUR
Norwegian	NAURN, NWAOEJ
not	
not	NOT
not guilty	N–G
not proper	NOPT
not relevant	NEV
not responsive	NOERP, N*RP
not that I recall	NIRL
not that I recall the	NIRLT
notaries public	NOIPS
notary public	NOIP
notation	NOEGTS
nothing	
nothing	NOG
nothing else	NOLG, NOLGS
nothing further	NORT
notice	
notice	NOIT
notices	NOITS

BRIEF ENCOUNTERS — N

noticing	NOIGT
noticed	NOITD
noticeable	NOIBL
notification	NOIFGS

notify

notify	NOIF
notifies	NOIFS
notifying	NOIFG
notified	NOIFD
notoriety	NAOIRT
notorious	NOURS
notoriously	NOURL, NOURLS
notwithstanding	NANG

nourish

nourish	NOURB
nourishes	NOURBS
nourishing	NOURBG
nourished	NOURBD
nourishment	NOURMT
novel	NOVL
novelty	NOVLT
November	NOV
now	NOU
now,	NOURBGS
nowhere	NO*R, NOIR
nowhere else	NORLS, NO*RL
nozzle	NOFL
nubile	NAOUBL
nuclear	NAOUKL
nugget	NUGT
nuisance	NAOUNZ
nuisances	NAOUNZ/-S
null and void	NOIVD
nullification	NULGS

number

number	NUB
numbers	NUBS
numbering	NUBG
numbered	NUBD
number of times	NUBT
numeric	NAOURMG, NAO*URK
numerically	NAOURKL
numerous	NAOUMS
nun	NAUN
nuns	NAUNZ

nuptial	NUP
nurture	
nurture	NOURT
nurtures	NOURTS
nurturing	NOURGT
nurtured	NOURTD
nutrient	TRAOENT
nutrition	
nutrition	N*UGS, NU/TRIGS
nutritional	TRINL
nutritionally	TRAOENL
nystagmus	N*IS

O

obedience	BAOENS
obedient	BAOENT
obediently	BAOENL
obituary	OEB

object
- object ... OB
- objects ... OBZ
- objecting ... OBGT, OB/-G
- objected ... OB/-D, OBTD

object
- objection ... OX
- *objection is overruled* ... OX/SOEVRLD
- *objection overruled* ... KPOEVRLD
- *objection sustained* ... OS
- *objection, your Honor* ... ORN
- objective ... OBT
- objectively ... OBLT

obligate
- obligate ... BLIG
- obligates ... BLIGZ
- obligating ... BLIG/-G
- obligated ... BLIGD

obligation ... BLIGS
obligatory ... BLIGT, BLIG/TOR

oblige
- oblige ... BLAOIJ
- obliges ... BLAOIJS
- obliging ... BLAOIJ/-G, BLAOIG
- obliged ... BLAOIJD

oblique
- oblique ... BLAOEK
- *oblique angle* ... BLAOEG, BLAOEN
- obliquely ... BLAOEL
- obliqueness ... BLAOENS
- *oblique triangle* ... BLAOEKT

obliterate
- obliterate ... BLAET
- obliterates ... BLAETS
- obliterating ... BLAEGT
- obliterated ... BLAETD

obliteration ... BLAEGS
obliterator ... BLAERT

oblivion	BLIFN, BLIV/YON
oblivious	BLIVS, BLIV/YOUS
obnoxious	NOUX, SNOX

obscure
obscure	SKAOUR
obscures	SKAOURS
obscuring	SKAOURG
obscured	SKAOURD

obscurity	SKAOURT

observe
observe	OBS
observes	OBSZ
observing	OBS/-G
observed	OBS/-D, OBD

observer	ORBS
obsolescence	BLENS
obsolescent	BLENT
obsolete	BLAOET
obstacle	STAKL
obstacles	STAKLZ
obstetric	STREK, OBS/TRIK
obstetrician	STREGS, OBS/TRIGS

obstreperous
obstreperous	STRERP, STREP/ROUS
obstreperously	STRERL
obstreperousness	STRERPS

obstruct
obstruct	BRUK
obstructs	BRUKZ
obstructing	BRUK/-G, BRUG
obstructed	BRUKD

obstruction	BRUX
obstruction of justice	STRAOJ, BR*UJ, BR-J

obtain
obtain	BAIN
obtains	BAINS
obtaining	BAING
obtained	BAIND

obtuse	STAOUS
obvious	OUB
obviously	OUBL
occasion	KAIRB
occasional	KAIRBL
Occident	SDON
Occidental	SDONL

O

occupancy	OUPZ, OUP/SI
occupant	OUPT
occupation	OUPGS
occupier	OURP

occupy
- occupy . . . OUP
- occupies . . . OUPS
- occupying . . . OUPG
- occupied . . . OUPD

occur
- occur . . . KUR
- occurs . . . KURZ
- occurring . . . KURG
- occurred . . . KURD

occurrence	KURNS
o'clock	KL-K
October	TOEB
ocular	AUK
oddball	OBL
ode	YOED, O*ED
odometer	DOEMT

of
- *of* . . . OF
- *of course* . . . F-K
- *of the* . . . OFT
- *of them* . . . OFM
- *of these* . . . OFZ

off
- *off* . . . AUF
- *off and on* . . . FAUN
- *off and on the* . . . FAUNT
- *off the* . . . AUFT
- *off the top of my head* . . . TPOPD
- *off the top of your head* . . . TPURPD
- *off these* . . . AUFZ
- *off those* . . . AUFS

offend
- offend . . . OFND
- offends . . . OFNDZ
- offending . . . OFNGD, OFNG
- offended . . . OFND/-D

offense . . . OFNS

offer
- offer . . . AUFR
- offers . . . AUFRS

O

offering	AUFRG
offered	AUFRD
offer of proof	FRAOF
offers of proof	FRAOFS
offhand	FAUND
office	OFS
officer	SAUFR
official	FIRBL
officially	FOIRBL
offset	SAUFT
often	AUFN, AUFRN
oh,	OERBGS
Ohio	HO*
ointment	OIMT
O.J.	OJ
Oklahoma	KLOEM, O*K/O*K
Oklahoma City	KLOEMS
older	OERLD
Oldsmobile	OEBL
olfactory	FLAOK
ombudsman	OM/BUD
ombudswoman	OM/BAM
omission	OEMGS

omit

omit	OEMT
omits	OEMTS
omitting	OEMGT, OEMG
omitted	OEMTD

on

on	ON
on and off	NAUF
on and off the	NAUFT
on and off them	NAUFM
on and off these	NAUFZ
on and off those	NAUFS
on behalf of	BAOF
on behalf of the	BAOFT
on behalf of them	BAOFM
on behalf of these	BAOFZ
on behalf of those	BAOFS
on one hand	WHAND
on or about	OERB
on or about the	OERBT
on the	ONT
on the ground	OG

BRIEF ENCOUNTERS

O

on the grounds	OGS
on the one hand	TWAND
on the other hand	TWRAND, OERND
on these	ONZ
on those	ONS
on top of the	NOFPT
once in a while	SWHAOIL, WHUNS

one

one	WUN
one-and-a-quarter	NAERT, WA*RT
one and two	WAOT, WAONT
one-eighth	WA*IT
one-fourth	WO*URT
one-half	WAF
one-half of the	WAFT
one-half of them	WAFM
one-half of these	WAFZ
one-half of those	WAFS
one-ninth	WAO*INT
one of	WUF
one of the	WUFT
one of them	WUFM
one of these	WUFZ
one of those	WUFS
one or two	WAORT
one quarter	WAERT
ones and twos	WAOTS, WAONTS
oneself	W*UNS
one-seventh	WEVNT
one-sixth	W*IX
ones or twos	WAORTS
one-tenth	W*ENT
one time	WAOIM
one-upmanship	WUPS
one way or the other	WUFR

ongoing	NONG

only

only	ONL
only the	ONLT
only these	ONLZ
only those	ONLS

onto

onto	AONT
onto the	AONTD
onto these	AONTSZ

O

onto those	AONTS

open
open	OEP
opens	OEPS
opening	OEPG
opened	OEPD

opener	O*ERP
operability	PRAIBLT
operable	PRAIBL

operate
operate	PRAIT
operates	PRAITS
operating	PRAIGT
operated	PRAITD

operating room	OERM
operation	PRAIGS
operational	PRAILGS
operative	PRAIV, PRAIF
operatively	PRAIVL, PRAIFL
operator	PRAIRT
ophthalmological	MOFLT
ophthalmologist	MOLT
ophthalmology	MOLG
opinion	P–N
opinionated	P–ND
opponent	POENT
opportunity	TUNT
opposite	OPS
opposition	OIPGS, AUPGS, OP/SIGS
optic	AUPT
optician	A*UPGS, OPGTS
optimism	OPT/MIFM
optometrist	TOMT
optometry	TROMT

or
or	OR
or the	ORT
or them	ORM
or these	ORZ
or those	ORS

oral
oral	ORL
oral deaf	AURLD
orally	OERL

orange	ORNG

orbit
- orbit . . . . ORBT
- orbits . . . . ORBTS
- orbiting . . . . ORBGT
- orbited . . . . ORBTD

orbital . . . . ORBL
orchestra . . . . OERK
orchestras . . . . OERKZ
orchestrate
- orchestrate . . . . ORK
- orchestrates . . . . ORKZ
- orchestrating . . . . ORK/-G
- orchestrated . . . . ORKD

orchestration . . . . ORK/STRAIGS
order
- order . . . . OD
- orders . . . . ODZ
- ordering . . . . OGD
- ordered . . . . OD/-D

order to show cause . . . . SHOERK
ordinance . . . . ORNS
ordinarily . . . . ORLD
ordinary . . . . ORD
ordnance . . . . AORNS
ore . . . . YO*ER
Oregon . . . . O*R
organ
- organ . . . . GORN
- organic . . . . GANK
- organism . . . . GOFM, GIFM

organization . . . . ORGS
organizational . . . . ORLGS
organize
- organize . . . . ORG
- organizes . . . . ORGZ
- organizing . . . . ORG/-G
- organized . . . . ORGD

organizer . . . . GRORN
orgasm . . . . GAFM
orgy . . . . O*ERJ
orient
- orient . . . . OERNT
- orients . . . . OERNTS
- orienting . . . . OERNGT, OERNG
- oriented . . . . OERNTD

O

oriental	OERNL
orientate	
orientate	TOERNT
orientates	TOERNTS
orientating	TOERNGT
orientated	TOERNTD
orientation	OERNGS
origin	
origin	AURJ
original	ORJ
originality	ORJT
originally	OERJ
origination	AURJS
origins	AURJZ
originate	
originate	AURJT
originates	AURJTS
originating	AURJT/-G
originated	AURJTD, AURJD
ornament	ORNT
ornamental	ORNL
orphanage	FAJ
orthodontic	THONK
orthodontist	THONT
orthopedic	ORPD, ORP
orthopedist	ORPT
Oscar	SKAOR
osmosis	SMOES, SMOEZ
ostensible	STENL
ostensibly	STAOENL
osteopath	TWOEPT
osteoporosis	TWOEP
ostrich	STRIFP
other	
other	OER
other side	OID
other than	OERT, OEFRN
other than the	OERTD
otherwise	OIS
otolaryngologist	LARNT
otolaryngology	LARN
ought	AUT
our	
our	OUR
ours	OURS

BRIEF ENCOUNTERS   O

```
         ourself ................................... OURZ
         ourselves ...................... OURSZ, O*URS
out ........................................... OUT
outage ............................... OUJ, OU/TAJ
outboard ................................... OURBD
*outboard motor* ............................. OURM
outbound ........................... OUBD, TBOUN
outbreak .................................. TBRAEK
outcast ..................................... OUKT
outburst ................. OURB, TBURS, TB*URS, T*URS
outcome ..................................... OUK
outer ....................................... OURT
outfit
         outfit ................................... OIFT
         outfits ................................. OIFTS
         outfitting .............................. OIFGT
         outfitted ............................... OIFTD
outgoing ..................................... OUG
outgrow
         outgrow ................................ TROE
         outgrows .............................. TROES
         outgrowing ............................ TROEG
         outgrew .............................. TRAO*U
         outgrown .............................. TROUN
outgrowth .................................. TRO*ET
outhouse .................................... THOUZ
outlandish ................................... TLAND
outlaw
         outlaw .................................. TLAU
         outlaws ............................... TLAUS
         outlawing ............................. TLAUG
         outlawed .............................. TLAUD
outlay ....................................... TLAE
outlet ........................................ OLT
outline
         outline ......................... OULT, TLAOIN
         outlines ...................... OULTS, TLAOINS
         outlining .............. OULGT, OULG, TLAOING
         outlined ..................... OULTD, TLAOIND
outlive
         outlive ................................. TLIV
         outlives .............................. TLIVS
         outliving .............................. TLIVG
         outlived .............................. TLIVD
outlook .................................... TLAOK
```

out loud . . . . TLOUD
outlying. . . . . TLAOIG
outmaneuver
    outmaneuver . . . . NAOUVR
    outmaneuvers . . . . NAOUVRS
    outmaneuvering . . . . NAOUVRG
    outmaneuvered . . . . NAOUVRD
outnumber
    outnumber. . . . . OUN
    outnumbers . . . . OUNZ
    outnumbering. . . . . OUNG
    outnumbered . . . . OUND
out of
    out of . . . . OUF
    out of the . . . . OUFT
    out of them . . . . OUFM
    out of these . . . . OUFZ
    out of those . . . . OUFS
outpatient. . . . . TAIRB, TAIRBT
outpouring . . . . TPOURG
outrage
    outrage . . . . TRAIJ
    outrages . . . . TRAIJS
    outraging. . . . . TRAIJ/-G, TRAIG
    outraged . . . . TRAIJD
outrageous. . . . . TRAIJZ
outrageously . . . . TRAOEJZ
outreach . . . . TRAEFP
outright . . . . TR–T
outside
    outside . . . . OUD
    outsider. . . . . OIRD, OUD/ER
    outside of. . . . . OUFD
    outside of the . . . . OUFTD
    outside of these . . . . OUFDZ
    outside the. . . . . OUTD
outskirt . . . . TIRT
outstanding . . . . OUS
outward
    outward. . . . . OURD
    outwardly. . . . . OURLD
    outwardness. . . . . OURNS
ovarian. . . . . OIV, OIVN, OIVRN
ovary. . . . . OEV
ovation . . . . OEVGS

BRIEF ENCOUNTERS O

over	OEFR
overall	OUVRL, OVR/AUL
overboard	VORD
overbook	
overbook	VBAOK
overbooks	VBAOKS
overbooking	VBAOG, VBAOK/-G
overbooked	VBAOKD
overburden	
overburden	VURD
overburdens	VURDZ
overburdening	VURGD
overburdened	VURD/-D
overcautious	VAURB
overcharge	
overcharge	VAURJ, VA*RJ
overcharges	VAURJS, VARJS
overcharging	VAURJ/-G, VARJ/-G
overcharged	VAURJD, VARJD
overcome	
overcome	VUM
overcomes	VUMS
overcoming	VUMG
overcame	VA*IM
overcome	VUM
overdo	
overdo	VOD
overdoes	VODZ
overdoing	VOGD
overdid	OVR/DID
overdone	VON
overdose	
overdose	VOEZ
overdoses	VOEFS, VOESZ
overdosing	VOEFG
overdosed	VOEFD
overdraw	
overdraw	VAU
overdraws	VAUS
overdrawing	VAUG
overdrew	VAO*U
overdrawn	VAUN
overhaul	
overhaul	VA*UL
overhauls	VAULS

O   BRIEF ENCOUNTERS

    overhauling . . . . VAULG
    overhauled . . . . VA*ULD
overhead . . . . VED
overlook
    overlook . . . . VAOK
    overlooks . . . . VAOKS
    overlooking . . . . VAOK/−G
    overlooked . . . . VAOKD
overly . . . . OVRL, OFRL
overnight . . . . OVRNT
overpower
    overpower . . . . VAUR
    overpowers . . . . VAURS
    overpowering . . . . VAURG
    overpowered . . . . VAURD
overrate
    overrate . . . . VA*ET
    overrates . . . . VAETS
    overrating . . . . VAEGT
    overrated . . . . VAETD
overrule
    overrule . . . . OEFRL, VAO*UL
    overrules . . . . OEFRLS, VAOULS
    overruling . . . . OEFRLG, VAOULG
    overruled . . . . OEFRLD, VAOULD
overseas . . . . VAES
oversight . . . . VAO*IT
oversimplification . . . . VIFRPGS
oversimplify
    oversimplify . . . . VIFRP
    oversimplifies . . . . VIFRPS
    oversimplifying . . . . VIFRPG
    oversimplified . . . . VIFRPD
overstep
    overstep . . . . VEP
    oversteps . . . . VEPS
    overstepping . . . . VEPG
    overstepped . . . . VEPD
over-the-counter . . . . VOUNT, VOURNT
over-the-counter sale . . . . VOUNTS, VOURNTS
overtime . . . . VAOIM, OMT, OEFRMT
overtone . . . . VOEN
overture . . . . VOURT
overturn
    overturn . . . . VURN

BRIEF ENCOUNTERS   O

```
overturns . . . . . . . . . . . . . . . . . . . . . . . . . . . . . . . . . . . VURNS
overturning . . . . . . . . . . . . . . . . . . . . . . . . . . . . . . . . VURNG
overturned . . . . . . . . . . . . . . . . . . . . . . . . . . . . . . . . . VURND
overwhelm
    overwhelm. . . . . . . . . . . . . . . . . . . . . . . . WHOEM, OVR/WHEM
    overwhelms . . . . . . . . . . . . . . . . . . . . . . WHOEMZ, OVR/WHEMS
    overwhelming . . . . . . . . . . . . . . . . . . . . WHOEMG, OVR/WHEMG
    overwhelmed . . . . . . . . . . . . . . . . . . . . . WHOEMD, OVR/WHEMD
overwhelmingly . . . . . . . . . . . . . . . . . . . . . . . . . . . . . . . WHOEJ
overwork
    overwork . . . . . . . . . . . . . . . . . . . . . . . . . . . . . . . . . . . VORK
    overworks . . . . . . . . . . . . . . . . . . . . . . . . . . . . . . . . . . VORKZ
    overworking . . . . . . . . . . . . . . . . . . . . . . . . . VORK/-G, VORG
    overworked . . . . . . . . . . . . . . . . . . . . . . . . . . . . . . . . . VORKD
overwrought. . . . . . . . . . . . . . . . . . . . . . . . . . . . . . . . . . . VAUT
ovulate
    ovulate. . . . . . . . . . . . . . . . . . . . . . . . . . . . . . . . . . . . . OVLT
    ovulates . . . . . . . . . . . . . . . . . . . . . . . . . . . . . . . . . . . OVLTS
    ovulating . . . . . . . . . . . . . . . . . . . . . . . . . . . . . OVLGT, OVLG
    ovulated. . . . . . . . . . . . . . . . . . . . . . . . . . . . . . . . . . . OVLTD
ovulation . . . . . . . . . . . . . . . . . . . . . . . . . . . . . OVLGS, OEVLGS
ovum . . . . . . . . . . . . . . . . . . . . . . . . . . . . . . . . . . . . . . OEVM
owner . . . . . . . . . . . . . . . . . . . . . . . . . . . . . . . . . . . . . . OERN
ownership. . . . . . . . . . . . . . . . . . . . . . . . . . . . . . . . . . . . OERP
oxen . . . . . . . . . . . . . . . . . . . . . . . . . . . . . . . . . . . . . . . O*XZ
oxide . . . . . . . . . . . . . . . . . . . . . . . . . . . . . . . . . . . . . . KPAOID
oxygen . . . . . . . . . . . . . . . . . . . . . . . . . . . . . . . SHEN, OX/JEN
oxygenate
    oxygenate . . . . . . . . . . . . . . . . . . . . . . . . . . . . . . . . . . SHAIT
    oxygenates . . . . . . . . . . . . . . . . . . . . . . . . . . . . . . . . . SHAITS
    oxygenating. . . . . . . . . . . . . . . . . . . . . . . . . . . . . . . . . SHAIGT
    oxygenated . . . . . . . . . . . . . . . . . . . . . . . . . . . . . . . . . SHAITD
oxygenation. . . . . . . . . . . . . . . . . . . . . . . . . . . . . . . . . . SHAIGS
ozone. . . . . . . . . . . . . . . . . . . . . . . . . . . . . . . . . . . . . . . OEZ
*ozone layer* . . . . . . . . . . . . . . . . . . . . . . . . . . . . . . . . . . . OELZ
```

P

pacer	PAIFR
Pacific	PAF
Pacific Ocean	POEF
pacifier	PAOIFR
pacifism	PAIFM, PA*FM
pacifist	PAFT
pacify	
pacify	PAOIF
pacifies	PAOIFS
pacifying	PAOIFG
pacified	PAOIFD
package	
package	PAJ
packages	PAJS
packaging	PAJ/-G
packaged	PAJD
packet	PAEKT
paddle	
paddle	PALD
paddles	PALDZ
paddling	PALGD
paddled	PALD/-D
pageant	PAJT
pager	PAIRJ
pain	
pain and suffering	PAIFRG
painful	PAIF
painfully	PAIFL
painless	PAINLS, PAINL
painter	PAIRNT
pajama	JAUM
palate	PLA
palates	PLA/-S
palatial	PLAIRBL
palette	PLELT
pallet	PALT
palm	PAUM
palpate	
palpate	PAPT
palpates	PAPTS
palpating	PAPGT
palpated	PAPTD

BRIEF ENCOUNTERS P

palpitation	PALGS
paltry	PAULT
pancreas	PAENK, PAN/KRAS
pandemonium	PAMD

pander
pander	PAND
panders	PANDZ
pandering	PANGD
pandered	PAND/-D
panderer	PRAND
panel	PANL
panelist	PANLT

panic
panic	PANK
panics	PANKS
panicking	PANK/-G
panicked	PANKD

paper
paper	PAIP, PAIRP
paperback	PAIRPB
paper bag	PAG
paper bags	PAGZ
paperwork	PAURK, PAIRK

parade
parade	PRAID
parades	PRAIDZ
parading	PRAIGD
paraded	PRAID/-D
paradigm	PAOIM
paradox	PAUX

paragraph
paragraph	PRAF
paragraphs	PRAFS
paragraphing	PRAFG
paragraphed	PRAFD
paralegal	PLAEL

parallel
parallel	PAERL
parallels	PAERLS
paralleling	PAERLG
paralleled	PAERLD
paralysis	PRALS

paralyze
paralyze	P-RL
paralyzes	P-RLS

P

paralyzing	P-RLG
paralyzed	P-RLD
paramedic	PAIRM
parameter	PRAMT
paramount	PAIRMT
paraphernalia	PAIRL
paraplegia	PLAOEJ
paraplegic	PLAOEK
parasite	PROIT

pardon
pardon	PARD
pardons	PARDZ
pardoning	PARGD
pardoned	PARD/-D

pardon me	PARM

parent
parent	PARNT
parents	PARNTS
parenting	PARNGT, PARNG
parented	PARNTD

parental	PARNLT
parenthood	PARND
parentheses	PRAENS
parenthesis	PRAEN
pariah	PRAOI/YA

parking
parking	PARG
parking lot	PLART
parking meter	P-RMT
parking ticket	PARKT

Parkinson's	PARNZ
Parkinson's disease	PARNDZ
parliament	PAERMT
parlor	PLAOR
parochial	PROEKL
parochial school	PROEKLS

parole
parole	PROEL
paroles	PROELS
paroling	PROELG
paroled	PROELD

parotid	PROTD

part
part of	PAFR
part of the	PAFRT

BRIEF ENCOUNTERS   P

part of them	PAFM
part of these	PAFRZ
parts of	PAFRS
part time	P-MT
partake	
partake	PAIK
partakes	PAIKS
partaking	PAIK/-G
partook	PAOK
partaken	PA*EN, PAR/TAEN
partial	
partial	PARB
partiality	PARBLT
partially	PARBL
participant	PARPT
participate	
participate	PARP
participates	PARPS
participating	PARPG
participated	PARPD
participation	PARPGS
particle	PARL
particular	
particular	PLAR
particularity	PLAERT
particularly	PLARL
partition	
partition	PARGS
partitions	PARGSZ
partitioning	PARGS/-G
partitioned	PARBD, PARGS/-D
partitioner	PRARGS
partly	PARLT
partner	PARN
partnership	PIP
party	
party	PAERT
parties	PAERTS
partying	PAERGT
partied	PAERTD
pass	
passable	PABL
passage	PAUJ, PA*J
passenger	PAENG, PAURJ
passerby	PAERB

© 1997 White-Boucke Publishing.   ILLEGAL TO PHOTOCOPY

passersby . . . . PAERBS
passion
    passion . . . . PAGS
    passionate . . . . PARBT
    passionately . . . . PAERBT
passive
    passive . . . . PAV
    passively . . . . PAVL
    passiveness . . . . PAVNS
passivity. . . . . PAVT
password . . . . P–RD
pastor . . . . PAORS
patella. . . . . PAT/LA
patellar . . . . PAT/LAR
patent
    patent . . . . PAENT
    patents. . . . . PAENTS
    patenting . . . . PAENGT
    patented. . . . . PAENTD
patent & trademark . . . . PAERK
patent & trademark attorney . . . . PAERKT
paternal . . . . PARNL
paternity . . . . PIRNT
pathetic . . . . TH*EKT
pathetically. . . . . THAOEKL
pathologic
    pathologic. . . . . THOJ
    pathological . . . . THAJ
    pathological liar . . . . THOL, THAOIR
    pathologically . . . . THAOJ
pathologist . . . . THOLT, THAOLT
pathology. . . . . THOLG, THAOLG
patience. . . . . PAIRBS
patient
    patient . . . . PAIRB, PAIRBT
    patiently. . . . . PAIRBL
    patients. . . . . PAIRBZ, PAIRBTS
patriot
    patriot . . . . PAIT/YOT
    patriotic . . . . PAIT/YOK
    patriotism . . . . PAIT/TIFM
patrol
    patrol . . . . PROL, TROL
    patrols . . . . PROLS, TROLS
    patrolling . . . . PROLG, TROLG

BRIEF ENCOUNTERS — P

patrolled	PROLD, TROLD

patrol
patrol car	TROEK
patrolman	TROM
patrolmen	TREM

pattern
pattern	PAERN
patterns	PAERNZ
patterning	PAERNG
patterned	PAERND
paucity	PAUFT
pauper	PAUP, PAURP
pauperism	PAUFM

pause
pause	PAUZ
pauses	PAUFS, PAUSZ
pausing	PAUFG
paused	PAUFD
pavement	PAIVMT, PAIFMT

pay
pay	PAI
pays	PAIZ
paying	PAIG
paid	PAID

pay
payable	PAIBL
payment	PAIMT
pay phone	PAIFN

pay back
pay back	PAIB
pays back	PAIBS
paying back	PAIB/−G
paid back	PAIBD
PC	P*K
PE	PE

peace
peaceable	PAEBL
peaceably	PAOEBL
peaceful	PAEF
peacefully	PAEFL, PAOEFL
peace officer	PEFR
peanut	PAOENT
peculiar	PEK
peculiarity	PEKT
pecuniary	PUK

pedal
    pedal . . . . PELD
    pedals . . . . PELDZ
    pedaling . . . . PELGD
    pedaled . . . . PELD/-D
pedestrian . . . . PED
pedigree . . . . PREGD
pejorative . . . . PORJ
pelvic . . . . PEFK, PEVK
pelvis . . . . PEFL, PEVL
penal
    penal . . . . PAOENL
    Penal Code . . . . P-K
    Penal Code Section . . . . P*X
penalize
    penalize . . . . PENL
    penalizes . . . . PENLS
    penalizing . . . . PENLG
    penalized . . . . PENLD
penalty . . . . PENLT
penalty of perjury . . . . POP
penchant . . . . PAEFP
pencil
    pencil . . . . SNIL
    pencils . . . . SNILS
    penciling . . . . SNILG
    penciled . . . . SNILD
penis . . . . PAOEN
penitentiary . . . . P-NT
Pennsylvania . . . . PA*
penultimate . . . . P*ULT
people
    people . . . . PAOEPL
    people's . . . . PAOEPLS
    People's . . . . PAOEPLZ
    People's exhibit . . . . PEX
    People's 1 . . . . PUN
    People's 1 and 2 . . . . PAOT
    People's 1 and 2 for identification . . . . PAOTD
    People's 1 for identification . . . . PUND
    People's 1 or 2 . . . . PAORT
    People's 1 or 2 for identification . . . . PAORTD
    People's 2 . . . . PAO
    People's 2 for identification . . . . PAOD
    People's 3 . . . . PAOE

BRIEF ENCOUNTERS — P

People's 3 for identification . . . . PAOED
People's 4 . . . . PO*ER
People's 4 for identification . . . . POERD, PO*ERD
People's 5 . . . . PAOIV
People's 5 for identification . . . . PAOIVD
People's 6 . . . . POIX, P*IX
People's 6 for identification . . . . POIKD, P*IX/–D
People's 7 . . . . PEV
People's 7 for identification . . . . PEVD
perceive
    perceive . . . . SPAOEV
    perceives . . . . SPAOEVS
    perceiving . . . . SPAOEVG
    perceived . . . . SPAOEVD
percent . . . . *P
percentage . . . . PARJ
percept
    percept . . . . SPEPT
    perceptibility . . . . SPIBLT
    perceptible . . . . SPIBL
    perceptibly . . . . SPOIBL
    perception . . . . SPEPGS
    perceptive . . . . SPIV
    perceptively . . . . SPIVL
    perceptivity . . . . SPIVT
percipience . . . . SPIPS
percipiency . . . . SPIPSZ
percipient . . . . SPIPT, SPIP
percipient witness . . . . SWIP
peremptory . . . . PRERMT
peremptory challenge . . . . PRAJ
perfect
    perfect . . . . P–F
    perfects . . . . P–FS
    perfecting . . . . P–FG
    perfected . . . . P–FD
perfect
    perfection . . . . P–FGS
    perfectionism . . . . P–FM
    perfectionist . . . . PEFT
    perfectly . . . . P–FL
perforate
    perforate . . . . FRAET, PRA*ET
    perforates . . . . FRAETS, PRAETS
    perforating . . . . FRAEGT, PRAEGT

P — BRIEF ENCOUNTERS

```
perforated . . . . . . . . . . . . . . . . . . . . . . . . . . . . . . FRAETD, PRAETD
perforation . . . . . . . . . . . . . . . . . . . . . . . . . . . . . . . . . . . . . . FRAEGS
perform
    perform . . . . . . . . . . . . . . . . . . . . . . . . . . . . . . . . . . . . . . . PORM
    performs . . . . . . . . . . . . . . . . . . . . . . . . . . . . . . . . . . . . . PORMS
    performing . . . . . . . . . . . . . . . . . . . . . . . . . . . . . . . . . . . PORMG
    performed . . . . . . . . . . . . . . . . . . . . . . . . . . . . . . . . . . . PORMD
performance . . . . . . . . . . . . . . . . . . . . . . . . . . . . . . . . . . . . . . POM
perfume . . . . . . . . . . . . . . . . . . . . . . . . . . . . . . . . . . . . . . PAOURM
perfusion . . . . . . . . . . . . . . . . . . . . . . . . . . . . . . . . . . . . . . PUFGS
perhaps . . . . . . . . . . . . . . . . . . . . . . . . . . . . . . . . . . . . . . . PRAPS
peril
    peril . . . . . . . . . . . . . . . . . . . . . . . . . . . . . . . . . . . . . . . . . . PIRL
    perilous . . . . . . . . . . . . . . . . . . . . . . . . . . . . . . . . . . . . . . PLOUS
    perilously . . . . . . . . . . . . . . . . . . . . . . . . . . . . . . . . . . . . PLOULS
    perilousness . . . . . . . . . . . . . . . . . . . . . . . . . . . . . . . . . PLOUNS
perimeter . . . . . . . . . . . . . . . . . . . . . . . . . . . . . . . . . . . . . PRIRMT
period
    period . . . . . . . . . . . . . . . . . . . . . . . . . . . . . . . . . . . . . . . . PERD
    periodic . . . . . . . . . . . . . . . . . . . . . . . . . . . . . . . . . . . . . . PERGD
    periodicity . . . . . . . . . . . . . . . . . . . . . . . . . . . . . . . . . . . . PEFRT
    *period of time* . . . . . . . . . . . . . . . . . . . . . . . . . . . . . . . . . P-FT
    *periods of time* . . . . . . . . . . . . . . . . . . . . . . . . . . . . . . . P-FTS
peripheral
    peripheral . . . . . . . . . . . . . . . . . . . . . . . . . . . . . . . . . . . . . . PRIF
    peripherally . . . . . . . . . . . . . . . . . . . . . . . . . . . . . . . . . . . PRIFL
    *peripheral vision* . . . . . . . . . . . . . . . . . . . . . . . . . . . . . PRIFGS
periphery . . . . . . . . . . . . . . . . . . . . . . . . . . . . . . . . . . . . . PRAOEF
perish
    perish . . . . . . . . . . . . . . . . . . . . . . . . . . . . . . . PROIRB, PR*IRB
    perishes . . . . . . . . . . . . . . . . . . . . . . . . . . . . . . PROIRBS, PRIRBZ
    perishing . . . . . . . . . . . . . . . . . . . . . . . . . . . . PROIRBG, PRIRBG
    perished . . . . . . . . . . . . . . . . . . . . . . . . . . . . . PROIRBD, PRIRBD
perishable . . . . . . . . . . . . . . . . . . . . . . . . . . . . . PROIBL, PR*IRBL
perishables . . . . . . . . . . . . . . . . . . . . . . . . . . . . PROIBLS, PRIRBLS
perjure
    perjure . . . . . . . . . . . . . . . . . . . . . . . . . . . . . . . . . . . . . . . . . P-J
    perjures . . . . . . . . . . . . . . . . . . . . . . . . . . . . . . . . . . . . . . . P-JS
    perjuring . . . . . . . . . . . . . . . . . . . . . . . . . . . . . . . . . . . . P-J/-G
    perjured . . . . . . . . . . . . . . . . . . . . . . . . . . . . . . . . . . . . . . . P-JD
perjurer . . . . . . . . . . . . . . . . . . . . . . . . . . . . . . . . . . . . . . . . PRERJ
perjury . . . . . . . . . . . . . . . . . . . . . . . . . . . . . . . . . . . . . . . . . PERJ
perm . . . . . . . . . . . . . . . . . . . . . . . . . . . . . . . . . . . . . . . . . P*ERM
permanence . . . . . . . . . . . . . . . . . . . . . . . . . . . . . . . . . . . . PAMS
permanency . . . . . . . . . . . . . . . . . . . . . . . . . . . . . . . . . . . PAMSZ
```

BRIEF ENCOUNTERS P

permanent . . . . PAMT, PERM
permanently . . . . PAEMT, PAOERM
permeate
    permeate . . . . PAERM
    permeates . . . . PAERMS
    permeating . . . . PAERMG
    permeated . . . . PAERMD
permeation . . . . PAERMGS
permissive
    permissive . . . . PIV
    permissively . . . . PIVL
    permissiveness . . . . PIVNS
permissibility . . . . PIBLT
permissible . . . . PIBL
permission . . . . PIGS
permit
    permit . . . . PERMT
    permits . . . . PERMTS
    permitting . . . . PERMGT, PERMG
    permitted . . . . PERMTD
permutation . . . . PERMGS
perpendicular . . . . PERP
perpetrate
    perpetrate . . . . PERPT
    perpetrates . . . . PERPTS, PERPS
    perpetrating . . . . PERPGT, PERPG
    perpetrated . . . . PERPTD, PERPD
perpetration . . . . PERPGS
perpetrator . . . . PRERP
perpetual . . . . PEFP
perpetually . . . . PEFPL
perpetuate
    perpetuate . . . . PEFPT
    perpetuates . . . . PEFPTS, PEFPS
    perpetuating . . . . PEFPGT, PEFPG
    perpetuated . . . . PEFPTD, PEFPD
perpetuation . . . . PEFPGS
persecute
    persecute . . . . SKWAOT
    persecutes . . . . SKWAOTS
    persecuting . . . . SKWAOGT, SKWAOG
    persecuted . . . . SKWAOTD
persecution . . . . SKWAOGS
persecutive . . . . SKWAOV
persecutor . . . . SKWAOR

© 1997 White-Boucke Publishing.   ILLEGAL TO PHOTOCOPY

persecutory. . . . . SKWOIR
perseverance. . . . . PAOEVRNS, PAOEFRNS
persevere
    persevere . . . . PAOEVR, PAOEFR
    perseveres . . . . PAOEVRS, PAOEFRS
    persevering. . . . . PAOEVRG, PAOEFRG
    persevered . . . . PAOEVRD, PAOEFRD
Persia . . . . PERZ
Persian . . . . PERGS
persist
    persist . . . . PIFT
    persists . . . . PIFTS
    persisting. . . . . PIFGT
    persisted . . . . PIFTD
persist
    persistence. . . . . PINS, PER/SINS
    persistency. . . . . PINSZ
    persistent. . . . . PINT, PER/SINT
    persistently . . . . PINL, PER/SINL
person
    person . . . . PERN
    persona . . . . P*ERN, POIRN
    personage. . . . . PERNG
    personages . . . . PERNGZ
    personal . . . . PERNL
    personality. . . . . PERNLT
    personally . . . . POIRNL, POINL
    personification. . . . . PERNGS
    personnel . . . . SNEL
perspective . . . . SPEVT, SPEK/TIV
perspiration . . . . SPIRGS
persuade
    persuade. . . . . PRAED
    persuades. . . . . PRAEDZ
    persuading . . . . PRAEGD
    persuaded . . . . PRAED/-D
persuasion . . . . PRAEGS
persuasive
    persuasive . . . . PRAEV
    persuasively . . . . PRAEVL
    persuasiveness . . . . PRAEVNS, PRAEFNS
pertain
    pertain . . . . PRAIN
    pertains. . . . . PRAINS
    pertaining . . . . PRAING

BRIEF ENCOUNTERS   P

pertained	PRAIND
pertinence	PERNTS
pertinency	PERNTSZ
pertinent	PERNT
perturb	
perturb	PERB
perturbs	PERBS
perturbing	PERB/-G
perturbed	PERBD
Peru	PRAO*U
Peruvian	PRAOUVN
perusable	PRAOUFBL
perusal	PRAOUFL
peruse	
peruse	PRAOUF
peruses	PRAOUFS
perusing	PRAOUFG
perused	PRAOUFD
peruser	PRAOUFR
pervasive	
pervasive	PAIV, PER/VAIV
pervasively	PAIVL, PER/VAIVL
pervasiveness	PAIVNS, PER/VAIVNS
perverse	P-VRS, P-FRS
perversion	P-VRGS, P-FRGS
pervert	
pervert	P-VRT, P-FRT, PEVRT
perverts	P-VRTS, P-FRTS, PEVRTS
perverting	P-VRGT, P-FRGT, PEVRGT
perverted	P-VRTD, P-FRTD, PEVRTD
pervious	
pervious	PEFRB
perviously	PEFRBL
perviousness	PEFRBS
pessimism	PIFM
pessimist	P*IS, PEMT
petal	PA*ELT
petition	PIRB
petitioner	PRIRB
petroleum	TROEL
pharmaceutical	FARL, FAURL
pharmacist	FARMT, FAURMT
pharmacology	FAURM
pharmacy	FARMZ, FAURMS
Ph.D.	H-PD

phenomena . . . . FON/NA
phenomenal . . . . FONL
phenomenon . . . . FON
Philadelphia . . . . F–LD, FIL/DEFL
Philippines . . . . FIPS
philosopher . . . . FLOFR
philosophical . . . . FLOFL
philosophically . . . . FLOEFL
philosophize
    philosophize . . . . FLAOIF
    philosophizes . . . . FLAOIFS
    philosophizing . . . . FLAOIFG
    philosophized . . . . FLAOIFD
philosophizer . . . . FLAOIFR
philosophy . . . . FLOF
phobia . . . . FOEB
phone
    phone call . . . . FOENK
    phone conversation . . . . F–FRGS
    phone number . . . . FUB
phonetic . . . . FOENT
phonetically . . . . FOENL
phoney . . . . FO*IN
phosphorus . . . . FOSZ
photocopier . . . . FOIRK
photocopy
    photocopy . . . . FOIK
    photocopies . . . . FOIKS
    photocopying . . . . FOIK/–G, FOIG
    photocopied . . . . FOIKD
photograph
    photograph . . . . FRAF
    photographs . . . . FRAFS
    photographing . . . . FRAFG
    photographed . . . . FRAFD
photograph
    photographer . . . . FRAFR
    photographic . . . . FRAFK
    photographically . . . . FRAFL, FRAEFK
    photography . . . . FRAEF
photostat . . . . FOIT, FOET/STAT
physical
    physical . . . . F–L
    physical education . . . . FEJ, PE/PE
    physical evidence . . . . FEVLD

BRIEF ENCOUNTERS P

physically . . . . FEFL, F*EL
physical therapist . . . . FAERPT
physical therapy . . . . FAERP
physician . . . . F-GS
physicians and surgeons . . . . FURNZ
physics . . . . FWIX
physiological . . . . FLOJ
physiology . . . . FOJ, FILZ
pianist . . . . PAONT
piano . . . . PAON
picket
    picket . . . . PIKT
    pickets . . . . PIKTS
    picketing . . . . PIKT/-G
    picketed . . . . PIKTD
picketer . . . . PIRKT
pickle
    pickle . . . . PIKL
    pickles . . . . PIKLS
    pickling . . . . PILG, PIKL/-G
    pickled . . . . PIKLD
pick up
    pick up . . . . PUP
    picks up . . . . PUPS
    picking up . . . . PUPG
    picked up . . . . PUPD
pictorial . . . . PIK/TORL
pictorially . . . . PIK/TOERL
picture
    picture . . . . PIR
    pictures . . . . PIRS
    picturing . . . . PIRG
    pictured . . . . PIRD
pidgin . . . . PIJD
pigeon . . . . PIJ
pigment . . . . PIMT
pilaf . . . . PLAUF
pilgrimage . . . . PLIJ
pillow . . . . PLO
pilot
    pilot . . . . PAOIT
    pilots . . . . PAOITS
    piloting . . . . PAOIGT
    piloted . . . . PAOITD
pilot light . . . . PAOILT

pimple	PIM
pinball	P-BL
pineapple	PAOINL
pioneer	
pioneer	PAOIRN
pioneers	PAOIRNS
pioneering	PAOIRNG
pioneered	PAOIRND
piracy	PAOIRS
pirate	
pirate	PAOIRT
pirates	PAOIRTS
pirating	PAOIRGT
pirated	PAOIRTD
pistol	STOL
pitcher	PRIFP
pitiful	PIFLT
pitifully	PAOEFLT
pituitary	PIRT, PIT/WIT
pivot	
pivot	PIVT
pivots	PIVTS
pivoting	PIVGT, PIVG
pivoted	PIVTD
pivotal	PIVLT
pixel	SPIX
placard	
placard	PLARD
placards	PLARDZ
placarding	PLARGD
placarded	PLARD/-D
place	
placement	PLAIFMT
place of business	PLAIBS
place of employment	PLAIMT
places of business	PLAIBSZ
places of employment	PLAIMTS
placebo	PLAOEB
plagiarism	PLAIFM
plagiarize	
plagiarize	PLAIJ
plagiarizes	PLAIJS
plagiarizing	PLAIJ/-G
plagiarized	PLAIJD
plagiarizer	PLAIRJ

BRIEF ENCOUNTERS   P

plague
    plague .... PLAEG
    plagues .... PLAEGZ
    plaguing .... PLAEG/-G
    plagued .... PLAEG/-D
plain
    plainclothes .... PLAIK
    plainly .... PLAINL
    plainness .... PLAINZ
plaintiff
    plaintiff .... PL-F
    plaintiff's attorney .... PL-FT
    plaintiff's exhibit .... PL-X
    Plaintiff's Exhibit .... P-X
plaintive
    plaintive .... PLAIV
    plaintively .... PLAIVL
    plaintiveness .... PLAIVNS
planet
    planet .... PLAENT
    planetarium .... PLAERM
    planetary .... PLAERNT
planner .... PLARN
plantation .... PLANGS
planter .... PLARNT
plastic
    plastic .... PLAS, PLAFK
    plastic bag .... PLAG
    plastic bottle .... PLAB
    plastic surgeon .... PLURN
    plastic surgery .... PLURG
platform .... PLAFRM
platitude .... PLATD
platoon .... PLAON
plausibility .... PLAUBLT
plausible .... PLAUB
plausibleness .... PLAUNS
plausibly .... PLAUBL
play
    play .... PLAI
    plays .... PLAIZ
    playing .... PLAIG
    played .... PLAID
play
    player .... PLAIR

playful	PLAIF
playfully	PLAIFL
playfulness	PLAIFNS
playground	PLAIGD
plaza	PLAUZ

plea

plea agreement	PLAEMT
plea of	PLEF
plea of guilty	PLOG
plea of no contest	PLOEK
plea of not guilty	PLENG

plea bargain

plea bargain	PLEB
plea bargains	PLEBS
plea bargaining	PLEBG
plea bargained	PLEBD
pleading	PLAEGD

pleasant

pleasant	PLEZ
pleasantly	PLELZ
pleasantness	PLENZ

please

please	PLES, PLAOES
pleases	PLEFS, PLAOEFS
pleasing	PLEFG, PLAOEFG
pleased	PLEFD, PLAOEFD
please be seated	PAOETD
please the Court	PLOURT
pleasurable	PLERBL
pleasure	PLERB
pledge of allegiance	PLAOEJS
plenipotentiary	PLEN

plentiful

plentiful	PLEFL
plentifully	PLAOEFL
plentifulness	PLEFNS

plenty

plenty	PLENT
plenty of the	PLEFT
plenty of them	PLEFM
plenty of these	PLEFZ
plethora	PL*ET
plexus	PLEKZ

plumb

plumb	PLUM, PLUB

BRIEF ENCOUNTERS — P

plumbs	PLUMS, PLUBS
plumbing	PLUMG, PLUB/-G
plumbed	PLUMD, PLUBD
plumber	PLOIRM, PL*URM

plummet
plummet	PLUMT
plummets	PLUMTS
plummeting	PLUMGT
plummeted	PLUMTD

plunder
plunder	PLUND
plunders	PLUNDZ
plundering	PLUNGD
plundered	PLUND/-D

plunderer	PLURND

plunge
plunge	PLUJ
plunges	PLUJS
plunging	PLUJ/-G, PLUNG
plunged	PLUJD

plunger	PLURJ
plural	PLURL
plurality	PLURLT
plus or minus	PLURM, PLURMS
p.m.	P-M
PMS	P-MS
pneumatic	NAOUMT
pneumonia	NAOUM

pocket
pocket	POKT
pockets	POKTS
pocketing	POKT/-G
pocketed	POKTD

podium	POEMD, POED
poet	POET
poetic	POEGT
poignance	POINZ
poignant	POIT
poignantly	POILT

point
pointer	POIRNT
pointless	POINLT
point of law	POIFL
point of view	POIF
points of law	POIFLS

P

points of view	POIFS
poison	
poison	POI
poisons	POIS
poisoning	POIG
poisoned	POID
poisoner	POIR
poker	POERK
Poland	PLOEND
polar	
polar	POERL
polarity	PLAIRT
polarization	POELGS
polarize	
polarize	POELT
polarizes	POELTS
polarizing	POELGT, POELG
polarized	POELTD
police	
police	PLOIF, PLIS
polices	PLOIFS
policing	PLOIFG
policed	PLOIFD
police	
police department	PLEPT
police dog	PLAUG
police force	PLORS
policeman	PLAM
policemen	PLEM
police officer	PLOFR
police report	PLORT
police station	PLAIGS
policy	POIL
polish	
polish	PLORB
polishes	PLORBS
polishing	PLORBG
polished	PLORBD
Polish	POERB, PLOERB
polite	
polite	PLOIT
politely	PLOILT
politeness	PLOINS
politic	
politic	PLOK

BRIEF ENCOUNTERS P

political . . . . PLIL
politically. . . . . PLAOEL
politician. . . . . POLGS
politics . . . . PLOX
politicize
    politicize. . . . . PLIT
    politicizes . . . . PLITS
    politicizing. . . . . PLIT/-G
    politicized. . . . . PLITD
pollen. . . . . PLON
pollutant. . . . . PLAOUNT
pollution. . . . . PLAOUGS
polygamist . . . . PLIGT
polygamy. . . . . PL*IG
pomegranate. . . . . PRANT
ponder
    ponder. . . . . PORND
    ponders . . . . PORNDZ
    pondering. . . . . PORNGD
    pondered. . . . . PORND/-D
pontificate
    pontificate . . . . PAUNT
    pontificates . . . . PAUNTS
    pontificating . . . . PAUNGT
    pontificated . . . . PAUNTD
pontification. . . . . PAUNGS
pontificator. . . . . PAURNT
poor
    poor . . . . PAOR
    poorer . . . . PRAOR
    poorly . . . . PAORL
poplar. . . . . PLAP
poplar tree. . . . . PLAPT
populace. . . . . PLAZ
popular. . . . . PLARP
popularity . . . . POPT, PLARPT
population . . . . POPGS
porch . . . . POFP
porn
    porn. . . . . PORN
    porno. . . . . POERN
    pornography. . . . . PORNG, PO*RN
porpoise . . . . POERP
porridge . . . . POERJ
portability . . . . PORBLT

portable	PORBL
portal	PORLT
portrait	P–RT
portray	
portray	POR
portrays	PORS
portraying	PORG
portrayed	PORD
portrayal	PORL
Portugal	PORGT
Portuguese	PORGZ
position	
position	POGS
positions	POGSZ
positioning	POGS/–G, POG
positioned	POGS/–D, POGD
positive	
positive	POF, POV, POZ
positively	POFL, POVL
positiveness	POFNS, POVNS
possess	
possess	PES
possesses	PEFS, PESZ
possessing	PEFG
possessed	PEFD
possession	PEGS
possibility	POBLT
possible	POBL
possibly	POEBL
post	
postage	POEJ
postal	POEFL
posterior	PAO*R
posteriorly	PAO*RL
posthumous	PAOUM
postmortem	PORMT
post office	POFS
postponement	POEMT
postpone	
postpone	POEN
postpones	POENS
postponing	POENG
postponed	POEND
postulate	
postulate	POFLT

BRIEF ENCOUNTERS   P

postulates	POFLTS
postulating	POFLGT, POFLG
postulated	POFLTD
postulation	POFLGS
potable	POEBT
potassium	PAUT, PO/TAS
potato	POE
potatoes	POEZ
potential	
potential	POERBL
potentiality	POERBLT
potentially	PAOERBL
poultry	POULT
poverty	POVRT
powder	
powder	PAUD
powders	PAUDZ
powdering	PAUGD
powdered	PAUD/-D
power	
power	PAUR
powers	PAURS
powering	PAURG
powered	PAURD
power	
powerful	PAUF
powerfully	PAUFL
powerless	PAURL
power of attorney	PAURN, PAUFRT
PR	P-R
practicability	PRAKLT
practicable	PRAKL
practicableness	PRAKLS
practicably	PRAEKL
practical	
practical	PRAK
practicality	PRAKT
practically	PRAEK
practice	
practice	PRA
practices	PRAS
practicing	PRAG
practiced	PRAD
practitioner	PRAR
pragmatic	PRAGT

© 1997 White-Boucke Publishing.

precarious
- precarious . . . . PRAERK, PRAIRK
- precariously. . . . . PRAERL
- precariousness. . . . . PRAERNS

precaution . . . . PRAUGS
precautionary . . . . PRAURGS
precautious
- precautious. . . . . PRAURB
- precautiously. . . . . PRAURBL
- precautiousness . . . . PRAUNS

precede
- precede. . . . . PROID
- precedes . . . . PROIDZ
- preceding. . . . . PROIGD, PROIG
- preceded . . . . PROID/-D

precedence. . . . . PR-NS
precedency. . . . . PR-NSZ
precedent . . . . PR-NT
precedential. . . . . PR-NL
precept . . . . PREPT
precinct. . . . . PRINGT
precious. . . . . PR-RB, PR*ERB
preciously. . . . . PR-RBL, PRERBL
precipitate
- precipitate . . . . PRIP
- precipitates. . . . . PRIPS
- precipitating. . . . . PRIPG
- precipitated . . . . PRIPD

precipitation. . . . . PR*IPGS, PRAIPGS
precise
- precise . . . . PRAOIF
- precisely . . . . PRAOILS
- preciseness. . . . . PRAOINS, PRAOIFNS

precision . . . . PRIGS
preclude
- preclude. . . . . PLAOU
- precludes . . . . PLAOUS
- precluding . . . . PLAOUG
- precluded . . . . PLAOUD

preclusion. . . . . PLAO*UGS, PLAOGS
preclusive. . . . . PLAOUV
preclusively. . . . . PLAOUVL
precocious
- precocious . . . . PROERB
- precociously . . . . PROERBL

BRIEF ENCOUNTERS P

precociousness	PROENS, PROERNS
predator	PRED
predict	
predict	PRIKT
predicts	PRIKTS
predicting	PRIKT/-G, PRIG
predicted	PRIKTD
predict	
predictability	PRIBLT
predictable	PRIBL
prediction	PRIX
preempt	
preempt	PREMT
preempts	PREMTS
preempting	PREMGT, PREMG
preempted	PREMTD
preempt	
preemption	PREMGS, PREM
preemptive	PREVMT
preemptive strike	PRAOIKT
preface	PREF
prefaces	PREFZ
prefect	PREFK
prefer	
prefer	PREFR
prefers	PREFRS
preferring	PREFRG
preferred	PREFRD
prefer	
preferability	PREFRBLT
preferable	PREFRBL
preferably	PRAEFRBL
preference	PREFRNS
preferential	PREFRNL
prefix	PRAOEFX, PREFX
pregnancies	PRAEGZ
pregnancy	PRAEG
pregnant	PREG
prejudice	PREJ
prejudicial	PRIRBL
prelim	
prelim	PL*IM
preliminary	PLIM
preliminary examination	PLEX
preliminary hearing	PLEG

preliminary hearings	PLEGZ
premature	
premature	PRAUR
prematurely	PRAURL
prematureness	PRAURNS
prematurity	PRAURT
premeditate	
premeditate	PRAEMT
premeditates	PRAEMTS
premeditating	PRAEMGT, PRAEMG
premeditated	PRAEMTD
premeditation	PRAEMGS
premier	PRAOERM
premiere	PRERM
premise	PR-M, PREMS
premium	PRAOEM
prenuptial	NUPT
preoccupation	PROUPGS
preoccupy	
preoccupy	PROUP
preoccupies	PROUPS
preoccupying	PROUPG
preoccupied	PROUPD
preordain	
preordain	PRORN
preordains	PRORNS
preordaining	PRORNG
preordained	PRORND
preordainment	PRORMT
preparation	PREPGS
preparatory	PRAEPT, PREP/TOIR
prepare	
prepare	PRAOEP
prepares	PRAOEPS
preparing	PRAOEPG
prepared	PRAOEPD
preponderance	P-P
preponderance of the evidence	P-PD
preponderate	
preponderate	P-PT
preponderates	P-PTS
preponderating	P-PGT, P-PG
preponderated	P-PTD
prerequisite	PREKT, PRIFT
prerogative	PROGT

BRIEF ENCOUNTERS   P

Presbyterian . . . . PRAOERN
preschool . . . . PRAOL
preschooler . . . . PRAORL
prescience . . . . PRERBZ
prescient . . . . PRERBT
prescribe
    prescribe . . . . PRAOIB
    prescribes . . . . PRAOIBS
    prescribing . . . . PRAOIBG
    prescribed . . . . PRAOIBD
prescription . . . . PRIPGS
presence . . . . PRENS
present
    present . . . . PRENT
    presents . . . . PRENTS
    presenting . . . . PRENGT, PRENG
    presented . . . . PRENTD
present
    presentable . . . . PREBL
    presentation . . . . PREGS, PRENGS
    presenter . . . . PRERNT
    presently . . . . PRENL
preservation . . . . PREFRX
preservative . . . . PREFRBT
preserve
    preserve . . . . PREFRB
    preserves . . . . PREFRBS
    preserving . . . . PREFRBG
    preserved . . . . PREFRBD
presidency . . . . P–TSZ
president . . . . P–T
presidential . . . . P–LT
press
    press conference . . . . PR–FRNS
    press release . . . . PRAOES
    press room . . . . PRAOM
pressure
    pressure . . . . PRERB
    pressures . . . . PRERBS
    pressuring . . . . PRERBG
    pressured . . . . PRERBD
prestige . . . . PRAOEJ
prestigious . . . . PRAOEJS
presumable . . . . PRUL
presumably . . . . PRUBL

presume
- presume . . . . PRAOUM
- presumes . . . . PRAOUMS
- presuming . . . . PRAOUMG
- presumed . . . . PRAOUMD

presumed innocent . . . . PRAOUNT
presumption . . . . PRUMGS, PRUM
presumption of innocence . . . . PRUJ
pretend
- pretend . . . . PREND
- pretends . . . . PRENDZ
- pretending . . . . PRENGD
- pretended . . . . PREND/-D

pretense . . . . PRETS
pretty
- pretty . . . . PRET
- ***pretty good*** . . . . PRAOG, PRAOGD
- ***pretty hard*** . . . . PRARD
- ***pretty much*** . . . . PREFP

pretrial . . . . PRAOIL
pretrials . . . . PRAOILZ
prevail
- prevail . . . . PRAIL
- prevails . . . . PRAILS
- prevailing . . . . PRAILG
- prevailed . . . . PRAILD

prevailer . . . . PRAIRL
prevalence . . . . PREFLS, PREVLS
prevalent . . . . PREFLT, PREVLT
prevalently . . . . PRAOEFLT, PRAOEVLT
prevent
- prevent . . . . PREFNT, PREVNT
- prevents . . . . PREFNTS, PREVNTS
- preventing . . . . PREFNG, PREVNG
- prevented . . . . PREFNTD, PREVNTD

prevent
- preventative . . . . PRAEFN, PRAEVN
- prevention . . . . PREFNGS, PREVNGS
- preventive . . . . PREFN, PREVN
- preventively . . . . PREVNL

preview
- preview . . . . PRAOUV
- previews . . . . PRAOUVS
- previewing . . . . PRAOUVG
- previewed . . . . PRAOUVD

BRIEF ENCOUNTERS   P

previous
- previous . . . PREV
- previously . . . PREVL
- *previous to* . . . PREVT

prickle
- prickle . . . PRIKL
- prickles . . . PRIKLS
- prickling . . . PRILG, PRIKL/-G
- prickled . . . PRIKLD

prima facie . . . PRAIRB, PRIM/FAIRB

primary . . . PROIRM

prime
- *prime minister* . . . PROIMT, PROIM
- primer . . . PRAOIRM
- *prime time* . . . PRAOIMT

princess . . . PRES

princesses . . . PRES/-S

principal
- principal . . . PRAL
- principality . . . PRINLT
- principally . . . PRINL

principle . . . PREL

printer . . . PRIRNT

printout . . . PROUT

prior
- prior . . . PRAOIR
- *prior inconsistent statement* . . . PRIMT
- priority . . . PROIRT, PRAO*IRT
- *prior to* . . . PRAOIRT
- *prior to the* . . . PRAOIRTD

prioritize
- prioritize . . . PROIR
- prioritizes . . . PROIRS
- prioritizing . . . PROIRG
- prioritized . . . PROIRD

prism . . . PRIFM

prison
- prison . . . PRIN, PRIZ
- prisoner . . . PRIR
- prisons . . . PRINZ, PRISZ

privacy . . . PRAOIVZ

private
- private . . . PRAOIVT
- privately . . . PRAOIVLT, PRAOIVL
- *private school* . . . VAOL

privatization . . . . PRAOIFGS
privation . . . . PRIVGS
privilege. . . . . PRIV
privileged. . . . . PRIVD
probability . . . . PROBLT
probable . . . . PROBL
probable cause . . . . PRAUZ
probably . . . . PRAOEBL, PROEBL
probate
    probate . . . . PRAIB
    probates . . . . PRAIBS
    probating. . . . . PRAIBG
    probated . . . . PRAIBD
probate court. . . . . PRAIBT, PRAIKT
probative value . . . . PROEV
probation
    probation. . . . . PRAIX
    probationer . . . . PRAIRX
    probation officer . . . . PRAIFR
problem . . . . PROB
problematic. . . . . PROBT
procedural. . . . . PRAOERL
procedure. . . . . PRAOER
proceed
    proceed . . . . PRAOED
    proceeds . . . . PRAOEDZ
    proceeding. . . . . PRAOEGD, PRAOEG
    proceeded . . . . PRAOED/-D
proceedings . . . . PRAOEGS
process
    process . . . . PROS
    processes . . . . PROFS, PROSZ
    processing . . . . PROFG
    processed. . . . . PROFD
processor. . . . . PRORS
proclaim
    proclaim . . . . PLAIM
    proclaims. . . . . PLAIMS
    proclaiming . . . . PLAIMG
    proclaimed . . . . PLAIMD
proclaimer. . . . . PLAIRM
proclamation . . . . PLAIMGS
proclivity . . . . PLIVT
procrastinate
    procrastinate. . . . . PRAFT

procrastinates	PRAFTS
procrastinating	PRAFGT
procrastinated	PRAFTD
procrastination	PRAFGS
procrastinator	PRAFRT
procurable	PRAOURBL
procurance	PRAOURNS

procure
procure	PRAOUR
procures	PRAOURS
procuring	PRAOURG
procured	PRAOURD

procurement	PRAOURMT
prodigy	PRAUJ

produce
produce	PRU
produces	PRUS
producing	PRUG
produced	PRUD

producer	PRUR

product
product	PRUT
production	PRUX, PRUGS
productive	PRUV
productively	PRUVL
productiveness	PRUVNS, PRUFNS
productivity	PRUVT

profess
profess	PROEF
professes	PROEFS
professing	PROEFG
professed	PROEFD

profession
profession	PROEFGS, PROFGS, PR–FGS
professional	PROEFL, PR–FL
professionalism	PR–FM
professionally	PRAOEFL

professor	PROFR, PROEFR

proffer
proffer	PRAUFR
proffers	PRAUFRS
proffering	PRAUFRG
proffered	PRAUFRD

profile
profile	PROIL

profiles	PROILS
profiling	PROILG
profiled	PROILD
profit	
profit	PROFT
profits	PROFTS
profiting	PROFGT
profited	PROFTD
profound	PROFND
profoundly	PROFNL
profundity	PROFNT, FUNT, FUNTD
prognoses	PROEGS
prognosis	PROEG
prognostic	PROEGT
program	
program	PRAM
programs	PRAMS
programming	PRAMG
programmed	PRAMD
program	
programmability	PRABLT
programmable	PRABL
programmer	PRARM
progress	
progress	PROG
progresses	PROGZ
progressing	PROG/-G
progressed	PROGD
progress	
progression	PROGS
progressive	PROF
progressively	PROFL
progressiveness	PROFNS
prohibit	
prohibit	HIB, HIBT
prohibits	HIBS, HIBTS
prohibiting	HIB/-G, HIBGT
prohibited	HIBD, HIBTD
prohibition	HIX
prohibitive	
prohibitive	HIVB, HIFB
prohibitively	HIVBL, HIFBL
prohibitiveness	HIVNS, HIBNS
project	
project	PROJ

projects	PROJS
projecting	PROJ/-G
projected	PROJD
projection	PROEJ
pro-life	PLAOIF
pro-lifer	PLAOIFR

proliferate
proliferate	PLIF
proliferates	PLIFS
proliferating	PLIFG
proliferated	PLIFD

proliferation	PLIFGS
proliferous	PLOUFS
prolific	PLIFK

prolong
prolong	PLONG
prolongs	PLONGZ
prolonging	PLONG/-G
prolonged	PLONGD

prolongate
prolongate	PLONGT
prolongates	PLONGTS
prolongating	PLONGT/-G
prolongated	PLONGTD

prolongation	PLONGS
prolonger	PLORNG
prom	PRAUM, PRO*M
prominent	PRONT
prominently	PRONLT, PRONL
promiscuity	SKMAOUT

promiscuous
promiscuous	SKMOUS, PROUS
promiscuously	SKMOUL, SKMAOEL
promiscuousness	SKMOUNS

promise
promise	PROM
promises	PROMS
promising	PROMG
promised	PROMD

promissory note	PROET

promote
promote	PROEMT
promotes	PROEMTS
promoting	PROEMGT, PROEMG
promoted	PROEMTD

P

promotion	PROEMGS
pronounce	
pronounce	PROUN
pronounces	PROUNS
pronouncing	PROUNG
pronounced	PROUND
pronouncement	PROUMT
pronunciation	PROUNGS
proof	PRAOF
propaganda	PROPGD
proper	
proper	PROR
properly	PRORL
property	PROT
property rights	PRORTS
prophet	PROEFT
prophylactic	FLAKT
proponent	PROENT
proportion	
proportion	PRORGS, PRORPGS
proportional	PRORLGS
proportionate	PRORNT
proportionately	PRORNLT, PRORNL
proposal	PROEPL
propose	
propose	PROEP
proposes	PROEPS
proposing	PROEPG
proposed	PROEPD
proposition	PROPGS
proprietarily	PR–LT
proprietary	PR–T, PRAERT
proprietor	PR–RT, PROPT
proprietorship	PRORP
propriety	PRAOIT, PRAOIPT
propulsion	PRULGS
prosecute	
prosecute	PR–
prosecutes	PR–S
prosecuting	PR–G
prosecuted	PR–D
prosecution	PR–GS
prosecutor	PR–R
prosecutorial	PR–L

- prospect
  - prospect . . . . PR–P
  - prospects . . . . PR–PS
  - prospecting . . . . PR–PG
  - prospected . . . . PR–PD
- prospective . . . . PR–VP
- prospector . . . . PR–RP
- prosper
  - prosper . . . . PRER
  - prospers . . . . PRERS
  - prospering . . . . PRERG
  - prospered . . . . PRERD
- prosper
  - prosperity . . . . PRERT
  - prosperous . . . . PRERZ
  - prosperously . . . . PRERL
  - prosperousness . . . . PRERNS
- prostate . . . . PRAET
- prosthetic . . . . PRO*T
- prostitute
  - prostitute . . . . PRAOT
  - prostitutes . . . . PRAOTS
  - prostituting . . . . PRAOGT
  - prostituted . . . . PRAOTD
- prostitution . . . . PRAOGS
- protect
  - protect . . . . PREK
  - protects . . . . PREKZ
  - protecting . . . . PREK/–G
  - protected . . . . PREKD
- protection . . . . PREX
- protective . . . . PREVK
  - ***protective custody*** . . . . PREVD, PRUVD
  - protectively . . . . PRAOEVK
  - protectiveness . . . . PREVNS
- protegé . . . . PRAIJ
- protein . . . . PROIN
- protest
  - protest . . . . PREFT
  - protests . . . . PREFTS
  - protesting . . . . PREFGT
  - protested . . . . PREFTD
- protester . . . . PREFRT
- protocol . . . . KPROET
- prototype . . . . PRAOIP

protrusion	PRAOUGS
proudly	PROULD
provable	PROVBL
prove	
prove	PROV
proves	PROVS
proving	PROVG
proved / proven	PROVD / PROVN
provide	
provide	VAOID
provides	VAOIDZ
providing	VAOIGD
provided	VAOID/-D
provision	PROIGS
provocative	VOK
provocation	PROVGS
provoke	
provoke	PROEK, PROEFK
provokes	PROEKS, PROEFKS
provoking	PROEK/-G, PROEFK/-G
provoked	PROEKD, PROEFKD
prowler	PROURL
proximate	
proximate	PR-KT, PRAUK
proximate cause	PR-K, PRAUS
proximately	PROX/LI, PRAUL
proximity	PR-MT, PRAUT
proxy	PRO*X, PRAUX
prudence	PRUNS
prudent	
prudent	PRUNT
prudently	PRUNL, PRUNLT
prudent person	PRUP
Prussia	PRURB
Prussian	PRURN
psalm	ZAUM
pseudo	SWAO
pseudonym	SWOIM
psyche	SKPAOE
psychedelic	SDEL
psychedelically	SDELG
psychiatric	SKAOIK
psychiatrist	SKAOIT
psychiatry	SKRAOE
psychic	SK*IK, SKOIK

BRIEF ENCOUNTERS   P

psychically . . . . SKOIL
psycho
    psycho . . . . SKOE
    psychological . . . . SKOJ
    psychologically . . . . SKOEJ
    psychologist . . . . SKOLT
    psychology . . . . SKOLG
    psychopath . . . . SKPA*T, SKPAT
    psychoses . . . . SKAOEZ
    psychosis . . . . SKOEZ
    psychotherapist . . . . STHAERPT, STHAIRPT
    psychotherapy . . . . STHAERP, STHAIRP
    psychotic . . . . SKOK
puberty . . . . PAOUBT
public
    public . . . . PUB
    publication . . . . PUX
    public defender . . . . PUD
    Public Defender's Office . . . . PUD/OFS
    publicist . . . . PUBLT
    publicity . . . . PUBT
    publicly . . . . PUBL
    public relations . . . . PRELGS, P-RS
    public school . . . . PLAOL
    Public Utilities Commission . . . . POIKZ, POIK/POIK
publicize
    publicize . . . . PLAOIZ
    publicizes . . . . PLAOIFS
    publicizing . . . . PLAOIFG
    publicized . . . . PLAOIFD
publish
    publish . . . . PL-RB
    publishes . . . . PL-RBS
    publishing . . . . PL-RBG
    published . . . . PL-RBD
publisher . . . . PLIR
PUC . . . . POIK
pudding . . . . PUGD
Puerto Rico . . . . P*R
Puerto Rican . . . . P*RN, P-RN
pull out
    pull out . . . . PLOUT
    pulls out . . . . PLOUTS
    pulling out . . . . PLOUGT
    pulled out . . . . PLOUTD

P — BRIEF ENCOUNTERS

pull over
   pull over . . . . PLOVR
   pulls over . . . . PLOVRS
   pulling over . . . . PLOVRG
   pulled over . . . . PLOVRD
pull up
   pull up . . . . PLUP
   pulls up . . . . PLUPS
   pulling up . . . . PLUPG
   pulled up . . . . PLUPD
pulp . . . . PL*UP, POUP
pump
   pump . . . . PUM
   pumps . . . . PUMS
   pumping . . . . PUMG
   pumped . . . . PUMD
punch
   punch . . . . PUFP
   punches . . . . PUFPS
   punching . . . . PUFPG
   punched . . . . PUFPD
punctual . . . . PUNL
punctuate
   punctuate . . . . PUNGT
   punctuates . . . . PUNGTS
   punctuating . . . . PUNGT/–G
   punctuated . . . . PUNGTD
punctuation . . . . PUNGS
puncture
   puncture . . . . PUNG
   punctures . . . . PUNGZ
   puncturing . . . . PUNG/–G
   punctured . . . . PUNGD
punish
   punish . . . . P–RB
   punishes . . . . P–RBS
   punishing . . . . P–RBG
   punished . . . . P–RBD
punishable . . . . P–RBL
punishment . . . . P–RBT, PUMT
punitive
   punitive . . . . PAOUV
   punitive damages . . . . PAOUVD, P–DZ
   punitively . . . . PAOUVL
pupil . . . . PAOUP

BRIEF ENCOUNTERS   P

puppy . . . . POIP
purchase
    purchase . . . . PR-FP
    purchases . . . . PR-FPS
    purchasing . . . . PR-FPG
    purchased . . . . PR-FPD
purchaser . . . . PR-FRP
purely . . . . PAOURL
purification . . . . PURGS
purism . . . . PAOUFM, PAOUFRM
purist . . . . PAOUFT, PAOUFRT
puritan . . . . PAOURN
puritanical . . . . PAOURNT, PAOURNL
purity . . . . PAOURT
purple . . . . PURPL
purport
    purport . . . . PURPT
    purports . . . . PURPTS
    purporting . . . . PURPGT, PURPG
    purported . . . . PURPTD
purpose
    purpose . . . . PURP
    purposeful . . . . PUFRL
    purposefully . . . . PAOEFRL
pursuance . . . . PURNS
pursuant . . . . PURNT
pursuant to . . . . PURNTD
pursue
    pursue . . . . PRAOU
    pursues . . . . PRAOUS
    pursuing . . . . PRAOUG
    pursued . . . . PRAOU/-D
pursuit . . . . PRAOUT
purulent . . . . PAOURLT
purview . . . . PAOUF
put
    put . . . . PUT
    puts . . . . PUTS
    putting . . . . PUGT
    put . . . . PUT
putative . . . . PAOUVT
puzzle
    puzzle . . . . PUFL
    puzzles . . . . PUFLS
    puzzling . . . . PUFLG

puzzled .... PUFLD
pyramid .... PIRMD

Q

quadriceps	KWEPS
quadriplegia	KWAOEJ
quadriplegic	KWAOEK
quadruple	
quadruple	DRAOUPL
quadruples	DRAOUPLS
quadrupling	DRAOUPLG
quadrupled	DRAOUPLD
quadruplet	DRAOUPLT, KRAOUPT
qualification	KW-FGS
qualifier	KW-FR
qualify	
qualify	KW-F
qualifies	KW-FS
qualifying	KW-FG
qualified	KW-FD
quality	KWALT
quandary	KWAND
quantitative	
quantitative	KWAIV
quantitatively	KWAIVL
quantitativeness	KWAIVNS
quantity	KWANT
quantum	KWAN
quarantine	
quarantine	KWAURNT, KWARN
quarantines	KWAURNTS, KWARNS
quarantining	KWAURNGT, KWAURNG, KWARNG
quarantined	KWAURNTD, KWARND
quarrel	
quarrel	KWARL
quarrels	KWARLS
quarreling	KWARLG
quarreled	KWARLD
quarrelsome	KWARM
quarry	KWAUR
quarter	KWAERT
quarterly	KWAERL, KWAERLT
quartz	KWARZ, KWA*RTS, KWARTSZ
quay	KWAE
queasy	KWAOEZ

Q BRIEF ENCOUNTERS

Quebec .... KWEB
quench
    quench .... KWEFP
    quenches .... KWEFPS
    quenching .... KWEFPG
    quenched .... KWEFPD
querulous .... KWERL
question
    question .... KWE
    questions .... KWES
    questioning .... KWEG
    questioned .... KWED
question
    questionability .... KWEBLT
    questionable .... KWEBL
    questionably .... KWAEBL
    questioner .... KWER
    questioners .... KWERZ
    question mark .... KWARK
    question of fact .... KWEFT
    question of law .... KWEFL
    questions? .... KWEZ
    questions of fact .... KWEFTS
    questions of law .... KWEFLS
queue
    queue .... KWAOU
    queues .... KWAOUS
    queuing .... KWAOUG
    queued .... KWAOUD
quibble
    quibble .... KWIBL
    quibbles .... KWIBLS
    quibbling .... KWIBLG
    quibbled .... KWIBLD
quibbler .... KWIRBL
quicken
    quicken .... KWEN
    quickens .... KWEN/-S
    quickening .... KWENG
    quickened .... KWEND
quid pro quo .... KW-P
quiet
    quiet .... KWAET
    quieter .... KWAOIRT
    quieter than .... KWAOIRN

BRIEF ENCOUNTERS   Q

quieter than the . . . . KWAOIRNT
quieter than these . . . . KWAOIRNZ
quieter than those . . . . KWAOIRNS
quietly . . . . KWAOILT
quintessence . . . . KWENZ
quintessential . . . . KWINT
quintuple . . . . KWUP
quintuplet . . . . KWUPT
quit
   quit . . . . KWIT
   quits . . . . KWITS
   quitting . . . . KWIGT
   quit . . . . KWIT
quitter . . . . KWIRT
quite a
   quite a bit . . . . KWAOIB
   quite a bit of . . . . KWAOIFB
   quite a bit of the . . . . KWAOIFBT
   quite a bit of these . . . . KWAOIFBZ
   quite a bit of those . . . . KWAOIFBS
   quite a few . . . . KWAOIF
   quite a few of the . . . . KWAOIFTD
   quite a few of them . . . . KWAOIFM
   quite a few of these . . . . KWAOIFZ
   quite a few of those . . . . KWAOIFS
   quite a few times . . . . KWAIOFT
   quite a while . . . . KWAOIL
   quite a while ago . . . . KWAOILG
quiver
   quiver . . . . KWIVR
   quivers . . . . KWIVRS
   quivering . . . . KWIVRG
   quivered . . . . KWIVRD
quorum . . . . KWOERM
quota . . . . KWA
quotable . . . . KWOEBL
quotas . . . . KWAZ
quotation . . . . KWOEGS
quotient . . . . KWOERB, KWOERBT

R

rabbit . . . . RABT
rabid . . . . RABD
rabies . . . . RAIB, RAIBS
racial . . . . RAIRB
racially . . . . RAIRBL
racism . . . . RAIFM
racket . . . . RAEKT
racquetball . . . . KWABL
radar . . . . DAR
radiance . . . . RAINZ
radiant . . . . RAINT
radiantly . . . . RAINL, RAINLT
radiate
    radiate . . . . YAET
    radiates . . . . YAETS
    radiating . . . . YAEGT
    radiated . . . . YAETD
radiation . . . . YAEGS
radiator . . . . YAERT
radical . . . . RALD
radically . . . . RAELD
radio
    radio . . . . RAO
    radioactive . . . . RAOV
    radioactively . . . . RAOVL
    radioactivity . . . . RAOVT
    radiologist . . . . ROLT, RAOLT
    radiology . . . . RAOLG
    radio show . . . . RAOZ
    radio shows . . . . RAOSZ
    radio station . . . . RAOGS
radius . . . . RUS
railroad
    railroad . . . . R–R
    railroad crossing . . . . R–RK
    railroad crossings . . . . R–RKZ
    railroad track . . . . R–RT
rainfall . . . . RAIFL
raise
    raise . . . . RAIZ
    raises . . . . RAIFS
    raising . . . . RAIFG

BRIEF ENCOUNTERS R

raised	RAIFD
raiser	RAIRZ
raise your right hand	RURD
RAM	RA*M
ramification	RAMGS, RAM/F-X
rampant	RAMT

ranch
ranch	RAFP
ranches	RAFPS
ranching	RAFPG
ranched	RAFPD

random
random	RAON
randomly	RAONL
randomness	RAONS

range
range	RAENG, RAING
ranges	RAENGS, RAINGS
ranging	RAENG/-G, RAING/-G
ranged	RAENGD, RAINGD

ranger	RAERNG

rapid
rapid	ROIP
rapidly	ROIPL
rapid transit	ROIPT

rapist	RAIPT
rapport	RART, RARP, RAORP, RAORPT
rarely	RAIRL
rareness	RAIRNS, RAERNS
raring	RAERG
raring to	RAERGT
rarity	RAERT, RAIRT
ratchet	RAFPT

rather
rather	RAFR
rather than	RAFRN
rather than the	RAFRNT
rather the	RAFRT

ratification	RAFGS, RAT/F-X
ratio	RAERB

rational
rational	RAL
rationale	RA*L
rationalization	RALGS

raucous	RAUK

R

raven	RAIVN
ravenous	RAVNS
ravine	RAVN
ravines	RAVNZ
razer	RAERZ

razor

razor	RAS, RAZ
razor blade	RABZ
razor blades	RABSZ
razors	RASZ
re	RAOE
reachable	RAOEFBL

react

react	RAKT
reacts	RAKTS
reacting	RAKT/-G
reacted	RAKTD

react

reaction	RAX
reactive	RAVK
reactor	RARKT

read

read	RAED
reads	RAEDZ
reading	RAEGD
read	RAED
reader	RAERD
readership	RAERP
readily	R-LD

readjust

readjust	RAUF
readjusts	RAUFS
readjusting	RAUFG
readjusted	RAUFD
readjustment	RAUFMT
ready	R-D
ready to proceed	RAOEG
Reagan	RAEG

real

real estate	REA
real estate agent	RAEJT
real good	RAELG, RAELGD
realism	RAEFM
realization	ROIFGS
really	REL

BRIEF ENCOUNTERS R

realtime	ELT
realtime captioning	RAPGS
realtime captionist	RARPGS
realty	RAOELT

realize
realize	ROIF
realizes	ROIFS
realizing	ROIFG
realized	ROIFD

rear view mirror	RAEM

reason
reason	R-N
reasons	R-NS
reasoning	R-NG
reasoned	R-ND

reason
reasonability	R-NLT
reasonable	R-NL
reasonable doubt	-RD
reasonableness	R-NLS

reassignment	RAOIMT

rebut
rebut	REBT
rebuts	REBTS
rebutting	REBT/-G
rebutted	REBTD

rebuttal	R-B, R-BT
REBUTTAL	R-B/R-B, R-BT/R-BT

recall
recall	RAUL
recalls	RAULS
recalling	RAULG
recalled	RAULD

recant
recant	KRANT
recants	KRANTS
recanting	KRANGT
recanted	KRANTD

recantation	KRANGS
receipt	RET
receivable	SEFBL

receive
receive	SEF
receives	SEFS
receiving	SEFG

received	SEFD
received in evidence	SNEVD
receiver	SEFR
recency	RAOENSZ

recent
recent	RAOENT
recently	RAOENL
recentness	RAOENZ

receptacle	REPT
reception	SEPGS
receptor	SOERPT

recess
recess	RES
recesses	REFS
recessing	REFG
recessed	REFD

recharge
recharge	RARJ
recharges	RARJS
recharging	RARJ/-G
recharged	RARJD

rechargeable	RAERBL
recipient	RIPT
reciprocal	RIRPL

reciprocate
reciprocate	RIRP
reciprocates	RIRPS
reciprocating	RIRPG
reciprocated	RIRPD

reciprocation	RIRPGS
reciprocity	RIRPZ

reckless
reckless	R-LS, REKL
recklessly	RAOEKL
recklessness	REKLS

recognition	R-GS
recognizance	KROGS, KWOG

recognize
recognize	REK
recognizes	REKZ
recognizing	REK/-G
recognized	REKD

recollect
recollect	R-K
recollects	R-KZ

BRIEF ENCOUNTERS   R

recollecting	R–K/–G
recollected	R–KD
recollection	REX
recommend	
recommend	R–M
recommends	R–MS
recommending	R–MG
recommended	R–MD
recommendation	R–MGS
reconcile	
reconcile	SKAOIL
reconciles	SKAOILS
reconciling	SKAOILG
reconciled	SKAOILD
reconciliation	SILGS, RAOILGS, RILGS
reconnoiter	
reconnoiter	NOIRT
reconnoiters	NOIRTS
reconnoitering	NOIRGT
reconnoitered	NOIRTD
record	
record	RORD
records	RORDZ
recording	RORGD
recorded	RORD/–D
recorder	ROERD
recount	
recount	ROUNT
recounts	ROUNTS
recounting	ROUNGT, ROUNG
recounted	ROUNTD
recover	
recover	ROFR, ROVR
recovers	ROFRS, ROVRS
recovering	ROFRG, ROVRG
recovered	ROFRD, ROVRD
recover	
recoverable	ROFRBL, ROVRBL
recovery	ROIFR, ROIVR
recovery room	R–RM
recriminate	
recriminate	RIMT
recriminates	RIMTS
recriminating	RIMGT
recriminated	RIMTD

© 1997 White-Boucke Publishing.   ILLEGAL TO PHOTOCOPY

recrimination . . . . RIMGS, RE/KRIJ
recross
    recross. . . . . ROF, ROS
    recrosses . . . . ROFS
    recrossing. . . . . ROFG
    recrossed . . . . ROFD
recross-examination . . . . R-X
RECROSS-EXAMINATION. . . . . R-X/R-X
recruit
    recruit . . . . KRAOUT
    recruits . . . . KRAOUTS
    recruiting. . . . . KRAOUGT
    recruited . . . . KRAOUTD
recruiter . . . . KRAOUR, KRAOURT
recruitment . . . . KRAOUMT
rectangle . . . . RANL
rectangular . . . . RARNL
recumbent . . . . RUBT
recuperate
    recuperate . . . . RAOUPT
    recuperates . . . . RAOUPTS
    recuperating. . . . . RAOUPGT, RAOUPG
    recuperated . . . . RAOUPTD
recuperation. . . . . RAOUPGS
recyclable . . . . ROIBL
recycle
    recycle. . . . . ROIK, RAOIKL
    recycles . . . . ROIKS, RAOIKLS
    recycling. . . . . ROIK/-G, ROIG, RAOIKL/-G
    recycled. . . . . ROIKD, RAOIKLD
red
    red blood cell . . . . REBLZ
    red blood count . . . . REBLT
    redder . . . . RERD
    red light . . . . R-LT
    red light district . . . . R-LTD
    redness . . . . R-NZ
redact
    redact . . . . DAK
    redacts . . . . DAKZ
    redacting. . . . . DAK/-G
    redacted . . . . DAKD
redaction . . . . DAX
redirect examination. . . . . R-RD
REDIRECT EXAMINATION . . . . R-RD/R-RD

BRIEF ENCOUNTERS   R

reduce
    reduce .... RAOUS
    reduces .... RAOUFS
    reducing .... RAOUFG
    reduced .... RAOUFD
reduction .... RAOUGS
redundancy .... DRUNZ, DRUNTS
redundant .... DRUNT
redundantly .... DRUNLT, DRUNL
refer
    refer .... REFR
    refers .... REFRS
    referring .... REFRG
    referred .... REFRD
reference
    reference .... REFRNS
    references .... REFRNSZ
    referencing .... REFRNG
    referenced .... REFRND
referral .... REFRL
referring to .... REFRGT
refinement .... FAOIMT
reflect
    reflect .... LEK, REFL
    reflects .... LEKZ, REFLS
    reflecting .... LEK/-G, REFLG
    reflected .... LEKD, REFLD
reflection .... LEX, REFLGS
reflex .... R-FX
reform
    reform .... REFM
    reforms .... REFMS
    reforming .... REFMG
    reformed .... REFMD
reformation .... REFRMGS
refract
    refract .... FRAEK
    refracts .... FRAEKZ
    refracting .... FRAEK/-G
    refracted .... FRAEKD
refraction .... FRAEX
refractive .... FRAEVK
refrain
    refrain .... FRAIN
    refrains .... FRAINS

refraining..FRAING
refrained...FRAIND
refrainment...FRAIMT
refresh
    refresh..RERB
    refreshes..RERBS
    refreshing...RERBG
    refreshed..RERBD
refreshment............................RERBT, FRERMT, FREMT

refresh my recollection
    refresh my recollection...............................RIR
    refreshes my recollection............................RIRS
    refreshing my recollection...........................RIRG
    refreshed my recollection............................RIRD

refresh your recollection
    refresh your recollection.............................RUR
    refreshes your recollection..........................RURS
    refreshing your recollection.........................RURG
    refreshed your recollection...............RUR/-D, R*URD

refrigerate
    refrigerate..FRAIJ
    refrigerates..FRAIJZ
    refrigerating....................................FRAIJ/-G
    refrigerated.......................................FRAIJD
refrigeration..FRAIJS
refrigerator...FRIR
refuge..RAOUJ
refund
    refund..RUND
    refunds..RUNDZ
    refunding..RUNGD
    refunded..RUND/-D
refusal..R-FL
refuse
    refuse...R-F
    refuses...R-FS
    refusing..R-FG
    refused..R-FD
refutation...REFGS
refute
    refute...FAOUT
    refutes...FAOUTS
    refuting..FAOUGT
    refuted...FAOUTD

BRIEF ENCOUNTERS — R

regard
    regard .... RAR
    regards .... RARS
    regarding .... RARG
    regarded .... RARD
regarding the .... RARGT
regardless .... RARLS
regent .... RAOEJT
regime .... JAOEM
region .... RAOEJ
regional .... RAO*EJ
register
    register .... REJ
    registers .... REJS
    registering .... REJ/-G
    registered .... REJD
registrar .... STRAR
registrar's office .... STROFS
registration .... RAEJ
regret
    regret .... GRET
    regrets .... GRETS
    regretting .... GREGT
    regretted .... GRETD
regular
    regular .... REG
    regularity .... REGT
    regularly .... RELG
regulate
    regulate .... RAIG
    regulates .... RAIGS
    regulating .... RAIG/-G
    regulated .... RAIGD
regulation .... REGS
regulator .... R-GT
regulatory .... R-RGT
regurgitate
    regurgitate .... GURJ
    regurgitates .... GURJZ
    regurgitating .... GURJ/-G
    regurgitated .... GURJD
regurgitation .... GURJS
rehab .... RAB
rehabilitate
    rehabilitate .... RABLT

© 1997 White-Boucke Publishing.   ILLEGAL TO PHOTOCOPY

R

rehabilitates. . . . . RABLTS
rehabilitating . . . . RABLT/-G, RABLG
rehabilitated . . . . RABLTD
rehabilitation. . . . . RABLGS
reimburse
   reimburse. . . . . KBURS
   reimburses . . . . KBUFS, KBURSZ
   reimbursing. . . . . KBUFG
   reimbursed . . . . KBUFD
reimbursement . . . . KBURMT
reinvent
   reinvent . . . . REFT
   reinvents. . . . . REFTS, REVTS
   reinventing . . . . REVG
   reinvented . . . . REVTD
reinvention. . . . . RIFGS
reiterate
   reiterate. . . . . RIT
   reiterates. . . . . RITS
   reiterating . . . . RIGT
   reiterated . . . . RITD
reiteration . . . . RIGS
reject
   reject . . . . JEKT
   rejects. . . . . JEKTS, JEKZ
   rejecting. . . . . JEG, JEKT/-G, JEK/-G
   rejected . . . . JEKTD, JEKD
rejection . . . . JEX
rejoinder . . . . ROIRN
rejuvenate
   rejuvenate . . . . JAOUV
   rejuvenates. . . . . JAOUVS
   rejuvenating . . . . JAOUVG
   rejuvenated . . . . JAOUVD
rejuvenation. . . . . JAOUVGS
relapse
   relapse. . . . . RAPZ
   relapses . . . . RAPSZ
   relapsing . . . . RAPGZ, RAPZ/-G
   relapsed. . . . . RAPZ/-D
relate
   relate . . . . RELT
   relates. . . . . RELTS
   relating . . . . RELGT
   related . . . . RELTD

relation	RELGS
relationship	HRELGS, RAEP
relative	REVLT
relatively	RAOEVLT

relax
- relax . . . RAEK
- relaxes . . . RAEKZ
- relaxing . . . RAEK/-G
- relaxed . . . RAEKD

relaxation . . . RAEX

relay
- relay . . . LAE
- relays . . . LAES
- relaying . . . LAE/-G, LA*EG
- relayed . . . LAE/-D, LA*ED

release
- release . . . RAOES
- releases . . . RAOEFS, RAOESZ
- releasing . . . RAOEFG
- released . . . RAOEFD

relevance	REVS
relevancy	RAEV, RAEVS
relevant	REV, REVT
reliability	RAOIBLT
reliable	RAOIBL
relief	RAOEFL

relieve
- relieve . . . RAOEVL
- relieves . . . RAOEVLS
- relieving . . . RAOEVLG
- relieved . . . RAOEVLD

religion	R-J
religious	LIJ

relinquish
- relinquish . . . RIRB
- relinquishes . . . RIRBS
- relinquishing . . . RIRBG
- relinquished . . . RIRBD

relinquishment	RIRBT
reluctance	LUNS, LUKZ
reluctancy	LUNSZ
reluctant	LUNT, LUKT
reluctantly	LUNL

remain
- remain . . . RAIM

R — BRIEF ENCOUNTERS

remains	RAIMS
remaining	RAIMG
remained	RAIMD
remainder	RAIRM, RAIRMD
remain silent	–RS

remand
remand	RAMD
remands	RAMDZ
remanding	RAMGD
remanded	RAMD/–D

remark
remark	RARK
remarks	RARKS
remarking	RARK/–G
remarked	RARKD

remarkable	RARBL
remarkably	RAOERBL
remedial	RAOELD, RAOEMD

remedy
remedy	ROIMD
remedies	ROIMDZ
remedying	ROIMGD
remedied	ROIMD/–D

remember
remember	REM
remembers	REMS
remembering	REMG
remembered	REMD

remembrance	REMZ

remind
remind	RAOIMD
reminds	RAOIMDZ
reminding	RAOIMGD
reminded	RAOIMD/–D

reminder	RAOIRMD

reminisce
reminisce	REM/NIS
reminisces	REM/NIFS, REM/NISZ
reminiscing	REM/NIFG
reminisced	REM/NIFD

reminiscence	REM/NINTS
reminiscent	REM/NINT
remission	REMGS, RE/MIGS

remit
remit	REMT

BRIEF ENCOUNTERS R

remits	REMTS
remitting	REMGT
remitted	REMTD
remittance	MANTS, RE/MANTS
remittent	RE/MENT
remnant	RAEMT
remodel	
remodel	ROELD
remodels	ROELDZ
remodeling	ROELGD
remodeled	ROELD/–D
remorse	
remorse	ROERS
remorseful	ROEFL, ROEFLS
remorseless	ROERL, ROERLS
remote	RAOEMT, ROEMT
remunerate	
remunerate	MAOUMT
remunerates	MAOUMTS
remunerating	MAOUMGT
remunerated	MAOUMTD
remuneration	MAOUMGS
renaissance	RENZ
renal	RAENL
rendezvous	RAUND
renewal	RAOUNL
renounce	
renounce	ROUNS
renounces	ROUFS, ROUNSZ
renouncing	ROUFG
renounced	ROUFD
renouncement	ROUMT
renouncer	ROURNS
renovate	
renovate	RAIVT
renovates	RAIVTS
renovating	RAIVGT
renovated	RAIVTD
renovation	RAIVGS
rental	R*ENL, RENLT
renunciation	RUNGS
reorganization	RORGS
reorganizational	RORLGS
reorganize	
reorganize	RORG

reorganizes	RORGZ
reorganizing	RORG/-G
reorganized	RORG/-D
reorganizer	ROERG

reorient
reorient	ROERNT
reorients	ROERNTS
reorienting	ROERNGT, ROERNG
reoriented	ROERNTD
reorientation	ROERNGS

repair
repair	RAIR
repairs	RAIRS
repairing	RAIRG
repaired	RAIRD

repeat
repeat	RAOEPT
repeats	RAOEPTS
repeating	RAOEPGT
repeated	RAOEPTD
repercussion	RERPGS
repertoire	TWAR
repertory	TWOIR

repetitious
repetitious	T*IRB, REP/TIRB
repetitiously	TIRBL, REP/TIRBL
repetitiousness	TIRNS
repetitive	RAOEVPT, TEV

rephrase
rephrase	FRAIR
rephrases	FRAIRS
rephrasing	FRAIRG
rephrased	FRAIRD
replevin	PLEV

replicate
replicate	KPAET, REP/KAIT
replicates	KPAETS, REP/KAITS
replicating	KPAEGT, REP/KAIGT
replicated	KPAETD, REP/KAITD
replication	KPAEGS, REP/KAIGS

reply
reply	PLI
replies	PLIZ
replying	PLIG
replied	PLID

BRIEF ENCOUNTERS   R

report
    report. . . . . RORT
    reports. . . . . RORTS
    reporting . . . . RORGT
    reported. . . . . RORTD
reportage . . . . RORJ
reporter . . . . ROERT
reprehend
    reprehend. . . . . REND, REP/HEN
    reprehends. . . . . RENDZ, REP/HENS
    reprehending . . . . RENGD, REP/HENG
    reprehended . . . . REND/–D, REP/HEND
reprehensible. . . . . R*ENL, REP/HENL
reprehension . . . . RENGS, REP/HENGS
represent
    represent . . . . REP
    represents. . . . . REPS
    representing . . . . REPG
    represented. . . . . REPD
represent
    representation . . . . REPGS
    representative . . . . REVP
    representatively . . . . REVPL
reprieve
    reprieve. . . . . RAOEV
    reprieves . . . . RAOEVS
    reprieving. . . . . RAOEVG
    reprieved . . . . RAOEVD
reprisal. . . . . PRAOIFL
reproach
    reproach. . . . . ROFP, RO*EFP
    reproaches. . . . . ROFPS, ROEFPS
    reproaching. . . . . ROFPG, ROEFPG
    reproached . . . . ROFPD, ROEFPD
reproachable. . . . . ROFPL, ROEFPL
reproductive. . . . . RAOUF
republic . . . . REB
republican. . . . . REN
repudiate
    repudiate . . . . PAOU
    repudiates . . . . PAOUS
    repudiating. . . . . PAOUG
    repudiated . . . . PAOUD
repudiation. . . . . PAOUGS

R   BRIEF ENCOUNTERS

repulse
- repulse . . . . RUL
- repulses . . . . RULS
- repulsing . . . . RULG
- repulsed . . . . RULD

repulsion . . . . RULGS, PULGS

repulsive
- repulsive . . . . PUV
- repulsively . . . . PUVL
- repulsiveness . . . . PUVNS

reputation . . . . R-PGS

repute
- repute . . . . PAOUT
- reputes . . . . PAOUTS
- reputing . . . . PAOUGT
- reputed . . . . PAOUTD

request
- request . . . . KW-
- requests . . . . KW-S
- requesting . . . . KW-G
- requested . . . . KW-D

requester . . . . KW-R

require
- require . . . . RAOIR
- requires . . . . RAOIRS
- requiring . . . . RAOIRG
- required . . . . RAOIRD

requirement . . . . RAOIRMT

requisite . . . . KWIFT

requisition
- requisition . . . . KWIFGS
- requisitions . . . . KWIFGSZ
- requisitioning . . . . KWIFGS/-G
- requisitioned . . . . KWIFGD, KWIFGS/-D

rescuable . . . . SKWUBL

rescue
- rescue . . . . SKWU
- rescues . . . . SKWUS
- rescuing . . . . SKWUG
- rescued . . . . SKWUD

rescuer . . . . SKWUR

rescue team . . . . SKWUT

research
- research . . . . REFP
- researches . . . . REFPS

BRIEF ENCOUNTERS R

researching .... REFPG
researched .... REFPD
researcher .... REFRP
reservation .... REFRBGS, REVRBGS
reserve
    reserve .... REFRB, REVRB
    reserves .... REFRBS, REVRBS
    reserving .... REFRBG, REVRBG
    reserved .... REFRBD, REVRBD
reservoir .... ROIFRB
res gestae .... JEZ, RES/JES
reside
    reside .... ROID
    resides .... ROIDZ
    residing .... ROIGD
    resided .... ROID/-D
residence .... -RZ
residences .... -RSZ
residency .... RAOEZ
resident
    resident .... REZ
    residential .... R-RBL
    residents .... RESZ, R-SZ
resign
    resign .... RAOIN
    resigns .... RAOINS
    resigning .... RAOING
    resigned .... RAOIN/-D
resignation .... RAOINGS, REZ/NAIGS
resist
    resist .... R*IS
    resists .... RIFS
    resisting .... RIFG
    resisted .... RIFD
resist
    resistance .... RA*NS, R*INS
    resistant .... RA*NT, RINT
    resistibility .... RIBLT
    resistible .... RIBL
    resistor .... RIFR
res judicata .... JAOUD, REZ/JAOUD
resolution .... ROLFGS
resolve
    resolve .... ROFL
    resolves .... ROFLS

resolving	ROFLG
resolved	ROFLD
resonance	RANS
resource	SRORS

respect
respect	R–P, –RP
respects	R–PS, –RPS
respecting	R–PG, –RPG
respected	R–PD, –RPD

respect
respectability	R–PT, R–BLT
respectable	R–BL
respectful	R–FP
respectfully	R–FPL

respiration	SPAOIRX
respirator	SPRAOIRT
respiratory	SPAOIRT

respond
respond	SPOND
responds	SPONDZ
responding	SPONGD
responded	SPOND/–D

respondent	DANT
respondent's exhibit	R–PX
responder	SPRON
response	SPONS
responsibility	SPONT
responsible	SPON
responsibly	SPONL

responsive
responsive	SPOIV
responsively	SPOIVL
responsiveness	SPOIVNS

rest
rest	R*ES
rests	R*ESZ
resting	REFGT
rested	REFTD

restaurant	STRANT, STRAUNT
restauranteur	STRARNT, STRAURNT

restitute
restitute	STAOT
restitutes	STAOTS
restituting	STAOGT
restituted	STAOTD

BRIEF ENCOUNTERS   R

restitution . . . . STAOGS
restoration . . . . RAURGS
restrain
    restrain. . . . . STR–N
    restrains . . . . STR–NS
    restraining . . . . STR–NG
    restrained . . . . STR–ND
restraining order . . . . STRO, RO
restraining orders. . . . . STROS, ROZ
restraint . . . . STR–NT, STRAENT
restrict
    restrict . . . . RIKT
    restricts. . . . . RIKTS
    restricting . . . . RIKT/–G
    restricted . . . . RIKTD, RIKD
restriction . . . . RIX
restrictive
    restrictive . . . . RIV
    restrictively . . . . RIVL
    restrictiveness . . . . RIVNS
restroom . . . . STRAOM
result
    result . . . . RULT
    results . . . . RULTS
    resulting . . . . RULGT
    resulted . . . . RULTD
resumé . . . . SMAE
resume
    resume . . . . RAOUM
    resumes . . . . RAOUMS
    resuming . . . . RAOUMG
    resumed . . . . RAOUMD
resumption . . . . RUMGS
resumptive . . . . RUMT
resuscitate
    resuscitate . . . . RUFT
    resuscitates. . . . . RUFTS, RUFS
    resuscitating . . . . RUFGT, RUFG
    resuscitated . . . . RUFD
resuscitation . . . . R*UFGS, RUFGTS
retail
    retail . . . . TRAEL
    retails . . . . TRAELS
    retailing . . . . TRAELG
    retailed . . . . TRAELD

retailer	TROIL, TROIRL
retaliation	TALGS
retard	
retard	TARD
retards	TARDZ
retarding	TARGD
retarded	TARD/-D
retardation	TARGS
retina	RAENT
retire	
retire	RERT
retires	RERTS
retiring	RERGT
retired	RERTD
retiree	RAOERT
retirement	TAOIRMT
retouch	
retouch	RUFP
retouches	RUFPS
retouching	RUFPG
retouched	RUFPD
retreat	
retreat	TRA*ET
retreats	TRAETS
retreating	TRAEGT
retreated	TRAETD
retribution	BAOUX
retrievable	TRAOEVBL
retrieval	TRAOEVL
retrieve	
retrieve	TRAOEV
retrieves	TRAOEVS
retrieving	TRAOEVG
retrieved	TRAOEVD
retriever	TRAOEVR
return	
return	RURN
returns	RURNS
returning	RURNG
returned	RURND
returnable	RURNL
Reuters	ROIRZ
reveal	
reveal	VAOEL
reveals	VAOELS

BRIEF ENCOUNTERS — R

revealing	VAOELG
revealed	VAOELD
revealer	VAOERL
reveler	REVRL
revenge	RENG
reverence	REVRNS
reverend	REVRND
reverent	REVRNT, REFRNT
reverently	REVRNL
reversal	RERL
reversals	RERLZ

reverse
reverse	RERS
reverses	RERSZ
reversing	RERGS
reversed	RERS/-D

reversely	RERLS
reversibility	RERBLT
reversible	RERBL
reversibly	RAOEBL

review
review	RAOUV
reviews	RAOUVS
reviewing	RAOUVG
reviewed	RAOUVD

reviewer	RAOUVR
revival	VAOIFL, VAOIVL

revive
revive	VAOIF
revives	VAOIFS
reviving	VAOIFG
revived	VAOIFD

revocation	ROFGS, ROVGS, ROEFGS, ROEVGS

revoke
revoke	ROEK
revokes	ROEKS
revoking	ROEK/-G
revoked	ROEKD

revolt
revolt	ROELT
revolts	ROELTS
revolting	ROELGT
revolted	ROELTD

revolution	REVGS
revolutionary	REVN

revolve
    revolve . . . . ROVL
    revolves . . . . ROVLS
    revolving . . . . ROVLG
    revolved . . . . ROVLD
revolver . . . . R–V
revulsion . . . . VULGS
revulsive . . . . VUV, VIV
reward
    reward . . . . RAUR
    rewards . . . . RAURS
    rewarding . . . . RAURG
    rewarded . . . . RAURD
rhetoric
    rhetoric . . . . WRET
    rhetorical . . . . WROL
    rhetorically . . . . WROEL
    rhetorical question . . . . WROLG
rheumatic . . . . ROIMT
rheumatism . . . . RAOUMT, RAOUFM
Rhode Island . . . . R*I
rhyme
    rhyme . . . . RAOIM
    rhymes . . . . RAOIMS
    rhyming . . . . RAOIMG
    rhymed . . . . RAOIM/–D
rhythm
    rhythm . . . . THIM
    rhythmic . . . . THIMG
    rhythmical . . . . THIL
riddle
    riddle . . . . RILD
    riddles . . . . RILDZ
    riddling . . . . RILGD
    riddled . . . . RILD/–D
ride
    ride . . . . RAOID
    rides . . . . RAOIDZ
    riding . . . . RAOIGD
    rode . . . . RO*ED
    ridden . . . . RIND
ridicule
    ridicule . . . . KAOUL, R*IL
    ridicules . . . . KAOULS, RILS
    ridiculing . . . . KAOULG, RILG

BRIEF ENCOUNTERS R

ridiculed	KAOULD, RIL/-D, R*ILD
ridiculer	KAOURL
ridiculous	RIL, RID/KLOUS

riffle

riffle	RIFL
riffles	RIFLS
riffling	RIFLG
riffled	RIFLD

right

right	-RT
right arm	RARM
right hand	-RND
right-hand lane	R-NLD, -RNL
right-hand side	R-NDZ, -RNDZ
right-hand turn	-RNT
right lane	R-L, -RL
right lanes	R-LZ
right leg	R-LG
rightly	-RLT
rightly or wrongly	RORNL
right now	ROUN
right or wrong	RORNG
right side	R-DZ
right to remain silent	R-RS
right turn	*RT

righteous

righteous	RAOIFP
righteously	RAOIFPL
righteousness	RAOIFNS

rigid	RIJD
rigor mortis	GORMT

ring

ring	RING
rings	RINGS
ringing	RING/-G
rang	RANG
rung	RUNG

Rio de Janeiro	R*J, RAOE/DAOEJ

riot

riot	ROIT
riots	ROITS
rioting	ROIGT
rioted	ROITD
rioter	ROIRT

R

rise
- rise . . . RAOIZ
- rises . . . RAOIFS, RAOISZ
- rising . . . RAOIFG
- rose . . . ROEZ
- risen . . . RINZ

ritual . . . RIFPL

rival
- rival . . . R–VL
- rivals . . . R–VLS
- rivaling . . . R–VLG
- rivaled . . . R–VLD

rivalry . . . ROIVL

rivet
- rivet . . . RIVT
- rivets . . . RIVTS
- riveting . . . RIVGT
- riveted . . . RIVTD

roadway . . . ROI

robber
- robber . . . RORB
- robbery . . . ROIB
- robbery-murder . . . RORM, ROIRM

robot . . . ROEBT
robust . . . BRUFT, BR*US
rocker . . . RORK
rocket . . . ROKT
rodent . . . ROEND
roller . . . RORL
ROM . . . ROM
romance . . . ROMS
romantic . . . ROMT
roommate . . . RAOMT
rotary . . . RAORT

rotate
- rotate . . . TROET
- rotates . . . TROETS
- rotating . . . TROEGT
- rotated . . . TROETD

rotation . . . TROEGS
rotational . . . TROELGS
rotative . . . TRAIV
rotatively . . . TRAIVL
rotator . . . TROERT
rotten . . . ROENT

BRIEF ENCOUNTERS   R

roughly	RUFL
round table	ROUNL
routine	ROIN
routinely	ROINL
rubber	BRUB
rubber-stamp	
rubber-stamp	BRAFRP
rubber-stamps	BRAFRPS
rubber-stamping	BRAFRPG
rubber-stamped	BRAFRPD
rubbery	BRAOEB
ruby	RAOUB
rudiment	RUMD
ruffle	
ruffle	ROIFL, RUF/-L
ruffles	ROIFLS, RUFLS
ruffling	ROIFLG, RUFLG
ruffled	ROIFLD, RUFLD
rugged	RUGD
ruination	RAOUNGS
rule	
rule of law	RAUFL
ruler	RAOURL
rules and regulations	R-RZ
rules of law	RAUFLS
rummage	
rummage	RUJ
rummages	RUJS
rummaging	RUJ/-G
rummaged	RUJD
rummage sale	RUJZ
rumor	
rumor	RAORM, RAOURM
rumors	RAORMS, RAOURMS
rumoring	RAORMG, RAOURMG
rumored	RAORMD, RAOURMD
run	
run	RUN
runs	RUNS
running	RUN/-G
ran	RAN
runway lights	RUNLTS
rupture	
rupture	RUPT
ruptures	RUPTS

© 1997 White-Boucke Publishing.   ILLEGAL TO PHOTOCOPY

```
rupturing . . . . . . . . . . . . . . . . . . . . . . . . . . . . . . . . . . . RUPGT
    ruptured . . . . . . . . . . . . . . . . . . . . . . . . . . . . . . . . . . . RUPTD
rural . . . . . . . . . . . . . . . . . . . . . . . . . . . . . . . . . . . . . . . . . . . RURL
*rush hour* . . . . . . . . . . . . . . . . . . . . . . . . . . . . . . . . . . . . . . . ROUR
Russia . . . . . . . . . . . . . . . . . . . . . . . . . . . . . . . . . . . . . . . RAOURB
Russian . . . . . . . . . . . . . . . . . . . . . . . . . . . . . . . . . . . . . RAOURN
ruthless
    ruthless . . . . . . . . . . . . . . . . . . . . . . . . . . . . R*UT, RAO*ULT
    ruthlessly . . . . . . . . . . . . . . . . . . . . . . . . . . . . . . . . . . . R*ULT
    ruthlessness . . . . . . . . . . . . . . . . . . . . . . . . . . . . . . . . R*UNS
```

S

sabbath	SBA*T
sabbatical	SBAT
sabotage	
sabotage	SBAUJ
sabotages	SBAUJS
sabotaging	SBAUJ/-G
sabotaged	SBAUJD
saboteur	SBAURJ, SAB/TUR
sacral	SKRAL
sacrament	SKRAMT
Sacramento	SAKT
sacred	SKRAID
sacredly	SKRAILD
sacrifice	
sacrifice	SKRAOIF
sacrifices	SKRAOIFS
sacrificing	SKRAOIFG
sacrificed	SKRAOIFD
sacrificer	SKRAOIFR
sacrificial	SKRAOIFL
sacrilege	SKLIJ, SKLEJ, SKREJ
sacrilegious	SKLIJS, SKLEJS, SKREJS
sacrum	SKRUM
sadism	SDIFM
sadist	
sadist	SD*IS
sadistic	SDIFK
sadistically	SDAOEFK, SDIFL
sadomasochism	SMAOFM
sadomasochist	SMAOFT
safe	
safe-deposit box	SD-B
safeguard	SAIFGD
safely	SAIFL
safe sex	SAIFX
safety	SAIFT
safety-deposit box	SDEB
safety feature	SFAOEFP
saga	SGA
sailor	SAIRL
salacious	
salacious	SLAIRB

S

salaciously	SLAIRBL
salaciousness	SLAIRBS
salacity	SLAIRBT
salad	SLAD
salad dressing	SLAGD
salary	SAL, SARL
sales	
saleslady	SLAED
salesman	SMAN
salesmanship	SMIP
salesmen	SMEN
saleswoman	SWOM
saleswomen	SWEM
salience	SAILZ, SAILTS
salient	SAILT
saline	SLAOEN
saliva	SLAOIV
Salmonella	SAUL
salon	SLON
saloon	SLAON
salsa	SAULZ, SALZ
Salt Lake City	SLAIKS
salutation	SALGS
salute	
salute	SLAOUT
salutes	SLAOUTS
saluting	SLAOUGT
saluted	SLAOUTD
Salvadoran	SAFRN
salvage	
salvage	SWAJ
salvages	SWAJS
salvaging	SWAJ/-G
salvaged	SWAJD
salvageable	SWABL
salvager	SWARJ
salvation	SWALGS
salve	SAV
Samaritan	SMAIRN
same	
same as	SAIMS
same day	SAIMD
same objection	SAIMGS, SAOB
same old	SMOELD
same time	SAIMT

BRIEF ENCOUNTERS — S

same time as .... SAIMTS
Samoa .... SMOE
Samoan .... SMO*EN
San
    San Bernardino .... SBAERN, BAERN
    San Diego .... SDAIG, DAIG
    San Francisco .... SFRAN
    San Jose .... S*J
sanatarium .... SNAIRM
sanction
    sanction .... SANGS
    sanctions .... SANGSZ
    sanctioning .... SANGS/-G
    sanctioned .... SANGD, SANGS/-D
sandal .... SDAL
sandbag
    sandbag .... SBAG
    sandbags .... SBAGS
    sandbagging .... SBAG/-G
    sandbagged .... SBAGD
sand dune .... SDAON, SDAOUN
sandwich
    sandwich .... SDWIFP, DWIFP
    sandwiches .... SDWIFPS, DWIFPS
    sandwiching .... SDWIFPG, DWIFPG
    sandwiched .... SDWIFPD, DWIFPD
sanitarium .... SNIRM
sanitary .... SNAIRT
sanitation .... SAINGS
sanitize
    sanitize .... SAN/TAOIS, SAN/TAOIZ
    sanitizes .... SAN/TAOIFS, SAN/TAOISZ
    sanitizing .... SAN/TAOIFG
    sanitized .... SAN/TAOIFD
sanity .... SANT
Santa
    Santa Ana .... SNAN
    Santa Barbara .... SPWARB
    Santa Claus .... SKLAUS
    Santa Cruz .... SKRUZ
    Santa Fe .... SFE
sarcasm .... SKAFM
sarcastic .... SARKT, SKARKT
sarcoma .... SKOEM
sarge .... SA*RJ, SAERJ

S

satchel	SAFPL
satellite	STLAOIT
satellite dish	STLAOITD, STLIRB, SDIRB
satiability	SAIRBLT
satiable	SAIRBL
satiably	SAOERBL
satiate	
satiate	SAIRB
satiates	SAIRBS
satiating	SAIRBG
satiated	SAIRBD
satiation	SAIRBGS
satire	STAOIR
satirical	STIRL
satirically	STAOERL
satisfaction	SAFX
satisfactorily	SAEFL
satisfactory	SAEF
satisfiable	SAFBL
satisfier	SAFR
satisfy	
satisfy	SAF
satisfies	SAFS
satisfying	SAFG
satisfied	SAFD
saturate	
saturate	SAFP
saturates	SAFPS
saturating	SAFPG
saturated	SAFPD
saturation	SAFPGS
Saturday	SATD
Saturdays	SADZ
Saturn	STAURN
saucer	SAURS
Saudi	
Saudi	SAUD
Saudi Arabia	SA*, SAUD/SAUD
Saudi Arabian	SA*N
sauna	SNAUN
sausage	SAUJ
savior	SYOER
savor	
savor	SWAOR
savors	SWAORS

BRIEF ENCOUNTERS S

savoring	SWAORG
savored	SWAORD
savory	SWOIR
savvy	SWAV

saw
saw	SAU
saws	SAUZ
sawing	SAUG
sawed	SAU/-D
sawed / sawn	SAU/-D / SAUN

sawed-off	SAUFD
sawed-off shotgun	SAUFG

say
say	SAI
says	SAIS
saying	SAIG
said	SAID

SBA	SBA

scaffold
scaffold	SKAFLD
scaffolds	SKAFLDZ
scaffolding	SKAFLGD, SKAFLG
scaffolded	SKAFLD/-D

scalability	SKAIBLT
scalable	SKAIBL
scallop	SKLAOP
scalp	SKAP
scalpel	SKLEP

scandal
scandal	SKANLD
scandalization	SKLAOIGS
scandalizer	SKLAOIRS, SKLAOIRZ

scandalize
scandalize	SKLAOIS, SKLAOIZ
scandalizes	SKLAOIFS, SKLAOISZ
scandalizing	SKLAOIFG
scandalized	SKLAOIFD

scandalous
scandalous	SKLOUS
scandalously	SKLOULS
scandalousness	SKLOUNS

Scandinavia	SKAIV
Scandinavian	SKAIVN

scant
scant	SKRANT

scantly	SKRANL, SKRANLT
scantness	SKRANS

scapegoat
scapegoat	SKAIPT
scapegoats	SKAIPTS
scapegoating	SKAIPGT
scapegoated	SKAIPTD

scarce
scarce	SKAIRS
scarcely	SKAIRL, SKAIRLS
scarceness	SKAIRNS

scarcity	SKAIRTS
scarf	SKAF
scary	SKRAIR
scathing	SKA*IGT

scatter
scatter	SKART
scatters	SKARTS
scattering	SKARGT
scattered	SKARTD

scavenge
scavenge	SKAVJ, SKAFJ
scavenges	SKAVJS, SKAFJS
scavenging	SKAVJ/-G, SKAVG, SKAFJ/-G, SKAFG
scavenged	SKAVJD, SKAFJD

scavenger	SKRAVJ, SKRAFJ
scenario	SNAR

scene
scene of the accident	SNAX
scene of the crime	SKRAOIM
scenery	SAO*ERN

scenic	SAENG, SAENK

scent
scent	SKRENT
scents	SKRENTS
scenting	SKRENGT, SKRENG
scented	SKRENTD

schedule
schedule	SKED
schedules	SKEDZ
scheduling	SKEGD
scheduled	SKED/-D

schema	SKMA
schematic	SKMAK
schizoid	SKOID

BRIEF ENCOUNTERS S

schizophrenia	SKIZ, FR*EN
schizophrenic	SKIKZ, FRENK
schmooser	SMAORZ

schmooze
schmooze	SMAOZ
schmoozes	SMAOFS, SMAOSZ
schmoozing	SMAOFG
schmoozed	SMAOFD

scholar
scholar	SKLAR
scholarliness	SKLARNS
scholarly	SKLARL
scholarship	SKLARP

scholastic	SKLAS, SKLAK
school district	SDRIK
school teacher	STRAOEFP
scienter	SAOENT
scientific	SAOIFK, SAOIN/TIFK
scientifically	SAOIFL
scientist	SAOINT

scissor
scissor	SIFR
scissors	SIFRS
scissoring	SIFRG
scissored	SIFRD

scope of
scope of	SKOEFP
scope of the	SKOEFPT
scope of them	SKOEFPL
scope of these	SKOEFPZ
scope of those	SKOEFPS

scornful	SKOFL
scornfully	SKOEFL
scorpion	SKORP, SKOERP

Scot
Scotland	SKLAND, SKOND
Scotland Yard	SKLARD
Scottish	SKORB

scoundrel	SKOUNL, SKOUND

screen
screener	SKRAOERN
screenplay	SKRAOEP
screenwriter	SKRAOER

screw
screwball	SKRAOUBL

screwdriver . . . . SKRAOIVR, SDRAOIVR
  screwer . . . . SKRAOUR
screw up
  screw up . . . . SKRUP
  screws up . . . . SKRUPS
  screwing up . . . . SKRUPG
  screwed up . . . . SKRUPD
scribble
  scribble . . . . SKRIB
  scribbles . . . . SKRIBS
  scribbling . . . . SKRIBG
  scribbled . . . . SKRIBD
scribbler . . . . SKRIRB
scripture . . . . SKRIRT
scriptwriter . . . . SKWIR
scrotum . . . . SKROET
scrounge
  scrounge . . . . SKROUJ
  scrounges . . . . SKROUJS
  scrounging . . . . SKROUJ/-G, SKROUNG
  scrounged . . . . SKROUJD
scrounger . . . . SKROURJ
scrubber . . . . SKRURB
scrunch
  scrunch . . . . SKRUN, SKRUFP
  scrunches . . . . SKRUNS, SKRUFPS
  scrunching . . . . SKRUNG, SKRUFPG
  scrunched . . . . SKRUND, SKRUFPD
scruple . . . . SKRAOUP, SKRAOUPL
scrutinize
  scrutinize . . . . SKRAOUT, SKRAOUN
  scrutinizes . . . . SKRAOUTS, SKRAOUNS
  scrutinizing . . . . SKRAOUGT, SKRAOUNG
  scrutinized . . . . SKRAOUTD, SKRAOUND
scrutiny . . . . SKRAOUNT
scuba . . . . SKAOB
scuba diver . . . . SKAOBD
sculpt
  sculpt . . . . SKUPLT
  sculpts . . . . SKUPLTS
  sculpting . . . . SKUPLGT
  sculpted . . . . SKUPLTD
sculptor . . . . SKUPT
sculpture . . . . SKUP
scythe . . . . SYAO*IT

BRIEF ENCOUNTERS   S

search
    search . . . . SEFP
    searches . . . . SEFPS
    searching . . . . SEFPG
    searched . . . . SEFPD
search
    search and seizure . . . . S-Z
    searches and seizures . . . . S-SZ
    searchlight . . . . SEFPLT
    search warrant . . . . SW-
season
    season . . . . S-N
    seasons . . . . S-NS
    seasoning . . . . S-NG
    seasoned . . . . S-ND
seasonable . . . . S-NL
seasonably . . . . SAOENL
seat belt . . . . KRELT
Seattle . . . . SYALT
seclude
    seclude . . . . SKLAO, SK-L
    secludes . . . . SKLAOS, SK-LS
    secluding . . . . SKLAOG, SK-LG
    secluded . . . . SKLAOD, SK-LD
seclusion . . . . SKLAOGS, SK-LGS
second
    second . . . . SEK
    seconds . . . . SEKZ
    seconding . . . . SEK/-G, SEG
    seconded . . . . SEKD
second
    second class . . . . SLAS
    second degree . . . . S-D
    second-degree burn . . . . S-BD
    second-degree murder . . . . S-MD
    secondhand . . . . SK*END, SKREND
    secondhand smoke . . . . SKOEK
secrecy . . . . SKRES
secret
    secret . . . . SKRET
    secretive . . . . SKREV
    secretively . . . . SKREVL
    secretiveness . . . . SKREVNS
    secretly . . . . SKREL
    Secret Service . . . . SK-FS, SKEFRBZ

S — BRIEF ENCOUNTERS

secretary . . . . SAEK
secrete
    secrete. . . . . SKRAO*ET
    secretes . . . . SKRAOETS
    secreting . . . . SKRAOEGT
    secreted. . . . . SKRAOETD
secretion . . . . SKRAOEGS
section. . . . . S–X
sector . . . . STEK, SERKT
secure
    secure . . . . SKUR
    secures . . . . SKURS
    securing. . . . . SKURG
    secured . . . . SKURD
securement . . . . SKURMT
Securities and Exchange Commission . . . . SKAEJS, SKAEJ
security . . . . SKURT
sedan . . . . SDAN
sedans. . . . . SDANZ
sedate
    sedate . . . . SDAET
    sedates . . . . SDAETS
    sedating. . . . . SDAEGT
    sedated . . . . SDAETD
sedation. . . . . SDAEGS
sedative. . . . . SDAEV
sedentarily . . . . SDAIRL, SDAERL
sedentariness. . . . . SDAIRNS, SDAERNS
sedentary . . . . SDAIR, SDAER
sediment
    sediment . . . . SD–MT
    sedimentary. . . . . SD–RMT
    sedimentation. . . . . SD–MGS
sedition . . . . SDERB
seditious
    seditious. . . . . SDERBS
    seditiously. . . . . SDERBL
    seditiousness . . . . SDERNS
seduce
    seduce . . . . SDAOUS
    seduces. . . . . SDAOUFS, SDAOUSZ
    seducing . . . . SDAOUFG
    seduced. . . . . SDAOUFD
seduction. . . . . SDUX

seductive
    seductive . . . . SDUV
    seductively . . . . SDUVL
    seductiveness . . . . SDUVNS
see
    see . . . . SAOE
    sees . . . . SAOE/-S
    seeing . . . . SAOEG
    saw . . . . SAU
    seen . . . . SAOEN
Seeing Eye dog . . . . SDAUG
seek
    seek . . . . SAOEK
    seeks . . . . SAOEKS
    seeking . . . . SAOEK/-G
    sought . . . . SAUT
seeker . . . . SAOERK
seemed to me . . . . SMAOED, SM*ED
seems to me . . . . SMAOE, SM*E
segment . . . . SAEMT
segregate
    segregate . . . . SGRAIT
    segregates . . . . SGRAITS
    segregating . . . . SGRAIGT
    segregated . . . . SGRAITD
segregation . . . . SGRAIGS
seismological . . . . SMOJ
seismologist . . . . SMOLT
seismology . . . . SMOLG
seizure . . . . SHAOEZ, SHAOES
seizures . . . . SHAOESZ
seldom . . . . SELD, SLOM, SDOM
seldomly . . . . SLOL, SDOL
select
    select . . . . SLEK
    selects . . . . SLEKZ
    selecting . . . . SLEK/-G, SLEG
    selected . . . . SLEKD
selection . . . . SLEX
selective
    selective . . . . SLEV, SLEVK
    selectively . . . . SLEVL
    selectiveness . . . . SLEVNS
self
    self . . . . SEVL

self-	SEFL
self-confessed	SFEFD
self-confidence	SK–FD
self-confident	SK–FT
self-conscious	SKONZ
self-defense	SD–FS
self-employed	SPLOID
self-employment	SPLOIMT
self-esteem	SFAOEM
self-explanatory	SPLARNT
Self Help for Hard of Hearing People	SH–D, SH/SH
self-hypnosis	SNOEPZ
self-incrimination	SK–RMGS, SK–RJ, SKR–J, SKR–MGS
self-inflicted	SFLIKD
self-interest	SFINT
selfish	SFIRB
selfishly	SFIRBL
selfishness	SFINS, SFIRNS
selfless	SF–LS
self-respect	S–RP
self-respecting	S–RPG
self-serving	S–VG
self-serving declaration	S–VD

self-incriminate

self-incriminate	SKR–M, SK–RM
self-incriminates	SKR–MS, SK–RMS
self-incriminating	SKR–MG, SK–RMG
self-incriminated	SKR–MD, SK–RMD

sell

sell	SEL
sells	SELS
selling	SELG
sold	SOLD

semantic	SMANT
semblance	SBLANS
semester	SMEFT, SM*ES
semi-	SEM
semiconductor	SMUK
seminar	SMAR
Semite	SMOIT
Semitic	SMIK
Semitism	SMEFM
senate	SNAT
senator	SNOR
senatorial	SNORL

BRIEF ENCOUNTERS S

send
    send . . . . SEND
    sends . . . . SENDZ
    sending . . . . SENGD
    sent . . . . SENT
sender . . . . SERND
senile . . . . SNAOIL
senility. . . . . SNILT
senior. . . . . S-R
seniority . . . . S-RT
sensation . . . . SENGS, SAERB
sensational. . . . . SENL, SAERBL
sense
    senseless . . . . SENLS
    sense of proportion . . . . SNORPGS
    sense of purpose . . . . SPURP
sensibility. . . . . SNIBLT
sensible . . . . SNIBL
sensibly . . . . SNAOEBL
sensitive . . . . SNIV
sensitiveness . . . . SNIVNS
sensitivity . . . . SNIVT
sensitization . . . . STAOIFGS, SNAOIFGS
sensitize
    sensitize . . . . STAOIS
    sensitizes . . . . STAOIFS, STAOISZ
    sensitizing . . . . STAOIFG
    sensitized . . . . STAOIFD
sensitizer. . . . . STAOIFR
sensor . . . . SOERN, SORNS
sensors . . . . SOERNZ, SORNSZ
sensual
    sensual . . . . SWUL
    sensualism . . . . SWUFM
    sensuality . . . . SWULT
sensuous
    sensuous. . . . . SWOUS
    sensuously. . . . . SWOULS
    sensuousness . . . . SWOUNS
sentence
    sentence . . . . SNENS
    sentences . . . . SNEFS, SNENSZ
    sentencing . . . . SNEFG
    sentenced. . . . . SNEFD
sentencer . . . . SNEFR, SNERNS

sentiment
- sentiment . . . . SMENT
- sentimental . . . . SMENL
- sentimentality . . . . SMENLT
- sentimentally . . . . SMAOENL

sentinel . . . . SNELT
sentry . . . . SNENT
separability . . . . SPRAIBLT
separable . . . . SPRAIBL
separably . . . . SPRAOEBL
separate
- separate . . . . SPRAIT
- separates . . . . SPRAITS
- separating . . . . SPRAIGT
- separated . . . . SPRAITD

separately . . . . SPRAIL
separate property . . . . SPROT
separation . . . . SPRAIGS
separatism . . . . SPRAIFM, SPRIFM
separatist . . . . SPRAIFT, SPRIFT
separator . . . . SPRAIRT
September . . . . SEPT
septic . . . . SPEP, SPEPG
septic tank . . . . SPEPGT
sequel . . . . SKWEL
sequence . . . . SKW-NS, SKWUNS
sequent
- sequent . . . . SKW-NT, SKWUNT
- sequential . . . . SKW-NL, SKWUNL
- sequentially . . . . SKWUNLT, SKWAOENL

sequester
- sequester . . . . SKWER
- sequesters . . . . SKWERS
- sequestering . . . . SKWERG
- sequestered . . . . SKWERD

sequestration . . . . SKWERGS
sequin . . . . SKWIN
Serb
- Serb . . . . SWERB
- Serbro-Croatia . . . . SKROERB
- Serbro-Croatian . . . . SKROEN

serendipitous . . . . SERPTS
serendipity . . . . SERPT
serf . . . . SWEF
sergeant . . . . SARJ

BRIEF ENCOUNTERS   S

serial	SAOERL
serialize	
serialize	SLAOERL, SLAOERLS
serializes	SLAOERLZ, SLAOERLSZ
serializing	SLAOERLG
serialized	SLAOERLD
serial port	SAOERP, SAOERPT
series	SERZ
serious	
serious	SERS, SAOERZ
serious bodily harm	SBARM
serious bodily injury	SBOJ, SB-J
seriously	SERLS, SAOERLZ
sermon	SERM
serpent	SERP
serum	SAOERM
servant	SEVRNT, SEFRNT
serve	
serve	SEFRB
serves	SEFRBS
serving	SEFRBG
served	SEFRBD
server	SR-VR, SR-FR
service	
service	S-FS
services	S-FSZ
servicing	S-FG
serviced	S-FD
service station	SEFRBGS
set	
set	SET
sets	SETS
setting	SEGT
set	SET
setback	STBAK
settle	
settle	SELT
settles	SELTS
settling	SELGT
settled	SELTD
settlement	ST-MT
settler	SERLT
set up	
set up	STUP
sets up	STUPS

setting up . . . . STUPG
set up . . . . STUP
set up the . . . . STUPT
seven
    seven . . . . SEVN, SEFN
    sevenfold . . . . SEVLD
    seven-piece . . . . SEVP
    seven-time . . . . SFAOIM
    seven times . . . . SFAOIMS
seventy
    seventy . . . . SFI
    seventy of the . . . . SFIFT
    seventy of them . . . . SFIFM
    seventy of these . . . . SFIFZ
    seventy of those . . . . SFIFS
several
    several . . . . SEFRL, SEVRL
    several days . . . . SEFRLD, SEVRLD
    several of the . . . . SEVRLTD
    several of them . . . . SEVFM
    several of these . . . . SEVRLZ
    several of those . . . . SEVRLS
    several times . . . . SEFRLT
    several years . . . . SYEVRL, SYEVRLS
    several years ago . . . . SYEVRLGS, SEVRLGS
severance . . . . SEVRNS
severe . . . . SWAOER
severely . . . . SWAOERL
severity . . . . SWAOERT
sew
    sew . . . . SOE
    sews . . . . SOES
    sewing . . . . SOE/-G
    sewed . . . . SOE/-D
    sewn . . . . SAOUN
sewage . . . . SAOUJ
sewer . . . . SAOUR
sewerage . . . . SAOURJ
sex
    sex . . . . SEX
    sexual activity . . . . SWIVT
    sexism . . . . SEFM
    sexist . . . . SEFT
    sexual . . . . SWAL
    sexual abuse . . . . SWAOUS

BRIEF ENCOUNTERS   S

sexual act .... SWAKT
sexual assault. .... SWALT
sexual harassment. .... SWAMT, SWARMT, SHARMT
sexual intercourse .... SWOURS
sexuality .... SWAELT
sexually .... SWAEL
sexual orientation. .... SWOERNGS
sexual partner. .... SWARNT, SWARN
sexual partners .... SWARNTS, SWARNZ
sexual preference .... SWEFRNS
sexual relation .... SWRELGS
shabbily .... SHAEBL
shabbiness .... SHAENS
shabby. .... SHAEB
shackle
   shackle. .... SHAKL
   shackles. .... SHAKLS
   shackling. .... SHALG, SHAKL/-G
   shackled. .... SHAKLD
shadow .... SHAOD
shake
   shake .... SHAIK
   shakes .... SHAIKS
   shaking. .... SHAIK/-G, SHAIG
   shook .... SHAOK
   shaken .... SHAIN
shaker. .... SHAIRK
shall
   shall be .... SH-B
   shall believe .... SH-BL
   shall feel .... SH-FL
   shall get. .... SH-GT
   shall go .... SH-G
   shall happen .... SH-P
   shall have. .... SHAF
   shall have been .... SH-FB
   shall have had. .... SH-FD
   shall have known. .... SH-FN
   shall live. .... SH-V
   shall mean .... SH-M
   shall recall. .... SH-RL
   shall recollect .... SH-RK
   shall remember. .... SH-RM
   shall say. .... SH-S
   shall see. .... SH-Z

shall think	SH-NG
shall think so	SH-NGS
shall understand	SH-NDZ
shall want	SH-PT
shallow	SHAOL
shallowness	SHAONS

shampoo
shampoo	SHAOP, SHAOM, SMAO
shampoos	SHAOPS, SHAOMS, SMAOS
shampooing	SMAOG, SHAOPG, SHAOMG
shampooed	SMAOD, SHAOPD, SHAOMD

shareholder	SHAIRLD

sharp
sharpener	SHAIRP
sharper	SHAERP, SHRARP
sharper than	SHAERN
sharper than the	SHAERNT
sharper than these	SHAERNZ
sharper than those	SHAERNS

sharpen
sharpen	SHAURN, SHAURP
sharpens	SHAURNS, SHAURPS
sharpening	SHAURNG, SHAURPG
sharpened	SHAURND, SHAURPD

shatter
shatter	SHART, SHAERT
shatters	SHARTS, SHAERTS
shattering	SHARGT, SHAERGT
shattered	SHARTD, SHAERTD

she
she	SHE
she be	SHEB
she been	SH*EB
she believe	SHEBL
she believed	SHEBLD
she believes	SHEBLS
she believing	SHEBLG
she can	SHEK
she can't	SHEKT, SHEK/-NT, SHE/K-NT
she could	SHEKD
she couldn't	SHEKTD, SHEKD/-NT, SHE/KUNT
she'd	SH*ED
she ever	SHEFR, SHEVR
she feel	SHAOEFL
she feels	SHEFLS

BRIEF ENCOUNTERS   S

she felt	SHEFLT
she get	SHEGT
she gets	SHEGTS
she go	SHEG
she goes	SHEGS
she hadn't	SHED/-NT, SHE/H-NT
she happen	SHEP
she happened	SHEPD
she happens	SHEPS
she is	SHES
she isn't	SHES/-NT, SHE/S-NT
she lived	SHEVD
she lives	SHEVS
she living	SHEVG
she'll	SH*EL
she mean	SHEM
she means	SHEMS
she means to	SHEMT
she means to say	SHEMTS
she recall	SHERL
she recalled	SHERLD
she recalling	SHERLG
she recalls	SHERLS
she recollect	SHERK
she recollected	SHERKD
she recollects	SHERKS
she remember	SHERM
she remembered	SHERMD
she remembering	SHERMG
she remembers	SHERMS
she's	SH*ES
she says	SHESZ
she sees	SHEZ
she shall	SHERB
she should	SHERBD
she shouldn't	SHERBTD, SHERBD/-NT, SHE/SH-NT
she think	SHENG
she thinks	SHENGS
she thinks so	SHENGSZ
she understand	SHEND
she understands	SHENDZ
she want	SHEPT
she wanted	SHEPTD
she wanting	SHEPGT
she wants	SHEPTS

S — BRIEF ENCOUNTERS

```
she was . . . . . . . . . . . . . . . . . . . . . . . . . . . . . . . . . . . . . . . . SHEFS
she wasn't . . . . . . . . . . . . . . . . . . . . . . . . . SHEFS/-NT, SHE/WUNT
she were . . . . . . . . . . . . . . . . . . . . . . . . . . . . . . . . . . . . . . . . SHERP
she weren't . . . . . . . . . . . . . . . . SHERPT, SHERP/-NT, SHE/W-RNT
she would . . . . . . . . . . . . . . . . . . . . . . . . . . . . . . . . . . . . . . . SHELD
she wouldn't . . . . . . . . . . . . . . . . . . . . . . . SHELD/-NT, SHE/WONT
she would say . . . . . . . . . . . . . . . . . . . . . . . . . . . . . . . . . . . SHELDZ
```
shear
```
    shear . . . . . . . . . . . . . . . . . . . . . . . . . . . . . . . . . . . . . . . SHAER
    shears . . . . . . . . . . . . . . . . . . . . . . . . . . . . . . . . . . . . . . SHAERS
    shearing . . . . . . . . . . . . . . . . . . . . . . . . . . . . . . . . . . . . SHAERG
    sheared . . . . . . . . . . . . . . . . . . . . . . . . . . . . . . . . . . . . SHAERD
    sheared / shorn . . . . . . . . . . . . . . . . . . . . . . . SHAERD / SHORN
```
shed
```
    shed . . . . . . . . . . . . . . . . . . . . . . . . . . . . . . . . . . . . . . . . SHED
    sheds . . . . . . . . . . . . . . . . . . . . . . . . . . . . . . . . . . . . . . . SHEDZ
    shedding . . . . . . . . . . . . . . . . . . . . . . . . . . . . . . . . . . . . SHEGD
    shed . . . . . . . . . . . . . . . . . . . . . . . . . . . . . . . . . . . . . . . . SHED
```
sheik . . . . SHAOEK
shellac
```
    shellac . . . . . . . . . . . . . . . . . . . . . . . . . . . . . . . . . . . . . . SLAEK
    shellacs . . . . . . . . . . . . . . . . . . . . . . . . . . . . . . . . . . . . . SLAEKS
    shellacking . . . . . . . . . . . . . . . . . . . . . . . . . SLAEG, SLAEK/-G
    shellacked . . . . . . . . . . . . . . . . . . . . . . . . . . . . . . . . . . SLAEKD
```
shelter
```
    shelter . . . . . . . . . . . . . . . . . . . . . . . . . . . . . . . . . . . . . . SHELT
    shelters . . . . . . . . . . . . . . . . . . . . . . . . . . . . . . . . . . . . . SHELTS
    sheltering . . . . . . . . . . . . . . . . . . . . . . . . . . . . . . . . . . . SHELGT
    sheltered . . . . . . . . . . . . . . . . . . . . . . . . . . . . . . . . . . . SHELTD
```
shenanigans . . . . SHANS
shepherd
```
    shepherd . . . . . . . . . . . . . . . . . . . . . . . . . . . . . . . . . . . . SHERD
    shepherds . . . . . . . . . . . . . . . . . . . . . . . . . . . . . . . . . . . SHERDZ
    shepherding . . . . . . . . . . . . . . . . . . . . . . . . . . . . . . . . . SHERGD
    shepherded . . . . . . . . . . . . . . . . . . . . . . . . . . . . . . . SHERD/-D
```
sheriff
```
    sheriff . . . . . . . . . . . . . . . . . . . . . . . . . . . . . . . . . . . . . . . SH-F
    sheriff's deputy . . . . . . . . . . . . . . . . . . . . . . . . . . . . . . . SHEFD
    sheriff's office . . . . . . . . . . . . . . . . . . . . . . . . . . . . . . . . SHOFS
```
shine
```
    shine . . . . . . . . . . . . . . . . . . . . . . . . . . . . . . . . . . . . . . SHAOIN
    shines . . . . . . . . . . . . . . . . . . . . . . . . . . . . . . . . . . . . . SHAOINS
    shining . . . . . . . . . . . . . . . . . . . . . . . . . . . . . . . . . . . . SHAOING
    shined / shone . . . . . . . . . . . . . . . . . . . . . . . SHAOIND / SHOEN
```
shingle . . . . SHING

BRIEF ENCOUNTERS S

shingles	SHINGS
shipment	SHIMT
shipper	SHIRP
shoot	
shoot	SHAOT
shoots	SHAOTS
shooting	SHAOGT
shot	SHOT
shooter	SHAORT
shoplift	
shoplift	SHOPT
shoplifts	SHOPTS
shoplifting	SHOPGT
shoplifted	SHOPTD
shoplifter	SHORPT
short	
shortage	SHORJ
shortcoming	SHORG
short cut	SHORK
shorter	SHOERT
shorter than	SHOERNT
shorter than the	SHOERNTD
shorter than those	SHOERNTS
shorthand	SHAND
short-lived	SHIVD
shortly	SHORL
shortness	SHORNS
shortness of breath	SHORB
short-term	SHORM
shortwave	SWAEV
shortwave radio	SWAEVR
shorten	
shorten	SHORNT, SHOERN
shortens	SHORNTS, SHOERNS
shortening	SHORNGT, SHOERNG
shortened	SHORNTD, SHOERND
shotgun	SHOG
should	
should	SHUD
should be	SHOUB
should believe	SHOUBL
should ever	SHOUFR, SHOUVR
should feel	SHOUFL
should get	SHO*UGT
should go	SHOUG

should happen	SHOUP
should have	SHOUF
should have been	SHOUFB
should have believed	SHOUFBLD
should have felt	SHOUFLT
should have gone	SHOUFG
should have had	SHOUFD
should have happened	SHOUFPD
should have known	SHOUFN
should have lived	SHOUVD
should have recalled	SHOUFRLD
should have recollected	SHOUFRKD
should have remembered	SHOUFRMD
should have said	SHOUFS
should have seen	SHOUFZ
should have understood	SHOUFND
should have wanted	SHOUFPTD
should know	SHO*UN
should live	SHOUV
should mean	SHOUM
should mean to	SHOUMT
should mean to say	SHOUMTS
shouldn't	SH-NT
should recall	SHOURL
should recall the	SHOURLT
should recollect	SHOURK
should recollect the	SHOURKT
should remember	SHOURM
should remember the	SHOURMT
should say	SHOUS
should see	SHOUZ
should think	SHOUNG
should think so	SHOUNGS
should understand	SHOUNDZ
should want	SHOUPT

shoulder
shoulder	SHOELD
shoulders	SHOELDZ
shouldering	SHOELGD
shouldered	SHOELD/-D

show
show	SHOE
shows	SHOES
showing	SHOEG
showed	SHOED

BRIEF ENCOUNTERS — S

shown.	SHOUN
show	
show business	SHOEB, SHOEBS
show cause	SHOEK
showdown.	SHOUND
shower	
shower	SHAUR
showers.	SHAURS
showering	SHAURG
showered.	SHAURD
show off	
show off.	SHOEF
shows off	SHOEFS
showing off	SHOEFG
showed off.	SHOEFD
show-off	SHAUF
show up	
show up.	SHOEP
shows up	SHOEPS
showing up.	SHOEPG
showed up	SHOEPD
shown up	SHOUN/UP
show up the	SHOEPT
show you are innocent	SHOURNT
shrapnel	SHREL
shred	
shred	SHROI, SHRED
shreds.	SHROIS, SHREDZ
shredding	SHROIG, SHREGD
shredded	SHROID, SHRED/-D
shredder	SHROIR, SHRERD
shriek	
shriek.	SHRAO*EK
shrieks.	SHRAOEKS
shrieking	SHRAOEG
shrieked.	SHRAOEKD
shrink	
shrink.	SHRINK
shrinks	SHRINKS
shrinking	SHRINK/-G
shrank.	SHRANK
shrunk.	SHRUNK
shrug	
shrug.	SHR*UG, SH-R
shrugs.	SHR*UGS, SH-RS

S — BRIEF ENCOUNTERS

shrugging . . . . SHR*UG/-G, SH-RG
shrugged . . . . SHR*UGD, SH-RD
shtick . . . . SHIK
shudder
    shudder . . . . SH*UD
    shudders . . . . SHUDZ
    shuddering . . . . SHUGD
    shuddered . . . . SHUD/-D
shut
    shut . . . . SHUT
    shuts . . . . SHUTS
    shutting . . . . SHUGT
    shut . . . . SHUT
shut up
    shut up . . . . SHUP
    shuts up . . . . SHUPS
    shutting up . . . . SHUPG
    shut up . . . . SHUP
shut up the . . . . SHUPT
Siamese . . . . SAOIMZ, SMAOEZ
Siamese twins . . . . SMINS, SWINZ
sibling . . . . SIBLG
sic . . . . SWIK
sickle . . . . S*IKL
sickness . . . . SNES
side
    sidebar . . . . SBAER
    side effect . . . . SEFK
    sideline . . . . SDLAOIN
    side of . . . . SAOIF
    side of the . . . . SAOIFT
    side of them . . . . SAOIFM
    sides of . . . . SAOIFS
    sides of the . . . . SAOIFTS
    sidewalk . . . . SWAUK
    sidewall . . . . SWAUL
    sideway . . . . SWA*I
    sideways . . . . SWAIZ
sigh
    sigh . . . . SAOI
    sighs . . . . SAOIS
    sighing . . . . SAOIG
    sighed . . . . SAOI/-D
signal
    signal . . . . SNAL

BRIEF ENCOUNTERS S

signals	SNALS
signaling	SNALG
signaled	SNALD
signature	SIG
signed English	SGLIRB
signifiable	SFABL, SFIBL
significance	SFANS
significant	SFANT
significantly	SFANL
signification	SFANGS, SFIVGS
significative	SFAV, SFIV
signify	
signify	SG-F
signifies	SG-FS
signifying	SG-FG
signified	SG-FD
sign language	S-L
sign language interpreter	S-LT
silence	SLENS
silencer	SLERNS
silent	SLENT, SAOILT
silhouette	SWHET
silicon	SKON
silicone	SKOEN
Silicon Valley	SKOV
silk	SILG
silks	SILGZ
silliness	SLAOENS
silly	SLAOE
silver	S-V
similar	
similar	SIM
similarity	SIMT
similarly	SLARL
simple	SM-L, SIFRP
simplicity	SM-LT, SIFRPT, SPLIFT
simplification	SM-GS, SM-LGS, SM-FGS, SIMGS
simplistic	SPLIFK
simply	SIFRPL
simulate	
simulate	SMAIT
simulates	SMAITS
simulating	SMAIGT
simulated	SMAITD
simulation	SMAEGS, SMA*IGS

simulator	SMAIRT
simultaneous	
simultaneous	SMULT
simultaneously	SMUL
simultaneousness	SMUNS
sincere	S-S
sincerity	S-FT
sine qua non	SKWAN, SIN/NON
sing	
sing	SING
sings	SINGS
singing	SING/-G
sang	SANG
sung	SUNG
Singapore	SPOERG
singer	SIRNG
single	SINLG
singularity	SLIRT, SING/LART
singularly	SLIRL, SING/LARL
sink	
sink	SINK
sinks	SINKS
sinking	SINK/-G
sank	SANK
sunk	SUNK
sinus	SNUS
Sioux	SWAOU
siren	SAOIRN
sister	
sister	SIS
sisterhood	SAOD
sister-in-law	SINL
sisters-in-law	SINLS
sit	
sit	SIT
sits	SITS
sitting	SIGT
sat	SAT
situate	
situate	SWAIT
situates	SWAITS
situating	SWAIGT
situated	SWAITD
situation	SWAIGS

BRIEF ENCOUNTERS　　　　　　　　　　　　　　　　　　　S

six
   sixfold... SWIFLD
   six of .... SWIF
   six of them .... SWIFM
   six of these .... SWIFZ
   six-piece .... SW*IP, SWAOES
   six-time .... SKAOIM
   six times.. SKAOIMS
   sixty .... SKI
sizable... SAOIFBL
sizableness .... SAOIFNS
sizably .... SAOEFBL
size
   size.. SAOIZ
   sizes .... SAOIFZ, SAOISZ
   sizing .... SAOIFG
   sized.. SAOIFD
skater .... SKAIRT
skaters .... SKA*IRTS
skeletal... SKALT, SKAELT
skeleton .... SKELT
skeptic
   skeptic .... SKEPT
   skeptical .... SKEPLT
   skepticism .... SK-FM
ski
   ski.. SKAO*E
   skis... SKAOES
   skiing... SKAOEG
   skied.. SKAOE/-D
skid mark .... SKARK
skier .... SKAOER
skillful
   skillful .... SKIFL
   skillfully .... SKAOEFL
   skillfulness .... SKIFLS
skipper .... SKIRP
skirmish
   skirmish .... SKIRM
   skirmishes.. SKIRMS
   skirmishing .... SKIRMG
   skirmished... SKIRMD
sky
   skydiver .... SDAOIVR
   skylight .... SKAOILT

S   BRIEF ENCOUNTERS

skyline .... SKLAOIN
skydive
   skydive .... SDAOIV
   skydives .... SDAOIVS
   skydiving .... SDAOIVG
   skydived .... SDAOIVD
skyrocket
   skyrocket .... SKROKT
   skyrockets .... SKROKTS
   skyrocketing .... SKROKT/-G
   skyrocketed .... SKROKTD
slander
   slander .... SLARN
   slanders .... SLARNZ
   slandering .... SLARNG
   slandered .... SLARND
slander
   slanderous .... SLARNS
   slanderously .... SLARNL
   slanderer .... SLAERN
slate
   slate .... SLAET
   slates .... SLAETS
   slating .... SLAEGT
   slated .... SLAETD
slaughter
   slaughter .... SLAURT, SLAUT
   slaughters .... SLAURTS, SLAUTS
   slaughtering .... SLAURGT, SLAUGT
   slaughtered .... SLAURTD, SLAUTD
slavery .... SLOIVR
Slavic .... SLAFK, SLAVK
slay
   slay .... SLAI
   slays .... SLAIS
   slaying .... SLAIG
   slew .... SLAOU
   slain .... SLAIN
sled
   sled .... SL*ED
   sleds .... SL*EDZ
   sledding .... SL*EGD
   sledded .... SL*ED/-D
sledder .... SL*ERD

BRIEF ENCOUNTERS   S

sleep
- sleep . . . . SLAOEP
- sleeps. . . . . SLAOEPS
- sleeping . . . . SLAOEPG
- slept . . . . SLEPT

sleeper . . . . SLAOERP

sleigh
- sleigh . . . . SLA*IG
- sleighs. . . . . SLAIGZ
- sleighing. . . . . SLAIG/-G
- sleighed. . . . . SLAIGD

slender . . . . SLEND

slenderize
- slenderize . . . . SLERN
- slenderizes . . . . SLERNZ
- slenderizing. . . . . SLERNG
- slenderized . . . . SLERND

slicker
- slicker . . . . SLIRK
- *slicker than* . . . . SLIRN
- *slicker than the*. . . . . SLIRNT
- *slicker than these* . . . . SLIRNZ
- *slicker than those* . . . . SLIRNS

slide
- slide . . . . SLAOID
- slides . . . . SLAOIDZ
- sliding. . . . . SLAOIGD
- slid . . . . SLID

slightly . . . . SLAOIL, SLAOILT

sling
- sling . . . . SLING
- slings . . . . SLINGS
- slinging . . . . SLING/-G
- slung. . . . . SLUNG

slink
- slink. . . . . SLAOENG, SLAOENK
- slinks. . . . . SLAOENGS, SLAOENKS
- slinking . . . . SLAOENG/-G, SLAOENK/-G
- slunk . . . . SLOING, SLOINK

slip and fall . . . . SLIFL
slipper . . . . SLIRP
slogan . . . . SLOG
sloven
- sloven . . . . SLOVN, SLOFN
- slovenly. . . . . SLOVNL, SLOFNL

S — BRIEF ENCOUNTERS

slovenliness . . . . SLOVNS, SLOFNS, SLOVNLS, SLOFNLS
slow
    slower . . . . SLOER
    slower than . . . . SLOERN
    slower than the . . . . SLOERNT
    slower than them . . . . SLOERM
    slower than these . . . . SLOERNZ
    slower than those . . . . SLOERNS
    slow motion . . . . SLOEGS
    slowness . . . . SLOENS
slow down
    slow down . . . . SLOUN
    slows down . . . . SLOUNS
    slowing down . . . . SLOUNG
    slowed down . . . . SLOUND
slyly . . . . SLAO*IL
small
    Small Business Administration . . . . SBAM, SBA/SBA
    small claim . . . . SMAIM
    small claims court . . . . SMAIMG
    smaller . . . . SMAURL
    smaller than . . . . SMAURN, SMAUNL
    smaller than the . . . . SMAURNT, SMAUNLT
    smaller than these . . . . SMAURNZ
    smaller than those . . . . SMAURNS
    smallest . . . . SMALS, SMAELS
    smallpox . . . . SMAUX
smarter
    smarter . . . . SMAERT
    smarter than . . . . SMAERN, SMARNT
    smarter than the . . . . SMAERNT, SMARNTD
    smarter than these . . . . SMAERNZ
    smarter than those . . . . SMAERNS, SMARNTS
smartest . . . . SMA*RTS
smell
    smell . . . . SMEL
    smells . . . . SMELS
    smelling . . . . SMELG
    smelled / smelt . . . . SMELD / SMELT
smite
    smite . . . . SMAOIT
    smites . . . . SMAOITS
    smiting . . . . SMAOIGT
    smote . . . . SMOET
    smote / smitten . . . . SMOET / SMINT

smoke
    smoke detector . . . . SD-RK, SMEKT
    smoke detectors . . . . SD-RKZ, SMEKTS
    smoker . . . . SMOERK
    smoke screen . . . . SMAOEM
smoking . . . . SMOEG
smolder
    smolder . . . . SMOUL
    smolders . . . . SMOULS
    smoldering . . . . SMOULG
    smoldered . . . . SMOULD
smooth
    smoother . . . . SMAO*RT, SMAORT
    smoother than . . . . SMAORN
    smoother than the . . . . SMAORNT
    smoother than these . . . . SMAORNZ
    smoother than those . . . . SMAORNS
    smoothly . . . . SMAO*LT
    smoothness . . . . SMAONS
smorgasbord . . . . SMORGD
smother
    smother . . . . SMOFR
    smothers . . . . SMOFRS
    smothering . . . . SMOFRG
    smothered . . . . SMOFRD
smuggle
    smuggle . . . . SMULG
    smuggles . . . . SMULGS
    smuggling . . . . SMULG/-G
    smuggled . . . . SMULGD
smuggler . . . . SMURL, SMURLG
snafu . . . . SNAOU
snazzy . . . . SNAZ
sneaker . . . . SNAOERK
sneeze
    sneeze . . . . SNAOEZ
    sneezes . . . . SNAOEFS, SNAOESZ
    sneezing . . . . SNAOEFG
    sneezed . . . . SNAOEFD
snicker
    snicker . . . . SNIK
    snickers . . . . SNIKS
    snickering . . . . SNIK/-G
    snickered . . . . SNIKD
sniper . . . . SNAOIRP

S   BRIEF ENCOUNTERS

snippet . . . . SNIPT
snob
    snobbery . . . . SNORB
    snobbish . . . . SNIRB
    snobbishly . . . . SNIRBL
    snobbishness . . . . SNIRBS
    snobbism . . . . SNOFM
snooker
    snooker . . . . SNAORK
    snookers . . . . SNAORKZ
    snookering . . . . SNAORG
    snookered . . . . SNAORKD
snowball
    snowball . . . . SNOEBL
    snowballs . . . . SNOEBLS
    snowballing . . . . SNOEBLG
    snowballed . . . . SNOEBLD
snowboard
    snowboard . . . . SNOERB
    snowboards . . . . SNOERBS
    snowboarding . . . . SNOERBG
    snowboarded . . . . SNOERBD
snowboarder . . . . SNROERB
snowfall . . . . SNOEFL
snowmobile . . . . SNOEB
snowplow
    snowplow . . . . SNOEP, SNOU
    snowplows . . . . SNOEPS, SNOUS
    snowplowing . . . . SNOEPG, SNOUG
    snowplowed . . . . SNOEPD, SNOUD
snowstorm . . . . SNORM
so
    so . . . . SO
    so be it . . . . SBIT
    so-called . . . . SAULD
    so far as . . . . SOFRS
    so good . . . . SOGD
    so help you God . . . . SOEG
    so marked . . . . SARK, SARKD
    so much . . . . SOFP
    so much as . . . . SOFPS
    so much the . . . . SOFPT
    so to speak . . . . SOPT
sober . . . . SOEB
sobriety . . . . SOEBT, SBRAOIT, SOBT

BRIEF ENCOUNTERS   S

soccer
- soccer . . . . SKR-, SO*RK
- *soccer ball* . . . . SKR-BL
- *soccer field* . . . . SKR-FLD

social
- social . . . . SORBL
- socialism . . . . SOEFM
- socialist . . . . SOEFT
- socialistic . . . . SOEFK, SOEFKT
- socialization . . . . SLOIFGS, SOLGS
- socially . . . . SOERBL
- *social security* . . . . SKORBL, SKOERBL
- *Social Security Administration* . . . . SKORBLGS, SKOERBLGS
- *social work* . . . . SWORK
- *social worker* . . . . SWRORK

socialize
- socialize . . . . SLOIF, SLAOIZ
- socializes . . . . SLOIFS
- socializing . . . . SLOIFG
- socialized . . . . SLOIFD

societal . . . . SOELT
society . . . . SOET

socio-
- socio- . . . . SKO
- sociological . . . . SOJ
- sociologically . . . . SOEJ
- sociologist . . . . SOLT
- sociology . . . . SOLG
- sociopath . . . . SOEPT

socket . . . . SOKT
soda . . . . SOED
sofa . . . . SOEF
sofas . . . . SOEFZ

soft
- soft . . . . SOFT, SOF
- softball . . . . SOFBL, SOFB
- *soft drink* . . . . SOFTD
- softener . . . . SROFN
- softly . . . . SOFL
- software . . . . SWAER

soften
- soften . . . . SOFN
- softens . . . . SOFNS
- softening . . . . SOFNG
- softened . . . . SOFND

S — BRIEF ENCOUNTERS

so he

so he believed	SOEBLD
so he believes	SOEBLS
so he can	SO*EK
so he can't	SOEKT, SOEK/-NT
so he could	SO*EKD
so he couldn't	SOEKTD, SO*EKD/-NT, SOEKD/-NT
so he feels	SOEFLS
so he felt	SOEFLT
so he gets	SOEGTS
so he goes	SOEGS
so he got	SOEGT
so he had	SO*ED
so he hadn't	SO*ED/-NT, SOED/-NT
so he happened	SOEPD
so he happens	SOEPS
so he imagined	SOEJD
so he imagines	SOEJS
so he is	SO*ES
so he isn't	SO*ES/-NT, SOES/-NT
so he lived	SOEVD
so he lives	SOEVS
so he means	SOEMS
so he means to	SOEMT
so he means to say	SOEMTS
so he recalled	SOERLD
so he recalls	SOERLS
so he recollected	SOERKD
so he recollects	SOERKZ, SO*ERKS
so he remembered	SOERMD
so he remembers	SOERMS
so he says	SOESZ
so he sees	SOEZ
so he shall	SO*ERB
so he should	SO*ERBD
so he shouldn't	SOERBTD, SO*ERBD/-NT, SOERBD/-NT
so he thinks	SOENGS
so he thinks so	SOENGSZ
so he understands	SOENDZ
so he understood	SOEND
so he wanted	SOEPTD
so he wants	SOEPTS
so he was	SOEFS
so he wasn't	SOEFS/-NT
so he will	SO*EL

BRIEF ENCOUNTERS S

so he would	SO*ELD
so he wouldn't	SOELTD, SO*ELD/-NT, SOELD/-NT
so he would say	SOELDZ

so I

so I	SOI
so I am	SOIM
so I believe	SOIBL
so I believed	SOIBLD
so I can	SOIK
so I can't	SOIKT, SOIK/-NT, SOI/K-NT
so I could	SOIKD
so I couldn't	SOIKTD, SOIKD/-NT, SOI/KUNT
so I feel	SOIFL
so I felt	SOIFLT
so I get	SOIGT
so I go	SOIG
so I had	SO*ID
so I hadn't	SOID/-NT, SOI/H-NT
so I happen	SOIP
so I happened	SOIPD
so I have	SOIF
so I have been	SOIFB
so I have believed	SOIFBLD
so I have had	SOIFD
so I have known	SOIFN
so I haven't	SOIFT, SOIF/-NT, SOI/V-NT
so I imagine	SOIJ
so I imagined	SOIJD
so I know	SO*IN
so I live	SOIV
so I lived	SOIVD
so I mean	SO*IM
so I mean to	SO*IMT
so I mean to say	SO*IMTS
so I recall	SOIRL
so I recalled	SOIRLD
so I recollect	SOIRK
so I recollected	SOIRKD
so I remember	SOIRM
so I remembered	SOIRMD
so I say	SOIS
so I see	SOIZ
so I shall	SOIRB
so I should	SOIRBD
so I shouldn't	SOIRBTD, SOIRBD/-NT, SOI/SH-NT

so I think	SO*ING
so I think so	SOINGS
so I understand	SOINDZ
so I understood	SO*IND
so I want	SOIPT
so I wanted	SOIPTD
so I was	SOIFS
so I wasn't	SOIFS/-NT, SOI/WUNT
so I will	SO*IL
so I would	SO*ILD
so I wouldn't	SOILTD, SOILD/-NT, SOI/WONT
so I would say	SOILDZ

sojourn
    sojourn . . . . SOURN
    sojourns . . . . SOURNS
    sojourning . . . . SOURNG
    sojourned . . . . SOURND
sojourner . . . . SROURN
solace . . . . SLAOS
solar . . . . SLAOR
solar heating . . . . SLAORG
soldier . . . . SOL
solemn
    solemn . . . . SLEM
    solemnity . . . . SLEMT
    solemnly swear . . . . SLAER
sole proprietorship . . . . SPRIP
solicit
    solicit . . . . SLIFT, SLIS
    solicits . . . . SLIFTS, SLIFS
    soliciting . . . . SLIFGT, SLIFG
    solicited . . . . SLIFTD, SLIFD
solicitation . . . . SLIGS
solicitor . . . . SLIFRT, SLIFR
solidarity . . . . SDAIRT
solubility . . . . SOBLT
soluble . . . . SOBL
solution . . . . SLAOUGS
solvability . . . . SOVBLT, SOFBLT
solvable . . . . SOVBL
solve
    solve . . . . SOVL
    solves . . . . SOVLS
    solving . . . . SOVLG
    solved . . . . SOVLD

BRIEF ENCOUNTERS   S

solvency . . . . SOFLS
solvent . . . . SOFLT
Somalia . . . . SMOL
Somalian . . . . SMONL
some
    some . . . . SOM
    somebody . . . . SM-B
    somebody else . . . . SM-BL
    somebody else's . . . . SM-BLS
    somebody like that . . . . SM-BLT, SM-BT
    somebody like this . . . . SM-BS
    somebody's . . . . SM-BZ
    someday . . . . SDAI
    somehow . . . . SMOU
    some kind of . . . . SKAOIF
    some more . . . . SMOR
    some of . . . . SM-F
    some of the . . . . SM-FT
    some of them . . . . SM-FM
    some of these . . . . SM-FS
    some of those . . . . SM-FZ
    someone . . . . SWUN
    someone else . . . . SWUNL
    someone else's . . . . SWUNLS
    someone like that . . . . SWUNT, SWUNLT
    someone like this . . . . SWUNS
    someone's . . . . SWUNZ
    someplace . . . . SPLAIS
    someplace else . . . . SPLAISZ, SPLEL
    someplace like that . . . . SPLAILT
    someplace like this . . . . SPLAILS
    something . . . . SM-G
    something else . . . . SM-LG
    something like that . . . . SL-T
    something like this . . . . SL-S
    sometime . . . . STAOIM, STOIM
    sometime the . . . . STAOIMT, STOIMT
    sometimes the . . . . STAOIMTS, STOIMTS
    somewhat . . . . SMA
    somewhere . . . . SM-R
    somewhere else . . . . SM-RL, SM-RS
    somewhere like that . . . . SM-RLT
    somewhere like this . . . . SM-RLZ
so move
    so move . . . . SMOV

so moves	SMOVS
so moving	SMOVG
so moved	SMOVD
son	
son-in-law	SONL
son of a bitch	SIFP
sons-in-law	SONLS
sons of bitches	SIFPS
sonar	SNAOR
soon	
soon	SAON
sooner	SAORN
sooner or later	SAORNL, SAONL
sooner or later the	SAORNLT, SAONLT
sooner than	SAORNT
sooner than the	SAORNTD
sooner than these	SAORNZ
sooner than those	SAORNS
soonest	SAOFT, SAO*NS
so order	
so order	SORD
so orders	SORDZ
so ordering	SORGD
so ordered	SORD/-D
sophisticate	
sophisticate	SFIF
sophisticates	SFIF/-S
sophisticating	SFIFG
sophisticated	SFIFD
sophistication	SFIGS
sordid	SDOD
sordidly	SDOLD
sore	
sorely	SOERL
soreness	SOERNS
sore throat	SOERT
sorrow	
sorrow	SWO
sorrowful	SWOF, SWOL
sorrowfully	SWOFL
sorrowfulness	SWOFNS, SWONS
sorry	SOR
sort of	SOFRT
sorts of	SOFRTS
SOS	SOS

BRIEF ENCOUNTERS   S

so stipulate
    so stipulate .... STOIP
    so stipulates .... STOIPS
    so stipulating .... STOIPG
    so stipulated .... STOIPD
sought .... SAUT
sound
    sound .... SOUN
    sounds .... SOUNS
    sounding .... SOUNG
    sounded .... SOUND
soundproof
    soundproof .... SPRAOF
    soundproofs .... SPRAOFS
    soundproofing .... SPRAOFG
    soundproofed .... SPRAOFD
south
    South Africa .... SFAK
    South African .... SFAN
    South Africans .... SFANZ
    South America .... SERK, SA
    South American .... SAN, SARN
    southbound .... SOUB
    South Carolina .... S*K
    South Dakota .... S*D
    southeast .... SAO*ES
    southeasterly .... SERL
    southeastern .... SAOERN
    southerly .... SORL
    southern .... SORN
    southerner .... SRORN
    south side .... S-DZ
    southwest .... SW*ES
    southwesterly .... SWERL
    southwestern .... SWERN
souvenir .... SAOUVR
sovereign
    sovereign .... SOVRN
    sovereignly .... SOVRNL, SOFRNL
    sovereignty .... SOVRNT, SOFRNT
Soviet .... SOVT
Soviet Union .... S*U
sow
    sow .... SO*U
    sows .... SOUZ

sowing . . . . SOU/-G
sowed . . . . SOUD
sowed / sown . . . . SOUD / SO*UN

so waive
   so waive . . . . SAEV, SWAIV
   so waives . . . . SAEVS, SWAIVS
   so waiving . . . . SAEVG, SWAIVG
   so waived . . . . SAEVD, SWAIVD

so you
   so you . . . . SOU
   so you are . . . . SO*UR
   so you aren't . . . . SOURNT, SOUR/-NT, SOU/R-NT
   so you believe . . . . SOUBL
   so you believed . . . . SOUBLD
   so you can . . . . SOUK
   so you can't . . . . SOUKT, SOUK/-NT, SOU/K-NT
   so you could . . . . SOUKD
   so you couldn't . . . . SOUKTD, SOUKD/-NT, SOU/KUNT
   so you feel . . . . SOUFL
   so you felt . . . . SOUFLT
   so you get . . . . SOUGT
   so you go . . . . SOUG
   so you had . . . . SO*UD
   so you hadn't . . . . SOUD/-NT, SOU/H-NT
   so you happen . . . . SOUP
   so you happened . . . . SOUPD
   so you have . . . . SOUF
   so you have been . . . . SOUFB
   so you have believed . . . . SOUFBLD
   so you have had . . . . SOUFD
   so you have known . . . . SOUFN
   so you haven't . . . . SOUFT, SOUF/-NT, SOU/V-NT
   so you imagine . . . . SOUJ
   so you imagined . . . . SOUJD
   so you live . . . . SOUV
   so you lived . . . . SOUVD
   so you mean . . . . SOUM
   so you mean to . . . . SOUMT
   so you mean to say . . . . SOUMTS
   so you recall . . . . SOURL
   so you recalled . . . . SOURLD
   so you recollect . . . . SOURK
   so you recollected . . . . SOURKD
   so you remember . . . . SOURM
   so you remembered . . . . SOURMD

so you shall	SOURB
so you should	SOURBD
so you shouldn't	SOURBTD, SOURBD/-NT, SOU/SH-NT
so you think	SO*UNG
so you think so	SOUNGS
so you understand	SOUNDZ
so you understood	SO*UND
so you want	SOUPT
so you wanted	SOUPTD
so you were	SOURP
so you weren't	SOURPT, SOURP/-NT, SOU/W-RNT
so you will	SO*UL
so you would	SOULD
so you wouldn't	SOULTD, SOULD/-NT, SOU/WONT
so you would say	SOULDZ
spacious	
spacious	SPAIRB
spaciously	SPAIRBL
spaciousness	SPAINS
spaghetti	SPAG
Spaniard	SPAURD
Spanish	SPARB
Spanish interpreter	**SPANT**
spare part	**SPAURT**
sparkle	
sparkle	SPARL
sparkles	SPARLZ
sparkling	SPARLG
sparkled	SPARLD
sparkler	SPRARL
sparsely	SPARLS
spasm	
spasm	SPAFM
spasmodic	SMOD
spasmodically	SMOLD
spastic	SPAS
spatial	SPAIL, SPAL
spatially	SPAEL
spatter	
spatter	SPART
spatters	SPARTS
spattering	SPARGT
spattered	SPARTD
speak	
speak	SPAOEK

```
speaks .................................... SPAOEKS
speaking .................................. SPAOEG
spoke ..................................... SPOEK
spoken .................................... SPOEN
```
speak about
```
    speak about ........................... SPEB
    speak about the ....................... SPEBT
    speak about them ...................... SPEFM
    speak about these ..................... SPEBZ
    speak about those ..................... SPEBS
speaker ................................... SPAOERK
```
speak of
```
    speak of .............................. SPAOEFK
    speaks of ............................. SPAOEFKS
    speaking of ........................... SPAOEFG
    spoke of .............................. SPOEFK, SPOEF
    spoken of ............................. SPOEFN
speaks for itself ......................... SPIS
```
speak up
```
    speak up .............................. SPUP
    speaks up ............................. SPUPS
    speaking up ........................... SPUPG
    spoke up .............................. SPUPD, SPOEK/UP
    spoken up ............................. SPOEND
spearmint ................................. SPAOERMT
spec ...................................... SP-K
special
    special ............................... SPERB
    special interest ...................... SPINT
    special interest group ................ SPINGT
    specialist ............................ SPERBT
    speciality ............................ SPERBLT
    specialization ........................ SPERBLGS, SPAOILGS
    specially ............................. SPERBL
specialize
    specialize ............................ SPAOIL
    specializes ........................... SPAOILS
    specializing .......................... SPAOILG
    specialized ........................... SPAOILD
specialty ................................. SPAERBLT
species ................................... SPAOES
specific
    specific .............................. SPEF
    specifically .......................... SPEFL
    specification ......................... SPEFX, SPEFGS
```

BRIEF ENCOUNTERS S

specificity . . . . SPEFT
specify
   specify. . . . . SPIF
   specifies. . . . . SPIFS
   specifying . . . . SPIFG
   specified . . . . SPIFD
specimen . . . . SPEM
specious. . . . . SPAOERB
speck . . . . SPAEK, SP*EK
speckle
   speckle . . . . SPEKL
   speckles . . . . SPEKLS
   speckling . . . . SPEKL/-G
   speckled . . . . SPEKLD
spectacle . . . . SPAEKT, SPAKL, SPAEKL
spectacular . . . . SPLAR
spectacularly . . . . SPLARL
spectator. . . . . SPERKT
spectrum . . . . SPRUM
speculate
   speculate . . . . SPLAIT
   speculates . . . . SPLAITS
   speculating. . . . . SPLAIGT
   speculated . . . . SPLAITD
speculation. . . . . SPLAIGS
speculative
   speculative. . . . . SPLAIV, SPLAIF
   speculatively. . . . . SPLAIVL, SPLAIFL
   speculativeness . . . . SPLAIVNS, SPLAIFNS
speculator . . . . SPLAIRT
speech
   speech impaired . . . . SPIRD
   speech impairment . . . . SPAIRMT, SPIRMT
   speech impediment . . . . SPEFMT
   speechless. . . . . SPAOEFPLS
   speechread . . . . SPRAOEFP
   speechreader. . . . . SPRAOEFRP
   speechreading . . . . SPRAOEFPG
   speech therapist. . . . . SPAERPT
   speech therapy . . . . SPAERP
speed
   speed. . . . . SPAOED
   speeds . . . . SPAOEDZ
   speeding . . . . SPAOEGD
   sped / speeded . . . . SPED / SPAOED/-D

speed
- speedboat . . . . SPAOEB, SPAOEBT
- speedily . . . . SPAOELD
- *speed limit* . . . . SPLIMT
- *speed of* . . . . SPAOEF
- *speed of the* . . . . SPAOEFT
- *speed of them* . . . . SPAOEFM
- *speed of these* . . . . SPAOEFZ
- *speed of those* . . . . SPAOEFS
- speedometer . . . . SPOMT
- speedy . . . . SPOID
- *speedy trial* . . . . SPRAOIL

spell
- speller . . . . SPERL
- *spell your last name* . . . . SPLAIM
- *spell your name* . . . . SPAIM
- *spell your name for the record* . . . . SPAIMD

spend
- spend . . . . SPEND, SPEN
- spends . . . . SPENDZ
- spending . . . . SPENGD, SPENG
- spent . . . . SPENT

sphincter . . . . SFING, SFINGT
sphincters . . . . SFINGZ, SFINGTS
sphinx . . . . SFINGS
spigot . . . . SPIKT

spin
- spin . . . . SPIN
- spins . . . . SPINS
- spinning . . . . SPING
- spun . . . . SPUN

spinach . . . . SPIFP

spinal
- spinal . . . . SPAOINL
- *spinal column* . . . . SPLUM
- *spinal cord* . . . . SKORD

spindle . . . . SPINL

spirit
- spirit . . . . SPIRT
- spirits . . . . SPIRTS
- spiriting . . . . SPIRGT, SPIRG
- spirited . . . . SPIRTD

spiritual
- spiritual . . . . SPUL
- spirituality . . . . SPULT

S

```
    spiritually .................................... SPIRLT
spit
    spit .......................................... SPIT
    spits ......................................... SPITS
    spitting ....................................... SPIGT
    spit / spat ................................. SPIT / SPAT
spiteful ........................................ SPAOIFL
splatter
    splatter ....................................... SPLART
    splatters ..................................... SPLARTS
    splattering .................................... SPLARGT
    splattered .................................... SPLARTD
splendid
    splendid ...................................... SPLEND
    splendidly .................................... SPLENLD
    splendidness .................................. SPLENS
splendor ................................... SPLEN, SPLOR
splinter
    splinter ....................................... SPLIRNT
    splinters ..................................... SPLIRNTS
    splintering ..................... SPLIRNGT, SPLIRNG
    splintered .................................... SPLIRNTD
split
    split .......................................... SPLIT
    splits ......................................... SPLITS
    splitting ...................................... SPLIGT
    split .......................................... SPLIT
```
split up
```
    split up ...................................... SPLUP
    splits up ..................................... SPLUPS
    splitting up ................................... SPLUPG
    split up ...................................... SPLUP
spokesman .................................... SPOEM
spokesperson ........................... SPOEP, SPERN
spokeswoman ................................. SPOM
sponge
    sponge .............................. SPUNG, SPONG
    sponges ........................... SPUNGS, SPONGS
    sponging ..................... SPUNG/-G, SPONG/-G
    sponged ..................... SPUNGD, SPONG/-D
sponsor
    sponsor ....................................... SPORN
    sponsors ..................................... SPORNS
    sponsoring .................................... SPORNG
    sponsored .................................... SPORND
```

sponsorship	SPOP
spontaneity	SPAENT
spontaneous	
spontaneous	SPAEN
spontaneous combustion	SKBUGS
spontaneously	SPAENL
spontaneousness	SPAENS
sporadic	SPRAK, SPORK
sporadically	SPRAEK, SPOERL, SPRAKL, SPORKL
sportsmanship	SPORP
spotlight	SPOLT, SPLAOIT
spousal	SPOULS
spousal abuse	SPAOUS
sprayer	SPRAIR
spread	
spread	SPRED
spreads	SPREDZ
spreading	SPREGD
spread	SPRED
spread	
spread-eagle	SPRAOEG, SPRAOELG
spreader	SPRERD
spreadsheet	SPRAOET
spring	
spring	SPRING
springs	SPRINGS
springing	SPRING/-G
sprang	SPRANG
sprung	SPRUNG
springtime	SPRINGT
springer	SPRIRNG
sprinkle	
sprinkle	SPRINL
sprinkles	SPRINLS
sprinkling	SPRINLG
sprinkled	SPRINLD
sprinkler	SPRIRNL
sprocket	SPROK
spunk	
spunk	SPUNK
spunkily	SPOINL
spunkiness	SPOINKS, SPOINGS
spunky	SPOINK
spurious	
spurious	SPRUS, SPROUS

BRIEF ENCOUNTERS S

spuriously	SPRULS, SPROULS
spuriousness	SPRUNS, SPROUNS
squadron	SKWAOD
squalor	SKWARL, SKWAORL
squander	
squander	SKWAND
squanders	SKWANDZ
squandering	SKWANGD, SKWANG
squandered	SKWAND/-D
squanderer	SKWRAND
square	
square feet	SKWAOEFT
square foot	SKWAOFT
square footage	SKWAOJ
square inch	SKWIFP
squarely	SKWAIRL
square meter	SKWAOERM, SKWAOERMT
square mile	SKWAIM, SKWAOIL
squareness	SKWAIRNS
square one	SKWON
square root	SKWRAOT
square yard	SKWARD
squeamish	SKWAOEM
squelch	
squelch	SKWEFP
squelches	SKWEFPS
squelching	SKWEFPG
squelched	SKWEFPD
Sr.	S*R
Sri Lanka	SLAUNG
St.	ST-FPLT
stability	STABLT
stabilization	STABLGS
stabilize	
stabilize	STLAOIZ, STLAOIS
stabilizes	STLAOIFS, STLAOISZ
stabilizing	STLAOIFG
stabilized	STLAOIFD
stadium	STAIM
stagnant	STAGT, SNAGT
stagnate	
stagnate	STAEG
stagnates	STAEGZ
stagnating	STAEG/-G
stagnated	STAEGD

stagnation	STAEGS, STAGS
stainless	STAINL
stainless steel	STAINLS
staircase	STAIRK
stairway	STWAI
stalactite	STLAK
stalagmite	STLAM
stalk	
stalk	STAUK
stalks	STAUKS
stalking	STAUG, STAUK/-G
stalked	STAUKD
stalker	STAURK
stalwart	
stalwart	STLART, SWART
stalwartly	STLARL, SWARL
stalwartness	STLARNS, SWARNS
stammer	
stammer	STARM
stammers	STARMS
stammering	STARMG
stammered	STARMD
stammerer	STRARM
stamp	
stamp	STAM
stamps	STAMS
stamping	STAMG
stamped	STAMD
stanchion	STANGS
stand	
stand	STAND
stands	STANDZ
standing	STANGD, STANG
stood	STAOD
stand	
stand-alone	STLOEN
standard	ST-D
standardization	ST-RGS
standard of living	STLIV, STLIVG
stand-off	STAUF
standpoint	ST-PT
standardize	
standardize	ST-RD
standardizes	ST-RDZ
standardizing	ST-RGD

BRIEF ENCOUNTERS S

standardized . . . . ST-RD/-D
stand up
    stand up. . . . . STAP
    stands up . . . . STAPS
    standing up. . . . . STAPG
    stood up . . . . STAOD/UP
stare decisis. . . . . STAIRD
star
    starlight . . . . STARLT
    starling. . . . . STA*RLG, STAURLG
    starlit. . . . . STLIT
starter . . . . STRART
startle
    startle. . . . . STARL
    startles . . . . STARLS
    startling . . . . STARLG
    startled. . . . . STARLD
starvation . . . . STARGS, STAFRBGS
starve
    starve. . . . . STAFRB
    starves . . . . STAFRBS
    starving . . . . STAFRBG
    starved. . . . . STAFRBD
state
    State Attorney . . . . STOERN
    State Attorney General. . . . . STOERNG, STOERNGT
    state capitol. . . . . STPOL, SKPOL
    state capitols. . . . . STPOLZ
    state constitution . . . . STAO*GS, STAOUGS
    State Department. . . . . SD-PT
    state highway . . . . STHOI
    state law . . . . STLA
    stately. . . . . STAILT
    statement . . . . STAIMT
    statement of rights . . . . STAIRTS
    state of . . . . STAIF
    state of emergency. . . . . STERJ
    state of mind. . . . . STAIMD
    state of the . . . . STAIFT
    state of the art. . . . . STAIRT
    state of them. . . . . STAIFM
    state of these . . . . STAIFZ
    state of those . . . . STAIFS
    state patrol . . . . STROL
    state police. . . . . STLIS

S — BRIEF ENCOUNTERS

- *state prison* . . . . STIN
- *state prisons* . . . . STINZ
- *state requirement* . . . . STAIRMT, STAOIRMT
- *state trooper* . . . . STRAORP
- statewide . . . . STWAOID
- *state your* . . . . STUR
- *state your business* . . . . STURBS
- *state your full name* . . . . STUFRN
- *state your name* . . . . STURN
- *state your opinion* . . . . STURP
- static . . . . STAKT
- stationary . . . . STAIRN
- stationery . . . . STAERN
- *station wagon* . . . . STWAG
- statistic
  - statistic . . . . STAT, STAFK
  - statistical . . . . STALT, STAFL
  - statistician . . . . STIGS
- statue . . . . STAOUFP
- stature . . . . STAUR
- status . . . . STAUS
- *status quo* . . . . SKWOE
- statute . . . . STAFP
- *statute of limitations* . . . . STIMS
- statutorily . . . . STRAFPL
- statutory
  - statutory . . . . STRAFP
  - *statutory rape* . . . . STRAEP
  - *statutory right* . . . . STRAFPT
- staunch
  - staunch . . . . STAUFP
  - staunchly . . . . STAUFPL
  - staunchness . . . . STAUNS
- stave
  - stave . . . . STAIV
  - staves . . . . STAIVS
  - staving . . . . STAIVG
  - staved / stove . . . . STAIVD / STOEV
- steadfast . . . . STEFD
- steadfastly . . . . STEFL
- steal
  - steal . . . . STAEL
  - steals . . . . STAELS
  - stealing . . . . STAELG
  - stole . . . . STOEL

BRIEF ENCOUNTERS   S

stolen	STOENL
steamer	STAOERM
steering wheel	STWAOEL
stellar	STLAR
stench	STEFP

stenograph
stenograph	SGRAF
stenographer	SGRAFR
stenographic	SGRAFK
stenographically	SGRAEFK
stenography	SGRAEF

step
stepbrother	STBRO
stepfather	SFA, SFAU, STEFR
stepfathers	SFAZ, SFAUS, STEFRS
step forward	STEFRD
stepmother	SMOER, SMOEFR, SMEFR
stepsister	STEPZ
stepsisters	STEPSZ

step down
step down	SDOUN
steps down	SDOUNS
stepping down	SDOUN/-G
stepped down	SDOUND

stereo	STER

stereotype
stereotype	STERP
stereotypes	STERPS
stereotyping	STERPG
stereotyped	STERPD

stereotypic	STERPT
stereotypical	STERPL
sterile	STERL
sterility	STERLT
sterilization	STERLGS
steroid	STERD
stevedore	STAOEVD
stewardess	SDESZ

stick
stick	STIK
sticks	STIKS
sticking	STIK/-G, STIG
stuck	STUK

sticker	STIRK

stickle
- stickle . . . . STIKL
- stickles . . . . STIKLS
- stickling . . . . STIKL/-G
- stickled . . . . STIKLD

stickler . . . . STIRKL, STLIK

stiffen
- stiffen . . . . STIFN
- stiffens . . . . STIFNZ
- stiffening . . . . STIFN/-G
- stiffened . . . . STIFND

stiffly . . . . STIFL
stiffness . . . . STIFNS

stifle
- stifle . . . . STAOIFL
- stifles . . . . STAOIFLS
- stifling . . . . STAOIFLG
- stifled . . . . STAOIFLD

stigmatism . . . . SMIFM

stigmatize
- stigmatize . . . . SMIG, STIGT
- stigmatizes . . . . SMIGZ, STIGTS
- stigmatizing . . . . SMIG/-G, STIGT/-G
- stigmatized . . . . SMIGD, STIGTD

stiletto . . . . STLET
stimulant . . . . STLANT

stimulate
- stimulate . . . . STLAIT
- stimulates . . . . STLAITS
- stimulating . . . . STLAIGT
- stimulated . . . . STLAITD

stimulation . . . . STLAIGS
stimuli . . . . STLAOI
stimulus . . . . STLUS

sting
- sting . . . . STING
- stings . . . . STINGS
- stinging . . . . STING/-G
- stung . . . . STUNG

stink
- stink . . . . STINK
- stinks . . . . STINKS
- stinking . . . . STINK/-G
- stank / stunk . . . . STANK / STUNK

BRIEF ENCOUNTERS   S

stipulate
    stipulate . . . . STIP
    stipulates . . . . STIPS
    stipulating . . . . STIPG
    stipulated . . . . STIPD
stipulation . . . . STIPGS
stirrup . . . . STIRP
St. Louis . . . . STLAOUS
stock
    stock and bond . . . . STOND
    stockbroker . . . . SBROER, SBROERK
    stock exchange . . . . SKPAING, STAEJ
    stockholder . . . . STOLD
    stock market . . . . STMAERK, SMAERK
    stock option . . . . STOPGS
    stocks and bonds . . . . STONS
stodgy . . . . STOJ
stoic
    stoic . . . . STWIK, STWOEK
    stoically . . . . STWIL, STWOEL
    stoicism . . . . STOEFM, STWOEFM
stomach . . . . STUM
stop
    stop light . . . . ST-LT
    stopper . . . . STORP
    stop sign . . . . STOIN
    stopwatch . . . . STWAFP
storage . . . . STORJ
story . . . . STROR, STROER
straddle
    straddle . . . . STRAD
    straddles . . . . STRADZ
    straddling . . . . STRAGD
    straddled . . . . STRAD/-D
straddler . . . . STRARD
straighten
    straighten . . . . STRAINT
    straightens . . . . STRAINTS
    straightening . . . . STRAINGT
    straightened . . . . STRAINTD
straightener . . . . STRAIRNT
straightforward
    straightforward . . . . STRAIFRD
    straightforwardly . . . . STRAIFRLD
    straightforwardness . . . . STRAIFRNS

straightjacket
- straightjacket . . . STRAIK
- straightjackets . . . STRAIKS
- straightjacketing . . . STRAIK/-G
- straightjacketed . . . STRAIKD

strange . . . STRAIJ, STRAING
stranger . . . STRAIRJ, STRAIRNG
strangle
- strangle . . . STRANG
- strangles . . . STRANGS
- strangling . . . STRANG/-G
- strangled . . . STRANGD

strangle hold . . . STHOLD
strangler . . . STRARNG
strangulate
- strangulate . . . SGLAIT
- strangulates . . . SGLAITS
- strangulating . . . SGLAIGT
- strangulated . . . SGLAITD

strangulation . . . SGLAIGS
strategic . . . STRAOEJ
strategist . . . STRAGT
strategy . . . STRAJ, STRAG
strawberry . . . STRAUB
streamer . . . STRAOERM
street . . . STR-T
street light . . . STR-LT, STRAOELT
strength . . . STRENG
strengthen
- strengthen . . . STREN, STRENT
- strengthens . . . STRENS, STRENTS
- strengthening . . . STREN/-G, STRENGT
- strengthened . . . STREND, STRENTD

strengthener . . . STRERN, STRERNT
strenuous
- strenuous . . . STRUS
- strenuously . . . STRULS
- strenuousness . . . STRUNS

strep throat . . . STREPT
stress
- stress . . . STRES
- stresses . . . STREFS, STRESZ
- stressing . . . STREFG
- stressed . . . STREFD

BRIEF ENCOUNTERS   S

stress
- ***stress and trauma*** .... STRAUM
- stressful .... STREFL
- stressfully .... STRAOEFL
- stretcher .... STREFRP
- ***stretch of the imagination*** .... STREJ

strew
- strew .... STRAOU
- strews .... STRAOUS
- strewing .... STRAOUG
- strewed / strewn .... STRAOUD / STRAOUN
- stricken .... STRIN
- strictly .... STRIKL

stride
- stride .... STRAOID
- strides .... STRAOIDZ
- striding .... STRAOIGD
- strode .... STROED
- stridden .... STRIND

stride
- stridence .... STRAOINS
- stridency .... STRAOINSZ
- strident .... STRAOINT
- stridently .... STRAOINLT, STRAOINL

strike
- strike .... STRAOIK
- strikes .... STRAOIKS
- striking .... STRAOIK/-G, STRAOIG
- struck .... STRUK
- struck / stricken .... STRUK / STRIN

strike
- striker .... STRAOIRK
- ***strike out*** .... STROUT
- ***strike that*** .... STRAT
- ***strike the*** .... STRAOIKT

string
- string .... STRING
- strings .... STRINGS
- stringing .... STRING/-G
- strung .... STRUNG
- stringent .... STRINT, STRIJ
- stringently .... STRINLT, STRINL
- stripper .... STRIRP

strive
- strive .... STRAOIV

strives	STRAOIVS
striving	STRAOIVG
strove	STROEV
striven / strived	STRIVN / STRAOIVD
strobe light	STROEBLT
stroller	STRORL, STROERL
strong	
stronger	STRORNG
stronger than	STRORN
stronger than the	STRORNT
stronger than these	STRORNZ
stronger than those	STRORNS
strongest	STRONGS
structural	
structural	STRURL
structuralization	STRULGS
structurally	STRAOERL
structure	
structure	STRUR
structures	STRURS
structuring	STRURG
structured	STRURD
struggle	
struggle	STRUG
struggles	STRUGS
struggling	STRULG, STRUG/-G
struggled	STRUGD
stubborn	
stubborn	STORN
stubbornly	STORNL
stubbornness	STORNS
student	STAOUN
studio	STAOUD
study	
study	STOI
studies	STOIS
studying	STOIG
studied	STOID
stuff like that	STUFT
stuff like this	STIFT
stupid	
stupid	STAOUP, STAOUPD
stupidity	STAOUPT, STAOUPTD
stupidly	STAOUPL, STAOUPLD
stupor	STAOURP

BRIEF ENCOUNTERS   S

stutter
    stutter .... STURT
    stutters .... STURTS
    stuttering .... STURGT
    stuttered .... STURTD
stutterer .... STRURT
sua sponte .... SWANT, SWAONT
subcommittee .... SKMAOET
subconscious .... SKONS
subconsciously .... SKONL
subcontract
    subcontract .... SKR-T
    subcontracts .... SKR-TS
    subcontracting .... SKR-GT
    subcontracted .... SKR-TD
subcontractor .... SKR-RT
subdivide
    subdivide .... SDWI
    subdivides .... SDWIS
    subdividing .... SDWIG
    subdivided .... SDWID
subdivision .... SDWIGS
subdue
    subdue .... SDAOU
    subdues .... SDAOUZ
    subduing .... SDAOUG
    subdued .... SDAOUD
subdural .... SDURL
subgroup .... SGRAOUP
subhuman .... SHAOUM
subject
    subject .... SUJ
    subjects .... SUJS
    subjecting .... SUJ/-G
    subjected .... SUJD
subjugate
    subjugate .... JAOG
    subjugates .... JAOGZ
    subjugating .... JAOG/-G
    subjugated .... JAOGD
subjugation .... JAOGS
subjugator .... JAORG
sublease
    sublease .... SLAOES
    subleases .... SLAOEFS, SLAOESZ

subleasing . . . . SLAOEFG
subleased . . . . SLAOEFD
sublet
   sublet . . . . SLET
   sublets . . . . SLETS
   subletting . . . . SLEGT
   sublet . . . . SLET
sublime
   sublime . . . . SBLAOIM
   sublimely . . . . SBLAOIL
   sublimeness . . . . SBLAOIMS
subliminal . . . . SBLIM
subliminally . . . . SBLIL
sublimity . . . . SBLIMT
submachine gun . . . . SM-RBG
submarine . . . . SMARN
submerge
   submerge . . . . SMERJ
   submerges . . . . SMERJS
   submerging . . . . SMERJ/-G
   submerged . . . . SMERJD
submerse
   submerse . . . . SMERB
   submerses . . . . SMERBS
   submersing . . . . SMERBG
   submersed . . . . SMERBD
submersible . . . . SMERBL
submersion . . . . SMERGS, SMERBGS
submission . . . . SMIGS
submissive
   submissive . . . . SMIV
   submissively . . . . SMIVL
   submissiveness . . . . SMIVNS
submit
   submit . . . . SMIT
   submits . . . . SMITS
   submitting . . . . SMIGT
   submitted . . . . SMITD
submittal . . . . SMIL
submitter . . . . SMIRT
subordinate
   subordinate . . . . SBORN
   subordinates . . . . SBORNZ
   subordinating . . . . SBORNG
   subordinated . . . . SBORND

BRIEF ENCOUNTERS   S

subordinately	SBORNL
subordination	SBORNGS
subordinative	SBOV
subpoena	
subpoena	S-P
subpoenas	S-PS
subpoenaing	S-PG
subpoenaed	S-PD
subpoena duces tecum	SP-D, S-P/D-T
subrogate	
subrogate	SBROG, BROG
subrogates	SBROGZ, BROGZ
subrogating	SBROG/-G, BROG/-G
subrogated	SBROGD, BROGD
subrogation	SBROGS, BROGS
sub rosa	SPWROES
subscribe	
subscribe	SKRI
subscribes	SKRIS
subscribing	SKRIG
subscribed	SKRID
subscriber	SKRIR
subscription	SKRIGS
subsequence	SKWENS
subsequent	SKWENT
subsequently	SKWENLT, SKWENL
subside	
subside	SWAOI
subsides	SWAOIS
subsiding	SWAOIG
subsided	SWAOI/-D
subsidiary	SWID
subsidies	SDAOEZ
subsidize	
subsidize	SDAOIS
subsidizes	SDAOIFS, SDAOISZ
subsidizing	SDAOIFG
subsidized	SDAOIFD
subsidy	SDAOE
subsist	
subsist	SWIS
subsists	SWIFS
subsisting	SWIFG
subsisted	SWIFD
subsistence	SWINS

S

subsistent	SWINT
substance	SUBS
substance abuse	SBAOUBS
substantial	STANL
substantially	STAENL
substantiate	
substantiate	STAENT
substantiates	STAENTS
substantiating	STAENGT
substantiated	STAENTD
substantiation	STAENGS
substitute	
substitute	STUT
substitutes	STUTS
substituting	STUGT
substituted	STUTD
substitution	STUGS
subtitle	STAOILT
subtle	SULT
subtlety	SUBLT
subtly	SAOELT, SAOEBLT
subtotal	
subtotal	STOLT
subtotals	STOLTS
subtotaling	STOLGT, STOLG
subtotaled	STOLTD
subtract	
subtract	STRAKT, SWAK
subtracts	STRAKTS, SWAKZ
subtracting	STRAKT/-G, SWAK/-G
subtracted	STRAKTD, SWAKD
subtraction	STRAEX, SWAX
subtropical	STROP
subtropics	STROX
suburb	SBURB, SB-B
suburban	SBURN, SBAN
subversion	SWERGS
subvert	
subvert	SWERT
subverts	SWERTS
subverting	SWERGT
subverted	SWERTD
subway	SWAIB
subway train	SWAIBT

BRIEF ENCOUNTERS   S

succeed
- succeed . . . . S-KD
- succeeds . . . . S-KDZ
- succeeding . . . . S-KD/-G, S-GD
- succeeded . . . . S-KD/-D

success
- success . . . . S-K
- successes . . . . S-KZ
- successful . . . . S-FL
- successfully . . . . SAOEFL
- successor . . . . S-RK, SKEFR
- successors . . . . S-RKZ, SKEFRS

succinct . . . . SINGT
succinctly . . . . SINLGT

succumb
- succumb . . . . SKOM
- succumbs . . . . SKOMS
- succumbing . . . . SKOMG
- succumbed . . . . SKOMD

such
- such . . . . SUFP
- *such as* . . . . SUFPS
- *such as the* . . . . SUFPT
- *such as these* . . . . SUFPZ

sucker . . . . SURK

suckle
- suckle . . . . SUKL
- suckles . . . . SUKLS
- suckling . . . . SULG, SUKL/-G
- suckled . . . . SUKLD

sudden
- sudden . . . . SUD
- suddenly . . . . SULD
- suddenness . . . . SUNS

suede . . . . SWED

suffer
- suffer . . . . SUFR
- suffers . . . . SUFRS
- suffering . . . . SUFRG
- suffered . . . . SUFRD

sufferable . . . . SUFRBL
sufferance . . . . SUFRNS

suffice
- suffice . . . . FAOIS
- suffices . . . . FAOIFS, FAOISZ

sufficing . . . . FAOIFG
sufficed. . . . . FAOIFD
sufficiency . . . . SUFS
sufficient
   sufficient . . . . SUF
   sufficiently . . . . SUFL
   sufficient proof . . . . SAOF
suffix . . . . SFIX
suffocate
   suffocate . . . . SUFT
   suffocates. . . . . SUFTS
   suffocating . . . . SUFGT
   suffocated . . . . SUFTD
suffocation. . . . . SUFGS
suffrage . . . . SFRAJ
sugar. . . . . SHUG
suggest
   suggest . . . . SUG
   suggests . . . . SUGZ
   suggesting . . . . SUG/-G
   suggested . . . . SUGD
suggestion . . . . SUGS
suicidal. . . . . SWAOIL
suicide. . . . . SWAOID
sui generis. . . . . SWAOEG
sui juris . . . . SWAOEJ
suit
   suitability . . . . SAOUBLT
   suitable . . . . SAOUB
   suitably . . . . SAOUBL
   suitcase. . . . . SAOK
   suite . . . . SWAET
   suitor. . . . . SAOURT
sulfate . . . . SUFLT
sulfide . . . . SUFLD
sulfur. . . . . SUFRL
sulfur dioxide. . . . . SUFRLD
sulk
   sulk . . . . SLUK
   sulks . . . . SLUKS
   sulking . . . . SLUK/-G
   sulked . . . . SLUKD
sullen
   sullen. . . . . SLUN
   sullenly. . . . . SLUNL

sullenness	SLUNZ
sum	SUM
summarily	SMAIRL

summarize
summarize	SMAOIS
summarizes	SMAOIFS, SMAOISZ
summarizing	SMAOIFG, SMAOIG
summarized	SMAOIFD, SMAOID

summary	SMAIR
summary judgment	SMUMT
summation	SMAIGS

summer
summer	SMER
summer camp	SMAFRP
summer school	SAOL
summertime	SMERT
summery	SMRER

summon
summon	SMON
summons	SMONS
summoning	SMONG
summoned	SMOND

sunbathe
sunbathe	SBA*IT
sunbathes	SBA*ITS
sunbathing	SBA*IGT
sunbathed	SBA*ITD

sunbather	SBA*IRT
sundae	SDAE
Sunday	SUND
Sunday school	SDAOL
sunglasses	SGLAFS
sunlight	SUNLT
super	SPR–, SAOURP
superb	SPR–B
superbly	SPR–BL
superficial	SPR–RBL
superficially	SPRAOERBL

superfluous
superfluous	SFLOUS, FLOUS
superfluously	SFLOULS, FLOULS
superfluousness	SFLOUNS

superimpose
superimpose	SPROES
superimposes	SPROEFS, SPROESZ

superimposing . . . . SPROEFG
superimposed . . . . SPROEFD
superintend
    superintend. . . . . SUPD
    superintends . . . . SUPDZ
    superintending . . . . SUPGD
    superintended . . . . SUPD/–D
superintendent . . . . SUPT
superior
    superior . . . . SYOR, SAOR
    superior court . . . . SYORT
    superiority . . . . SYO*RT, SY–RT, SAO*RT
    superiorly . . . . SYORL, SAORL
superlative. . . . . SPR–LT
supermarket . . . . SPR–M
supernatural . . . . SPR–NL
superstition . . . . SPRIGS
superstitious . . . . SPRIRB
superstitiously . . . . SPRIRBL
supervise
    supervise . . . . SPR–F
    supervises . . . . SPR–FS
    supervising . . . . SPR–FG
    supervised. . . . . SPR–FD
supervision . . . . SPR–GS
supervisor . . . . SPR–FR
supervisory . . . . SPROIFR, SPROIR
supplement
    supplement . . . . SPLEMT
    supplemental . . . . SPLENL
    supplementally . . . . SPLAENL, SPLAOENL
supplicate
    supplicate . . . . SPLAET
    supplicates . . . . SPLAETS
    supplicating . . . . SPLAEGT
    supplicated . . . . SPLAETD
supplication . . . . SPLAEGS
supplier . . . . SPLAOIR
supply
    supply . . . . SPLI, SPLAOI
    supplies . . . . SPLIS, SPLAOIZ
    supplying . . . . SPLIG, SPLAOIG
    supplied . . . . SPLID, SPLAOID
supply and demand . . . . SPLAND

BRIEF ENCOUNTERS   S

support
- support .... SPOR
- supports .... SPORS
- supporting .... SPORG
- supported .... SPORD

support
- supportable .... SPORL, SPORBL
- supportably .... SPAOERL
- supporter .... SPROR
- supportive .... SPOV

suppose
- suppose .... SPOES
- supposes .... SPOEFS, SPOESZ
- supposing .... SPOEFG
- supposed .... SPOEFD

supposition .... SPOEGS

suppress
- suppress .... SPRES
- suppresses .... SPREFS, SPRESZ
- suppressing .... SPREFG
- suppressed .... SPREFD

suppress
- suppression .... SPREGS
- suppressive .... SPREF
- suppressor .... SPRER, SPRERS

supra .... SAORP, SPRA
supremacist .... SPREFT
supremacy .... SPREMS
supreme .... SPRAOEM, SPREM
supreme court .... SPREMT, SPEMT

surcharge
- surcharge .... SKHARJ, SAURJ
- surcharges .... SKHARJS, SAURJS
- surcharging ...... SKHARJ/-G, SKHARG, SAURJ/-G, SAURG
- surcharged .... SKHARJD, SAURJD

sure
- sure .... SHAOUR
- surely .... SHURL, SHAOURL
- sureness .... SHAOURNS
- surety .... SHURT, SHAOURT

surf
- surf .... SWUF
- surfs .... SWUFS
- surfing .... SWUFG
- surfed .... SWUFD

surf
    surfboard . . . . SUFB, SWUFB
    surfer . . . . SWUFR
    surf the Web . . . . SWEB
surface
    surface. . . . . SFAS
    surfaces . . . . SFAFS, SFASZ
    surfacing . . . . SFAFG
    surfaced . . . . SFAFD
surgeon . . . . SURN
Surgeon General . . . . SURNG
surgery . . . . SURG
surgical. . . . . SURL
surgically . . . . SURLG
Suriname . . . . SNAM
Surinamese. . . . . SNAO*ES
surmise
    surmise . . . . S-RM
    surmises . . . . S-RMS
    surmising. . . . . S-RMG
    surmised . . . . S-RMD
surmount
    surmount . . . . SMOUN
    surmounts. . . . . SMOUNS
    surmounting . . . . SMOUNG
    surmounted . . . . SMOUND
surmountable . . . . SMOUNL
surname . . . . SNAIM
surpass
    surpass. . . . . SPAF
    surpasses . . . . SPAFS
    surpassing . . . . SPAFG
    surpassed . . . . SPAFD
surplus . . . . SPLUS
surprise
    surprise. . . . . SPRAOIS, SUR
    surprises . . . . SPRAOIFS, SPRAOISZ, SURS
    surprising . . . . SPRAOIFG, SUR/-G
    surprised . . . . SPRAOIFD, SUR/-D
surrebuttal . . . . SURB, SURBL
SURREBUTTAL. . . . . SURB/SURB, SURBL/SURBL
surrender
    surrender . . . . SURD
    surrenders . . . . SURDZ
    surrendering . . . . SURGD

BRIEF ENCOUNTERS S

surrendered	SURD/-D
surrogacy	SGAOE
surrogate	SGAT
surround	
surround	SROUN
surrounds	SROUNS
surrounding	SROUNG
surrounded	SROUND
surroundings	SROUNGS
surveil	
surveil	SWAIL
surveils	SWAILS
surveilling	SWAILG
surveilled	SWAILD
surveillance	SWAINS
surveillant	SWAINT
survey	
survey	SWAE
surveys	SWAES
surveying	SWAEG
surveyed	SWAED
survival	SWAOIVL
survive	
survive	SWAOIV
survives	SWAOIVS
surviving	SWAOIVG
survived	SWAOIVD
survivor	SWAOIVR
susceptibility	STIBLT
susceptible	STIBL
suspect	
suspect	S-PT
suspects	S-PTS
suspecting	S-PGT
suspected	S-PTD
suspend	
suspend	SWEN
suspends	SWENZ
suspending	SWENG
suspended	SWEND
suspense	SPENZ
suspenseful	SPUFL
suspension	SWENGS
suspicion	SPIGS
suspicious	SPIRB

S — BRIEF ENCOUNTERS

suspiciously .... SPIRBL
sustain
    sustain .... STAEN
    sustains .... STAENS
    sustaining .... STAENG
    sustained .... STAEND
suture
    suture .... SAOUFP
    sutures .... SAOUFPS
    suturing .... SAOUFPG
    sutured .... SAOUFPD
svelte
    svelte .... SFELT
    sveltely .... SFAOELT
    svelteness .... SFELS
    svelter .... SFERLT
    sveltest .... SFELTS
swallow
    swallow .... SWAOL
    swallows .... SWAOLS
    swallowing .... SWAOLG
    swallowed .... SWAOLD
swamp
    swamp .... SWAUM, SWAFRP
    swamps .... SWAUMS, SWAFRPS
    swamping .... SWAUMG, SWAFRPG
    swamped .... SWAUMD, SWAFRPD
swap meet .... SWAPT
swastika .... SWA*S, SWAZ
swear
    swear .... SWER
    swears .... SWERS
    swearing .... SWERG
    swore .... SWOER
    sworn .... SWORN
sweater .... SWAERT
sweat pants .... SWANTS
sweat shirt .... SWIRT
Swede .... SWAOED
Sweden .... SWAOE
Swedish .... SWAOERB
sweep
    sweep .... SWAOEP
    sweeps .... SWAOEPS
    sweeping .... SWAOEPG

BRIEF ENCOUNTERS S

swept .... SWEPT
sweepstake .... SWAIK
sweet
   sweetener .... SWAOERN
   sweeter .... SWRAOET
   sweeter than .... SWRAOEN, SWAOERNT
   sweeter than the .... SWRAOENT, SWAOERNTD
   sweeter than these .... SWRAOENZ, SWAOERNZ
   sweeter than those .... SWRAOENTS
   sweetheart .... SWHART
sweeten
   sweeten .... SWAOEN
   sweetens .... SWAOENS
   sweetening .... SWAOENG
   sweetened .... SWAOEND
swell
   swell .... SWEL
   swells .... SWELZ
   swelling .... SWELG
   swelled .... SWELD
   swelled / swollen .... SWELD / SWOEN, SWOENL
swelter
   swelter .... SWELT
   swelters .... SWELTS
   sweltering .... SWELGT
   sweltered .... SWELTD
swerve
   swerve .... SWEFRB, SW-V
   swerves .... SWEFRBS, SW-VS
   swerving .... SWEFRBG, SW-VG
   swerved .... SWEFRBD, SW-VD
swiftly .... SWIFLT
swiftness .... SWIFNS
swim
   swim .... SWIM
   swims .... SWIMS
   swimming .... SWIMG
   swam .... SWAM
   swum .... SWUM
swimming pool .... SMAOL, SWAO*L
swindle
   swindle .... SWINL
   swindles .... SWINLS
   swindling .... SWINLG
   swindled .... SWINLD

swindler	SWIRNL

swing
swing	SWING
swings	SWINGS
swinging	SWING/-G
swung	SWUNG
switchboard	SBAORD

switch off
switch off	SWAUF
switches off	SWAUFS
switching off	SWAUFG
switched off	SWAUFD

switch on
switch on	SWON
switches on	SWONZ
switching on	SWONG
switched on	SWOND

Switzerland	SWITS
swollen	SWOEL, SWOEN, SWOENL
syllable	SIBL
syllabus	SBUS
symbiosis	SBOES

symbol
symbol	SBOL
symbolic	SBLIK
symbolically	SBLOIK

symmetric
symmetric	SMEK
symmetrical	SMET
symmetrically	SMAET

symmetry	SMAOET
sympathetic	STHIK

sympathize
sympathize	STHAOIS, STHAOIZ
sympathizes	STHAOIFS, STHAOISZ
sympathizing	STHAOIFG, STHAOIG
sympathized	STHAOIFD

sympathizer	STHAOIR
sympathy	STHI
symphony	SNAOE
symposium	SPUM
symptom	STOM
symptomatic	STOMT
synagogue	SGOG
synchronization	SKROIFGS

BRIEF ENCOUNTERS   S

synchronize
    synchronize . . . . SKROIF
    synchronizes . . . . SKROIFS
    synchronizing. . . . . SKROIFG
    synchronized . . . . SKROIFD
synchronizer. . . . . SKROIFR
syndicate
    syndicate . . . . SKAET
    syndicates . . . . SKAETS
    syndicating. . . . . SKAEGT
    syndicated . . . . SKAETD
syndication . . . . SKAEGS, SKAIGS
syndicator. . . . . SKAERT
syndrome. . . . . SDROEM
synergism . . . . SNERM
synergy. . . . . SNERJ
synonym. . . . . SNIM
synopsis. . . . . SNOPS
syntheses . . . . STHESZ
synthesis . . . . STHES
synthetic . . . . STHEK
syphilis. . . . . SIFLS
syringe . . . . SRING
syrup. . . . . SIRP
system
    system . . . . S-M
    systematic . . . . S-MT
    systematically . . . . S-M/KLI

T

tablespoon	TAIBLZ
tablespoons	TAIBLSZ
tablet	TABLT
tabloid	BLOID, TBLOID
taboo	TBAO
tabular	TBLAR
tabulation	TABLGS

tackle
tackle	TAKL
tackles	TAKLZ
tackling	TALG, TAKL/-G
tackled	TAKLD

tact
tactful	TAFL
tactfully	TAEFL
tactic	TWAK
tactical	TAKLT
tactical alert	TLERT
tactile	TWOIL, TWAO*IL

tagger	TARG
taggers	TARGZ

tail
tail	TAIL
tailbone	TWOEN
taillight	TAILT

tailgate
tailgate	TAILGT
tailgates	TAILGTS
tailgating	TAILGT/-G
tailgated	TAILGTD, TAILTD

tailor
tailor	TAIRL, TLOR
tailors	TAIRLS, TLORS
tailoring	TAIRLG, TLORG
tailored	TAIRLD, TLORD

Taiwan
Taiwan	TWAUN
Taiwanese	TWAUNZ
Taiwan's	TWAUNS

take
take	TAIK
takes	TAIKS

```
taking .................................... TAIK/-G, TAIG
took ............................................. TAOK
taken ............................................ TAEN
take
    take-off ....................................... TAUF
    takeover ...................................... TOEVR
    taker ......................................... TAIRK
take into consideration
    take into consideration ...................... TAIRGS
    takes into consideration .................... TAIRGSZ
    taking into consideration ..................... TAIRG
    took into consideration ..................... TAORGS
    taken into consideration ........... TAERGS, TAERNGS
take over
    take over ...................................... TOVR
    takes over .................................... TOVRS
    taking over ................................... TOVRG
    took over .................................... TAOVR
    taken over .................................. TAEVRN
take place
    take place ..................................... TAEP
    takes place ................................... TAEPS
    taking place .................................. TAEPG
    took place ................................... TAOPS
    taken place ............................. TAEN/PLAIS
take the stand
    take the stand ................................ TAND
    takes the stand .............................. TANDZ
    taking the stand ............................. TANGD
    took the stand .............................. TAOND
    taken the stand ........................... TA*END
talent ................................... TAELT, TLENT
talented ............................... TAELTD, TLENTD
talk
    talk .......................................... TAUK
    talks ........................................ TAUKS
    talking ............................... TAUK/-G, TAUG
    talked ....................................... TAUKD
talk
    talk about .................................... TAUB
    talk about the .............................. TAUBT
    talk about these ............................ TAUBZ
    talk about those ............................ TAUBS
    talkative ..................................... TAUV
    talkatively .................................. TAUVL
```

T BRIEF ENCOUNTERS

talkativeness . . . . TAUVNS
talker. . . . . TAURK
tall
   taller . . . . TAURL
   taller than. . . . . TAURN
   taller than the . . . . TAURNT
   taller than these . . . . TAURNZ
   taller than those . . . . TAURNS
   tallest. . . . . TAULS
talon . . . . TLAON
tamper
   tamper . . . . TAFRP
   tampers . . . . TAFRPS
   tampering. . . . . TAFRPG
   tampered . . . . TAFRPD
tangibility . . . . TANLT
tangible . . . . TANL
tangibly . . . . TAOENL
tantrum . . . . TRUM
taper
   taper. . . . . TAIRP
   tapers . . . . TAIRPS
   tapering. . . . . TAIRPG
   tapered . . . . TAIRPD
tape recorder . . . . TROERD
tape recording . . . . TRORG, TRORGD, TROERG
target
   target. . . . . TARGT
   targets. . . . . TARGTS
   targeting. . . . . TARGT/-G, TAERGT
   targeted. . . . . TARGTD
tariff . . . . TAIF
tarmac. . . . . TARM
tarnation . . . . TARNGS
tarnish
   tarnish. . . . . TARN
   tarnishes . . . . TARNS
   tarnishing. . . . . TARNG
   tarnished . . . . TARND
tarnishable . . . . TARNL
taser . . . . TAIRZ
task . . . . TAF, TAFK
tatter
   tatter. . . . . TRAT
   tatters . . . . TRATS

BRIEF ENCOUNTERS   T

tattering	TRAGT
tattered	TRATD
tattoo	
tattoo	TWAOT
tattoos	TWAOTS
tattooing	TWAOGT
tattooed	TWAOTD
Taurus	TAURZ
tavern	TAVRN, TAFRN
tawny	TAUN
taxi	
taxi	TAEX
taxis	TAEXZ
taxiing	TAEX/-G
taxied	TAEX/-D, TAEKD
taxpayer	TAIR
tax return	TRURN
TDD	TAOED
teach	
teach	TAOEFP
teaches	TAOEFPS
teaching	TAOEFPG
taught	TAUT
teacher	TRAOEFP
teamwork	TWERK
tear	
tear	TAER
tears	TAERS
tearing	TAERG
tore	TOER
torn	TORN
teaspoon	TAEPZ
teaspoons	TAEPSZ
tech	
tech	T*EK
technical	TEK
technicality	TEKT
technique	TAOEK, NAOEK
technological	TOJ
technologically	TAOEJ
technologist	TOKT
technology	T-J
teenage	TAEJ
teenager	TAERJ

telecommunication
    telecommunication . . . . TELGS
    telecommunications device . . . . TELD
    Telecommunications Device for the Deaf . . . . TAOEDZ
teleconference. . . . . T-FRNS
teleconferencing . . . . T-FRNG
telegram . . . . TEG
telepathic . . . . TLAPG
telepathy. . . . . TLAP
telephone
    telephone . . . . TEFL
    telephones. . . . . TEFLS
    telephoning . . . . TEFLG
    telephoned. . . . . TEFLD
telephone conversation . . . . TEFK, T-FRGS
telephonic . . . . FONG
TelePrompTer . . . . TLOMT
telescope . . . . TLOEP
teletypewriter . . . . TWOI, TWAOI/TWAOI
televise
    televise . . . . TWAOIZ
    televises. . . . . TWAOIFS, TWAOISZ
    televising . . . . TWAOIFG
    televised. . . . . TWAOIFD
television
    television . . . . TWIGS
    television set . . . . TWET
    television station . . . . TWAIGS
tell
    tell . . . . TEL
    tells . . . . TELS
    telling. . . . . TELG
    told . . . . TOLD
teller . . . . TLER
temp
    temp. . . . . TEFRP, T*EM
    temper . . . . TEP
    temperament. . . . . TEM/PRAMT
    temperamental. . . . . TEM/MENL
    temperature . . . . TEM
    temporarily . . . . TRAERL
    temporary. . . . . TRAER
    temporary injunction . . . . TRUNGS
    temporary restraining order. . . . . TRO
    temptation . . . . TEMGS

tempt
    tempt . . . . TEMT
    tempts . . . . TEMTS
    tempting . . . . TEMGT
    tempted . . . . TEMTD
tenacious
    tenacious . . . . TAERB
    tenaciously . . . . TAERBL
    tenaciousness . . . . TAERBS
tenant . . . . TANT
tender
    tender . . . . TERND
    tenders . . . . TERNDZ
    tendering . . . . TERNGD
    tendered . . . . TERND/-D
tendon . . . . TOIN
Tennessee . . . . T*N
tennis . . . . SNIS
tennis ball . . . . TEBL
tentative
    tentative . . . . TAEV
    tentatively . . . . TAEVL
    tentative ruling . . . . TRAOULG
tenure . . . . TAOR
tenured . . . . TAORD
tepid . . . . TEPD
tequila . . . . TWAOEL
terminal . . . . TAERL
terminate
    terminate . . . . TERMT
    terminates . . . . TERMTS
    terminating . . . . TERMGT
    terminated . . . . TERMTD
termination . . . . TERGS, TERMGS
terminator . . . . TRERMT
terminology . . . . TERLG
terrace . . . . TRAS
terrain . . . . TRAEN
terrible . . . . TERBL
terribly . . . . TAOERBL
terrific . . . . TRIF
terrifically . . . . TRIFL
terrify
    terrify . . . . TER
    terrifies . . . . TERZ

T   BRIEF ENCOUNTERS

    terrifying . . . . TERG
    terrified . . . . TERD
territorial . . . . TRORL, TRAOEL
territory . . . . TERT
terror
    terror . . . . TROR
    terrorism . . . . TRIFM
    terrorist . . . . TRIFT
terrorize
    terrorize . . . . TRAOIZ
    terrorizes . . . . TRAOIFS
    terrorizing . . . . TRAOIFG
    terrorized . . . . TRAOIFD
testate . . . . TAET, TWEFT
testator . . . . TAERT, TWEFRT
testatrix . . . . TRIKZ
testify
    testify . . . . TEF
    testifies . . . . TEFS
    testifying . . . . TEFG
    testified . . . . TEFD
testimony . . . . T–M
tether
    tether . . . . T*ERT
    tethers . . . . T*ERTS
    tethering . . . . T*ERGT
    tethered . . . . T*ERTD
Texas . . . . T*X
text . . . . TEX
Thai . . . . THAO*I
Thailand . . . . THAOIL, THAOILD
than
    than . . . . THAN
    than the . . . . THANT
    than these . . . . THANZ
    than those . . . . THANS
thank
    thank . . . . THANG
    thanks . . . . THANGS
    thanking . . . . THANG/-G
    thanked . . . . THANGD
thank
    thankful . . . . THAFL
    Thanksgiving . . . . THAFG
    thank you . . . . THAUNG

BRIEF ENCOUNTERS T

thank you, sir	THAUNGS
thank you very much	THAUFP
thank you, your Honor	THAURN

that
that	THA
that afternoon	THAFRN
that are	THAR
that aren't	THARNT, THAR/-NT, THA/R-NT
that be	THAB
that believe	THABL
that believed	THABLD
that believes	THABLS
that believing	THABLG
that can	THAK
that can't	THAKT, THAK/-NT, THA/K-NT
that could	THAKD
that couldn't	THAKTD, THAKD/-NT, THA/KUNT
that evening	THAENG
that ever	THAFR, THAVR
that feel	THA*FL
that feeling	THAFLG
that feels	THAFLS
that felt	THAFLT
that get	THAGT
that gets	THAGTS
that go	THAG
that goes	THAGS
that had	THAD
that hadn't	THAD/-NT, THA/H-NT
that happen	THAP
that happened	THAPD
that happening	THAPG
that happens	THAPS
that have	THAF
that have been	THAFB
that have had	THAFD
that have known	THAFN
that haven't	THAFT, THAF/-NT, THA/V-NT
that is	THAS
that is all	THAUL
that is correct	THARK
that isn't	THAS/-NT, THA/S-NT
that is right	THART
that is to say	THAISZ
that live	THAV

that lived	THAVD
that lives	THAVS
that living	THAVG
that'll	THA*L
that means	THAMS
that means to	THAMT
that means to say	THAMTS
that morning	THAM, THAORNG
that much	THAFP
that recall	THARL
that recalled	THARLD
that recalling	THARLG
that recalls	THARLS
that recollect	THA*RK
that recollected	THARKD
that recollects	THARKS
that remember	THARM
that remembered	THARMD
that remembers	THARMS
that's	THA*S
that says	THASZ
that's correct	THAERK
that shall	THARB
that should	THARBD
that shouldn't	THARBTD, THARBD/-NT, THA/SH-NT
that's right	THA*RT, THAERT
that the	THAT
that understand	THANDZ
that understood	THAND
that want	THAPT
that wanted	THAPTD
that wanting	THAPGT
that wants	THAPTS
that was	THAFS
that wasn't	THAFS/-NT, THA/WUNT
that were	THARP
that weren't	THARPT, THARP/-NT, THA/W-RNT
that will	THAL
that would	THALD
that wouldn't	THALTD, THALD/-NT, THA/WONT
that would say	THALDZ

that he

that he	THAE
that he believe	THAEBL
that he believed	THAEBLD

BRIEF ENCOUNTERS
T

that he believes	THAEBLS
that he can	THAEK
that he can't	THAEKT, THAEK/-NT, THAE/K-NT
that he could	THAEKD
that he couldn't	THAEKTD, THAEKD/-NT, THAE/KUNT
that he ever	THAEFR, THAEVR
that he feel	THAEFL
that he feels	THAEFLS
that he felt	THAEFLT
that he gets	THAEGTS
that he go	THAEG
that he goes	THAEGS
that he got	THAEGT
that he had	THAED
that he hadn't	THAED/-NT, THAE/H-NT
that he happen	THAEP
that he happened	THAEPD
that he happens	THAEPS
that he imagined	THAEJD
that he imagines	THAEJS
that he is	THAES
that he isn't	THAES/-NT, THAE/S-NT
that he know	THAEN
that he knows	THAENS
that he live	THAEV
that he lived	THAEVD
that he lives	THAEVS
that he mean	THAEM
that he means	THAEMS
that he means to	THAEMT
that he means to say	THAEMTS
that he recall	THAERL
that he recalled	THAERLD
that he recalls	THAERLS
that he recollect	THA*ERK
that he recollected	THAERKD
that he recollects	THAERKS
that he remember	THAERM
that he remembered	THAERMD
that he remembers	THAERMS
that he says	THAESZ
that he sees	THAEZ
that he shall	THAERB
that he should	THAERBD
that he shouldn't	THAERBTD, THAERBD/-NT, THAE/SH-NT

that he thinks	THAENGS
that he thinks so	THAENGSZ
that he understands	THAENDZ
that he understood	THAEND
that he want	THAEPT
that he wanted	THAEPTD
that he wants	THAEPTS
that he was	THAEFS
that he wasn't	THAEFT, THAEFS/-NT, THAE/WUNT
that he were	THA*ERP
that he weren't	THA*ERPT, THAERP/-NT, THAE/W-RNT
that he will	THAEL
that he would	THAELD
that he wouldn't	THAELTD, THAELD/-NT, THAE/WONT
that he would say	THAELDZ

that I

that I	THAI
that I am	THAIM
that I believe	THAIBL
that I believed	THAIBLD
that I can	THAIK
that I can't	THAIKT, THAIK/-NT, THAI/K-NT
that I could	THAIKD
that I couldn't	THAIKTD, THAIKD/-NT, THAI/KUNT
that I ever	THAIFR, THAIVR
that I feel	THAIFL
that I felt	THAIFLT
that I get	THAIGT
that I go	THAIG
that I had	THAID
that I hadn't	THAID/-NT, THAI/H-NT
that I happen	THAIP
that I happened	THAIPD
that I have	THAIF
that I have been	THAIFB
that I have had	THAIFD
that I have known	THAIFN
that I haven't	THAIFT, THAIF/-NT, THAI/V-NT
that I imagine	THAIJ
that I imagined	THAIJD
that I know	THAIN
that I live	THAIV
that I lived	THAIVD
that I mean	THA*IM
that I mean to	THAIMT

that I mean to say	THAIMTS
that I recall	THAIRL
that I recalled	THAIRLD
that I recollect	THAIRK
that I recollected	THAIRKD
that I remember	THAIRM
that I remembered	THAIRMD
that I say	THAIS
that I see	THAIZ
that I shall	THAIRB
that I should	THAIRBD
that I shouldn't	THAIRBTD, THAIRBD/-NT, THAI/SH-NT
that I think	THAING
that I think so	THAINGS
that I understand	THAINDZ
that I understood	THAIND
that I want	THAIPT
that I wanted	THAIPTD
that I was	THAIFS
that I wasn't	THAIFS/-NT, THAI/WUNT
that I were	THA*IRP
that I weren't	THAIRP/-NT, THAI/W-RNT
that I will	THAIL
that I would	THAILD
that I wouldn't	THAILTD, THAILD/-NT, THAI/WONT
that I would say	THAILDZ

that you

that you	THAU
that you are	THAUR
that you aren't	THAURNT, THAUR/-NT, THAU/R-NT
that you believe	THAUBL
that you believed	THAUBLD
that you can	THAUK
that you can't	THAUKT, THAUK/-NT, THAU/K-NT
that you could	THAUKD
that you couldn't	THAUKTD, THAUKD/-NT, THAU/KUNT
that you ever	THAUFR, THAUVR
that you feel	THAUFL
that you felt	THAUFLT
that you get	THAUGT
that you go	THAUG
that you had	THAUD
that you hadn't	THAUD/-NT, THAU/H-NT
that you happen	THAUP
that you happened	THAUPD

T

BRIEF ENCOUNTERS

that you have	THAUF
that you have been	THAUFB
that you have had	THAUFD
that you have known	THAUFN
that you haven't	THAUFT, THAUF/-NT, THAU/V-NT
that you imagine	THAUJ
that you imagined	THAUJD
that you know	THAUN
that you live	THAUV
that you lived	THAUVD
that you mean	THAUM
that you mean to	THAUMT
that you mean to say	THAUMTS
that you recall	THAURL
that you recalled	THAURLD
that you recollect	THAURK
that you recollected	THAURKD
that you remember	THAURM
that you remembered	THAURMD
that you say	THAUS
that you see	THAUZ
that you shall	THAURB
that you should	THAURBD
that you shouldn't	THAURBTD, THAURBD/-NT, THAU/SH-NT
that you think	THA*UNG
that you think so	THA*UNGS
that you understand	THAUNDZ
that you understood	THAUND
that you want	THAUPT
that you wanted	THAUPTD
that you were	THAURP
that you weren't	THAURPT, THAURP/-NT, THAU/W-RNT
that you will	THA*UL
that you would	THAULD
that you wouldn't	THAULTD, THAULD/-NT, THAU/WONT
that you would say	THAULDZ

the

the	T-
the fact of the matter	FAFMT
the fact of the matter is	FAFMTS
the first time	T-FRT
the last time	T-LT
The Netherlands	N*ELT
the only	TONL

BRIEF ENCOUNTERS   T

the only time	TONLT
the president	T-PT
the question and answer were read	KWARD
the question was read	KWERD
the reason	TR-N, T-RN
the reasoning	TR-NG, T-RNG
the record	TRORD
the right	T-RT
the rights	T-RTS
the truth, the whole truth and nothing but the truth	TR*UT/TR*UT
the very first time	T-VRT
the whole time	TW-T
the witness may answer	TWAM
the witness will answer the question	NERB/NERB
theater	THAOERT
theatrical	THAOERK
theatrically	THAOERKL
theatrics	THAOERKS
their	THAIR
them	THEM
themselves	THOIM, THOIMS, THEMS
then	
then	THEN
then the	THENT
then these	THENZ
theologian	THOEJ, THOELGS
theology	THAOELG
theorem	THAOERM
theoretical	THAOERLT
theoretically	THAOERL
theoretician	THAOERGS
theory	THAOER
therapeutic	
therapeutic	THAOUP, THAOUPT
therapeutical	THAOUL, THAOUK
therapeutically	THAOEL, THAOUKL
therapist	THAERPT, THAIRPT
therapy	THAERP, THAIRP
there	
there	THR-
thereabout	THR-BT
thereafter	THRAF
thereafter the	THRAFT
there are	THR-R
there aren't	THR-RNT, THR-R/-NT, THR-/R-NT

thereat	THRAT
there be	THR-B
thereby	THR*B
there can	THR-K
there can't	THR-KT, THR-K/-NT, THR-/K-NT
there could	THR-KD
there couldn't	THR-KTD, THR-KD/-NT, THR-/KUNT
there ever	THREVR, THR-VR
therefor	THREFR
therefore	THR-FR
therefore the	THR-FRT
therefrom	THR-FM
there go	THR-G
there goes	THR-GS
there had	THR-D
there hadn't	THR-D/-NT, THR-/H-NT
there happen	THR-P
there happened	THR-PD
there happens	THR-PS
there have	THR-F
there have been	THR-FB
there have had	THR-FD
there haven't	THR-FT, THR-F/-NT, THR-/V-NT
there he goes	THREGS
there I go	THRIG
therein	THRIN
there is	THR-S
there isn't	THR-S/-NT, THR-/S-NT
there lived	THR-VD
there lives	THR-VS
there'll	THR*L
thereof	THROF
thereon	THRON
there's	THR*S
there shall	THR-RB
there should	THR-RBD
there shouldn't	THR-RBTD, THR-RBD/-NT, THR-/SH-NT
thereto	THR-T
thereupon	THRUP
there've	THR-V
there want	THR-PT
there wanted	THR-PTD
there wants	THR-PTS
there was	THR-FS
there wasn't	THR-FS/-NT, THR-/WUNT

BRIEF ENCOUNTERS   T

there were	THR-RP
there weren't	THR-RPT, THR-RP/-NT, THR-/W-RNT
there will	THR-L
therewith	TW*IT
there would	THR-LD
there wouldn't	THR-LTD, THR-LD/-NT, THR-/WONT
there you are	THRUR
there you go	THRUG
thermal	TH*ERM
thermometer	THERMT
these	THEZ
theses	THAOESZ
thesis	THAOEZ
they	
they	THE
they are	THER
they aren't	THERNT, THER/-NT, THE/R-NT
they be	THEB
they believe	THEBL
they believed	THEBLD
they believing	THEBLG
they can	THEK
they can't	THEKT, THEK/-NT, THE/K-NT
they could	THEKD
they couldn't	THEKTD, THEKD/-NT, THE/KUNT
they'd	TH*ED
they ever	THEFR, THEVR
they feel	THEFL
they feeling	THEFLG
they felt	THEFLT
they get	THEGT
they go	THEG
they had	THED
they hadn't	THED/-NT, THE/H-NT
they happen	THEP
they happened	THEPD
they have	THEF
they have been	THEFB
they have believed	THEFBLD
they have had	THEFD
they have known	THEFN
they haven't	THEF/-NT, THE/V-NT
they'll	TH*EL
they mean to	THEMT
they mean to say	THEMTS

they're	TH*ER
they recall	THERL
they recalled	THERLD
they recalling	THERLG
they recollect	THERK
they recollected	THERKD
they recollecting	THERK/-G
they remember	THERM
they remembered	THERMD
they remembering	THERMG
they shall	THERB
they should	THERBD
they shouldn't	THERBTD, THERBD/-NT, THE/SH-NT
they think	THENG
they think so	THENGS
they understand	THENDZ
they understood	THEND
they've	THEV
they've been	THEVB
they've had	THEVD
they've known	THEVN
they want	THEPT
they wanted	THEPTD
they wanting	THEPGT
they were	THERP
they weren't	THERP/-NT, THE/W-RNT
they will	THEL
they would	THELD
they wouldn't	THELTD, THELD/-NT, THE/WONT
they would say	THELDZ
thimble	THIM

thin

thinly	THINL
thinner	THIRN
thinness	THINS
thing	THING

think

think	THI
thinks	THIS
thinking	THIG
thought	THOT, THAUT
thinkable	THIBL

third

third class	THIRK
third degree	TH-RD

BRIEF ENCOUNTERS   *T*

third-degree burn . . . . TH–BD, THR–BD
third party . . . . THIRP
thirsty . . . . THIRS, THAO*ERS
thirty
    thirty . . . . THRI
    thirty of them . . . . THRIFM
    thirty of these . . . . THRIFZ
    thirty of those . . . . THRIFS
this
    this . . . . TH–
    this afternoon . . . . TH–FRN
    this are . . . . TH–R
    this aren't . . . . TH–RNT, TH–R/-NT, TH–/R–NT
    this be . . . . TH–B
    this can . . . . TH–K
    this can't . . . . TH–KT, TH–K/-NT, TH–/K–NT
    this could . . . . TH–KD
    this couldn't . . . . TH–KTD, TH–KD/-NT, TH–/KUNT
    this evening . . . . THAOENG
    this ever . . . . TH–FR, TH–VR
    this feel . . . . TH–FL
    this feeling . . . . TH–FLG
    this feels . . . . TH–FLS
    this felt . . . . TH–FLT
    this get . . . . TH–GT
    this gets . . . . TH–GTS
    this go . . . . TH–G
    this goes . . . . TH–GS
    this had . . . . TH–D
    this hadn't . . . . TH–D/-NT, TH–/H–NT
    this happen . . . . TH–P
    this happened . . . . TH–PD
    this happening . . . . TH–PG
    this happens . . . . TH–PS
    this have . . . . TH–F
    this have been . . . . TH–FB
    this have had . . . . TH–FD
    this is . . . . TH–S
    this isn't . . . . TH–S/-NT, TH–/S–NT
    this mean . . . . TH–M
    this means . . . . TH–MS
    this means to . . . . TH–MT
    this means to say . . . . TH–MTS
    this morning . . . . THORNG
    this much . . . . TH–FP

this recall	TH-RL
this recalled	TH-RLD
this recalling	TH-RLG
this recalls	TH-RLS
this say	TH*S
this says	TH-SZ
this shall	TH-RB
this should	TH-RBD
this shouldn't	TH-RBTD, TH-RBD/-NT, TH-/SH-NT
this the	TH-T
this want	TH-PT
this wanted	TH-PTD
this wanting	TH-PGT
this wants	TH-PTS
this was	TH-FS
this wasn't	TH-FT, TH-FS/-NT, TH-/WUNT
this were	TH-RP
this weren't	TH-RPT, TH-RP/-NT, TH-/W-RNT
this will	TH-L
this would	TH-LD
this wouldn't	TH-LTD, TH-LD/-NT, TH-/WONT
this would say	TH-LDZ
Thomas	THOMS
thorax	THORX, THOERX

thorough
    thorough . . . . THOR
    thoroughbred . . . . THORB, THORBD
    thoroughfare . . . . THOFR
    thoroughly . . . . THORL
though . . . . THO
thought
    thought . . . . THAUT
    thoughtful . . . . THAULT, THOFL
    thoughtfully . . . . THAOEFL
    thoughtless . . . . THAULS
    thoughtlessness . . . . THAUNS
thousand
    thousand . . . . THOU
    thousand dollar . . . . THOUD
    thousand of the . . . . THOUFT
    thousand of them . . . . THOUFM
    thousand of these . . . . THOUFZ
    thousand of those . . . . THOUFS
    thousands . . . . THOUS
    thousandth . . . . THO*UT

BRIEF ENCOUNTERS   T

threaten
- threaten . . . . THREN
- threatens . . . . THRENS
- threatening . . . . THRENG
- threatened . . . . THREND

three
- threefold . . . . THREFLD
- *three of the* . . . . THREFT
- *three of them* . . . . THREFM
- *three of these* . . . . THREFZ
- *three of those* . . . . THREFS
- three-piece . . . . THREP
- threesome . . . . THREM
- three-time . . . . THRAOIM
- *three times* . . . . THRAOIMS

threshold . . . . THRERB, THOLD
thriftiness . . . . THRIFNS
thrifty . . . . THROIFT
thriller . . . . THRIRL

thrive
- thrive . . . . THRAOIV
- thrives . . . . THRAOIVS
- thriving . . . . THRAOIVG
- thrived / throve . . . . THRAOIVD / THROEV
- thrived / thriven . . . . THRAOIVD / THRIVN

throttle
- throttle . . . . THROT
- throttles . . . . THROTS
- throttling . . . . THROGT
- throttled . . . . THROTD

through
- through . . . . THRU
- throughout . . . . THROUT
- *throughout the* . . . . THROUTD
- *through the* . . . . THRUT
- *through them* . . . . THRUM
- *through these* . . . . THRUZ
- *through those* . . . . THRUS

throw
- throw . . . . THROE
- throws . . . . THROES
- throwing . . . . THROEG
- threw . . . . THRAOU
- thrown . . . . THROUN

© 1997 White-Boucke Publishing.   ILLEGAL TO PHOTOCOPY

throw up
   throw up . . . . THROUP
   throws up . . . . THROUPS
   throwing up . . . . THROUPG
   threw up . . . . THRAOUP
   thrown up . . . . THROUN/UP
thrust
   thrust . . . . THRUFT
   thrusts . . . . THRUFTS, THRUFS
   thrusting . . . . THRUFGT, THRUFG
   thrust . . . . THRUFT
thruster . . . . THRUFRT
thump
   thump . . . . THUP
   thumps . . . . THUPS
   thumping . . . . THUPG
   thumped . . . . THUPD
thumper . . . . THURP
thunder
   thunder . . . . THURND, THUND
   thunders . . . . THURNDZ, THUNDZ
   thundering . . . . THURNGD, THUNGD
   thundered . . . . THURND/-D, THUND/-D
thunderstorm . . . . THORM
Thursday . . . . THURS, THURZ
thwart
   thwart . . . . TWART, THAURT
   thwarts . . . . TWARTS, THAURTS
   thwarting . . . . TWART/-G, TWARG, THAURGT
   thwarted . . . . TWART/-D, THAURTD
thy . . . . THOI
thyme . . . . TAO*IM, THAO*IM
thyroid . . . . THAOIRD, THROID
thyroid gland . . . . THAOIRG, THAOIRGD
tibia . . . . TIB
tibial . . . . TIBL
ticker . . . . TIRK
ticket . . . . TIKT
tickle
   tickle . . . . TIKL
   tickles . . . . TIKLS
   tickling . . . . TIKL/-G
   tickled . . . . TIKLD
tickler . . . . TIRKL
ticklish . . . . TLIRB

BRIEF ENCOUNTERS   T

tidal	TALD, TAO*ILD
tidal wave	TAIV
tidy	TOID
tiger	TIRG
tighten	
tighten	TAOINT
tightens	TAOINTS
tightening	TAOINGT, TAOING
tightened	TAOINTD
tight	
tightener	TAOIRNT, TAOIRN
tight-lipped	TLIPD
tightwad	TWAD
Tijuana	TWAN
timber	TBER
time	
time	TAOIM
times	TAOIMS
timing	TAOIMG
timed	TAOIMD
timer	TAOIRM
timers	TAOIRMZ
timid	TIMD
tinker	
tinker	TIRNG
tinkers	TIRNGS
tinkering	TIRNG/-G
tinkered	TIRNGD
tire	
tireless	TAOIRL
tirelessly	TAOIRLZ
tirelessness	TAOIRLS
tiresome	TAOIRMS
tissue	TIRB
title	
title	TAOILT
titles	TAOILTS
titling	TAOILGT
titled	TAOILTD
to	
to	TO
to a certain extent	TAERX
to a great extent	TRAEX
to be	TOB
to believe	TOBL

to believe so	TOBLS
to do	TOD
to do so	TODZ
to feel	TOFL
to get	TOGT
to go	TOG
to have	TOF
to have been	TOFB
to have believed	TOFBLD
to have gone	TOFG
to have had	TOFD
to have known	TOFN
to have recalled	TOFRLD
to have recollected	TOFRKD
to have remembered	TOFRMD
to have wanted	TOFPTD
to live	TOV
to recall	TORL
to recollect	TO*RK
to remember	TORM
to say	TOS
to see	TOZ
to the	TOT
to think	TONG
to think so	TONGS
to understand	TONDZ
to want	TOPT
to your attention	TOURNGS
to your knowledge	TOURJ
tobacco	TBAK
today	TAI
toddler	TAUD
together	TOEG
toilet	TOILT
token	TOENG, TOENK
tolerability	TLABLT
tolerable	TLABL
tolerance	TLANS
tolerant	TLANT
tolerantly	TLANLT, TLANL
tolerate	
tolerate	TLAIT
tolerates	TLAITS
tolerating	TLAIGT, TLAIG
tolerated	TLAITD

BRIEF ENCOUNTERS   T

toleration .... TLAIGS
tomato .... TOEMT
tomatoes .... TOEMTS
tomorrow
    tomorrow .... TW–
    tomorrow afternoon .... TWAFRN
    tomorrow evening .... TWAOENG
    tomorrow morning .... TWORNG
    tomorrow night .... TWAOIT
tonal .... TOENL
tonality .... TOENLT
tonight .... TONT
tonsil .... TAUNL
too
    too bad .... TAOBD
    too big .... TAOB, TAOG
    too deep .... TAOP
    too far .... TAOFR
    too fast .... TAOFT
    too few .... TAOF
    too good .... TAOGD
    too great .... TAOGT
    too important .... TAORNT
    too large .... TAORJ
    too late .... TAOLT
    too long .... TAONG
    too many .... TAOM
    too many days .... TAOMD
    too many times .... TAOMT
    too much .... TAOFP
    too often .... TAOFN
    too old .... TAOLD
    too soon .... TAON
    too wide .... TAOD
took place .... TAOPS
toothbrush .... TBRURB
topic .... TAUP
topical .... TAUPL
top of the .... TOFPT
top of these .... TOFPZ
topper .... TORP
torch
    torch .... TOFP
    torches .... TOFPS
    torching .... TOFPG

torched . . . . TOFPD
torment
    torment . . . . TORMT
    torments . . . . TORMTS
    tormenting . . . . TORMGT, TORMG
    tormented . . . . TORMTD
tormentor. . . . . TRORMT
tornado . . . . TORND
torpedo
    torpedo . . . . TWORP
    torpedoes . . . . TWORPS
    torpedoing. . . . . TWORPG
    torpedoed . . . . TWORPD
torrent . . . . TORNT
torrential. . . . . TRENL
torrid . . . . TORD
torture
    torture. . . . . TAOUR
    tortures . . . . TAOURS
    torturing . . . . TAOURG
    tortured. . . . . TAOURD
total
    total. . . . . TOLT
    totalitarian . . . . TORLT
    totality. . . . . TALT
    totally. . . . . TOELT
to the best of
    to the best of my knowledge . . . . TAOIJ
    to the best of my recollection . . . . TAOIX
    to the best of your knowledge. . . . . TURJ
    to the best of your recollection . . . . TURX
toughen
    toughen . . . . TUFN
    toughens . . . . TUFNZ
    toughening. . . . . TUFNG
    toughened . . . . TUFND
toughly. . . . . TUFL
toughness. . . . . TUFNS
tourism . . . . TOURM
tourist . . . . TOURT
tournament . . . . TOURMT
tourniquet . . . . TOURNT, TOURK
toward
    toward . . . . TWARD
    toward the. . . . . TWARTD

BRIEF ENCOUNTERS   T

    toward them . . . . TWARM
    toward these . . . . TWARZ
    toward those . . . . TWARS
town hall . . . . TOUNL
township . . . . TWIP
toxic . . . . TOK
toxin . . . . TOX
toxins . . . . TOKZ, TOXZ
Toyota . . . . YOET
trace
    traceability . . . . TRAIBLT, TRAIFBLT
    traceable . . . . TRAIBL, TRAIFBL
    tracer . . . . TRAIFR
trackball . . . . TRABL
tracker . . . . TRARK
traction . . . . TRAX
tractor . . . . TRAOK
trade
    trademark . . . . TRAIRK
    trader . . . . TRAIRD
    trade school . . . . TRAOL
    trade union . . . . TROIN
tradition
    tradition . . . . TRIRB
    traditional . . . . TRIRBL
    traditionally . . . . TROIRBL, TRAOERBL
traffic
    traffic . . . . TRAF
    traffic jam . . . . TRAFM
    traffic light . . . . TR-LT
    traffic warrant . . . . TWARNT
tragedy . . . . TRAJ
tragic . . . . TRIJ
tragically . . . . TRIL, TRAOEJ
trailer
    trailer . . . . TRAIRL
    trailer park . . . . TRAIP, TRAIRP
    trailer parks . . . . TRAIPZ, TRAIRPS
trainer . . . . TRAIRN
train station . . . . TRAINGS
traitor . . . . TRAIRT
traject
    traject . . . . TRAJT
    trajects . . . . TRAJTS
    trajecting . . . . TRAJT/-G, TRAG

T   BRIEF ENCOUNTERS

trajected	TRAJTD
trajection	TRAGS
trajectory	TRARJ, TRARJT
trample	
trample	TRAFRPL
tramples	TRAFRPLS
trampling	TRAFRPLG
trampled	TRAFRPLD
trance	TRAENS
tranquil	TWIL
tranquility	TWILT
tranquilize	
tranquilize	TRAENK
tranquilizes	TRAENKS
tranquilizing	TRAENK/-G
tranquilized	TRAENKD
tranquilizer	TRANK
transact	
transact	TR-K
transacts	TR-KZ
transacting	TR-K/-G
transacted	TR-KD
transaction	TR-X
transatlantic	TRANLT
transcribe	
transcribe	TRIB
transcribes	TRIBS
transcribing	TRIB/-G
transcribed	TRIBD
transcript	TRIPT
transcription	TRIPGS
transfer	
transfer	TR-FR
transfers	TR-FRS
transferring	TR-FRG
transferred	TR-FRD
transferable	TR-FRBL
transference	TR-FRNS
transform	
transform	TR-FM
transforms	TR-FMS
transforming	TR-FMG
transformed	TR-FMD
transformation	TR-FMGS, TR-GS
transformer	TR-FRM

BRIEF ENCOUNTERS   T

transfuse
- transfuse .... TR-FS, TRAOUZ
- transfuses .... TR-FSZ, TRAOUFS
- transfusing .... TR-FG, TRAOUFG
- transfused .... TR-FD, TRAOUFD

transfusion .... TR-FGS, TRAOUFGS
transience .... TRAENZ
transient .... TRAENT

transit
- transit .... TRIT
- transition .... TRIGS
- transitional .... TRILGS
- transitoriness .... TRINTS
- transitory .... TRIRT

translate
- translate .... TRAN
- translates .... TRANZ
- translating .... TRANG
- translated .... TRAND

translation .... TRANGS
translator .... TRARN
translucence .... LAOUNS
translucency .... LAOUNSZ
translucent .... LAO*UNT, LOUNT
translucently .... LAOUNL, LAOUNLT
transmission .... TR-MGS

transmit
- transmit .... TR-MT
- transmits .... TR-MTS
- transmitting .... TR-MGT, TR-MG
- transmitted .... TR-MTD

transmitter .... TR-RMT
transparence .... TR-PS
transparencies .... TR-PSZ
transparency .... TR-PZ
transparent .... TR-P

transplant
- transplant .... TRAPT
- transplants .... TRAPTS
- transplanting .... TRAPGT
- transplanted .... TRAPTD

transplantation .... TRAPGS
transplanter .... TRARPT

transport
- transport .... TR-PT

© 1997 White-Boucke Publishing.   ILLEGAL TO PHOTOCOPY

T — BRIEF ENCOUNTERS

```
    transports . . . . . . . . . . . . . . . . . . . . . . . . . . . . . . . . . . . . . . TR-PTS
    transporting . . . . . . . . . . . . . . . . . . . . . . . . . . . . . . . . . . . . TR-PGT
    transported . . . . . . . . . . . . . . . . . . . . . . . . . . . . . . . . . . . . . TR-PTD
transportation . . . . . . . . . . . . . . . . . . . . . . . . . . . . . . . . . . . . . . TR-PGS
transporter . . . . . . . . . . . . . . . . . . . . . . . . . . . . . . . . . . . . . . . . . TR-RPT
transpose
    transpose . . . . . . . . . . . . . . . . . . . . . . . . . . . . . . . . . . . . . . . . TROEP
    transposes . . . . . . . . . . . . . . . . . . . . . . . . . . . . . . . . . . . . . . TROEPS
    transposing . . . . . . . . . . . . . . . . . . . . . . . . . . . . . . . . . . . . . TROEPG
    transposed . . . . . . . . . . . . . . . . . . . . . . . . . . . . . . . . . . . . . . TROEPD
transposition . . . . . . . . . . . . . . . . . . . . . . . . . . . . . . . . . . . . . . . TROEPGS
transverse
    transverse . . . . . . . . . . . . . . . . . . . . . . . . . . . . . . . . . . . . . . . TRAFRB
    transversely . . . . . . . . . . . . . . . . . . . . . . . . . . . . . . . . . . . . . TRAFRBL
    transverseness . . . . . . . . . . . . . . . . . . . . . . . . . . . . . . . . . . TRAFRNS
transvestism . . . . . . . . . . . . . . . . . . . . . . . . . . . . . . . TREVM, TREFM
transvestite . . . . . . . . . . . . . . . . . . . . . . . . . . . . . . . . . TREVT, TREFT
trauma . . . . . . . . . . . . . . . . . . . . . . . . . . . . . . . . . . . . . . . . . . . . . TRAUM
traumatic . . . . . . . . . . . . . . . . . . . . . . . . . . . . . . . . . . . . . . . . . . TRAUMT
travel
    travel . . . . . . . . . . . . . . . . . . . . . . . . . . . . . . . . . . . . . . . . . . . . TRAFL
    travels . . . . . . . . . . . . . . . . . . . . . . . . . . . . . . . . . . . . . . . . . . TRAFLS
    traveling . . . . . . . . . . . . . . . . . . . . . . . . . . . . . . . . . . . . . . . . TRAFLG
    traveled . . . . . . . . . . . . . . . . . . . . . . . . . . . . . . . . . . . . . . . . . TRAFLD
traveler . . . . . . . . . . . . . . . . . . . . . . . . . . . . . . . . . . . . . . . . . . . . TRAFRL
treacherous . . . . . . . . . . . . . . . . . . . . . . . . . . . . . . . . . . . . . . . . TRAFPS
treacherousness . . . . . . . . . . . . . . . . . . . . . . . . . . . . . . . . . . . TRAFPZ
treachery . . . . . . . . . . . . . . . . . . . . . . . . . . . . . . . . . . . . . . . . . . TRAFP
tread
    tread . . . . . . . . . . . . . . . . . . . . . . . . . . . . . . . . . . . . . . . . . . . . . TRED
    treads . . . . . . . . . . . . . . . . . . . . . . . . . . . . . . . . . . . . . . . . . . . TREDZ
    treading . . . . . . . . . . . . . . . . . . . . . . . . . . . . . . . . . . . . . . . . . TREGD
    trod . . . . . . . . . . . . . . . . . . . . . . . . . . . . . . . . . . . . . . . . . . . . . TROD
    trod / trodden . . . . . . . . . . . . . . . . . . . . . . . . . . . TROD / TROND
treason . . . . . . . . . . . . . . . . . . . . . . . . . . . . . . . . . . . . . . . . . . . . TRAOENZ
treasure
    treasure . . . . . . . . . . . . . . . . . . . . . . . . . . . . . . . . . TR-Z, TRERB
    treasures . . . . . . . . . . . . . . . . . . . . . . . . . . . . . . . TR-SZ, TRERBS
    treasuring . . . . . . . . . . . . . . . . . . . . . . . . . . . . . . TR-GZ, TRERBG
    treasured . . . . . . . . . . . . . . . . . . . . . . . . . . . . . . . TR-DZ, TRERBD
treasurer . . . . . . . . . . . . . . . . . . . . . . . . . . . . . . . . . . . . . . . . . . . TR-RZ
treasury . . . . . . . . . . . . . . . . . . . . . . . . . . . . . . . . . . TRERZ, TRERBZ
treat
    treatable . . . . . . . . . . . . . . . . . . . . . . . . . . . . . . . . . . . . . . . . TRAOEBL
    treater . . . . . . . . . . . . . . . . . . . . . . . . . . . . . . . . . . . . . . . . . . TRAOERT
```

treatment	TREMT, TRAOEMT
tremble	
tremble	TR-M
trembles	TR-MS
trembling	TR-M/-G
trembled	TR-MD
tremendous	TRE
tremendously	TREL
tremor	TRERM
trench	TREFP
trepidation	TREPGS
trespass	
trespass	TREP
trespasses	TREPS
trespassing	TREPG
trespassed	TREPD
trespasser	TR*ERP, TREP/ER
trial de novo	TROEV
triangle	TRING
triangles	TRINGZ
triangular	
triangular	TLAR
triangularity	TLAIRT
triangularly	TLARL
triangulate	
triangulate	TRINGT
triangulates	TRINGTS
triangulating	TRINGT/-G
triangulated	TRINGTD
triangulation	TRINGS
tribal	TRAOIBL
tribulation	TRIBLGS
tribunal	BAOUNL
tribune	BAOUN
tribute	TRAOUT
trickle	
trickle	TRIKL
trickles	TRIKLZ
trickling	TRIKL/-G
trickled	TRIKLD
trident	TRAOINT
trier	
trier	TRAOIR
trier of fact	TRAOIFT
triers of fact	TRAOIFTS

T BRIEF ENCOUNTERS

trigger
    trigger . . . . TRIRG
    triggers . . . . TRIRGS
    triggering . . . . TRIRG/-G
    triggered . . . . TRIRGD
trigonometry . . . . TRIGT
trillion
    trillion . . . . TR-L
    trillion dollar . . . . TR-LD
    trillionth . . . . TR*LT, TR*ILT
trimester . . . . TRAOIM
Trinidad . . . . TRIND
trinity . . . . TRINT
triplet . . . . TLIPT
tripod . . . . TROPD
triumph
    triumph . . . . TRUFM
    triumphs . . . . TRUFMS
    triumphing . . . . TRUFMG
    triumphed . . . . TRUFMD
triumphant . . . . TRUFMT
trivia
    trivia . . . . TRIV
    trivial . . . . TRIVL
    triviality . . . . TRIVLT
Trojan . . . . TROJ
trooper . . . . TRAORP
trophy . . . . TROEF
tropic . . . . TROPG
tropical . . . . TROP
troubleshoot
    troubleshoot . . . . TRAOT
    troubleshoots . . . . TRAOTS
    troubleshooting . . . . TRAOGT
    troubleshot . . . . TRUBLT, TRUBL/SHOT
troubleshooter . . . . TRAORT
truancy . . . . TRAOUNS
truant . . . . TRAOUNT
trucker . . . . TRURK
true name . . . . TRAOUN, TRUN
trueness . . . . TRUNS
truism . . . . TRAOUFM
truly . . . . TRAOUL
truly yours . . . . TURS

BRIEF ENCOUNTERS T

trumpet
    trumpet . . . . TRUMT
    trumpets . . . . TRUMTS
    trumpeting . . . . TRUMGT, TRUMG
    trumpeted . . . . TRUMTD
trumpeter . . . . TRURMT
truncate
    truncate . . . . TRUNT
    truncates . . . . TRUNTS
    truncating. . . . . TRUNGT
    truncated . . . . TRUNTD
truncation. . . . . TR*UNGS
trust
    trusteeship . . . . TRUFP
    trust fund . . . . TRUND
    trustworthily . . . . TWORL
    trustworthiness . . . . TWORNS
    trustworthy. . . . . TWORT, TWO*RT
truthful
    truthful. . . . . TRUF
    truthfully. . . . . TRUFL
    truthfulness. . . . . TRUFNS
T-shirt . . . . TWIRT
TTY. . . . . TWAOI
TTY user . . . . TWAOURS
tubercular . . . . BERL
tuberculosis. . . . . BERK
tubal
    tubal . . . . TUBL
    tubal ligation . . . . TUBLGS, TAOUBLGS
    tubal pregnancy . . . . TUBLG, TRAEG
tubular . . . . TAOURBL
tubule . . . . TAOUBL
Tuesday . . . . TAOUS, TAOUZ
tuition . . . . TWAOUGS
tumor . . . . TAOURM
tumult . . . . TMULT
tumultuous . . . . TMOUS
tune-up . . . . TUP
tunnel
    tunnel . . . . TUNL
    tunnels. . . . . TUNLS
    tunneling . . . . TUNLG
    tunneled. . . . . TUNLD
tunic . . . . TAOUNK

© 1997 White-Boucke Publishing.   ILLEGAL TO PHOTOCOPY

T — BRIEF ENCOUNTERS

turban . . . . TBUN, TBA*N
turbid . . . . TURBD
turbidity . . . . TURBTD
turbine . . . . TBAOIN
turbo
    turbo . . . . TBO
    turbocharged . . . . TBARJD
    turbocharger . . . . TBRAURJ
    turbojet . . . . TBOJ
    turboprop . . . . TBOP
turbulence . . . . TURBL
turbulent . . . . TURBLT
turf . . . . TWUF
Turk
    Turk . . . . TURK
    Turkey . . . . TO*IRK
    Turkish . . . . TRURB
turkey . . . . TOIRK
turmoil . . . . TURM
turnaround . . . . TWA*RN
turn around
    turn around . . . . TWARN
    turns around . . . . TWARNS
    turning around . . . . TWARNG
    turned around . . . . TWARND
turn down
    turn down . . . . TWOUN
    turns down . . . . TWOUNS
    turning down . . . . TWOUNG
    turned down . . . . TWOUND
turn off
    turn off . . . . TWAUF
    turns off . . . . TWAUFS
    turning off . . . . TWAUFG
    turned off . . . . TWAUFD
turn-off . . . . TWA*UF
turn on
    turn on . . . . TWON
    turns on . . . . TWONS
    turning on . . . . TWONG
    turned on . . . . TWOND
turn-on . . . . TWO*N
turnout . . . . TWO*UT
turn out
    turn out . . . . TWOUT

BRIEF ENCOUNTERS T

turns out . . . . TWOUTS
turning out . . . . TWOUGT
turned out . . . . TWOUTD
turnover . . . . TWOEVR
turn over
    turn over . . . . TWOVR
    turns over . . . . TWOVRS
    turning over . . . . TWOVRG
    turned over . . . . TWOVRD
turpentine . . . . TURPT
turpitude . . . . TURP
turquoise . . . . TWOIS
turtle . . . . TURLT
tutor
    tutor . . . . TWOR, TAOURT
    tutors . . . . TWORS, TAOURTS
    tutoring . . . . TWORG, TAOURGT
    tutored . . . . TWORD, TAOURTD
tuxedo . . . . TWUX, TUX/TUX
TV set . . . . TWEVT
TV station . . . . T-VGS, TWAIVGS
tweezers . . . . TWAOEZ, TWAOERZ
twelve . . . . TWEFL, TWEVL
twenty
    twenty . . . . TWI
    twenty-four hour . . . . TWOUR
    twenty-four-hour period . . . . TWOURP
    twenty of the . . . . TWIFT
    twenty of them . . . . TWIFM
    twenty of these . . . . TWIFZ
    twenty of those . . . . TWIFS
twiddle
    twiddle . . . . TWILD
    twiddles . . . . TWILDZ
    twiddling . . . . TWILG, TWILGD
    twiddled . . . . TWILD/-D
twilight . . . . TWAOILT
twinkle
    twinkle . . . . TWINL, TWIKL
    twinkles . . . . TWINLS, TWIKLS
    twinkling . . . . TWINLG, TWIKL/-G
    twinkled . . . . TWINLD, TWIKLD
twit . . . . TWOIT
two
    two . . . . TWO

twofold	TWOFLD
two of the	TWOFT
two of them	TWOFM
two of these	TWOFZ
two of those	TWOFS
two-piece	TWOP
twosome	TWOM
two-thirds	TWIRDZ
two-timer	TWAOIRM
two times	TWAOIMS
two-time	
two-time	TWAOIM
two-times	TWAOIMZ
two-timing	TWAOIMG
two-timed	TWAOIMD
tycoon	TWAON
Tylenol	TLAOIL
type	
type of	TAOIFP
type of the	TAOIFPT
type of these	TAOIFPZ
types of	TAOIFPS
types of the	TAOIFPTS
typewriter	TRIR, TWAOIR
typewritten	TRIN
typical	TOIP
typically	TOIPL, TAOEP
typist	TAOIPT
typographic	
typographic	TAOIFK
typographical	TAOIF
typographically	TAOIFL
tyrannical	TRANL
tyrannosaur	
tyrannosaur	TRAN/SAUR
tyrannosaurus	TRAN/SAURS
tyrannosaurus rex	TRAN/SAURZ
tyranny	TIRN
tyrant	TRANT

U

UCLA	YUK
Uganda	YAOUGD
Ugandan	YAOUNGD
uglier	OIRG
ugliness	OINS
ugly	OIG
uh	H*U
uh-huh (= yes)	HUP
uh-uh (= no)	H*UP, H*U/H*U
ulcer	ULS
ultimate	ULT
ultimatum	*ULT, ULT/MAIM
ultra	URLT
umbrella	BREL
um-hmm	H-M, UM/H-M
U.N.	*UN
unable	NAIBL
unacceptability	SNEBLT
unacceptable	SNEBL
unadulterated	NURLTD
unanimous	NAN
unanimously	NANL
unarmed	NARMD
unavailability	NAIVBLT, NAIFBLT
unavailable	NAIVBL, NAIFBL
unavoidable	NWOIBL
unbelievable	NEFBL
unbelievably	NAOEFBL
uncertain	
uncertain	SNERN
uncertainly	SNERNL
uncertainty	SNERNT
uncle	UNK
uncomfortable	N-FRBL, NUFRBL
uncomfortableness	N-FRBLS, NUFRBLS
uncomfortably	NEFRBL
unconditional	N-KL
unconditionally	NOIKL
unconstitutional	NAOULGS, NAOLGS
uncover	
uncover	NOVR
uncovers	NOVRS

uncovering . . . . NOVRG
uncovered . . . . NOVRD
under
   under . . . . N–R
   underage . . . . NAIJ
   under all the circumstances . . . . ULTS
   undercover . . . . NOEVR
   undergraduate. . . . . N–RGD
   underground . . . . N–RG
   underling . . . . NIRLG
   underlying . . . . NAOIRLG
   underpass . . . . N–RPS
   under the . . . . N–RT
   under the assumption . . . . NUGS
   under the circumstance . . . . UTS
   under the circumstances . . . . UTSZ
   under the influence . . . . NUFL
   under the influence of alcohol . . . . NUFK
   under these . . . . N–RZ
   under those . . . . N–RS
undergo
   undergo . . . . NR–G
   undergoes . . . . NR–GS
   undergoing . . . . NR–G/–G
   underwent . . . . NR–T
   undergone . . . . NR–N
underline
   underline. . . . . N–RL
   underlines . . . . N–RLS
   underlining . . . . N–RLG
   underlined. . . . . N–RLD
understand
   understand. . . . . UNS
   understands . . . . UNSZ
   understanding. . . . . UNGS
   understood. . . . . UND
undoubtedly . . . . NOULT
unemployment . . . . NOIMT
unethical. . . . . NEKL
uneven
   uneven. . . . . UN/AOEN
   unevenly . . . . UN/AOENL
   unevenness. . . . . UN/AOENS
unfold
   unfold . . . . NOFLD

BRIEF ENCOUNTERS U

unfolds . . . . NOFLDZ
unfolding . . . . NOFLG, NOFLGD
unfolded . . . . NOFLD/-D
unfortunate . . . . UFRN
unfortunately . . . . UFRNL
unification . . . . UFGS, AOUFGS, YAOUFGS
Unified School District . . . . YUKT, YAOKT
uniform . . . . UFRM
uniformity . . . . UFRMT
unify
    unify . . . . YAOI
    unifies . . . . YAOIS
    unifying . . . . YAOIG
    unified . . . . YAOID
unincorporated . . . . NOURPD, UN/NORPD, UN/KORPD
uninterrupted . . . . NUPTD
union . . . . YOIN
unionization . . . . YOINGS
unique
    unique . . . . YAOEK
    uniquely . . . . YAOEL, YAOEKL
    uniqueness . . . . YAOENS
unit . . . . UNT
unite
    unite . . . . YAOUN
    unites . . . . YAOUNS
    uniting . . . . YAOUNG
    united . . . . YAOUND, UTD
United
    United Kingdom . . . . YINGD
    United Nations . . . . *UNS, *UN/*UN
    United Parcel Service . . . . UPS/UPS
    United States . . . . USZ, *US/*US
    United States mail . . . . YAOUM/YAOUM
    United States of America . . . . UMS, *US/MERK
    United States Postal Service . . . . YAOL/YAOL
    United States Post Office . . . . YAOPS/YAOPS
unity . . . . YAOUNT
universal . . . . YAOUFRL
universally . . . . YOIFRL
universe . . . . YAOUFRS, YAOUFRNS
university . . . . UVT
unjust . . . . N*US
unlawful . . . . NAUFL
unlawfully . . . . NOIFL

U   BRIEF ENCOUNTERS

unless	N-LS
unnecessarily	UN/NEL
unofficial	NOIRB
unofficially	NOIRBL
unreasonable	N-RNL, NR-NL
unsafe	SNAIF
unsatisfactory	SNAF
unspeakable	SPAOEBL
unstable	SNAIBL
unsuccessful	SN-FL
until	
until	N-L
until the	N-LT
until these	N-LZ
untold	NOLD
unusual	NURB
unusually	NURBL
unwanted	NAUNTD
unwarranted	NARNTD
unwavering	NAIVRG
unwilling	N-LG
up	
up	UP
up and down	POUN
up and down the	POUNT
up or down	POURN
up or down the	POURNT
up or down these	POURNZ
up or down those	POURNS
ups and downs	POUNZ
up these	UPZ
upcoming	POMG
update	
update	PAIT
updates	PAITS
updating	PAIGT
updated	PAITD
upgrade	
upgrade	UPGD
upgrades	UPGDZ
upgrading	UPGD/-G
upgraded	UPGD/-D
upheaval	HAOEVL
uphold	
uphold	POELD

```
upholds......................................... POELDZ
upholding ....................................... POELGD
upheld.......................................... UP/HELD
upholder .......................................... POERLD
upload
    upload ........................................ PLOED
    uploads........................................ PLOEDZ
    uploading ..................................... PLOEGD
    uploaded ..................................... PLOED/-D
upon
    upon ........................................... PON
    *upon the* ....................................... PONT
    *upon the ground* ................................. POEG
    *upon the grounds*................................ POEGZ
    *upon these* ..................................... PONZ
    *upon those* ..................................... PONS
upper ..................................... OIRP, *URP
uproar ........................................... PROER
UPS ...................................... *UPS, UPSZ
upset
    upset .......................................... SPET
    upsets ......................................... SPETS
    upsetting ...................................... SPEGT
    upset .......................................... SPET
*upside down*........................... SPOU, UPS/DOUN
upstairs ............................................ UPS
urbanization ................................. URB/SAIGS
urbanize
    urbanize...................................... URB/NAOIZ
    urbanizes ..................................... URB/NAOIFS
    urbanizing .................................... URB/NAOIFG
    urbanized..................................... URB/NAOIFD
urgency .......................................... URGS
urgent ............................................ URGT
urgently .......................................... URNL
urinate
    urinate........................................ YAOURNT
    urinates....................................... YAOURNTS
    urinating.......................... YAOURNGT, YAOURNG
    urinated....................................... YAOURNTD
urination ....................................... YAOURNGS
urine ............................................ YAOURN
urologist......................................... YAOURLT
urology ......................................... YAOURLG
Uruguay ................................. YOURG, YAOURG
```

Uruguayan	YOURNG
us	US
U.S.	
U.S.	*US
U.S.A.	UZ
U.S. mail	YAOUM
U.S. Postal Service	YAOL
U.S. Post Office	YAOPS
usable	YAOUBL, AOUBL
usage	YAOUJ
use	
use	AOUS, AOUZ
uses	AOUFS, AOUSZ
using	AOUFG
used	AOUFD
use	
useful	YAOUF
usefully	YAOUFL
usefulness	YAOUFNS
useless	YAOULS
user	AOURS, YAOURS
USSR	S*U/S*U
usual	URB
usually	URBL
Utah	*UT
uterine	YAOURT
uterus	YAOUT
utility	YAOULT
utopia	YAOUP
utter	
utter	URT
utters	URTS
uttering	URT/-G, UT/ERG
uttered	URTD
Uzi	AO*UZ

V

vacancy	VAIKZ
vacant	VAIK
vacate	
vacate	VAIKT
vacates	VAIKTS
vacating	VAIKT/-G, VAIK/-G
vacated	VAIKTD, VAIKD
vacation	VAIGS, VAIX
vaccinate	
vaccinate	VAKT
vaccinates	VAKTS
vaccinating	VAKT/-G
vaccinated	VAKTD
vaccination	VAGS
vaccine	VAO*EN
vaccines	VAO*ENS, VAOENZ
vacillate	
vacillate	VAFLT
vacillates	VAFLTS
vacillating	VAFLGT, VAFLG
vacillated	VAFLTD
vacillation	VAFLGS
vacuum	
vacuum	VAK
vacuums	VAKS
vacuuming	VAK/-G, VAG
vacuumed	VAKD
vagabond	VBOND
vagina	VAJ
vague and ambiguous	VAIM
vainly	VAINL
Valentine	VA*LT
Valentine's Day	VA*LTD
valid	VALD
validate	
validate	VAILT
validates	VAILTS
validating	VAILGT
validated	VAILTD
validation	VAILGS
validity	VALTD
valley	VAEL

V   BRIEF ENCOUNTERS

valor . . . . VAORL
valuable . . . . VABL
valuation . . . . VALGS
value
    value . . . . VAL
    values . . . . VALS
    valuing . . . . VALG
    valued . . . . VALD
value of
    value of . . . . VAF
    value of the . . . . VAFT
    value of these . . . . VAFZ
    value of those . . . . VAFS
valve . . . . VAFL, VAVL
vandal . . . . VANL
vandalism . . . . VAFM
vandalize
    vandalize . . . . V–NL
    vandalizes . . . . V–NLS
    vandalizing . . . . V–NLG
    vandalized . . . . V–NLD
vane . . . . VA*EN
vanguard . . . . VAND, VANGD
vanilla . . . . VINL
vanish
    vanish . . . . VARB
    vanishes . . . . VARBS
    vanishing . . . . VARBG
    vanished . . . . VARBD
vanity . . . . VANT
vapor . . . . VAIP
vaporization . . . . VAIRPGS
vaporize
    vaporize . . . . VAIRP
    vaporizes . . . . VAIRPS
    vaporizing . . . . VAIRPG
    vaporized . . . . VAIRPD
variable . . . . VAIRBL
variant . . . . VAIRNT
variation . . . . VAIRGS
varicose . . . . VAIRKS
varicose veins . . . . V–VS
variety . . . . VAIRT
various . . . . VAIRB
varsity . . . . VAURT

BRIEF ENCOUNTERS   V

vary
    vary .... VAIR
    varies .... VAIRS
    varying .... VAIRG
    varied .... VAIRD
vas deferens .... VAFD
vasectomy .... VEKT
Vatican .... VAFK
vaudeville .... VAUD
vaudevillian .... VAULD
VCR .... VAOES
vector .... VERKT
Vegas .... VEG
vegetation .... VEGS
vehemence .... VAOEMS
vehemency .... VAOEMSZ
vehement .... VAOEM, VAOEMT
vehicle
    vehicle .... VEK, VAOEK
    Vehicle Code .... V-K
    Vehicle Code Section .... V-X
    vehicles .... VEKZ, VAOEKS
vehicular .... VELG, VEKL, VAOEKL
vehicular homicide .... VEKLS, VEKLD, VAOEKLS, VAOEKLD
velocity .... VOFT, VOS/TI
velvet .... VEFLT, VEVLT
vendetta .... VAENT
vendor .... VERND
veneration .... VERNGS
venereal disease .... VAIRLD
Venezuela .... VENZ
Venezuelan .... VAENZ
vengeance .... VAENG
venom .... VEM
ventilate
    ventilate .... VELT
    ventilates .... VELTS
    ventilating .... VELGT
    ventilated .... VELTD
ventilation .... VELGS
ventral .... VARL
venture
    venture .... VUR
    ventures .... VURS
    venturing .... VURG

V   BRIEF ENCOUNTERS

ventured	VUR/-D
venue	VAOUN
veracity	VAEFT
verbal	VERBL
verbalization	V-RBLGS, VOIRBLGS
verbalize	
verbalize	V-RBL
verbalizes	V-RBLS
verbalizing	V-RBLG
verbalized	V-RBLD
verbally	VOIBL
verbatim	VERM
verdict	VERD, VERK
verification	VAERGS, VEFRGS
verify	
verify	VAER
verifies	VAERS
verifying	VAERG
verified	VAERD
veritable	VERLT
veritableness	VERLTS
veritably	VERBLT
Vermont	V*T
vernacular	VERN
versatile	V-RT
versatility	V-RLT
version	VERGS
versus	V-RS, VERZ
vertebra	
vertebra	VA
vertebrae	VAE
vertebral	BRAL
vertical	VERL
vertically	VAERL
vertigo	VERG, VERGT
very	
very	V-R
very bad	VAD
very big	VIG
very calm	VAUM
very deep	VAOEP
very far	VAR
very fast	V-F
very few times	V-FT, V-FTS
very good	VAOG

very good time	VAOGT
very hard	VARD
very hot	VOT
very important	VORNT
very importantly	VORNL
very kind	VAOIND
very large	VARJ
very little	VILT
very long	VONG
very long time	VONGT
very many	V-M
very most	VO*S
very much	V-FP
very nice	V-N
very often	V-FN
very old	VOLD
very small	VAUL
very soon	VAON
very sorry	VOR
very strong	VONGS
very truly yours	V-T/URS
very well	VEL
very young	VUNG
vessel	VEFL
vestibule	VEFBL
veteran	VERT
veterinarian	VAIRN
veterinarians	VAIRNZ
veto	
veto	VAOET
vetoes	VAOETS
vetoing	VAOEGT
vetoed	VAOETD
VGA	VAOEJ
via	VAOEV
viability	VAOIBLT
viable	VAOIBL
viably	VAOEBL
vibrant	VAOIBT
vibrate	
vibrate	VAOIB
vibrates	VAOIBS
vibrating	VAOIB/-G
vibrated	VAOIBD
vibration	VAOIBGS

vibrator	VAOIRBT
vicarious	VAOIK
vice	
vice chairperson	VAOIRP
vice president	V-PT
vice verse	V-V
vicinity	VINT
vicious	
vicious	VIRB
viciously	V*IRBL
viciousness	VIRBS, V*IRNS
victim	VIM
victimization	VIMGS
victory	VIKT
video	
video	VAOD
video game	VAOGD
videographer	VAOFR
videography	VAOEF, VAEF
videotape	
videotape	VAOP
videotapes	VAOPS
videotaping	VAOPG
videotaped	VAOPD
Vietnam	VAM, V*N
Vietnamese	VAOEZ
view	
viewer	VAOUR
viewership	VAOURP
view of	VAOUF
view of the	VAOUFT
view of the fact	VAOUFK
view of them	VAOUFM
view of these	VAOUFZ
view of those	VAOUFS
viewpoint	VAOUPT
vigilance	VIJS
vigilant	VIJ
vigilante	VIJT
vigor	
vigor	VIRG
vigorous	VIRGS
vigorously	VIRLG, VIRLS
vilification	VIFLGS
village	VIL

BRIEF ENCOUNTERS   V

vindicate
- vindicate . . . . VIND
- vindicates . . . . VINDZ
- vindicating . . . . VINGD
- vindicated . . . . VIND/-D

vindication . . . . V-NGS
vinyl . . . . VAOINL
violate
- violate . . . . VAOILT
- violates . . . . VAOILTS
- violating . . . . VAOILGT, VAOILG
- violated . . . . VAOILTD

violation
- violation . . . . VILGS, VAOILGS
- ***violation of law*** . . . . VIFL
- ***violation of section*** VIX
- ***violation of the law*** . . . . VIFLT

violence . . . . V-L
violent . . . . V-LT
viper . . . . VOIRP
viral . . . . VAOIRL
virgin
- virgin . . . . VIRJ
- Virginia . . . . VA*
- Virgin Islands . . . . V*I
- virginity . . . . VIRJT, VIRGT

virile . . . . VIRL
virility . . . . VIRLT
virtual
- virtual . . . . VIFP
- virtuality . . . . VIFPT
- virtually . . . . VIFPL

virtue . . . . VIR
virtuoso . . . . VOEFP
virtuous . . . . VIFPS
virus . . . . VAOIR
visible . . . . VIFBL
visibility . . . . VIFBLT
vision . . . . VIGS
vision loss . . . . VOS
visit
- visit . . . . VIFT, VIF
- visits . . . . VIFTS
- visiting . . . . VIFGT
- visited . . . . VIFTD

visitation	VIFGS
visitor	VIFR
visual	
visual	VIRBL
visual impairment	VIRT
visually impaired	VIRD
visualization	VIRBLGS
vital	VALT
vitamin	VAOIMT
vituperate	
vituperate	VIPT
vituperates	VIPTS
vituperating	VIPGT
vituperated	VIPTD
vituperation	VIPGS
vituperative	
vituperative	VIVP
vituperatively	VIVPL
vituperativeness	VIVPS
vivacious	
vivacious	VAERB
vivaciously	VAERBL
vivaciousness	VAERBNS
vivid	VIVD
vividly	VIVLD
vocabulary	VOEB
vocal	VOEFK, VOEKL
vocalization	VOELGS
vocalize	
vocalize	VOEL
vocalizes	VOELS
vocalizing	VOELG
vocalized	VOELD
vocally	VOIKL
vocation	
vocation	VOEGS
vocational	VORBL, VOEXL
vocationalism	VOFM
vocationally	VOERBL
vociferate	
vociferate	VOEFT
vociferates	VOEFTS
vociferating	VOEFGT
vociferated	VOEFTD
vociferation	VOEFGS

BRIEF ENCOUNTERS   V

vociferous	VOEF
vociferously	VOEFL
voice	
voice	VOIS
voices	VOIFS, VOISZ
voicing	VOIFG
voiced	VOIFD
voir dire	
voir dire	V-RD, VOIRD
voir dire examination	VOIRX
VOIR DIRE EXAMINATION	V-RD/V-RD
volatile	VOIL
volatility	VOILT
volcano	VOLG
volcanos	VOLGZ
volition	VOLGS
Volkswagen	VO*EX
volley ball	VOB, VOBL
voltage	VOJ
volume	VAOUM
voluntarily	VOL
voluntariness	VONS
voluntary	VO
voluntary manslaughter	VOM
volunteer	
volunteer	VOE
volunteers	VOES
volunteering	VOE/-G
volunteered	VOED
volunteerism	VOEFM
vomit	
vomit	VOMT
vomits	VOMTS
vomiting	VOMGT, VOMG
vomited	VOMTD
voracious	VORB
vortex	VORX
voter	VOERT
votership	VOERP
votive	VOEV
voucher	VOUFRP
vowel	VOUL
voyage	
voyage	VOIJ
voyages	VOIJS

V — BRIEF ENCOUNTERS

voyaging	VOIJ/-G
voyaged	VOIJD
voyeur	VOIR
V.P.	V-P
vs.	V-S
vulgar	VULG
vulgarity	VULGT
vulnerability	VUBLT
vulnerable	VUBL
vulture	VURT

W

wager
- wager . . . . WAIRJ
- wagers . . . . WAIRJS
- wagering . . . . WAIRJ/-G
- wagered . . . . WAIRJD

wagerer . . . . WRAIRJ
wagon . . . . WHAG
wagons . . . . WHAGZ
Waikiki . . . . WAOIK

wait a
- *wait a minute* . . . . WIMT
- *wait a moment* . . . . WOMT
- *wait a second* . . . . WAK, WAIKT

waiter . . . . WAIRT
wake
- wake . . . . WAIK
- wakes . . . . WAIKS
- waking . . . . WAIK/-G, WAIG
- woke / waked . . . . WOEK / WAIKD
- woken / waked . . . . WOENG / WAIKD

Wales . . . . WAELS
walk
- walk . . . . WAUK
- walks . . . . WAUKS
- walking . . . . WAUK/-G, WAUG
- walked . . . . WAUKD

walker . . . . WAURK
wallet . . . . WALT
wallop
- wallop . . . . WAOP, WLOP
- wallops . . . . WAOPS, WLOPS
- walloping . . . . WAOPG, WLOPG
- walloped . . . . WAOPD, WLOPD

Wall Street . . . . WRAOET
Wall Street Journal . . . . WRAOEJ, WOURNL
wand . . . . WAUND
wander
- wander . . . . WAURND
- wanders . . . . WAURNDZ
- wandering . . . . WAURNGD
- wandered . . . . WAURND/-D

wanderer . . . . WRAURND

wanton
    wanton . . . . WAON
    wantonly . . . . WAONL
    wantonness . . . . WAONS
war crime . . . . WRAOIM
warden . . . . WAERND
wardrobe . . . . WROEB
warehouse
    warehouse . . . . WROUS
    warehouses . . . . WROUFS, WROUSZ
    warehousing . . . . WROUFG
    warehoused . . . . WROUFD
warmer
    warmer . . . . WRARM
    warmer than . . . . WRARMT
    warmer than the . . . . WRARMTD
    warmer than these . . . . WRARMZ
    warmer than those . . . . WRARMS
warranty . . . . WAERNT
warrior . . . . WOR, WAOR
warriors . . . . WORZ, WAORS
was . . . . WUZ
washer . . . . WRARB
Washington . . . . WA*
Washington, D.C. . . . . WARBDZ
wasn't . . . . WUNT
watch the . . . . WAFPT
water
    water . . . . WART
    waters . . . . WARTS
    watering . . . . WARGT
    watered . . . . WARTD
waterproof
    waterproof . . . . WRAOF
    waterproofs . . . . WRAOFS
    waterproofing . . . . WRAOFG
    waterproofed . . . . WRAOFD
wattage . . . . WAJ
waver
    waver . . . . WAEVR
    wavers . . . . WAEVRS
    wavering . . . . WAEVRG
    wavered . . . . WAEVRD
way
    way . . . . WAI

BRIEF ENCOUNTERS   W

way, shape, manner or form . . . . WOFRM
way, shape or form . . . . WOFM
we
    we . . . . WE
    we are. . . . . WER
    we aren't . . . . WERNT, WER/-NT, WE/R-NT
    we believe . . . . WEBL
    we believed . . . . WEBLD
    we believing . . . . WEBLG
    we can . . . . WEK
    we can't . . . . WEKT, WEK/-NT, WE/K-NT
    we could . . . . WEKD
    we couldn't . . . . WEKTD, WEKD/-NT, WE/KUNT
    we'd . . . . W*ED
    we ever. . . . . WEFR, WEVR
    we feel. . . . . WEFL
    we feeling . . . . WEFLG
    we felt . . . . WEFLT
    we get . . . . WEGT
    we go . . . . WEG
    we hadn't . . . . WE/H-NT, WED/-NT
    we happen . . . . W*EP
    we happened . . . . WEPD
    we have. . . . . WEF
    we have been . . . . WEFB
    we have believed. . . . . WEFBLD
    we have had . . . . WEFD
    we have known . . . . WEFN
    we haven't . . . . WEFT, WEF/-NT, WE/V-NT
    we know . . . . WEN
    we'll . . . . W*EL
    we mean. . . . . W*EM
    we mean to . . . . WEMT
    we mean to say . . . . WEMTS
    we're . . . . W*ER
    we recall . . . . WERL
    we recalled. . . . . WERLD
    we recalling . . . . WERLG
    we recollect . . . . WERK
    we recollected . . . . WERKD
    we remember . . . . WERM
    we remembered. . . . . WERMD
    we remembering . . . . WERMG
    we say . . . . WES
    we see . . . . WEZ

W — BRIEF ENCOUNTERS

we shall . . . . WERB
we should . . . . WERBD
we shouldn't . . . . WERBTD, WERBD/-NT, WE/SH-NT
we think . . . . WENG
we think so . . . . WENGS
we understand . . . . WENDZ
we understood . . . . W*END
we've . . . . WEV
we've been . . . . WEVB
we've believed . . . . WEVBLD
we've had . . . . WEVD
we've known . . . . WEVN
we want . . . . WEPT
we wanted . . . . WEPTD
we wanting . . . . WEPGT
we was . . . . WEFS
we wasn't . . . . WEFS/-NT, WE/WUNT
we were . . . . WERP
we weren't . . . . WERPT, WERP/-NT, WE/W-RNT
we would . . . . W*ELD
we wouldn't . . . . WELTD, WELD/-NT, WE/WONT
weaken
   weaken . . . . WAOEN
   weakens . . . . WAOENS
   weakening . . . . WAOENG
   weakened . . . . WAOEND
weaker . . . . WAERK
weakly . . . . WAEKL
wean
   wean . . . . WAO*EN
   weans . . . . WAO*ENS
   weaning . . . . WAO*ENG
   weaned . . . . WAO*END
weapon . . . . WEP
wear
   wear . . . . WAER
   wears . . . . WAERS
   wearing . . . . WAERG
   wore . . . . WOER
   worn . . . . WORN
weather
   weather . . . . W*ET
   weathers . . . . W*ETS
   weathering . . . . W*EGT
   weathered . . . . W*ETD

BRIEF ENCOUNTERS W

weave
    weave .... WAOEV
    weaves... WAOEVS
    weaving .... WAOEVG
    wove .... WOEV
    woven .... WOEVN
weaver .... WAOEVR
Web
    Web page .... WAEJ
    Web server.......................... WEFRB, WREFRB
    Web site .... WAOIB
wed
    wed .... WED
    weds.. WEDZ
    wedding .... WEGD
    wedded .... WED/-D
    wedded / wed .... WED/-D / WED
wedlock .... WLOK
Wednesday .... WENS
week
    weekday...................................... WAOEKD
    weekend .... WEND
    weekly .... WAOEKL
weep
    weep .... WAOEP
    weeps... WAOEPS
    weeping .... WAOEPG
    wept .... W*EPT
weigh
    weigh .... WAE
    weighs .... WAES
    weighing .... WAEG
    weighed .... WAES
weight.. WAET
welfare .... WAEFL
well
    well .... WEL
    wells .... WELS
    welling... WELG
    welled... WEL/-D
Welsh .... WERBL, WELZ
wench .... WEFP
were .... W-R
weren't .... W-RNT

west
- westbound .... WAOEB, W-B
- **west coast** .... WO*ES, WOEFT
- westerly .... WAOERL
- western .... WERN
- westerner .... WRERN
- **west side** .... W-DZ
- West Virginia .... W-V

wet
- wet .... WET
- wets .... WETS
- wetting .... WET/-G
- wet / wetted .... WET / WETD

whale .... WHA*EL
wharf .... WAUR

what
- what .... WHA
- *what about* .... WHAB
- *what about the* .... WHABT
- *what am* .... WHAM
- *what are* .... WHAR
- *what aren't* .... WHARNT, WHAR/-NT, WHA/R-NT
- *what can* .... WHAK
- *what can't* .... WHAKT, WHAK/-NT, WHA/K-NT
- *what could* .... WHAKD
- *what couldn't* .... WHAKTD, WHAKD/-NT, WHA/KUNT
- whatever .... WAFR, WHAEFR
- *what evidence* .... WHAEVD
- *what feeling* .... WHAFLG
- *what feels* .... WHAFLS
- *what felt* .... WHAFLT
- *what gets* .... WHAGTS
- *what goes* .... WHAGS
- *what good* .... WHAOGD
- *what got* .... WHAGT
- *what had* .... WHAD
- *what hadn't* .... WHAD/-NT, WHA/H-NT
- *what happened* .... WHAPD
- *what happening* .... WHAPG
- *what happens* .... WHAPS
- *what have* .... WHAF
- *what have been* .... WHAFB
- *what haven't* .... WHAFT, WHAF/-NT, WHA/V-NT
- *what if anything* .... WHAFG, WAFG

BRIEF ENCOUNTERS   W

what is	WHAS
what isn't	WHAS/-NT, WHA/S-NT
what'll	WHA*L
what part	WHAPT
what parts	WHAPTS
what're	WHA*R
what recalled	WHARLD
what recalls	WHARLS
what's	WHA*S
what says	WHASZ
what shall	WHARB
what should	WHARBD
what shouldn't	WHARBTD, WHARBD/-NT, WHA/SH-NT
whatsoever	SWAFR, SWAVR
what the	WHAT
what time	WHAOIM
what've	WHAV
what was	WHAFS
what wasn't	WHAFS/-NT, WHA/WUNT
what were	WHARP
what weren't	WHARPT, WHARP/-NT, WHA/W-RNT
what will	WHAL
what will the	WHALT
what would	WHALD
what wouldn't	WHALTD, WHALD/-NT, WHA/WONT

what he

what he	WHAE
what he believed	WHAEBLD
what he believes	WHAEBLS
what he can	WHAEK
what he can't	WHAEKT, WHAEK/-NT, WHAE/K-NT
what he could	WHAEKD
what he couldn't	WHAEKTD, WHAEKD/-NT, WHAE/KUNT
what he feels	WHAEFLS
what he felt	WHAEFLT
what he gets	WHAEGTS
what he got	WHAEGT
what he had	WHAED
what he hadn't	WHAED/-NT, WHAE/H-NT
what he happened	WHAEPD
what he happens	WHAEPS

what he imagined	WHAEJD
what he imagines	WHAEJS
what he is	WHAES
what he isn't	WHAES/-NT, WHAE/S-NT
what he knows	WHAENS
what he means	WHAEMS
what he means to	WHAEMT
what he means to say	WHAEMTS
what he recalled	WHAERLD
what he recalls	WHAERLS
what he recollected	WHAERKD
what he recollects	WHAERKS
what he remembered	WHAERMD
what he remembers	WHAERMS
what he says	WHAESZ
what he sees	WHAEZ
what he shall	WHAERB
what he should	WHAERBD
what he shouldn't	WHAERBTD, WHAERBD/-NT, WHAE/SH-NT
what he thinks	WHAENGS
what he understands	WHAENDZ
what he understood	WHAEND
what he wanted	WHAEPTD
what he wants	WHAEPTS
what he was	WHAEFS
what he wasn't	WHAEFT, WHAEFS/-NT, WHAE/WUNT
what he will	WHAEL
what he would	WHAELD
what he wouldn't	WHAELTD, WHAELD/-NT, WHAE/WONT
what he would say	WHAELDZ

what I
what I	WHAI
what I am	WHAIM
what I believe	WHAIBL
what I believed	WHAIBLD
what I can	WHAIK
what I can't	WHAIKT, WHAIK/-NT, WHAI/K-NT
what I could	WHAIKD
what I couldn't	WHAIKTD, WHAIKD/-NT, WHAI/KUNT
what I feel	WHAIFL
what I felt	WHAIFLT

BRIEF ENCOUNTERS W

what I get	WHAIGT
what I had	WHAID
what I hadn't	WHAID/-NT, WHAI/H-NT
what I happen	WHAIP
what I happened	WHAIPD
what I have	WHAIF
what I have been	WHAIFB
what I have had	WHAIFD
what I have known	WHAIFN
what I haven't	WHAIFT, WHAIF/-NT, WHAI/V-NT
what I'll	WHA*IL
what I imagine	WHAIJ
what I imagined	WHAIJD
what I know	WHAIN
what I mean	WHA*IM
what I mean to	WHAIMT
what I mean to say	WHAIMTS
what I recall	WHAIRL
what I recalled	WHAIRLD
what I recollect	WHAIRK
what I recollected	WHAIRKD
what I remember	WHAIRM
what I remembered	WHAIRMD
what I say	WHAIS
what I see	WHAIZ
what I shall	WHAIRB
what I should	WHAIRBD
what I shouldn't	WHAIRBTD, WHAIRBD/-NT, WHAI/SH-NT
what I think	WHAING
what I understand	WHAINDZ
what I understood	WHAIND
what I've	WHAIV
what I've been	WHAIVB
what I've believed	WHAIVBLD
what I've had	WHAIVD
what I've known	WHAIVN
what I want	WHAIPT
what I wanted	WHAIPTD
what I was	WHAIFS
what I wasn't	WHAIFS/-NT, WHAI/WUNT
what I will	WHAIL
what I would	WHAILD

W — BRIEF ENCOUNTERS

what I wouldn't .... WHAILTD, WHAILD/-NT, WHAI/WONT
what I would say .... WHAILDZ
what if anything .... WAFG
what is
    what is .... WHAS
    what is your business .... WHAURBS
    what is your business or occupation .... BORK/BORK, WHAS/UR/BORK
    what is your full name .... WHAUFRN
    what is your name .... WHAURN
    what is your occupation .... WHAURPGS
    what is your occupation and assignment .... WOS
what kind
    what kind .... WHAOIND
    what kind of .... WHAOIF
    what kinds of .... WHAOIFS
what type
    what type .... WHAOIP
    what type of .... WHAOIFP
    what types of .... WHAOIFPS
what you
    what you .... WHAU
    what you are .... WHAUR
    what you aren't .... WHAURT, WHAUR/-NT, WHAU/R-NT
    what you believe .... WHAUBL
    what you believed .... WHAUBLD
    what you can .... WHAUK
    what you can't .... WHAUKT, WHAUK/-NT, WHAU/K-NT
    what you could .... WHAUKD
    what you couldn't .... WHAUKTD, WHAUKD/-NT, WHAU/KUNT
    what you feel .... WHAUFL
    what you felt .... WHAUFLT
    what you get .... WHAUGT
    what you had .... WHAUD
    what you hadn't .... WHAUD/-NT, WHAU/H-NT
    what you happen .... WHAUP
    what you happened .... WHAUPD
    what you have .... WHAUF
    what you have been .... WHAUFB
    what you have believed .... WHAUFBLD
    what you have had .... WHAUFD

BRIEF ENCOUNTERS   W

    what you haven't .... WHAUFT, WHAUF/-NT,
                                                             WHAU/V-NT
    what you imagine .... WHAUJ
    what you imagined .... WHAUJD
    what you know .... WHAUN
    what you mean .... WHAUM
    what you mean to .... WHAUMT
    what you mean to say .... WHAUMTS
    what you recall .... WHAURL
    what you recalled .... WHAURLD
    what you recollect .... WHAURK
    what you recollected .... WHAURKD
    what you remember .... WHAURM
    what you remembered .... WHAURMD
    what you say .... WHAUS
    what you see .... WHAUZ
    what you shall .... WHAURB
    what you should .... WHAURBD
    what you shouldn't .... WHAURBTD, WHAURBD/-NT,
                                                     WHAU/SH-NT
    what you think .... WHAUNG
    what you understand .... WHAUNDZ
    what you understood .... WHAUND
    what you've .... WHAUV
    what you've been .... WHAUVB
    what you've believed .... WHAUVBLD
    what you've had .... WHAUVD
    what you've known .... WHAUVN
    what you want .... WHAUPT
    what you wanted .... WHAUPTD
    what you were .... WHAURP
    what you weren't .... WHAURPT, WHAURP/-NT,
                                                    WHAU/W-RNT
    what you will .... WHAUL
    what you would .... WHAULD
    what you wouldn't .... WHAULTD, WHAULD/-NT,
                                                    WHAU/WONT
    what you would say .... WHAULDZ
wheelchair .... WHAIR
when
    when .... WH-, WHEN
    when are .... WH-R
    when aren't .... WH-RNT, WH-R/-NT, WH-/R-NT
    when can .... WH-K
    when can't .... WH-KT, WH-K/-NT, WH-/K-NT

W   BRIEF ENCOUNTERS

when could .... WH–KD
when couldn't .... WH–KTD, WH–KD/–NT, WH–/KUNT
whenever .... WHEFR, WHEVR
when had .... WH–D
when hadn't .... WH–D/–NT, WH–/H–NT
when have .... WH–F
when haven't .... WH–FT, WH–F/–NT, WH–/V–NT
when is .... WH–S
when isn't .... WH–S/–NT, WH–/S–NT
when's .... WH*S
when shall .... WH–RB
when should .... WH–RBD
when shouldn't .... WH–RBTD, WH–RBD/–NT,
                                         WH–/SH–NT
when the .... WH–T
when was .... WH–FS
when wasn't .... WH–FS/–NT, WH–/WUNT
when were .... WH–RP
when weren't .... WH–RPT, WH–RP/–NT,
                                         WH–/W–RNT
when will .... WH–L
when will the .... WH–LT
when would .... WH–LD
when wouldn't .... WH–LTD, WH–LD/–NT,
                                         WH–/WONT

when he
    when he .... WHE
    when he believed .... WHEBLD
    when he believes .... WHEBLS
    when he can .... WHEK
    when he can't .... WHEKT, WHEK/–NT, WHE/K–NT
    when he could .... WHEKD
    when he couldn't .... WHEKTD, WHEKD/–NT,
                                          WHE/KUNT
    when he feels .... WHEFLS
    when he felt .... WHEFLT
    when he gets .... WHEGTS
    when he goes .... WHEGS
    when he got .... WHEGT
    when he had .... WHED
    when he hadn't .... WHED/–NT, WHE/H–NT
    when he happened .... WHEPD
    when he happens .... WHEPS
    when he imagined .... WHEJD
    when he imagines .... WHEJS

BRIEF ENCOUNTERS   W

when he is	WHES
when he isn't	WHES/-NT, WHE/S-NT
when he lived	WHEVD
when he lives	WHEVS
when he means	WHEMS
when he means to	WHEMT
when he means to say	WHEMTS
when he recalled	WHERLD
when he recalls	WHERLS
when he recollected	WHERKD
when he recollects	WHERKS
when he remembered	WHERMD
when he remembers	WHERMS
when he says	WHESZ
when he sees	WHEZ
when he shall	WHERB
when he should	WHERBD
when he shouldn't	WHERBTD, WHERBD/-NT, WHE/SH-NT
when he thinks	WHENGS
when he thinks so	WHENGSZ
when he understands	WHENDZ
when he understood	WHEND
when he wanted	WHEPTD
when he wants	WHEPTS
when he was	WHEFS
when he wasn't	WHEFT, WHEFS/-NT, WHE/WUNT
when he will	WHEL
when he will go	WHELG
when he would	WH*ELD
when he wouldn't	WHELTD, WHELD/-NT, WHE/WONT
when he would say	WHELDZ
when I	
when I	WHI
when I am	WHIM
when I believe	WHIBL
when I believed	WHIBLD
when I can	WHIK
when I can't	WHIKT, WHIK/-NT, WHI/K-NT
when I could	WHIKD
when I couldn't	WHIKTD, WHIKD/-NT, WHI/KUNT
when I feel	WHIFL

W — BRIEF ENCOUNTERS

when I felt	WHIFLT
when I get	WHIGT
when I go	WHIG
when I had	WHID
when I hadn't	WHID/-NT, WHI/H-NT
when I happen	WH*IP
when I happened	WH*IPD
when I have	WHIF
when I have been	WHIFB
when I have believed	WHIFBLD
when I have had	WHIFD
when I have known	WHIFN
when I haven't	WHIFT, WHIF/-NT, WHI/V-NT
when I imagine	WHIJ
when I imagined	WHIJD
when I know	WHIN
when I live	WHIV
when I lived	WHIVD
when I mean to	WHIMT
when I mean to say	WHIMTS
when I recall	WHIRL
when I recalled	WHIRLD
when I recollect	WHIRK
when I recollected	WHIRKD
when I remember	WHIRM
when I remembered	WHIRMD
when I say	WHIS
when I see	WHIZ
when I shall	WHIRB
when I should	WHIRBD
when I shouldn't	WHIRBTD, WHIRBD/-NT, WHI/SH-NT
when I think	WHING
when I think so	WHINGS
when I understand	WHINDZ
when I understood	WHIND
when I've been	WHIVB
when I've believed	WHIVBLD
when I've known	WHIVN
when I want	WHIPT
when I wanted	WHIPTD
when I was	WHIFS
when I wasn't	WHIFS/-NT, WHI/WUNT
when I will	WHIL
when I will go	WHILG

BRIEF ENCOUNTERS   W

when I would .... WHILD
when I wouldn't .... WHILTD, WHILD/-NT,
                                                    WHI/WONT
when I would say .... WHILDZ
when you
   when you .... WHU
   when you are .... WHUR
   when you aren't .... WHURNT, WHUR/-NT,
                                           WHU/R-NT
   when you believe .... WHUBL
   when you believed .... WHUBLD
   when you can .... WHUK
   when you can't .... WHUKT, WHUK/-NT,
                                           WHU/K-NT
   when you could .... WHUKD
   when you couldn't .... WHUKTD, WHUKD/-NT,
                                           WHU/KUNT
   when you feel .... WHUFL
   when you felt .... WHUFLT
   when you get .... WHUGT
   when you go .... WHUG
   when you had .... WHUD
   when you hadn't .... WHUD/-NT, WHU/H-NT
   when you happen .... WHUP
   when you happened .... WHUPD
   when you have .... WHUF
   when you have been .... WHUFB
   when you have believed .... WHUFBLD
   when you have had .... WHUFD
   when you have known .... WHUFN
   when you haven't .... WHUFT, WHUF/-NT,
                                           WHU/V-NT
   when you imagine .... WHUJ
   when you imagined .... WHUJD
   when you know .... WHUN
   when you live .... WHUV
   when you lived .... WHUVD
   when you mean .... WHUM
   when you mean to .... WHUMT
   when you mean to say .... WHUMTS
   when you recall .... WHURL
   when you recalled .... WHURLD
   when you recollect .... WHURK
   when you recollected .... WHURKD
   when you remember .... WHURM

when you remembered	WHURMD
when you say	WHUS
when you see	WHUZ
when you shall	WHURB
when you should	WHURBD
when you shouldn't	WHURBTD, WHURBD/-NT, WHU/SH-NT
when you think	WHUNG
when you think so	WHUNGS
when you understand	WHUNDZ
when you understood	WHUND
when you've been	WHUVB
when you've believed	WHUVBLD
when you've known	WHUVN
when you want	WHUPT
when you wanted	WHUPTD
when you were	WHURP
when you weren't	WHURPT, WHURP/-NT, WHU/W-RNT
when you will	WHUL
when you will go	WHULG
when you would	WHULD
when you wouldn't	WHULTD, WHULD/-NT, WHU/WONT
when you would say	WHULDZ

where
where	WR-
whereabout	WRABT, WR-BT
where are	WR-R
where aren't	WR-RNT, WR-R/-NT, WR-/R-NT
whereas	WRAZ
whereat	WRAT
whereby	WR-B
where can	WR-K
where can't	WR-KT, WR-K/-NT, WR-/K-NT
where could	WR-KD
where couldn't	WR-KTD, WR-KD/-NT, WR-/KUNT
where did you live	WRUV
where do you live	WROUV
where do you reside	WROURD
wherever	WREFR, WREVR
wherefore	WR-FR
where had	WR-D
where hadn't	WR-D/-NT, WR-/H-NT
where have	WR-F

BRIEF ENCOUNTERS   W

where haven't	WR-FT, WR-F/-NT, WR-/V-NT
wherein	WRIN, WR-N
where is	WR-S
where isn't	WR-S/-NT, WR-/S-NT
whereof	WROF
whereon	WRON
where's	WR*S
where shall	WR-RB
where should	WR-RBD
where shouldn't	WR-RBTD, WR-RBD/-NT, WR-/SH-NT
where the	WR-T
whereupon	WROP
where was	WR-FS
where wasn't	WR-FS/-NT, WR-/WUNT
where were	WR-RP
where weren't	WR-RPT, WR-RP/-NT, WR-/W-RNT
where will	WR-L
where will the	WR-LT
where would	WR-LD
where wouldn't	WR-LTD, WR-LD/-NT, WR-/WONT

where he

where he	WRE
where he believed	WREBLD
where he believes	WREBLS
where he can	WR*EK
where he can't	WREKT, WREK/-NT, WRE/K-NT
where he could	WR*EKD
where he couldn't	WREKTD, WREKD/-NT, WRE/KUNT
where he feels	WREFLS
where he felt	WREFLT
where he gets	WREGTS
where he goes	WREGS
where he got	WREGT
where he had	WRED
where he hadn't	WRED/-NT, WRE/H-NT
where he happened	WREPD
where he happens	WREPS
where he imagined	WREJD
where he imagines	WREJS
where he is	WRES
where he isn't	WRES/-NT, WRE/S-NT
where he knows	WRENS
where he lived	WREVD
where he lives	WREVS

where he means.	WREMS
where he means to.	WREMT
where he means to say	WREMTS
where he recalled	WRERLD
where he recalls	WRERLS
where he recollected	WRERKD
where he recollects	WRERKS
where he remembered	WRERMD
where he remembers	WRERMS
where he says	WRESZ
where he sees	WREZ
where he shall	WRERB
where he should	WRERBD
where he shouldn't	WRERBTD, WRERBD/-NT, WRE/SH-NT
where he thinks	WRENGS
where he thinks so	WRENGSZ
where he understands	WRENDZ
where he understood	WREND
where he wanted	WREPTD
where he wants	WREPTS
where he was	WREFS
where he wasn't	WREFT, WREFS/-NT, WRE/WUNT
where he will	WREL
where he will go	WRELG
where he would	WRELD
where he wouldn't	WRELTD, WRELD/-NT, WRE/WONT
where he would say	WRELDZ

where I

where I	WR*I
where I am	WRIM
where I believe	WRIBL
where I believed	WRIBLD
where I can	WRIK
where I can't	WRIKT, WRIK/-NT, WRI/K-NT
where I could	WRIKD
where I couldn't	WRIKTD, WRIKD/-NT, WRI/KUNT
where I feel	WRIFL
where I felt	WRIFLT
where I get	WRIGT
where I go	WR*IG
where I had	WRID
where I hadn't	WRID/-NT, WRI/H-NT

BRIEF ENCOUNTERS W

where I happen	WRIP
where I happened	WRIPD
where I have	WRIF
where I have been	WRIFB
where I have had	WRIFD
where I haven't	WRIFT, WRIF/-NT, WRI/V-NT
where I imagine	WRIJ
where I imagined	WRIJD
where I live	WRIV
where I lived	WRIVD
where I mean	WR*IM
where I mean to	WRIMT
where I mean to say	WRIMTS
where I recall	WRIRL
where I recalled	WRIRLD
where I recollect	WRIRK
where I recollected	WRIRKD
where I remember	WRIRM
where I remembered	WRIRMD
where I see	WRIZ
where I shall	WRIRB
where I should	WRIRBD
where I shouldn't	WRIRBTD, WRIRBD/-NT, WRI/SH-NT
where I think	WR*ING
where I think so	WR*INGS
where I understand	WRINDZ
where I understood	WRIND
where I want	WRIPT
where I wanted	WRIPTD
where I was	WRIFS
where I wasn't	WRIFS/-NT, WRI/WUNT
where I will	WRIL
where I will go	WRILG
where I would	WRILD
where I wouldn't	WRILTD, WRILD/-NT, WRI/WONT
where I would say	WRILDZ
where you	
where you	WRU
where you are	WRUR
where you aren't	WRURNT, WRUR/-NT, WRU/R-NT
where you believe	WRUBL
where you believed	WRUBLD

© 1997 White-Boucke Publishing.   609   ILLEGAL TO PHOTOCOPY

W — BRIEF ENCOUNTERS

where you can	WRUK
where you can't	WRUKT, WRUK/-NT, WRU/K-NT
where you could	WRUKD
where you couldn't	WRUKTD, WRUKD/-NT, WRU/KUNT
where you feel	WRUFL
where you felt	WRUFLT
where you get	WRUGT
where you go	WRUG
where you had	WRUD
where you hadn't	WRUD/-NT, WRU/H-NT
where you happen	WRUP
where you happened	WRUPD
where you have	WRUF
where you have been	WRUFB
where you have had	WRUFD
where you haven't	WRUFT, WRUF/-NT, WRU/V-NT
where you imagine	WRUJ
where you imagined	WRUJD
where you know	WRUN
where you mean	WRUM
where you mean to	WRUMT
where you mean to say	WRUMTS
where you recall	WRURL
where you recalled	WRURLD
where you recollect	WRURK
where you recollected	WRURKD
where you remember	WRURM
where you remembered	WRURMD
where you say	WRUS
where you see	WRUZ
where you shall	WRURB
where you should	WRURBD
where you shouldn't	WRURBTD, WRURBD/-NT, WRU/SH-NT
where you think	WRUNG
where you think so	WRUNGS
where you understand	WRUNDZ
where you understood	WRUND
where you want	WRUPT
where you wanted	WRUPTD
where you were	WRURP
where you weren't	WRURPT, WRURP/-NT, WRU/W-RNT

where you will	WRUL
where you will go	WRULG
where you would	WRULD
where you wouldn't	WRULTD, WRULD/-NT, WRU/WONT
where you would say	WRULDZ

whether

whether	WHR-
whether every	WHR-FR
whether or not	WHRONT
whether the	WHR-T
whether these	WHR-Z
whether those	WHR-S

whether he

whether he	WHRE
whether he believed	WHREBLD
whether he believes	WHREBLS
whether he can	WHREK
whether he can't	WHREKT, WHREK/-NT, WHRE/K-NT
whether he could	WHREKD
whether he couldn't	WHREKTD, WHREKD/-NT, WHRE/KUNT
whether he ever	WHREFR, WHREVR
whether he feels	WHREFLS
whether he felt	WHREFLT
whether he gets	WHREGTS
whether he goes	WHREGS
whether he got	WHREGT
whether he had	WHRED
whether he hadn't	WHRED/-NT, WHRE/H-NT
whether he happened	WHREPD
whether he happens	WHREPS
whether he imagined	WHREJD
whether he imagines	WHREJS
whether he is	WHRES
whether he isn't	WHRES/-NT, WHRE/S-NT
whether he knows	WHRENS
whether he lived	WHREVD
whether he lives	WHREVS
whether he means	WHREMS
whether he means to	WHREMT
whether he means to say	WHREMTS
whether he recalled	WHRERLD
whether he recalls	WHRERLS

whether he recollected	WHRERKD
whether he recollects	WHRERKS
whether he remembered	WHRERMD
whether he remembers	WHRERMS
whether he says	WHRESZ
whether he sees	WHREZ
whether he shall	WHRERB
whether he should	WHRERBD
whether he shouldn't	WHRERBTD, WHRERBD/-NT, WHRE/SH-NT
whether he thinks	WHRENGS
whether he thinks so	WHRENGSZ
whether he understands	WHRENDZ
whether he understood	WHREND
whether he wanted	WHREPTD
whether he wants	WHREPTS
whether he was	WHREFS
whether he wasn't	WHREFT, WHREFS/-NT, WHRE/WUNT
whether he were	WHRERP
whether he weren't	WHRERPT, WHRERP/-NT, WHRE/W-RNT
whether he will	WHREL
whether he will go	WHRELG
whether he would	WHRELD
whether he wouldn't	WHRELTD, WHRELD/-NT, WHRE/WONT
whether he would say	WHRELDZ

whether I

whether I	WHRI
whether I am	WHRIM
whether I believe	WHRIBL
whether I believed	WHRIBLD
whether I can	WHRIK
whether I can't	WHRIKT, WHRIK/-NT, WHRI/K-NT
whether I could	WHRIKD
whether I couldn't	WHRIKTD, WHRIKD/-NT, WHRI/KUNT
whether I ever	WHRIFR, WHRIVR
whether I feel	WHRIFL
whether I felt	WHRIFLT
whether I get	WHRIGT
whether I go	WHRIG
whether I had	WHRID
whether I hadn't	WHRID/-NT, WHRI/H-NT

BRIEF ENCOUNTERS — W

whether I happen	WHRIP
whether I happened	WHRIPD
whether I have	WHRIF
whether I have been	WHRIFB
whether I have had	WHRIFD
whether I have known	WHRIFN
whether I haven't	WHRIFT, WHRIF/-NT, WHRI/V-NT
whether I imagine	WHRIJ
whether I imagined	WHRIJD
whether I know	WHRIN
whether I live	WHRIV
whether I lived	WHRIVD
whether I mean	WHR*IM
whether I mean to	WHRIMT
whether I mean to say	WHRIMTS
whether I recall	WHRIRL
whether I recalled	WHRIRLD
whether I recollect	WHRIRK
whether I recollected	WHRIRKD
whether I remember	WHRIRM
whether I remembered	WHRIRMD
whether I say	WHRIS
whether I see	WHRIZ
whether I shall	WHRIRB
whether I should	WHRIRBD
whether I shouldn't	WHRIRBTD, WHRIRBD/-NT, WHRI/SH-NT
whether I think	WHRING
whether I think so	WHRINGS
whether I understand	WHRINDZ
whether I understood	WHRIND
whether I want	WHRIPT
whether I wanted	WHRIPTD
whether I was	WHRIFS
whether I wasn't	WHRIFS/-NT, WHRI/WUNT
whether I were	WHRIRP
whether I weren't	WHRIRPT, WHRIRP/-NT, WHRI/W-RNT
whether I will	WHRIL
whether I will go	WHRILG
whether I would	WHRILD
whether I wouldn't	WHRILTD, WHRILD/-NT, WHRI/WONT
whether I would say	WHRILDZ

whether or not .... WHORNT
whether or not he
   whether or not he .... WHROE
   whether or not he believed .... WHROEBLD
   whether or not he believes .... WHROEBLS
   whether or not he can .... WHROEK
   whether or not he can't .... WHROEKT, WHROEK/-NT, WHROE/K-NT
   whether or not he could .... WHROEKD
   whether or not he couldn't .... WHROEKTD, WHROEKD/-NT, WHROE/KUNT
   whether or not he ever .... WHROEFR, WHROEVR
   whether or not he feels .... WHROEFLS
   whether or not he felt .... WHROEFLT
   whether or not he gets .... WHROEGTS
   whether or not he goes .... WHROEGS
   whether or not he got .... WHROEGT
   whether or not he had .... WHROED
   whether or not he hadn't .... WHROED/-NT, WHROE/H-NT
   whether or not he happened .... WHROEPD
   whether or not he happens .... WHROEPS
   whether or not he imagined .... WHROEJD
   whether or not he imagines .... WHROEJS
   whether or not he is .... WHROES
   whether or not he isn't .... WHROES/-NT, WHROE/S-NT
   whether or not he knows .... WHROENS
   whether or not he lived .... WHROEVD
   whether or not he lives .... WHROEVS
   whether or not he means .... WHROEMS
   whether or not he means to .... WHROEMT
   whether or not he means to say .... WHROEMTS
   whether or not he recalled .... WHROERLD
   whether or not he recalls .... WHROERLS
   whether or not he recollected .... WHROERKD
   whether or not he recollects .... WHROERKS
   whether or not he remembered .... WHROERMD
   whether or not he remembers .... WHROERMS
   whether or not he says .... WHROESZ
   whether or not he sees .... WHROEZ
   whether or not he shall .... WHROERB
   whether or not he should .... WHROERBD
   whether or not he shouldn't .... WHROERBTD, WHROERBD/-NT, WHROE/SH-NT
   whether or not he thinks .... WHROENGS
   whether or not he thinks so .... WHROENGSZ

BRIEF ENCOUNTERS   W

whether or not he understands.	WHROENDZ
whether or not he understood	WHROEND
whether or not he wanted	WHROEPTD
whether or not he wants	WHROEPTS
whether or not he was	WHROEFS
whether or not he wasn't	WHROEFT, WHROEFS/-NT, WHROE/WUNT
whether or not he were	WHROERP
whether or not he weren't	WHROERPT, WHROERP/-NT, WHROE/W-RNT
whether or not he will	WHROEL
whether or not he will go	WHROELG
whether or not he would	WHROELD
whether or not he wouldn't	WHROELTD, WHROELD/-NT, WHROE/WONT
whether or not he would say	WHROELDZ
whether or not I	
whether or not I	WHROI
whether or not I am	WHROIM
whether or not I believe	WHROIBL
whether or not I believed	WHROIBLD
whether or not I can	WHROIK
whether or not I can't	WHROIKT, WHROIK/-NT, WHROI/K-NT
whether or not I could	WHROIKD
whether or not I couldn't	WHROIKTD, WHROIKD/-NT, WHROI/KUNT
whether or not I ever	WHROIFR, WHROIVR
whether or not I feel	WHROIFL
whether or not I felt	WHROIFLT
whether or not I get	WHROIGT
whether or not I go	WHROIG
whether or not I had	WHROID
whether or not I hadn't	WHROID/-NT, WHROI/H-NT
whether or not I happen	WHROIP
whether or not I happened	WHROIPD
whether or not I have	WHROIF
whether or not I have been	WHROIFB
whether or not I have had	WHROIFD
whether or not I have known	WHROIFN
whether or not I haven't	WHROIFT, WHROIF/-NT, WHROI/V-NT
whether or not I imagine	WHROIJ
whether or not I imagined	WHROIJD
whether or not I know	WHROIN

© 1997 White-Boucke Publishing.   615   ILLEGAL TO PHOTOCOPY

whether or not I live	WHROIV
whether or not I lived	WHROIVD
whether or not I mean	WHRO*IM
whether or not I mean to	WHROIMT
whether or not I mean to say	WHROIMTS
whether or not I recall	WHROIRL
whether or not I recalled	WHROIRLD
whether or not I recollect	WHROIRK
whether or not I recollected	WHROIRKD
whether or not I remember	WHROIRM
whether or not I remembered	WHROIRMD
whether or not I say	WHROIS
whether or not I see	WHROIZ
whether or not I shall	WHROIRB
whether or not I should	WHROIRBD
whether or not I shouldn't	WHROIRBTD, WHROIRBD/-NT, WHROI/SH-NT
whether or not I think	WHROING
whether or not I think so	WHROINGS
whether or not I understand	WHROINDZ
whether or not I understood	WHROIND
whether or not I want	WHROIPT
whether or not I wanted	WHROIPTD
whether or not I was	WHROIFS
whether or not I wasn't	WHROIFS/-NT, WHROI/WUNT
whether or not I were	WHROIRP
whether or not I weren't	WHROIRPT, WHROIRP/-NT, WHROI/W-RNT
whether or not I will	WHROIL
whether or not I will go	WHROILG
whether or not I would	WHROILD
whether or not I wouldn't	WHROILTD, WHROILD/-NT, WHROI/WONT
whether or not I would say	WHROILDZ
whether or not you	
whether or not you	WHROU
whether or not you are	WHROUR
whether or not you aren't	WHROURNT, WHROUR/-NT, WHROU/R-NT
whether or not you believe	WHROUBL
whether or not you believed	WHROUBLD
whether or not you can	WHROUK
whether or not you can't	WHROUKT, WHROUK/-NT, WHROU/K-NT
whether or not you could	WHROUKD

BRIEF ENCOUNTERS W

whether or not you couldn't	WHROUKTD, WHROUKD/-NT, WHROU/KUNT
whether or not you ever	WHROUFR, WHROUVR
whether or not you feel	WHROUFL
whether or not you felt	WHROUFLT
whether or not you get	WHROUGT
whether or not you go	WHROUG
whether or not you had	WHROUD
whether or not you hadn't	WHROUD/-NT, WHROU/H-NT
whether or not you happen	WHROUP
whether or not you happened	WHROUPD
whether or not you have	WHROUF
whether or not you have been	WHROUFB
whether or not you have had	WHROUFD
whether or not you have known	WHROUFN
whether or not you haven't	WHROUFT, WHROUF/-NT, WHROU/V-NT
whether or not you imagine	WHROUJ
whether or not you imagined	WHROUJD
whether or not you know	WHROUN
whether or not you live	WHROUV
whether or not you lived	WHROUVD
whether or not you mean	WHROUM
whether or not you mean to	WHROUMT
whether or not you mean to say	WHROUMTS
whether or not you recall	WHROURL
whether or not you recalled	WHROURLD
whether or not you recollect	WHROURK
whether or not you recollected	WHROURKD
whether or not you remember	WHROURM
whether or not you remembered	WHROURMD
whether or not you say	WHROUS
whether or not you see	WHROUZ
whether or not you shall	WHROURB
whether or not you should	WHROURBD
whether or not you shouldn't	WHROURBTD, WHROURB/-NT, WHROU/SH-NT
whether or not you think	WHROUNG
whether or not you think so	WHROUNGS
whether or not you understand	WHROUNDZ
whether or not you understood	WHROUND
whether or not you want	WHROUPT
whether or not you wanted	WHROUPTD
whether or not you were	WHROURP
whether or not you will	WHROUL

whether or not you will go	WHROULG
whether or not you would	WHROULD
whether or not you wouldn't	WHROULTD, WHROULD/-NT, WHROU/WONT
whether or not you would say	WHROULDZ
whether the	WHR-T

whether you
whether you	WHRU
whether you are	WHRUR
whether you aren't	WHRURNT, WHRUR/-NT, WHRU/R-NT
whether you believe	WHRUBL
whether you believed	WHRUBLD
whether you can	WHRUK
whether you can't	WHRUKT, WHRUK/-NT, WHRU/K-NT
whether you could	WHRUKD
whether you couldn't	WHRUKTD, WHRUKD/-NT, WHRU/KUNT
whether you ever	WHRUFR, WHRUVR
whether you feel	WHRUFL
whether you felt	WHRUFLT
whether you get	WHRUGT
whether you go	WHRUG
whether you had	WHRUD
whether you hadn't	WHRUD/-NT, WHRU/H-NT
whether you happen	WHRUP
whether you happened	WHRUPD
whether you have	WHRUF
whether you have been	WHRUFB
whether you have had	WHRUFD
whether you have known	WHRUFN
whether you haven't	WHRUFT, WHRUF/-NT, WHRU/V-NT
whether you imagine	WHRUJ
whether you imagined	WHRUJD
whether you know	WHRUN
whether you live	WHRUV
whether you lived	WHRUVD
whether you mean	WHRUM
whether you mean to	WHRUMT
whether you mean to say	WHRUMTS
whether you recall	WHRURL
whether you recalled	WHRURLD
whether you recollect	WHRURK

BRIEF ENCOUNTERS W

whether you recollected	WHRURKD
whether you remember	WHRURM
whether you remembered	WHRURMD
whether you say	WHRUS
whether you see	WHRUZ
whether you shall	WHRURB
whether you should	WHRURBD
whether you shouldn't	WHRURBTD, WHRURBD/-NT, WHRU/SH-NT
whether you think	WHRUNG
whether you think so	WHRUNGS
whether you understand	WHRUNDZ
whether you understood	WHRUND
whether you want	WHRUPT
whether you wanted	WHRUPTD
whether you were	WHRURP
whether you weren't	WHRURPT, WHRURP/-NT, WHRU/W-RNT
whether you will	WHRUL
whether you will go	WHRULG
whether you would	WHRULD
whether you wouldn't	WHRULTD, WHRULD/-NT, WHRU/WONT
whether you would say	WHRULDZ

which
which	WI, KH-
which are	KH-R
which aren't	KH-RNT, KH-R/-NT, WI/R-NT
which are the	KH-RT
which can	KH-K
which can't	KH-KT, KH-K/-NT, WI/K-NT
which could	KH-KD
which couldn't	KH-KTD, KH-KD/-NT, WI/KUNT
whichever	WIFR, WIVR
which get	KH-GT
which gets	KH-GTS
which go	KH-G
which goes	KH-GS
which had	KH-D
which hadn't	KH-D/-NT, WI/H-NT
which happen	KH-P
which happened	KH-PD
which happens	KH-PS
which have	KH-F
which have been	KH-FB

W   BRIEF ENCOUNTERS

```
which have had . . . . . . . . . . . . . . . . . . . . . . . . . . . . . . . . . KH-FD
which haven't . . . . . . . . . . . . . . . . . . . . . . . . KH-F/-NT, WI/V-NT
which have the . . . . . . . . . . . . . . . . . . . . . . . . . . . . . . . . . KH-FT
which is . . . . . . . . . . . . . . . . . . . . . . . . . . . . . . . . . . . . . . . KH-S
which isn't . . . . . . . . . . . . . . . . . . . . . . . . . . KH-S/-NT, WI/S-NT
which of them . . . . . . . . . . . . . . . . . . . . . . . . . . . . . . . . . . WIFM
which of these . . . . . . . . . . . . . . . . . . . . . . . . . . . . . . . . . . WIFZ
which of those . . . . . . . . . . . . . . . . . . . . . . . . . . . . . . . . . . WIFS
which shall . . . . . . . . . . . . . . . . . . . . . . . . . . . . . . . . . . . . KH-RB
which should . . . . . . . . . . . . . . . . . . . . . . . . . . . . . . . . . KH-RBD
which shouldn't . . . . . . . . . . . . . KH-RBTD, KH-RBD/-NT, WI/SH-NT
which the . . . . . . . . . . . . . . . . . . . . . . . . . . . . . . . . . . . . . . KH-T
which want . . . . . . . . . . . . . . . . . . . . . . . . . . . . . . . . . . . . KH-PT
which wanted . . . . . . . . . . . . . . . . . . . . . . . . . . . . . . . . . KH-PTD
which wants . . . . . . . . . . . . . . . . . . . . . . . . . . . . . . . . . . KH-PTS
which was . . . . . . . . . . . . . . . . . . . . . . . . . . . . . . . . . . . . KH-FS
which wasn't . . . . . . . . . . . . . . . . . . . . . . . KH-FS/-NT, WI-/WUNT
which were . . . . . . . . . . . . . . . . . . . . . . . . . . . . . . . . . . . . KH-RP
which weren't . . . . . . . . . . . . . . . . KH-RPT, KH-RP/-NT, WI/W-RNT
which will . . . . . . . . . . . . . . . . . . . . . . . . . . . . . . . . . . . . . . KH-L
which would . . . . . . . . . . . . . . . . . . . . . . . . . . . . . . . . . . . KH-LD
which wouldn't . . . . . . . . . . . . . . . . KH-LTD, KH-LD/-NT, WI/WUNT
which would say . . . . . . . . . . . . . . . . . . . . . . . . . . . . . . . . KH-LDZ
which he
    which he . . . . . . . . . . . . . . . . . . . . . . . . . . . . . . . . . . . . . . KHE
    which he believed . . . . . . . . . . . . . . . . . . . . . . . . . . . . . KHEBLD
    which he believes . . . . . . . . . . . . . . . . . . . . . . . . . . . . . . KHEBLS
    which he can . . . . . . . . . . . . . . . . . . . . . . . . . . . . . . . . . KH*EK
    which he can't . . . . . . . . . . . . . . . . . . . KHEKT, KHEK/-NT, KHE/K-NT
    which he could . . . . . . . . . . . . . . . . . . . . . . . . . . . . . . . . KH*EKD
    which he couldn't . . . . . . . . . . . . . . KHEKTD, KHEKD/-NT, KHE/KUNT
    which he ever . . . . . . . . . . . . . . . . . . . . . . . . . . . KHEFR, KHEVR
    which he feels . . . . . . . . . . . . . . . . . . . . . . . . . . . . . . . . KHEFLS
    which he felt . . . . . . . . . . . . . . . . . . . . . . . . . . . . . . . . . KHEFLT
    which he gets . . . . . . . . . . . . . . . . . . . . . . . . . . . . . . . . KHEGTS
    which he goes . . . . . . . . . . . . . . . . . . . . . . . . . . . . . . . . . KHEGS
    which he got . . . . . . . . . . . . . . . . . . . . . . . . . . . . . . . . . . KHEGT
    which he had . . . . . . . . . . . . . . . . . . . . . . . . . . . . . . . . . . KHED
    which he hadn't . . . . . . . . . . . . . . . . . . . . . . KHED/-NT, KHE/H-NT
    which he happened . . . . . . . . . . . . . . . . . . . . . . . . . . . . . KHEPD
    which he happens . . . . . . . . . . . . . . . . . . . . . . . . . . . . . . KHEPS
    which he imagined . . . . . . . . . . . . . . . . . . . . . . . . . . . . . . KHEJD
    which he imagines . . . . . . . . . . . . . . . . . . . . . . . . . . . . . . KHEJS
    which he is . . . . . . . . . . . . . . . . . . . . . . . . . . . . . . . . . . . . KHES
    which he isn't . . . . . . . . . . . . . . . . . . . . . . . . KHES/-NT, KHE/S-NT
```

which he knows	KHENS
which he lived	KHEVD
which he lives	KHEVS
which he means	KH*EMS
which he means to	KHEMT
which he means to say	KHEMTS
which he recalled	KHERLD
which he recalls	KHERLS
which he recollected	KHERKD
which he recollects	KHERKS
which he remembered	KHERMD
which he remembers	KHERMS
which he says	KH*ESZ
which he sees	KHEZ
which he shall	KHERB
which he should	KHERBD
which he shouldn't	KHERBTD, KHERBD/-NT, KHE/SH-NT
which he thinks	KHENGS
which he understands	KHENDZ
which he understood	KHEND
which he wanted	KHEPTD
which he wants	KHEPTS
which he was	KHEFS
which he wasn't	KHEFT, KHEFS/-NT, KHE/WUNT
which he will	KHEL
which he would	KHELD
which he wouldn't	KHELTD, KHELD/-NT, KHE/WONT
which he would say	KHELDZ

which I

which I	KHI
which I am	KHIM
which I believe	KHIBL
which I believed	KHIBLD
which I can	KH*IK
which I can't	KHIKT, KHIK/-NT, KHI/K-NT
which I could	KHIKD
which I couldn't	KHIKTD, KHIKD/-NT, KHI/KUNT
which I ever	KHIFR, KHIVR
which I feel	KHIFL
which I felt	KHIFLT
which I get	KHIGT
which I had	KHID
which I hadn't	KHID/-NT, KHI/H-NT
which I happen	KH*IP

which I happened	KH*IPD
which I have	KHIF
which I have been	KHIFB
which I have had	KHIFD
which I have known	KHIFN
which I haven't	KHIFT, KHIF/-NT, KHI/V-NT
which I imagine	KHIJ
which I imagined	KHIJD
which I know	KH*IN
which I live	KHIV
which I lived	KHIVD
which I mean	KH*IM
which I mean to	KHIMT
which I mean to say	KHIMTS
which I recall	KHIRL
which I recalled	KHIRLD
which I recollect	KHIRK
which I recollected	KHIRKD
which I remember	KHIRM
which I remembered	KHIRMD
which I say	KHIS
which I see	KHIZ
which I shall	KHIRB
which I should	KHIRBD
which I shouldn't	KHIRBTD, KHIRBD/-NT, KHI/SH-NT
which I think	KHING
which I understand	KHINDZ
which I understood	KHIND
which I want	KHIPT
which I wanted	KHIPTD
which I was	KHIFS
which I wasn't	KHIFS/-NT, KHI/WUNT
which I would	KHILD
which I wouldn't	KHILTD, KHILD/-NT, KHI/WONT
which I would say	KHILDZ

which you

which you	KHU
which you are	KHUR
which you aren't	KHURNT, KHUR/-NT, KHU/R-NT
which you believe	KHUBL
which you believed	KHUBLD
which you can	KH*UK
which you can't	KHUKT, KHUK/-NT, KHU/K-NT
which you could	KHUKD
which you couldn't	KHUKTD, KHUKD/-NT, KHU/KUNT

BRIEF ENCOUNTERS   W

which you ever	KHUFR, KHUVR
which you feel	KHUFL
which you felt	KHUFLT
which you get	KHUGT
which you had	KHUD
which you hadn't	KHUD/-NT, KHU/H-NT
which you happen	KH*UP
which you happened	KH*UPD
which you have	KHUF
which you have been	KHUFB
which you have had	KHUFD
which you have known	KHUFN
which you haven't	KHUFT, KHUF/-NT, KHU/V-NT
which you imagine	KHUJ
which you imagined	KHUJD
which you know	KHUN
which you live	KHUV
which you lived	KHUVD
which you mean	KH*UM
which you mean to	KHUMT
which you mean to say	KHUMTS
which you recall	KHURL
which you recalled	KHURLD
which you recollect	KHURK
which you recollected	KHURKD
which you remember	KHURM
which you remembered	KHURMD
which you say	KHUS
which you see	KHUZ
which you shall	KHURB
which you should	KHURBD
which you shouldn't	KHURBTD, KHURBD/-NT, KHU/SH-NT
which you think	KHUNG
which you understand	KHUNDZ
which you understood	KHUND
which you want	KHUPT
which you wanted	KHUPTD
which you were	KHURP
which you weren't	KHURPT, KHURP/-NT, KHU/W-RNT
which you will	KHUL
which you would	KHULD
which you wouldn't	KHULTD, KHULD/-NT, KHU/WONT
which you would say	KHULDZ

W — BRIEF ENCOUNTERS

while
- *while ago* . . . . WHAOILG
- *while the* . . . . WHAOILT
- *while these* . . . . WHAOILZ
- *while those* . . . . WHAOILS

whisper
- whisper . . . . WHIR
- whispers . . . . WHIRS
- whispering . . . . WHIRG
- whispered . . . . WHIRD

whistle
- whistle . . . . WH*IFL
- whistles . . . . WHIFLS
- whistling . . . . WHIFLG
- whistled . . . . WHIFLD

white
- *white blood cell* . . . . WHAOIBL
- *white blood count* . . . . WHAOIBLT
- *white house* . . . . WHO*US
- *White House* . . . . WHOUS
- whiter . . . . WHAOIRT
- *whiter than* . . . . WHAOIRN
- *whiter than the* . . . . WHAOIRNT
- *whiter than them* . . . . WHAOIRM
- *whiter than these* . . . . WHAOIRNZ
- *whiter than those* . . . . WHAOIRNS
- whitest . . . . WHAO*ITS

whitewash
- whitewash . . . . WHAOIRB
- whitewashes . . . . WHAOIRBS
- whitewashing . . . . WHAOIRBG
- whitewashed . . . . WHAOIRBD

whittle
- whittle . . . . WHILT
- whittles . . . . WHILTS
- whittling . . . . WHILGT
- whittled . . . . WHILT/-D

who
- who . . . . WHO
- *who are* . . . . WHOR
- *who aren't* . . . . WHORNT, WHOR/-NT, WHO/R-NT
- *who believe* . . . . WHOBL
- *who believed* . . . . WHOBLD
- *who believes* . . . . WHOBLS
- *who can* . . . . WHOK

BRIEF ENCOUNTERS   W

who can't	WHOKT, WHOK/-NT, WHO/K-NT
who could	WHOKD
who couldn't	WHOKTD, WHOKD/-NT, WHO/KUNT
who'd	WHO*D
who else	WHOELS
whoever	WHOEFR, WHOEVR
who feel	WHOFL
who feels	WHOFLS
who felt	WHOFLT
who get	WHOGT
who gets	WHOGTS
who go	WHOG
who goes	WHOGS
who had	WHOD
who hadn't	WHOD/-NT, WHO/H-NT
who happen	WHOP
who happened	WHOPD
who happens	WHOPS
who have	WHOF
who have been	WHOFB
who have had	WHOFD
who have known	WHOFN
who haven't	WHOFT, WHOF/-NT, WHO/V-NT
who imagine	WHOJ
who imagined	WHOJD
who imagines	WHOJS
who is	WHOS
who isn't	WHOS/-NT, WHO/S-NT
who know	WHON
who knows	WHONS
who live	WHOV
who lived	WHOVD
who lives	WHOVS
who'll	WHO*L
who mean	WHO*M
who mean to	WHO*MT
who mean to say	WHO*MTS
who means	WHOMS
who means to	WHOMT
who means to say	WHOMTS
who're	WHO*R
who recall	WHORL
who recalled	WHORLD
who recalls	WHORLS
who recollect	WHORK

who recollected	WHORKD
who recollects	WHORKS
who remember	WHORM
who remembered	WHORMD
who remembers	WHORMS
who's	WHO*S
who shall	WHORB
who should	WHORBD
who shouldn't	WHORBTD, WHORBD/-NT, WHO/SH-NT
whosoever	WHO/SOEFR, WHO/SOEVR
who the	WHOT
who think	WHONG
who thinks	WHONGS
who think so	WHONGSZ
who understand	WHONDZ
who understood	WHOND
who want	WHOPT
who wanted	WHOPTD
who wants	WHOPTS
who was	WHOFS
who wasn't	WHOFS/-NT, WHO/WUNT
who were	WHORP
who weren't	WHORPT, WHORP/-NT, WHO/W-RNT
who will	WHOL
who would	WHOLD
who wouldn't	WHOLTD, WHOLD/-NT, WHO/WUNT
who would say	WHOLDZ

who he

who he	WHOE
who he believed	WHOEBLD
who he believes	WHOEBLS
who he can	WHOEK
who he can't	WHOEKT, WHOEK/-NT, WHOE/K-NT
who he could	WHOEKD
who he couldn't	WHOEKTD, WHOEKD/-NT, WHOE/KUNT
who he felt	WHOEFLT
who he feels	WHOEFLS
who he gets	WHOEGTS
who he goes	WHOEGS
who he got	WHOEGT
who he had	WHOED
who he hadn't	WHOED/-NT, WHOE/H-NT

who he happened	WHOEPD
who he happens	WHOEPS
who he imagined	WHOEJD
who he imagines	WHOEJS
who he is	WHOES
who he isn't	WHOES/-NT, WHOE/S-NT
who he knows	WHOENS
who he lived	WHOEVD
who he lives	WHOEVS
who he means	WHOEMS
who he means to	WHOEMT
who he means to say	WHOEMTS
who he recalled	WHOERLD
who he recalls	WHOERLS
who he recollected	WHOERKD
who he recollects	WHOERKS
who he remembered	WHOERMD
who he remembers	WHOERMS
who he says	WHOESZ
who he sees	WHOEZ
who he shall	WHOERB
who he should	WHOERBD
who he shouldn't	WHOERBTD, WHOERBD/-NT, WHOE/SH-NT
who he thinks	WHOENGS
who he understands	WHOENDZ
who he understood	WHOEND
who he wanted	WHOEPTD
who he wants	WHOEPTS
who he was	WHOEFS
who he wasn't	WHOEFT, WHOEFS/-NT, WHOE/WUNT
who he will	WHO*EL
who he would	WHO*ELD
who he wouldn't	WHOELTD, WHOELD/-NT, WHOE/WONT
who he would say	WHO*ELDZ

who I

who I	WHOI
who I am	WHOIM
who I believe	WHOIBL
who I believed	WHOIBLD
who I can	WHOIK
who I can't	WHOIKT, WHOIK/-NT, WHOI/K-NT
who I could	WHOIKD

who I couldn't	WHOIKTD, WHOIKD/-NT, WHOI/KUNT
who I feel	WHOIFL
who I felt	WHOIFLT
who I get	WHOIGT
who I go	WHOIG
who I have	WHOIF
who I have been	WHOIFB
who I have had	WHOIFD
who I have known	WHOIFN
who I haven't	WHOIFT, WHOIF/-NT, WHOI/V-NT
who I imagine	WHOIJ
who I imagined	WHOIJD
who I know	WHOIN
who I mean	WHO*IM
who I mean to	WHOIMT
who I mean to say	WHOIMTS
who I live	WHOIV
who I lived	WHOIVD
who I recall	WHOIRL
who I recalled	WHOIRLD
who I recollect	WHOIRK
who I recollected	WHOIRKD
who I remember	WHOIRM
who I remembered	WHOIRMD
who I say	WHOIS
who I see	WHOIZ
who I should	WHOIRBD
who I shouldn't	WHOIRBTD, WHOIRBD/-NT, WHOI/SH-NT
who I think	WHOING
who I understand	WHOINDZ
who I understood	WHOIND
who I want	WHOIPT
who I wanted	WHOIPTD
who I was	WHOIFS
who I wasn't	WHOIFS/-NT, WHOI/WUNT
who I will	WHOIL
who I would	WHOILD
who I wouldn't	WHOILTD, WHOILD/-NT, WHOI/WONT
who I would say	WHOILDZ
wholesale	WAEL
wholesaler	WAERL
wholly	WHOIL

BRIEF ENCOUNTERS — W

whom
    whom . . . . WHOM
    whomsoever . . . . WHOM/SOEFR, WHOM/SOEVR
    whom the. . . . . WHAOMT
    whom these . . . . WHOMZ, WHAOMZ
    whom those . . . . WHAOMS
whorehouse . . . . WHORS, WHOERZ
whose . . . . WHOZ
who you
    who you. . . . . WHOU
    who you are . . . . WHOUR
    who you aren't. . . . . WHOURNT, WHOUR/-NT, WHOU/R-NT
    who you believe. . . . . WHOUBL
    who you believed . . . . WHOUBLD
    who you can. . . . . WHOUK
    who you can't . . . . WHOUKT, WHOUK/-NT, WHOU/K-NT
    who you could . . . . WHOUKD
    who you couldn't. . . . . WHOUKTD, WHOUKD/-NT, WHAOU/KUNT
    who you feel . . . . WHOUFL
    who you felt . . . . WHOUFLT
    who you get . . . . WHOUGT
    who you go . . . . WHOUG
    who you have . . . . WHOUF
    who you have been . . . . WHOUFB
    who you have had . . . . WHOUFD
    who you have known . . . . WHOUFN
    who you haven't. . . . . WHOUFT, WHOUF/-NT, WHOU/V-NT
    who you imagine . . . . WHOUJ
    who you imagined . . . . WHOUJD
    who you know . . . . WHOUN
    who you live. . . . . WHOUV
    who you lived . . . . WHOUVD
    who you mean . . . . WHOUM
    who you mean to . . . . WHOUMT
    who you mean to say . . . . WHOUMTS
    who you recall . . . . WHOURL
    who you recalled . . . . WHOURLD
    who you recollect . . . . WHOURK
    who you recollected. . . . . WHOURKD
    who you remember . . . . WHOURM
    who you remembered . . . . WHOURMD

W   BRIEF ENCOUNTERS

who you see .... WHOUZ
who you shall .... WHOURB
who you should .... WHOURBD
who you shouldn't .... WHOURBTD, WHOURBD/-NT, WHOU/SH-NT
who you think .... WHOUNG
who you understand .... WHOUNDZ
who you understood .... WHOUND
who you want .... WHOUPT
who you wanted .... WHOUPTD
who you were .... WHOURP
who you weren't .... WHOURPT, WHOURP/-NT, WHOU/W-RNT
who you will .... WHOUL
who you would .... WHOULD
who you wouldn't .... WHOULTD, WHOULD/-NT, WHOU/WONT
who you would say .... WHOULDZ

wicked .... WIKD
widen
    widen .... W*ND
    widens .... W-NDZ
    widening .... W-NGD
    widened .... W-ND/-D
widget .... WIJ
widow
    widow .... DWO
    widower .... DWOR
    widowers .... DWORZ
width .... W*ID
wildcard .... WAOIKD
wildlife .... WAOIFLD
will
    will .... L-, WIL
    wills .... L-Z, WILS
    willing .... L-G, WILG
    willed .... L*D, WILD
will
    will be .... L-B
    will believe .... L-BL
    will ever .... L-FR, L-VR
    will have .... L-F
    will have been .... L-FB
    will have believed .... L-FBLD
    will have had .... L-FD

BRIEF ENCOUNTERS   W

    will recall .... L-RL
    will recollect .... L-RK
    will remember .... L-RM
    will the .... L-T
    will you .... LU
    will you be .... LUB
    will you please .... LUP
    will you please tell .... LUPT
    will you please tell us .... LUPTS
    will you repeat .... L*URP
    will you repeat the .... LURPT
    will you repeat the question .... LURPTS
    will you rephrase .... LUFR
    will you rephrase the .... LUFRT
    will you rephrase the question .... LUFRTS
    will your Honor .... LURN
    will your Honor please .... LURP
    will you tell .... LUT
    will you tell us .... LUTS
    will want .... L-PT
willful .... WIFL
willfully .... WAOEFL
win
    win .... WIN
    wins .... WINZ
    winning .... WIN/-G
    won .... WON
wind
    wind .... WAOIND
    winds .... WAOINDZ
    winding .... WAOINGD
    wound .... WOUN
wind
    window .... WID
    windshield .... WIRBLD
    windshield wiper .... WIP, WAOIRBL
winner .... WIRN
winter .... WIRNT
wireless .... WAOIRLS
Wisconsin .... W*I
wisdom .... WIZ
wiser .... WAOIRZ
wish to .... WIRBT
*wish to sa*y .... WIRBTS

W — BRIEF ENCOUNTERS

with
  with .... W-
  with my knowledge .... WAOIJ
  with reference .... WREFRNS
  with regard............................. WRARD, WRAR
  with regards .... WRARDZ
  with regard to .... WRART
  with regard to these .... WRARZ
  with regard to those .... WRARS
  with respect....................................... WR-P
  with respect to .... WR-PT
  with the.. W-T
  with your knowledge .... WOURJ
withdraw
  withdraw .... WRAU
  withdraws.. WRAUS
  withdrawing .... WRAUG
  withdrew .... WRAOU
  withdrawn... WRAUN
withdrawal .... WRAUL
wither
  wither .... WIRT
  withers.. WIRTS
  withering .... WIRGT
  withered.. WIRTD
withhold
  withhold .... WHOELD
  withholds.. WHOELDZ
  withholding................... WHOELGD, WHOELG
  withheld .... WHELD
within
  within... W-N
  within the .... W-NT
  within these...................................... W-NZ
without
  without.. WOUT
  without foundation............................. WOUNGS
  without the...................................... WOUTD
  without these.................................. WOUTSZ
  without those .... WOUTS
withstand
  withstand .... WHAN, WAN
  withstands............................... WHANS, WANS
  withstanding .... WHANG, WANG
  withstood .... WHAOD

witness
- witness . . . . W-NS
- witnesses . . . . W-NSZ
- witnessing . . . . W-NG
- witnessed . . . . W-ND

witness be excused . . . . WAOUFD
witness stand . . . . WAND
woman . . . . WOM
woman's . . . . WOMS
women . . . . WIM
women's . . . . WIMS
wonder
- wonder . . . . WOND
- wonders . . . . WONDZ
- wondering . . . . WONGD
- wondered . . . . WOND/-D

wonderful . . . . WUFL
wonderfully . . . . WOIFL
won't . . . . WOENT
wood . . . . WAOD
wooden . . . . WAOND
word processing . . . . W-PG
word processor . . . . W-P
work
- work . . . . WORK
- works . . . . WORKS
- working . . . . WORK/-G, WORG
- worked . . . . WORKD

work
- workaholic . . . . WROK
- worker . . . . WRORK
- workout . . . . WROUT
- workplace . . . . WRAIS
- *workers' compensation* . . . . W-K

World Wide Web . . . . WAOIBD
worriment . . . . WOIRMT
worry
- worry . . . . WOIR
- worries . . . . WOIRS
- worrying . . . . WOIRG
- worried . . . . WOIRD

worse
- worse . . . . WORS
- *worse than* . . . . WORNS
- *worse than the* . . . . WORNT

W   BRIEF ENCOUNTERS

    worse than these . . . . WORNZ
worsen
    worsen . . . . WOERN
    worsens . . . . WOERNS
    worsening . . . . WOERNG
    worsened . . . . WOERND
worship
    worship . . . . WORP
    worships . . . . WORPS
    worshipping . . . . WORPG
    worshipped . . . . WORPD
    worshiper . . . . WRORP
worth
    worth . . . . WO*RT
    worthier . . . . WRO*IRT, WROIRT
    worthily . . . . WO*IRLT, WOIRLT
    worthiness . . . . WOIRNS
    worthless . . . . WORLS
    worthwhile . . . . WRAOIL
    worthy . . . . WO*IRT, WOIRT
would
    would . . . . WO, WOULD
    would be . . . . WOUB
    would believe . . . . WOUBL
    would believe the . . . . WOUBLT
    would be the . . . . WOUBT
    would be these . . . . WOUBZ
    would be those . . . . WOUBS
    would ever . . . . WOUVR
    would feel . . . . WOUFL
    would feel the . . . . WOUFLT
    would get . . . . WOUGT
    would go . . . . WOUG
    would happen . . . . WOUP
    would have . . . . WOUF
    would have been . . . . WOUFB
    would have been the . . . . WOUFBT
    would have believed . . . . WOUFBLD
    would have believed the . . . . WOUFBLTD
    would have gone . . . . WOUFG
    would have had . . . . WOUFD
    would have had the . . . . WOUFTD
    would have known . . . . WOUFN
    would have recalled . . . . WOUFRLD
    would have recollected . . . . WOUFRKD

BRIEF ENCOUNTERS   W

would have remembered	WOUFRMD
would have the	WOUFT
would have them	WOUFM
would have these	WOUFZ
would have those	WOUFS
would imagine	WOUJ
would it be	WIB
would it be accurate to say	WOKTS
would it be accurate to state	WOKT
would it be fair	WIFB
would it be fair to	WIBT, WIFBT
would it be fair to do	WIBTD, WIFBTD
would it be fair to say	WIBTS, WIFBTS, WOFRTS
would it be fair to state	WOFRT
would mean	WOUM
would mean to	WOUMT
would mean to say	WOUMTS
wouldn't	WONT
would recall	WOURL
would recall the	WOURLT
would recollect	WOURK
would recollect the	WOURKT
would remember	WOURM
would remember the	WOURMT
would say so	WOUSZ
would see	WOUZ
would seem to me	WO/SME
would the	WOT
would think	WO*UNG
would think so	WO*UNGS
would've	WOUV
would've been	WOUVB
would've had	WOUVD
would've known	WOUVN
would want	WOUPT
would you	WOU
would you please	WUP
would you please tell	WUPT
would you please tell us	WUPTS
would you repeat	WOURP
would you repeat the	WOURPT
would you repeat the question	WOURPTS
would you rephrase	WOUFR
would you rephrase the	WOUFRT
would you rephrase the question	WOUFRTS

would you say . . . . WOUS
would you tell . . . . WUT
would you tell us . . . . WUTS
wrangle
    wrangle. . . . . WRAN
    wrangles. . . . . WRANS
    wrangling . . . . WRANG
    wrangled. . . . . WRAND
wrangler . . . . WRARN
wrapper. . . . . WRARP
wreak havoc
    wreak havoc . . . . WRAVK
    wreaks havoc . . . . WRAVKS
    wreaking havoc . . . . WRAVG
    wreaked havoc . . . . WRAVKD
wreckage . . . . WREJ
wring
    wring. . . . . WRING
    wrings . . . . WRINGS
    wringing . . . . WRING/-G
    wrung. . . . . WR*UNG
wrinkle
    wrinkle. . . . . WRINL
    wrinkles . . . . WRINLS
    wrinkling . . . . WRINL/-G
    wrinkled . . . . WRINLD
wristwatch. . . . . WRAFP
write
    write . . . . WRI
    writes. . . . . WRIS
    writing . . . . WRIG
    wrote . . . . WRO
    written . . . . WREN
write-off. . . . . WRAOIF
write off
    write off . . . . WRAUF
    writes off. . . . . WRAUFZ
    writing off . . . . WRAUFG
    wrote off. . . . . WRO/AUF, WROEF
    written off . . . . WREN/AUF, WREFN
write-protect. . . . . WRAOIK
write-protection . . . . WRAOIX
writ of certiorari . . . . WRAIRB
writ of habeus corpus . . . . WRAIB, WHAIB

BRIEF ENCOUNTERS **W**

wrong
    wrongdoer . . . . WRORN
    wrongdoing . . . . WROND
    wrongful . . . . WROFL
    wrongfully . . . . WROEFL
    wrongly . . . . WRONLG
Wyoming . . . . WAO*I, WOEM

X

X-chromosome . . . . KPOEM
xenophobe . . . . KPOB, SFOB
xenophobia . . . . KPOEB, SFOEB
xenophobic . . . . KPOEK, SFOEK
Xerox
    Xerox . . . . ZOX
    Xeroxes . . . . ZOXZ
    Xeroxing . . . . ZOX/-G, ZOG
    Xeroxed . . . . ZOX/-D, ZOKD, ZOGD
Xerox copier . . . . ZOIRK
Xerox copy . . . . ZOIK, ZOP
x-ray
    x-ray . . . . KPRAI
    x-rays . . . . KPRAIS
    x-raying . . . . KPRAIG
    x-rayed . . . . KPRAID
xylophone . . . . ZAOIFL

Y

y'all	YAL
yardage	YARJ
yeah	YAE
year	
year	YAOER
year after year	YAOEFR
year ago	YAOERG
yearbook	YAOERK
year by year	YAOERB
year-end	YAOERND
year in, year out	YOUT
yearly	YAOERL
year old	YERLD
year-olds	YERLDZ
years ago	YAOERGS
yearn	
yearn	YAERN, Y*ERN
yearns	YAERNS, YERNS
yearning	YAERNG, YERNG
yearned	YAERND, YERND
yellow	
yellow	YOEL
yellows	YOELS
yellowing	YOELG
yellowed	YOELD
yellow	
yellower	YOERL
yellowest	YOELT
yellow light	Y-LT
yellow line	YAOIN
yellow zone	YOEN
yes	
yes	YE
yes,	YERBGS
yes.	YEFPLT
yeses	YE/-S
yes, ma'am	YEM
yes or no	YOERN
yes, sir	YER
yes, your Honor	YEN
yesterday	
yesterday	YED

Y — BRIEF ENCOUNTERS

yesterday afternoon . . . . YAFRN
yesterday morning . . . . YORNG
yogurt . . . . YOEGT
yokel . . . . YOEKL
you
   you . . . . U
   you allege . . . . ULG
   you alleged . . . . ULGD
   you aren't . . . . URNT, U/R–NT
   you be . . . . UB
   you believe . . . . UBL
   you believed . . . . UBLD
   you believe so . . . . UBLS
   you believing . . . . UBLG
   you can . . . . UK
   you can't . . . . UKT, UK/–NT, U/K–NT
   you could . . . . UKD
   you couldn't . . . . UKTD, UKD/–NT, U/KUNT
   you'd . . . . *UD
   you ever . . . . UFR, UVR
   you feel . . . . UFL
   you feeling . . . . UFLG
   you felt . . . . UFLT
   you get . . . . UGT
   you go . . . . UG
   you had . . . . UD
   you hadn't . . . . UD/–NT, U/H–NT
   you have . . . . UF
   you have a right to remain silent . . . . TR*RS
   you have been . . . . UFB
   you have believed . . . . UFBLD
   you have had . . . . UFD
   you have known . . . . UFN
   you haven't . . . . UFNT, UF/–NT, U/V–NT
   you have the . . . . UFT
   you have the right to remain silent . . . . TR–RS
   you imagine . . . . UJ
   you imagined . . . . UJD
   you'll . . . . *UL
   you may proceed . . . . MAOEG
   you mean . . . . *UM
   you mean to . . . . UMT
   you mean to say . . . . UMTS
   you're . . . . *UR
   you recall . . . . URL

BRIEF ENCOUNTERS   Y

you recalled . . . . URLD
you recalling . . . . URLG
you recollect . . . . URK
you recollected . . . . URKD
you recollecting . . . . URK/-G
you remember . . . . URM
you remembered . . . . URMD
you remembering . . . . URMG
you shall . . . . *URB
you should . . . . URBD
you shouldn't . . . . URBTD, URBD/-NT, U/SH-NT
you think . . . . UNG
you think so . . . . *UNGS, UNGZ
you've . . . . UV
you've been . . . . UVB
you've had . . . . UVD
you've known . . . . UVN
you want . . . . UPT
you wanted . . . . UPTD
you wanting . . . . UPGT
you were . . . . URP
you weren't . . . . URPT, URP/-NT, U/W-RNT
you will . . . . UL
you would . . . . ULD
you wouldn't . . . . ULTD, ULD/-NT, U/WONT
you would say . . . . ULDZ
young
    young . . . . YUNG
    younger . . . . YURNG
    youngest . . . . YUNGS
    youngster . . . . Y*UNGS
your
    your . . . . UR
    your Honor . . . . URN
    your Honor's . . . . URNS
    yours . . . . URS
    yourself . . . . *URS, URSZ
    yourselves . . . . *URSZ, *URS/-S
youth authority . . . . YORT
youthful . . . . YOUFL
Yugoslavia . . . . YAOUG
Yugoslavian . . . . YAO*UNG, YAOUVG

Z

Zaire.. ZAOIR
Zambia... ZAFRP
Zambian.. ZAFRN
zealot.. ZELT
zealous.. ZEL
zebra..................................... ZAOEB, ZEB
zenith... ZAOENT
zilch.. ZICH
zillion
    zillion....................................... Z–L
    zillion dollar............................... Z–LD
    zillionth............................. Z–LT, ZILT
Zimbabwe.. ZIFRP
zip code.. ZIK
zipper
    zipper....................................... ZIRP
    zippers..................................... ZIRPS
    zippering................................... ZIRPG
    zippered.................................... ZIRPD
zombie.. ZOM
zonal... ZAUNL
zonation........................... ZOENGS, ZAUNGS
zoo
    zoological.................................. ZAOL
    zoologist.................................. ZAOLT
    zoology................................... ZAOLG
zucchini.. ZAOUK
Zulu.. ZAOUL
Zurich... ZAOURK

BRIEF ENCOUNTERS — numbers

numbers

	0	ZER
	1	WUN
	2	TWO
	3	THRE
	4	FOUR
	5	FAOIV
	6	SIX
	7	SEV
	8	AIT
	9	NAOIN
	10	TEN
	11	LEV
	12	TWEL
....AOEN	13	THRAOEN
	14	FRAOEN
	15	FAOEN
	16	SKAOEN
	17	SFAOEN
	18	AO*EN
	19	NAOEN
TW....	20	TWI
	21	TWUN
	22	TWAO
	23	TWAOE
	24	TWOER
	25	TWAOIV
	26	TWIK
	27	TWEV
	28	TWAI
	29	TWAEN
THR....	30	THRI
	31	THRUN
	32	THRAO
	33	THRAOE
	34	THROER
	35	THRAOIF
	36	THRIK
	37	THREV
	38	THRAI
	39	THRAEN
FR....	40	FRI
	41	FRUN
	42	FRAO
	43	FRAOE
	44	FROER
	45	FRAOIV
	46	FRIK
	47	FREV
	48	FRAI
	49	FRAEN

V....	50	VI
	51	VUN
	52	VAO
	53	VAOE
	54	VOER
	55	VAOIV
	56	VIK
	57	VEV
	58	VAI
	59	VAEN
SK....	60	SKI
	61	SKUN
	62	SKAO
	63	SKAOE
	64	SKO*ER
	65	SKAOIV
	66	SKIK
	67	SKEV
	68	SKAI
	69	SKAEN
SF....	70	SFI
	71	SFUN
	72	SFAO
	73	SFAOE
	74	SFOER
	75	SFAOIV
	76	SFIK
	77	SFEV
	78	SFAI
	79	SFAEN
Y....	80	Y*I
	81	YUN
	82	YAO*
	83	YAOE
	84	YOER
	85	YAOIV
	86	YIK
	87	YEV
	88	YAI
	89	YAEN
N....	90	NAOI
	91	N*UN
	92	NAO*
	93	NAO*E
	94	NOER
	95	NAOIV
	96	N*IK
	97	NEF
	98	NAI*
	99	NAEN

numbers

911 . . . . NEN, NO*IN

1995 . . . . NOIV
1996 . . . . NOIK
1997 . . . . NEVN, NEFN
1998 . . . . NAENT
1999 . . . . NOIN
2000 . . . . TWOU
2001 . . . . TWAOUN
2002 . . . . TWAOU
2003 . . . . TWE
2004 . . . . TWAOUR
2005 . . . . TWIV
2006 . . . . TWOUX, TWAOUX
2007 . . . . TWEVN, TWEFN
2008 . . . . TWAE
2009 . . . . TWOIN
2010 . . . . TWEN

special characters

.	(decimal point, between two numbers)	P*
-	(hyphen, attached to both words)	HIF
-	(hyphen, attached to first word only)	HIFS
-	(hyphen, attached to second word only)	SHIF
-	(space–hyphen–space)	SHIFS
—	(dash–attached to both words)	D-RB
—	(space–dash–space)	D*RB
(	(opening parenthesis)	PREN
)	(closing parenthesis)	PRENZ
	(character space)	SP-
$	(dollar symbol, attached to first digit) . . . . -D (with number bar)	
¢	(cents symbol)	S-TS
&	(ampersand)	M-PD
!	(exclamation mark)	STPH-FPLT
;	(semicolon)	-FRBGS
:	(colon)	-FPLTD
:	(colon, attached both sides)	KL-N
*	(asterisk)	STR-K
¶	(new paragraph)	PRAEF
¶¶	(line space and new paragraph)	PRAEF/PRAEF
'	(opening single quote)	SKW-T
'	(closing single quote)	SKW-TS
[	(opening bracket)	BR-K
]	(closing bracket)	BR-KS
...	(ellipsis mark)	LIPZ

APPENDIX

SPEAKER IDENTIFICATION SHORTCUTS

If RIGHT1 or RIGHT2 is going to ask a question after colloquy, *K–* (for "question") can be used with the right-bank speaker identification. Same system applies for left bank.

BY RIGHT1:	K–EURBGS
Q	
BY RIGHT2:	K–EUFPLT
Q	
BY LEFT1:	SKWRAO–K
Q	
BY LEFT2:	STPHAO–K
Q	

The first letter of speaker's name or title can be used with the answer bank. Names should be entered into a "case" dictionary as they vary from job to job.

MS. DAVIS:	D–FRPBLGTS
THE DEFENDANT:	D–FRPBLGTS
THE WITNESS:	W–FRPBLGTS
THE JUROR:	J–FRPBLGTS
PROSPECTIVE JUROR NO. 1:	J–FRPBLGTS/1

For conferences, lectures and meetings, names and/or titles of speakers can be written in a variety of ways. Again, these should be entered into a "case" dictionary only. Some examples:

PROFESSOR BLACK:	SKWRAO–B
PROFESSOR BLACK:	SKWRAO/BLAK
PROFESSOR BLACK:	BLAK/BLAK

or

BILL BLACK:	SKWRAO–B
BILL BLACK:	SKWRAO/BLAK
BILL BLACK:	BLAK/BLAK

"Q" (QUESTION) SHORTCUTS

Q: Yes . . . . STKPWHR-ES
Q: Yes, sir . . . . STKPWHR-IR
Q: Yeah . . . . STKPWHR-AE

Q: No . . . . STKPWHR-O
Q: No, ... STKPWHR-N
Q: No, sir . . . . STKPWHR-OIR

Q: Oh, ... STKPWHR-OE
Q: Right . . . . STKPWHR-R
Q: All right . . . . STKPWHR-RT
Q: Well, ... STKPWHR-L
Q: And . . . . STKPWHR-A
Q: But . . . . STKPWHR-UT
Q: Okay . . . . STKPWHR-K

Q: Now, ... STKPWHR-OU
Q: Now, sir, ... STKPWHR-OUS

Q: Mr. . . . . STKPWHR-M
Q: Mrs. . . . . STKPWHR-S
Q: Miss . . . . STKPWHR-SZ
Q: Ms. . . . . STKPWHR-Z

Q: He . . . . STKPWHR-E
Q: You . . . . STKPWHR-U

"A" (ANSWER) SHORTCUTS

A: **Yes** .... YE-FRPBLGTS
A: **Yes, sir** .... YI-FRPBLGTS
A: **Yeah** .... YAE-FRPBLGTS

A: **No** .... NO-FRPBLGTS
A: **No,** .... O-FRPBLGTS
A: **No, sir** .... NOI-FRPBLGTS

A: **Oh,** .... OE-FRPBLGTS
A: **Right** .... R-FRPBLGTS
A: **All right** .... TR-FRPBLGTS
A: **Well,** .... L-FRPBLGTS
A: **And** .... A-FRPBLGTS
A: **But** .... B-FRPBLGTS
A: **Okay** .... K-FRPBLGTS

A: **Now** .... OU-FRPBLGTS
A: **Now, sir,** .... SOU-FRPBLGTS

A: **Mr.** .... M-FRPBLGTS
A: **Mrs.** .... S-FRPBLGTS
A: **Miss** .... SM-FRPBLGTS
A: **Ms.** .... Z-FRPBLGTS

A: **He** .... E-FRPBLGTS
A: **You** .... U-FRPBLGTS

APPENDIX
BRIEF ENCOUNTERS

SPEAKER + FOLLOW-ON SHORTCUTS

Each example consists of (i) speaker identification and (ii) a commonly used word or phrase.

LEFT1:	*Objection*	SKWRAOBGS
		(SKWRAO + BGS)
LEFT2:	*Objection*	STPHAOBGS
		(STPHAO + BGS)
LEFT1:	*Objection, your Honor*	SKWRAORBGS
		(SKWRAO + RBGS)
LEFT2:	*Objection, your Honor*	STPHAORBGS
		(STPHAO + RBGS)
RIGHT1:	*Objection*	KWREURBGS
		(KWR + EURBGS)
RIGHT2:	*Objection*	KWREUFPLT
		(KWR + EUFPLT)
RIGHT1:	*Objection, your Honor*	SKWREURBGS
		(SKWR + EURBGS)
RIGHT2:	*Objection, your Honor*	SKWREUFPLT
		(SKWR + EUFPLT)

Examples of some variations:

RIGHT1:	*Objection*	OEURBGS
		("O" for **Objection**)
RIGHT2:	*Objection*	OEUFPLT
		("O" for **Objection**)
RIGHT1:	*Objection*	KPEURBGS
		("KP" for **Objection**)
RIGHT2:	*Objection*	KPEUFPLT
		("KP" for **Objection**)

CATegorically Speaking

CATEGORICALLY SPEAKING contains information and briefs that are outside the scope of BRIEF ENCOUNTERS. The two books complement each other in many ways, and both use a common philosophy to construct conflict-free briefs and phrases.

CATEGORICALLY SPEAKING is designed to help court reporters and students perfect their realtime writing skills while increasing their speed and accuracy. Where applicable, it will facilitate the change to realtime writing. Categorical listings cover a variety of subjects including:

alphabets • blind and visually impaired • computer and internet • deaf and hearing impaired • geography • medical (over 1,250 entries) • numbers

The 120-page "numbers" category contains an extensive selection of number-writing styles, from the bare essentials to advanced and complex numbering techniques, catering for values from zero to the trillions. Most numbering systems are given both with and without use of the number bar, and include the following number formats:

words • figures • numbers followed by a comma or in parentheses • plurals • decimals and fractions • ordinals • Roman numerals • U.S. currency • time, date and year

A 160-page lexicon contains various forms of word association that can be used to resolve conflicts and facilitate the learning of briefs. It includes homonyms, stenonyms, "soundalikes," "look-alikes," easily confused words (*accelerate, exhilarate*), antonyms (*honesty, dishonesty*) and word families.

The sections on word-compacting strategies and brief-form prefixes and suffixes will enable the user to become more fluent in the creation and incorporation of briefs.

Published 1996, list price $37.50. For further information, contact:

WHITE-BOUCKE PUBLISHING
PO BOX 400, LAFAYETTE, CO 80026
tel: (303) 604-0661, fax: (303) 604-0662

MEDICAL BRIEFS

a dictionary of realtime medical briefs for court reporters

The book every court reporter has been waiting for: a dictionary of over 45,000 easy-to-remember medical briefs.

Volume 1 (the main dictionary) is arranged alphabetically by English and provides one-stroke and two-stroke, conflict-free medical briefs. It contains terminology ranging from lay medical terms to highly specialized vocabulary.

Volume 2 lists brief-form prefixes, suffixes and other combining forms listed alphabetically by English and also by steno.

All steno suffixes are written in one stroke. The steno suffix KLAOJ represents four separate building blocks (chol + angio + jejuno + stomy) and potentially nine syllables and nine steno strokes. Suffix variations such as tomy/otomy, emesis/temesis, lysis/olysis and metry/ometry/imetry are given.

English entries are largely based on definitive reference works such as ***Stedman's Medical Dictionary, Dorland's Illustrated Medical Dictionary*** and ***Taber's Cyclopedic Medical Dictionary***.

> "*Medical Briefs uses the concept of building blocks to construct conflict-free steno outlines. And there's a healthy dose of what I think is tantamount to steno-outline genius in the simplicity of the theory.*"
>
> Journal of Court Reporting
> (Brooks on Books - January 1999)

Published 1998, list price $75.00. For further information, contact:

WHITE-BOUCKE PUBLISHING
PO BOX 400, LAFAYETTE, CO 80026
tel: (303) 604-0661, fax: (303) 604-0662